THE PAPERS OF
WOODROW WILSON

VOLUME 34
JULY 21–SEPTEMBER 30, 1915

SPONSORED BY THE WOODROW WILSON
FOUNDATION
AND PRINCETON UNIVERSITY

THE PAPERS OF

WOODROW WILSON

ARTHUR S. LINK, *EDITOR*

DAVID W. HIRST, *SENIOR ASSOCIATE EDITOR*

JOHN E. LITTLE, *ASSOCIATE EDITOR*

ANN DEXTER GORDON, *ASSISTANT EDITOR*

PHYLLIS MARCHAND AND MARGARET D. LINK,
EDITORIAL ASSISTANTS

Volume 34
July 21–September 30, 1915

PRINCETON, NEW JERSEY
PRINCETON UNIVERSITY PRESS
1980

Note to scholars: Princeton University Press
subscribes to the Resolution on Permissions of
the Association of American University Presses,
defining what we regard as "fair use" of copyrighted works. This Resolution, intended to encourage scholarly use of university press publications and to avoid unnecessary applications
for permission, is obtainable from the Press or
from the A.A.U.P. central office. Note, however,
that the scholarly apparatus, transcripts of
shorthand, and the texts of Wilson documents
as they appear in this volume are copyrighted,
and the usual rules about the use of copyrighted materials apply.

   Publication of this book has been aided by a
grant from the National Historical Publications
and Records Commission.

Printed in the United States of America
by Princeton University Press
Princeton, New Jersey

INTRODUCTION

THE first document in this volume is a press release dated July 21, 1915, announcing that Wilson and his cabinet are undertaking a broad review looking toward "a reasonable and adequate naval programme." It signals one of the main themes of this volume: the preparation of programs of military and naval preparedness that Wilson will present to Congress in his Annual Message of 1915.

Meanwhile, Wilson, after a refreshing vacation in New Hampshire with Mrs. Galt and members of his family, is overwhelmed by three major crises. The first is the new eruption of the submarine crisis when a German submarine sinks a British passenger ship, *Arabic*, without warning and with loss of American lives on August 19. Eager to avoid a break in diplomatic relations and war, Wilson negotiates patiently. The result is the so-called *Arabic* pledge of September 1 in which the German government promises not to torpedo passenger liners without warning them and providing for the safety of their passengers and crews.

The second problem is war-torn Mexico, long a source of perplexity to the Washington administration. Unknown to Wilson, a cabal in the State Department, led by Secretary Lansing, works out a plan for comprehensive intervention by the United States, the ouster of Venustiano Carranza, and the installation of a new government—all behind the screen of Pan-American cooperation. The Pan-American conferences begin on August 5. The conferees first appeal to the revolutionary chiefs to combine and next plan to install their own regime in Mexico City. Then Wilson intervenes dramatically on August 11 by instructing Lansing not to insist upon the elimination of Carranza. During the following weeks, Wilson sets negotiations in progress that will lead to the *de facto* recognition of the Carranza government.

A third crisis breaks out when violence explodes in Port-au-Prince, the climax of the most recent of many revolutions in Haiti. Wilson intervenes reluctantly but firmly in a rescue mission. He occupies Port-au-Prince with sailors and marines and then imposes upon the Haitian government a treaty that makes Haiti a protectorate of the United States.

This volume continues the series of letters between Wilson and Mrs. Galt which we have characterized in an earlier volume. Wilson's letters to Mrs. Galt printed in this volume are, if anything, more revealing than those in preceding volumes. We see

Wilson, the statesman, in agony over the possibility of war with Germany and trying desperately to find alternatives to belligerency. We also see Wilson, the man, confronting public humiliation and the termination of his engagement to Mrs. Galt on account of the possible publication of his letters to Mrs. Hulbert; confessing to Mrs. Galt that he had had some kind of affair with Mrs. Hulbert; and triumphing over his fiancée's shock and dismay.

"VERBATIM ET LITERATIM"

In earlier volumes of this series we have said something like the following: "All documents are reproduced *verbatim et literatim*, with typographical and spelling errors corrected in square brackets only when necessary for clarity and ease of reading." The following essay explains our textual methods and review procedures.

We have never printed and do not intend to print critical, or corrected, versions of documents. We print them exactly as they are, with a few exceptions which we always note. We never use the word *sic* except to denote the repetition of words in a document; in fact, we think that a succession of *sics* simply defaces a page.

We repair words in square brackets when letters are missing. As we have said, we also repair words in square brackets for clarity and ease of reading. Our general rule is to do this when we ourselves cannot read the word without stopping to determine its meaning. Jumbled words and names misspelled beyond recognition of course have to be repaired. We are usually able to correct the misspelling of a name in the footnote identifying the person.

However, when an old man writes to Wilson saying that he is glad to hear that Wilson is "comming" to Newark, or a semiliterate farmer from Texas writes phonetically, we see no reason to correct spellings in square brackets when the words are perfectly understandable. We do not correct Wilson's misspellings unless they are unreadable, except to supply in square brackets letters missing in words. For example, for some reason he insisted upon spelling "belligerent" as "belligerant." Nothing would be gained by correcting "belligerant" in square brackets.

We think that it is very important for several reasons to follow the rule of *verbatim et literatim*. Most important, a document has its own integrity and power, particularly when it is not written in perfect literary form. There is something very moving in seeing a Texas dirt farmer struggling to express his feelings in words, or a semiliterate former slave doing the same thing. Second, in Wilson's case it is crucially important to reproduce his errors in letters that he typed himself, since he always typed badly when he was in an agitated state. Third, since style is the essence of the person, we would never correct grammar or make tenses consistent, as one correspondent has urged us to do. Fourth, we think that it is obligatory to print typed documents *verbatim et literatim*. For example, we think that it is very important that we print exact transcripts of Charles L. Swem's copies of Wilson's letters. Swem made many mistakes (we correct them in footnotes from a reading of his shorthand books), and Wilson let them pass. We thus have to assume that Wilson did not read his letters before signing them, and this, we think, is a significant fact. Finally, printing letters and typed documents *verbatim et literatim* tells us a great deal about the educational level of the stenographical profession in the United States during Wilson's time.

We think that our series would be worthless if we produced unreliable texts, and we go to some effort to make certain that the texts are authentic.

Our typists are highly skilled and proofread their transcripts carefully as soon as they have been typed. The Editor sight proofreads documents once he has assembled a volume and is setting the annotation. The editors who write the notes read through documents several times and are careful to check any anomalies. Then, once the manuscript volume has been completed and all notes checked, the Editor and Senior Associate Editor orally proofread the documents against the copy. They read every comma, dash, and character. They note every absence of punctuation. They study every nearly illegible word in written documents.

Once this process of "establishing the text" is completed, the manuscript volume goes to our editor at Princeton University Press, who checks the volume carefully and sends it to the printing plant. The volume is set by linotype by two typographers who have been working on the Wilson volumes for years. The galley proofs go to the proofroom, where they are read orally against copy. And we must say that the proofreaders at the Press are extraordinarily skilled. Some years ago, before we found a way to ease their burden, they used to query every misspelled word, absence of punctuation, or other such anomalies. Now we write "O.K." above such words or spaces on the copy.

We read the galley proofs three times. Our copyeditor gives them a sight reading against copy to look for remaining typographical errors and to make sure that no line has been dropped. The Editor and the Senior Associate Editor sight read them against documents and copy. We then get the page proofs, which have been corrected at the Press. We check all the changes twice. In addition, we get *revised* pages and check them twice.

This is not the end. Our indexer of course reads the pages word by word. Before we return the pages to the Press, she comes in with a list of queries, all of which are answered by reference to the documents.

Our rule in the Wilson Papers is that our tolerance of error is zero. No system and no person can be perfect. We are sure that there are errors in our volumes. However, we believe that we have done everything humanly possible to avoid error; the chance is remote that what looks at first glance like a typographical error is indeed an error.

We should offer a special word of explanation about our transcripts of Mrs. Galt's letters. Her punctuation and capitalization were eccentric, to say the least. For example, she rarely used the period mark or commas and relied on flicks of the pen for most punctuation. The reproduction, *literatim*, of her punctuation would, in many cases, render her letters virtually incomprehensible. Hence, we have tried to follow what we thought were her intentions and have converted her dashes or half dashes into commas, periods, and so on. A comparison of our transcript of her letter to Wilson of August 3, 1915, with the reproductions of these pages in the illustration section will show our method.

It is obvious that Mrs. Galt never had much instruction in penmanship and spelling. We have not corrected in square brackets her spelling errors unless absolutely necessary for clarity of meaning. We think that we have succeeded in deciphering her script, some of which is virtually illegible.

We are greatly indebted to Professors John Milton Cooper, Jr., William H. Harbaugh, and Richard W. Leopold and to Katharine E. Brand for reading the manuscript of this volume and making helpful suggestions. We take this occasion to thank Professor Wilton B. Fowler for his cheerful help in finding documents for us in the House Papers. And we continue to benefit from the careful work of Judith May, our editor at Princeton University Press.

THE EDITORS

Princeton, New Jersey
June 6, 1979

CONTENTS

Collateral Materials

ILLUSTRATIONS

Following page 268

Wilson with Francis Bowes Sayre and Francis, Jr.
Princeton University Library

Mrs. Galt's letter to Wilson of August 3, 1915
Library of Congress

At a World Series Game with Mrs. Galt in Philadelphia
Princeton University Library

Robert Lansing
Library of Congress

Theobald von Bethmann Hollweg
National Archives

ABBREVIATIONS

AL	autograph letter
ALI	autograph letter initialed
ALS	autograph letter signed
CC	carbon copy
CCL	carbon copy of letter
CCLS	carbon copy of letter signed
CLS	Charles Lee Swem
CLSsh	Charles Lee Swem shorthand
CLST	Charles Lee Swem typed
EAW	Ellen Axson Wilson
EBG	Edith Bolling Galt
EBW	Edith Bolling Wilson
EMH	Edward Mandell House
FR	*Papers Relating to the Foreign Relations of the United States*
FR-LP	*Papers Relating to the Foreign Relations of the United States, The Lansing Papers*
FR-WWS 1915	*Papers Relating to the Foreign Relations of the United States, 1915, Supplement, The World War*
Hw	handwriting, handwritten
HwC	handwritten copy
HwCL	handwritten copy of letter
HwLS	handwritten letter signed
HwS	handwritten signed
JD	Josephus Daniels
JPT	Joseph Patrick Tumulty
JRT	Jack Romagna typed
LMG	Lindley Miller Garrison
MS	manuscript
RG	record group
RL	Robert Lansing
T	typed
T MS	typed manuscript
TC	typed copy
TCL	typed copy of letter
TL	typed letter
TLI	typed letter initialed
TLS	typed letter signed
TS	typed signed
WGM	William Gibbs McAdoo
WHP	Walter Hines Page
WW	Woodrow Wilson
WWhw	Woodrow Wilson handwriting, handwritten
WWsh	Woodrow Wilson shorthand
WWT	Woodrow Wilson typed
WWTC	Woodrow Wilson typed copy
WWTCL	Woodrow Wilson typed copy of letter
WWTL	Woodrow Wilson typed letter
WWTLI	Woodrow Wilson typed letter initialed
WWTLS	Woodrow Wilson typed letter signed

ABBREVIATIONS FOR COLLECTIONS
AND REPOSITORIES

Following the National Union Catalog of the
Library of Congress

CtY	Yale University
CSt-H	Hoover Institution on War, Revolution and Peace
DLC	Library of Congress
DNA	National Archives
EBR	Executive Branch Records
FO	British Foreign Office
GFO-Ar	German Foreign Office Archives
MH	Harvard University
MH-Ar	Harvard University Archives
NcD	Duke University
NjP	Princeton University
PRO	Public Record Office
PSC	Swarthmore College
RSB Coll., DLC	Ray Stannard Baker Collection of Wilsoniana, Library of Congress
SDR	State Department Records
WC, NjP	Woodrow Wilson Collection, Princeton University
WHi	State Historical Society of Wisconsin
WP, DLC	Woodrow Wilson Papers, Library of Congress

SYMBOLS

[Sept. 28, 1915]	publication date of a published writing; also date of document when date is not part of text
[*July 26, 1915*]	composition date when publication date differs
[[Aug. 3, 1915]]	delivery date of speech if publication date differs
* * *	text deleted by author of document

THE PAPERS OF

WOODROW WILSON

VOLUME 34

JULY 21–SEPTEMBER 30, 1915

THE PAPERS OF
WOODROW WILSON

A Press Release[1]

July 21, 1915

The President, ⟨of course⟩ in association with the heads of Departments, regardless of present day conditions or controversies, has ⟨given⟩ *long been giving* a great deal of consideration to the preparation of a reasonable and adequate naval programme, which he intends to propose to Congress at the proper time.

That is one of the ⟨very⟩ things he is now considering in the quiet of Cornish. He feels, now that the note has been dispatched, that it is best, for the time being, to drop the discussion of it as far as he is concerned, *and is turning to questions of permanent national policy.*

Of course, he realizes that he must have the best practical advice obtainable in this matter and is seeking for it from every available professional source. In fact, it is known that the best minds of the various departments of the Government, both of the Army and the Navy, are now and have been at work on these important matters for sometime; that is, he is seeking advice from the men in those departments who have been most directly in touch with the new conditions of defense that have been evolved out of modern experience. He not only wishes advice from those who have a knowledge of actual modern conditions of warfare, but he is seeking light from those who are able to understand and comprehend the altered conditions of land and naval warfare. He wishes the Navy to stand upon an equality with the most efficient and serviceable.

As to the Army, it is known here that he is preparing to incorporate in his next message to Congress a programme in regard to the development and equipment of the Army and a proper training of the citizens of the United States to arms which, while in every way consistent with American traditions and national policy, will be of such a character as to commend itself to every patriotic and practical mind. In this matter he is working with the Secretary of War and his professional associates, who, it is understood, have reached some very definite conclusions on these

exceedingly important matters. He is anxious to have a programme that will be definite and positive, and wishes to have
the information in hand before laying the matter before the Committees of the Senate and the House.

T MS (WP, DLC).
¹ The following statement was drafted by Tumulty, sent to Cornish, and
emended by Wilson. An unknown person added the date. Wilson's deletions are
printed in angle brackets; his additions in italics. The statement was printed or
paraphrased in the newspapers on July 24.

To Lindley Miller Garrison

My dear Mr. Secretary: [The White House] July 21, 1915

I have been giving scarcely less thought than you yourself have
to the question of adequate preparation for national defense, and
I am anxious, as you know, to incorporate in my next message
to Congress a programme regarding the development and equipment of the Army and a proper training of our citizens to arms
which, while in every way consistent with our traditions and our
national policy, will be of such a character as to commend itself
to every patriotic and practical mind.

I know that you have been much in conference with your
professional associates in the department and that you have
yourself come to some very definite conclusions on these exceedingly important matters. I shall be away from Washington for a
few days, but I would be very much obliged if you would be kind
enough to prepare for me a programme, with estimates, of what
you and the best informed soldiers in your counsels think the
country ought to undertake to do. I should like to discuss this
programme with you at as early a time as it can be made ready.
Whether we can reasonably propose the whole of it to the Congress immediately or not we can determine when we have studied
it. The important thing now is to know and know fully what we
need. Congress will certainly welcome such advice and follow it
to the limit of its opportunity.

Cordially and faithfully yours,   Woodrow Wilson¹

TLS (Letterpress Books, WP, DLC).
¹ There are WWT drafts of this and the following letter in the C. L. Swem
Coll., NjP.

To Josephus Daniels

My dear Mr. Secretary: [The White House] July 21, 1915

I have been giving, as I am sure you have also, a great deal of
thought to the matter of a wise and adequate naval programme,

to be proposed to the Congress at its next session, and I would like to discuss the whole subject with you at the earliest possible date.

But first we must have professional advice. I would be very much obliged if you would get the best minds in the department to work on the subject: I mean the men who have been most directly in contact with actual modern conditions, who have most thoroughly comprehended the altered conditions of naval warfare, and who best comprehend what the Navy must be in the future in order to stand upon an equality with the most efficient and most practically serviceable. I want their advice, a programme by them formulated in the most definite terms. Whether we can reasonably propose the whole of it to the Congress immediately or not we can determine when we have studied it. The important thing now is to know and know fully what we need. Congress will certainly welcome such advice and follow it to the limit of its opportunity.

It should be a programme planned for a consistent and progressive development of this great defensive arm of the nation, and should be of such a kind as to command itself to every patriotic and practical man.

I shall return to Washington in a few days and shall be glad to take this important matter up with you at your early convenience.

Cordially and faithfully yours,   Woodrow Wilson

TLS (Letterpress Books, WP, DLC).

To Edward Mandell House

My dear Friend,   The White House 21 July, 1915.

Lansing will go to you the latter part of the week commissioned to discuss several matters of the utmost importance, and I know that you will talk to him freely. I dare not seek you out myself just at this time for fear of making the impression on the country that I am not really finding Lansing satisfactory. But I need not explain anything to you. You know as well as I do what my motives are, so soon as I form them.

It happens that instructions practically identical with those you suggest to Page (I mean about the change of opinion in this country as a result of the British treatment of cotton, oil, etc.) went forward to Page from Lansing several days ago, and we already have Page's answer.[1] He saw Sir Edward, who comprehended, as usual, and who realized the gravity of the situation, but said that to open trade to Germany or to the neutral countries about her for us would be practically to remove all the present economic pressure and therefore to greatly prolong the war. That is perhaps true, but it will not satisfy the United States. Sir Edward immediately undertook conferneces [conferences] with his colleagues, to acquaint them with the situation and to consider what could be done in the circumstances. How far do you think they will yield? I should like to press for the utmost and yet I should wish to be sensible and practical.

Affectionately Yours,   Woodrow Wilson

I enclose some things from Gerard.[2]

WWTLS (E. M. House Papers, CtY).
[1] See RL to WHP, July 16, 1915, and WHP to RL, July 19, 1915, Vol. 33.
[2] One of them is printed as an Enclosure with EMH to WW, July 22, 1915; the others were the telegrams cited and summarized in RL to WW, July 7, 1915, ns. 1 and 2, Vol. 33; and in WW to RL, July 7, 1915 (second letter of that date), n. 3, *ibid.*

To Robert Latham Owen

Personal.

My dear Senator: [The White House] July 21, 1915

I have your telegram of the nineteenth[1] and appreciate its significance. I do not feel that we can abate any of our rights, but you may be sure I shall try to handle the whole matter in a way that will make peace possible if there is the least reason on the other side of the sea.

Cordially and sincerely yours,   Woodrow Wilson

TLS (Letterpress Books, WP, DLC).
[1] It is missing.

From Franklin Knight Lane

My dear Mr President,   Washington [July 21, 1915]

Perhaps you should know this. Burleson called me up yesterday after my conference with you[1] and said that he thought that he could bring about some adjustment if I could get my New York friend[2] to call on him. I wired New York & this morning Mr Strong called on Burleson. The result I know nothing of, but I believe we should not let this thing grow if it can be stopped.[3]

Is there any sanity in this thought—that we narrate to Germany her conduct since the beginning of the war, the invasion of Belgium, the tales of atrocities, the Thrasher, Gulflight & Lusitania cases. And say that in her present mind & mood we can have nothing to do with her,—that we will not go to war with her for what she has done—but will treat her as one who by her hysterical acts of outlawry deserves to be boycotted until sense returns to her.   Lane

The country will take your advice & leadership. It is splendid to see how in a real day of trial your attitude, spirit & judgement are understood and accepted.

ALS (WP, DLC).
¹ Lane saw Wilson at the White House at 8 P.M. on Tuesday, July 20. They talked at length about the Alaska Railroad and other matters, particularly the cotton crisis and southern demands for strong action against Great Britain.
² Benjamin Strong, Governor of the Federal Reserve Bank of New York.
³ That is, the panic in the South.

From Edith Bolling Galt

                                              Cornish, New Hampshire
My own Dearest: July 21st, 1915 10. A.M.

What a long time it seemed between the time I said goodby to you Sunday and late yesterday afternoon when I could read your dear note written at 9:50 Monday morning.

Thank you for writing me the minute you reached the White House, and I am oh! so glad it did not seem an empty house! I was there to welcome you and [be] with you every minute during the hours that followed.

Yesterday when Frank, Jessie, Helen and I were motoring along over these beautiful roads from eleven to one, I thought of you deep in a Cabinet meeting, and probably bored and worried, and I did so long to *really* come and put my arms about you when it was over, and pet you and bring you a sense of my love, and make you rest. I trust the German note will not have to be discussed until you are weary and that Mr. Lansing will be a real help. I miss so terribly our delicious *working* hours, and all the interesting things you let me share and am crazy for the second chapter of the "note" and other questions of the day.

I am wondering if you will go to Richmond? And if you can really come back here the end of the week. As much and as ardently as I want you Sweetheart, I would not have you come if it means any but the *wise* thing for you. And you know I will always understand.

Our picnic yesterday was a charming one. We went up the River Road toward Hanover—and then out that good road toward Lake Sunapee.

We found an ideal spot in a pine grove beside the lake to lunch, and the day was perfect. We had to hurry back on account of the "Discussion Club," and, as we were 20 minutes behind time in reaching home I could not read your letter—so dressed and rushed off again with Jessie and Helen, leaving my thoughts behind safe put away with your letter until I could get back. The "Discussion" was about the most amusing thing I have heard in a long time, and no one knew a bit more when we left than when we arrived. But lots of the women had talked a great deal.

We got back at six, and I found another letter from *old* Mr. Wilson, and so I came up to my room and read—which do you think first? And re-read it before opening the other. And I was so happy to know Washington did not seem hot and that you were well. Bless your heart, please stay strong and free from anything that would cause you unhappiness.

Today we have guests for lunch, so Helen and I are starting in a few minutes for our walk.

This brings you all my love, and I am

always yours,   Edith.

ALS (WP, DLC).

To Edith Bolling Galt

[The White House] Wednesday,

My precious Sweetheart,   21 July, 1915 6.50 P.M.

My pen will hardly obey me at all, because I am tired and a good deal out of spirits, but I simply *must* talk to you a little, my heart needs you so. I am tired, not because of the *amount* of work I have done to-day, but because of the kind. The German note is completed and will probably go off to-night or early to-morrow morning: to-day we made all the final decisions of phrase and subject-matter. It is so direct and emphatic and un-compromising (I did not see how, in the circumstances, to make it anything else) that it brings us to the final parting of the ways, unless Germany yields—which, I fear, is most unlikely. That is why, besides being very tired, I am out of spirits and so desperate-ly need my Darling,—the touch of her hand, the love light in her eyes, the consciousness of her sweet sympathy and comprehen-sion! And so I must speak *to* her, at least.

10 P.M.

I was interrupted by the coming in of the Secretary of State for a last word or two about the note. He stayed until 7.30, when your brother came in for dinner, and since then I have had the pleasure of being with *him*. We have just come back from a ride in the park and he has gone home in the car. I thoroughly enjoyed being with him—and shall try to get him to come again some time. I did not tell Robinson[1] what route to follow, but he took us through the ford beyond the Miller cottage, and I had the thrill of one of the sweetest memories a lover could have. My adorable Sweetheart! How it would have interested your brother if he could have known what my thoughts were at that moment! Lansing left me a copy of the note, my Darling, and I am enclosing it.[2] It will not be given to the public till Saturday morning, but of course you may privately read it to the little circle of Students of American history whose departure for bed used to be our introduction to paradise.

To-night you are dining with the Fitches and will meet a man much more vital and interesting than "the wonderful person whom you love" and to whom you generously ascribe such perfections. I am glad your heart is engaged. He is very wonderful!

Thursday, 22, 7 A.M.

I broke off here last night because I was so sleepy that I could not quite see the paper and could not go on rationally—sheer reaction from the strain of the day. The ride had soothed me without resting me. It was a heavenly night, the air a little heavy with moisture but cool and refreshing, the moon prevailing over all and shining with a sort of calm lustre that seemed a sort of rebuke to disturbed and anxious thoughts. And yet it could not cure the ache at my heart because you were not there, but rather increased it with its calm beauty, which made me feel nature unsympathetic and my need for another kind of beauty, the beauty of human love and comradeship, all the greater. I talked freely, and enjoyed talking, with your brother and hope that he did not see that I was out of sorts, but *you* would have noticed the difference, for it was an effort and I did not wholly overcome the mood before the ride was over. This morning nothing is left of it except a very solemn sense of the momentous decision I have made and of all the consequences which may be involved for this great country we love and for the millions of people in it who so generously trust me and so confidingly depend on me to keep them out of the hor[r]ors of this war. Cannot my Darling pray for *me*, that I may be guided and all things overruled for the good of the world? I would be willing to sacrifice myself at any time, but how can any man think with even tolerable composure about sacrificing millions of his fellow men to his own individual, almost unaided judgment? In the midst of all these anxieties and perplexities, my precious Darling, only one light burns steadily for me, and that is the light of your dear love. In the midst of the whole confused scene stands your dear noble figure. Your starry eyes and that wonderful smile of yours, full of love and reassurance and light, seem to me to be my beacons and to show me how to steer. I never needed you more—needed you close in my arms, to whisper into my lips the sweet love that gives me life—than I did last night—than I do at this moment! I know that your dear spirit is with me—I feel it every hour of the day; but, alas! things do so crowd and distract! You ask whether I came to the sofa for a few moments rest in your arms before lunch on Monday. No, Sweetheart, your instinct was right. I was think-ing of you intensely, but things press hardest and most insistently just at one o'clock, just at the culmination of the forenoon's work, and would not *let* me come. The connections *were* im-perfect: I could not speak to you or hear you speak. But the wires were not *crossed* and there was no obstacle or impediment between your heart and mine. Business may be imperious and *command* my attention, but my heart is with you every minute of the twenty-four hours. And how deeply, with what eagerness and joy do I love you and claim you for my own! These days of heart-breaking responsibility, in which each twenty-four hours seems to count more than a decade of an ordinary life-time, are binding us so close together by every kind of tie that some day we shall be grateful for them and look back to them as to the days when we really read one another's souls and *knew* that love and sympathy and comprehension had grown perfect between us,— the time when the real marriage of our hearts was consummated and we were made sure of all that was to follow in the sweet days when we were to be constantly together and always and in everything united. It is my strength that you love me, and my joy that I love you, my precious, my incomparable Darling! How deep do the foundations of our happiness go!

Your own   Woodrow

ALS (WP, DLC).
    [1] Francis Robinson, the President's chauffeur.
    [2] RL to J. W. Gerard, July 21, 1915, CCL (WP, DLC).

To Walter Hines Page

My dear Page: [The White House] July 22, 1915

The invitation to your daughter's wedding[1] leads me to send you a word of personal greeting and, through you, to Mr. Loring[2] a message of sincere congratulation. I am glad that a little ray of genuine happiness is coming into your life just at this time to relieve the terrible strain and gloom of these months of anxiety.

Please give my warmest messages of friendship to your daughter with my sincere hope that her future will be in every way bright and happy. I wish with all my heart that I might be present at the wedding.

I want you to know, my dear Page, how deeply I have valued your letters and with what genuine interest I look forward to receiving them. They have thrown lights upon the situation which I am sure I could have got from no other quarter and have been immensely serviceable to my thought and to the forming of my purposes in these perplexing and amazing times.

I feel that I can make no adequate return for them in kind, because it seems literally impossible for me to write letters into which I can put my thought and set out in order the impressions that come crowding upon me nowadays. I can only send you in return such messages as this of genuine friendship and gratitude.

Cordially and faithfully yours,   Woodrow Wilson

TLS (Letterpress Books, WP, DLC).
  1 The invitation to the wedding of Katherine Alice Page is missing.
  2 Charles Greely Loring, architect of Boston, married Katherine A. Page on August 4, 1915. At the insistence of King George and Queen Mary, the wedding took place in the Chapel Royal of St. James's Palace.

To Charles William Eliot

My dear Doctor Eliot: The White House July 22, 1915

Your letter of the sixteenth of July[1] has made a deep impression on my mind, but it seems to me that a diplomatic note is hardly the utterance in which to express the feelings which have stirred the country and the world. It seems to me that it is necessary in such a document to be as restrained and as reserved as is consistent with the object of the communication itself.

I quite appreciate the force of what you urge and you may be sure am always glad to receive such frank expressions of your opinion in matters in which I feel that I greatly need counsel and guidance.

Cordially and sincerely yours,   Woodrow Wilson

TLS (C. W. Eliot Papers, MH-Ar).
  1 C. W. Eliot to WW, July 16, 1915, Vol. 33.

From Edward Mandell House, with Enclosure

                                        Manchester, Massachusetts.
Dear Governor: July 22nd, 1915.

In regard to our shipping troubles with Great Britain, I believe that if we press hard enough they will go to almost any limit rather than come to the breaking point. But in doing so, we would gain their eternal resentment for having taken advantage of their position, and our action would arise to haunt us, not only at the peace conference, but for a century to follow.

This, I think, is the actual situation. Just how far we should go and just how far we must necessarily go is perhaps the most difficult problem that confronts you.

If it came to the last analysis and we placed an embargo upon munitions of war and foodstuffs to please the cotton men, our whole industrial and agricultural population would cry out against it.

I hope you read the letter from Gerard. I asked him to leave his communications open so you might read them before they came to me. For fear you did not read it I am enclosing a copy.

I am glad Lansing is coming for the week end. I always understand your motives. You do not know what a comfort it is that there is such a perfect understanding between us and to feel that our friendship is beyond the reach of mischief-makers.

Affectionately yours,   E. M. House

TLS (WP, DLC).

E N C L O S U R E

James Watson Gerard to Edward Mandell House

My dear Colonel: Berlin, Germany, July 6th, 1915.

You will find three cable despatches sent July 3rd, 4th and 5th[1] interesting as giving drafts of German note and possibilities.

It is, of course, entirely for the President to decide. If he sticks to the letter of the law, why it may be that Germany will not agree to give up submarine war and the trouble will be on. If all that is wanted is some reasonable compromise by which Americans can travel even on belligerent ships, then that can be negociated. A mere exchange of formal notes will lead to a break.

I suppose it is my duty to try to prevent war, but the Germans have certainly developed a degree of poisonous hate against us which it is hard to view equably.

The Germans are having great successes against the Russians. Will probably get Warsaw soon.

The harvest is rather dried up and will fall below normal.

Undercurrent for peace. Think the plain people will be heard from if they have to go in trenches another winter.

Kaiser seems to have disappeared as a factor. It seems extraordinary. He is entirely in power of military.

The great news of peace or war or breach will be made this week.

Am very curious about the Bryan matter.

Yours as ever,   Jas. W. Gerard.

TCL (WP, DLC).
    1 See RL to WW, July 7, 1915, ns. 1 and 2, and WW to RL, July 7, 1915 (second letter of that date), n. 3, all in Vol. 33.

From Morris Sheppard

My dear Mr. President: Texarkana, Texas, July 22, 1915.

The cotton growers are again facing a crisis. Unless Great Britain respects our right as a neutral to ship cotton, a non-contraband article, to neutral ports and countries even though some of it may ultimately reach Germany and Austria cotton prices will again be destructively low and intense distress will again be the lot of the South.

I am opposed on principle to the traffic in munitions of war but our government has taken the position that an embargo at this time would be a violation of neutrality and an act of war. I am doing everything within my power to uphold our government in this critical period and I would not knowingly advocate any course that might embarass it. But the conduct of Great Britain and the allies in taking half their war supplies from us while holding up our cotton on the high seas is so inconsistent and so unjust as to demand immediate, vigorous and effective action. Not only are cotton shipments to neutral countries of Northern Europe detained but the delays in the matter of payment amount in large degree to confiscation and the situation is rapidly becoming such as to make shipments this fall exceedingly hazardous, very costly, and inevitably limited. Personally I would notify Great Britain and the other allies that if they expect to exercise the neutral privilege of buying war munitions from us they must accord us the neutral right of selling our great, non-contraband export staple, on which so many of our people depend, to neutral countries without interference.

It is said that cotton is a material for explosives. That was known when the leading nations met in the Conference of London in 1907 and put raw cotton at the head of the list of articles universally agreed to be non-contraband. Last October the British Ambassador at Washington transmitted to our State Department the assurance of Sir Edward Grey, the British minister of foreign affairs, that cotton would not be seized, that it was on Britain's non-contraband list and would remain there.

Commending this matter to your usual careful and serious consideration, I am,

Very sincerely,   Morris Sheppard.

TLS (WP, DLC).

From Edith Bolling Galt

My precious One:

Cornish, New Hampshire
July 22nd 1915, 10 a.m.

It seems almost too good to be true that tomorrow night you will be starting back again, and that this is the last letter before you come.

Your dear letter of Tuesday came yesterday while we had four guests to lunch so, again, I had to wait before I could read it—but, at last, they departed and I took it out in the hammock (where we have spent so many happy hours) and read it. You sounded so busy and so content that it did my heart good. You were well, things were going forward, and you were coming home. Could any one ask for more—with the strong, tender assurance of your love for me running through every word. *I* am so happy, Sweetheart, that you are, and so proud to feel that it is I that make you so.

Your description of the house was so forlorn that I almost got blue picturing how dreary a homecoming it made for you. And then a great wave of happiness came over me that, in spite of such surroundings, you still felt my love and that its very warmth cheered bare rooms. I read Helen what you said about the Landaulette and she was so amused. By the way, she is quite herself again, and so sweet and thoughtful for every one.

The lunch party was a great success and after they left Helen and I went to call on the *other* Miss Slade[1] (one of them came to lunch) and we had a very nice time and a wonderful view.

Then at seven we went to dine with Dr. Fitch and his wife, and had a very stimulating evening.

As soon as I saw him I realized that I had heard him preach at New Haven last February. I don't know why I had never associated him with the Dr. Fitch I heard except that I thought Frank said this one lived in New York.

His sermon was splendid at New Haven, and I would so like to hear him again.

We have not yet heard whether Margaret is coming today, but Helen and Jessie think she will. Frank has gone for the walk we were discussing before you left. Jessie and I decided we were not quite up to such a climb, and besides it is still raining, in spots, and we are going with Helen for a more modest tramp.

I have to get a letter off to Randolph by this mail so must stop. But my thoughts and love flow onward, and you are never really far away from me.

So take very tender care of your precious self, and know that I will be waiting for you with open arms.

Always yours,   Edith.

ALS (WP, DLC).
[1] There were four Misses Slade living in Cornish at this time: Elizabeth, Fannie, Emily, and Augusta. See the index references in Vol. 28 of this series.

To Robert Lansing

My dear Mr. Secretary: The White House July 23, 1915

I know you will be interested in reading the two letters enclosed.[1] They seem to me unusually interesting. I did not show them to you before the note was formulated because it did not seem to me necessary.

Cordially and sincerely yours,   Woodrow Wilson

TLS (SDR, RG 59, 763.72/1978½, DNA).
[1] G. F. Williams to WW, July 15, 1915, TLS, and G. W. Kirchwey to WW, July 15, 1915, TLS, enclosing T memorandum, all in SDR, RG 59, 763.72/1978½, DNA. The lengthy and rambling letter from George Fred Williams, the Boston lawyer and long-time supporter of William Jennings Bryan, argued essentially that the American government was using very dubious logic in demanding of Germany that the concept of war zones and the use of the submarine, both of which were unknown heretofore in international law, should somehow be made to conform to the requirements of that law. The administration had further weakened its position by failing to protest when the British, in November 1914, had mined much of the North Sea and the English Channel, declared it a war zone, and warned neutral vessels that they traveled therein at their own risk. It thus had been highly illogical for the United States to hold Germany to a "strict accountability" for doing much the same thing in February 1915. As for the submarine, even the American note to Germany of May 13 had admitted that it was impossible for this instrument of war to conform to the traditional requirements of visit and search. To demand that it do so was in effect to deny Germany of her only effective naval weapon. If the United States continued such impossible demands on Germany, Germany could only respond with defiance. Since an American declaration of war against Germany was "unthinkable," the only possible outcome of the present negotiations was either an impasse or "some method of reaching diplomatically an arrangement for safe carriage of Americans and American goods by the consent of all the belligerents."
The letter and memorandum from George Washington Kirchwey, professor at and former dean of the Columbia University School of Law, advocated that the United States propose to Germany the immediate calling of an international conference to consider "the proper limits of belligerent as against neutral rights to be observed in the future conduct of the present war and in future wars"; "how the lives and interests of non-combatants and the principles of humanity can best be secured against invasion in time of war"; "whether the time has not come for the general acceptance of the principle of the absolute freedom of the seas to innocent commerce, whether destined to belligerent or to neutral ports and whether carried in enemy or in neutral bottoms"; and, finally, the enactment of rules for the regulation of submarine warfare. Pending the

completion of this large program, the United States and Germany should agree to a *modus vivendi* by which Germany would modify its submarine warfare to permit "free and unobstructed passage" to American and all other neutral ships not carrying contraband, assure the lives and safety of all persons on neutral ships even though carrying contraband, and assure the lives and safety of all persons on enemy ships not carrying munitions. The United States, in return, should recognize the principle that enemy ships carrying munitions of war were "quasi-military" in character and thus not entitled to immunity from capture or destruction because of the presence of neutral or other non-combatant passengers and would undertake to inspect enemy merchant vessels leaving its ports and mark "in some proper way" those which carried no munitions. Kirchwey added the thought that a conference called for this "specific and limited purpose might easily grow into a conference to settle the peace of the world," under Wilson's guidance.

To Giles D. Jackson

My dear Sir: [The White House] July 23, 1915

It is with the keenest and most sincere regret that I find it impossible for me to be present at any time during the Negro Exposition and Celebration in Richmond. The fact is that I have been so engrossed by the many matters calling upon my serious and immediate attention that it has not been possible for me to address my mind to what I should like to say if I come to Richmond on this important occasion. I feel that for me merely to attend would be a very slight and indifferent service to those who are conducting this Exposition, and yet it is impossible for me to come as I should wish to come, prepared to say what would be worth saying in regard to so interesting an occasion and all that it signifies.

With much regret,
                          Sincerely yours,   Woodrow Wilson

TLS (Letterpress Books, WP, DLC).

To Charlotte Everett Wise Hopkins

My dear Mrs. Hopkins: [The White House] July 23, 1915

I hope that you will pardon me for not having replied sooner to your letter of June twenty-first.[1] It has not been because it did not receive my immediate attention but only because I was necessarily so absorbed in other matters that I could not make the sort of reply I wished to make.

It gives me great pleasure to say that your plans for model tenements have my very warm approval. I do not feel that I am entitled to any expert judgment in these matters, but the plans seem to me very admirable indeed and my heart, I need hardly say, is very much engaged in the enterprise. If there is any way

in which I can help that is appropriate and in good taste, I hope
that you will not hestitate to call upon me.

Cordially and sincerely yours,   Woodrow Wilson

TLS (Letterpress Books, WP, DLC).
  [1] Charlotte E. W. Hopkins to WW, June 21, 1915, Vol. 33.

From Josephus Daniels

Dear Mr. President: Washington. July 23, 1915.

The questions you asked me yesterday gave me a new point of
view and I decided to act upon your suggestion and will not make
the designation about which we talked. For the service demanded
at this time we must have the best obtainable advice on the General Board. Every time I talk with you about policies and administration your point of view is so sound that I am tempted to ask
more frequent conferences.

Your letter suggesting the making of a naval policy will be
acted upon. I have already taken it up with Badger and Benson
and will be ready to talk with you about it when you return. Hope
you will have a pleasant stay and come back improved and
strengthened for your tasks.

Sincerely   Josephus Daniels

ALS (WP, DLC).

From Walter Hines Page

Dear Mr. President: London, July 23. 1915

I write you these sheets chiefly of gossip, which I cannot
vouch for, because they may in a measure indicate the kind of
atmosphere we live and work in. I hear hundreds of such things
every week. People tell me—in the clubs, at my house—everywhere; they drink Mrs. Page's tea & give pay in tales; and much
I hear indirectly—things they do not flatly say *to* me. The censor-
ship and the habit of secrecy have revived the ancient practice,
wh. existed before newspapers, of making things known by word
of mouth. Certain rumors will curiously break out all over London at about the same hour on the same day. Most of them are
nonsense or mare's nests, but now and then a profound secret
slips out as naïfly as a child sometimes reveals a family skeleton.

The story got loose several days ago that Warsaw had already
been taken (it isn't quite taken yet), that the retreating Russians
suffered a nervous breakdown and killed a lot of English and
French who were trying to leave Warsaw for Moscow. Why?

Because the Russians had the notion that the English and the French were doing nothing in the war. Then last night a military man told me that the Russian Grandduke sent one of his staff here a month or more ago to inform the English that they wd. have to give up Warsaw in time & to ask the English not to put too much value on this incident.

There is frequent talk here not only of a row between the Germans and the Turks, which is probably true, but a very bad row also between the Germans and the Austrians; and the German plan is to annex the Austrian Germans and to throw over all the other Austrian national[i]ties, thus bringing practically all the Germans into one Empire and under one central government.

Lichnowsky, the recent German Ambassador to this Gov't, a few weeks ago wrote a letter to one of his closest friends here, wh. was brought from Berlin by one of our men, in wh. he said that the Emperor is merely drifting, that Germany has had no fixed plan since the attempt on Paris failed, and that thoughtful Germans know perfectly well that Germany is beaten. You may, perhaps, hear more of this letter. And this paragraph is not gossip. I've read the letter—under bonds of profound secrecy.

The only chance the Allies have of taking the Dardanelles is that the Turks shall run out of ammunition. If Roumania continues to forbid ammunition to go thro' her territory, the Allies will succeed: otherwise not.

Tales multiply of graft in the Russian army and among contractors—high and low. There are stories even of English corruption in the army here, among contractors and ammunition-makers. And it is said that one of the largest shell-manufacturers in England accepted a very big contract at the beginning of the war from the Russian Government; that the price left so large a profit that they were unwilling to divide the work; that the pressure of work for the British army became so great that they put off beginning the Russian work time and again, and that they have just now begun it.

You hear fresh reasons every week why Lloyd George will become Prime Minister. How Asquith is to be got rid of does not appear. Certainly things happen wherever George is—first in the Exchequer, then as Minister of Munitions, then as the settler of the big coal-strike in Wales.

The quarrel between Kitchener and French—talk about that has for the moment died down. A little while ago it was said on every side that it had been definitely decided to remove French from the command of the army in France.

Now, instead of the imminent plan to break through the German line in France, you hear that the programme for the autumn and winter is the present programme of gradual attrition—there will be no effort at a general forward movement till next Spring.

There is much talk, quiet and discreet, about Japan—enough to betray a general fear of friction when the new settlement of the world comes. She will want Pacific islands, wh. were German; and the Australians in particular will object. The great self-governing colonies are consulted more than ever by the British Gov't and they have been promised a voice in the peace-agreement. Very many Englishmen have always disliked the Anglo-Japanese treaty; and you hear now much talk about a Japanese-Russian treaty to be made on [in] some early year, with an anti-British leaning. But there are other stories of failures to agree now—that is, failures between Japan and Russia. For example, it is said that Japan offered to supply large quantities of ammunition to Russia if Russia would cede her part of Sakhalin Island. Russia refused and Japan sent no more ammunition. I know that Japan wishd. to send troops to France, but askd. such a price that the French and English declined.

It must be the idlest talk in the whole world, but I hear many predictions that other wars will quickly follow the Great War. The whole world will be broken to pieces—sawed into bits like a gig-saw puzzle—and no matter how it is put together, somebody will be violently dissatisfied. In much of this talk suspicion of Japan crops out. In certain moods the Italian and the Spanish Ambassadors[1] become recklessly frank with me—almost as frank as the neutral Ministers. But, tho' I often see His Excellency the Jap.,[2] and tho' his wife[3]—a very remarkable and amazingly well-informed little lady—runs in & out of my house constantly and gives us her confidence on all unimportant things most charmingly, they *never* talk politics or diplomacy. There are loose-tongued women in the diplomatic corps and not a few men who love to air their knowledge; but these Japs are inscrutable. The Chinaman[4] is loquacity itself in comparison. Even the Jap. secretaries and attachés are *all* prudence incarnate; and so much can be said about no other group in this city. I'd undertake to find out something about anything in 24 hours thro' the back-door of any other Embassy or legation in London; but the Jap. —nothing about nothing! A diplomatic corps, after a year or two of common acquaintance, becomes a sort of union or guild; and, being human, they talk shop with one another, and their women, like all other women, lapse on occasion into surprising gossip,

[1] Marquis Guglielmo Imperali and Alfonso Merry del Val y Zulueta.
[2] Katsunosuke Inouye.
[3] Suye Ozawa Inouye, daughter of Seiji Ozawa and niece of Marquis Inouye, father of the Ambassador.
[4] Sao-Ke Alfred Sze.

and the chief coin they pass is, of course, international oracular deliverances. Not so our Jap. friends and close neighbors—not on your life. But the Australians (each of the Colonies has a sort of diplomatic corps here—able men, too) are not tongue-tied on the subject. They talk as if they were Californians.

Other wars to follow this, tho' 5 million men are already dead? Nothing sounds more foolish. Yet I hear talk about such a probability every week. I am reminded how this experience of cumulative horrors is changing everybody on this side the world. Men are becoming reconciled to war. Perhaps, they'll tell you—it is just as well to kill a generation of men. How else can the monarchs and dictatorial parties and the many kinds of groups & of men who enjoy wrong and ancient privileges be shaken loose? In all the years of our democracy only two democracies have come in Europe—Switzerland & France. And absolute monarchy has held its own in Russia and Germany. How else shake the world into liberalism? Men who abhor war and who feel about it as we feel ask you such questions as these. In a sense the more horrible it becomes, the less horror it gives men in it and close to it. A wounded Canadian in a hospital here said the other day: "the war's damned dangerous but it's the finest sport in the world"—not an uncommonly expressed opinion.

Other gossip and conjectures run thus: The war will be won at last by aircraft. We are just beginning to prove the value of the aeroplane—especially the big aeroplane. Send 1000 of them every day for a week over Essen and we cd. destroy it. The 5,000 aeroplanes and the 10,000 men required cost less than a new dreadnought & her crew, & the dreadnought may be blown up by a mine. Or, send a dozen aeroplanes every day to drop bombs on the headquarters of the enemy, so that the generals wd. have to seek underground quarters. You hear, in fact, that the English are making plans for an aerial army, all the aircraft work done hitherto being mere experiments. The Germans working under the sea, the English and French in the air, and all underground— that's the life of men in this year of grace on this side the world.

Of course there's a lot of gossip about us, our attitude and our activities. As considerable a man as Lord Cromer,[5] for example, is saying that our objection to the Order in Council of March 11 is all captiousness, that we are sticklers for the forms of things and lovers of the dollar. And many lesser men say similar things. They say, too, that we are valiant writers of Notes, but that we'll do nothing till we take the gun down from over the

5 Evelyn Baring, 1st Earl of Cromer, best known for his service in Egypt from 1883 to 1907, during which, though nominally only the British consul-general, he was the virtual ruler of the country.

door. I dare say the volume of criticism of us that is gossiped about is enormous, judging from what I hear and read. It all comes to this: Have we any spunk in us? Nothing counts now but shooting.

Yet—leaving mere gossip and coming to what I know—the Government and the governing class are very greatly disturbed about the cotton situation. I talk it over *in extenso* with the Government; members of both Houses of Parliament come to see me every day; and I think I have managed—purely privately—at least to bring them to consider the advisability of rescinding the Order in Council. You will perhaps read the article that I enclose from this morning's *Times*,[6] wh. was written with my knowledge. The writer doesn't *know* that cotton will be made contraband. I thought it worth while, since he was forced to advocate *that*, that he shd. advocate also the rescinding of the Order in Council. That article bro't old Bryce to see me this morning & Lord Charnwood[7] & others. With my knowledge of the situation (whatever that may be worth) the programme to (1) make cotton contraband (which they will do anyhow), (2) to buy as much as they will at as high a price as they will, and (3) at the same time rescind the Order in Council—that's as good as we can hope for; and that wd. remove our legal difficulties. Having set the *Times* on this rescinding tack, I confess I have more or less hope: I do not know just how much to have.

As regards British opinion of our controversy with the Germans—it is unanimous, I think, that we'll get nowhere by more notes or by any form of controversy, that they will surely blow up more ships with Americans on board; and that we had as

[6] "Cotton. The American Point of View. A Suggested Solution," *The Times*, July 23, 1915. This article by "a Correspondent" began with a discussion of the economic, social, and political significance of cotton in the United States, a significance which no administration, least of all a Democratic one, could ignore. Beyond this, the writer asserted, both the American government and the American people shared the conviction that the British Order in Council of March 11, 1915, under the authority of which the British navy was preventing any cotton from reaching Germany and her allies, was "illegal and unwarrantable." This conviction, together with the justifiable fear of the cotton growers that they faced continuing economic disaster, was leading the American government and people toward a direct confrontation with Great Britain. The writer warned that this might well take the form of a law banning the export of munitions of war. The writer proposed as a solution that the British government declare cotton absolute contraband, thus putting its interdiction of cotton to central Europe on a much more acceptable legal basis, and, at the same time, arrange to buy that portion of the American cotton crop which would normally have gone to Germany and her allies. The author estimated that the cost of this purchase might run as high as £35,000,000. The reader should note that this proposal was essentially the same as the so-called Crawford plan, about which see EMH to WW, Aug. 6, 1915, printed as an Enclosure with WW to RL, Aug. 6, 1915.

[7] Godfrey Rathbone Benson, 1st Baron Charnwood, active as a Liberal member of the House of Lords; soon to be best known for his biographies of Abraham Lincoln (1916) and Theodore Roosevelt (1923).

well face the necessity of war with them; that they want no great nation fresh when the war ends, but that they prefer that all shd. be crippled alike, so that no one will have an advantage in trade & industry & capital. The English regard the Germans as mad and as wholly incapable of understanding any other people. And it must be said that the English did not start out with this idea —they refused to believe it themselves till they had been at war nearly a year.

There is, therefore, no thought (to say nothing of talk) of peace here. They say that there's no use in stopping under conditions that will require another war at an early time. The English loan was taken by all classes of society—even servants subscribing in incredible numbers and for incredible sums. They can raise 3 billion dollars several times more; men continue to enlist, without conscription (wh., however, may come later), and the Colonies continue to raise men and money. The present mood is for a fight to a finish; and they will suspect any peace "feelers" the Germans may put forward.

To go back to cotton: the feeling is deep that the South is worked up by the German propagandists, that demagogues seem to flourish there, that the cotton men do not seem to appreciate the fact that it is the war in general that has ruined the cotton-market rather than the English blockade of Germany. Since England is the biggest buyer of cotton, the English think that the cotton-grower ought to be more patient and considerate. There will be a stronger movement than ever, after the war, to develop cotton on British territory. The cotton-spinners here constantly recall how the U. S. Gov't kept them without cotton during the civil war and they pride themselves on having endured this hardship with a minimum of complaint. They constantly ask why we can't be patient and considerate now in their time of trouble.

As to the general situation—as looked at from this much-censored capital, it seems certain that the war will end with an unfriendly feeling between the U. S. and Germany. If it end with an unfriendly feeling also between the U. S. and the Allies, we shall have an isolation in fact. For France and Russia and Italy will take the cue from England, and Japan wd. use our "unfriendliness" to the Allies as an excuse for whatever feeling she wishd. to stir up in her population.

My anonymous mail, cartoons here and there, anti-American pamphlets etc. etc. indicate a considerable body of opinion that coincides with Lord Cromer's

But gossip and conjecture enough. We are in deep enough water in fact. I confess to a dread of the long, long time of controversy and adjustment that is still to come. But I take up the task of every day as it presents itself and do the best I can, hoping for as favourable an issue at last as can be got out of this utter breakdown of the world.

Yours faithfully,   Walter H. Page

ALS (WP, DLC); P.S. omitted.

To Edith Bolling Galt

[The White House] Friday,
My precious Darling,   23 July, 1915 7.15 A.M.

It seems absurd to write you a letter that will get to you at the same time that I will myself, but somehow it is necessary to ease the impatience of my heart; and, besides, I never believe in my good fortune till it actually comes. I have my travelling clothes on this minute and know of nothing that *can* prevent my starting for Cornish this afternoon—possibly on the very train that will carry this letter—but I know that *something* might turn up any moment to stop me—and you will not *have* to read this if I come myself! There will be nothing new or novel in it. The necessity that is on me this morning is laid upon me by my heart *every* morning, and will be till I die,—the necessity to pour out my love to you. In spite of myself, I have been sad the past two days, or, rather, oppressed with the consciousness of many things in whose presence I *cannot* be gay or light-hearted, and never before have I felt the need of you, of your care and love and companionship, so poignantly, so as if to be without it were a constant handicap, a momentary loss of force. I cannot work at my best (it has been so all my life) unless my heart is satisfied and at ease. It is not that the work I do is inferior—I could not prove that—but it is done at infinitely greater cost to me, and I cannot doubt that it lacks the spontaneity and colour of life that it would otherwise have. My eagerness to get back to you is simply the crying out of every part of me for added life; my mind, which finds yours its satisfying partner, my heart, which feels at every turn of the day and of our sweet intercourse the exquisite response in kind of your own,—the boy that is in me and who has found a perfect playmate, the lover in me who has found love like his own, only more subtle and pervasive, like the perfume of a flower, and the man of affairs, who finds in you a woman fit to be a man's counsellor, "to warm, to comfort, and command"—and yet "not too bright or good for human nature's daily food; for transient sorrows, simple wiles, praise, blame, love, kisses, tears and smiles." You satisfy, delight, *and complete me*, and I cannot for a moment be wholly happy while separated from you! And this is the love message that goes before me. I shall have the exquisite pleasure of *saying* all this to you,—but that will be to-morrow, and my heart must have ease to-day—as much as I can give it.

Your own   Woodrow

I am perfectly well.

ALS (WP, DLC).

Charles Lee Swem to the White House Staff

Windsor, Vermont, July 25, 1915.

Please order from Tokalon Wine Company, F. Street, Washington, one dozen bottles American Sauterne for use in making punch. Have it expressed to Brooks early Monday morning. Important that it reach here Wednesday.   Swem.

T telegram (WP, DLC).

From Edward Mandell House

Manchester, Massachusetts,

Dear Governor: July 25th, 1915.

We are all pleased at the Note and its reception by the country. I have never known a public document give such general satisfaction.

I have had a delightful two days with Lansing. I believe he will be a great comfort to you. The things that are open, like the Mexican situation, the South American proposal and the treaty with Russia will, I think, be closed with celerity. He knows what you want done and he is familiar with the machinery for doing it.

His Department is your most important instrument at present and everything should be done to perfect it so that your policies may be carried through in the shortest time and most efficient manner. If good men can be selected for Counsellor and First and Second Secretaries, things will move as never before.

Lansing very much hopes you will not insist upon Palmer[1] for Counsellor. He feels he is not the type of man that can serve the Department best. He is, however, open minded about it and if you decide that you want him, he will accept your decision cheerfully.

He was wondering whether Palmer would not do for Santo

Domingo. That is a $12 ooo. place and has large possibilities for conspicuous service.

I am glad you are back in Cornish and I hope you will remain there as long as you did before.

Affectionately yours,   E. M. House

TLS (WP, DLC).
¹ That is, A. Mitchell Palmer. About the pressure put upon Lansing to accept Palmer, see Stanley Coben, *A. Mitchell Palmer: Politician* (New York, 1963), pp. 117-18.

From James Ford Rhodes

My dear Mr. President   Seal Harbor, Maine. July 25 1915

I approve thoroughly your despatch of July 21 and I think that it will be approved by everybody except the German-Americans and pro-Germans. I believe your entire conduct of foreign affairs has been sound and just and that ten or twenty years hence it will look very fine.

With the expression of my high respect I remain

Very truly yours   James F. Rhodes

Please do not take the trouble to answer this.

ALS (WP, DLC).

From Paul Samuel Reinsch

My dear Mr. President: N. Y. July 25 [1915].

It was a matter of the deepest regret to me that on account of my sickness I should not have been able to come to Washington in time to see you. The hospital treatment, which under these circumstances I underwent much against my will, was however it seems entirely successful.

An opportunity to discuss with you briefly the situation which now confronts us in China would have been of the greatest value to me. The matter presents itself roughly as follows: Shall China, hitherto bent on peaceful industry and genuinely friendly to us be forced into a militarist policy and into a position where she will not be free to manifest good will toward the U. States? What program of action can we adopt to prevent such a result? It seems to me that the only promise of safety for the future lies in attempting to do certain concrete things—to develop every individual American interest in China quickly and with energy while there is yet time; to oppose at every point all attempts to establish an exclusive policy; and to have if possible a clear understanding with Gt Britain and Russia as to means for averting the common danger. Such cooperation seems to me to be possible at present; though if the attempt to subjugate China should be allowed to succeed, then indeed the first thought of the European powers would naturally be how to protect *their own* countries against the new menace.

The Chinese people itself still remains a factor. Bitterly resenting the unjust attempt at foreign domination, more than ever anxious to be free to follow the example of the American people, they still constitute a great moral force, though unorganized for slaughter. Any action or word that will help them to keep heart, that will preserve their sense of the dignity of their country, will help to avert enslavement. The Chinese are very anxious to have a voice, at least, in the conferences which are likely to follow the war, aside from a special conference of the belligerents. If some concrete action could be prepared, tending to guarantee the existence of smaller or weaker nations against direct aggression, there would be new hope for China. China is weak only in centralized organization, in every other respect she is strong and her strength rests in true social justice. Thus the Chinese question is intimately connected with the possibility of rehabilitating justice as a controlling force in human affairs, after this war is over. And it would seem that at that time with the bitter experience recently gathered, humanity might be predisposed to a more effective organization of international justice.

These are some of the problems I had hoped to discuss with you, Mr. President, and such a discussion would have given me heart and courage and wise guidance in my attempts to work towards a solution which would preserve for the present and for the future, when we shall need them, those opportunities for independent and fruitful work which our people have thus far enjoyed in China, together with the deep and spontaneous good will of the Chinese.

Should you consider it desirable to summon me for a brief discussion, I shall hold myself in readiness to come. However, as the latest date on which I can leave New York for San Francisco is Monday Aug 2, I would respectfully request that you would kindly cause your desire to be communicated to me in New York (Union Club) if possible by Wednesday, in order that I may plan my necessary work here and in Washington.

With the highest regard and the best wishes for your continued well-being I am, Dear Mr. President,

Faithfully yours   Paul S. Reinsch

ALS (WP, DLC).

From Edwin Forrest Sweet

Washington DC July 26 1915

On account of unseemly effort of labor and vessel interests to make capital out of Eastland catastrophe[1] this department subjected to gross misrepresentation   Secretary Redfield and Solicitor Thurman[2] arrive Chicago Blackstone Hotel eight tomorrow morning. Files show Eastland allowed in 1906 carry three thousand passengers and more than once carried nearly that number without accident. Am advised she has since been remodeled in direction of greater safety notwithstanding newspaper report to contrary. Department has from start urged need of searching and absolutely impartial investigation in addition to the inquiry already begun according to law by Steamboat Inspection Service   If legal authority can be found think investigation should be conducted by men whose professional standing would be an assurance to the country of our determination to bring out all facts and to punish any found guilty.

E F Sweet, Acting Secretary

T telegram (WP, DLC).

1 The Great Lakes excursion steamship, *Eastland*, capsized at its pier in the Chicago River on the morning of July 24, 1915, with the loss of 812 souls. About 2,500 Western Electric Company employees and their families had boarded the ship for their annual outing across Lake Michigan. The Steamboat Inspection Service of the Department of Commerce launched an investigation, as provided by law, to determine whether faulty inspection contributed to the accident. However, charges arose immediately that the service could not be impartial in the circumstances. The Chicago Federation of Labor, for example, sent a "most emphatic protest" to Wilson on the evening of July 24, reiterating charges made since 1914 that the inspectors "acted more like shipping agents than public officials." The *Chicago Tribune* telegraphed to Wilson on the morning of July 26, citing charges by the Cook County state's attorney, of "avarice and collusion, involving officials of the Federal inspection service," and asking for a special commission to investigate the disaster. E. N. Nockels to WW, July 24-25, 1915, T telegram (WP, DLC), and *Chicago Tribune* to WW, July 26, 1915, T telegram (WP, DLC). See also American Red Cross, Chicago Chapter, *Eastland Disaster Relief, American Red Cross, 1915-1918* (n.p., 1918), and Graham Taylor, "The Eastland Disaster," *Survey,* XXXIV (Aug. 7, 1915), 410-13.

2 Albert L. Thurman, solicitor of the Department of Commerce.

To Joseph Patrick Tumulty

Dear Tumulty: [Cornish, N. H. July 26, 1915]

There is something in the suggestion made at the end of this telegram. I wish you would ascertain from the Department of Justice, perhaps, whether I have the right to associate such persons with this inquiry?   The President. C.L.S.

TL (WP, DLC).

From Cleveland Hoadley Dodge

My dear Mr. President: New York July 26, 1915.

I was off on the yacht over Saturday and Sunday, and it is needless to say that I thought a great deal about you and your last splendid letter to Germany, which puts the position of the American people in such unequivocal and definite shape. With the exception of a few strong pro-Germans, I have not met any-one who did not thoroughly approve of the letter, and I think that most people are glad that the time is coming when we will have to line up pretty decidedly with the Allies.

I have just received a letter from my sister Mary,[1] who lives in England, stating that Mr. McKenna,[2] the Chancellor of the Exchequer, had been spending Sunday with her just after Germany's last note was sent. She quotes a remark of his to this effect that "he would rather be in anyone's position than our President's" which shows how thinking men on the other side realize the serious position in which you have been placed.

I earnestly trust and pray that in spite of the work which you expect to do at Cornish, you may get some good golf, and get new health and vigor for any further contingencies which may arise.

With dearest love to all the family,
                    Yours affectionately,   C H Dodge

P.S. I know you are very busy, so please do not take the trouble of replying.

TLS (WP, DLC).
  [1] Mary Hoadley Dodge.
  [2] Reginald McKenna.

From Henry Lee Higginson

Dear Mr. President: Boston. July 26, 1915.

It is to be hoped that you know how hearty and fully the people who come within my circle endorse your letter to Germany, and how ready they are to stand behind it.

The Germans have not yet taken in what we are and what we mean, and, being very thick-headed, a new idea gets inside their heads with great difficulty.

But another point pleases the men whom I see, viz: that you are calling for reports about the army and the navy. To my mind, there is not a question that we should have some system of education for our population like the Swiss system, where all boys are obliged to drill, go into camp for a certain time to learn their lesson, and then to go each year for a few days or so. Nothing would do our people more good than to acquire the habits of obedience and respect, and the physical training would be excellent for them. But, beyond that, we need a larger army and a great deal better navy, and we need them now. A considerable lot of the best men here from thirty to forty years of age have arranged to go to the camp at Plattsburg—[1] men of position, of large duties, men whose time is valuable. That spirit has been awakened, and it will do much good.

I hear constantly the talk about peace, and no one who has ever had the honor to serve in the army doubts the wisdom and the rightfulness of peace. But if the great nations threaten us, or may threaten us, we cannot talk about peace. Our condition really is pitiable in that regard, and if anybody supposes that militia are of any use against regular soldiers, they are greatly mistaken. When we first went out in 1861, we saw a considerable body of militia, and they were an absolute hindrance and interference with carrying out our duties and with the habits of the three-year volunteers whom we were trying to make into soldiers, and who made an excellent army—on both sides. Until men learn to move instinctively and without thinking of their movements, to obey instantly without question and to treat their officers with absolute respect and confidence, they will not be soldiers. And, with the present warfare conducted by machinery, we have a great deal to learn and a great deal to do.

You know all this, but, talking with Colonel House the other day, I received the impression that you were not sorry to hear from men situated as I am, who want nothing except the welfare of their country.

We all note the newspaper comments in Germany on your last letter to Berlin. The Germans are very thick-headed, and they cannot get a new idea without a surgical operation.

I had much pleasure in seeing Mr. and Mrs. Lansing last Saturday, and was glad to think of such a man in your Cabinet.

I am, with great respect,

Very truly yours,   Henry L. Higginson

TLS (WP, DLC).
[1] About this, see EMH to WW, Aug. 8, 1915, n. 1.

From Charles William Eliot

Dear Mr. President: Asticou, Maine 26 July, 1915

May I say that your last Note to Germany is altogether admirable in matter, style, and spirit. So far as I can judge, you have the whole American people behind you, except a few people who thought that you should have seized Northern Mexico, more than a year ago, with intent to keep it, and who now think that the United States should declare war on Germany, Austria-Hungary, and Turkey at the earliest moment which our constitutional process will permit. This minority seems to me insignificant.

I still hope, however, that you will find or make opportunity to tell Germany just what the neutral Powers think of her mode of making war, and of her prospects in this terrible convulsion. This would not be a diplomatic paper; but it would be in the truest sense a friendly communication and a paper in advocacy of peace. In your present Note you have dealt conclusively with several of the points mentioned in my letter of July 16th; but is there not an effective plea for the cessation of hostilities which you as President of the United States could make better than any other person in the world? It seems to me possible to present simultaneously an argument for peace to both Germany and Great Britain, always provided that the territorial status of last July be first re-established by common consent. It would not be a diplomatic document, or in accordance with diplomatic custom, but it would surely be a humane effort, and it might prove to be effective sooner or later. It would be a restrained document, although it would try to express "the feelings which have stirred this country and the world," to quote a phrase from your cordial note to me of July 22nd.

Sincerely yours,   [C. W. Eliot]

CCL (C. W. Eliot Papers, MH-Ar).

A Telegram and a Letter to Robert Lansing

EXTREMELY CONFIDENTIAL.

Windsor, Vermont July 27, 1915.

Instructions of Sir Edward Grey to Ambassador about cotton[1] gives me deep concern. Am I mistaken in my recollection that the British Government formally notified us that cotton would be regarded as not already contraband and would be continued to be so treated.   **Woodrow Wilson**

T telegram (SDR, RG 59, 763.72112/1399½, DNA).
   [1] See WHP to RL, July 22, 1915, printed as an Enclosure with WW to EMH, July 27, 1915 (second letter of that date).

My dear Mr. Secretary,   [Cornish, N.H.] 27 July, 1915.

Thank you sincerely for letting me see this letter from Thomas Nelson Page.[1] The information he gives us from the insid[e] viewpoint of the recent indiscretion of the Pope[2] is most interesting, and shows where many currents are running.

Faithfully Yours,   W.W.

WWTLI (SDR, RG 59, 763.72119/89½, DNA).

1 T. N. Page to RL, June 30, 1915, TLS (SDR, RG 59, 763.72119/88½, DNA).

2 On June 21, the Paris newspaper, *La Liberté*, published an interview with Pope Benedict XV by Louis Latapie, a member of its staff. In general, the Pope expressed opinions that were noticeably pro-German. However, the Pontiff's principal indiscretion was in voicing complaints critical of the Italian government and people. He criticized the government for mobilizing part of his security guard for national service and for allegedly opening mail intended for the Vatican. He also suggested that defeat in the war might lead the Italian people to revolution, one which would directly affect the papacy. The interview created a furor in Italy and stirred up much anti-clerical sentiment. In an interview published in Rome on June 28, Cardinal Pietro Gasparri, the papal Secretary of State, disavowed much of the interview as being totally inaccurate, specifically including the portions dealing with the relations of the papacy to the Italian government and people. In the letter cited in n. 1 above, Page stated that Gasparri had taken this course as the only way out of an awkward and potentially dangerous situation. In addition to Page's letter, see the *New York Times*, June 22, 25, 26, and 29, 1915.

To Edward Mandell House

My dear Friend,   [Cornish, N. H.] 27 July, 1915.

It has given me a great deal of satisfaction to think of you and Lansing in conference, and I am heartily glad that your impression of him has been confirmed by his visit.

He need not fear that I will insist on Palmer unless he is entirely convinced that he is the best man in sight. Personally I am inclined to think that he is; but I want Lansing to sati[s]fy himself of that; and in the meantime I am more than willing to discuss anyone else. Houston thinks that his department Solicitor, Caffey,[1] would make an admirable choice, and is generous enough to be willing to let us have him for the State Department if it is thought best to transfer him.

I feel very keenly the difficulties of dealing with Great Britain in regard to her present treatment of neutral trade, and think of it just as you do. I wonder if you and Lansing discussed, in your talk the other day, a line of action at once practicable and effective that would escape the consequences you (and I) would dread and deplore?[2] I would deeply appreciate any suggestions you may have thought out on this infinitely difficult matter. We cannot long delay action. Our public opinion clearly demands it.

With deep affection,

Faithfully Yours,   Woodrow Wilson

WWTLS (E. M. House Papers, CtY).

1 Francis Gordon Caffey.

2 As soon will become evident, Wilson was beginning to search for alterna-

tives to war, the principal one of which was the effective re-establishment of international law governing maritime warfare by a conference of the neutral nations, which the United States would head.

To Edward Mandell House, with Enclosure

Dear Friend   [Cornish, N. H., July 27, 1915]

This came to me after I had sealed my letter of this morning. It seems to me very serious indeed. Do you think it would be of any use to get into direct communication with Sir Edward?

In haste   Affy   W.W.

ALI (E. M. House Papers, CtY).

ENCLOSURE

London July 22, 1915.

2510. Confidential. Sir Edward Grey has just informed me that he has telegraphed his Ambassador at Washington that the British Government will make cotton contraband before the new crop gets to market. The British Commercial Attache at Washington[1] is instructed to confer with the cotton interests and to (#) to some satisfactory working arrangement whereby this country will buy large quantities at a good price. Whatever arrangement is made will be announced when the announcement is made that cotton will be contraband.

American Ambassador, London.

T telegram (E. M. House Papers, CtY).
  [1] Sir Richard Frederick Crawford, commercial adviser to the British Embassy in Washington.

To Henry Lee Higginson

My dear Major: Cornish, N. H., July 27, 1915

Your letter of July twenty-sixth is most welcome and I have read it with the greatest appreciation and accord with your own thinking.

Cordially and sincerely yours,   [Woodrow Wilson]

CCL (Letterpress Books, WP, DLC).

To Cleveland Hoadley Dodge

My dear Cleve: Cornish, N. H., July 27, 1915

Thank you with all my heart for your letter of July twenty-sixth. I know that wherever you are, you are thinking of me and I want you to know also that that knowledge gives the greatest comfort.

These are indeed trying and perplexing days and a message like this from you is just what I need.

With warmest affection,

Faithfully yours,   Woodrow Wilson

TLS (WC, NjP).

From Robert Lansing

Dear Mr. President: Washington July 27, 1915.

I enclose a copy of the English note we have received in reply to ours of March 30th.[1] It was intended to have this note published simultaneously in England and the United States Wednesday morning, but last night I received a telegram from Mr. Page, saying that Sir Edward Grey would have ready within a week another note dealing with the practical questions relating to shipping, and he therefore requested that publication be delayed until the latter note had been delivered.

Faithfully yours,   Robert Lansing

TLS (WP, DLC).
[1] WHP to RL, July 24, 1915, T telegram (WP, DLC), printed in *FR-WWS 1915*, pp. 168-71. In this note, Sir Edward Grey defended at length the British blockade and made no significant concessions to the point of view set forth in the American note of March 30, 1915.

From Robert Lansing, with Enclosure

Dear Mr. President: Washington July 27, 1915.

I have just received from Ambassador Page at London, the enclosed telegram which is addressed to you and me.

Faithfully yours,   Robert Lansing

TLS (WP, DLC).

E N C L O S U R E

London July 27, 1915.

2536. Very confidential. To the Secretary and the President.

The public and private and official and unofficial comment on our latest note to Germany is practically unanimous in approval. Most of it is of very hearty commendation. The very general opinion as far as I can gather it is that war is inevitable between the United States and Germany. Nobody seems to believe that Germany will meet our demands nor that she will cease her unlawful submarine acts.

American Ambassador, London.

T telegram (WP, DLC).

To Morris Sheppard

Personal.

My dear Senator: Cornish, N. H., July 28, 1915

Thank you for your letter of July twenty-second. I think I realize the seriousness of the situation of our cotton as keenly as any man in the United States, but I am none the less obliged for reminders about this all-important matter.

The whole subject is surrounded with complexities and difficulties which I should not like to put in a letter but which I should like some day to discuss with you. It does not seem as if we ought to go the length of involving the country in war and so cut off the market for cotton altogether, and yet there are many serious offences being committed on the other side of the water.

Cordially and sincerely yours,   [Woodrow Wilson]

CCL (Letterpress Books, WP, DLC).

From Robert Lansing

[Washington] July 28, 1915

Confidential. Your telegram of twenty-seventh concerning cotton. Your recollection as to British assurance that cotton was a non-contraband and would continue so is correct. The language of Sir Edward Grey's telegram to British Ambassador, a copy of which was handed me on October twenty-sixth, contained the following regarding cotton:

"It is therefore as far as we are concerned in the free list and will remain there."

On the same day Mr. Page telegraphed, "Sir Edward Grey makes the positive declaration to me that cotton is not contraband and as far as the British Government is concerned will not be." Similar assurances were given by the French Government in December.

These declarations were given wide publicity in the department through letters and the Press.

The change of policy which is evidently determined upon by the British Government as shown by the telegram received yesterday afternoon from Mr. Page (which I will repeat to you) will cause intense dissatisfaction in this country and the demands for retaliatory measures which will undoubtedly be made will embarrass us seriously. I am afraid that the question will become a political rather than a diplomatic one.

I had a talk with Spring-Rice on the subject Monday in which I told him that for his government to put cotton on the contraband list was a confession that their alleged blockade was ineffective; that if it was effective and their theory of blockade was correct, it was needless to declare cotton contraband, since all articles regardless of their character would be prevented from entering or leaving Germany. I said that if cotton was made contraband at this time, we should have to assume that their theory of blockade as far as neutral ports were concerned had been abandoned and we would proceed on that assumption, which would create a very difficult situation. I also pointed out to him the resentment which would be caused in this country by the proposed action and by the feeling that Great Britain had broken her promise, and that his government could not hold us responsible for the consequences.[1]

I am telegraphing Page the substance of my statements to Spring-Rice.

The following is the telegram received from Page yesterday afternoon:

"July twenty-seventh, 3 P.M. Confidential. I had another long informal private conversation with Sir Edward Grey yesterday which might almost be intimate, about the whole relation between the United States and Great Britain. I explained to him with candor and frankness the whole political situation in the United States. He is alive to the dangers and difficulties and he will try in the additional note he is now preparing to clear away as many difficulties as possible. I advised him, since the Cabinet has decided to make cotton contraband, to announce this fact soon, because cotton is sold long in advance of delivery. He will probably include this announcement in his forthcoming note. Sir Edward will go to the limit of his ability to make British action bear as lightly on American interests as possible."

Robert Lansing.

T telegram (WP, DLC).

[1] Spring Rice reported fully on this conversation in C. A. Spring Rice to E. Grey, July 28, 1915, T telegram (FO 382/464, No. 103289, PRO).

From Edward Mandell House, with Enclosure

Manchester, Massachusetts.

Dear Governor: July 28th, 1915.

I am enclosing you a copy of a letter I have just received from Bernstorff.

I did not arrange to see him as I first planned because he was conferring with Lansing and I did not think it necessary in these circumstances, to do so. I am trying to plan a way to see him without it becoming known.

Your autograph note, enclosing a memorandum from Page, came this morning, but not the other letter of which you speak. The postmaster assorted the mail himself and he says there was but one letter in a White House envelope. If it comes during the day I will add a line to this.

I think the time has come for me to get in touch with Sir Edward direct and I shall do so at once. I have a feeling that as far as the cotton producer is concerned, the proposal to purchase it would be more to our advantage than the present arrangement. This though, would not satisfy the people that are creating this agitation. I see evidences of a systematic and well financed campaign in the South. Papers that formerly took one view have turned almost in a night to a contrary one, and I notice one after the other joining the cry.

The[re] are some curious things going on in this country and I received some information the other day that may give us some light. I also have some information concerning the leakage in the State Department, and the names of two men (both of them, by the way, Bryan men) are given. I am arranging to let Lansing have this information so he may run it down.

Delano and Governor Strong of the New York Federal reserve Bank, were here yesterday to see me concerning the serious condition that confronts us in regard to foreign exchange. They believe that unless the Federal Reserve System broadens its basis of credits that another month or two will bring about a crisis and almost a complete breakdown of our foreign trade.

They told me that three of the Reserve Board are in favor of broadening the credits, but that two are opposed to it. They did not give the names for it was not necessary.[1]

My advice was that while we were living under abnormal conditions we should have the courage to meet them in a way that will redound to the advantage of our country, and that credits should be broadened as far as perfect safety would permit. I hope this view meets with your approval.

Affectionately yours,   E. M. House

6 P.M. The letter has not yet come.[2]

TLS (WP, DLC).
  [1] About this matter, see WGM to WW, Aug. 21, 1915.
  [2] It had been mistakenly sent to the White House and mailed from there.

E N C L O S U R E

Count Johann Heinrich von Bernstorff to Edward Mandell House

My dear Colonel House: Washington, D. C. July 27th, 1915.

Many thanks for your kind letter of 12th inst. The present situation is not pleasant. In the last American note such strong language was used that I am afraid I will not be able to do much in the matter. Nevertheless I am doing my best, but my efforts will certainly fail, if the expected American note to England does not use just as strong a language as that employed towards us.

At present nobody in Germany believes in the impartiality of the American Government. That is the great difficulty of the situation. Very much ill feeling has been created on both sides of the ocean and any—not "deliberately unfriendly," but unintended unfortunate, incident may bring about war any moment.

Nevertheless I have taken up the matter and, if my efforts are successful, I hope it will be possible for me to negotiate informally and confidentially with the Secretary of State with regard to the contents of our answer. If this is feasible, we may be able to give an answer which satisfies both sides and opens the way for negociations about the "freedom of the sea." We must *certainly* stop publishing sharp and unsatisfactory notes. I do not think that public opinion in either country can stand that much longer. If I cannot persuade my Government to give an answer, we will have to trust to our good luck and hope that no incident will occur which brings about war.

Very sincerely yours,   J. Bernstorff.

TCL (WP, DLC).

From Albert Sidney Burleson, with Enclosure

My dear Mr. President: [Washington] July 28, 1915.

Enclosed please find a letter from Representative James Hay, of Virginia.[1] I beg to suggest that I think it would be wise, as soon as you can find time, to ask Mr. Hay to confer with you about the administration of the proposed military program. I feel sure that Mr. Hay is anxious to cooperate with you in any plan you will propose looking toward preparedness in the Military Establishment.

I also enclose an editorial from the St. Louis Republic, and two letters which I think may prove of interest to you. When you have read the letters you may destroy them.[2]

I sincerely hope you may continue to enjoy your well earned rest.   Sincerely yours,   A. S. Burleson

TLS (WP, DLC).
[1] He was chairman of the House Military Affairs Committee.
[2] Wilson apparently did so. The editorial is also missing.

E N C L O S U R E

James Hay to Albert Sidney Burleson

My dear Albert: [Madison, Va.] July 27, 1915.

I have seen in the newspapers, with a great deal of satisfaction, that the President has taken up the question of national defense and proposes to give it his personal attention. I would like very much to see you and talk with you about this question, as it is one of an intricate character in very many of its aspects. I see that the War Department is counting on raising an army of 500,000 men, either as part of the regular army or as reserves. I have had, as you know, a long experience with propositions offered to Congress by the War Department. Such a proposition as the one above referred to is impossible of being practically worked out for the reason that, without compulsory military service, it is impossible in this country to get a large number of men to enlist in the army, either as regular soldiers or as reservists. This is one of the questions that I would like to talk to you about.

I also would like to call your attention to the fact that the proposition to increase the coast artillery is not a practical or useful one. It is not necessary for me to go into the reasons, but I could convince you, I am sure, in a very few minutes that it will not be useful or practical to do this. I believe that it would be wise to increase the regular army to the extent of providing that its organization be kept to war strength in times of peace and that we should increase our filed [field] artillery. Something must also be done for the organized militia.

When it will be convenient for you to see me, let me know, and I will come down here any time.

Sincerely yours,   James Hay

TLS (WP, DLC).

From Horace Herbert Clark,[1] with Enclosure

Dear Mr. President: Los Angeles, Calif July 28/15.

Conforming with our conversation of the 19th inst. I am enclosing a promisory note for $7,500. signed by Mrs. Mary Allen Hulbert, bearing interest at 6% and maturing in six months.

May I ask you to kindly sign the enclosed receipt for the mortgages and forward to me at your convenience.

Greatly appreciating the courtesy and honor extended to me both at Windsor and at the White House, I am,

Very sincerely yours   H. H. Clark

ALS (WP, DLC).
[1] A businessman of Los Angeles, who was a financial agent for Mrs. Hulbert.

ENCLOSURE

July 19/15

Received from Mary Allen Hulbert the following Mortgages and bonds covering the properties listed below:

Property located in the Bronx and designated, house numbers 1988 and 1990 Cruger Ave; property known as 419 East 239th Street; lots known as 148 and 149 on the west side of Macomb's Road about 63.32 feet south of 174th St.

Woodrow Wilson[1]

HwS MS (WP, DLC).
[1] Wilson signed and returned the receipt. It was later returned to him when he purchased the mortgages.

Frank Buchanan[1] to Joseph Patrick Tumulty

My Dear Mr. Tumulty: Chicago, Ill., July 28, 1915.

Your favor of the 24th inst. duly received, and, to put the situation mildly, was decidedly disappointing in character. The information it contained, though courteously phrased, could not, and did not, alter the inference forced by the statement made.

Your intimation that the President's time was so fully taken up with matters of pressing importance that he could not grant an audience to representatives of labor, that has made the United States of America the proud nation that it is, in order to permit them in person to demonstrate that the subsidized press, representing organized dollars in America, which is seeking to serve as the volunteer adviser of the President, was misrepresenting labor's attitude in the present crisis, is tantamount to a declaration that the President is more concerned about the desires of big business than he is to discover the heartfelt sentiment of the common people.

As is well known, I, by the vote of the people, was taken from the ranks of America's toilers to serve them in the Hall of Congress, and as their representative to voice their opinion on national questions. As a trade unionist I found that the first lesson taught by organized labor was to implant in the hearts and minds of its members the ethics of humanity and the sacredness of human life.

War is generally regarded by the common people, who are its only victims, as legalized murder on a wholesale plane, which all the sophistry of questionable patriots and demagogues can never invest, and yet, the President cannot find time to listen to the people who desire peace, because his time is completely occupied by those who apparently desire war.

I thank you, Mr. Tumulty, for your candor. My duty to those I serve leaves me no alternative but to say that so long as they, the people whom I serve, continue to be united in their belief that progress and prosperity is dependent upon religious observance of the scriptu[r]al admonition, "And they shall beat their swords into ploughshares and their spears into pruning hooks; nation shall not lift up sword against nation, neither shall they learn war any more," just so long shall I continue to rap at the door of the President's private chambers to secure admittance for a delegation of workers, who not only desire peace at home but peace abroad as well.

I again urge upon you to kindly present to the President my desire for a conference and inform him that, if I am to be denied the courtesy so liberally extended to Congressmen speaking for Big Business, I shall be reluctantly forced to advise the public of my position in the premises through the medium of an open letter.

Awaiting your reply, I have the honor to be,

Very truly yours,   Frank Buchanan.

Printed in the *New York Times*, Aug. 10, 1915.
 1 Democratic congressman from Illinois and former president of the International Union of Bridge and Structural Iron Workers. He was president of the
Labors' National Peace Council, organized in Washington on June 21, 1915,
with generous German money behind it, to agitate for an arms embargo and
other policies favorable to Germany. Buchanan, along with Franz Rintelen von
Kleist and others, were indicted by a federal grand jury in New York on December 28, 1915, for instigating strikes, interfering with interstate and foreign
commerce, and bribery. Rintelen and two other defendants were convicted on
May 20, 1917, but the jury failed to agree on Buchanan and other defendants.
They were never re-tried.
 Buchanan wrote his letter of July 28 to Tumulty in response to a letter from
the latter stating that he had had no time during Wilson's brief return to
Washington from Cornish to put before the President Buchanan's earlier request for an appointment at the White House.

To Robert Lansing

My dear Mr. Secretary,   [Cornish, N. H.] 29 July, 1915.

The many distressing and disturbing despatches pouring in
from Mexico[1] perplex me sadly as to what our immediate duty is.
I note the messages you are sending to Villa and indirectly to
Zapata, and I suppose that they represent all that we can do for
the present.[2] If *any*thing else should occur to you as practicable,
will you not let me have the suggestion to think over. I feel that
a final crisis at Mexico City might make more deliberate plans
at any moment next to impossible.

                              Faithfully Yours,   W.W.

WWTLI (SDR, RG 59, 812.00/15629½, DNA).
 1 RL to WW, July 29, 1915, three T telegrams, two in WP, DLC, the third in
EBR, RG 130, DNA. The first two embodied messages from John R. Silliman
reporting continued severe food shortages and resulting starvation in Mexico
City. The third contained a report from William W. Canada about an assault
upon a United States diplomatic courier carrying messages from Puebla to
Mexico City and about other outrages allegedly perpetrated by followers of
Emiliano Zapata.
 2 RL to WW, July 29, 1915, T telegram (EBR, RG 130, DNA). Lansing herein
quoted dispatches which he had just sent to various American agents in Mexico
embodying messages to Zapata, urging him to cease his attacks on foreigners
and diplomatic couriers; to Villa, requesting that he use his influence to restrain
Zapata; and to Carranza, demanding that he reopen the railway to Mexico City
in order that succor might reach that afflicted capital.

Two Letters from Edward Mandell House

                              Manchester, Massachusetts.
Dear Governor: July 29th, 1915.

Your letter of July 27th which should have come yesterday
reached me today via Washington.

I am glad you have an open mind about the Counsellor for
the State Department. Dudley Malone was here yesterday and
he said he had noticed from the press that you intended to appoint Palmer. He expressed a warm liking for Palmer, but said

he was sure the same condition would follow his appointment as existed between Mr. Bryan and John Bassett Moore.

I understand that Burleson will be here for this week end and I will see if something cannot be worked out for Palmer that will satisfy him, provided Lansing still feels as he does.

Caffey seems to me to be a good thought and while I do not know him I have confidence in Houston's judgment concerning his fitness.

I think within a week or ten days I may be able to advise you more intelligently as to the best course to take with Great Britain. In this connection I have called Lansing's attention to the fact that in dealing with England we are dealing just as directly with France, Italy and Russia. That while England is assuming the responsibility yet she has the entire sympathy of her allies. I know that the feeling in France is even more insistent than it is in England, and if the latter were not to the fore, France would be.

I suggested to Lansing also that he get Houston to give out some facts in regard to the cotton situation, particularly in regard to the export of that commodity, which do not seem to be generally known. The people of the South are being misinformed and misled and should be set right by the proper authorities.

Affectionately yours,   E. M. House

Dear Governor:

Manchester, Massachusetts.
July 29th, 1915.

Page's Secretary, young Carver,[1] writes me an exceedingly interesting letter.

In lunching with the Cahncellor [Chancellor] of the Exchequer he met Lord Fisher and Lady Ian Hamilton.[2] Fisher said at the luncheon that a new gas had been discovered by an English chemist, far heavier than air, which clings to the ground in great clouds and is to be used in timed explosive shells. The shells are to be used first in the Dardanelles.

Fisher also remarked that the adventure of the Dardanelles had been one of the greatest tragedies of his life.

Another thing that came out was that at the present moment the British coast is practically unprotected, as far as submarines are concerned. All the available destroyers and torpedo boats have been sent to the Dardanelles.

Carver adds "It is a dangerous moment for the country should the Germans discover this, and I firmly believe that an almighty fear is at the bottom of the hearts of the Cabinet as to permanent blockade of these parts being established as a result of this action. In fact, Lord Fisher said without hesitation that he believed that English shipping and the neutral shipping had never been endangered to the extent it is at the present moment."

The recklessness with which the English officials talk is beyond understanding. I have a feeling that Lord Fisher is piqued and is given to criticizing the Admiralty.

Your affectionate,　E. M. House

TLS (WP, DLC).
1 Clifford Nickels Carver, Princeton 1913, private secretary to Walter Hines Page.
2 Jean Miller Muir Hamilton, wife of General Sir Ian Standish Monteith Hamilton, commander of the British army at Gallipoli.

Two Telegrams from Robert Lansing

Washington, D. C., July 29, 1915

I have received the following telegram from Gama:

"Have cabled twice to Rio de Janeiro since our last conversation, so far receiving no answer, Considering situation. I venture to suggest that you begin work while I cable again explaining matter. Am writing."

Shall I proceed with the others or wait a few days?

Robert Lansing.

T telegram (WP, DLC).

Washington, D. C. July 29-15

Owing to Naon's telling me that he is going to leave for Buenos Aires in about twenty days, I have decided to go ahead with the conference of the six Latin Americans and so have called an informal conference for Thursday, August fifth, at two thirty PM., at which probably all will be present except perhaps Da Gama.

Robert Lansing

T telegram (SDR, RG 59, 812.00/15627½A, DNA).

To Robert Lansing

My dear Mr. Secretary,　　　　[Cornish, N. H.] 29 July, 1915.

I entirely approve of this suggestion, and hope that you will act upon it at once.　　　　Faithfully Yours, ˌ W.W.

WWTLI (SDR, RG 59, 812.00/15628½, DNA).

From Robert Lansing

Washington, D. C., July 29, 1915

I have received the following telegram from Gerard, dated July 27th 11 A.M.:

"I gather that German Government will endeavor to let submarine controversy drag along as long as possible without coming to a definite break. The Germans are making prodigious efforts to bring war to a close before entering upon another winter campaign and they now hope and expect to take Warsaw in near future and to shorten their lines in Poland so that one or two million men can be spared for the West front, in order to break through to Calais or Paris. They would, therefore, be glad to avoid further complications at present. At the same time, both Press and Foreign Office are extremely angry at the American note and there is much bluster about continuing the submarine warfare without restriction. It is not yet possible to gauge whether this is bluff or in earnest, but from present indications I am inclined to think that the 'deliberately unfriendly' act specified in the American note will be avoided."

Robert Lansing.

T telegram (WP, DLC).

To Edward Mandell House

My dear Friend,   [Cornish, N. H.] 29 [30] July, 1915.

Thank you for your letters of the twenty-eighth and twenty-ninth.

I am glad that you feel that within a week or so you will have something in your mind to suggest as to the best way of dealing with the English. I feel as fully as you do the various difficulties of the situation, and the acute difficulty of our own public opinion, which is being deliberately framed against us.

I do not feel that Bernstorff is dealing frankly with us, somehow, and, if you have the opportunity, you might see what you can do to make him feel that it is up to him to do more than he has done to make his Government realize facts as they are.

I am glad that you are to talk with Burleson about Palmer. The case worries me a good deal.

WWTL (E. M. House Papers, CtY).

To Joseph Patrick Tumulty

[Cornish, N. H. July 30, 1915]

Please see the Acting Secretary of Commerce and the Secretary of the Navy and see what they think of the feasibility and the advisability of an investigation by a board of inquiry constituted of naval officers and whether I have the authority under law to constitute such a board for such a purpose.[1]

Woodrow Wilson.

WWT telegram (WP, DLC).
[1] That is, to investigate the *Eastland* disaster. Tumulty replied that Daniels and Sweet agreed with Wilson's plan but thought that Redfield should be consulted. To this end, Sweet was going to Chicago "to present the matter . . . and to try to induce the Secretary himself to request you to take this action." He added: "Personally, I think this plan is an excellent one and that it ought to be carried out at all cost." JPT to WW, July 30, 1915, T telegram (WP, DLC).

To Charles William Eliot

My dear Doctor Eliot: Cornish, N. H., July 30, 1915

Thank you for your letter of July twenty-sixth. It gives me deep gratification that our last note to Germany should have met with your warm approval.

I think I appreciate the occasion as you describe it for making a more comprehensive and less formal statement of the feeling of the country about some of the aspects of the war. I can only say that I shall watch my opportunities very carefully and it may be that some opening that will be natural and obvious will occur when I can express myself with greater freedom than in official documents.

With warm regard,

Cordially and sincerely yours, Woodrow Wilson

TLS (C. W. Eliot Papers, MH-Ar).

From Josephus Daniels

Washington, D. C. July 30-15

Report from admiral Caperton Portauprince says in attack 8 P.M. last night by sniping in outskirts two seamen were killed[1] attack repulsed quiet and order maintained in town throughout no cause for alarm am sending Connecticut with 500 marines at request of Admiral Caperton

Josephus Daniels

T telegram (WP, DLC).
[1] Rear Admiral William Banks Caperton, U.S.N., commander of the Cruiser

Squadron of the Atlantic Fleet, had spent much of his time since January 1915 in Haitian waters on board his flagship, *U.S.S. Washington*, keeping close watch on revolutionary activity in Haiti. An insurrection broke out in Port-au-Prince against the incumbent President, Vilbrun Guillaume Sam, on July 27. With his regime tottering, Sam ordered the execution of some one hundred and seventy political prisoners. The order was carried out in very brutal fashion. The news of this slaughter led to a frenzy of mob violence in which the prison commandant was shot to death and, on the following day, President Sam was dragged from his refuge in the French legation and literally torn to pieces. In response to this storm of violence, severe even by contemporary Haitian standards, and to demands by the entire diplomatic corps for protection of foreigners, Admiral Caperton landed a force of 330 sailors and marines on the evening of the twenty-eighth, an action which was soon backed up by a direct order from Washington and which marked the beginning of a lengthy occupation of Haiti by American forces. The two sailors mentioned in the above telegram died on the second night of the occupation; subsequent investigation suggested that they might have been killed by the gunfire of their own nervous comrades. See Arthur S. Link, *Wilson: The Struggle for Neutrality, 1914-1915* (Princeton, N. J., 1960), pp. 532-34, and David Healy, *Gunboat Diplomacy in the Wilson Era: The U. S. Navy in Haiti, 1915-1916* (Madison, Wisc., 1976), pp. 54-67.

To Robert Lansing, with Enclosure

My dear Mr. Secretary,   Cornish, N. H. 31 July, 1915.

This is really a very interesting report, and the paper enclosed is little less than amazing in its detailed revelation of the whole German state of mind as (I have no doubt truthfully) represented by these various associations.

Faithfully Yours,   W. W.

WWTLI (SDR, RG 59, 763.72119/83, DNA).

E N C L O S U R E

James Watson Gerard to Robert Lansing

Confidential.

Sir: Berlin, July 13, 1915.

I have the honor to acknowledge the receipt of the Department's instruction of June 17th, (File No. 763.72119/68; Serial No. 927) relative to certain conditions in Germany, and to reply as follows.

I. The Foreign Office complains bitterly that it is under the control to a great extent of the Military and Naval authorities. Von Jagow told me that Bismarck had the same difficulty in 1870 and that he speaks of it in his memoirs. In this war there has been added the influence of the Marine Department, headed by von Tirpitz a popular character (largely on account of his aggressiveness and his beard) and the Marine Staff and Marine Kabinet all independent and all reporting direct to the Kaiser. In fact all measures are agreed on by a sort of Junta consisting of the Chancellor and Foreign Office, von Tirpitz, von Müller, (naval Kabinet) Behncke[1] (naval staff Berlin) von Falkenhayn (General Staff), the Emperor, and sometimes, on commercial questions, Delbrück of the Interior Department, and people like Ballin[2] (of the Hamburg-American Line) and von Gwinner[3] and others of big banks. The influence of von Tirpitz is great; Falkenhayn is a courtier and has the ear of the Emperor, while the Chancellor bores the Emperor to death. On the submarine warfare question von Tirpitz wanted to establish a blockade of individual English ports, while the Admiralty Staff, of which von Pohl[4] was the head, at that time, succeeded in carrying through the proposition of a war-zone and the general submarine war as now carried on. The Admiralty people have a very effective press bureau. The War Ministry has taken a purely administrative place.

II. The Socialist party had agreed to "bury the hatchet" during the war. Liebknecht himself told me that they were united and relied on the army and that they must stand against Russian "Czarismus." This was before the "Gott strafe England" craze. There is now quite a split, the party leaders like Haase, Bernheim,[5] and others being ready to criticize the Government and ask about the object of the war; but I am convinced the majority is against them; they cannot however be read out of the party except in a general assembly which they are not allowed to hold. A small number are in favor of annexing Belgium. I think it is safe to say that the Socialists are for the war but against annexation of more territory.

III. The more prosperous Germans are divided into two groups; one composed of "Junkers" (country squires) and the ultra conservatives and royalists is for an understanding with Russia after the war. The other group consisting of shipowners, manufacturers and bankers and business men are for an understanding with England. The Bund Neues Vaterland represents the latter group; an abstract of a leaflet issued by this "Bund" to its members, confidentially, is enclosed.[6]

IV. The spirit of the people is absolutely unbroken; they believe in ultimate victory and certainly have had no defeats. The wonderful organization takes care of everyone; money is plentiful, in fact there is a period of inflation. Wives of soldiers get a war allowance and so much per child and are better off than in peace times.

Public works such as extending the underground railroad in Berlin are being carried on. Small towns and villages feel the war more than Berlin; but there are no signs of failure of war spirit. Perhaps if the war means another winter campaign there may be a different spirit. I have heard many hints to that effect.

As to Germany's war methods, they have the full approval of the people; the sinking of the "Lusitania" was universally approved, and even men like von Gwinner, head of the German Bank, say they will treat the "Mauretania" in the same way if she comes out.

V. The general public want to keep Belgium. They say the sacrifices of the war demand a compensation. They are led by the official opinion. Only the Socialists want no new territory and there is a dissenting party even among them. People in Government circles say that to give up Belgium would be to invite a revolution and the expulsion of the Hohenzollerns. The whole German people is dangerously mad. I cannot give you in detail the sources of my information—most of it is confidential, but I have personal relations with all classes.

I have the honor to be, Sir,

Your obedient servant,   James W. Gerard.

TLS (SDR, RG 59, 763.72119/83, DNA).
  [1] Admiral Paul L. Gustav Behncke, deputy head of the German Admiralty.
  [2] Albert Ballin, managing director of the Hamburg-American Line and an important informal adviser to the German government.
  [3] Arthur von Gwinner, head of the Deutsche Bank.
  [4] Admiral Hugo von Pohl, head of the Admiralty.
  [5] Hugo Haase and Eduard Bernstein, leaders of the radical pacifist wing of the Social Democratic Party.
  [6] Circular of the "Neus Vaterland" League, June 20, 1915, T MS (SDR, RG 59, 763.72119/83, DNA). Gerard was confused about the Bund Neues Vaterland. It was founded in November 1914 by liberal intellectuals and socialists. The abstract that Gerard enclosed was a summary of a petition addressed to the Imperial Chancellor on May 20, 1915, by six organizations representing the largest industrial and business interests of Germany. The Bund replied in a petition addressed to Bethmann Hollweg on June 20, 1915. Both petitions are printed in S. Grumbach, *Das Annexionistische Deutschland* (Lausanne, 1917), pp. 123-31, 375-409.

To William Cox Redfield

My dear Mr. Secretary: Cornish, N. H., July 31, 1915

I have received your several messages about the Eastland investigation[1] and am sincerely obliged to you for keeping me in touch with it. I have never for a moment doubted that you were doing everything that it was possible to do, and doing it with your usual thoroughness and fair spirit.

Mr. Sweet will have told you what occurred to me as a method of supplementing your investigation and relieving the intolerable pressure upon you, and I shall be very much interested to know what you think of the suggestion.

With warmest regard and genuine regret that this burden should have suddenly come upon you,
        Cordially and sincerely yours,   [Woodrow Wilson]

CCL (Letterpress Books, WP, DLC).
    1 W. C. Redfield to WW, July 26, 2:06 P.M. and 2:40 P.M., and July 30, 1915, T telegrams; and P. J. Stevenson to WW, July 27, 1915, TLS (WP, DLC).

To Paul Samuel Reinsch

Windsor Vt Jul 31 [1915]

Your letter was greatly appreciated and it is a matter of genuine regret with me that a personal interview should have proved impracticable and particularly that your illness should have been [the cause] because I think I understand three [the] great questions you refer to and am deeply appreciative of your exposition of them   I shall seek to keep in touch with you in Pekin[1]
        Woodrow Wilson

T telegram (P. S. Reinsch Papers, WHi).
    1 Actually, Wilson saw Reinsch at the White House for an hour on August 18, 1915.

From Robert Lansing, with Enclosure

My Dear Mr. President: Washington July 31, 1915.

I have been studying the proposed Colombian treaty, of which I have had a very superficial knowledge since Mr. Bryan handled the matter without discussing it with me. As a result I know very little of the objections raised by the Senate. Whatever they were they seem to have been effective thus far in preventing consent.

As I recall the press reports, one of the objections, of which much was made, was the so-called "apology" (expression of regret) by this Government; and another was that the amount to be paid to Colombia was considered excessive.

The first objection might possibly be removed by an expression of *mutual* regret instead of one by our Government alone. Perhaps it will not be thought politic to do this, but I am so anxious to see the treaty accepted by the Senate that any suggestion which would remove objections seems to me worthy of consideration. I append a tentative redraft of Article I in line with this suggestion.

In view of the known opposition in this country to the amount to be paid to Colombia might not the consent of that government be obtained to reduce it? Would it be worth while to attempt to have that government agree to such reduction? I believe that in view of the present financial situation of this Government as a result of the European War, the objection as to amount will be stronger than before. I would suggest, therefore, that whatever the total sum may be, this objection would be weakened by amending the terms of payment in some manner such as the following:

(a) Change method of payment of the indemnity in Article III. Instead of payment being made "within six months" the article to read "immediately upon the exchange of ratifications etc. the sum of five million dollars gold, U. S. money, and a similar sum on the same day of *three* successive years thereafter." If necessary, this might be changed to *four* successive years; again making the total twenty-five millions.

(b) To pay the indemnity not in U. S. gold but in Panama Canal Bonds.

(c) Make the following a condition precedent to the payment of any indemnity; by stipulating that

(1) the "material reparation" consist in the United States presenting Colombia with certain public works to be jointly agreed upon; such as the sanitation of Buenaventura and/or Cartagena; and/or the construction of a railway to link the capital with a port on the Pacific and/or the Atlantic; and/or a railway between Cucuta and Tamalamque; and/or a railway from Bogotá to deep water on the Magdalena River; or

(2) The indemnity to be paid to Colombia under United States supervision. An American Financial Adviser will be appointed who shall jointly approve and countersign drafts on the money which the United States will pay by instalments into the Colombian Government's account with some reputable Trust Company in the United States.

I am writing you at this time in regard to possible changes in the treaty because as you know I am sending Mr. Leland Harrison to Colombia to convey to our Minister certain confidential information. Nominally he is going there to take the place of the Secretary of Legation[1] who left on leave a few days ago. I am afraid, however, that the Colombian Government will doubt whether that is the real object of his mission and will be suspicious of his purpose. If he was charged with the duty of assisting Mr. Thomson in sounding confidentially and unofficially the government leaders on certain modifications of the treaty in order to secure its speedy approval by the Senate when it meets, they would not speculate as to other reasons for his visit.

Mr. Harrison is especially well equipped for a delicate mission of this sort. He speaks Spanish fluently and knows more or less intimately all the principal men of Colombia as he was stationed there for three years. He is very discreet, tactful and absolutely trustworthy, and would be of great aid to Mr. Thomson. I feel convinced that he would perform his mission well and would be able on his return to tell us more accurately as to the situation and the possibility of obtaining modifications of the treaty, than would be possible by correspondence.

Colombia we know needs money. She cannot borrow from Europe. Fifteen millions will look much bigger today than twenty-five millions looked fourteen months ago. On the other hand, I am afraid that the Senate's vision will be much the same in view of the decrease in our revenues. But Colombia's need may be so great that she will make concessions in order to obtain the ratification of the treaty early in the next session of Congress.

If the foregoing suggestions meet with your approval, I would like to be advised as soon as possible as I think Harrison should proceed on his secret mission without delay. In any event, if the modifications cannot be obtained, no harm will have been done as the entire affair can be kept secret.

Faithfully yours,   Robert Lansing.

TLS (SDR, RG 59, 711.21/328A, DNA).
¹ Charles B. Curtis.

ENCLOSURE

ARTICLE I.

The Government of the United States of America and the Government of the Republic of Colombia, wishing to put at rest all controversies and differences that may unhappily exist between them by reason of the events from which the present situation on the Isthmus of Panama resulted, express, in their own names and in the names of their respective peoples, sincere regret that anything should have occurred to interrupt or to mar the relations of cordial friendship that had so long subsisted between them, in the full assurance that every obstacle to the restoration of complete harmony between the two nations will thus disappear.

T MS (SDR, RG 59, 711.21/328A, DNA).

From Robert Lansing

Washington D C July 31 [1915]

Six latin American diplomats have agreed to be here Thursday, August fifth for informal conference. When do you think it would be well to make public announcement that conference is to take place. Believe that announcement will have beneficial effect in Mexico and in this country, as indicating intention to proceed.

Robert Lansing

T telegram (SDR, RG 59, 812.00/15629½A, DNA).

From Joseph Patrick Tumulty

Dear Governor:　　　　　　　Avon, New Jersey July 31, 1915.

I am sending you herewith a copy of a letter from Congressman Buchanan of Illinois.[1] I think that the time has arrived when you ought to show in some way your resentment of the intolerant attitude of this gentleman. It seems to me you will find sufficient reason for it in the last paragraph of his letter, which I have underlined.

I think it would be more effective if you would write Buchanan direct or if you do not feel like doing so, you could prepare a letter for my signature. The letter might emphasize this fact,—that no one is more sincerely desirous of bringing about peace than the President himself; that every effort of the Administration since the beginning of this unfortunate war has been given toward the accomplishment of that end; that the only thing that has embarrassed the President in handling these difficult matters has been the attitude of men like Mr. Buchanan himself who had been giving this impression that the Administration and the President in his foreign policy have not behind them a united country, and that the President in his foreign policy has acted as the mouthpiece of Big Business. (See the first page of Mr. Buchanan's letter.)

I think this is a fine opportunity to deliver a scathing rebuke to men of the Buchanan type. The country is waiting for a pronouncement from you on this subject. The statement made by Buchanan is on all fours with the statement uttered by Weismann at Utica a few days ago.[2] You will recall that he referred to you as the mouth-piece of Wall Street and as a political bankrupt. The threat at the very end of Buchanan's letter is sufficient reason why he ought to be publicly rebuked.

Cordially yours,　J. P. Tumulty

TLS (WP, DLC).
[1] This enclosure is missing; Buchanan's letter is printed at July 28, 1915.
[2] At a "Volksfest" in Utica, N. Y., on July 27, Henry Weismann of Brooklyn, president of the New York State German-American Alliance, bitterly attacked Wilson and the supporters of military preparedness, charging that Wall Street was behind the movement. He declared that Wilson's latest note to Germany was an ultimatum and continued:

"I feel that I must differ from the President in any act that brings on danger. I accuse him of having violated his oath of office by transgressing the Constitution that defines the powers of the Executive and separates them from the legislative and other departments. His one-sided neutrality is bringing on war with Germany. His policy closes the door to further discussion. . . .

"This political bankrupt has dared to assume powers that belong to Congress alone. As President he has, by his policies, forfeited his re-election, and unless some grave situation should arise that would require it, his re-election is doomed. Under the Constitution how can the President . . . send an ultimatum to Europe? By this he has created a situation that if Germany by chance should kill a single American, Congress, to uphold his hand and protect him, would put forth the most unjust declaration of war ever penned." *New York Times*, July 27, 1915.

From Edward Mandell House

Dear Governor: Manchester, Mass. July 31st, 1915.

Only the first page of your letter of July 29th came this morning It is not signed or closed so I suppose there must have been another sheet.

Burleson and Tumulty telephoned yesterday from Asbury Park about Palmer. Burleson could not come here because of Mrs Burleson's illness.

I promised him to write Lansing advising him to give up hope of Davis,[1] but I could not agree to urge anybody else. Their main argument for Palmer was that he was a good stump speaker which they said Davis was not, and that he could present the Administration's views upon questions which they seemed to think essential to anyone occupying that office.

If Lansing does quickly and well the two or three things you have in mind for him to do, there will be no need for anyone to defend the Administration for the people will do it themselves.

The main thing I think is always to do the job better than anyone else has ever done it, and the political end will take care of itself. This has always been my theory and I have found it satisfactory and successful.

Affectionately yours,   E. M. House

TLS (WP, DLC).
[1] That is, John W. Davis.

From Hatton William Sumners[1]

Dallas, Texas, July 31, 1915.

I have just returned from a tour over my district. Find a state of general apprehension and rapidly growing resentment because of England's probable attitude towards cotton from neutral with strong ally leaning. Definite and aggressive anti-England sentiment is rapidly developing. My judgment is that if marketing conditions of last season result from England's action President will probably lose control over the south. In dealing with the present situation, I cannot too strongly emphasize gravity of the probable consequences in so far as the south can control.

Hatton W. Sumners.

T telegram (WP, DLC).
    1 Democratic congressman from Dallas, Tex.

To Robert Lansing

My dear Mr. Secretary,   [Cornish, N. H.] 1 August, 1915.

I am very glad of this, and write to ask whether you think it would be best for me to be in Washington at that time or to wait until the deliberations and actions of this group seem to be approaching a point where they can offer practical advice. I should like to do what will best assist psychologically as well as practically.

I think that it will be wise to announce at once the approach of this conference and its objects, in general terms, not too fully disclosing what we wish to leave a little vague, vis. just what we expect the procedure and the action of the U. S. towards what the conference advises to be.   Faithfully Yours,   W.W.

WWTLI (SDR, RG 59, 812.00/15630½, DNA).

From Robert Lansing

Washington, D. C., August 1, 1915

Have received following from Page, London:

"July 31; 2 P.M. Strictly confidential; for the Secretary. I have received an indirect message from the President that conference with you and him might be advantageous under present conditions and I think it is desirable. I can arrange for a visit home almost immediately. If instructed by you to go, I shall have a full conference with Sir Edward Grey about all subjects of present controversy with direct reference to my subsequent conference with you and the President. If you instruct me to go, please give no publicity to my forthcoming visit. I will leave London for a vacation in the country a few days before I sail and let my going, if it should be discovered here, appear merely as a part of my vacation."

What reply shall I make?   Robert Lansing.

T telegram (R. Lansing Coll., NjP).

Two Letters to Robert Lansing

My dear Mr. Secretary,   [Cornish, N. H.] 2 August, 1915.

I do not understand this at all. No one was authorized by me to convey any such intimation to Page,[1] and, as a matter of judgment, I think it would be very unwise for him to come to America just at this time. It would create the impression that something unusually critical was in the wind and that it was of too confidential a nature to be safely handled by correspondence.

I would be very much obliged if you would convey this information to him.   Faithfully Yours,   W.W.

WWTLI (R. Lansing Coll., NjP).
  [1] In fact, Colonel House, without consulting the President, had conveyed "the intimation" to Page through his son, Arthur W. Page. See John Milton Cooper, Jr., *Walter Hines Page: The Southerner as American, 1855-1918* (Chapel Hill, N. C., 1977), pp. 312-13.

My dear Mr. Secretary,   [Cornish, N. H.] 2 August, 1915.

The Colombian Government is, of course, very sensitive about this matter and we, on our part, are, I think, pledged to the utmost to stand by the terms of the treaty as drawn. I think, moreover, that it is likely that the views of some Senators will prove to have been a good deal modified since the last session by a fuller knowledge of all that is involved.

At the same time I see the necessity of furnishing Harrison with an ostensible mission, and the wisdom of knowing exactly what we may count on, should insuperable difficulties arise in the Senate at the next session. Moreover, it is perfectly natural that you should seek, for yourself, to get into close touch with a matter which you did not personally handle while it was in its formative stage; and I dare say the Colombian people would so interpret Harrison's errand.

I think, however, that it would not be wise to act in this matter as you suggest until you can have an interview with Senator Stone and find out exactly what the obstacles in the Senate were, and how they are likely to be most successfully dealt with. It would hardly do to act on the newspaper versions of what they were.

I wonder if you could obtain such an interview in time, or whether, lacking that, you could get from Senator Stone a letter giving the whole case as it stands in his view?

I did not understand that Harrison's mission (his real mission) was to be a secret one as regards his object, except to the outside world. Official-dom would have to know pretty promptly, and might be sobered by knowing, if they had been tempted to lose their sobriety.   Faithfully Yours,   W.W.

WWTLI (SDR, RG 59, 711.21/328½, DNA).

To Robert Lansing, with Enclosure

My dear Mr. Secretary,   [Cornish, N. H.] 2 August, 1915.

This is truly extraordinary. Thank you for letting me see it.[1]
                    Faithfully Yours,   W.W.

WWTLI (SDR, RG 59, 812.001 H 87/52, DNA).
[1] Wilson was replying to RL to WW, July 31, 1915, TLS (SDR, RG 59, 812.001 H 87/52, DNA). Bernstorff had sent Huerta's appeal (without taking notice of or answering it) in J. H. von Bernstorff to RL, July 28, 1915, TLS (SDR, RG 59, 812.001 H 87/52, DNA).

ENCLOSURE

El Paso, Texas, July 26, 1915.

I am at Fort Bliss and my household consisting of thirty or thirty five persons who are at the city of El Paso are not accorded guarantees of any kind. I wish to know whether the Government of His Imperial Majesty you so worthily represent in Washington can do me the favor of protecting my wife and children, as the officers of the Federal American Justice in that city do not let them sleep or eat and search my home at will.

I respectfully beg reply.   V. Huerta

Hw translation of telegram (SDR, RG 59, 812.001 H 87/52, DNA).

To Josephus Daniels

My dear Daniels: Cornish, N. H., August 2, 1915

Thank you warmly for your letter about the Chicago investigation.[1] Your argument convinces me, but since I asked Tumulty to see you I have myself come to the conclusion that Redfield had gone too far to justify me in insisting upon a substitute course of action which might seem to discredit him before I had even gained knowledge of the results of the investigation or had been fully apprised of the methods by which it had been conducted.

I believe, as you do, that he is trying to make the investigation strictly and truly impartial and I cannot help hoping that out of this melée of misrepresentation and excitement calmer counsels will come and the whole matter be seen in the full light of impartial information.

Always   Affectionately yours,   Woodrow Wilson

TLS (J. Daniels Papers, DLC).
   1 J. Daniels to WW, July 31, 1915, ALS (WP, DLC), reassessing the proposal for an independent investigation of the *Eastland* disaster, which Redfield had strongly opposed. Daniels wrote: "I know he is guided by the best motives, but fear he is making a mistake. His loyalty to subordinates does credit to his heart, but it seems to me that he runs the risk of making the public believe he is championing their cause while they are under fire more than should be done since they are, in a sense, under the charge of manslaughter because of negligence." Daniels concluded, however, that nothing could be done.

To Frederick A. Duneka

My dear Mr. Duneka: Cornish, N. H., August 2, 1915

I have your letter of July twenty-ninth about the proposal to make film stories out of my little essay, "When a Man Comes to Himself," and out of my History of the American People.[1]

There are many things to make the idea interesting and attractive, but I must say that I am old-fashioned enough to have an inveterate prejudice against this sort of thing. It seems to me that it would seem a rather cheap exploitation of both books. I would feel a[l]most as if I had gone on the stage myself to advertise my wares and my judgment is against it, profitable though I dare say it could easily be made.

I hope that you will pardon this attitude of mine towards commercial matters. I have an instinctive feeling that the people of the country would not like it, particularly at this time, and that it is unwise to undertake it.

May I not say how deeply and warmly I appreciate the personal words you were kind enough to add to your letter and how proud it makes me to have such generous friends?

Cordially and sincerely yours,   [Woodrow Wilson]

CCL (WP, DLC).
   1 F. A. Duneka to WW, July 29, 1915, TLS, enclosing J. F. Byrnes to F. A. Duneka, July 26, 1915, TCL, both in WP, DLC. Byrnes proposed to pay $6,000 in advance royalties for the motion picture rights to "When a Man Comes to Himself," with the further understanding that he was also to have the motion picture rights to *A History of the American People* for $5,000 in advance, plus 10 per cent of the gross receipts. Byrnes further noted that Samuel G. Blythe had expressed his willingness to write the scenario for "When a Man Comes to Himself." Duneka, in his covering letter, commented that Harper & Brothers was "inclined to think that this may be a desirable thing to do from many points of view." He noted also that in such cases the publishing firm customarily collected all monies at a charge of 20 per cent.

To James Hay

My dear Mr. Hay: Cornish, N. H., August 2, 1915

I am sure you have had as much in mind as I have the whole matter of what it is wise and necessary to do in the matter of national defence. I have been taking steps to get full recommendations from the War and Navy Departments and I am hoping that after I get back to Washington it may be convenient for you to come up and have a talk with me as to the best way in which the whole thing can be handled, so that we shall all have a single judgment in the matter and a single programme of action. I shall value your advice in the matter very much indeed.

Cordially and sincerely yours,   [Woodrow Wilson][1]

CCL (Letterpress Books, WP, DLC).
[1] Wilson wrote the same letter on the same date to Representative Lemuel P. Padgett and Senators George E. Chamberlain and Benjamin R. Tillman. Padgett and Tillman were the chairmen of the naval affairs committees of their respective houses as were Hay and Chamberlain of the military affairs committees of the House and Senate.

To Hatton William Sumners

My dear Mr. Sumners: Cornish, N. H., August 2, 1915

I have received your telegram of July thirty-first and read it with close attention.

I think I understand the gravity and importance of the cotton situation and you may depend upon it I shall handle it with the sincere desire to serve the interests of the cotton states in every way that it is possible to serve them. I wish that I could alter the circumstances of the war which are so seriously affecting our whole national life.

Cordially and sincerely yours,   [Woodrow Wilson]

CCL (Letterpress Books, WP, DLC).

To Emily Greene Balch[1]

My dear Miss Balch: Cornish, N. H., August 2, 1915

I am in receipt of your interesting letter of July nineteenth.[2] I am not making engagements to see anyone while I am here in Cornish, but I take it for granted that I shall soon be called back to Washington upon some one or other of the many important pieces of business now pending, and when I do return I shall be glad to make arrangements for an interview with you, to which I shall look forward with the most sincere pleasure.

Cordially and sincerely yours,   [Woodrow Wilson]

CCL (Letterpress Books, WP, DLC).
1 Professor of Political Economy and Political and Social Science at Wellesley College. She had recently been a delegate to the International Congress of Women at The Hague and had subsequently visited various European statesmen on behalf of that body.
2 It is missing.

A Telegram and Two Letters from Robert Lansing

Washington, August 2, 1915.

Do not think it necessary for you to be in Washington at first informal conference of Diplomats. Will telegraph you on Thursday after conference on this subject. I am giving to the press tonight a brief announcement of the conference.

Robert Lansing

TS telegram (SDR, RG 59, 812.00/24277c, DNA).

My Dear Mr. President: Washington August 2, 1915.

In view of the making public of the Austrian statement in regard to the exportation of arms and ammunition,[1] I hasten to send you a draft of reply.[2] I have not had time to review it with the care I should like to give to it.

You will observe in reading it that it is presented in a popular rather than a technical manner because I think it will be more valuable for the public here in the United States than for its effect upon Austria-Hungary.

I hope you can pass upon it speedily because I believe it would, at the present moment, have a very beneficial effect on public opinion. It is our first opportunity to present in a popular way the reasons why we should not restrict the exportation of munitions of war. If you have noticed in the papers meetings are being held under various auspices looking to the imposition of an embargo on arms and ammunition. The propaganda is being conducted in various parts of the country and if continued may become very embarrassing.   Faithfully yours,   Robert Lansing.

TLS (SDR, RG 59, 763.72111 EM 1/26, DNA).
1 About which see WW to RL, July 7, 1915, n. 2, Vol. 33. The Austro-Hungarian Embassy made public the full text on August 1. See, e.g., the *New York Times*, Aug. 2, 1915.
2 It was a twenty-four page typed draft prepared by Lester Hood Woolsey, at this time serving as a legal adviser to Robert Lansing, and bears the same file number as Lansing's letter.

Dear Mr. President: Washington August 2, 1915.

In regard to the present situation in Mexico I do not think of anything further to be done with reference to relieving the very distressing conditions which exist, other than the action already taken. It is very possible when it becomes public that we are holding a conference with other American countries in regard to Mexico that the Mexican authorities will make a more earnest effort to relieve the suffering of the people. For that reason, I believe the announcement of the conference should be made as soon as possible. Faithfully yours, Robert Lansing.

TLS (WP, DLC).

From Robert Lansing, with Enclosure

My Dear Mr. President: Washington August 2, 1915.

I enclose a despatch which we have received from Port au Prince.

This morning I had a conference with Mr. Paul Fuller, Jr. in regard to Haitian affairs. As you know, in his report,[1] he advocated very strongly the temporary occupation of Haiti by our military forces and the adoption of a course similar to that which was followed in the case of Cuba. That is, he believes we should take over all governmental functions and confide them to the War Department, providing for an honest election and an arrangement by which a more or less permanent peace might be secured in the Republic. I have not yet been able to reach a conclusion as to the course this Government should pursue. Our Naval forces are in control of the city and I believe they should remain there until a definite policy in regard to the Republic can be reached.

Mr. Farnam of the City National Bank has asked for a conference with Mr. Fuller and myself. It will take place tomorrow. I confess that I am a little suspicious as to the City Bank's attitude toward the Republic of Haiti. Certain actions taken by them are at least criticizable, I also find that Mr. Farnam, who has visited the Island several times, is not liked by the Haitian people, and that he has shown more or less arrogance in treating with them. I do not wish to be unjust to the bank, but at the same time statements in their behalf must be received with caution.

Faithfully yours, Robert Lansing.

TLS (WP, DLC).
[1] See WW to RL, July 2, 1915 (fourth letter of that date), n. 1, Vol. 33.

ENCLOSURE

Port au Prince July 31, 1915.

Disarming of citizens and soldiers continues. Situation critical but being well handled by forces and authorities of landing force. Revolutionary committee seemingly acting in good faith and practically under Admiral's direction. Existence of great number of armed troops in the north constitute a menace to Port au Prince and establishment of peace and imperatively demands sufficient troops here to control situation in an emergency.

Davis.[1]

T telegram (WP, DLC).
[1] Robert Beale Davis, Jr., Secretary of Legation.

From Josephus Daniels

My dear Mr. President: Washington. August 2, 1915.

You have doubtless noted in the press that after conferences with Secretary Lansing, I wired Admiral Caperton at Port au Prince to permit a small number of French troops to land at the French legation. I am in receipt of the following telegram from Admiral Caperton showing that the French authorities appreciate this action:

"At 7 a.m. today (August 2nd) DES CARTES landed legation guard. The French Minister called this morning to thank me and the United States Government for protection by our landing force to his legation."

In addition to sending the CONNECTICUT down with 500 marines, so that our sailors and marines will not have to be on duty too long in that climate, the SOLACE, our hospital ship, was ordered down and is now on the way. The CONNECTICUT will reach there Wednesday.

Admiral Caperton reports food is very scarce and suffering among the poor is probable. I wired him to get in touch with the Haitiens, advise that they organize a relief committee and let them have such supplies as they may desire at Navy prices. It is very dangerous to begin to supply provisions because many Haitiens are like the negroes in the South after the war and would quit work entirely, deserting plantations if our Government undertakes to feed them. Admiral Caperton has sent a commission on the JASON to Cape Haitien and seems to have the matter in Hayti as well in hand as possible.

In all these matters with reference to Hayti, I have had daily conferences with Secretary Lansing and we are taking action after agreement.

News from Naval commanders both in the East and West of Mexico report no change in conditions.

                    Faithfully yours,   Josephus Daniels

TLS (WP, DLC).

From Edward Mandell House

Dear Governor: Manchester, Mass. August 2nd, 1915.

Spring-Rice has just left. We went over the cotton question from beginning to end. He confirmed my opinion as to the length Great Britain would go in the event you brought sufficient pressure and he also confirmed my opinion as to the ultimate result of such a policy.

He will be at Prides for the next ten days and I am talking with Sir Edward through him and will be able to let you have the net result before you are ready to answer the British Note.

He tells me they know of the propaganda that is being carried on in the South and by whom and that he was informed that for a sufficient sum a certain Senator[1] could be diverted. His Government refused to indulge in such tactics. They will try and arrange the matter in an honorable way and in a way that will be satisfactory to the Southern planter.

He believes the trouble is not at all with the planter, but with the agitators. The plan contemplates at least ten cents per pound f.o.b. ship and all to go directly to the farmer. I advised him to bring France, Italy and Russia to the fore. This will make it easier for us. The prejudice is largely being centered against Great Britain and that Government is taking the entire responsibility when, as a matter of fact, France, Russia, Belgium and Italy are more concerned than she is, for they have a deeper and more intimate interest in the outcome of the war. If the war goes against the Allies, England will suffer least because of her navy and insular protection.

If our people realized that this was not a one nation policy, but one which involved half of Europe, they would not be so eager to give affront.

Spring-Rice said the Germans have marked for destruction light-houses, tunnels and important bridges etc. etc. in this country and that they have men upon every one of our battle-ships.

He also said the German propaganda was financed largely by German-American citizens who did not know how the money they were contributing was being used.

W. J. Burns, the detective, was here the other day and confirmed this. Burns said, by the way, that he thought the time had come when this Government should have accurate knowledge of every suspicious character in the country. He thought it could be gotten with comparative ease.

Spring-Rice thought the money that the Allies were spending here for munitions of war would increase our plants to such an extent that it would give us a reasonable amount of safety within another year. He said the Allies were not pressing conclusions on the Western front because of insufficient shells, that they could not make headway until they had as much as the Germans. He did not seem at all discouraged as to the final outcome.

Affectionately yours,   E. M. House

TLS (WP, DLC).
[1] Hoke Smith, as Spring Rice reported to Grey in C. A. Spring Rice, Aug. 12, 1915, T telegram (FO 115/1920, p. 284, PRO). According to Dewey W. Grantham, Jr., *Hoke Smith and the Politics of the New South* (Baton Rouge, La., 1958), pp. 287-88, there is no evidence to support Spring Rice's assertion.

From Edith Bolling Galt

Manchester Vt. Hotel Equinox

My precious Sweetheart: August 2nd 1915 10 P.M.

It does not seem possible that only *twelve* hours ago we were on the porch together. I did not know a day *could* be so long! Tonight when I heard your dear voice on the telephone I wanted to cry out all my love and longing for you, and, instead, I had to be conventional and say only the things neither of us wanted to. I am so glad though your beloved "Nell" has been with you tonight and I know what· a radiant presence hers is—and I wish I could have seen her.

You haven't been very lonely have you Precious? And you are going to try to put sadness from you and think of only the happy days before us. I have thought of you every minute—all along those roads that seemed almost ugly because you were not there. Every foot of the way to Springfield was familiar ground, and yet how strange and empty and unfriendly it seemed. It was a positive relief to me when we got beyond Springfield and the constant reminders of our rides together were left behind, for there was such an ache in my heart, I felt I could not look on things that spoke of you. We went to the "Adna Brown" Hotel for lunch, and Mr. & Mrs. Rose[1] said the *food* was good. But as it was *not* "spiritual food" I could not eat it and talked to cover my lack of appreciation. Just after leaving there we ran into a heavy storm, and the going was bad until we reached Chester. From there on we seemed to run out of the storm, and the rest of the trip was lovely. This place (Manchester) is really awfully pretty—great mountains surround it on all sides, and the houses are quaint and attractive, and the proverbial trees & grass of this country in most luxurious perfection. The Hotel is very attractive and spotlessly clean, but oh! how I do long for my blue nest at Harlakenden and find myself listening for a dear footstep in the hall, or the sound of a vibrant tone, that finds its echo in my heart.

We reached here at 4.20 brushed up and went for a walk. Back to the Hotel for "Tea," which we had on the porch—surrounded by the usual crowd that makes up a Summer Resort Company. About 6:30 the men began coming in from golf and Mr. Rose found a friend of his, so he is going out to play tomorrow morning. Then we will leave after early lunch and go to Troy. Since talking to Helen we find Saratoga is packed with the crowd who follow the Races that began there today. So we decided to go to Troy—from there I dont know the next stop—but we plan to reach Geneva on Thursday.

With what eagerness will I scan my mail, and oh what joy it will be to talk to you again.

This is just the time I miss you most—the hour when you were all the world contained. And I am wondering if you are already in your little *room under the roof* and if you are missing me as keenly as I am you? Helen said you drove to Woodstock this afternoon. So you did carry out our plan and tried, and I feel sure, succeeded in keeping up your spirits.

If I wrote all night, my precious Woodrow I could not tell you of the perfect happiness of these past weeks, or thank you for the infinite tenderness and thought I felt you always surrounded me with. So I leave it to your unfailing intuition and comprehension and only tell you that I love you with all my heart—and that I am with you *now* and *always*.

Goodnight my wonderful Sweetheart,

Your own,   Edith.

ALS (WP, DLC).
    [1] Mrs. Galt spent the month of August traveling with her friends, Hugh Lawson Rose and Mary Francesca Granville Delaney Rose, of Geneva, N.Y. Rose had retired from farming.

Two Letters to Joseph Patrick Tumulty

My dear Tumulty: Cornish, N. H., August 3, 1915

I doubt if any attention should be paid to letters like this of Buchanan's. I think that nothing would benefit them more than to get into a controversy with me. Their attacks return upon themselves by their very violence and their evident injustice, and I think that if I should make any pronouncement upon these matters, it should be issued not upon a provocation but upon some occasion when it could be done with greater dignity and therefore with greater effect.

It occurs to me that a letter such as you outline in yours of July thirty-first might very well be written by yourself, and the very outline you submit is in itself sufficient, but I hope that you will think over even that a little further before you do it, because I am inclined to believe that the greatest service we can do men of this sort is to take them seriously.[1]

Always   Affectionately yours,   [Woodrow Wilson]

CCL (Letterpress Books, WP, DLC).
[1] See JPT to WW, Aug. 6, 1915, n. 1.

My dear Tumulty: Cornish, N. H., August 3, 1915

Thank you for letting me see the enclosed.[1] My own opinion is that there are already so many bodies independently investigating this distressing disaster in Chicago that the best and only thing we can do for the present is to let these investigations proceed in the hope that the investigation by the Federal Grand Jury in particular will result in something that will be conclusive in the public view. I think it very likely that Secretary Redfield is doing everything he can, despite minor mistakes of judgment, to make the investigation thorough and impartial, and that it would be very unjust to him if we were to override him in any way before he has brought his investigation to a conclusion. It will be time then to judge whether further inquiry is necessary in order to satisfy reasonable public opinion. The attacks upon him have been of a very passionate sort, if I may judge from those which have come to me, and I cannot discredit an eminent colleague by acting upon them at this time. Secretary Sweet will have conveyed to Mr. Redfield the advice of those of us who have been looking at the matter from this distance and I think that we shall, for the present at any rate, do well to be guided by Mr. Redfield's reply to Mr. Sweet.

Always   Affectionately yours,   Woodrow Wilson

TLS (J. P. Tumulty Papers, DLC).
[1] R. Forster to JPT, July 31, 1915, TCL (WP, DLC), conveying "confidential information" about Redfield's investigation of the *Eastland* calamity, obtained from the Chicago *Daily News* correspondent, Leroy Tudor Vernon. According to Vernon, many state and city officials thought that Redfield had laid himself open to the charge of trying to whitewash his subordinates. Vernon also quoted at length from a *Daily News* editorial which characterized Redfield as possessing "an abundance of egotism and a general feeling of complacency in which all things connected with his department are comfortably submerged like sardines

in oil." The editorial concluded with an appeal for an inquiry of a broader and more searching nature. Vernon himself thought that the situation in Chicago should be met "quickly and conclusively."

From Robert Lansing, with Enclosure

My Dear Mr. President: Washington August 3, 1915.

I enclose a letter which I have just received from Mr. James P. McDonald,[1] who is the capitalist at the back of the Haitian Railroad.[2] I think you will find some interesting suggestions in his letter. Will you please return the letter after reading it?

Faithfully yours,   Robert Lansing.

TLS (SDR, RG 59, 838.00/1418, DNA).
[1] Connected with the National Railroad Co. of Haiti through the Caribbean Construction Co. His address was 42 Broadway, New York.
[2] About this ill-fated project, see Dana G. Munro, *Intervention and Dollar Diplomacy in the Caribbean, 1900-1921* (Princeton, N. J., 1964), pp. 255-56, 362-63.

E N C L O S U R E

James P. McDonald to Robert Lansing

Personal and confidential.

Sir: New York August 2, 1915.

In accordance with that part of the conversation I had with you Friday last in which you suggested that I put into a letter my views of a solution of the problems in Haiti, I submit to you the following:

First: President.

Have the Chamber of Deputies and Senate, as now constituted, elect a Provisional President for a term of not more than 30 days, so that the present congress and Provisional President will constitute a Government through whom our Government may negotiate and enter into a treaty. The man to be suggested to the Haitan Congress for Provisional President should be selected with some care. He should be an educated man, kindly disposed to the United States and should have as his chief aim the proper salvage and development of Haiti. There are a number of men with these qualifications in Haiti who have the courage of their convictions and are not of the old grafting type; I will be glad to suggest to you the names of a number of men who I believe would acceptably fill this office.

The Cabinet chosen by the Provisional President should also be selected with great care.

Second: Treaty.

During the thirty days of the Provisional Government a treaty should be ratified between Haiti and the United States which should contain the following provisions:

(1) The United States should assist the Haitian Government in administering its Finances. That is, it should lend its assistance to installation of an honest and efficient system of collecting the export and import duties and their transfer to a proper custodian to be disbursed (a) in the payment of the interest and sinking fund of the Haitian Government's Foreign and Domestic loans, and guaranteed bonds, (b) in setting aside a certain percent. for paying the operating expenses of the Government, (c) in setting aside a certain portion for necessary internal improvements and in establishing a department for instructing and aiding the natives in agricultural pursuits and development.

(2) The United States should agree to use its armed forces to enforce order and tranquility throughout the Republic. This may be brought about by disarming and disbanding the present military system and placing in its stead a civil head supported by a rural police or constabulary. I am confident that the present class of so-called "Generals" in Haiti would be glad to be drafted into this rural guard and thus put themselves in a position where they would receive a regular wage for their services. This would go far in putting an end to the Revolutionary disease with which the country is infected.

In other words, I think a combination of the two treaties now existing between the United States and San Domingo and United States and Cuba if put into operation in Haiti with the addition of a Controller of the Haiti Treasury of your appointment to assist in installing a proper system of accounts and to keep proper check on the disbursements of Government money would result in establishing a machine which will insure stability and progress.

(3) In order that the Haitian Government may not get into any more difficulties with Foreign Governments similar to the Lueders and the Peters affairs,[1] I suggest that a consular Court be established to which all questions arising between Foreigners and the Haitian Government be referred as a Court of last Appeal.

(4) In view of the fact that Haiti is sadly in need of money to meet its present obligations some of which are for a considerable time in default, the United States should provide the Haitian Government with money either through a lease of the Mole St. Nicholas or by arranging a loan with Bankers on proper terms so

as to put the credit of Haiti where it will be unassailable. Haitian currency should be placed on a gold basis with a ratio of not less than five to one.

(5) The Haitian Government should be required to confirm and recognize all lawfully existing contracts and agreements between itself and Foreigners and to settle all proper claims suffered by Foreigners on account of the many revolutions and the unauthorized actions of the numerous de facto Governments of the past few years.

Third: Permanent Government.

At the end of the thirty days Provisional Government, a treaty with the foregoing provisions having been consummated the Chamber of Deputies and Senate shall elect a President for the constitutional period (7 years).

The foregoing plan contains certain suggestions of mine hastily formulated which may suggest some new thoughts to you.

The one thing more than any other needed to alleviate the present conditions in Haiti, is to provide employment for its people. Due to the frequent revolutionary movements during the past few years no public work of consequence has been done, and the native has almost entirely neglected the cultivation of the soil, because his crops were either stolen or destroyed by the various contending parties. As soon as the United States Government takes affirmative action that will alleviate the deplorable conditions now prevailing in Haiti and protect investments of capital, I expect to immediately begin work to complete the construction of the National Railroad of Haiti, which consists of about 400 miles of road, 10 miles of which has already been constructed and equipped.

In this construction work I expect to give employment to 25,000 to 50,000 Haitian laborers and I also intend to interest the natives living along the line of the road in various commercial and agricultural enterprises through the cultivation of bananas, cotton, coffee, cocoa, etc. and the mining of coal, copper and iron ore and intend to provide facilities through which the natives will have a cash market for all their products. I am satisfied that within 10 or 12 years Haiti will be able to pay off all its national debt through the legitimate income from its custom duties.

I hold myself entirely at your disposal in case you wish to call me.

I am, sir, your most obedient servant,

Jas. P. McDonald

TLS (SDR, RG 59, 838.00/1418, DNA).

[1] About the Lüders affair, see Ludwell Lee Montague, *Haiti and the United States, 1714-1938* (Durham, N. C., 1940), pp. 178-79. Nothing can be found about the Peters affair.

From Robert Lansing

My Dear Mr. President: Washington August 3, 1915.

The situation in Haiti is distressing and very perplexing. I am not at all sure what we ought to do or what we can legally do.

I had an hours conference this morning with Mr. Paul Fuller, Junior, Mr. Farnam of the National City Bank, and Mr. Casenave[1] of the National Bank of Haiti. The latter represents the French interests in the Republic. I think all three are of one mind and that is that in some way this Government should maintain the foothold which it gained at Port au Prince by landing marines, and exercise some form of provisional government until arrangements can be made for a government which will insure peace in the Republic.

I do not see how anything could be accomplished if we do not have some form of administration which will conserve the customs and prevent their receipt by irresponsible persons. The Committee of Safety which has been established seems to have ceased operations because the National Bank declined to advance funds with which to bribe the rioters. The city is in a state of great excitement and the suffering of the people, even the middle class, is very acute on account of the lack of food. I believe it to be a fact that people are starving to death in Port au Prince because the country people are afraid to bring in food. This is a condition which has been increasing during the past month and is now very acute.

We have no excuse of reprisal as we had at Vera Cruz, to take over the city government and administer the offices. There would appear to me to be but one reason which could be given for our doing so, and that is the humane duty of furnishing means to relieve the famine situation. If our naval authorities should take over the collection of customs on imports and exports these might be expended on the grounds of dire necessity for the relief of the starving people. If such a course should be adopted I think we would have to go further and convey, at least unofficially to the foreigners who have in the past financed revolutions, that this Government would not permit the debts incurred in that manner to be paid.

The great difficulty with the entire situation is that while there are many intelligent Haitians who would like to support the United States in its endeavor to prevent further revolutionary disorders, they do not dare take that position openly as they would be at once liable to assassination. When we consider that there are from two million to two million and a half inhabitants in Haiti, and that of that number probably not over fifty thousand can read or write or speak understandable French, the problem presented is one of great difficulty. The great mass of the people are clay in the hands of the small group of politicians who are quarreling for office simply because it gives them an opportunity to loot the people.

I do not think that we can let the present condition continue too long. The reported peace conference to be held at Cape Haitian is undoubtedly intended to restore, if possible, a corrupt and irresponsible government of some sort. Dr. Bobo, who appears to be the head or the figurehead of the present revolution, is, I am informed, mentally unbalanced and brutally savage in his treatment of his enemies when they fall into his hands.

I hope that you can give me some suggestion as to what course we should pursue. I am sure if it was not for the European War we would find France demanding of us the pacification of the Republic, or our consent that she pacify it. The German element in the Island is hostile to such course because they are the principal ones who have profited by the frequent revolutions in the matter of loans carrying rates of interest as high as fifty per cent. In fact, I believe that element is responsible for the failure of our efforts to secure treaty arrangements with the Haitian Government by slandering our Minister and by spreading false reports as to the intentions of the United States.

Faithfully yours,   Robert Lansing

TLS (SDR, RG 59, 838.00/1418, DNA).
    [1] Maurice Casenave, president of the Board of Directors of the National Bank of the Republic of Haiti.

From Josephus Daniels

Washington, D.C., August 3, 1915

After consultation with Secretary Lansing, we think election of President under present conditions would continue the disorder. Lansing tells me he has written you letter this afternoon dealing with situation. The following telegram has been received from Admiral Caperton at Port au Prince:

"Professional soldiers called Cacos are largely responsible for the existence of the large number of Haitian revolutionists. The Cacos are organized in bands under irresponsible and lawless chiefs who side with the party offering greatest inducement and only nominally recognize the government. All Haitians fear the Cacos and they practically control politics. There are now in Port au Prince about fifteen hundred Cacos retaining organization and believed to have hidden arms and ammunition but ostensibly disarmed. The election of Bobo as President has been demanded by them and Congress, terrorized by the mere demand, is on the point of complying, but my request restrained. No other man can be elected under present conditions on account of fear of Cacos. I believe that I can control Congress. After the arrival of the regiment of marines on the Connecticut I can prevent any Cacos outbreak at Port au Prince. A stable government in Haiti is not possible until Cacos bands are broken up and their power broken. If the United States desires to negotiate a treaty for financial control of Haiti, such action is now imperative in Port au Prince. Must have regiment of marines in addition to that on Connecticut in order to accomplish this. The majority of the populace are submissive and well disposed and will welcome disbanding Cacos and stopping revolutions. Recommend Captain Beach[1] appointed single Commissioner of the United States with full instructions and authority should agreement with Haiti be desired. My negotiations on shore have been conducted by him and I believe he has generally the confidence of Haitians. I earnestly request to be informed fully of the policy of the United States, as future relations between Haiti and the United States depend largely upon course of action taken at this time."

Josephus Daniels.

T telegram (WP, DLC).
[1] Edward Latimer Beach, U.S.N.

From William Cox Redfield

My dear Mr. President: Chicago, August 3, 1915.

I hand you copy of letter sent Secretary Daniels today, which will speak for itself.[1]

Matters have cleared up very much. The atmosphere is calmer and we know somewhat more of the miserable political movements which lie behind the campaign against me of the last week. You are the object at which they aim. I am the anvil on which the blows are struck. I am glad to be pounded in so good a cause, and yet I confess the blows have hurt. In the last day or two some of the great papers in other cities have come to the rescue, and there is a marked reaction. I have assured the public that in the fall there would be a searching examination of all the methods of the Steamboat-Inspection Service, and at that time I will form a committee to conduct that inquiry, which with your assistance we will make so strong that no one can condemn it.

Meanwhile I can again assure you that nothing that reflects discredit upon the service or any man in it has as yet been discovered. The Federal Grand Jury has its drag-net out and threatens in a day or two more to wind us up by an order of Judge Landis[2] forbidding witnesses to testify before us. It is possible, therefore, that we shall close by Thursday evening and leave the matter with the Federal Court. I doubt if the Federal District Attorney has sufficient technical knowledge to deal very intelligently with this accident, which is after all a problem in physics applied disastrously. Yet if he will proceed long enough and searchingly enough he will find the truth, which the record of our own inquiry will show rather clearly.

When our incident is closed I will report to you more fully.

Yours very truly,   William C. Redfield

TLS (WP, DLC).
[1] It is missing.
[2] Kenesaw Mountain Landis, United States district judge for the northern district of Illinois.

To Edith Bolling Galt

My own Darling,

[Cornish, N. H.] Tuesday,
3 Aug., 1915 7.15 A.M.

What a thrill it gave me to hear your dear voice over the telephone last night and what a struggle I had with myself to hold back from pouring out to you in words the love that was in my heart! I had made the day go well enough till lunch time,—so far as steadiness of spirits was concerned, but the afternoon had been a fight in which I cannot claim to have altogether won,— the whole *world* hereabouts was so desolately empty and devoid of beauty! I went to work immediately after your motor disappeared round the turn in the driveway—immediately after that lovely hand, waving its farewell, had been withdrawn the second time. The *regular* work, of correspondence, was done by twelve o'clock, as I had foreseen it would be, but I managed to eke out work enough to last till one by attacking the great pile of commissions and other papers they had sent up from Washington for my signature,—some two or three hundred of them. The time between lunch and four, when Helen and Jessie and I went for a ride (the Woodstock circle reversed) was the critical period in my fight for self-mastery, because there was nothing in particular to do. I was even reduced to playing pool by myself and trying to put more balls in for you (the alternate shots) than for myself! While we were out driving Mac. *and Nell* arrived. They had come in their own motor from Boston. The baby has been perfectly well now for four or five days and Mac. had prevailed upon my dear Nell to come with him. She is radiantly well, just her own vital and delightful self, and it was a joy to see her and hold her in my arms again. Miss Batten,[1] Margaret's friend, had also arrived, and we had quite a lively circle in the morning room after dinner. Four girls (and Frank on the arm by Jessie) sat on the lounge, and I sat in the desk chair. I took Nell into the music room after a while and told her of the great happiness that had come to us, my precious One, and I know you would have been touched and delighted if you could have seen and heard how she took it,—with unaffected joy that I should have found escape from my loneliness and comfort and support now and in the days to come, and even the little she had seen of you had given her an impression of you that made her glad that it was *you* she was to welcome. Isn't it wonderful how they all three understand and how their sweet love for me interprets the whole thing to them perfectly? I *knew* Nell would receive the news as she did. If anything could have made me love these dear girls more than ever, this experience of their power to comprehend and sympathize has done it—bless their hearts! And when, in the sweet months and years to come, they have a chance to know you in the intimacy of family life they will love you and trust you and admire you in a way that will complete our happiness, my Darling. I know that because I know them, and know that they love and admire the same qualities and gifts that I do,—and that I have found in you in such wonderful perfection. Mac. and Nell leave this morning at eleven, by motor, by one route, and Helen and Jessie and Frank at about the same hour by another. Mac. has not yet had a chance to disclose his business to me. This afternoon Sister Annie, "little" Annie, the baby Josephine, and George Howe arrive and the circle in the morning room will be changed altogether,—and Thursday afternoon the Carters from Williamstown.[2]

And so, my precious One, you are posted to date about all that is happening to the Wilsons at your home at Harlakenden. In public business nothing of new consequence has turned up. I am putting in another envelope one or two letters and messages which explain themselves. The most interesting and unexpected piece of news is that that unconscionable old scoundrel Huerta, who is in the steady clutches of the six-foot-four Scots Presbyterian elder down in the Lone Star State,[3] has appealed to the Imperial German Government to protect him and his followers against us! Lansing sent me a confidential letter from Bernstorff

[1] Clare W. Batten, daughter of Loring Woart Batten, a professor at the General Theological Seminary in New York.

[2] The Rev. John Franklin Carter, Alice Henry Carter, and perhaps other members of their family. See EAW to WW, July 2, 1913, n. 4, Vol. 28.

[3] Attorney General Gregory.

to him enclosing a copy of Huerta's message to him (B.).[4] The old fool seems still to look upon himself as a sovereign government and appeals to the German government to represent him at Washington—that's what it comes to. Did you ever hear anything more amazing? I've no doubt Bernstorff would have been dee-lighted, but didn't dare!

Tuesday, 12.45

The two motor parties have gone; Margaret, Miss Batten[,] the doctor and I have just taken an hour's turn with White and Murphy, to cool off from the hurry and confusion that preceded the two gettings off, and I am again alone with my thoughts of my darling Sweetheart. I spent an hour with Mac. in the music room after breakfast, to discuss business. It turned out to be something personal, indeed, as he had said, but not personal to himself or to me, but personal to Mr. Sam'l Untermyer, the New York lawyer, for whom Mac. has a very warm feeling of friendship—not a matter of general interest at all, but one in which he thought we might do Mr. Untermyer a good turn. That and a secret service matter[5] took up all of our hour. Nell was again as sweet as she could be about our happiness, my sweet Love, and Frank told me that after I told her last night she went and had a talk with Jessie about it and was as happy as possible in every way. And so you are taken into the Wilson family, my beloved Darling, with open arms and a welcome that is full of love, as unaffected and spontaneous as it is full-hearted and genuine! There is nothing but an added source of happiness for us there! And, with so much to give and confirm happiness, I am ashamed to be sad. Indeed I am not exactly *sad*. It's just that I *miss* you so that my heart aches and is infinitely heavy. How could it be

[4] It is printed as an Enclosure with WW to RL, Aug. 2, 1915 (third letter of that date).

[5] Actually, the "secret service matter" was of very great importance. McAdoo informed Wilson that, on an elevated train in New York City on July 24, a Secret Service operative, by a lucky chance, had been able to seize a large brief case belonging to Dr. Heinrich F. Albert, commercial attaché in the German Embassy in Washington and head of the German Purchasing Commission in New York. William James Flynn, chief of the Secret Service, immediately got in touch with McAdoo and, on the following day, brought the brief case to North Haven, Maine, where the McAdoos were vacationing. The contents of the brief case disclosed that Albert headed an important part of the German propaganda and undercover efforts in the United States and revealed many intimate details of these operations. While these activities were probably not indictable under American law, they did represent a vast, clandestine effort to influence American opinion and American foreign policy and even to divert American-produced war materials destined for the Allies. For further details of the Albert affair, see David W. Hirst, "German Propaganda in the United States, 1914-1917" (Ph.D. dissertation, Northwestern University, 1962), pp. 243-45; Link, *Struggle for Neutrality*, pp. 554-56, and William G. McAdoo, *Crowded Years* (Boston and New York, 1931), pp. 324-29. For the decision about the disposal of the Albert documents, see EMH to WW, Aug. 10, 1915, n. 1.

otherwise? Throughout these blessed weeks that I have had with you here I have enjoyed so deep and rare a happiness, my beloved Darling, that nothing but your own return to me in your own dear person can ever make up to me for the loss of it. I had not known before, for all I loved you so tenderly and so ardently and with such an abiding joy of admiration and devotion, how *perfectly* lovely you are, how completely enjoyable and satisfying you are to every faculty and need and desire of my mind and heart, or how delightfully and perfectly fitted to be the companion, whether as friend or sweetheart or wife, of every mood and thought and purpose. I had not known until the very last—until this last blessed week—(though I had thought I did) what an incomparable *personality* you are, rich in everything that delights and comforts and stimulates and makes life together worth while, in work, at play, in perplexity or in quiet content, with the world at my ears or alone with one another, all the world shut out. And the complete discovery made me so *happy*, made me feel so in love with life itself, created in my heart such a passion of devotion and admiration for you, my incomparable Darling, filled every moment I was with you with such a sense of *privilege* as well as pleasure, of stimulation and expansion as well as enjoyment, that to lose your companionship seems like losing the sweetest part of life itself. How wonderful the Fourth Chapter has been! It was so rounded out with sweet experiences, in their right and natural sequences, of what we meant to one another, and ended in a happiness so full of every element of perfect love that no doubt or fear or question of any kind could touch it with so much as a shadow. In the midst of my heaviness of heart because my darling is not here I know that I am the happiest man in this distracted world and that nothing can communicate that distraction to my thoughts, because, present or absent, you are mine.

9 P.M.

I have stolen away to the study, my precious One, to have a few minutes with you. Sister and the rest are in the morning room, but I could not stand it there without you,—particularly now that I have that blessed love letter you wrote last night in Manchester at my heart and the hour has come when we used to shut the world out (the curtains are drawn close in the morning room now, and the fire is lighted!) and look into our own hearts alone. How full the room seems of you! You said in your sweet note that you would be in Troy to-night, but Margaret and I have just called up *all* the hotels in Troy and been told that you are not registered at any of them, so I suppose Mr. Rose changed his plan again, and I shall have to deny myself even the sound of your dear voice to-night. Ah, my precious One, my Darling, my Darling, I wonder if you know what happiness your love has given me and how constantly and with what a passion of pure love my thoughts follow you all the day through and dwell with you in the quiet night. My heart aches because you are not here, but it rejoices and is full of joy and pride because you love me and have given me that supreme gift of love, your own dear, wonderful, delightful, adorable self, the noblest, most satisfying, most lovable woman in the world. I love you, I *love* you, I LOVE you, and *you love me*. What can touch me now? My thoughts will follow you every hour till we meet again, with, oh, such deep and yearning tenderness. My hopes are all in your keeping—and I know them to be safe there. I am full of strength and confidence because our lives are united and my Darling is happy, as I am, in their union. These weeks have been infinitely happy and have given me what my heart desired. My Darling has blessed me, and I love her with all my heart. I am always and altogether hers!

Wednesday morning 4 August, '15

My heart has been searching for you all night, my precious Sweetheart, because you were not in Troy and I could not conjecture where you were; and yet I have known all the time that you were with me, as you said you would be. A sweet peace seems to have come over my heart this morning! It is just three months to-day since I declared my love to my precious One, and now she is mine in every thought and purpose and has given me a love so tender, so full of her own penetrating charm, so warm with her own strength and sweetness, so compounded of all the delightful elements of her own wonderful mind and heart, that my heart is satisfied and at peace, and all my thoughts run forward to the blessed days that lie before us, in which lies the complete fulfilment of our happiness,—days in which I shall try to show by a *life* of love and devotion how *truly* I love her, with how sincere and genuine a devotion. You have changed the world for me, my darling Edith—changed *this mad* world into a place of peace and confident hope for me. All my thoughts centre in you, get their strength from my consciousness that you are mine and that I shall always have your love to sustain me and light my way. You blessed Darling! I feel as if you were actually close by my side as I write this morning, thinking of these wonderful three months as I am thinking of them. I can almost feel the warmth of your dear hand on mine and can fancy that at any moment I might turn and touch your lips with mine. Shall I ever be able to tell you,—to make you realize how I love you?

Your own   Woodrow

P.S. I am perfectly well—how could I be anything else, now that you have given yourself to me?

The doctor returned Monday evening in fine spirits. He has said nothing about his experience except that he was *so* sorry he could not see you. 'He had a number of pleasant little things to tell you—nothing very big, but a number of pleasant little things.' I think it must be all right. He said he had never before had so peaceful and happy a visit.

Helen went off in fine spirits and apparently feeling *very* well. W.

ALS (WP, DLC).

From Edith Bolling Galt

Schenectady, N. Y.

Dearest: August 3rd 1915 6 P.M.

I am at my window here at the "Edison Hotel" overlooking city streets and ugly brick houses and trolley cars. But, instead of looking out, I am dreaming of a big house in the centre of green terraces, and tall pine trees—and wondering if a certain pair of dear eyes are resting on the peace and beauty of this loved spot!

I am wondering if Helen and Jessie and Frank really started on their journey this morning, and if your Sister came. In fact I have held you so in my thoughts that each minute has been filled with questions I am longing to have answered.

Oh! Sweetheart there are no locked doors—or suitcases now—but instead all the gates are flung wide, and a perfect flood of longing rushes out to you.

I mailed a letter to "Margaret" last night at Manchester—about 11—and then I got to bed about 12:30.

This morning Mr. Rose played golf with 2 N. York men and said the course really was lovely, but terribly wet from the constant rains. We had lunch at 12:30 so as to get off early, and we had not gone 10 miles before it began to pour. So we had to run slowly but got to Troy so early decided to come on here, arriving about half an hour ago. The roads are fine most of the way, but very slippery. We are going off pretty early tomorrow—thinking we might reach Geneva by night—but it is 180 miles and if it is raining I don't think it will be possible. But we will be near enough to make an easy run on Thursday. I see in the paper

Mr. Lansing has given out about the A.B.C. Conference, and I read one very nice Editorial about your wisdom in inviting this consultation, and I am longing to know what new things have come to you since our last happy work hour. I don't believe I ever made you know how perfectly happy I was when you would let me share your work. And I thrill now when it comes back to me how—in the midst of all the whirring of the machinery, that seemed so complicated as to demand every part of brain and energy—you would turn to me with love on your lips, and whisper the tenderest secret in the world and make me glow with the assurance that nothing could crowd me out of your thoughts.

I had to stop here to join Mr. & Mrs. Rose and now it is nearly ten and I must get this mailed. I must tell you something Mrs. R. said to me last night in speaking of you and the girls. She said you all seemed so devoted to each other that she wondered if you should marry again if it would make the girls unhappy, adding that you were so charming and attractive she knew women would fall in love with you, but adding, in a comforted tone, but of course with all he has on his mind he can't give his thoughts or attention to any woman!

Goodnight my precious   Forgive writing and know that I am with all my heart   your own   Edith

ALS (WP, DLC).

To Robert Lansing

My dear Mr. Secretary,   [Cornish, N. H.] 4 August, 1915.

These are serious matters, and my own judgment is as much perplexed as yours.

I fear we have not the legal authority to do what we apparently ought to do; and that if we did do what is necessary it would constitute a case very like that of Mr. Roosevelt's action in Santo Domingo, and have very much the same issue.

I suppose there is nothing for it but to take the bull by the horns and restore order. A long programme such as the enclosed letter suggests involves legislation and the cooperation of the Senate in treaty-making, and must therefore await the session of our Congress.

In the meantime this is plain to me:

*1. We must send to Port au Prince a force sufficient to absolutely control the city not only but also the country immediately about it from which it draws its food. I would be obliged if you

would ascertain from the Secretary of the Navy whether he has such a force available that can reach there soon.

2. We must let the present Congress know that we will protect it but that we will not recognize any action on its part which does not put men in charge of affairs whom we can trust to handle and put an end to revolution.

3. We must give all who now have authority there or who desire to have it or who think they have it or are about to have it to understand that we shall take steps to prevent the payment of debts contracted to finance revolution: in other words, that we consider it our duty to insist on constitutional government there and will, if necessary (that is, if they force us to it as the only way) take charge of elections and see that a real government is erected which we can support. I would greatly value your advice as to the way in which all this can be done.

Number One can be done at once. How do you advise handling Numbers Two and Three?

In haste,　　　　　　　　　　Faithfully Yours,　W.W.

* This will probably involve making the city authorities virtually subordinate to our commanders. They may hand the city government over to us voluntarily.

WWTLI (SDR, RG 59, 838.00/1418, DNA).

To Edward Mandell House

Dearest Friend,　　　　　　　[Cornish, N. H.] 4 August, 1915.

I do not know what can have happened to me that I should have sent you only the first page of a letter. I cannot find another page lying here among my papers. Did it close with a complete sentence, and can it be that I did not have room to close with the type-writer and meant to *write* the closing words?

You are quite right about Lansing and Palmer. Lansing ought to have a man he can himself feel confidence in. I have written him this since I got your letter.[1]

I note what you say about your interview with Spring Rice and about your talk with Burns. I am not sure of the latter. Are you? But I am sure that the country is honeycombed with German intrigue and infested with German spies. The evidences of these things are multiplying every day, and we know a great deal more about them than Burns realizes.

I keep well, but find myself rather tired.

Just at the moment our acute difficulties are in Mexico and

Haiti. I know that you approve what we are doing in calling in the Latin-American diplomats to advise us with regard to Mexico. I hope with all my heart that something will come out of it.

With deep affection,   Woodrow Wilson

WWTLS (E. M. House Papers, CtY).
1 WW to RL, Aug. 2, 1915, WWTLI (R. Lansing Papers, NjP).

To Edward Mandell House, with Enclosure

Dearest Friend,   [Cornish, N. H.] 4 August, 1915.

Will you not expand this idea a little more?

I take it that we have no authority in law to put this Government under such obligations as you suggest without legislative action by both Houses and treaty action by the Senate, and that we are in danger of going a course not unlike that which Roosevelt followed on the isthmus.

Meanwhile, Congress not being in session, money will be needed for even the first and temporary arrangements made in Mexico. I do not like to risk a session of Congress just now, and yet Mexico cannot wait till December.

What is your idea as to an immediate modus vivendi that will safeguard the points that we must safeguard?

Affectionately Yours,   Woodrow Wilson

WWTLS (E. M. House Papers, CtY).

E N C L O S U R E

From Edward Mandell House

Manchester, Massachusetts.
Dear Governor: August 3rd, 1915.

There is one part of the Mexican program which I failed to discuss with Lansing but which should have attention and that is the financing of whatever government is recognized.

The idea has been to permit Americans having large interests in Mexico to undertake this task. I feel this would be a grave mistake and would bring the whole plan under suspicion. It would look too much like exploiting Mexico for the benefit of our people under our protection. Foreign governments would not view it with favor and it would be necessary for us to be constantly explaining.

Whatever government is recognized could be financed by our guarantee alone or in conjunction with the A.B.C. Powers. We could be amply protected by having a certain amount of the revenues pledged as security. This would give us an opportunity to have a representative in Mexico to look out for our interests and it could be arranged to make the consent of this representative necessary for the expenditure of the loan.

Unless this is done the plan may not work out well, for there is no one in sight in Mexico that would be able to successfully restore constitutional order in a way which would make it lasting.

We must, I think, either ourselves or jointly with the A.B.C. people keep a hand on the throttle for many years to come. Restoring order for the moment is only one part of the job. The other part is giving right direction to affairs so that your policy as a whole may be justified.

There have been many precedents for such a course. England, I believe, did it for Greece at one time and it has been done by other governments under like conditions.

Your affectionate,   E. M. House

TLS (E. M. House Papers, CtY).

To Josephus Daniels

My dear Daniels: Cornish, N. H., August 4, 1915

I thank you warmly for your letter of August second about what is going on in Haiti and entirely approve the several things you have done in consultation with Lansing.

I am expecting to hear from Lansing about the situation when the pouch comes in today and will write him in reply to his letter. In the meantime, let me thank you sincerely for what you are doing.   Faithfully yours,   Woodrow Wilson

TLS (J. Daniels Papers, DLC).

To William Cox Redfield

My dear Mr. Secretary: Cornish, N. H., August 4, 1915

I thank you sincerely for your letter of August first[1] giving a full account of the way in which you have sought to open the inquiry into the Eastland disaster very fully to everyone who can assist in making certain that the truth is got at. I appreciate the difficulties you have encountered and am sincerely sorry that the inquiry should have been in any degree prejudiced by premature judgments expressed either by individuals or the Press.

It has been my feeling from the first that you should be left free to follow the plain law in this matter which clearly prescribes the method of inquiry and the duty of the department in making it, and I shall look to see an attitude of confidence on the part of the public as to the impartiality of the inquiry succeed the present fears and doubts. The disaster was of so tragical and distressing a sort that it is not strange it should have caused deep excitement. It is very difficult in the midst of such excitement to judge with impartiality those who are supposed to have been at fault and the object of all of us should be to get at the facts without fear or favor. It seems to me that you organized the inquiry in a way to do this and that you have opened it as wide as it could be opened under the law to everyone who could assist in making the inquiry thorough and impartial.

These must have been very trying days for you and I sincerely hope a calmer atmosphere will prevail as this preliminary inquiry draws to its close.

Cordially and sincerely yours,   Woodrow Wilson

TLS (Letterpress Books, WP, DLC).

1 W. C. Redfield to WW, Aug. 1, 1915, ALS (WP, DLC), explaining the legal provisions for an inquiry by the Steamboat Inspection Service and the liberties that Redfield had taken to expand the hearings to include local officials and representatives of the press. Nonetheless, Redfield reported, the press had acted like "lunatics in a bedlam," and no labor leader could be found to participate in the hearings who had not "published his conclusions (chiefly denunciations) in advance." He had been told, Redfield continued, that the row had been stirred up by local politicians and the Hearst press in order "to damn the administration." The hearings had located no fault in the Inspection Service but had pinpointed necessary changes in the law. "Meanwhile," he concluded, "the suggestion of another commission is made to discredit the Department and myself and would be so hailed. I should of course regard it as an open rebuke. . . . I should greatly value a word of confidence. . . . The chief danger to be dreaded now is weakness at Washington. I think we can pull this situation off if we go along steadily another week."

To Emily Chapman Martin Yates

My dear Friend: Cornish, N. H., August 4, 1915

It was indeed delightful to get your letter of July twenty-second.[1] I believe our thoughts run more frequently across the sea to Rydal than to any other place where dear friends are, and we were all getting particularly hungry for news of you and Fred and Mary. This letter brings us just what we want.

We are struggling in the midst of many grave perplexities on this side of the water and I have a daily debate with myself what the real duty of the country is, but you can imagine these difficulties and doubts without my dwelling upon them. They keep me so absorbed that I have no time for personal letters but I cannot deny myself the pleasure of sending you our love.

It is delightful to hear that Mary is having so enjoyable an outing and that Fred is finding acceptable work to do. I know that always is a condition of his happiness.

We are spending the summer here in New Hampshire, in the same house we had last summer and the summer before, and become more and more attached to the place every year. Jessie and her husband, Frank Sayre, and their little boy are with me; so is Margaret; and my sister and her daughter are here. Nell ran over from Maine the other day for a few hours by motor to see us, and the glimpse we had of her refreshed and delighted us very much. She and her little daughter are getting on famously.

With delightful recollections and sincere affection, always
Faithfully yours,   Woodrow Wilson

P.S. Thank you for the extract from the New Statesman.

TLS (F. Yates Coll., NjP).
1 It is missing.

From Robert Lansing, with Enclosure

My Dear Mr. President: Washington August 4, 1915.

I have just received the enclosed confidential telegram from Berlin, which you will be interested in reading.
Faithfully yours,   Robert Lansing.

TLS (WP, DLC).

E N C L O S U R E

Berlin via Copenhagen, August 2, 1915.

2670. STRICTLY CONFIDENTIAL to be deciphered by a thoroughly confidential person.

A man who is at general headquarters informed a friend of mine of following conversation with the Emperor:

"The Emperor talked to him for an hour and a half on many subjects. He is very angry with America and Americans; thinks that President Wilson is absolutely pro-English; talked for a long time regarding the export of arms and ammunition; said that the war would have been over four months ago but for America's assistance to the Allies; said that we had forbidden the export of arms and ammunition to Mexico; we should do the same for the whole of Europe.

"Man interposed, 'But international law,' whereupon the Emperor angrily retorted, 'There is no international law!'

"Man remarked that Germany had given ammunition to Russia in the Russo-Japanese war. 'Yes,' said the Emperor; 'because the Russians were fighting against a yellow race.'

"He said it was a crime that his brave educated men were being killed by black and yellow men; that he was disappointed in the Anglo-Saxon race; that they were egging on the yellow races; that China was finished.

"England was responsible for the war. England fully intended to retain Calais after the war; the French Government recently went there and were flabbergasted to find it turned into a British colony; the French were afraid of the British fleet.

"Conscription in England was wholly ridiculous; this could only be built up after generations; it was absurd starting it in the middle of a was [war]. Man remarked that we had done this in our Civil war and it enabled us to defeat the South.

" 'Yes,' said the Emperor; 'but that was [war] lasted four years.'

"The Emperor seemed full of confidence; modestly said that after this war Europe would have to be entirely rebuilt and he was sixty years old.

"He seems to be so carefully surrounded by his officers that he is misinformed on many subjects."

Above is reliable but please do not inform anyone except the President as it might be traced to source and cause great trouble.

Gerard, Berlin.

T telegram (WP, DLC).

From Edward Mandell House, with Enclosure

Manchester, Massachusetts.

Dear Governor: August 4th, 1915.

Page is in a blue funk. So also is Sir Edward. To read Page's letters one would think the Germans were just outside London and moving rapidly westward upon New York.

As soon as our affairs with Great Britain become less acute, I think it would be well to send for Page and let him have thirty or forty days in this country. The war has gotten on his nerves and he has no idea what the sentiment of the people in this country is in regard to it.

Now that the fortunes of war are for the moment going against the Allies the feeling among them becomes more prevalent that we are not doing our share, and that which I feared might happen seems nearer today than ever, that we will soon be without friends anywhere.

They do not realize the diversity of races here, our isolation and consequent inability to see the bogies they set up. Nor do they altogether understand or appreciate the potential help we are giving them from an economic standpoint.

It is a difficult situation and gives me no little concern.

Your affectionate,   E. M. House

I inclose you a copy of my answer to Page. I have suggested that he show it to Sir Edward.

TLS (WP, DLC).

ENCLOSURE

Edward Mandell House to Walter Hines Page

Manchester, Massachusetts.

Dear Page: August 4th, 1915.

Your letters of the 20th and 21st come this morning to add something to the depression of the day.

Sir Edward and you cannot know the true situation here. I did not know it myself until I returned and began to plumb it. Ninety percent of our people do not want the President to involve us in war. They desire him to be firm in his treatment of Germany, but they do not wish him to go to such lengths that war will follow. He went to the very limit in his last note to Germany. If he had gone beyond that, he would have lost his influence with the American people.

Today he is the most popular President since Lincoln, and it is not altogether because of his firmness with Germany, but more particularly because he has not involved us in war. Roosevelt is utterly discredited as an extremist on the one hand, and Bryan is discredited as an extremist on the other.

If the President had followed any course other than the one he has, his influence would have been broken and he would not be able to steer the nation as he now is and which in the end, will be best for all. He sees the situation just as you see it and as I do, but he must necessarily heed the rocks.

His judgment and mine was that last Autumn was the time to discuss peace parleys and we both foresaw present possibilities. War is a great gamble at best and there was too much at stake in this one to take chances. I believe if we could have started peace parleys in November we could have forced the evacuation of both France and Belgium and finally forced a peace which would have eliminated militarism both on sea and land. The wishes of the Allies were heeded with the result that the war has now fastened itself upon the vitals of Europe, and what the end may be is beyond the knowledge of man.

I am sorry there is anyone in England who thinks so ill of the President as to write "A Merry Ballad of Woodrow Wilson."[1] It is the same sort of unjust criticism which is being leveled at England for not doing her share in this war. She has really done more than her share and is today the only obstacle between Germany and complete success. No one a year ago would have thought that England's part was more than to clear the seas and hold them free for the commerce of the Allies. But today she is criticized for not being able to cope with Germany on land.

And so it is with America. A year ago the Allies would have been content beyond measure if they could have been assured that munitions of war would go to them from here in such unrestricted volume, and if they had known that the President would demand of Germany a cessation of her submarine policy in regard to the sinking of merchantmen without warning, to the extent of a threat of war.

What neutral nation has done so much? The shipping of Holland, Sweden, Norway, Denmark and Spain have been sunk without warning and innumerable lives lost. Each of those nations, I take it, had passengers upon the Lusitania, and yet not one has raised a voice in protest and no criticism has come from the Allies. Holland today with her well equipped army and potential situation would be of more momentary value to the Allies than could the United States.

We are told that the Allies are fighting our battles. Be this as it may, are they not fighting more largely the battles of Holland and the smaller European states?

It is not altogether clear to Americans that we could not well take care of ourselves if needs be. Our hopes, our aspirations and our sympathies are closely woven with the democracies of France and England, and it is this that causes our hearts and potential economic help to go out to them and not the fear of what may follow for us in their defeat.

Your friend always,   [E. M. House]

TCL (WP, DLC).
[1] [Dugald Sutherland MacColl], *A Merry New Ballad of Dr. Woodrow Wilson, President of the United States in America: Embellished with Pictures by an Eminent Hand & Enriched with Historical Notes from the Original Sources* (Glasgow, 1915). Printed "for private circulation," this thirty-two-page doggerel was dated June 12, 1915, and signed with the initials "D.S.M." It concentrated on Wilson's diplomacy with regard to submarine warfare and the British blockade, although it also included a brief attack on his Mexican policy. A typical pair of stanzas ran as follows:

The President from prayerful thought
   Prolonged a day and night
Emerged like Moses from the Mount
   Dark with excess of light
Flags waved, and alien tears were shed
   "A nation, like a man" he said
     "May be too proud to fight"

But should an unregenerate Mob
Relieve him of a thankless job
   To hunt the sharks at sea
God send him favour in the crammed
Great College of the Faintly Damned
   Their President to be

MacColl was a painter, art critic, and art gallery director, who was at this time curator of the Wallace Collection in London.

From John Franklin Jameson

Glacier National Park

My dear Mr. President: August 4, 1915.

I wonder if anyone, except perhaps in some official report, has told you much about Lake Ellen Wilson. In the course of a three days' vacation walk here in this park, I came upon that lake this afternoon, with not a soul near; and, coming upon it at the time and angle I did, it was one of the great sensations of my life. It is surrounded by high mountains, perhaps 8000 or 9000 feet, partly verdant and partly of varie-colored rock and partly covered with patches of snow. The result was that, seen from a pass high above, it shone with color. Really, it was like an opal a mile long. It was so beautiful, so retired, so tranquil, that I could not think the lovely and gracious lady, if she could have seen it, would have been reluctant to have it bear her name.

Middletown memories were revived last month by meeting very pleasantly Professor Axson, whom I had not seen since those days, but who was lecturing to great and much-pleased audiences at the University of California.

Dear friend, I keep you daily in mind, wish you every success, enjoy deeply the noble record you are making.

Sincerely yours,   J. F. Jameson.

ALS (WP, DLC).

To Edith Bolling Galt

[Cornish, N. H.]

My precious Darling,   Wed. afternoon, 4 Aug., 1915

Your dear letter from Schenectady has just come and has filled my heart with such a deep flood of joy, (as that from Manchester

did) such a sweet abundance of content, that I must put everything else aside, close the door, take you in my arms, cover you
with kisses, and tell you how full to overflowing my thoughts
are with love for you, my wonderful Sweetheart! That "there
are no locked doors" in your dear heart any longer, that "all the
gates are flung wide open and a perfect flood of longing rushes
out" from its sweet thoughts to me, that you are indeed 'with all
your heart my own Edith,' fills me with an unutterable happiness
and sends my thoughts back to you more eager than ever to carry
you messages that will make you equally happy, equally content
with the present and yet eager,—oh, *so* eager, for the future. It
must be that the constant cry of my own heart for you is somehow conveyed to you across the spaces that seem (only seem)
to separate us, my Darling. Nothing—literally nothing—can put
you out of my thoughts, from day's end to day's end, my Beloved.
I long for you with an *unutterable* longing; and yet, all the while,
my heart is not heavy, but very light, because you seem to be
inseparably *by* me, your hand clasped within mine, your very lips
upon mine, your sweet self pressed close to my side, giving me
share of your life and consciousness of your very thoughts. It
was never quite so vivid or so real before, and the delight of it is
unspeakable. And my love for you—how can I put it into words!
—its tenderness; its deep influences dominating every part of
me, and every faculty; its power to put beauty into everything,
even the most commonplace, because everything is associated
with thoughts of you; its light-hearted joyfulness, because every
thought of you is so delightful, so full of exquisite memories and
of promises as sweet; its passion of loyalty and devotion, like a
new purpose in life. These things cannot be put into words. They
are too deep and real, too much stuff of the heart itself. One
would have to invent a new language; and, after all, the best
language for love such as ours is life itself. We do not merely
think and *say* that we belong to one another! Our hearts have in
fact become one,—and the joy of it all is that each of us *knows*
what is in the other's heart. We put it into words, not to prove
it or expound it, but to ease our longing and to delight one another,—just as our eyes speak when are together and kisses are
sweeter than words. My Darling, my Darling! A south-eastern
storm came up yesterday and the weather for two days has been
cold and bleak, but to me the whole world has seemed bright
because of you and your love. It brightens everything just to think
of you!

Thursday morning 5 Aug., 1915.
Business has gone on in a sort of routine, my precious Sweet-

heart, since you left, and has been *most* uninteresting because you were not here to share it. The critical matter just now is Haiti, and the complications of that we have not yet mastered. We are holding Port au Prince until we fully know what they are and get some key to them. It's a pretty mess! A long note from Germany about the sinking of the *Frye* (long ago)[1] gets us nowhere and affords additional proof how insincere and impossible they are. I am sending you, in a big envelope, Page's last letter,[2] just received. Keep it, Dearest, if it is not in your way, till we get back to Washington, unless you would rather return it and get rid of it.

Margaret and I laboured last night for about a quarter of an hour with "Central," to try to get a telephone connection with 10 Park Place, to see if you had reached there, and were told that Mr. Rose had no Bell telephone. Is that true? I did not believe it, but had to accept it, since I could not go and find out for myself. I take it for granted that you hardly undertook the whole 180 miles in such weather. It is so wet this morning that we shall be cut out of our golf. We played yesterday at Hanover, as per schedule, and were to have played this morning, as my sweet captain had commanded, at Claremont. The Carters arrived yesterday afternoon, Jessie and Frank got back from York Harbor (where they had left Helen well, and happy to be with her friends again) about five, and we had a most talkative evening. Mrs. Carter is very lively and attractive and is really great fun, and it was delightful, while she talked, to think of *you*,—of how much your charm surpasses that of any other woman, and how much more completely your mind interests and *grips* me. Indeed everything and everybody seems only to set me thinking more intensely and more delightedly of you. It is such *fun* to think of you, my charming, lovable, entrancing Darling, and of all that the sweet secret between us means. It does not make me proud to think of myself as the (temporarily) beloved President of the one hundred million people of a great nation, but it does make me proud to think of myself as the accepted and trusted lover of the sweet lady whom I adore. While Margaret and I were sitting here in the study last night working over the telephone connections with Geneva, Sweetheart, she told me of a conversation *she* had had with Nell about us, and said that Nell was evidently deeply and sincerely happy about it all. Then we fell to talking about you and I think it would have made you very happy to hear with what warm admiration and affection she spoke of you. I did not lead her on to it or invite it. It came with evident spontaneity and the tones of her voice meant more than the words themselves. You are going to be the idol of your household, my precious One, and will have to accept the fealty and worship of all of us, but I hope you will wish it chiefly from   Your own   Woodrow

My guests are demanding my attention. I *never* want to stop when I am talking with you and only wish this unmanageable pen would go as fast as my thoughts do. I love you, I love you, I love you!

ALS (WP, DLC).
¹ J. W. Gerard to RL, July 30, 1915, *FR-WWS 1915*, pp. 493-95.
² WHP to WW, July 23, 1915.

From Edith Bolling Galt

                                               10 Park Place, Geneva,
Dearest and best Beloved: N. Y. August 4, 1915

I have missed and wanted you so today that I know you have felt it. And I can hardly wait until tomorrow to get your blessed letter telling me of your self and

                                               August 5th, 10 am
My precious One,

I began this last night as you see, but could not finish it on account of one of those rare, but awful headaches I have. I had to stop and go to bed, and so before anything prevents this morning I am going to have a much-needed talk with my "other self"

I am quite well again this morning and think the headache was really neuralgia, as it has been so damp and rainy for days   But this morning is perfect, with floods of sunshine, and I am by a big window, with my purple writing case beside me and everything to make me happy *but, one great* lack.

How I did long for your tender fingers last night to rub away the pain in my eyes. After all I wondered if it was all physical pain or if the longing at my heart increased it ten fold. It was *our* anniversary of May 4th and that made the distance between us seem greater.

Just here the postman came, and I have just finished reading your beloved letter covering Tuesday and Wednesday and also the enclosurs in other envelope. You were sweet to send me such a long messenger when you had so many guests and things to claim you and every word has brought me happiness

I am so glad that you could tell "Nell" your self Dearest, for I know just how tenderly you two love each other and that coming from you directly made her understand far better. Bless her heart! I love her already, because you do, and appreciate all her sweetness and welcome to me more than I can express. I wish she could have stayed with you, but [am] so glad you have gotten such hold of yourself and that you are content and happy.

Thank you for sending me Mr. Lansing's telegram. I hope this means you can, at least, stay in Cornish until next week and know you will stay as long as possible. The letter enclosed from your admirer in California quite warms my heart toward him and makes me so glad other people appreciate you.

I see Mr. Crane has been appointed by Mr. Lansing,[1] so know that pleases you.

As to the Huerta development, I think it the most remarkable thing that gentleman has yet done and agree with you, that if the other party dared to, nothing would be more to their taste than what he suggests.

This is just the time we used to work, and I am wondering if you still take your work on the porch, or if you sit in the study or your own room. I am always with you, and love the way you put one dear hand on mine, while with the other you turn the pages of history.

I know how you miss Helen—and suppose Jessie and Frank are already home—and the Carters will arrive this afternoon. You have certainly had plenty of diversion in the way of guests, and I trust have enjoyed them.

I found 2 letters from Rolfe here, but nothing new in them except the fact that even if Powell[2] should come to Panama he thinks it would be too late to change things and [is] still hoping he, Rolfe, can leave at once. He had not gotten the letter *we* wrote in the morning room, but I don't think that will change his attitude.

We came 180 miles yesterday—most of the way in a downpour of rain—but at Syracuse the sun came out and smiled upon us for a brief interval to cheer us on our way.

I am so sorry I missed your telephone call at Troy, but you know now we went on to Schenectady. It would have been a joy to have talked to you—so glad the Dr. seems happy   I want to put a line in this to Margaret so must stop, but my love goes on my precious Woodrow, and I am   yours always   Edith.

P.S. I forgot to say my trunk got here on Tuesday and is unpacked and everything in nice shape. But you did not play fair on that, as you said you would have it sent *collect*. Thank you for this, but you know how I feel about such matters—and that it embarrasses me.   As always   E.

ALS (WP, DLC).
[1] Lansing had just appointed Richard Crane, son of Charles R. Crane, as his private secretary.
[2] Unidentified.

To Robert Lansing, with Enclosure

My dear Mr. Secretary,   [Cornish, N. H.] 5 August, 1915.

I have gone over this paper very carefully indeed, and these questions urge themselves upon me:

1. Can this argument not be taken as an argument in sympathy with the Allies and against militarism, which is Germany?

2. Are we not ourselves about to urge the control of the manufacture of arms and munitions by every government in our proposed understandings and undertakings with the Latin-American countries; and do we not wish ultimately to strive for the same thing in the final European settlement?

Of course we are arguing only to the special case, and are absolutely unanswerable in our position that these things cannot be done *while a war is in progress* as against the parties to it; but how far, do you think, the arguments we urge in this paper will estop us in future deliberations on the peace and security of the world?   Faithfully Yours,   W.W.

WWTLI (SDR, RG 59, 763.72111 EM 1/31½, DNA).

E N C L O S U R E[1]

Draft of reply to Austro-Hungarian Note
of June 29, 1915, regarding prohibition
of exportation of Arms and Ammunition.

The Government of the United States has given careful consideration to the statement of the Imperial and Royal Government in regard to the exportation of arms and ammunition from the United States to the countries at war with Austro-Hungary and Germany. ⟨It is a matter of satisfaction that the Imperial and Royal Government recognizes that the attitude of this Government in regard to such exportation emanates from no other than an intention⟩ *The Government of the United States notes with satisfaction the recognition by the Imperial and Royal Government of the undoubted fact that its attitude with regard to the exportation of arms and ammunition from the United States is prompted by its intention* to "maintain the strictest neutrality and to conform to the letter of the provisions of international treaties⟨.⟩" ⟨But⟩, *but is surprised to find* the Imperial and Royal Government implying that the observance of the ⟨letter of the⟩ *strict principle of the* law under the conditions⟨,⟩ which have

---

[1] The following document was a new draft written by Lansing. The text in angle brackets was deleted by Wilson; that in italics, except for the title, was inserted by him.

developed in the present war⟨,⟩ is insufficient, ⟨asserts⟩ *and asserting* that this Government should go beyond the long recognized rules governing ⟨the⟩ *such* traffic by neutrals ⟨in munitions of war⟩ and adopt measures to ⟨effect the "desire of the Federal Government to⟩ "maintain an attitude of strict parity with respect to both belligerent parties."

To this assertion of *an* obligation to change or modify the rules of international usage on account of special conditions the Government of the United States cannot accede. The recognition of an obligation of this sort, unknown to the international practice of the past, would impose upon every neutral nation a duty to sit in judgment on the progress of a war and to restrict its commercial intercourse with a belligerent whose naval successes prevented the neutral from trade with the enemy. The contention of the Imperial and Royal Government appears to be that the advantages gained to a belligerent by its superiority on the sea should be equalized by the neutral powers ⟨establishing⟩ *by the establishment of* a system of non-intercourse with the victor. The Imperial and Royal Government confines its comments to arms and ammunition, but, if the principle for which it contends is sound, it should apply with equal force to all articles of contraband. A belligerent controlling the high seas might possess an ample supply of arms and ammunition but be in want of food and clothing. On the novel principle that equalization is a neutral duty, neutral nations would be obliged to place an embargo on such articles because one ⟨belligerent⟩ *of the belligerants* could not obtain them through commercial intercourse.

But, if this principle, so strongly urged by the Imperial and Royal Government, *should be admitted to obtain* by reason of the superiority of a belligerent at sea, ought it not to operate equally as to a belligerent superior on land? Applying ⟨the⟩ *this* theory of equalization, a belligerent⟨,⟩ who lacks the necessary munitions to contend successfully on land⟨,⟩ ought to be permitted to purchase them from neutrals, while a belligerent with an abundance of war stores or with the power to produce them should be debarred from such traffic.

Manifestly the idea of ⟨a⟩ strict neutrality *now* advanced by the Imperial and Royal Government would involve a neutral nation in a mass of perplexities⟨,⟩ which would *obscure the whole field of international obligation*, produce economic confusion, and deprive ⟨its⟩ *all* commerce and industry of legitimate fields of enterprise already heavily burdened by the unavoidable restrictions of ⟨an international⟩ war.

In this connection it is pertinent to direct the attention of the Imperial and Royal Government to the fact that Austria-Hungary and Germany, particularly the latter, have during the years preceeding the present European war produced a great surplus of arms and ammunition, which they sold throughout the world and especially to belligerents. Never during that period did either of them suggest or apply the principle now advocated by the Imperial and Royal Government.

During the Boer War between Great Britain and *the* South African Republics the patrol of the coasts of neighboring neutral colonies by British naval vessels prevented arms and ammunition⟨s⟩ reaching the Transvaal or the Orange Free State. The Allied Republics were in a situation almost identical *in that respect* with that in which Austria-Hungary and Germany ⟨are⟩ *find themselves* at the present time. Yet, in spite of ⟨this⟩ *the* commercial isolation of one belligerent, Germany sold to *Great Britain*, the other belligerent, ⟨Great Britain,⟩ hundreds of thousands of kilos of explosives, gunpowder, cartridges, shot and weapons; and ⟨to a less degree⟩ *it is known that* Austria-Hungary *also* sold similar munitions to the same purchaser⟨.⟩, *though in smaller quantities.* While, *as* compared with the present war, the ⟨amounts are small⟩ *quan[ti]ties sold were small* (a table of the sales is appended), the principle of neutrality involved ⟨is⟩ *was* the same. If at that time Austria-Hungary and her present ally had refused to sell arms and ammunition to Great Britain on the ground that to do so would violate the spirit of strict neutrality, the Imperial and Royal Government might with greater consistency and greater force urge its present contention.

It might be further pointed out that during the Crimean War large quantities of arms and military stores were furnished to Russia by Prussian manufacturers; that during the recent war between Turkey and Italy, as this Government is advised, arms and ammunition were furnished to the Ottoman Government by Germany; and that during the Balkan wars the belligerents were supplied with munitions by *both* Austria-Hungary and Germany. While these latter cases are not analogous, as is the case of the South African War, to the ⟨present⟩ situation of Austria-Hungary and Germany⟨, it⟩ *in the present war, they nevertheless clearly* indicate⟨s⟩ the long-established practice of the two Empires in the matter of trade in war-supplies.

In view of the foregoing statements, this Government is reluctant to believe that the Imperial and Royal Government will ⟨imply unneutrality to⟩ *ascribe to* the United States *a lack of impartial neutrality* in continuing its legitimate trade in all kinds of supplies used to render the armed forces of a belligerent efficient, even though the ⟨fortunes of⟩ *circumstances of the present* war prevent Austria-Hungary from obtaining such supplies from the markets of the United States, which have been and ⟨are open to all belligerents alike.⟩ *remain, so far as the action and policy of this Government are concerned, open to all belligerants alike.*

But, in addition to the question of principle, there is a practical and substantial reason why the Government of the United States has from the foundation of the Republic to the present time advocated and practiced unrestricted trade in arms and military supplies. It has never been the policy of this country to maintain in time of peace a large military establishment or stores of arms and ammunition sufficient to repel invasion by a well equipped and powerful enemy. It has desired to remain at peace with all nations and to avoid any appearance of menacing such peace by the threat of its armies and navies. In consequence of this standing policy the United States would, in the event of attack by a foreign power, be at the outset of the war seriously, if not fatally embarrassed by the lack of arms and ammunition and by the means to produce them in sufficient quantities to supply the requirements of national defense. The United States has always depended upon the right and power to purchase arms and ammunition from neutral nations in case of foreign attack. This right, which it claims for itself, it cannot deny to others.

A nation⟨, relying⟩ *whose principle and policy it was to rely* upon international obligations and international justice to preserve its political and territorial integrity, ⟨would⟩ *might* become the prey of an aggressive nation ⟨which increases⟩ *whose policy and practice it was to increase* its military strength during times of peace with the design of conquest, unless the nation ⟨be⟩ attacked could, after war had been declared, go into the markets of the world and purchase the means to defend ⟨its national safety⟩ *itself* against the agressor.

The general adoption by the nations *of the world* of the theory that neutral powers ought to prohibit the sale of arms and ammunition to belligerents would compel all nations to have ⟨stored⟩ *in readiness* at all times sufficient munitions of war to meet any emergency which might arise and to erect and maintain establishments for the manufacture of arms and ammunition ⟨in⟩ sufficient ⟨number⟩ to supply the needs of ⟨the⟩ *her* military and naval forces ⟨during the⟩ *throughout the* progress of a war. Manifestly the application of this theory would result in every nation becoming an armed camp, ready to resist aggression and tempted to employ force in asserting its rights rather than appeal⟨ing⟩ to reason and justice for the settlement of international disputes.

⟨The Government of the United States perceives that the prohibition of the⟩ *Perceiving, as it does, that the adoption of the principle that it is the duty of a neutral to prohibit the* sale ⟨to a belligerent⟩ of arms and ammunition *to a belligerant* during the progress of a war⟨, as a neutral duty,⟩ would *inevitably* give the advantage to the belligerent which had encouraged the manufacture of munitions in time of peace⟨,⟩ and which had lai⟨n⟩*d* in vast stores of arms and ammunition in anticipation of war, *the Government of the United States is* is [*sic*] convinced that the adoption of the theory would force militarism on the world and work against that universal peace which is the desire and purpose of all nations which exalt justice and righteousness in their relations with one another.

While the practice of nations, so well illustrated by the practice of Austria Hungary and Germany during the South African War, and the manifest evil which would result from a change of that practice⟨,⟩ render compliance with the suggestions of the Imperial and Royal Government out of the question, certain assertions appearing in the Austro-Hungarian statement as grounds for its contentions cannot be passed over without comment. These assertions are substantially as follows: (1) that the exportation of arms and ammunition from the United States to belligerents contravenes the preamble of The Hague Convention No. 13 of 1907: (2) that it is inconsistent with the refusal of this Government to allow delivery of supplies to vessels of war on the high seas: (3) that, "according to all authorities on international law who concern themselves more properly with the question," exportation should be prevented "when this traffic assumes such a form or such dimensions that the neutrality of a nation becomes involved thereby."

As to the assertion that the exportation of arms and ammunition contravenes the preamble of The Hague Convention No. 13 of 1907, this Government presumes that reference is made to the last paragraph of the preamble, which is as follows:

> "Seeing that, in this category of ideas, these rules should not, in principle, be altered, in the course of the war, by a neutral Power, except in a case where experience has shown the necessity for such change for the protection of the rights of that Power."

Manifestly the only ground to change the rules laid down by the Convention, one of which, *it should be noted, explicitly* declares that a neutral is not bound to prohibit the exportation of contraband of war, is the necessity of a neutral power to do so in order to protect its *own* rights. ⟨The determination as to⟩ *The right and duty to determine when* this necessity *exists* rests with the neutral, not with a belligerent. It is discretionary, not mandatory. If a neutral power does not avail itself of the ⟨permission⟩ *right*, a belligerent is not privileged to complain, for in doing so it would be in the position of declaring to the neutral power what is necessary to protect ⟨its⟩ *that power's* own rights. The Imperial and Royal Government cannot but perceive that a complaint of this nature would invite just rebuke.

With reference to the asserted inconsistency of the course adopted by this Government in relation to the exportation of arms and ammunition and that followed in not allowing supplies to be taken from its ports to ships of war on the high seas, it is only necessary to point out that the prohibition of supplies to ships of war rests upon the principle that a neutral power must not permit its territory to become a naval base for either belligerent. A warship may under certain restrictions obtain fuel and supplies in a neutral port once in three months. To permit merchant vessels acting as tenders to carry supplies more often than three months and in unlimited amount would defeat the purpose of the rule, and constitute the neutral territory a naval base. Furthermore, this Government is unaware that any Austro-Hungarian ship of war has sought to obtain supplies from a port in the United States either directly or indirectly. ⟨The⟩ *This* subject has, ⟨been⟩ however, *already been* discussed with the Imperial German Government, to which the position of this Government was fully set forth December 24, 1914.

In view of the positive assertion in the statement of the Imperial and Royal Government as to the unanimity of the opinions of text-writers as to the exportation of contraband being unneutral this Government has caused a careful examination of the principal authorities on international law to be made. As a result of this examination it has come to the conclusion that the Imperial and Royal Government has been misled and *has* inadvertently made an erroneous assertion. Less than one fifth of the authorities consulted advocate unreservedly the prohibition of the export of contraband. Several of ⟨those writers⟩ *those who constitute this minority* admit that the practice of nations has been otherwise. It may not be inopportune to direct particular attention to the declaration of the German authority, Paul Einicke, who states that, at the beginning of a war, belligerents have never remonstrated against the enactment of prohibitions on trade in contraband, but adds "that such prohibitions may be considered as violations of neutrality, or at least as unfriendly acts, if they are enacted during a war with the purpose to close unexpectedly the sources of supply to a party which heretofore had relied on them."

The Government of the United States deems it unnecessary to extend further at the present time a consideration of the statement of the Austro-Hungarian Government. The principles of international law, the ⟨universal⟩ practice of nations, the national safety of the United States and other nations without great military and naval establishments, the prevention of increased armies and navies, the adoption of peaceful methods for the adjustment of international differences, and, finally, neutrality itself are opposed to ⟨a⟩ *the prohibition by a* neutral nation ⟨prohibiting⟩ *of* the exportation of arms, ammunition, or other munitions of war to ⟨the⟩ belligerent powers during the progress of the war.

T MS (SDR, RG 59, 763.72111 EM 1/31½, DNA).

To Edward Mandell House

Dearest Friend,   [Cornish, N. H.] 5 August, 1915.

A letter from Page, received yesterday, bearing date the twenty-third of July, suggests the following, which he is urging on the ministers in England: that, cotton being put on the list of contraband, the Order in Council of the eleventh of March be rescinded. Does it not seem to you that that is a good tip for Spring Rice, and that if they would clear away the so-called blockade and buy an unusual amount of our cotton our public would see that we were getting the best we could out of a bad situation?

I send you this for fear Page may not have written to you also about what he has been working on.

In haste,   Affectionately Yours,   Woodrow Wilson

WWTLS (E. M. House Papers, CtY).

From Robert Lansing

Washington, D. C., August 5, 1915

Confidential. Had a two-hours session with the six diplomats and Mr. Fuller in regard to Mexico. There was manifested unanimous feeling of gratification that this informal conference had been called as indicating the attitude of the Government toward Pan Americanism. We made decided progress toward an agreement as to identical views in regard to the character of government which should be recognized. The conference adjourned till tomorrow afternoon. I believe that a definite and practical plan will result. Of course, I shall agree to nothing nor take a definite attitude without fully consulting you. As, however, the meeting tomorrow will be a continuance of the preliminary discussion, I can see no reason for your immediate return to Washington. I will telegraph you if I should think it necessary or essential that you should be here.   Robert Lansing.

T telegram (WP, DLC).

From John Lowndes McLaurin

Mr. President: Columbia, S. C. August 5, 1915.

As you perhaps know, South Carolina has been operating a State Warehouse system since last October. Very valuable aid has been rendered in financing the warehouse receipts by Mr. Harding, of the Federal Reserve Board. I note with great satisfaction an Associated Press dispatch giving instructions to the banks how to proceed with regard to the certificates.

I have been in such close contact with the cotton situation for the past year that I am going to venture a suggestion:

The borrowing power of our cotton is in proportion to the market price, and if much cotton is offered for sale in the open market, under present conditions, the price is bound to be so low that we will not be able to borrow enough to meet the debts incurred in making the cotton. It seems to me that there are two practical methods which might be employed to give the price of cotton a boost about the time that the crop is coming on the market. This would fix the borrowing basis, and enable us to tide over the war situation.

First. I take it, from the statements which I have seen from Secretary Daniels and others, that this government will soon begin to place herself upon a broader military footing, and to do this will need large quantities of low grade cotton for the manufacture of explosives. This low grade cotton is the heaviest burden that there is upon the market, and, as a business proposition, its purchase at present prices would be a good investment, and relieve the pressure on the better grades.

Second. It must be realized that there is great dissatisfaction and a sharp division of sentiment in the United States over the action of England in shutting off the European markets from American cotton. The low grade cotton to which I refer is a necessity in the manufacture of explosives, and the Allies will continue to need it in large quantities. As a matter of diplomacy, it would seem that the purchase of this cotton would be a good thing for them to do in changing the trend of sentiment setting strongly against England, especially in the South. If England could corner the available supply of raw material for gun cotton, she would not only provide for the future of the Allies, but hold a tremendous advantage over her enemies.

If a reasonable price could be fixed, say ten cents net, to the present holders of cotton, England and the United States would hold a monopoly in low grade raw cotton which they could manufacture for war purposes or sell for future commerce at a profit. Neither country could lose by purchasing cotton at the price of production. Both countries would be acquiring supplies for war purposes, and would not be open to the charge of valorizing a commodity for political or other ends. I am of the opinion that two million bales of strict low middling cotton taken up in this way would establish a firm borrowing basis for the entire crop.

I have watched your efforts to maintain the neutrality of this country, and admired the calmness and wisdom with which you have acted. In my humble sphere I have been doing what I could to sustain you, and I am hoping that some way can be found to ameliorate conditions which are almost inevitable without some artificial aid to sustain the market. The October movement generally breaks the price, and now is the time to act. I regard the sharp advance yesterday as due primarily to the statement by the Federal Reserve Board, coupled with Mr. Harding's interview, rather than to crop news, as stated in the report from the New York Exchange. I do not think the price of any article of commerce is so much a matter of psychology as cotton. This is seen in the manner in which England maintained the price of Egyptian cotton last fall.

With assurances of my highest respect and confidence,

Respectfully,   Jno. L. McLaurin

TLS (WP, DLC).

From Mabel Thorp Boardman

Dear Mr. President: [Washington] Aug. 5th, 1915

My mother[1] and I greatly appreciated your and Miss Wilson's kindness in remembering my dear father[2] and sending the beautiful wreath yesterday.

After more than fifty years of the happiest and most perfect married life the separation is almost overwhelming for my dear mother, but with her brave and unselfish heart she tries to suppress her grief for our sakes. To all of us my father left such a blessed, beautiful memory that it is a great comfort.

With again many sincere thanks for thinking of us in the midst of your great burden of work, I am, Mr. President,

Yours respectfully,   Mabel T. Boardman.

ALS (WP, DLC).
1 Florence Sheffield Boardman.
2 William Jarvis Boardman, who had died on August 2.

To Edith Bolling Galt

[Cornish, N. H.]

My precious Darling,   Thursday evening 5 Aug., 1915

Every moment I *can* spend writing to you I must spend. I think of you so constantly, I long for you so passionately, that I am as restless as any caged tiger if I cannot at least be pouring out my heart to you when I am free to come to my desk at all, before and after business. And the intervals are not frequent or long enough at best (what with golf—which it would distress my sweet lady for me to omit—and business and auto. rides *and guests*) to give me time to write much, because this hand is so hard to manage when there's a pen in it and the pen lags so far behind the thoughts that run eagerly out to seek my Darling. It's a poor, slow substitute at best for the conversations with my sweet One that have filled the past weeks with joy and comfort. How I long for the sound of that dear voice, and, when evening comes, for those sweet tones of it that vibrated so with tenderness and the love that comprehends and transforms all! When I read your dear letters I seem actually to hear it, and am thrilled as nothing else conceivable could thrill me. The words of love you speak and write seem to me,—*are* to me—a veritable charter of happiness, and of freedom from the care that burdens the heart! What blessings you have brought me, my Love, my precious Darling! I took a drive over to Springfield this afternoon only to see the Adna Brown hotel where you had taken lunch on Monday. Only George Howe (I am in a hurry to have you know the dear chap) went with me, for our household has undergone to-day one of its kaleidoscopic changes. The Carters left early in the afternoon; Frank was to start for New York *and Labrador* at six (poor Jessie is very desolate to-night!); Margaret, the doctor, Miss Batten, and "little" Annie went horse-back riding; and, because little Annie was out, sister felt she had to stay at home and take care of Josephine. George and I were the residuum. We went "the Claremont round," with Springfield thrown in "on the side." I felt every foot of the way as you did—that nothing on the way looked as it had looked when my Darling had sat by my side and seen it with me, and could never look the same again, never have the same charm again, until we should again see it together. The association of every part of every familiar road with her is so poignant that it almost *hurts*; but *anything* associated with her is dear to me, draws me to it in spite of myself; and I am willing to pay the price for the sake of the sweet and vivid memories.

A cipher message from Lansing this evening says the A.B.C. conference opened very happily to-day and will continue to-morrow its work of determining exactly what it will seek to accomplish. He will telegraph me the minute he thinks that it would be best for me to come down and confirm, or direct, what it is doing. I fancy he will summon me for (say) Monday. The only other interesting things the day has brought me I am sending you, in another envelope.

I must go to bed now, it is late. Good night, Darling. I will come to you again early in the morning.

Friday morning, 6.30. 6 Aug. 1915.

I am just up, my precious One, and had such a strange experience in the night. At five minutes after two (I lighted the candle by my bedside and looked at my watch) I suddenly waked up with, oh, such a pang at my heart because *I could not find you*. I found myself exclaiming "Edith, my Darling, *where are you?*" It was as if you had been at my side but a moment before and had then gone utterly away both in person and in thought. The desolation and loneliness of it was unspeakable. I had to get up and wake myself thoroughly to recover myself and see things right again. I wonder if it all corresponded with any dream or experience of my Darling's? I hope not. I would not like to have her suffer so. And it was so strange, coming, as it did, in the midst of calm happiness! Perhaps it was only because no letter from my precious One reached me yesterday and I felt specially lonely. I can easily imagine how that happened because I have been finding out about the mails between here and northern New York and they are slow and roundabout. I fear my letters will not reach you till the second day after they are written. But, if I can only establish their unbroken sequence, you will at least know every day with what a deep, happy, and abiding love I think of you every moment of the day. And the love is combined with so many vivid and delightful things which I am sure I should feel whether I loved you or not,—with a deep admiration; with the consciousness of a *greatness* of character in you, a greatness not only of faculty and of feeling but also of personality which your extraordinary vitality and charm render irresistible. I so deeply *enjoy* every thought of what you are and so rejoice to have the stimulation of it, and the sense of beauty and sweetness, besides—of a wonderful woman, as trustworthy and capable and fit for counsel as any man, but quick with a power of love, of sympathy, of inspiration which no man could possess. I never feel so proud or so strong as when I know that I am

Your own   Woodrow.

ALS (WP, DLC).

From Edith Bolling Galt

My precious One: Geneva, August 5th, 1915 midnight

Will you forgive a pencil tonight? For I am in bed where I cannot use the ink without endangering some very lovely linen things in the way of sheets and pillow cases—and I must talk to you a little while before I put my light out.

Shall I give you a picture of my abode that you may better visualize me—Well this is a big square room with high old-fashioned mantlepiece between 2 big windows. The latter have white curtains with blue borders, and the walls are blue & white.

All the furnature is big and massive, and by one window is a writing desk, where you can sit and talk to loved ones far away or gaze out over a big green yard—full of big apple trees —and on into a vegetable garden beyond. But—to come back to the room. In the centre of the side wall is a wide, low, old timey bed with big pillows piled high. And just now, in the centre of these, rests a lonely lady who loves you very dearly and while she writes is almost deafened by the claps of thunder and torrents of rain that roar and clash without.

Just over her head is an electric light which makes even the vivid lightning less disturbing than it would be.

It is just the kind of night to carry out a plot or do some wild thing that needs the cover of storm and darkness.

I know you did not get a letter from me today and that is why you got Margaret to send the telegram tonight. Thank you for it, precious One. I would have answered it except I thought it

might be telephoned after you were all asleep, as it was nine
thirty when I got yours. But I wrote you, Margaret and Jessie
today so you will have them all tomorrow. And I think perhaps,
on account of publicity, I had better not telegraph. Oh, Woodrow,
how I did love every word in these twenty one pages I got from
you this morning. What a wealth of love was stored into them
and with what eagerness did my heart feed on all your dear
fingers had written! I read it all over again this afternoon, for I
had to hurry over it this morning as I wanted to get my letter off
to you while Mr. & Mrs. R. were downtown. And after they got
back I did not have a moment until late this afternoon.

Mrs. R. asked me in such a naive way this morning, when I
said I wanted to stay and write to Margaret and Helen to thank
them for all their sweet courtesy to me—"Oh but you won't have
to write to the President too will you?" that I almost laughed—
but managed to say "Well, I hardly suppose it is necessary, but
I might send him just a line" Then tonight when your telegram
came, Mrs. R. answered the phone and then called me and said
it was a telegram and she was afraid someone was sick. So, of
course, I told her it was just a message from Margaret saying she
hoped we had all arrived safely. When she said, "Oh! of course
they have read of these dreadful rains and have heard nothing
from you since you phoned the night you left, so they may have
felt uneasy."

I almost had to bite my tongue to keep from saying oh, yes
I have written every day except yesterday, but, fortunately,
caught myself in time, and instead said yes I suppose they have
and it was like Margaret to think of sending us a line of greeting.

Oh Sweetheart I almost die of internal combustion when the
Roses tell their friends of you and your charm and other people
ask questions and say how wonderful they think you are. I want
to go and hug them for appreciating you and then stagger them
by saying you love me and how perfectly I worship you. But of
course I can't do either of these things and just keep quiet for
fear if I do speak I will say too much.

Friday, 10 a.m.

The mail has just come, and brought me that which makes the
day bright—your letter of Wed. and Thursday and I have read
it through twice and will again when I finish this.

Thank you Dearest for all the love it brings and for the assurance that you are so happy in our perfect comprehension of each
other. I have just been reading the N. Y. Times—and wonder,

if what they say about the A.B.C. Conference is true? I suppose it is, as they say it is given out by Mr. Lansing. How much I hope you may be able to straighten out that problem at least, for Germany seems bent on giving us more and more trouble.

Thank you for sending me Mr. Page's letter. I expect it will come by the next mail, as it failed to with yours. I know I will enjoy it, and will keep it as you direct until I get home   But, Precious One, how much I wish we could read it together before the fire in the music room as we did the last one.

This is a gray rainy day and we had to give up our plan to go to the country club for a lesson in golf. But I hope to begin my lessons next week and work hard so someday I can play with you.

I knew from the Hanover postmark that you played there, as the letter was stamped 10 a.m., and I am sorry you could not get a game yesterday.

I have just asked Mrs. Rose about the telephone and she says there is no Bell telephone in the house as there are 2 local lines and they have these—so unless you go downtown you cannot get long distance   This is a nuisance but should there be any necessity I think you could ask the main office here to send a message to me and I could go to a public booth. Of course you would not want to do this except for important things

Give my dearest love to the girls and hug that blessed little Margaret for me. She was always so full of sympathetic comprehension.

Now I must stop and write to my family, but I would lots rather keep on talking to you.

Goodby until tomorrow and remember I am now—and always

Your own,   Edith.

ALS (WP, DLC).

To Robert Lansing, with Enclosure

My dear Mr. Secretary,   [Cornish, N. H.] 6 August, 1915.

Perhaps House sends you such pieces of information as this at the same time that he sends them to me, but, for fear he does not, I hand this on for what it is worth.

Faithfully Yours,   W.W.

WWTLI (WP, DLC).

E N C L O S U R E

From Edward Mandell House

Manchester, Massachusetts.

Dear Governor: August 6th, 1915.

I have just seen Spring-Rice. He had a cable from Sir Edward saying that he was now discussing with the French Government the policy of intercepting German goods in which the French and English Navies are acting in agreement.[1]

The other day, I gave Sir Edward, through Spring-Rice, something of your Mexican plan.[2] His reply to that is "I am much relieved to receive the message so kindly sent me regarding Mexico."

Sir Cecil tells me they are pleased with the plan and wish it every success.

I asked him what he thought of American interests in Mexico furnishing money to finance the government. He thought it would create a very bad impression in Europe, and he hoped we would find some other way out.

In reply to your letter about this, I think it can be done temporarily through American bankers with the understanding that you will try to get Congress, when it meets, to approve of the Government guaranteeing a loan which will have sufficient security back of it to make it safe. The temporary loan could be secured through banks or bankers in which the people having large holdings in Mexico are interested. This will be much the same thing, but will be less open to criticism.

I have gone into the cotton situation very fully today. First with Governor Strong[3] of the New York Federal Reserve Bank. He had many useful ideas in connection with it. I later took it up with Sir Cecil.

Sir Richard Crawford has this matter in hand[4] and I have arranged to bring him and Strong together.

Strong's idea is that if the British Government will put sufficient money back of a plan to take three million bales off the market, there will be no cotton problem to solve. S. R. says American bankers have expressed a willingness to handle the transaction[5] and to hold the cotton for two years if necessary, in this country, so it will not come in competition with foreign shipments or with present consumption. The British Government are to take what loss, if any, and the bankers have the privilege of selling the cotton above ten cents f.o.b. and make whatever profit they can. The British Government do not want to be in a position of making a profit out of it.

Strong's idea is that this plan should be carried out quietly. If anything is said about it, the reply should be that it is a matter between the British Government and the American planter and the German, or any other Government, can make a similar arrangement if they desire.

Governor Hamlin, of the Federal Reserve Board, lunched with me day before yesterday. I think the matter of credits, about which I wrote you, will work out satisfactorily. Hamlin said that both Warburg and Miller had not allowed their German sympathies to influence them in the slightest in their actions. I was glad to hear this and I know you will be.

I told Vick sometime ago that it would not do for an appointment to be given him because Mr. Bryan and his friends would resent it. He thought, perhaps, Mr. Bryan would endorse him. I suggested that he try. That was about a month ago and he has not mentioned it since.

The unfinished letter was probably sent that way because there was no room to close it with the typewriter. The sentence was finished.   Your affectionate,   E. M. House

TLS (WP, DLC).
    [1] It is E. Grey to C. A. Spring Rice, Aug. 5, 1915, T telegram (FO 382/464, No. 105854, PRO).
    [2] It is C. A. Spring Rice to E. Grey, Aug. 3, 1915, T telegram (E. Grey Papers, FO 800/85, PRO), saying that the American plan was "to recognise provisional Coalition Government, cut off supplies of money and arms from all others, obtain recognition from South American Governments, then from Europe, guarantee loan with control, and thus pacify without using force."
    [3] That is, Benjamin Strong.
    [4] Crawford's negotiations are related in C. A. Spring Rice to E. Grey, July 28 and 30, 1915, T telegrams (FO 382/464, Nos. 103200, 104511, PRO); and E. Grey to C. A. Spring Rice, July 30, 1915, T telegram (FO 382/464, No. 103290, PRO). For further discussion of the so-called "Crawford plan," see Link, *Struggle for Neutrality*, pp. 606-16.
    [5] Spring Rice conveyed this information in C. A. Spring Rice to E. Grey, July 28, 1915, T telegram (FO 382/464, No. 103290, PRO).

To John Sharp Williams

My dear Senator: Cornish, N. H., August 6, 1915

Your letter of August second[1] has caused me deep and genuine grief. Surely, my dear Senator, you know me better and know my personal feeling for you better than to suppose that there was any intention to put the least slight upon you or to do anything that would wound you in the matter of the appointments in the District Attorney's office, and I am sure I can speak for the Attorney General to the same effect. There is no one in public life for whom I have a warmer personal feeling or a more genuine admiration than I have for you, and I am sure that if you did not learn of the appointment of Mr. George[2] directly from the department it was only because it was taken for granted at the first that your recommendation in that matter would be followed.

As to the Assistant District Attorney, I had a long conference with the Attorney General. I did not suppose that you felt that this, which has generally been regarded as strictly a departmental appointment, lay within the field of what you felt you had a right to claim, and I have not at any time supposed, my dear Senator, that you took the position that you desired your recommendations accepted without my exercising the privilege of forming a personal judgment about the qualifications of the nominee for myself. I am sure now that that is not the position that you wish to take. The truth of the matter, if I may say it in the utmost kindness and confidence, is that young Mr. Lee's[3] personal habits are such, if I am correctly informed, as to make me doubt very seriously the wisdom of appointing him to the place at his present age; and I hoped, my dear Senator, that you would understand and share my desire to appoint Mr. Alexander's son,[4] who, of course you understand, did not directly or indirectly solicit the place and to whom so far as I know our idea of appointing him is even yet unknown.

As to your retiring from public life, I think that would be nothing less than a public misfortune and I beg that you will consider nothing of the kind. This whole matter will be handled with the utmost consideration for yourself, and I am writing this letter to beg that you will reconsider the whole matter in the light of what I have said and let me know what you would suggest,—whether it is your desire, in fact, that I should appoint young Mr. Lee when personally I do not believe that it would be wise either for him or for the public service that I should do so. I know that you will speak to me with the utmost frankness about this, as you have always about all things, and I know that I can count upon your friendship for me as well as your unswerving devotion to the public service to deal with this matter in a way which will lead to nothing so distressing as a personal difference between us, or anything that would deprive the country of your services as Senator.

Please let me hear from you again, and say anything that you please.

Cordially and sincerely yours,   Woodrow Wilson

TLS (J. S. Williams Papers, DLC).

[1] It is missing in WP, DLC; there is a HwCL in the J. S. Williams Papers, DLC.

[2] Joseph Warren George, of Yazoo City, Miss., had been nominated on July 20 to a recess appointment as United States attorney for the southern district of Mississippi. He was confirmed by the Senate on January 10, 1916.

[3] Richard Charles Lee, Jr., of Jackson, Miss., son of the recently deceased United States attorney for the southern district of Mississippi.

[4] Julian Power Alexander, Princeton 1908, of Jackson, whose father, Charlton Henry Alexander, also a lawyer of Jackson, had died suddenly of a stroke just after delivering a speech on Wilson's behalf at the Democratic state convention in May 1912. See William F. Holmes, *The White Chief: James Kimble Vardaman* (Baton Rouge, La., 1970), pp. 263-64. Eventually, young Alexander did receive the appointment as assistant attorney.

To Sophia Gompers[1]

My dear Madam: Cornish, N. H., August 6, 1915

I have read your letter of August third[2] with the deepest sympathy. I feel like congratulating you on having had a son[3] whose dignity[4] it was to die in the service of his country, but my heart goes out to you none the less in profound sympathy.

I am sure that it would be the desire of everyone connected with the public service to see that you did not suffer need because of your son's death. I am sending your letter to the Secretary of the Navy to inquire whether there is any possibility under the law as it stands of assisting you.[5] I fear that there is not, but I am sure the Secretary of the Navy will wish to consider the matter very fully.

         Cordially and sincerely yours,   Woodrow Wilson

CCL (Letterpress Books, WP, DLC).

[1] Of 107 Stockton Street, Brooklyn.

[2] Sophia Gompers to WW, Aug. 3, 1915, ALS (J. Daniels Papers, DLC).

[3] William C. Gompers, killed in Port-au-Prince on July 29. He was a nephew of Samuel Gompers.

[4] Wilson dictated "duty."

[5] WW to J. Daniels, Aug. 6, 1915, TLS (J. Daniels Papers, DLC).

Two Letters from Robert Lansing

My Dear Mr. President: Washington August 6, 1915.

I return to you Colonel House's letter of the 2d, in which he states the substance of an interview with the British Ambassador.

Sir Cecil has in the past presented to me very similar ideas to those which he gave to Colonel House, particularly referring to the cotton question.

In regard to the German activity in this country, I believe that Sir Cecil is very much affected by any rumor or report which comes to him from whatever source. That has been my experience with him and with our endeavors to find out the truth of his suspicions.

In regard to finding out about suspicious characters in this country I ought to tell you that about a month ago I called the matter to the attention of Mr. Warren, of the Department of Justice, and since then have spoken to him upon the subject and he tells me that they have been preparing a full list of such persons. As soon as I receive it I will forward it to you.

Faithfully yours,   Robert Lansing.

My Dear Mr. President: Washington August 6, 1915.

I enclose for your consideration a paper which was handed to me this morning by Mr. Oswald G. Vallard [Villard] of the New York Evening Post. He requested me to lay the matter before you as I declined to express any opinion in regard to the proposals submitted.[1]

Faithfully yours,   Robert Lansing.

TLS (WP, DLC).

[1] "Formulation of August 4, 1915," T MS (WP, DLC). This statement, signed by Villard, Jane Addams, Emily Greene Balch, George W. Kirchwey, and other leaders of the American peace movement, asserted that the civilian leaders of the belligerent nations desired action by the neutral powers to end the war, and that the United States should take the lead in mediation. The signers therefore urged that an international committee be formed to seek out and propose to the belligerents some workable basis upon which peace negotiations might begin. They added that the American members of the international committee, while having no diplomatic credentials, "should have the sanction of President Wilson."

From Robert Lansing, with Enclosures

PERSONAL AND CONFIDENTIAL.

My dear Mr. President: Washington August 6, 1915.

I did not write you of the conference yesterday on Mexico as the session today was in continuance. Yesterday's session lasted two hours; today's three hours.

All the conferees were enthusiastic over the meeting, primarily on account of the evidence of the Administration's friendliness to the Pan-American idea. Should it fail in every other way, it has already done much to draw Latin-America near to us.

I explained fully at the opening of the first session that the conference was informal and advisory and that there was no purpose of joint action, but that it might result in identical action which would, however, be independent. I said that this Government had no intention to invade the sovereignty of Mexico but merely to aid the Mexican people in the present distressing condition by seeking to recognize a government which would restore peace, secure individual rights, and perform its international obligations; that we recognized the right of revolution against injustice and tyranny; that we recognized that the principle of the revolution, the restoration of constitutional government, had triumphed a year ago; that the factions of the revolutionists, which were now quarreling, were joint possessors of the sovereignty; that personal ambition and personal greed were the causes of the factions; that no one faction represented the revolution, but that all of them combined did represent it; and that, therefore, we must seek for a new government among the factions and see if their differences could not be adjusted at least sufficiently to have the greater part unite on a provisional government strong enough and honest enough to command respect at home and abroad and to obtain recognition.

To the foregoing statement all the conferees gave assent, and we proceeded to discuss the means to accomplish the end sought.

Without entering into the long discussions upon abstract subjects, such as the nature of sovereignty, liberty, etc., which delights the Latin mind and in which one must share to win their respect, the first session decided upon two definite steps: *First*, to send a communication to the factions inviting them to an immediate conference, the communication to be signed by all the conferees independently and severally, not jointly: *Second*, to work out at once a plan of selecting a government to be recognized by the countries represented in case the first step failed.

At the session today Mr. Suárez submitted a draft communication in Spanish to be sent to the factions, which he prepared at my request. After some correction and considerable discussion it was approved by all. I stated to the conference that before I could act, the plan and communication must be submitted to you. I, therefore, enclose a translation for your consideration.

After a general expression of views, which again wandered into the field of abstraction, I suggested that a committee of three, Mr. Náon, Mr. Calderón,[1] and Mr. Fuller, prepare the details of the course to be taken in case the first step failed. This seemed the only way of practical suggestion. I enclose a written declaration prepared by Mr. Naón which was approved by all. The report will be supplemental to the latter part of this declaration.

I believe the committee are to work upon it tonight and it will be presented to the conference, which is to meet in New York on Tuesday or Wednesday. The change of the place of meeting was at the request of the conferees and was due to the heat here.

I do not think that the first step will succeed. Suárez was the originator. On account of the difficulty in dealing with him I gave immediate approval because the step could do no harm. As to the second step he approved without demur. In the second step lies our hope.

In the discussions I found that there was unanimous agreement that Carranza was impossible, that even if he triumphed it would mean continued disorder. The disposition was to eliminate from consideration as the head of a government to be recognized all the present heads of factions and to seek a man who would draw the secondary chiefs to him. It was felt too that the man to establish the government must be named to us by Mexicans and, if possible, should be one with a measure of constitutional right. All were impressed with the necessity of haste on account of the distress in Mexico. For a conference composed largely of Latin-Americans we made rapid progress.

I would be gratified if you would telegraph your approval of the Suárez' communication to the factions, if you do approve, so I can notify the conferees and also call the meeting in New York to consider the committe's report on the second step.

I forgot to say that it is intended to send the communication not only to the heads of the factions but to the principal military and political chiefs as well.

Secretary McAdoo telegraphed me asking me to meet him in New York on Sunday, the 8th, as you desired us to confer. I shall, therefore, be at The Biltmore Sunday morning.

Faithfully yours,   Robert Lansing.[2]

TLS (WP, DLC).
[1] Ignacio Calderón, Bolivian Minister to the United States.
[2] Wilson sent this letter and its enclosure to Mrs. Galt (WW to EBG, c. Aug. 7, 1915, ALI [WP, DLC]) with the following comment:
"I think this will give you a better idea than anything else could of the way these people have to be steered and of L's ability in steering them. You will also see (I am afraid I do) their lack of sympathy with the revolution and their sympathy with the exiled reactionaries."

E N C L O S U R E   I

AMBASSADOR NAÓN: It seems to me this has been accepted: The recognition of a provisional government *de facto* in Mexico to be constituted by the agreement between all the factions within a reasonable time. If that government, from the agreement of all the factions, cannot be constituted, then to recognize a government organized by any of these factions strengthened by the concurrence of public opinion outside of the factions and on the basis of guarantees upon the life and property of foreigners and nationals.

ENCLOSURE II

(DRAFTED BY MR. SUÁREZ)

The undersigned, acting severally and independently, unanimously send to you the following communication: Inspired by the most sincere spirit of American fraternity, and convinced that they rightly interpret the earnest wish of the entire Continent, have met informally at the suggestion of the Secretary of State of the United States, to consider the Mexican situation and to ascertain whether their friendly and disinterested help could be successfully employed to re-establish peace and constitutional order in our sister Republic.

In the heat of the frightful struggle which for so long has steeped in blood the Mexican soil, doubtless all may well have lost sight of the dissolving effects of the strife upon the most vital conditions of the national existence, not only upon the life and liberty of the inhabitants, but on the prestige and security of the country. We cannot doubt, however—no one can doubt—that in the presence of a sympathetic appeal from their brothers of America, recalling to them these disastrous effects, asking them to save their mother land from an abyss—no one can doubt, we repeat—that the patriotism of the men who lead or aid in any way the bloody strife, will not remain unmoved; no one can doubt that each and every one of them, measuring in their own conscience their share in the responsibilities of past misfortune and looking forward to their share in the glory of the pacification and reconstruction of the country, will respond, nobly and resolutely, to this friendly appeal and give their best efforts to opening the way to some saving action.

We, the undersigned, believe, that if the men directing the armed movements in Mexico—whether political or military chiefs —should agree to meet, either in person or by delegates, far from the booming of cannon, and with no other inspiration save the thought of their afflicted land, there to exchange ideas and to determine the fate of the country—from such action would undoubtedly result the strong and unyielding agreement requisite to the creation of a provisional Government, which should adopt the first steps necessary to the constitutional reconstruction of the country—and to issue the first and most essential of them all, the immediate call to general elections.

In order to bring about a conference of this nature the undersigned, or any of them, will willingly, upon invitation, act as intermediaries to arrange the time, place, and other details of such conference, if this action can in any way aid the Mexican people.

The undersigned expect a reply to this communication within a reasonable time; and, if none is received within ten days after the communication is delivered, the indication will be that none may be expected.

T MSS (WP, DLC).

From Robert Lansing, with Enclosure

My dear Mr. President:　　　　　Washington August 6, 1915.

I am in receipt of your letter returning in revised form the proposed answer to the Austrian statement regarding arms and ammunition, and I think the changes improve the language very much.

The questions which you raise as to the possibility of the reply being taken as an argument in sympathy with the Allies and against German militarism applies, I presume, to that part of the draft which advances the practical and substantial reason—being on page 6.

I think the question is justified. The argument might, and I have no doubt would by pro-German sympathizers, be construed as you suggest by your question. But, if we do not mean it, do we not run the risk of resting our whole case on the principle that to change our laws in time of war would be unneutral and also on the past usage of nations, and especially the practice of Germany and Austria?

While probably that argument is sufficient to meet the contention of Austria, it may be held to be technical and will not, I am afraid, satisfy the humanitarians. For that reason, it seemed to me politic to insert the practical reason against prohibition and to show that it would compel general armament and so make for war rather than peace. Mr. Bryan and I talked this subject over on several occasions and I am sure that he considers that the prohibition of the sale of arms upon the advancement of peace would have this effect.

Would it be advisable, if this portion of the argument remains, to insert a paragraph disavowing any purpose of insinuating that Austria and Germany were aggressors?

Would that cure the objection or would it aggrevate it? I am not at all sure in my own mind what the effect would be.

I enclose such a paragraph for consideration. It could be inserted between lines 2 and 3 on page 9.

I do not think that the argument would seriously affect the program in regard to the American Republics or to a similar program for Europe. The principle is for governmental regulation and control of arms and ammunition, but with it goes the guaranty of political and territorial integrity. In case an American nation was attacked by a transoceanic nation, or another American nation, would it not be the duty of the guarantors to furnish the nation attacked not only with arms, but with men and ships?

Furthermore, I understand that the regulation of the manufacture and sale of arms is limited to trade between the contracting parties and would not apply to other nations unless they entered into a similar guaranty and agreement to regulate. Without the guaranty of integrity of territory and political independence I believe that an agreement restricting in general the sale of arms and ammunition would be inadvisable. With the guaranty the agreement is practical and will make for peace.

Unless, therefore, Europe sees fit to adopt the guaranty and to enter into the agreement about munitions, the argument advanced in the draft would remain and this country would be as free as it is today to trade in arms and ammunition with belligerents, and would be justified, as a neutral, in doing so.

One other thought in this connection suggests itself. If the guaranty should be adopted by the American Republics, an invasion by one of the territory of another would make every guarantor a belligerent, so that the question of the *neutral* right to sell arms and ammunition could never arise.

Faithfully yours,   Robert Lansing.

TLS (SDR, RG 59, 763.72111 EM 1/31½, DNA).

E N C L O S U R E[1]

PROPOSED INSERT AFTER LINE "TWO" PAGE 9.

The Government of the United States in the foregoing discussion of the practical reason why it has advocated and practiced trade in munitions of war, (distinctly disavows any purpose to suggest that Austria-Hungary and Germany are aggressive powers inspired with purposes of conquest. It makes this disavowal in order that no misconstruction may be placed upon its statements and that it may not be credited with imputations which it had no intention of making.⟩ *wishes to be understood as speaking with no thought of expressing or implying any judgment with regard to the circumstances of the present war, but as merely putting very frankly the argument in this matter which has always been conclusive in determining the policy of the United States.*

T MS (SDR, RG 59, 763.72111 EM 1/31½, DNA).
1 Words in angle brackets in this document deleted by Wilson: those in italics, added by him.

From Joseph Patrick Tumulty

Dear Governor: Avon, New Jersey August 6, 1915.

I received your letter with reference to Mr. Buchanan and was very much interested in all that you had to say. I will write him a purely formal reply and allow the incident so far as I am personally concerned, to rest.[1] I still think the conduct of men of the Buchanan and Weismann type ought to meet with a public rebuke at your hands in some dignified way. I agree with you that to reply to any of these would seem to be paying too much deference to them. If the Buchanan reply to my letter and the aspersions cast upon you were an isolated instance, I would not think it worth your while to indulge in any controversy; but the point I wish to make in this letter is this: that the attitude of such men is but a proof of a propaganda which is growing in intensity day by day, and which is creating a situation that is, to say the least, intolerable to all Americans not in the hyphen class. Only this morning we take up the papers to read the attacks made on you in San Francisco at a meeting presided over by Mr. Hexamer.[2]

However, I know that you are considering these matters and will act at the proper time.

With affectionate regards,   J. P. Tumulty

TLS (WP, DLC).
1 Tumulty wrote a brief note to Buchanan on August 6. He stated that he resented the tone of Buchanan's letter of July 24 and "the unwarrantable inferences" contained in it. Tumulty added that he had no objection to the publication of the correspondence. *New York Times*, Aug. 10, 1915.
2 Charles John Hexamer, a civil engineer of Philadelphia, had been president since 1901 of the National German-American Alliance, an organization claiming in 1915 a membership of over two and a half million. On August 4, during the Alliance's biennial meeting in San Francisco, one Henry C. Bloedel of Pittsburgh submitted a draft of a letter to President Wilson. It bitterly denounced his conduct of public affairs and blamed his administration for the diplomatic controversy with Germany. Hexamer, despite the fact that he himself had denounced the administration's policies in his opening speech on August 1, now urged that the Bloedel letter be dropped. The convention then passed a substitute resolution which demanded that the United States "adopt the same standard of treatment" in dealing with all belligerent nations. *New York Times*, Aug. 2, 1915; New York *World*, Aug. 5, 1915. See also Clifton

James Child, *The German-Americans in Politics, 1914-1917* (Madison, Wisc., 1939), pp. 79-80. This book contains much about the activities of the National German-American Alliance.

From Horace Herbert Clark

Dear Mr. President: Los Angeles, Calif., August 6th 1915.

Referring to the matter of Mrs. Hulbert's mortgages, I repeated to her your suggestion of purchasing them outright, and she has asked me to write to you to say that she would find it most agreeable if it is convenient to you to do so.

In most cases of transferring mortgages, it is the custom to make a concession to the purchaser, and in view of the early maturities of these mortgages, I have suggested that a discount of 2½% or $375.00 would be the discount which any commission house would approve of, and Mrs. Hulbert is entirely agreeable to this arrangement.

In the event of you desiring to buy the mortgages on this basis, the amount of the check which you would remit to Mrs. Hulbert, after deducting the discount and interest to date on the $7,500. loan, would be $7,097.50. The interest would be 22 days at 6%, or $27.50.

The mortgages as you have them are a perfect delivery, and it is only necessary for you to have them transferred and registered in your name to complete the transaction and vest ownership with you.

Thanking you for your kind attention to this matter,[1] I am,
Very sincerely yours,   H. H. Clark

TLS (WP, DLC).
[1] Wilson bought the mortgages.

To Edith Bolling Galt

[Cornish, N. H.]
My precious Darling,   Friday evening, 6 August, 1915

It was a great comfort to get your letter to-day from Geneva and know that you were really safely there. There seems to be something strange and inaccessible about No. 10 Park Place! I've told you how we tried to telephone the night you arrived, Wednesday, and were told Mr. Rose had no Bell telephone connections. Well, last night, Thursday, Margaret telegraphed you, early in the evening "Hope you all arrived safe and well. Love from all" and not only got no reply but was unable this morning to obtain any assurance from the Western Union that the telegram had been delivered.* Is Mr. Rose at outs with the telephone and telegraph companies? I am very sorry, my Sweetheart, that you think I did not "play fair" about the charges on the trunk; but I did not prepay them in the spirit you think. It's true I *do* covet little privileges like that—to make me feel that we are one and not two—but I knew your feeling and took the liberty in this case only because I thought the trunk would arrive before you did—as it did—and feared there might be some difficulty about it's being delivered and being ready for you when you came if there was no one in the house to pay for it. You must forgive me for seeking to make sure of your comfort and convenience. I love to do you a service, however small.

I have no idea of the house or of the household at No 10,— apart from Mr. R's love of the motor and of golf and his passion for bridge in the evening, and find myself at a loss to follow my Darling with my thoughts through the day because I cannot picture what she does. Please give me a sample day or two and tell me something to think about concerning the people you meet— and an idea of what your own room is like, wont you, my precious One? I don't like to lose you in strange places. It is part of my happiness to be able to follow you very definitely in my thoughts.

No, I do not take my papers out to the porch to read now. That would be *too* lonely. I miss you at best almost more than I can bear. I cannot venture to accentuate my lack by working where I spent those happy hours working with you. I work in the study and up in my room, keeping to the part of the house which is *not* too vividly associated with you,—the part you did not frequent. If I should try to work on the porch or in the music room or in the morning room, I am afraid my thoughts would run off, in spite of me, into dreams of the dear, dear Sweetheart whose presence used to make work easy and romantic. The day has been barren of any mail of interest. Dudley Field Malone sends me a description of Zapata, prepared, he says, by General Angeles[1] (who was one of those who recently came to Windsor, you remember) and I am going to send it to you on the chance that it will interest you,—no, not on the 'chance,' for you are interested in *every*thing that is worth knowing about, you blessed thing. How I love you for it. Perhaps this paper has something in it about Zapata that you never read before. There has been nothing further about the conference even. If anything should come to-

*I take it back. Margaret had not told me that later she got a reply.

[1] D. F. Malone to RL, Aug. 5, 1915, TLS, enclosing F. Angeles, "Zapata," CC MS (a translation), both in the R. Lansing Papers, DLC.

morrow morning, I will put it in with the Angeles paper. I think
it very likely that I shall be off for Washington by Sunday afternoon. Do you know I am beginning to think of Washington with
a liking that I never had before, and I think it is altogether because it has been your home, *you* like it, and I found you there!
I can now think of it and feel about it otherwise than as merely
the seething centre of politics and personal intrigue.

We played golf this morning, Grayson, Geo. Howe, and I on
the Kennedy course (not being sure the rain was over) and this
afternoon Sister, Margaret, Miss Batten, the aforesaid gentlemen
and I (I on the front seat—relegating Murphy to the Secret Service car) rode to Hanover, there crossed the river and came home
down the Vermont side,—the sun still struggling with the clouds
and only now and then coming out with a vague smile to brighten
the bleak day. If we do not have a sunny day soon (we have had
only a few *hours* of the sun since you left on Monday) I foresee
that my brave show of good spirits is going to break down and
I shall have to go hastily to *Geneva, New York*, where I have
never been in my life, for a fresh supply of the genuine article.
I instinctively know that the sources of my happiness lie there,
on Park Place, a street I have never seen!

I wish with all my heart that you had better news from your
brother Rolfe. I am distressed to think that he does not change
his point of view or his purpose at all. You will let me know
what he says, if anything, in reply to, or comment on, *our* letter,
will you not, my Darling? I wish you could *talk* to him.

Saturday morning 7 Aug., 1915

It's all very well, dear little girl, to keep a steady heart and
'play the game' like a sport, and all the other heroics of it, but the
plain truth is that I miss you *desperately*, that the days are intolerably slow and long and empty without you, and that the real
living will not begin again until I am once more with you. No
doubt that will shorten life: the days will fly with wings then;
none of them will be long enough; but, oh, the happiness and
sweetness of it! I cannot bear to think of your having a distressing headache and I not there to do what I can with loving fingers
to conjure it away! I am sure I could do a great deal. If nothing
more, I could make you feel the deep love and sympathy that
makes even pain easy to bear. For my own part, I know that my
headaches (which come and go with thinking) would always be
chased away—they *have* always been chased away—by a loving
smile and gentle caress from you. It takes the pain out of anything
merely to tell you about it and feel the sweet response of your

love. Every day, my precious Sweetheart, I realize more and more how *deeply* and *tenderly* and *devotedly* I love you, and how constantly and entirely I depend on your love, not only for joy and strength but even for the hourly, momentary impulses that make the day's work possible and lift it above dull effort and more resolute fidelity. It is my solace and inspiration, and all that part of my motive power that carries me beyond duty and makes work seem a privilege,—the work that is for others and for the world. Our love transforms so many things! It makes me love my fellow men more and understand them better, and, because it gives me deep happiness and confidence, clears my head and makes it easier to see my duty and do it. Because my heart is at ease, my mind is freer to think for them. I am like a runner who has been training under weights and is at last free of them and runs light and elastic in the race itself. You have *added* so much to me, my dear One, by the sweet gift of your love. I can look at the world now with clear and lively eyes, as I could not before. In brief, my Darling, I love you, and you love me, and your love has made me free. It is such a pleasure to think of you, and these wonderful weeks we have spent together here at Harlakenden have stored my heart with memories that would make any man rich beyond computation. I *know* you to be the most stimulating, helpful, comprehending, charming, fascinating, entrancing chum, partner, and Sweetheart my heart could desire, and I am more happy every day to be   Your own   Woodrow.

ALS (WP, DLC).

To Joseph Patrick Tumulty

Dear Tumulty: Cornish, N. H., August 7, 1915

I have your letter of August sixth about what we should do in the case of men of the Buchanan and Weismann type and refer to it again only because I am not sure I gather from the letter what your personal judgment is,—whether you agree with me or not that the occasion has not yet offered itself when I can refer to them or reply to them with dignity and the greatest effect. You know how I would value any suggestion on your part as to when and how to handle this matter.

Always   Affectionately yours,   [Woodrow Wilson]

CCL (Letterpress Books, WP, DLC).

To John Lowndes McLaurin

My dear Mr. McLaurin: Cornish, N. H., August 7, 1915

Your letter of August fifth has been forwarded to me here and I have read it with genuine interest, finding it very suggestive indeed. I shall hope to discuss with those who understand these matters better than I do the feasibility of carrying out your suggestions.   Sincerely yours,   [Woodrow Wilson]

CCL (Letterpress Books, WP, DLC).

To Edward Mandell House

Dearest Friend,   [Cornish, N. H.] 7 August, 1915

I am enclosing a letter from Jno. L. McLaurin, of South Carolina making suggestions about which I should very much like your opinion. Do you think it feasible to act on them, and wise, if feasible?

This would seem in some degree at least to fit in with the suggestions you have been discussing with Mr. Strong. Your letter about that, and about your conversations with Spring Rice about cotton and other things came to-day. Thank you for those full reports. They serve to guide me in a way I deeply appreciate.
                          Affectionately Yours,   W.W.

WWTLI (E. M. House Papers, CtY).

From Robert Lansing, with Enclosure

My Dear Mr. President: Washington August 7, 1915

After a conference with Admiral Benson,[1] who is acting Secretary of the Navy, he has submitted to me a memorandum embodying instructions to be sent to Admiral Caperton at Port au Prince. If you approve the instructions will you wire him to that effect as soon as possible?

I had a lengthy interview this morning with the Haitian Minister[2] regarding affairs of that Republic. He tells me that the people there are doubtful as to our motives, although he personally realizes that we are acting in perfect good faith and are only attempting to assist Haiti. I assured him of our entirely unselfish motives and that in landing marines in Haiti we had acted on account of two reasons: first, that it was in the interest of humanity and, second, that in case we had not taken the step, in all probability some other nation would have felt called upon to do so. I further said to him that the intelligent Haitians should feel gratified that it was the United States rather than some other power whose motives might not be as unselfish as ours.

Faithfully yours,   Robert Lansing.

TLS (WP, DLC).
[1] Rear Admiral William Shepherd Benson, Chief of Naval Operations since May 11, 1915.
[2] Solon Ménos.

E N C L O S U R E

Washington, August 7, 1915.

MEMORANDUM

Organize customs service so that all moneys both for exports and imports shall be paid to some reliable Haytian and by him placed in a reliable bank. The withdrawal of any of this money only to be upon approval of such parties as you or the properly designated representative of the United States may designate.

Under no circumstances shall any of this money be paid out at present except for defraying necessary expenses of government, sanitation, and relieving cases of extreme need. It is desired that you utilize native reliable Haytians as far as possible in all these actions but properly safeguarded by cooperation of Naval Officers, particularly pay officers.

Take necessary steps to ensure free communication from country to towns, and if necessary and practicable see that order is maintained throughout country districts.

Lose no opportunity and spare no means to impress upon the people of Hayti the sincerity of the beneficent intentions of the United States and of the resolution to safeguard the independence of their country and to establish permanent peace and increase the general welfare, at the same time insisting that law and order shall be maintained now and in the future.

It is not desired that an election take place until conditions are more nearly normal. Assure people or their representatives that as soon as conditions are favorable every assistance will be rendered in holding elections and establishing normal governmental conditions.

In carrying on temporary government of affairs comply with established customs and Haytian law as far as possible.

T MS (WP, DLC).

From Robert Lansing, with Enclosure

PERSONAL AND CONFIDENTIAL.

My Dear Mr. President: Washington August 7, 1915.

I received today a letter from the German Ambassador in regard to cotton. I enclose a copy, which I think you will find of extreme interest. I confess that I am unable to say what the German point of view is. It, however, may be of great value in clearing up the troubles of our cotton states.

Faithfully yours,   Robert Lansing

TLS (WP, DLC).

E N C L O S U R E

Count Johann Heinrich von Bernstorff to Robert Lansing

Personal and confidential.

My dear Mr. Secretary: Cedarhurst, N. Y. August 6, 1915

According to rumors current in New York the British Government has declared cotton contraband and has, at the same time, made the offer to the Government of the United States to buy at the price of 10 Cents two and a half million bales of cotton, which would remain deposited in this country until after the end of the war. Such an arrangement would naturally tend to lower the price of cotton for the next years. I assume that for reasons of principle the Government of the United States will not accept the British offer. Should I, however, be wrong and there is any chance of this offer being accepted by the Government of the United States, I beg to inform you personally and confidentially, that the Imperial Government will at any moment be ready to buy three million bales of cotton at the normal price regulated by supply and demand, if this cotton can be transported to Germany through neutral countries according to the rules of international law.

I remain, my dear Mr. Lansing,

Very sincerely yours,   J. Bernstorff.[1]

TCL (WP, DLC).
[1] Wilson sent this letter to Mrs. Galt with the following comment (AL, WP, DLC): "Is not this extraordinary? It's an ingenious bribe, is it not?"

From Edith Bolling Galt

[Geneva, N. Y.]

My own Precious One: Saturday 9:45 August 7, 1915

I need and want you so today I have had such disturbing news from Panama. Old Mr. Wilson is still on the trail, as you will see from the enclosed letters[1] (just destroy them after you read) and I am heartsick for the dearest, tenderest Sweetheart in the world. If your letter of Thursday and early yesterday morning had not come by the same mail to comfort and bless me, I dont know what I should do, but I have it here close beside me and I am getting the calm help that your presence always brings.

I am so sorry you were so unhappy in the night Thursday. It came from no cause I can ascribe, for I was with you and had not even gone to sleep after finishing the penciled letter I wrote you after midnight. And I have been with you all the time. I am so glad you are playing golf and taking rides. It will do you lots of good—and I want you to be so well and so happy.

Mr. Page's letter[2] came yesterday at noon—and I read it with such keen interest. It is full of amazing things and if the war is to be in the *air* as he suggests I hope they won't put it off too long but get the awful thing done.

I wanted you so to tell me what you thought of what he wrote, and if the "gossip" really throws any light on things.

Thank you for getting the German note[3] from Frank. In the rush of things I really forgot to ask him for it, and it was like you to remember it. I will take care of Mr Page's letter until I can give it back to you.

I see in the paper this evening that the A.B.C. Conference is adjourned to meet again next week probably in N. Y.

I hope you will motor down and please try to see the oculist in Phil. about those dear, splendid eyes.

The news from Panama is from my brother's wife and she writes that Rolfe is on the verge of a collapse mental and physical, and that she is waked at night by his sobbing and thinks if Elizabeth[4] does carry out her plans it will kill him. Still tells me nothing about the man or why it is so awful—and that she has telegraphed her brother,[5] who is a doctor (and a Jackass, I think) to come down and thinks if his influence avails nothing she will have him give the girl something to make her unconscious and put her on a boat for home though first he is to *threaten* the man. Did you ever hear of such a dime-novel plot?

She is keeping this from Rolfe, as she thinks he would go mad if he should have further anxiety. She has also written another man friend of E's to come, and she has taken the Edwards'[6] into her confidence and Gen. Edwards' suggestion is as mad as hers. It is to have Rolfe pretend to collapse in the Bank, be carried to a hospital and have her told the Drs think him in a hopeless state unless she gives up her plan.

That this could easily be carried out for he looks so terrible that even Elizabeth wrote him a letter telling him how dreadfully she felt to see him so distressed and that she would do anything or give up anything *but* the man to try to restore him.

Forgive me for writing you so much stuff, but I know you agree with me that they are all crazy and there is nothing to appeal to in such a state. Rolfe did not see the above letter, but he wrote me that E. had written Margaret—so please explain to her what the letter means, as she was away and knew nothing of your invitation. Rolfe said E. was so pleased and flattered and showed more appreciation than about anything else.

The Roses are planning to go to Dansville, N. Y. on Monday by motor, returning Tuesday night—and I hope we will not start before the mail comes on Monday, for otherwise I won't know where to write to you

I think there will be no chance of mail tomorrow as it is Sunday unless you think to put a Special Delivery on it. So I will have to wait until Monday for another one of our dear talks.

I will write you tomorrow anyway and send it to Windsor & the same on Monday unless I hear from you to the contrary.

I did not get an extra envelope from you this morning, so may have that by the noon delivery.

I must stop now and get this in the mail. Bless your heart for going just to look at that Hotel in Springfield—it is better inside than it looks.

My fond love to the girls and tell Jessie I know how she feels.

All my love to you my precious Woodrow—always

Your own   Edith

ALS (WP, DLC).

[1] N. Wilson to EBG, Aug. 4, 1915, ALS (WP, DLC). The other letter is missing.

[2] WHP to WW, July 23, 1915.

[3] That is, the *Frye* note referred to in WW to EBG, Aug. 4, 1915.

[4] Elizabeth Bolling, daughter of Rolfe E. and Annie Litchfield Bolling. She was engaged to Jorge Eduardo Boyd, a Panamanian identified in EBG to WW, Aug. 7, 1915, n. 3. Her parents were violently opposed to her impending marriage for reasons mentioned in Mrs. Galt's letters.

[5] George Victor Litchfield, Jr., physician of Abingdon, Va.

[6] Clarence Ranson Edwards, brigadier general, U.S.A., commander of United States troops in the Canal Zone; and Bessie Rochester Porter Edwards.

To Edith Bolling Galt

[Cornish, N. H.] Saturday evening
My precious, lovely Sweetheart,   7 Aug., 1915.

To-day's post brought me that sweet, sweet letter written in bed Thursday night and finished yesterday morning, and my heart is aglow with its love and tenderness and with the sense it conveys of your dear self. How ardently my love goes out to meet it, and what unspeakable delight it gives me to receive such adorable outpourings of my Darling's heart! "Forgive a pencil," indeed! What difference does it—can it—make to me what my precious Sweetheart writes *with* when I read in every line evidences of the love that is the breath of life to me? You sweet thing! I fancy I can see you (you would not mind, would you?) propped up in the "old-timey bed" in that stately spare room, writing to your lover, with a heavenly light in your sweet eyes! And how dear it was in you to divine that I would want to know what your room was like,—and what one can see from the windows. You always read what is in my thought, and always will, I am sure; for love is a wonderful wizard in such things, and my Darling's love is of the sort that makes divination easy. You manage, too, my sweet One, to get the *atmosphere* of love into your letters—*how* I do not quite make out—I suppose by the same magic by which you put your personality into everything you do and say. You succeed in thrilling me by everything you do and say. Your letters *make* the day for me.

To-day has been uneventful, except for your letter. The mail has for the rest been quite barren of anything of interest. I had a long letter from Lansing, in reply to one of mine, about the reply he has prepared to Austria's protest about the selling of arms and ammunition to the Allies; but you know the points of that controversy and there is nothing vital or critical in it anyhow. I am trying to see if there is anything workable in Page's suggestion to Sir Edward about a rescinding of the Order in Council of March 11th, in view of the declaration of cotton as contraband—and House is in communication with both Sir Edward and Spring Rice. I fear there may be a little irregularity, my Darling, about your receipt of my letters (though you may be sure that one will be despatched every day) because those contemptible spies, the newspaper men, are curious about every special visit either the doctor or I or anyone in the family makes to the P. O. and I do not like to send my letters by the messenger that carries the others from the house at regular intervals; and the big envelopes that contain the things I forward to you will often not come by the same post that brings my letters, because *they* (the big envelopes) go out with the regular official mail which Swem carries down every afternoon about four—just as we are starting out for our drive. By the way, do not trouble to return any of the documents I send, Sweetheart, unless I specially indicate that I should like to have them back at once.

We had intended to take George Howe over to Woodstock this morning for golf (and to post my letter), but the recent rains have almost flooded that course, I noticed the other day in passing there, and it had rained most of the night, so we went again to the Kennedy course. George left this afternoon for New York, though we tried very hard to keep him. He had promised to go back to that good-for-nothing wife[1] of his. I am very fond of the dear fellow. He is much too fine for her!

How jolly, my Sweetheart, that you are taking golf lessons (and how I envy the teacher—you will be adorable as a pupil!). Of course we shall have many and many a game together—as many as I can persuade you to play. I am so glad that that was what you thought of and that prompted you to consent to take the lessons! Remember "Ye must tak a fir-r-m hold on your cloob, but ye must'na sput on your hands." If you'll give yourself as free a swing in hitting the ball as you give yourself in walking, you'll beat me all to pieces. What jolly times we'll have together, bless your dear heart. You and the open fields and a good game all put together are surely all that a man's heart could desire when play time comes, as you and a good book or you and and an interesting piece of work, or you and a good long talk are all that a man's heart could desire when the hours come when one must take up the things of the mind and the tasks of business.

I can't get that fascinating picture of you in the midst of the pillows of the "big, low, old-timey bed" out of my head, or the longing out of my heart to stoop over you there and take you in my arms and cover you with kisses. *Do* the words of love I write make your heart glow, Edith, my precious Darling, and give you deep happiness? It must be because *some*thing of the *passion* of love that is in my heart as I write them—and at all other times of the day and night, too—gets into them, pale and inadequate as they seem to me as I write them. They are very poor coinage of my heart. I've never yet made the "image and superscription" of my soverign queen on them what I *wanted* them to be, or what my heart conceived. If I could, I fancy it would be impossible *My other paper gave out*[2]   for you to stay away from me longer

---

[1] His off and on wife, Margaret Smyth Flinn Howe.
[2] Here he began using presidential stationery. He usually used plain paper and envelopes.

than it would take for you to come to me from where you happened to be—and that not by motor but by train—for they would
speak my need as well as my love so eloquently that no woman
could resist the call. Ah, Sweetheart, how I *do* love you; and how
glad, how proud, I am that my love makes you happy,—brings
light into those dear eyes of yours, and fills the world with confident hope for both of us! To-day has been the first day of sunshine with us since you left (on black Monday) and our ride this
afternoon (Sister, Jessie, Miss Batten, the doctor, and I were the
company) was made delightful by soft airs very unlike the chill of
the last six days; but to-night, as I sit here in this quiet study, a
gentle rain is coming down outside again and there is thunder
on the distant hills. Margaret, Miss Batten, little Annie, and the
doctor have gone up to the Maxfield Parrish's to hear the Fuller
sisters[3] sing; Sister Annie is upstairs with Josephine; dear Jessie
is in her room not feeling very well; and I seem singularly
alone, except for the consciousness of you. I am dreaming of
those never-to-be forgotten evenings in the morning room, which
is now empty, with its curtains drawn as they have been every
evening, but no one to make it seem at once like home and like
a corner of Paradise. It is *too* full of dreams for me to sit alone
in it now. My heart would ache intolerably, just because the
memories that now fill it are so inexpressibly sweet and wonderful, with the sweetness and wonder of perfect love. It was there,
more than anywhere else in this dear house that is for me so full
of you, that we learned perfectly to see one another's hearts, that
all fear and questioning became impossible, like things that had
never been, and the tender links were formed that made us love
and comprehend perfectly. Whenever the evening comes now
I fall under the spell of those precious memories and my Darling
seems so close to me that it seems incredible to me that I cannot
put out my hand and touch hers, that I cannot turn about and
press my lips to hers. Ah, Edith, my own Darling, this has been
a very, very long week. We have not been before so long separated
since we knew the full depth and sweetness of our love for one
another. The separation is desolately hard to bear! We must make
our letters serve to ease the pain by making them the vehicles for
everything that is in our hearts, and so make *them* carry us on to
the blessed days to come!

Sunday, 10 A.M. 8 Aug., 1915

I was looking this morning, (with what emotion I need not

[3] Probably relatives of Henry Brown Fuller and Lucia Fairchild Fuller, artists,
who maintained a home in Cornish.

say) my beloved Sweetheart, at what is, I think, my most precious document—the little pledge written on the West Porch (do you remember the exact words of it: "I promise with all my heart absolutely to trust and accept my loved Lord and unite my life with his without doubts or misgivings") and noted that it was dated the twenty-ninth of June, the very beginning of our happy weeks here. I cannot tell you how it thrilled me to think how that sweet pledge has been fulfilled and with what tenderness and admiration it filled me to remember *how* you had fulfilled it in the days that followed—with what unstinted generosity and sweetness, with what incomparable charm and the unconscious grace that goes always with everything you do,—the grace of innate beauty and refinement,—and yet with what frank ardor of sheer love and devotion! It is like recalling a great poem, such as no man could write, for lack of adequate coinage of words. It fills me not only with gratitude and pride and unspeakable happiness but also with a sense of having myself been made finer and bigger, and given a truer, deeper insight into love and duty. You do everything the same way, everything little and big,—with largess of your own great nature. There is no touch of anything that is niggardly or petty or grudging in anything you do. With all your variety there is one invariable principle of unity,—the reality and directness and genuineness of everything that comes from you, whether sentiment or action. That is the reason I have said so often that you seem to me in the finest sense of the word *a great Woman*. Others have seen it and felt it—as Mr. Wilson has, for example—but only I know how deep the truth of the judgment goes, and what depths of sheer loveliness there are in this incomparable lady whom I love and honour with the best, whether of thought or purpose or devotion, that is in me. To be mated with *her* is to be something more than complete. It is to partake of her greatness and to be purified by her sweetness,—to partake of all her splendid genuineness and refinement and strength, and of the beauty of nature which is her special endowment. It will be my privilege and delight in the days to come, Edith, my Sweetheart, as it has been in the days we have already spent together, to show you how utterly I trust you and believe in you, but I love to put my admiration and love into words. I love to send you these outpourings of what is in my heart. Indeed I can't *help* doing it. And it makes me very happy that your dear heart is strengthened and cheered and helped through the days of waiting, as mine is, by these messengers of love and intimate confession.

Frank sailed yesterday from New York for Newfoundland and so no one seems inclined to day to go to church. He seems to have been the only persuasive guide thitherward. I was inclined to go (perhaps out of sheer loneliness) but reflected that it might look as if on previous Sundays *you* had been the object of my worship and kept me away! And so I slept later than usual and am sitting here and pouring out my adoration to you as usual.

If anything worth while that I can send you should turn up in the pouch when it comes to-day, I will enclose it under another cover and forward it to you. There seems to be a lull in things of first-rate consequence just at present. And my plans about returning to Washington are all uncertain. I have just sent a telegram to Lansing asking him if he expects and needs me there. I had expected a summons before this. Until you hear that I have actually started, please, Dearest, continue to send your letters here, under cover to Margaret.

I wonder if you realize how much *all* of this little household loves you. They want me to send you messages of love every day. If I do not actually do it—in my selfish absorption in my own love for you—please remember that it is my omission, not theirs.

Good-bye, my wonderful, delightful, satisfying Sweetheart till to-morrow—till to-night. You are all the world to me and I am in every thought of my heart   Your own Woodrow

ALS (WP, DLC).

From Edith Bolling Galt

My own Dearest:

[Geneva, N. Y.] Saturday.
11:40 P.M. August 7, 1915

I wonder if you are thinking of this time last Saturday night? and of our happiness together.

You have been so vividly with me today, and this afternoon, when the big envelope came with all its enclosures—I just could not feel that you were not coming in a moment to join me & read them together. Thank you Dearest for sending them to me—it is *such* fun keeping in touch with your work—and I am so pleased that you trust me so utterly. Shall I keep these for you or return them by mail? I have them safely locked up and will keep them so until you tell me what you wish me to do. Col. H's letter to Mr. Page interested me—'specially because you told me how English he got in his point of view, and that he thinks you had better let Mr. P. come home to get Americanized again. By the way, did you ever learn the source of the cable to Mr. Page suggesting his return? The one he thought came from you? Mr. G's[1] code message was food for thought—and rather unlike other things he has sent it seems to me

But oh! Sweetheart, there is so much for you to think of, about such absorbing things I don't see how you ever have time to give me even a tiny thought and yet what tender & absorbing thought you show me every day. I notice you spoke of your dear hand being slow—and as though it was an effort to write. Please don't do any thing that gives you pain and now that I understand, I really want you to use your typewriter. Do this for you have to sign so many things you must keep your hand for that. In describing my room to you the other night I forgot to tell you that right by my bed is a picture on a small dressing table that I love to look at. It is the one taken with Col. H. and I dared put it out because it was just a snapshot and that I might have of anyone. Besides being the two figures it is less conspicuous. You don't know what a joy & comfort it is to me. Did you see the "Times" Editorial today?[2] I thought it very good. Was the clipping you sent in regard to America being the "heir to Europe's fortune," sent to you? And do you really think anyone believes it? Of course I was pleased at the letter of appreciation of you. Such things delight me beyond measure, for I want everyone to know how splendid you really are. And oh Dearest I do love you so.

I am afraid my letter this morning was rather depressed, but I have got myself in hand now & given up worrying over the Panama situation

I wrote Elizabeth this afternoon & told her that I was utterly in the dark as to why her parents objected to the man[3] and only knew of the deep unhappiness that had come to them all. So I would reserve my judgment until I knew & hoped she would write me frankly & fully with the assurance that I would be loyal to her if I felt I possibly could. That by cutting herself off from those who loved her she was cheating herself and making what should be the happiest thing in her life a perfect tragedy. That, if Mr Boyd was what she thought him, he would love and admire her for following her father's wishes—long enough to prove to them by waiting—that he Boyd was ["]worthy of her"—or something along those lines. But I am afraid it will do no good, and I really feel anxious about Rolfe's health from what his wife writes.

Then I got another letter from old Mr. Wilson[4] which I will enclose in this & to which I replied that I would be glad to see him—if he thought necessary—but that I had nothing I *wanted* to tell him.

Sunday, 9 a.m.

Just a word more to tell you I love you and ask if you still love me? Your dear letters are so full of all I want to know, but this

morning I want you. I am going to church and will say *amen*
to one prayer that makes the service now for me—and perhaps
add a little prayer of my own for the dearest person in the world.
Goodbye until tomorrow—*forgive pencil*

Yours now and always   Edith

ALS (WP, DLC).
  [1] That is, Gerard.
  [2] "Mr. Wilson and National Defense," *New York Times*, Aug. 7, 1915, praising
Wilson's determination to formulate and recommend to Congress a program
for the enlargement of the army and navy. It expressed confidence that the
President would be able to overcome the considerable opposition to such a
program both in the Democratic party and in Congress: "His powers of temperate, convincing statement and triumphant suasion are famous." It also
called on Republican congressmen to support Wilson.
  [3] Jorge Eduardo Boyd, lawyer and diplomat of Panama, born in Panama City
in 1886 and holder of an LL.B. (1907) from the law school of the University
of Pennsylvania. He had already served as secretary, and often as chargé d'affaires, of the Panamanian legations in London, Paris, Brussels, and The Hague
and as chief counselor of the Panamanian legation in Washington, 1912-13. He
became an associate justice of the Supreme Court of Panama in 1916 and later
held many other high legal, judicial, and diplomatic offices, including that of
Ambassador to the United States, 1939-1943. For further information on Boyd's
background and character, see WW to E. B. Galt, Aug. 16, 1915.
  [4] N. Wilson to EBG, Aug. 5, 1915, ALS (WP, DLC).

From Robert Lansing

Washington, August 8, 1915.

Have just returned from conferring with Secretary McAdoo in
New York and find your telegram. Do not think it imperative you
should return early this week. If you approve communication
drawn by Conference and for session in New York to consider
second step I will call it for Wednesday. I think it politic for you
to delay return until after that session so as not to arouse belief
that there is a crisis.   Robert Lansing.

T telegram (SDR, RG 59, 812.00/15751½A, DNA).

To Robert Lansing

Windsor, Vt., August 8, 1915.

CONFIDENTIAL.

Approve communication drawn by Conference and plan for
session in New York on Wednesday to consider second step.
Would suggest, however, that this point be dwelt upon: the first
and most essential step in settling affairs of Mexico is not to call
general elections. It seems to me necessary that a provisional
government essentially revolutionary in character should take
action to institute reforms by decree before the full forms of the

constitution are resumed. This was the original program of the revolution and seems to me probably an essential part of it.

Approve instructions to Admiral Caperton.

Woodrow Wilson.

T telegram (SDR, RG 59, 812.00/15752½, DNA).

From Edward Mandell House, with Enclosure

Manchester, Massachusetts.

Dear Governor: August 8th, 1915.

I am sorry I could not get in conference with Lansing and McAdoo today in New York. I might have done this if I could have gotten in better touch with McAdoo. I thought up to the last moment he would come through Boston and telephone from there so I might meet him and determine how necessary it was to go to New York with him. Of course, unless it was a matter of imperative necessity I would not want to risk the heat of the trip.

I have just received a letter from Wallace at Tacoma, a copy of a part of which I enclose you. You will find it of interest as an index of Mr. Bryan's state of mind. I cannot quite understand Bryan's attitude towards Wallace. After antagonizing him in every way possible for the past two years, they wrote from San Francisco to them practically asking for an invitation to visit.

I was sure Bryan contemplated a trip to Europe in behalf of peace. If he goes he will return a sadder if not wiser man.

I believe I know the temper of the American people at this time to be certain that upon the question of preparedness, you will be able to lessen his ever diminishing influence.

General Wood was here yesterday. He gave some interesting information. He said the camp at Plattsburgh[1] was turning out far better than anyone could anticipate. That the material that came to them was of such a high order of intelligence that it took but little time to teach them the rudiments.

He is very anxious for you to fill the gaps in the regiments. He considers that the main thing to be done at present. He said this could be done by merely giving the order.

There are 32 000 men available in Continental United States. This leaves 20 000 lacking which he thinks should immediately be filled. He said if you had any trouble whatever with Mexico you would need this number at once. This would make the Army 52 000 and he said it could be brought up to 60 000 in Continental United States without authority from Congress and he believes it should be done.

If I were in your place, I would give this order at once. It will have a good effect.

He said the weakness of our position was largely because all our factories for munitions were located in a small territory lying between Boston and Philadelphia and running back scarcely more than fifty miles. He says he knows it is in the mind of the enemy, in the event of war, to occupy this territory as soon as possible, and that if they did it, all chance for further resistance would be at an end. He believes that some of these big munitions contracts for the Allies should be filled in the West so the country would not be dependent upon such a restricted territory, and that territory upon the seaboard.

He recommends strongly, of course, a modified Swiss System. He thinks if our young men from eighteen to twenty-two had two months a year for four years, we would soon have a citizen soldiery that would practically make it unnecessary for us to have a standing army.

Wood is anxious to go to Europe and see something of the war as it is conducted today, and I agree with him there, for there is not an American soldier of great ability who has the remotest idea of how war is carried on now. One cannot get it from reports, one must see it. He said he could go over without any publicity and he could get to the front without it being known.

While our people do not want war, I am satisfied that 80% of them see for the first time the danger of our position. New conditions have arisen that seem to me to make it the part of wisdom to heed.

Gregory is here today. He made it plain that it would be unwise to take Davis from him. He agrees with Lansing in regard to Palmer. He does not believe that Palmer would care for the place after he had seen just what was required of him. He thinks Caffey would be an admirable man, or he thinks Frank Polk would be equally good. I do not believe Polk would take it. Lansing spoke to me about Polk, but I told him that he was probably not available. He now thinks of suggesting for your consideration William M. Howard of Augusta, Georgia. He was a member of Congress from 1897 to 1911 and was on the Foreign Relations Committee.   Your affectionate,   E. M. House

TLS (WP, DLC).
¹ A military training camp for business and professional men held at the United States Army post at Plattsburgh, N. Y., from August 9 to September 5, 1915. Some 1,200 men, mostly college graduates and from the northeastern part of the country, learned the basics of military drill and science, engaged in a rigorous program of physical conditioning, and participated in maneuvers in the field. This camp, designed to provide an elite officer corps in case of war, was the nucleus of what became known as the Plattsburgh movement, that is, the establishment of similar camps throughout the country. See John Garry

Clifford, *The Citizen Soldiers: The Plattsburgh Training Camp Movement, 1913-1920* (Lexington, Ky., 1972), pp. 54-91.

E N C L O S U R E

August 2nd, 1915.

"The Bryans have come and gone. They reached here last evening and after he spoke for an hour and a half to twelve thousand people, they dined, spent the night with us and left at eleven this morning. Of the details of our talk I will tell you at some future time. We did not talk personalities. However, he said to me five or six times, "What a pleasure it has been to get really acquainted with you after all these years!!!"

The interesting and significant part of his speech was the evident intention to make a campaign against the demand for preparedness. I got the strong impression that his propaganda for peace would take concrete form against preparedness.

He fully believed he had his audience with him. I do not think so. I have observed for twenty years that he mistakes applause for sympathy and conviction.

He told me he was thinking of going abroad in behalf of peace. He said he could not think of a good excuse to justify his going but he believed that if he could see Lloyd-George and the Kaiser he could enter the wedge. I will tell you more about it when I see you.

I have been at considerable pains to sound public sentiment since I came West. My conclusion is that the country is behind the President to an extraordinary degree and that he is the most popular President we have had in a half century. Most of the old Bryanites are with the President as against anybody. I also believe the Democratic Party has not gained in strength or in the confidence of the people except through the President. I believe without the President there would not be a grease spot left of the party at the next election"

T MS (WP, DLC).

From Florence Jaffray Hurst Harriman

Personal & Private.

Dear Mr. President,   Lake Forest, Ill. Sunday Aug. 8. '15

My friend Mr. Norman Angell sent me the enclosed paper[1] the other day and I send it on to you as it seems to me interesting

& valuable. While open to attack, and doubtful as a practical program, it's main idea is so important that it seems worth the twenty minutes that it would take to read it.

Among a number of communications which have been addressed to me since the Eastland disaster is this letter from Mrs. Robins[2] and I pick it out to forward as it is the most comprehensive. It is very strong and one questions the taste of the writer in accusing a Department of "criminal negligence."

But, without being on the ground, and passing the scene of the disaster twice daily as I have, it would be hard for anyone to realize how intense and widespread has been the resentment against the manner of conducting the federal investigation. Even some of your personal friends have not hesitated to call the course pursued "unwise."

Being a stranger in Chicago I have no way of judging how much of the condemnation is sincere, & how much artificially stimulated for political reasons, nor would I, personally, criticize a member of your cabinet if I did know. But, I would not consider myself a friend of the Administration if I did not draw your attention to the fact that the feeling was not by any means confined to any one class of citizens.

May I take this opportunity of saying with what admiration I have followed the course of your negotiations with Germany. It is very wonderful to belong to a party whose leader, through problems & trials such as no other President has ever had to face, has won the respect and confidence of the whole country. Since I have been in Lake Forest I have seen a great deal of Messrs. David & Thomas Jones and Mr. & Mrs. Cyrus McCormack and we have enjoyed having political matters in common.

I fear that your holiday has not been a very real one, but I hope, sincerely, that the air & country life may have afforded you some rest.

The Commission[3] adjourns forever next week, and then Ethel[4] & I are going to spend two months in California. With best regards,   Very sincerely   Florence J. Harriman

ALS (WP, DLC).

[1] Norman Angell, "A New Kind of War," *New Republic*, III (July 31, 1915), 327-29, proposing that, in the event of a break in diplomatic relations between the United States and Germany, the former should cooperate with the Allies and the neutral powers to place world trade under international control. This would both hasten the defeat of German militarism and serve as the beginning of an international organization which could actually enforce international law.

[2] Margaret Dreier (Mrs. Raymond) Robins, president of the National Women's Trade Union League and member of the executive board of the Chicago Federation of Labor. Margaret D. Robins to Florence J. H. Harriman, Aug. 3, 1915, TLS (WP, DLC).

[3] That is, the Commission on Industrial Relations.

[4] Her daughter, Ethel Borden Harriman.

Sir Cecil Arthur Spring Rice to Sir Edward Grey

PERSONAL.   Washington. 8 August 1915.

My telegram of August 3. American Ambassador in London suggested to the President having cotton as contraband of war, with simultaneous palliative measures. Friend[1] has consulted United States Financial Adviser, Mr. Strong, who thinks that direct negotiations with the planters for option at minimum price could be made privately. (This is doubted by experts, who think that regular dealings must be used.) Friend's southern correspondents say that German inspired agitation is increasing. It is partly to be directed against northern States who are accused of making money by munitions of war and desiring cheap cotton. If price is kept up above non-paying rate, agitation will not be very dangerous.

Friend insists that his friend has gone as far as the country would stand, and going further would mean losing confidence of the country, which he now possesses. He hopes that England and France will appreciate this, and that you will understand, seeing that right is one thing and doing another.

President appears to desire to get rid of blockade by enlarging contraband list. I think that the principle involved in our restrictive measures is so important to the United States themselves in future that it will be appreciated here in time.

T telegram (E. Grey Papers, FO 800/85, PRO).
  [1] That is, House.

To Edith Bolling Galt

[Cornish, N. H.]
My precious Darling   Sunday evening, 9.30 8 Aug., 1915

It grieves me past all expression that you should have received such news from Panama,—and I not beside you to comfort you and counsel with you! It is *so* bad, so incredible, that I cannot believe that such mad counsels *can* prevail for long together. I *must* believe that they will all "come to" and see that they are making things worse, not better; and that Gen'l Edwards should join in the madness claps [caps] the climax. Apparently, however, my brains will not work upon the matter any better than theirs will—for I must admit that I am utterly at a loss to suggest *any*thing that can be done. Perhaps a letter of deep *sympathy* from you, combined with calm advice, would serve to calm and soothe your brother a little; and it may be that, since she has written to you and taken you into *her* confidence, a letter of warning from you to Mrs. Bolling as to the danger and folly of her course might cause her at least to pause and consider. You may use my name if you choose, since she happens to think so much of me. *Any* means of impressing her would be justified in the extraordinary and alarming circumstances, and I hope you will not hesitate to act upon this suggestion. God knows it's little enough! My heart *aches* to think of my Darling's sore distress and perplexity and my inability to help—even with serviceable counsel. To think of her lying stark awake all by herself with not so much as a hand to touch while she thinks her distresses out, while all the time my heart is full of her and everything in me that is fine yearns to do her service and help her to happiness and peace of mind and heart—while I would give anything in the world to go to her and give my life to her—is almost too much to bear in addition to *my* need of *her.* We are certainly being tested out, little girl! There is at least this solace in this letter of yours that tells of your increasing distress, that it shows that my love *does* help you, and that you feel it in hours of unhappiness as something that sustains you,—something that you can absolutely depend on. Indeed you can, my precious One! Your days of loneliness are over. All that I am is yours. And I have come to you for that very purpose,—to *help!* It makes me so *happy* to help. If only I *could* help—if only *any*body could help in this blind, mad business. All that I can give is my unbounded love and sympathy—my whole heart. I have thought about the dear people in Panama almost as much and as anxiously as you have, I venture to say, but alas! to no practical purpose. I can only give them, what you give them, my deep sympathy, and such counsel as you may be able and willing to convey for me. I wish with all my heart that they had some friend down there with more sense and force than that fool Edwards!

The mail is hard to get here on Sundays, as it is in Geneva, and I did not see your dear letter until just before I sat down to write this. Miss Batten, Margaret, the doctor, and I started out for a ride early this afternoon (two o'clock) and rode all the way over to Rutland and back, with the result that it was eight o'clock before we got back (it was half-past eight the last time, you remember) and I could not attract Sister's attention by keeping them waiting still longer for dinner till I read your letter. We took tea at the Otter Creek Tea House, and I looked up the entry, under June the 28th, on their visitors' book of "Woodrow Wilson and Party." Did you remember that it was so near the beginning of our happy weeks here that we were over there—just the day before that blessed pledge was written? Ah, my Love, how completely we have found ourselves, and our happiness, since then! And now I am privileged really to *share* all your thoughts and concerns and to know that my love, if nothing else, *does* help—as your precious love helps me in my gravest perplexities, in the presence of difficulties which seem insoluble, some of which *are*, no doubt, insoluble. *No* distress seems able now really to disturb my moorings. In everything my partnership has made me free. I delight myself by believing that it is the same with you. Your letters are *so* sweet, my Darling, and give me such a sense of our absolute *union* in heart and thought that they seem in every line to give me life and happiness. Thank you with all my heart for telling me all the trouble in Panama. It is that—the feeling that you *must* share everything with me if your heart is to carry the burden—that gives me the final proof of what has happened to us—"without benefit of clergy"! You make me happy in proportion as you show me, not only how *much* you love me, but also *how* you love me and how much you depend upon me. And I! I depend upon you for *every*thing that keeps a man's heart going, and feel a sense of identification with you which I am sure marriage itself cannot increase. My darling Sweetheart, my ideal Sweetheart, you are the intimate companion and inspiration of every act and thought of every day!

Monday, 6.30 A.M. 9 Aug., 1915

Last night, my Darling, I had a message from Lansing saying that he thought that it was probably best for me not to come down to Washington just now, for fear the newspapers might give the impression that there was some sort of a crisis in the Mexican conference. Always the newspapers! They make the normal and thorough conduct of the public business impossible. I feel that I *ought* to be down there: there are so many critical pieces of business, like that in Haiti, for example, the *small* guiding threads of which, the threads which really define the pattern of the whole transaction, I do not see clearly or at all, and I feel that I am rather blindly following the lead of the Secretary of State. I wonder what lead *he* is following? The A.B.C. conference has adjourned to New York for convenience and on account of the great heat in Washington. It will convene again on Wednesday. It's deliberations have been most harmonious and it is acting, Lansing says, with enthusiasm because of being consulted at all,—But I will send you L's letter about it. It is very interesting. If they do not get lost in a jungle of abstractions, they may make the journey we wish them to make. Lansing has been sensible in the selection of his committee to formulate a plan. They will probably report something concrete and definite—I hope also *workable*.

Yes, Sweetheart, Page's last letter does throw a good deal of light, it seems to me, not so much on the situation as on the state of mind in England and among the Allies. And, after all, it is the state of mind that we must be guided by, if we cannot change it. They are ready to believe *any*thing, evidently,—particularly the incredible. It would look as if Europe had finally determined to commit suicide, as Carlyle thought it had at the time of the French Revolution,—and the only way we can hope to save it is by changing the current of its thoughts. That's the only reason it's worth while to write Notes, to Germany or England or anybody else. They alter no facts; they change no plans or purposes; they accomplish nothing immediate; but they *may* convey some thoughts that will, if only unconsciously, affect opinion, and set up a counter current. At least such is my hope; and it is also the only hope for those distracted English!

Mr. Wilson certainly is on the trail still, hotter than ever, it seems to me; but he has at least accepted your programme,— because he knows he must—and is going to wait until you choose to tell him something. He has a good nose for the chase, and he is keen to find what he wants to find—and is *going* to find, God be praised!

My thought returns again to Panama this morning, my precious one, and the longing for you in my heart is, if possible, greater than ever. I still think that what your brother needs is, not counsel, not suggestions of plots and plans and escapes, but just deep, loving human sympathy *in the presence of the inevitable*, and especially an outpouring of it from the dear Sister he loves and trusts and depends upon so. Does his foolish wife think that if, by any trick they get Elizabeth away from the Isthmus, Boyd cannot and will not *follow* her at once; and does she not see that that would *hasten* the marriage—for he would certainly marry her the minute he found her. Indeed there is a sense in which he *ought* to, if he has a speck of spunk and gallantry in him. *I* would, if I were in his place in such circumstances. And that will be the first thing that will occur to her also. Is Edwards going to arrange to have *him* kidnapped and start another Panama revolution?

Did you *like* the idea of a motor trip to Dansville or were you kidnapped, too? It makes me far from happy to think of your going on long trips over all sorts of roads, driven by an amateur chauffer. You are all the world to me, and if anything should happen to you that would be the end for me. You are such a dead

game sport, bless you! that you have the capacity to enjoy anything you undertake. I hope that you will get fun, and a lot of
it, out of this trip—at the least a partial release from anxiety.

All the dear ones send their love. I send more than any letter
or any messenger could carry, for I am altogether and in everything   Your own   Woodrow

ALS (WP, DLC).

From Edith Bolling Galt

[Geneva, N. Y.]
Precious One: Sunday night August 8, 1915

It is so late I can only talk to you a little while tonight, and we
expect to get off pretty early tomorrow morning—unless it rains
and we have to put the trip off

However Mr. Rose said tonight he would wait for the mail,
which quite delighted me for I have been so hungry for your
letter all day, and tomorrow I may have two. I will try to read
them before mailing this so as to know where to send it, in case
you have decided to go back to Washington But, if I dont
answer questions you will understand why and I will answer
them in the next letter.

As I wrote you I went to church today and it was a curious
coincidence that the psalter for today was the same one you read
aloud to me the Sunday you went back to W. Do you remember
reading it on the crimson sofa in the Music Room?

This morning I could here the very intonations of your voice
as the whole day came back to me. And another curious thing
was that the minister who read was named *Wilson* and he afterward preached a very good sermon—which I had to listen to—
although I had intended just to think about you and not to mind
if the sermon was stupid.

Just after we got in from church I never saw more terrible
lightning and it grew so dark we could not see without lights. I
thought it might mean a tornado, as they had one here a few
years ago. But, fortunately, it was mostly rain, which came in
sheets for nearly two hours and enough wind to break the trees
and send all light things flying before it.

Tonight is much cooler and we hope the storm has cleared
things up to stay.

We have had guests all evening and some of them quite agreeable people—tomorrow a Mr. & Mrs. Grant[1] go with us to Dansville. He is English Canadian & she a New Yorker and both seem
very pleasant.

Do write me Sweetheart if you still feel well—and continue to take care of your precious self. This has been a long week without you and it has made me sure that there is no one else in the world to compare with you.

Goodnight, my pen must stop, but my thoughts go on and on and seek you way across the distance, and when you have made them welcome they rest content—secure in our perfect love,

Always your own   Edith

ALS (WP, DLC).
1 Probably Mr. and Mrs. William W. Grant, of Geneva, N. Y.

Two Letters to Robert Lansing

My dear Mr. Secretary,   [Cornish, N. H.] 9 August, 1915.

Bernstorff's letter to you about the purchase of cotton is, indeed, amazing. What crude blunderers they are! The idea of offering us a palpable bribe—or, rather, offering it to the southern planders [planters]. How little they understand us!

Faithfully Yours,   W.W.

WWTLI (SDR, RG 59, 763.72112/12696, DNA).

My dear Mr. Secretary,   [Cornish, N. H.] 9 August, 1915.

I am satisfied to let the note go out as altered, with the addition of the disavowal appended to be inserted on page 9. It is no doubt just as well to have the argument as candid as possible. I hope you think the disavowal, as altered, safe and unobjectionable.

Thank you for your letter in the matter. Your reply with regard to the pending American agreement is entirely convincing. Indeed, I had thought it out to that effect before your reply came.

Faithfully Yours,   W.W.

WWTLI (SDR, RG 59, 763.72111 EM 1/32½, DNA).

From Robert Lansing

Washington D. C. Aug 9th [1915]

The Navy Department received late Saturday the following message which I did not see until this morning quote General Bobo formally resigned the position Chief Executive power and dismissed his cabinet ministers before the landing at Port au Prince today. By his orders all his generals in the North were telegraphed to deposit their arms with the American forces at Cape Haytian. He promises to use every effort for good order.

Similar promises have been given by Vourand[1] and to his troops in the North have been sent similar instructions. Because it did not keep faith, I have curtailed the power of the revolutionary committee for this resulted in not having a serviceable committee. My orders are gladly accepted and executed by the civil officials of the late government. The immediate election of a President is clamored for by all classes of Haytians. For regular government, Congress with civil functionaries and all necessary organizations except President and Congress now legally exist. There are only two serious candidates, Bobo and Dartiguenave.[2] Congress will probably elect the latter. I have had daily conferences with the President of the Senate and Chamber of Deputies, with senators, deputies, ex-cabinet ministers and many leading Haytians. In the presence of congressmen, Dartiguenave, President of the Senate, stated that congressmen are agreed that Hayti must and will accede gladly to any terms proposed by the United States. Now, they say they will cede outright without restriction St Nicholas Mole, granting us the right to intervene when necessary, custom house control and any other terms. Only they beg to avoid as far as possible humiliation. They insist that no government can stand except through protection of the United States. Without this protection there would be nothing but anarchy in Hayti according to their statements. Most Haytians now fear that the Americans will withdraw their troops immediately.

It is extremely desirable to reestablish government. Next Thursday, unless otherwise directed, I will permit Congress to elect a President. end quote.

Admiral Benson informed me that he did not think we needed to occupy Mole St Nicholas. I asked him to submit the matter to the General Board of the Navy Department which was then in session. He did so and brought back a report that quote: the General Board sees no necessity for naval purposes to have a station at St Nicholas Mole unquote.

The report goes on to state the reasons for their decision which is substantially the same one which they reached on October seventeen last year.

In view of the telegram from Admiral Caperton above repeated, and the report of the Board, it is proposed to send the following telegram to Admiral Caperton if it meets with your approval.

Quote: Allow election of President to take place whenever Haitians wish. United States prefers election of Dartiguenave. United States appreciates generous disposition of Haitian people regarding cession of St Nicholas Mole, but wishes to assure them United States desires no Haitian teritory and has no other motive than the establishing of a firm and lasting voernment [government] by the Haytian people, and to assist them now and at all times in the future to maintain their political independence and territorial integrity unimpared. The United States will insist that the Haitian government will grant no territorial concession to any foreign governments. end quote.

I believe that the declaration in regard to Mole St Nicholas and also our willingness to have the election of President proceed will have a very salutary effect upon public opinion in Haiti. I do not see why it would not be as easy to control a government with a president as it is to control the Haitian Congress and administrative officers. I would advise, therefore, sending the proposed telegram.

If possible it is advisable that an answer should be received by wire from you today in order that Admiral Caperton receive his instructions promptly.   Robert Lansing.

T telegram (WP, DLC).
¹ General Darius Bourand, former Minister of the Interior in the Sam government, at this time commander of government troops in northeastern Haiti.
² Philippe Sudre Dartiguenave, President of the Haitian Senate.

To Robert Lansing

Windsor, Vermont. August 9, 1915.

Approve the message to Admiral Caperton except that I think it would be best instead of saying that we did not wish the cession of Mole St Nicholas to retain the rest of the message as you have sent it to me and add that the Government of the United States would take up the question of the cession of the Mole later along with the other questions to be submitted to the reorganized Government with regard to its relations to the United States.

Woodrow Wilson.

T telegram (SDR, RG 59, 838.00/1275½, DNA).

From Edward Mandell House, with Enclosure

Manchester, Massachusetts.

Dear Governor: August 9th, 1915.

I am enclosing you a copy of a letter which has just come to me from Sir Edward, and which is, as usual, full of interest. I do not know why it was so long in coming.

Your affectionate   E. M. House

TLS (WP, DLC).

Sir Edward Grey to Edward Mandell House

Private.

Dear Colonel House,   London, S. Wednesday, 14 July 1915.

I received your letter, sent from New York on the 17th of June, while I was away at Fallodon.

I have now returned to London, and take up work tomorrow. I am not yet fully in touch with all the latest details of current controversies; but it is clear that, at present, neither side of the belligerents is prepared to accept terms to which the other side would agree.

I see that it will naturally take very great provocation to force your people into war. If they do go to war, I believe it is certain that the influence of the United States on the larger aspects of the final conditions of peace will prevail, and I am very doubtful whether anything short of being actually involved in the war will stir your people sufficiently to make them exercise, or enable the President to exercise, on the terms of peace all the influence that is possible. Personally, I feel that the influence of the President would be used to secure objects essential to future peace that we all desire.

The more I have meditated on past events, the more continually I have come to the point that the refusal of a Conference in July last year was the fatal moment that decided the question of peace or war. Austria had presented a tremendous ultimatum to Serbia. Serbia had accepted nine tenths of that ultimatum. Russia was prepared to leave the outstanding points to a Conference of Germany, Italy, France and ourselves. France, Italy and ourselves were ready: Germany refused. After that came reports that Germany was mobilizing, the announcement that Russia had mobilized, the ultimatum from Germany to Russia, and all the rest.

The invasion of Belgium, I believe, decided the opinion of people in England, who were not thinking much of foreign policy or at all of war, to enter the war at the beginning; but the great question of peace or war for Europe was decided, and the death warrant of millions of men was signed, when the Conference was refused.

If neutral nations and the opinion of the world generally had been sufficiently alert to say that they would side against the party that refused a Conference, war might have been avoided. Peace in future years, after this war is over, seems to me to depend greatly upon whether the world takes this lesson to heart sufficiently to decide promptly if ever such a crisis occurs again.

I spent nearly the whole of June at my home in Northumberland, wearing dark glasses and not reading at all, but fishing a little and moving about constantly amongst flowers and trees, seeing for the first time shrubs and trees in flower, many of which I had planted with my own hands 25 or 26 years ago: for I had not been at home in June for 19 years. There was really something reassuring in the indifference of Nature to the war, and its unconsciousness of it when one was in the country away from the actual theater of the war. Now, I am feeling something of what I hear that wounded or invalided soldiers feel when the time comes for them to return to the trenches.

I greatly miss your presence in London, and should be much refreshed by a talk with you.

The immediate danger to my sight is removed for the present, and I am to try whether I can do my work, with a minimum of actual reading with my own eyes, without reviving the trouble.

Yours sincerely,   E. Grey.

TCL (WP, DLC).

From Edward Mandell House, with Enclosure

Manchester, Massachusetts.
Dear Governor: August 9th, 1915.

Here is a copy of another letter from Wallace[1] and the one to him of which he speaks.[2] I believe you will find them worth reading. I wonder how correctly Titlow has analyzed the situation.

I am enclosing some extracts from a letter which I have just received from Lincoln Steffens. John Lind thinks as Steffens does.

I give you the following extracts of a letter from Sir Gilbert Parker.

"There is a matter which causes great anxiety here—more indeed than the cotton question which I think you may assume will be settled in a way satisfactory to the United States. That is the question of German exports which is becoming acute because of the dyes previously exported from Germany.

It is strange, though, that there has been very little agitation in the American Press upon the matter, for I see about forty American newspapers every week, and the demand on the part of the United States has come like a thunder clap upon us.[3] I think it is the most difficult of all the questions we have yet tackled."

Sir Gilbert is the head of the British Publicity Bureau for the United States and Canada.

I shall see Sir Cecil today or tomorrow and will write you further concerning McLaurin's letter which you enclosed in yours of yesterday.   Your affectionate,   E. M. House

TLS (WP, DLC).
[1] H. C. Wallace to EMH, Aug. 3 [1915], TCL (WP, DLC), commenting further on the meeting with William Jennings Bryan described in his letter of August 2, printed as an Enclosure with EMH to WW, Aug. 8, 1915. Wallace was now more critical of Bryan, pointing out that, in his two-hour speech at Tacoma, he had mentioned Wilson only once and in conversation at Wallace's home had not mentioned the administration at all. Wallace now believed that Bryan, buoyed up by the size and apparent friendliness of the audiences on his speaking tour, was "building new hopes" about his own political future.
[2] A. R. Titlow to H. C. Wallace, Aug. 3, 1915, TLS (WP, DLC). Titlow, a lawyer of Tacoma and a prominent Democrat in the State of Washington, began by recalling that he had been a loyal supporter of Bryan since he, Titlow, had switched from the Republican to the Democratic party in 1896. However, he had been deeply disturbed by Bryan's speech in Tacoma, as well as by his speaking tour in general. Titlow asserted that Bryan was "on a reconnoitering tour, to feel the pulse of the people." If he deemed the results of the tour sufficiently satisfactory, Bryan would be a candidate for the Democratic presidential nomination in 1916. Even if the tour was not a large success, Bryan might still become the candidate of "a third party, on the platform of Peace, Prohibition and Woman Suffrage." Titlow firmly believed that Bryan would "seek to hold his personal popularity by any means, even at the expense of dividing the Democratic party."
[3] That is, RL to WHP, July 14, 1915.

E N C L O S U R E

Extracts from letter of Lincoln Steffens.   August 7th, 1915.

Carranza has practically conquered Mexico in the military sense * * * * In other words the revolution is coming to an end with Carranza and the Caranzistas on the top. I believe the dominating parties of that group are sincere, earnest radical. Their good conduct does not depend upon their good character. They are bound to do what is right, as all men with convictions are, simply because they see it. Therefore I trust they are like some of the best reformers we have ever known in this country.

And the opposition is perfectly comprehensible to me, for the same reason that I have seen the same opposition arise to reform movements in this country. The Church and the other privileged interests here and abroad and in Mexico are desperately bent upon robbing Carranza and the revolution of the fruits of their victory, and it must not be done.

And this conference, it seemed to me, was organized for that very purpose. It was made up of the representatives of South American governments which are in the state against which the

Mexican people have arisen in Mexico; that is to say, they were really the representatives of the Diaz regime. I understand that they failed to do what they met to do, and I am not even sure they are going to be able to meet again.

But those men were saved from smashing this revolution in Mexico simply by their suspicion of the United States. And it does seem to me that that South American suspicion is just. I have learned since I have been down here that Mr. Paul Fuller, who proposed this plan and was carrying it out is the chief counsel of the Catholic Church in the United States.

Now I was so worked up about all this that I sent word to Mr. Lansing, who would not see me, that I intended to write an article along these lines, giving the facts somewhat as I have stated them above, with my interpretation of them: as a move to betray the Mexican revolution. But I told him that if my interpretation was not right I would take a hint from him not to write the article and he sent me a word by Mr. Richard Crane, his private secretary, that made me decide not to write the article, at least not with the feeling that I wanted to put in it. I shall wait, but I do not intend to write this last chapter of the history of the Mexican revolution: the American chapter.

I cannot understand why our Administration does not recognize the Carranza Government. I heard that you felt that one could not deal with Carranza. Well, some men cant; Mr. Fuller can't when he wants him to make concessions to the Catholic Church—the Harvester Trust can't when it wants concessions; nobody can move Carranza backward. But when I was talking with him and he discovered that I was friendly to the purpose of the revolution, he showed himself to be a most suggestible mind. He is a slow-minded, honest, quick-tempered and determined revolutionist; a gentleman, but a radical.

T MS (WP, DLC).

From Samuel Gompers

Sir: Washington, D. C. Aug. 9, 1915.

Permit me to assure you that it causes me genuine regret to in the least disturb you in an effort to secure much needed rest or to even break in upon your time when there are other grave conditions with which you are required to deal, but there is a matter of such moment which should receive your early attention that I feel it incumbent upon me to present it to you in this communication.

After an absence from my office of several days upon important missions, and my return here today, I find awaiting a letter addressed to me by Mr. Edmund E. Martinez, a representative of the Mexican Federation of Labor, who came to the United States for the purpose of presenting to the people of our country, including me in my official capacity, the situation and conditions as they really prevail in Mexico. Mr. Martinez comes with duly authenticated credentials not only from the Mexican Federation of Labor, but also of several other organizations of that country. This afternoon I sent a messenger to Mr. Martinez and have just had a most interesting conference with him.

First, let me say that I was greatly impressed with the matters he submitted to me, as well as with the man himself.

I am enclosing herein a copy of Mr. Martinez' letter to me which I am sure you will read with much interest, and I hope sympathy.[1]

The newspapers publish statements so fraught with impending big events in so far as the attitude of the United States toward Mexico is concerned, that I hasten to lay this matter before you, for I am confident that you will welcome any contribution which may be even in the least helpful in the performance of the great responsibility and duty which devolves upon in this situation.

In addition to the above, may I suggest that if possible you will accord Mr. Martinez an opportunity of laying the entire Mexican situation before you? I have discussed this suggestion with him, and he would gladly undertake the trip to Cornish if you can accord him even but a half an hour of your time. He feels as I feel after going over this matter with him that what he has to present is of such transcendent importance that it ought to be communicated to you in person. A word by telegraph or otherwise addressed to Mr. Martinez either to 631 2d Street, N. W., Washington, D. C., or to the Mexican Constitutionalist headquarters at 14th and I Streets, or to him in my care, will be communicated to and responded by him at once.

Trusting that the above may commend itself to your favorable consideration and action, I have the honor to remain,

Yours very respectfully,   Saml. Gompers.

P. S. Mr. Martinez speaks English well.

TLS (WP, DLC).
[1] E. E. Martinez to S. Gompers, Aug. 5, 1915, TCL (WP, DLC), expressing strong support for Carranza, repudiating Villa and Zapata, and urging that the United States not intervene against the Carranza government but instead recognize it.

To Edith Bolling Galt

[Cornish, N. H.]

My precious Darling,   Monday evening 9 Aug., 1915

Your letters fill me with a delight to which I do not know how to give expression! They breathe the very spirit of intimate love and give me the sort of deep-seated exaltation and joy that came to me during those last evenings we spent together here, when our hearts seemed absolutely opened to one another without need of interpretation, and the satisfying delight came to us in full flood of complete comprehension and acceptance of the great love that revealed itself to us, like a blessing without stint and out of heaven itself. You ask, in this dear letter of Saturday night and Sunday morning which has just been handed to me, if my thoughts returned on Saturday night to the blessed hours we spent together the week before and our happiness was made perfect. They did indeed, my Darling—as much as I dared let them. I say 'dared' because I must confess that I have to keep these memories within bounds for fear I cannot bear the longing they bring with them, the immediate need of you, and the intolerable loneliness! Your letters interpret so perfectly—though quite unconsciously, I sometimes think—what is in my own heart that there is no necessity for me to put it into words,—supposing I could! These are times when I need you,—need *you*, the touch of your hand and of your sweet lips, the love and understanding that speak in your eyes and in every dear gesture and every accent of your voice; the thrill and delight of your actual presence and your exquisite caresses and endearments,—till my heart cries out with the sheer pain of it. Your letters make me feel more than I supposed it possible for words to convey, as if they actually spoke the ardor that was in your dear loving heart when you were writing, but, but—*you know*! I need not tell you! Having found and loved one another as we have, we cannot pretend to be wholly happy or satisfied when we are separated. There is not a moment of the day when I am not consciously with you in thought, and with every thought there goes the yearning that can be quieted only when you are in my arms or holding lovingly on to my hand or sitting close beside me and sharing everything that I think or do. Just now, after dinner, I was sitting with Jessie and the doctor in the morning room. I was in the deep chair that stands between the writing desk and the fireplace. As I looked at that dear lounge, the curtains closely drawn behind it, tears came into my eyes— very happy tears, for there my Darling had wholly surrendered her dear heart to me and endowed me with a love that makes me sure of every sweet and sacred and precious thing that my heart can desire—but tears of real pain, too, because she was not there but hundreds of miles away, longing for me as I for her, and yet kept away because those who do not and cannot understand command our lives and not we ourselves—and we must wait, for that which alone can make our lives complete! Yes, Sweetheart, there is an infinite deal for me to think about and give the best that is in me to—the papers I send you show you that, as you say, and they are only part of the day's work,—but business does not take my thought away from you. All the while I am dealing with it, all the while I turn the pages of letters and despatches and memoranda, my hand is on yours as it used to be on the west porch or beside the fire in the music room, and I seem to grow more conscious of you, not less. I cannot actually turn to you and speak words of love, and of pleasure that you should be there, but I seek your eyes with other messengers which I am sure must somehow find you.

It *is very* interesting to find how House is getting re-American-ized and now sees how much Walter Page also needs repatria-tion. I still cannot imagine who gave Page the tip to come home, and I am not yet sure that I want him to come; but House's judg-ment in the matter counts very heavily with me, and I shall probably, after talking with Lansing, send for him,—though I don't know exactly how to explain to him my sudden change of wish. For just the other day, you remember, I sent him word that he had been misinformed and that I did *not* want him to come!

Yes, I think the clipping about America now standing as likely heir to the influence and power hitherto possessed and ex[er]-cised by England and her continental neighbours and rivals does contain a thought that has been seriously entertained by a good many thoughtful men over seas—as, as you see by the comment House has written on the margin of the clipping, he thinks that it will become more and more prominent in the discussion of the effects of this suicidal war by European editorial writers and publicists. And is it not a pretty safe prediction, always supposing we succeed in keeping out of the deadly maelstrom ourselves?

I think you wrote the right, wise, and sweet thing to Elizabeth, my Darling. You always *think a thing straight,*—and I cannot help hoping that what you have written her will make the deep im-pression on E. it ought to make. It may be that her distress about her father will do not a little to open her heart to advice. She knows that she has always got the truth from you, and she knows that it comes in love and not in reproof—and that it comes, not from the heated air of Panama, but from a cool distance where people can keep their heads. How sweet and fine you are about it all, my splendid Darling! I am so much obliged to you for telling me about it—and I am so proud that such a lady loves and trusts me!

Ah, Sweetheart, how it touched and delighted me to have you say in the sweet letter that has made to-day bright for me that when you went to church you were not only going to say Amen with a full heart to the petition which 'makes the service for you' but were going to add a little prayer of your own. Nothing can make me happier than that—to open that door to you; and surely a prayer made in love such as yours must bring an answer that will make me rich in strength and fitness to do my work.

It is hard to go to bed when once I begin talking to you—as I think I have several times proved! It quiets me and stimulates me at one and the same time—quiets my restless longing and gives me the deep pleasure of putting my love into words. Sweet as my thoughts of you are, happy as they make me, they need some vent. If my voice could not sometimes reach you; if I could not at least pour out on paper what my heart contains of love for you; if my thoughts, which so need your companionship and response, could not go out and find you before the day was over, I think some sinew of my heart would snap. These evening hours and the first hours of the morning before the household is astir, when I can sit here in this quiet study and talk at will to you, are the sweetest of the day,—I had almost said the only sweet hours of the day,—now that you are not here; and, as I don't know where to begin, I do not know where or when to leave off. But I must say good-night now, my precious One, and go and *dream* of you. I am tired and you would scold me if I were to stay up any longer. I adore you. It makes me so happy to love you! You are so incomparably sweet to love. I'll see you bright and early in the morning. I wonder if you are in Dansville to-night and if your lover seems as near you there as you seem to him here. If his love for you can make him seem so, he must seem in your very arms. Good-night, my Precious. I hope that you are not *too* tired by your ride and that you are conscious how my thoughts hover about you and would fain make you as glad as they are tender!

Tuesday 6:30 A.M. 10 August, 1915

Good morning, my precious Sweetheart. I hope you are rested and refreshed this morning, even if you were worn out with your long ride last night. I have never seen you fresh out of bed. Breakfast and letters, maybe, and other transactions of the day had already been attended to before you sallied forth to meet your lover; but you looked so radiant with fresh strength and spirit then that I can imagine the beauty that is all about you when you first step out of bed. You used to look, as you came smiling down the stairs, like the very spirit of morning and of love, bless you! I wonder if the ride *was* all day long—and I wonder if you really took it? Not if the weather was like what we have had here. Not a day has gone by since you left without rain. I could almost fancy that Nature has known how I felt without you and has suited her mood to mine,—and yesterday we had a wild storm with the lightening striking, with fearful crashes, all about the house. Jessie, the baby, the doctor and I constituted the whole household, the others having all gone to escort Miss Batten to friends of hers away up by the Maine line, and it was nearly five before we could drive. We found a new way to Claremont through the dripping woods,—at least part of it was new,—for the rest, every object we passed was associated in my thoughts with the loveliest and most to be desired lady in the world. It was a chill, mysterious world we drove through. The clouds had come down to the very earth while the storm lasted and were still only slowly drawing off. They stalked like veritable wraiths through the trees about us as we threaded the wet roads. We had to light a fire as soon as we got back to get the creeping chill of their presence out of our bones. Miss Batten's escorts did not get back till long after I was in bed last night—I don't know what the hour was. Just before I turned in they telephoned ("from somewhere in the White Mountains," Dickson[1] vaguely reported) that they were all right but *might* not be home till after eleven. They had left here before eight in the morning! Think of taking that child Josephine on such a trip *for fun*. She had not been well for several days, and I shall probably hear this morning that she is quite done up. It is still dripping wet, the mist all through the valley, but we shall probably *try* the links anyhow.

My plans are still undecided. I ought to be in Washington, and yet there seem to be reasons (newspaper reasons) why I should not go down each particular day. Besides, I want to go down by motor, as my Sweetheart suggested, and the weather seems far from propitious for such a ride. Continue to direct your letters here to your home, my Darling, until you hear that I have started, please. They will get to Washington as soon as I do. Alas that I should have to do without them for a single day. That's the part of your plan for my journey that I dread. Those dear letters keep my heart going. Ah, Sweetheart, my *precious* Darling, how hard it is to have you so much from home, and to be exiled myself for week after week! I have no real home where you are not—and *you* need a home as much as I do. I am keeping one warm for you, and I know you *want* to come home,—do you not? to

Your own   Woodrow

All send love. M. and J. were pleased to the core of their hearts by your sweet notes to them.

ALS (WP, DLC).
[1] Presumably a White House employee or Secret Service agent. He is not in any official list.

From Edith Bolling Galt

Dansville, N. Y.

My precious One,   Jackson Health Resort, August 9th/1915

I was oh! so glad to get your 2 blessed letters this morning before we started—and could hardly wait to read them—but, beyond just a hurried peep to see if you were still to be at Cornish tomorrow long enough to get my letter, I had to wait until this afternoon to really read them. Then I sat at my window here—overlooking the most wonderful view of smiling valleys—full of ripe grain and green hills beyond, and read and reread your wonderful words of love, and my heart was just so full of love and yearning for you I felt you must feel it. I pictured you riding along (it was between 5 and 6) and that suddenly you would feel my hand steal under the ring and nestle a moment in yours, and then both arms would go 'round your neck and I would draw you close and say, Dearest, I have come—I *could* not stay away.

It is so hard not to tell the Roses how I love you—they are crazy about you—but of course don't know how hard it is for me to talk about you and seem disinterested. But I am trying to put up a good bluff.

We had a really lovely ride over here. It is only 80 miles and very good roads. Had lunch and went to the country club, where Mr. R. & Mr. Grant played golf. They say these are wonderfully good links. We sat on the porch and read or talked   Got to the Hotel, or "Health Resort" as it is called about 5, and of course I ran into some Wash. people. Then came the real happiness of the day when I could get by myself with my precious Sweetheart's letters. This took most of the time before getting ready for dinner. And I also had such a sweet note from "Nell"[1]—as soon as I answer it I will send it for you to see. It was awfully generous of her to write me, and when you see or write to her please tell her how much I appreciate it. You certainly should be proud Dearest of these three dear girls, as I know you are. Their devotion to you and generosity is unlike anything I have ever known, and I already love them as though they were my own. They are unusual in every sense. Please give Margaret and Jessie my tender love. Thank you for the 2 enclosures in the big envelope —both of which interested me deeply. The one from Berlin is I take it the one you sent me Col. H's reply to on Saturday,[2] and the Zapata one[3] very interesting. How splendid it will be if you can get that Mexican matter in hand. I have such infinite faith in you and your insight and control that I believe you will—if only you can depend on the A.B.C. support. And oh how proud I am of you and all that you mean to the world.

You already know you *mean* the world to me.

Tomorrow we are leaving here about 8.30 to go on to Letchworth's Park which everyone says is entrancingly lovely. It is a large tract of land owned by the State of N. Y. I think and containing wonderful trees and a waterfall thought by some to be more beautiful than Niagara. I don't see how that is possible, but I will tell you more about it after I have been there. We expect to get back to Geneva tomorrow, Tuesday night, where my heart will be made glad by your letter of today.

The letters do come very promptly and directly Dearest—so far one every morning by the 9.15 delivery—and the big envelopes by the noon, or 2 P.M. delivery and I hope mine go to you as promptly.

I am so glad, you sweet thing, that you are beginning to love Washington. Nearly half of my life has been spent there, and, while I would follow you where ever you went, I would always be a little hurt if you hated Washington. And if you can love it because I do—and because you found me there—it will make me proudly happy, and I will do all I can to make it from now on seem really like *home*. Thank you too Woodrow for all the tender things you say about the little document you call the "most precious in the world." How little we thought that day, when you were in the hammock and I by you with my writing, that you were seeing so straight into so near a future and directing my fingers as you will, from now on direct my life.

Have you tried, my dear Lord, to write our story? Or have you had time and heart to? Your letters are such love poems that I feel selfish to keep them just for myself. All though it would hurt to share them with anyone—but you—so, someday I am going to read them aloud to you to let you share the real joy I have in them. I am so sorry you were so alone Saturday night—my how

I wish I could have stolen in from the Billiard room and before you knew I was there, put my hands over those dear eyes and made you guess, who?

You will wonder why I am using this tiny paper. It is because I found these are the only envelopes small enough to go in the ones you addressed to Mr. Hoover, and when I packed this a.m. I thought I would have to send this to Washington, as I rather expected you would have to leave yesterday. But I am glad you can stay on and have as much rest as possible. 1308—is closed. A letter from my faithful Susan this a.m. tells me she started for Va. on Saturday.

Mr. & Mrs. Rose plan to take me in the car to Ocean City—where they will stay a week—and return home and I will go with Mother & my sister. We will take 2 days for the trip down, probably leaving here about the twentieth. But of course I will tell you of that later. I did not mean, my precious One, to hurt your feelings about the trunk, and I am deeply grateful for your dear thought in releiving me of all trouble regarding it.

The Roses household consists only of themselves & Mrs. R's brother[4]—who is a batchelor and a Dr. We have breakfast about 8.30 get the mail at 9.15 Then we go downtown about 10, and take a drive or go to Mr. R's farm about 4 miles out—home for lunch at 1 Then he plays golf, and Mrs. R. & I read or talk, or do as we please—and we play Bridge every night. As the Roses are not going to parties I have declined all invitations, though I have been asked to lunches, teas, etc. and it is good to get out of such so comfortably. I will post this here tomorrow morning and hope it will reach you Wed. Goodnight a real lovers kiss.

Your own   E.

ALI (WP, DLC).
    [1] Eleanor W. McAdoo to EBG, Aug. 7 [1915], ALS (WP, DLC).
    [2] She may have referred to J. W. Gerard to EMH, July 20, 1915, TCL (WP, DLC), but neither the Wilson Papers nor the House Papers contains a reply.
    [3] See WW to EBG, Aug. 6, 1915, n. 1.
    [4] John Pope Delaney, M.D.

Two Letters from Robert Lansing

My dear Mr. President: Washington August 10, 1915.

I am in receipt of your letter of yesterday in regard to the reply to the Austro-Hungarian statement. I approve very heartily of the change which you made as to the paragraph to be inserted on page 9. I will have our reply prepared and sent as soon as possible, and also arrange for its publication here,[1] as I think it will have a salutary effect upon public opinion which is undoubtedly being seriously affected by the propaganda against the exportation of arms and ammunition.

Faithfully yours,   Robert Lansing.

TLS (WP, DLC).
  [1] It was published, for example, in the *New York Times*, Aug. 16, 1915; also in *FR-WWS 1915*, pp. 794-99.

PERSONAL AND CONFIDENTIAL.

My dear Mr. President: Washington August 10, 1915.

I enclose you a stenographic report of our two conferences on Mexico held here in Washington.[1] I do not know as you will care to read them, but I thought you might wish to see the lines along which developed the definite understanding which we reached.

Necessarily the report is more or less fragmentary on account of the informal nature of the conference; separate conversations going on at the same time, and some of them in Spanish, prevented a full and accurate report.

I endeavored, at the outset, to clear away as far as possible the discussion of principles and abstractions, in order that we could get down to the practical points to be discussed.

I also enclose a printed copy of the communication to be sent to the chiefs of the factions.[2] You will observe that I put my name last, rather than first, in order to exalt, as far as possible, the interest of the other nations in the settlement of the Mexican question.   Faithfully yours,   Robert Lansing

TLS (SDR, RG 59, 812.00/15864A, DNA).
  [1] "Conference Held at the Office of the Secretary of State, between the Ambassadors of Brazil, Argentina and Chile, and the Ministers of Uruguay, Guatemala and Bolivia—August 5, 1915," T transcript (SDR, RG 59, 812.00/15714½, DNA) and "Continuation of Mexican Conference," Aug. 6, 1915, T transcript (SDR, RG 59, 812.00/15715½, DNA).
  [2] D. da Gama *et al.* to "the Chiefs of the Factions in Mexico," Aug. 6, 1915, printed L (SDR, RG 59, 812.00/15864A, DNA). Aside from one minor addition to the first sentence, this document was identical with the draft by E. Suárez-Mujica printed as an Enclosure with RL to WW, Aug. 6, 1915 (third letter of that date).

From Robert Lansing, with Enclosure

My dear Mr. President: Washington August 10, 1915.

I enclose to you a copy of the telegram which was sent last night by Admiral Benson to the Naval Commander at Port au Prince, after I had received your telegram and advised him of the change in the wording of the original draft.

We have had no further advices as to the situation, but I believe that unless there is a decided change we will be able to arrange matters very much as we please.

Faithfully yours,   Robert Lansing.

TLS (WP, DLC).

ENCLOSURE

Whenever the Haitians wish you may permit the election of a President to take place. The election of Dartiguenave is preferred by United States   You will assure the Haitians that the United States has no other motive than the establishing of a firm and lasting government by the Haitian people and wishes to assist them now and at all times in the future to maintain both their political independence and territorial integrity unimpaired. That the Haitian Government will grant no territorial concessions to any foreign governments will be insisted upon by the United States. The question of the session [cession] of Mole St. Nicholas will be taken up later by the government of the United States along with the other questions to be submitted to the reorganized government with regard to its relations to the United States. Acknowledge 21009   Benson Acting

TC telegram (WP, DLC).

From Edward Mandell House

Manchester, Massachusetts.

Dear Governor: August 10th, 1915.

McAdoo was here this morning and told me the story.[1] I think he has done fine work. The publication will cause excitement and deep feeling.

It may, in my opinion, even lead us into war, but I think the publication should go ahead. It will strengthen your hands enormously, and will weaken such agitators as Mr. Bryan and Hoke Smith. The people will see things as those of us that know the true conditions have long seen them, and it will make it nearly impossible to continue the propaganda.

Mr. Metcalf and Mr. Raeburn[2] of the Providence Journal lunched with me. You know, of course the work they are doing. They tell me that Hoke Smith is in the pay of the German Government. They are trying to prove it and think they can.

Dumba called this afternoon. He explained the Bryan episode[3] and hoped you did not think ill of him. He still talks of the possibility of peace along the lines of the status quo. When I told him the sentiment of Germany was against it, he said he thought the Government would try to soften public opinion. He said Austria wanted nothing except to curb Serbia so she might not give further trouble. He thought a kingdom should be constructed out of Poland so it might be a buffer between Austria-Germany and Russia. The idea was however, that it should be under the suzerainty of Austria-Germany.

I am merely repeating the conversation so you may know what he talked about, not that it is of the slightest value.

Your affectionate,   E. M. House

My thoughts are always with you and I pray for your health and happiness.

TLS (WP, DLC).
1 That is, of the exposure of Albert's activities, about which see WW to EBG, Aug. 3, 1915, n. 5. McAdoo had already conferred in New York with Lansing and with Frank I. Cobb, chief editorial writer of the New York *World*. The decision had been made to give the Albert documents to the *World* for publication, with the one condition that the newspaper should never disclose whence they came. Wilson had approved the decision, requesting only that McAdoo also get House's approval. The *World* published many of the documents from August 15 to August 23, and many other newspapers reprinted them. They stirred up an enormous amount of anti-German feeling in the country. See the House diary, Aug. 10, 1915, T MS (E. M. House Papers, CtY); McAdoo, *Crowded Years*, pp. 328-30; and Link, *Struggle for Neutrality*, pp. 555-56.
2 Stephen Olney Metcalf, president of the Providence Journal Co., and John R. Rathom, editor.
3 See WJB to WW, May 17, 1915, n. 2 and EMH to WW, May 24, 1915, n. 1, both in Vol. 33.

Two Letters to Edith Bolling Galt

Dearest,   Cornish, New Hampshire 10 Aug. '15

Since writing this morning, it has seemed to me my duty to go down to Washington to-morrow—and by train. They are putting so many things to me by telegram, without details, for decision that I feel it too serious a risk to remain away. I sh. be there Thursday at 9.35 a.m. I will go back to Phila. to the oculist almost at once.

In haste to catch the mail,
Lovingly   Your own   Woodrow.

Cornish, New Hampshire
My own Darling,   Tuesday evening, 10 August, 1915

I know that you understand why I am returning to Washington to-morrow afternoon notwithstanding the fact that I have not been summoned and that there is no *special* piece of business that I am going back to handle in person; for your mind acts as mine does in such matters of duty, and I instinctively feel that you think, as I do, that I *ought* to go. To-day, for example, I authorized the sending of the Atlantic fleet to Vera Cruz on Lansing's judgment that the moral effect would be good,—since it is said that the Carranza authorities there are countenancing mob violence against foreigners. No doubt he is right, but I do not know enough about the details upon which he has formed his judgment to be sure that he is, and the consequences of the presence of the fleet there are a bit incalculable. I ought to be at headquarters to guide the whole thing. And so of other matters, in Haiti and elsewhere: I am depending too much on other persons' judgment. I was at the White Sulphur, I can't help recalling, when the Tampico incident occurred which led eventually to the occupation of Vera Cruz. I shall be in Washington in time to direct matters after the arrival of the fleet at Fool Carranza's capital. Just because he is a fool a delicate situation will have to be very carefully watched and safeguarded. You will readily see, therefore, my Darling, that it is quite beyond planning or predicting whether I shall come back up here or not. I shall hope, but I shall not expect. I am going with my mind quite accommodated to the idea that I am going for good, so far as this summer is concerned—though I am not distressing the dear ones here by admitting that that is what is in my mind. Presently *you* will be in Washington, when September comes, and then how *can* I leave it—even though I never see you from one slow week's end to another? Ah, my Love, where you are I *must* be, and as near you as the stern Fates permit!

There is a story in the papers this morning which, I need hardly tell you, is chiefly not so. Yesterday after the storm, as we were driving along the river road between Windsor and Ascutneyville we came upon a little group of three or four automobiles which had stopped near a machine which had turned turtle over the bank at the side of the road, a bank not more than three feet high. The people who had been in the machine—two women and a man—were already safely out and quite unhurt. We stopped and made inquiries, of course, and made certain that nothing could be done until the wreckers came from the garage in Windsor to which another passing motorist was just starting off to carry word, and I left the secret service men and their car to take the women into Windsor and render any other service they could—that was all. There was no rescue or heroics of any kind—any more than there was when we found that car tipped against the sapling at Echo Lake one day. It was so commonplace an incident that I had actually forgotten all about it when I wrote of our ride in my last letter.

You will understand, by the way, that I am denying myself the pleasure of the motor trip to Washington because I must get there before the fleet reaches Vera Cruz. As I said in the little scribbled note of this morning, I shall come back as far as Phila. in a few days and consult the oculist. I have already made sure that he will be there—and not off on his vacation.

I was so much interested in what you had to tell of the church service last Sunday, my Darling. Of course I remember reading the morning service to you that Sunday before I last went back to Washington—and the psalter. I do not think that I shall ever forget anything we did this blessed summer here together, and it pleased me to think that the very next Sunday you went to church the same passages from the Psalms were repeated. And to think of my lovely Darling sitting there in all her vital beauty filled with thoughts of me makes me very happy. This dear tired letter of my Sweetheart's which lies here before me, written late Sunday night, seems touched with sadness, my precious One,— only because you were weary and the day with its racking storm and the long evening with company had worn you out? I have read it again and again, with my heart as well as with my eyes, and each time I have got the impression that you sorely needed to be taken into your lover's arms and petted and cheered and made over by the magic of love and tenderness. "This has been a long week without you"—what an echo that finds in my heart! All the strength in me seems to give way and leave nothing but infinite loneliness and longing. Ah, my Darling, my Darling, *how* long it has been—longer than the whole month that preceded it, which seemed like only a single happy week! And I can borrow the rest of the sentence as if my own heart had coined it: "it has made me sure that there is no one else in the world to compare with you,"—no one so dear, so incomparably dear and fine and delightful and interesting and lovable and altogether desirable. The words with which the little epistle closes are very, very dear to me, my dear little girl—"secure in our perfect love" How easily you find the perfect words for your thought, my wonderful Sweetheart, when your heart speaks! If, when you are weary or sad or lonely, you feel this perfect love that has come to us as the one secure and certain thing which nothing can disturb or invade or touch, we have found the same happiness. The flood of tender love that welled up in my heart as I read those words— that wells up in it each time I read them—was a flood of very *deep* happiness. It is strange how the bitter and the sweet mingle in my thoughts and emotions these long-drawn-out days of separation. It is a bitter thing to love so and be in such pressing need of one another, to be possessed with a great longing which cannot be satisfied, and be bidden keep still and wait, wait, wait for what the heart cannot too long do without; and yet it is sweet to find out how great the love is, how deep it flows, like a mighty tide of life, how it springs from the deepest and most permanent things in us, how separation but makes it the clearer every day and every hour that we must be united, how thought and memory and hope but make us dearer to one another,—how space itself seems to be cheated by love and makes us hourly more certain that the love we bear one another is true and permanent and perfect. It is so *sweet* to think of you, and yet, oh, the longing it brings! I think of you every moment—the days are full of you, and only you—and every moment the longing threatens to become intolerable. Yes, Darling, I am perfectly well, and you may count on me to take good care of myself. I love life now more than ever, because you are in it. Can I count on you to do the same—for my sake? You are strong and well (how happy it makes me to know that!) but you presume on the fact and often overtax yourself. *Please*, for our love's sake, be very careful, my Edith. What would become of me now, if anything should happen to you? *Are* you well, and do you feel that there is a new reason, and a very big reason, for taking better care of yourself?

Wed. morning 6.45

We shall not play golf this morning—there are too many little last things to pick up and see to before leaving to cut our time down by half a morning, but I shall try to take a little turn in the machine to get the air of afternoon out-of-doors in my lungs just before starting.

I must confess that I leave with a heavy heart. There is nothing but work down in Washington and the fussing and scheming and palavering of many minds—and that bare and empty house with its ghostly furniture is not a homelike place to go to. It will seem emptier than ever now. But I'm game for it. It is plainly my duty to go, and to stay long enough to get hold of things very thoroughly—it may be till *next* summer; and I shall get adjusted to it within twenty-four hours after I get there. Moreover, I shall [be] happier there than I've been for many and many a long day—for many and many a long *year*, if time were reckoned by events and anxieties. I shall have a peace of mind that will make me proof against all "the slings and arrows of outrageous fortune," for I shall rest "secure in our perfect love," with thoughts of my ador-

able Darling, my own Edith, that will fortify me against everything but longing for her sweet presence, the sound of her voice
and the touch of her lips. I'm secure against unhappiness now,
whatever else loneliness and yearning may bring upon me. And,
besides, September will be here now in less than three weeks and
Helen has promised to come down then and see that we do not
go crazy or lose our decorous self-control. Margaret will come,
too, for a week end or two, if we need her,—and come with joy,
bless her heart. So far from having anything ahead of me that I
have a right to complain of, I know that I am in fact the most
fortunate man in the whole world and the most graciously
blessed, for I have my heart's desire. I have the love, the unstinted,
limitless love of the sweet, the incomparable woman to whom I
have given my heart and devoted my life; and her love has
changed the world for me. For she is altogether lovely and beyond
compare, a fit mate for any great work or deep pleasure. My heart
and my mind both rejoice in her. It is stimulation enough to carry
the man she loves through any test merely to think of her—her
strength, her loveliness, her steadfastness, her capacity for great
experiences and deep counsels, and her infinite sweetness and
charm with it all! Ah, Sweetheart, you have made me rich indeed!
You may depend upon it that, whatever weak yielding to loneliness the sheer yearning of my heart may plunge me into, in spite
of myself, I shall never be really unhappy while I may think of
you and of all you have given me, all you are to me. It does hurt
to go still further away from you, but I have myself thoroughly in
hand and rejoice in you!

I am sorry there is so little to send you in the way of interesting
papers, but business has turned up nothing new the last day or
two, except in Haiti, and there are no documents about that. The
newspapers seem to have the facts substantially straight about
what is happening down there; but if any despatch or other paper
comes into my hands which really throws light on that benighted
place I will of course send it to you. It is very likely that I will
myself find out a lot of things about it when I get down to Washington that I do not now know. It's for that very purpose I am
going, and perhaps ought to have gone sooner. I am sending you
to-day a belated letter of Sir Edward Grey's to House

Good-bye, Sweetheart; I must get to work. I shall try to write
at least a few lines from the train, so that you may not go a day
without a love message from   Your own   Woodrow.

All join me in messages of dear love.

ALS (WP, DLC).

To Robert Lansing

Windsor, Vt. August 11, 1915. Rec'd. 10:23 A.M.

I think it would be unwise for the conference to take for granted or insist upon the elimination of Carranza.[1] It would be to ignore some very big facts. It seems to me very important that the plan now formed should leave the way of action open in any direction and not assume a beginning over again with a clean sheet of paper to write on. Carranza will somehow have to be digested into the scheme and above all the object of the revolution will have to be in any event conserved.

Woodrow Wilson.[2]

T decode of telegram (SDR, RG 59, 812.00/15753½, DNA).
[1] Wilson sent this telegram not only in response to Lansing's letter of August 6, but also after reading the minutes of the conference of August 5 and 6. The minutes revealed that it was Lansing himself, generally supported by Paul Fuller, Sr., who had led the other conferees to the conclusions that recognition of Carranza was both unwise and impossible, and that they should agree upon a man for provisional president who could unite all the factions in Mexico, preferably someone with some claim to constitutional legitimacy.
[2] There is a WWsh draft of this telegram in WP, DLC.

To Samuel Gompers

My dear Mr. Gompers: Cornish, N. H., August 11, 1915

I received your telegram[1] and your letter of August ninth and have given the matter my serious thought.

Unfortunately, it is not possible for me to see Mr. Martinez; if I were to do so, I would open the door to practically everybody who wishes to see me about Mexico (and their name is Legion) or else make discriminations and give serious offence. But his letter to you sets forth his case so fully that I think I take it all in as fully as if I were to have an interview with him, and you may be sure what he says will form part of my thought in discussing the all-important question of Mexico with the Secretary of State and the Latin-American conferees.

Cordially and sincerely yours,   Woodrow Wilson

TLS (photostat in RSB Coll., DLC).
[1] S. Gompers to WW, Aug. 9, 1915, T telegram (WP, DLC).

From William Banks Caperton

Port au Prince, Hayti. August 11th, 1915.

In conjunction with Charge d'Affaires have informed assembled senators and deputies and presidential candidates of the intentions and policies of the Government of the United States as set forth by the Secretary of State in his cable message of midnight August tenth. Senators and deputies cordial. Election will be held tomorrow. The day passed quietly at Port au Prince, but considerable uneasiness and some demonstrations, due to the approaching elections and the desperate attitudes of the Bobo and Zamor factions.

Revolutionary committee issued orders dissolving Congress today and attempted to seal doors of Chamber of Deputies, but anticipated their action by sending a force to the Chamber of Deputies and informed committee that their action was without authority. For this reason and on account of the hostile and disturbing influences of the Bobo and Zamor factions I have dissolved the revolutionary committee and informed them that they have no further authority in Port au Prince and would be considered public enemies of the United States if they attempted to give any further orders or to menace U. S. policies

I have taken extra precaution against disorder during the elections, and have placed U.S.S. Castine and U.S.S. Eagle at the wharf and have landed men from them to re-enforce the landing force.

Have assumed control of state telegraph office.

Petigoave quiet.

Connecticut today held a conference with ex-Bobo forces relative to surrender of arms at Cape Haitien.   Caperton

T telegram (WP, DLC).

From Edith Bolling Galt

10 Park Place, Geneva August 11, 1915 9.45 a.m.

Welcome home, my precious one, and oh! if I were only really there to throw my arms 'round you and make you *know* how welcome you really are—always. I have just gotten your delicious long letter of Monday night and Tuesday morning—every word of which thrills me with happiness—and the little hurried note telling me your plan to leave today for Washington. Dearest my thoughts will follow you every mile of the road and fly before to welcome your coming.

I believe, in a way, you will be happier in Washington and certainly more content that you are in direct touch with things that are so vital.

Bless your heart for wanting to do as I asked about the trip down. But if it is rainy and cold you would not enjoy the motor, so I am glad you are going by train. I will be at the station in

Windsor at 3 to bid you God speed and then by your side all the way in my thoughts. And I do hope this will reach you early tomorrow but am afraid it can't much before lunch time.

Please don't plunge into things so deep that you will wear yourself out, and do try to get out for golf and long rides. I read in your letter a certain restlessness to be back at the source of things, and that you were uncertain as to the full report submitted to you.

We got back from our trip to Dansville and thence to Letchworth Park late yesterday afternoon and found your precious letters of Sunday and Monday (Please pardon such a mixup)[1] waiting for me with the additional pleasure of the contents of the big envelope. I could hardly wait to get my things off and get rid of people, to come to you for our daily talk together. But at last I did close my door, and, refreshed from brushing up, and a hurried plunge in the tub, settle down on the big bed with your letter. I read it through three times without stopping—and wanted it to go on and on. It brought you so vividly to me, and I could feel your dear heart beating against mine as I held you close and told you all about our trip—and how glad I was to get *home*—to your arms again—and how safe I felt when they encircled me. The trip was nice, and the Park very beautiful. An old fashioned farm house—in the centre of a thousand acres of woodland from the windows of which you can see the Falls below in a deep ravine—roaring and tumbling from a great height. They are very lovely, but absurd in comparison to Niagara, and to my mind the trees are the feature of the place.

We enjoyed wandering around and seeing an old Indian camping ground and a rude sort of hut called the "Council House" where the Indians are supposed to have met to settle affairs.

This part of the country is really wonderful for farming and fruit growing and is a swelling, fertile landscape quite different from the ruggedness of Vermont and New Hampshire. We came all through the famous Genesee Valley and saw the Wadsworth's places,[2] and many others finer and much better kept up. Since the terrific storm I wrote you of on Sunday, we have had no rain, but really lovely weather and today is so fresh and invigorating

We have just come from a spin to Mr. Rose's farm (11.45) and he is calling me to come join him on the porch—so I can't write as long a letter as I wanted to. We are going to the country club tonight for dinner, and afterwards home for "Auction." I have not yet begun golf as we have been away the only days it has not rained, and someway I feel I would rather wait and have you teach me. Thank you for sending me Mr. L's letter regarding the A.B.C. It does sound as though they might accomplish what you want and you are the most marvelous person in the world if you can do this with those wretched Mexicans

I am awfully interested to know what reply Mr. L. made to the German gentleman in regard to his letter about "cotton." It is extraordinary to a degree, and shows how his country watches day and night. I am keeping all these things locked up and will return them at any time if you need them. I think what you say regarding Mr. Page is true, that there seems much more reason for him to stay *there* to keep you informed, than to come here to inform himself unless he is so steeped in the English point of view that he does not see straight.

Oh my precious Woodrow how I do want to talk to you and know if you are worried over things and just keeping up a show to me—to "play the game" as you say. Don't do this, always tell me frankly—will you—the true state of things? and if you are well and your eyes and head are behaving?

What a wild trip Margaret and your sister "et als" had. I hope little Josephine was none the worse for it. They will all feel desolate today without you I know.

Thank you again for all your sweet sympathy about Panama, and your permission to use your dear name. I have not written to either Rolfe or his wife again because I did not want any other letter to get there at the same time mine did to Elizabeth, for fear she would think they had asked me to write. I told her "if she wanted to get away where she could think things over quietly for awhile, to come to me, but not to let Mr. Boyd follow her, for that would defeat what she wanted, and I could not help her." Another letter from Rolfe said the uncle was to arrive the next day so I am holding my breath to see what happens. I am sorry you have really worried over it, but please don't any more, for "we" have done all we can. Now I must go—I will write tomorrow. My tender love and a welcoming kiss from

Your own   Edith

ALS (WP, DLC).
   1 She wrote "Monday Saturday," crossed them out, and wrote "Monday" above them.
   2 The estates of the several branches of the Wadsworth family of Geneseo, N. Y., especially those of former Congressman James Wolcott Wadsworth and his son, United States Senator James Wolcott Wadsworth, Jr.

To Edith Bolling Galt

Wednesday Evening, en route.

My precious Darling,   11 August, 1915.

I hate to write to you on my typewriter, but I simply cannot manage my pen at all on the train, and I do not want you to go a single day without a love message from me if I can help it. Knowing what your letters mean to me, I cannot help hoping and believing that mine mean as much to you: indeed I know that they do, for has not my darling Sweetheart told me what they mean to her? Her heart shall not wait for them in vain through any fault of mine.

We left Windsor this afternoon at three, or a little after (for the train was late), and are now passing Hartford, Connecticut. After doing all the work in sight this morning after breakfast, I took a drive with the two girls and Sister Annie, and a rather interesting thing happened. We were on a quiet, out-of-the-way road that we have been on only once before this summer, so far as I can remember, the road from Plainfield to Cornish Flat, when we met another machine. The road was so narrow that we stopped to let it pass. It was driven by a gentleman who looked very hard at me as he approached. When he got abreast of us he stopped and, rising in his machine, said, "Mr. President, I have here a little bunch of thirteen four-leaf clovers for you. I hoped I should have a chance to see you, and now a happy accident has thrown me in your path. I twice had the pleasure of giving similar bunches of clover to Mr. Cleveland while he was President, and take great satisfaction in finding you to give you these. There is also in the bunch a clover with seven leaves. I doubt if you have often seen one." I stood up in our machine, as he did in his, and thanked him very heartily. I was so taken by surprise at the whole thing that he had finished his little presentation and gone on his way before I realized that I had forgotten to ask his name, and knew only that he looked a thorough gentleman, and a very pleasant on[e] at that, and was accompanied by a lady with a face full of sweet good nature and quite unusually quick intelligence. Wasn't that an interesting little encounter; and was it not odd that our ride should have taken us on that particular road to-day? I am genuinely sorry I did not identify him. I liked his looks so much.

When we got back from the ride and I was feeling too blue for words at the immediate prospect of leaving the dear place where my sweet Love made me supremely happy, your letter from Dansville was handed to me. I wonder if I can tell you what it meant to me,—I wonder if you were yourself aware when you wrote it with how perfect and wonderful a revelation of your love for me you were blessing me? I [A] flood of tender happiness came over me as I read it that has robbed the day of every regret and every fatigue and made it seem a day of special joy instead of a day of sadness, as if it came at the beginning of a season of delight instead of at the end of it! For this precious letter breathes. It seems to speak with the very voice that you spoke with those last blessed evenings at Harlakenden, when our hearts were so perfectly opened to one another, the tones, unspeakably tender and sweet, that seemed to enter my very heart and thrill it with a happiness so poignant and complete that every sweet desire and every deepest need it had ever had was satisfied, and hopes fulfilled that it had seemed like wishing for something more ideal than the world had ever yielded even to entertain them. Here in this wonderful letter is that same blessed assurance of love made perfect. I know as I read it that you are indeed my very own, that my dream has come true, my heart's desire filled to the utmost. The sweet intimacy and confidence of it are as if they came out of my own thought. All your letters speak the same thing. Those happy days at Harlakenden took us the whole journey. But somehow this particular letter from Dansville seems the most intimate revelation of your dear heart of any of them. You speak of my letters in the same way, my precious One, but I am sure that they do not convey the very essence of love as this one does,—by what magic no analysis could determine,—just because it was written by you without reserve, to your lover, and your heart was full to overflowing when you wrote it of the love that only such natures as yours can feel and confess: a love that has made me happy and secure for the rest of my life. If I could do the same thing, if I could put into words the feeling I have for you, the love and tenderness and passionate devotion, I could make you as happy as you have made me. But you know, do you not, my Darling? If you did not, I could not have won you as I have. It is love that has won you, and no excellence in myself. I have given you my whole heart and that has moved you to give me yours in return, and I am in your debt, for you are more lovely and more to be desired than I. I am only a man, while you are that greatest and finest of all things, a greatly endowed Woman, compact of every sort of loveliness, capable of bestowing every sort of delight and comfort and guidance and inspiration. You help me to believe in myself by loving me so!

I am going back to Washington with the feeling, as you know, that the play days of the summer are over and that the days have come in which I must get back to the strenuous work of getting purposes put into action, not only in Mexico and Haiti and all the foreign field but also here at home, where the whole programme for the next session of Congress is yet to be formulated and the men who are to carry it through got into line; and that big empty House is going to seem very cheerless to me for a while;

but, do you know, Sweetheart, you have somehow transformed Washington for me! You have already made it home for me, because it is home for you. I once hated it; but now my feeling about it is changing altogether. This single sentence in your letter in which you promise that it shall always be home for me while you are there seems of itself to have altered it, or to have made me conscious that it is already altered. These have been wonderful weeks, my Darling. They have altered the whole world for us. We are not the same people we were when we went to Cornish! The world has been filled with light and certainty and peace for us! Why should Washington *not* be a different place for me? Will it not be a different place for you also? The old unhappy thoughts are cleared away. There is no haunting question mark hidden in anything. The days ahead of us will be bright with confident planning, reassuring trust, the sweetest intimacy and companionship of purpose; and it will be a brightness in which there will be no shadow. Love will shine in every nook and corner alike of the things we remember and of the things we do and of all that we plan and hope for. Washington used to be full, for me, only of selfish men: now it will be full of one lovely woman; and she will redeem it. She will give me the things that make any place a kingdom. And it has contained you all these years! I am so thankful, my precious Darling, that you have yourself found a new happiness there! I shall look at the place with new eyes to-morrow morning.

Good-night. I read to Margaret and Jessie what you said about them, and your sweet messages to them of tender love, and their faces glowed with genuine joy. They both spoke of you with deep admiration and affection. How happy all this makes me: your love for them and their love for you. Happiness has come upon me of late in a flood!

I shall mail this immediately on our arrival, and it will carry with it the whole heart of   Your own,   Woodrow

I would like to keep on indefinitely, but the swaying of the train as I write makes me a bit dizzy.

Arrived safe & well. Dearest love   W.

WWTLS (WP, DLC).

From Edith Bolling Galt

My precious One: August 11, 1915 Geneva N. Y.

The town clock is just striking midnight, and, while I lie here in my big bed with the windows wide open to the cool night air,

I am picturing you on a hot, dusty train rushing through the darkness, and I will stop to whisper a little prayer for your protection and safe arrival in the place that has been home to me for so many years.

I have thought of you all through the day and pictured your leaving, and all the longing in my heart has been rushing out to meet you. I do hope the faithful Mr. Hoover will have things ready for you tomorrow with flowers everywhere and the house with an air of home—to bid you welcome.

I sent my letter to Mr. Hoover today and trust you will get it promptly. I am so afraid you are going to find it terribly hot in Washington, so please Dearest, be careful.

After I finished my letter to you at noon I went down on the porch with Mr. Rose. He is really deeply distressed over the death of his brother and seems to dread living alone.

We got maps and tried to work out the best route toward Ocean City, for they have definitely decided to take me thence in their car and all remain a week before they come home and Mother Bertha and I go back to Washington

After lunch Mr. R. went to play golf and I wrote a lot of letters, among which was an answer to Nell's dear note to me. About four I got sleepy and took a little nap before reading the papers. We three went to the country club for dinner and as it (the Club House) is beautifully situated on a point running out into the Lake it is very lovely there, and there was a beautiful sunset. We got back a little after eight, and Mr. Wheat[1] came to play cards. We had an interesting game and did not stop until eleven. Three other people came to call, so we got started very late. I have had invitations for every afternoon and evening but as the Roses are not going anywhere I have been able to decline, and I am enjoying the freedom of doing as I please

Have you heard from Helen? I wrote her as soon as I got to Geneva but have heard nothing from her and do hope she is not sick but just taking a good rest.

I saw an account in three papers of your going to the rescue of the motorists in distress, and, allowing for newspaper exageration, I suppose there must really have been a "human interest" story this time. How your description of the little Otter Creek Tea House brought back our happy afternoon there, and after reading your dear letter I fell asleep and dreamed it all over again just as it really happened. Just in the midst of the dream Mr. Rose called me to give me a telephone message and I thought for one happy moment that it was you who had called me, and, not until I was fully awake, could I convince myself you were far away. You seemed *here—in the room*—and I could not let you go.

I will finish this in the morning after I get the mail. Goodnight my precious One—and a happy awakening when we get home!

Thursday, 12

The mail came a half hour ago (just as your train was due in Washington) and I hope you are not tired out and can get adjusted to the change of climate before you have to plunge into work.

Your dear letter seems sad and as though you felt the weight of things more acutely than you admit—even to me. I know it was hard to leave Cornish and all the dear ones there and feel that your real holiday may be over for months. But, I believe, (as I wrote you yesterday) you will worry less in Washington because you will have every thing under your own control.

Bless your precious heart! how I wish I could really be the help you say I am. Never before did I long for the wisdom of a well informed mind half so much for then I could be a staff for you to lean on. But if a keen sympathy and comprehension can lift the burden, even a little bit, then I am a help to the wisest and dearest person in the world. I am so interested in Sir Edward's letter—and the deep sorrow of the man speaks in every line. What he says of nature is very pretty and gives a strong light on the character of the man. As to the other letter about that *Traitor*[2] my blood boils when I think of him, and I am afraid if he were left in my hands by an inscrutable Fate, I would put him where the world would never be troubled with him or his "peace" *sheeps clothing* again. Oh, but I would love to publish this letter in every paper in the land! and add to it what I think of him. Thank you for the picture and the cartoon. That is so absurd it doesn't hurt, but this other thing is so low words can't reach it. You will think me a fire brand if I don't stop, so I will change the subject and tell you that I am ashamed of these badly written sheets after reading your letters, where even the clear, regular writing bespeaks perfection. But on the other hand the two letters are characteristic of our personalities and there is no use my trying to impress you with even a pretence of law and order. I am what I am—and as you love me you forgive the blots—and overlook the faults—and make me happy by your tender comprehension. Goodbye for today dear, tired little boy. Remember how I love you, and that I am yours with all my heart,   Edith.

ALS (WP, DLC).

[1] Probably Henry A. Wheat, president of the Summit Foundry Co., Geneva, N. Y.

[2] That is, Bryan.

From Josephus Daniels

My dear Mr. President: Washington. August 12, 1915

Your letter of the 6th, enclosing one from Mrs. Sophia Gompers, who lost her son at Haiti, arrived while I was in North Carolina, and my office immediately communicated with Mrs. Gompers and the State Department, informing her of such steps as she must take to obtain a gratuity, and requesting the State Department what adjustment can be arranged with the Haitian Government.

Believe me   Sincerely yours,   Josephus Daniels

TLS (WP, DLC).

From Lindley Miller Garrison

My dear Mr. President: Washington. August 12, 1915.

I herewith transmit to you an outline of the military policy which I recommend should be adopted.[1]

I desire to submit the following suggestions for your consideration as to the best way to proceed in this matter.

Whatever of value is to be accomplished will be in response to public opinion. The public knows this matter is being studied for the purpose of formulating and submitting a policy for consideration and adoption. It is not necessary that you should now reach or express any fixed determination upon the matter. It is sufficient if it be known that you are giving the whole subject matter full and deliberate consideration. Before final decision you should be advised of the trend of public opinion. The only way that I can see adequately to ascertain this is as follows. I can arrange for the fullest and most widespread publicity for this outline as that which has been recommended. This will result in fixing public attention upon the subject matter, giving it something to discuss and consider, and thus will elicit public opinion. In this way, you will be enabled to gather what that opinion is and to act advisedly.

If you agree with the suggested course, and will so inform me, I will promptly set about following it. My judgment is it should be done promptly. To secure adequate publicity, there should be at least a week, perhaps more, between the delivery of the matter to be published and the release.

If you desire to see me personally, and I happen to be at my cottage at Sea Bright, I can always reach Washington within a few hours after notification.

I sincerely trust you are refreshed and re-created by your

absence from the immediate pressure here, and that you will avail yourself of the first opportunity to return to the country.

Sincerely yours,   Lindley M. Garrison

TLS (WP, DLC).

¹ [L. M. Garrison] "An Outline of Military Policy" [c. Aug. 12, 1915], T memorandum (WP, DLC). After a lengthy introduction chiefly devoted to showing the inadequate strength of the regular army and to proving that the National Guard was not and could not be made an adequate force for national defense, Garrison recommended a modest increase in the size of the regular army and the creation of a trained reserve or "citizen force" of 400,000 men. He did not indicate how this policy might be implemented, and he provided no estimate whatever as to the cost. He said only that the "aggregate of cost . . . is being carefully worked out" and added that "the proper cost of a proper policy must be met."

From Edmundo E. Martinez

Sir: Washington, D. C., August 12, 1915.

I have come to the United states, primarily as the representative of the working people of Mexico: and as such, I deplore to learn that you could not accord me the privilege of laying the case of an oppressed people before your Excellency, when so many others assume the right to dispose of our future to their entire satisfaction.

In fact, I did not disclose in my letter, or orally, to Mr. Gompers what I intended to convey to you, and it is this.

Besides having been selected by the Mexican Federation of Labor as their spokesman in the United States, I was also sent by the Masons of that country to present the case as we think it really is. Also, I was entreated by the Evangelical (Protestant) Mexicans to try to secure for Mexico the same rights other people have.

If your Excellency will bear with me I will say this. Regardless of statements to the contrary, the Mexican people desire the leadership of Mr. Carranza, as he has put an end to the domination in Mexico by the Church of Rome. We consider that no matter what they are in this country, the Romanists have been a curse to our unfortunate country for the last four hundred years. The Mexicans have had for you the greatest esteem, as they know you are a Christian gentleman and though [thoroughly] in favor of the freedom of conscience, but opposed to the political domination of any church in the affairs of your or our nation. I still hope you hold this view, although the American Press reports indicate that by the course you intend to pursue, we will be handed over to Rome.

We understand that Rome is busy to hold her prey, and is using all her power to do so. I too am a Christian, a Methodist, and in the name of Jesus, I ask you to consider, before thousands of innocent lives are sacrificed on both sides.

You can help our unfortunate country, now that Mr. Carranza and the people have nearly won. The laying down of arms by Villa will prove it to you. Another thing, we want Mr. Carranza because he has been to us what you have been to the American people. The big corporations have not been able to buy him and he has conducted the revolution without the help of them. Permit me to assure you that the Evangelical people, the working people of Mexico, the Masons, and the country at large, have given him their undivided support. Mr. Carranza may have been misrepresented by some of his generals, but he always corrected the errors.

In the Carranza controlled territory, there is no more pulque being sold; no gambling is allowed; no cock fights or bull fights are permitted. I have documents to prove this.

Mr. Carranza has always helped honest American citizens, and has protected them in their lives and properties.

We don't think it just that people like Villa and Zapata, whom we consider as vile murderers, should be heard in the councils of the nation. The murder of an Englishman, Benton, and the blowing up of trains of defenceless passengers bear me witness to my statement.

Your Excellency has been aware that the slave drivers of this country have attacked you because they could not rob your nation. They have done the same with Mr. Carranza because he does not let them do as they please.

Therefore, I appeal to you, before I send word to the people who sent me here, for a word of hope. I would appreciate this as we Mexican Christians have put you up before our people as the model for a Christian gentleman and citizen, the one who could unite all America for the Master. Furthermore, I would like to tell them that your country has men like Mr. Samuel Gompers, who are going to extend to us the true hand of fellowship. We think a good deal of him in Mexico, and trust that with his fatherly advice, we will settle many a rough path. If the people there think that we Evangelical people and Masons have been untrue to them, it will be years before we can build up our work again. I consider that you can avert the war which your millionaires and the Church of Rome are bringing on.

Let us have what we want, freedom of worship. Don't deliver us into the hands of those who would oppress us by driving us into political, industrial and religious serfdom.

I beg, your Excellency, to remain, as a Mexican Mason and Christian, your obedient servant,

Respectfully yours,   Edmundo E. Martinez[1]

TLS (WP, DLC).

[1] Wilson wrote to Tumulty on August 17 (TL, WP, DLC): "Please say to Mr. Martinez that I have read this letter not only, but also the one transmitted to me from Mr. Gompers, and have read them with the greatest interest, being impressed by their earnestness and by the representations which they make. Assure him that they will constitute a part of my thought in handling this difficult matter."

To Edith Bolling Galt

[The White House] Thursday evening,
My precious Darling,   8 o'cl. 12 Aug., 1915

Your sweet, sweet little letter of yesterday, though the last part of it was not written till noon, reached me, to my great delight, a little before noon to-day. Hoover walked into the study here, where I sat alone, working, and handed it to me in his most sober and formal manner, but with an evident effort to make it seem as if it were a perfectly simple and merely routine thing for him to receive letters for me in that way. He's a brick. I respect him— his real tact and natural dignity—as much as I like and value him. He is going to be one of our best and truest friends. And what an exquisitely sweet letter it was he handed me! Ah, my Darling, there is no adequate way in which to tell you what these precious letters of yours mean to me, with their tender, intimate love, except to hold you close in my arms and cover you with kisses and whisper into your lips all the most endearing names that lovers ever invented to give their hearts ease. You *were* at the train at Windsor, precious Sweetheart; you were with me on the journey; and you were here to welcome me. You are everywhere for me, and the consciousness of you transforms all these familiar places, makes these empty rooms feel like home—a home mer[e]ly waiting for you, its mistress and glory, to come. And I can almost *touch* you when I read these dear, dear letters. It is almost as if you were speaking them in soft whispers in my ear and your breath were on my cheek. I thrill with the sense of your nearness and feel your exquisite charm and loveliness almost as vividly as if I actually held you close to my heart and were soothed and quickened by your sweet caresses. No, Sweetheart, I do not wear myself out or let worry upset my spirits. I am not keeping a calm face or "playing the game," to keep anxiety or distress away from you. I am well and do not chafe under the burden of the day. If you did not love me, I would,—the day's

anxieties would be intolerable. If you did not love me as you do,—
as you have loved me since those blessed days of perfect revelation at Harlakenden, when our spirits sprang together in a union
which nothing can ever sever or disturb,—if you did not give me
the wonderful, tender love spoken so sweetly in these letters
which are like your very self,—I think that worry would find me
out and wear me out. But there seems to be nothing to *distress*
myself about since you gave yourself to me. I think intensely
about the intricate and difficult matters that press upon me so
insistently and seem to afford no way out of perplexity; I give
the best that I have of intelligence and of labour of my [heart]
and conscience to them, and they tug mightily at my heart-strings
as well as at my mind; the day's work is always intense and
sometimes exhausting; but it touches no vital part of me. I
breathe an atmosphere now so sweet and tonic that nothing can
really hurt me or impair my vitality. It was not so only a few
weeks ago. It was not so when I was last here. It could not be
so until I was sure that the road ahead was clear and altogether
inviting to my Darling,—until I was sure that· her heart was
absolutely at ease and full of gladness and exhileration. I am sure
of that now. That is the reason why no anxiety, however great,
that does not touch her or her happiness, can impair my strength
or slacken my courage or affect my physical health for a moment.
I drank of the fountain of youth again when my Darling's brow
finally cleared, one of those wonderful evenings at Harlakenden,
never to be darkened again by anything affecting us, and I knew
that she saw her way to perfect, fearless happiness with her
chosen lover. Ah, Sweetheart, my own precious little girl, what an
emancipation that was for both of us! You made me safe then,
and can keep me safe by the simple act of letting yourself love
as only you can. I shall tell you the exact full truth about myself
in every letter. I shall not get ill from any malady of the mind.
If I did, you, and not Grayson, could cure me. I gave myself a
nervous headache writing at that swaying typewriter in my
state-room on the train last night (my special car is always attached to the rear end of the train, and whips about on the curves
and switches like the end of a whip lash) and I did not get wholly
rid of it till your letter came and I had lunch. But this afternoon
I have felt fine, and beat the doctor at golf for the first time
since you drove off with the Roses. This forenoon I cleared up
routine business and had a long conference with Lansing getting
thoroughly posted (nothing has gone wrong or too hastily, after
all, I find), and this afternoon early I had a long talk with the
Secretary of the Navy to make sure that the right orders about
Haiti and Vera Cruz had gone out. They had.

But I must not forget to tell you an amusing thing about Cornish. At the "Discussion Club" last Tuesday (this is gossip brought in by the doctor from the Shipman's—no one from Harlakenden attended) the subject was "Feminism: Is it a Menace?" and Mrs. Churchill[1] read a paper on "Love" which went on and on for the better part of two hours! She paid no attention to interruptions or comments. Twice Mrs. Adams,[2] in a sweet, gentle voice, said "May I ask a question?", but not the slightest notice was taken of her either by Mrs. Churchill or anybody else; and, when the paper seemed at last to be concluded, Mrs. Shipman said that, 'without meaning to imply the least criticism of what Mrs. Churchill had said,['] she would very much like to know just what the point was that Mrs. Churchill had been trying to make? But Mrs. Churchill paid no attention to the question and neither Mrs. Shipman nor anybody else, so far as she could learn by pointed inquiry ever did find out. I was dying to find out what Mrs. Churchill's idea of love is, and whether she thinks it works or not—but I could not—apparently because she herself could not tell. And whether feminism is a manace [menace] or not they seem to have forgotten to determine. What would I not have given to have had your account of it all, as we had your inimitable account of Mrs. Adams's spiritual assessment of the workman's task! I am so glad, my precious little girl, that you really enjoyed the Dansville trip. It must have been through delightful country— for I could visualize it from your descriptions of it. How I envied the Roses and the Grants! How I envied everybody who saw you. Geneva must be the happiest place in the world to be just now, if one knows the Roses and can have a few words with their lovely guest!

Margaret & Sister and little Annie and Josephine came through their ride (320 miles, it turned out to be) extraordinarily well, after all—and had a good time! They are tougher than I thought. And little Josephine got through fresher than them all! So much for the fears of a prudent elderly gentleman.

That was a lovely letter you wrote Elizabeth, my Darling,—just like you in generous thoughtfulness and practical good sense. I wish that she might, under its influence, have a lucid interval, accept the invitation, and come. Great a burden as it would entail upon you, that would be easier to bear than your present anxiety and perplexity about your brother. I, too, hold my breath for fear of what we shall next hear from that uncle!

I do not think Lansing made any reply to that amazing letter of Bernstorff's about cotton purchases—except simply to acknowledge its receipt. What *could* he say? The thing was unspeakable!

The A.B.C. (and B.U.G—Bolivia, Uruguay, and Guatamala) conference adjourned after their meeting yesterday until they could hear from the factional leaders whom they had addressed in their appeal (I sent you a printed copy of it to-day for your convenience, should you wish to refer to it). There was nothing further to discuss till they did. I do not expect much from the conference except a certain very valuable moral effect on Latin America as a whole, and, indirectly, on Mexico itself, because of what it so clearly indicates as to the *spirit* in which we are trying to act—not playing a rôle of selfish aggression nor even playing Big Brother to the hemisphere too arrogantly. And yet it may have some practical effects, too. I shall not give up hope of them until the whole programme is worked out and I can see just how far we can make them go along with us.

Good night, Edith, my precious little girl. How sweet it is to dream that you are actually close against my heart, giving me a long, true lover's kiss, and that I can feel the quick drawn breaths of happy excitement that shake us both when we are in each other's arms. Ah, my Darling, how sweet you are! How I love you! How happy it makes me to love you—and how happy beyond all words to have you love me—with sweet perfection, as you do!

Friday, 7 A.M. 13 Aug., 1915

The first thing my eyes rested on when I opened them this morning was your dear face. I had propped one of your photographs up against the pillow of the twin bed next to mine just before I put out the light on the little stand by my bedside last night, hoping that I would happen to be facing it when the morning came and I wake up,—and I was. Oh, the happy thrill it gave me! I began talking love to it before I was fairly awake and it gave me the most delicious sense of your actual presence. Ah, Sweetheart, the glass over a picture is a cold thing to kiss, but surely you must feel the kisses I give these lovely pictures of my beautiful Darling. If you had been there, instead of your "counterfeit presentment," I fear I should have smothered you with kisses. Your mere picture made me happy and started the day right for me. Your beauty, my Darling, so wonderfully represents your *self*: it is so vivid, so full of life, goes so much beyond mere beauty of form. It is a sort of *speaking* beauty, eloquent of a charm of heart and mind and spirit that hold and captivate. These dear pictures are a great comfort to me. They are really wonderful in having caught so much of your life and charm. It is hard to have to lock them up, and take them out only at night when I am safely alone in my bed room, as if I were *stealing* some pleasure I was ashamed of! I am so *proud* of your love that I want all the world to know about it!

There is to be no cabinet meeting to-day. There is nothing in shape to be formally discussed or finally decided, and I am never anxious to hear the *saltered* opinions of my dear colleagues of the Discussion Club. I see those who are acting on the things that need action—and when I see them every word said means business. That's what I like. That's what I get satisfaction out of. Except for *seeing* people, there is very little more regular business each day here than there was at Cornish—but the exception is a huge one. All sorts of demands for interviews will come crowding in now. The town is beginning to fill up with men of the restless, meddling sort. Some of them are southern congressmen with wild schemes, preposterous and impossible schemes to valorize cotton and help the cotton planter out of the Reserve Banks or out of the national Treasury—out of anything, if only they can make themselves solid with their constituents and seem to be "on the job." Hoke Smith is one of these. "Bob" Henry, of Texas, is another. The difference between these two in character is very great, however. Bob Henry is a fool, but he is honest—I need not complete the antithesis! I am going to send you to-day, in the big envelope, a letter from House which contains an interesting (!) item about Hoke Smith. Spring Rice intimated the same thing about him to House in a recent talk with him. If it's true, I hope they can prove it—and the sooner the better, for he is making a great deal of mischief.

It is hot here, of course, but not hot enough to be distressing—nothing like so hot as it was a few days ago, when they say the thermometers in the places of business on the street registered 106° and 107°. Heat apparently does not hurt me, though it sometimes makes me cross.

The duties of the day are calling, and I must go. My thoughts will be with you every moment and this letter carries with it to my precious Darling the tender, intimate, unbounded love of
Your own   Woodrow

Here are some larger envelopes, my precious Sweetheart.   W.

ALS (WP, DLC).
1 Mabel Harlakenden Hall (Mrs. Winston) Churchill.
2 Adeline Valentine Pond (Mrs. Herbert) Adams.

From Edith Bolling Galt

My precious One: [Geneva, N. Y.] August 12, 1915 11 P.M.

I have come to looking forward to this time with you every night when the rest of the household is asleep, as the happiest part of the day except when the Postman brings me your *part* of our blessed talks, and I sit by my window and read those dear pages on which the hand I love has so recently rested—and which brings you and your vital, stimulating mind in direct touch with mine

I am in bed—and have just finished reading over again your last letter from Harlakenden written "Tuesday evening" and yesterday morning at 6.45

Each letter I get Sweetheart is so full of tenderness and the old, old story that makes this dull earth glorified, that I fear the next one can not find new words in which to tell me what my ears long to hear, and yet the next day brings its own message more full, more rich, more satisfying, and I know that such prodigal wealth can only spring from depths whose foundations can never be disturbed—and from which comes only precious metal that will only become brighter by use.

I know how weary you must have been tonight after your long journey and I hope you got to bed early and will dream that I am with you and holding you safe in my arms, while, with very tender fingers, I press down your tired lids, and bid you sleep while I keep watch beside you.

Your letter was sad my dear Lord, and I trust the sadness came chiefly from your dread of leaving that dear house which is so full of memories for us both and the ending of your freedom from affairs that were not important enough to admit of transportation.

Even if I am in Washington for September I want you to go back to Cornish if you possibly can, for those nice *old* ladies will be there then and you will enjoy it and get another chance of refreshment. This afternoon I got a sweet letter from Dr. G. written aboard your car and posted at New Haven.

He tells me Altrude is in Washington so I suppose they are together tonight and his heart is at ease, if only for a few brief hours.

He says he wishes he could talk to me—that things are much better than they were early in the summer but still *unsettled*, which he knows will be a disappointment to me as well as to himself. Then he says some very lovely things about our happiness and how much it means to him—that it is too sacred for him to put on paper—but he will try to express it when he sees me.

Dear fellow, how I wish I could make him as happy. Tell him Dearest how I appreciate his letter and that I will answer soon.

You asked me if I was well, and reminded me to take care of myself, and I can promise you I will do this and that I love to feel you care. This afternoon Mrs. Endicott and Miss Seward[1] from N. Y. spent the afternoon and at 5:30 Mr Rose took them home in his car, and as Mrs. R. was tired, I went for a three mile walk by myself. It had poured rain all day and there was a high wind, but it cleared about four and was fine and bracing

The Lake was full of little white caps and looked awfully pretty in the pale sunlight   Tonight we went to a very nice place for a game of "Auction" but we stopped at ten and got home by half past. I see in the evening paper that Mr. Lansing thinks the ordering of the ships south a very grave mistake and has asked you to sidetrack them somewhere—as he fears the effect—and that the sending of them is a blunder in the Army or Navy Dept.

Of course, in view of what you said about the order being a request to you from Mr. Lansing, I can't credit the newspaper account of this and suppose it is as sensational as the account of the automobile accident in which you "stood ankle deep in mud" while you rescued 2 charming ladies—who failed to recognize you as the President

Sunday—11:30 a.m.

Your dear letter written en route came by the early mail bringing its own sweet welcome. I hope you did not weary your dear head by writing me such a long delicious letter, but if you knew what happiness it brought you would feel repaid. I am always so glad when you are off those nasty trains, and see from the morning paper that Washington had a pouring rain, so I trust it cooled things off and you had a restful night. We have been out all morning and as the mail is collected at 12 I have to hurry to get this posted so it will reach you tomorrow.

I had read in the papers the story of the clovers but it was not nearly so interesting as your own account of it, and it seems strange you should have taken that particular road, or that the number should have been your lucky 13. I am so glad, for even if it is a superstition, it is a happy one, and it must bring my precious One all happiness and good fortune.

My heart comes with this—and I am always

Your own   Edith.

ALS (WP, DLC).
[1] Caroline Seward (Mrs. Robert) Endicott and Alice D. Seward of New York.

To Robert Lansing, with Enclosure

Dear Mr. Secretary   [The White House, c. Aug. 13, 1915]

This is, I think, necessary and has my approval. Do you think it will affect Latin American opinion unfavourably?

W.W.

ALI (SDR, RG 59, 711.38/24½, DNA).

E N C L O S U R E

From Robert Lansing

My Dear Mr. President: Washington August 13, 1915.

I enclose for your consideration a telegram to our Legation at Port au Prince,[1] which directs our Chargé to negotiate and sign a treaty with the Haytien Government along the lines of the treaty which was sought to be negotiated a year ago last July. It, of course, makes several alterations and additions covering the ground far more thoroughly and granting to this Government a much more extensive control than the original treaty proposed. I enclose also the file copy of the instructions sent to our Minister July 2, 1914,[2] and also a draft of convention, with the alterations and additions included.

I believe that I informed you yesterday in our interview that the Haytien Congress adjourns next Tuesday and, therefore, if we intend to sign a treaty and have it ratified by that congress, which is so friendly to our Government, before our own Congress assembles in December, there is not time for delay. If it is to be done at all, it will have to be done immediately.

I confess that this method of negotiation, with our marines policing the Haytien Capital, is high handed. It does not meet my sense of a nation's sovereign rights and is more or less an exercise of force and an invasion of Haytien independence. From a practical standpoint, however, I cannot but feel that it is the only thing to do if we intend to cure the anarchy and disorder which prevails in that Republic. I believe it will be welcomed by the better element of the Haytien people, who now do not dare to take part in public affairs on account of the danger of assassination and massacre. It does not seem to me that the so-called Haytien revolutions are revolutions in fact, but, in reality, represent the struggle of bandits for control of the machinery of government which they utilize solely for the purpose of plunder. None of these so-called "generals" represent a principle or represent in any way the people of Haiti. The only possible way, it seems to me, of restoring to the Haytiens their political and personal rights and protecting them from the terrorism of unscrupulous military leaders is to obtain control, for a time at least, of the prize which these chieftans seek, namely, the public revenues of the Republic.

I have not been unmindful of the possible criticism which may be aroused in the Senate in case this treaty should be signed and submitted to them for action. As I said, it seems a high handed procedure, but I do not see how else we can obtain the desirable end of establishing a stable government in Haiti and maintaining domestic peace there.

I have seen the French Ambassador this morning in regard to the contractual obligations of the Haytien Government to the Bank of Haiti, which is a French corporation. In that connection I enclose, for your information, a memorandum of the provisions of the contract, which was submitted to the Department yesterday by Mr. Casenave, the President of the Bank. In case this treaty should become operative there would have to be an exchange of notes between the French Ambassador and this Department, in which we would state that the bank would continue to be the depository of the public funds of Haiti. While I did not disclose to the French Ambassador the text of the treaty, I suggested to him that we might feel compelled, in the interest of the Haytien people, to take charge of their finances and support the established government. With this he was heartily in accord, provided that we would protect the Bank of Haiti in its rights. The Ambassador evidenced a sentimental interest in the Republic and expressed the hope that we would not endeavor to change its language from French to English. As to that I gave him assurance that we had no such purpose.

This newly proposed treaty I prepared as soon as possible. I regret that I have not been able to send it to you sooner or to talk over the details of the plan, because I realize it is establishing a policy considerably in advance of our Dominican policy. The necessity of speedy action is my excuse for, if anything is to be done, a decision must be reached without delay in order that action may be taken before the adjournment of the Haytien Congress.   Faithfully yours,   Robert Lansing.

TLS (SDR, RG 59, 711.38/24A, DNA).

1 RL to Amlegation, Port-au-Prince, Aug. 12, 1915, T telegram (SDR, RG 59, 711.38/24A, DNA), printed in FR 1915, pp. 431-33. This telegram specified instructions for negotiation of the new treaty with Haiti. They consisted largely of changes to be made in the draft treaty referred to below. The new treaty did indeed provide for complete control of Haitian affairs by the United States: virtually total American control of Haitian finances; a Haitian-manned con-

stabulary, with American officers, to police the country; and sanitary and other public improvements to be carried out under the supervision of American engineers. The Haitian government was also to agree to the execution of a protocol with the United States for the settlement of all foreign debts; in addition, the Haitian government was to agree that it would not alienate any Haitian territory to a foreign power other than the United States. Article 13 was the most important. It stipulated: "The United States shall have authority to prevent any and all interferences with the attainment of any of the objects comprehended in this convention as well as the right to intervene for the preservation of Haitian independence and the maintenance of a government adequate for the protection of life, property and individual liberty." The treaty was to be in force for ten years, and for another ten years at the request of either party.

² It is printed in *FR 1914*, pp. 349-50.

To John Franklin Jameson

My dear Jameson: [The White House] August 13, 1915

I deeply appreciate your letter of August fourth. It gave me very keen pleasure.

I have some conception of the beauty of Lake Ellen Wilson because the Secretary of the Interior was kind enough to send me a glass transparency of it, very beautifully colored, which is hanging in my study window now. I am glad to say that Mrs. Wilson knew before she went that the beautiful lake had been named after her and saw this representation of it. She was, I think, greatly pleased and touched.

It was delightful to have your description of it.

I am glad you saw Axson. I am hoping that he will come to us in Washington for a little while this autumn. It is a real deprivation to me that I do not see friends like yourself in Washington. The absorption of my duties is one of the hardest things for me to bear.

Cordially and sincerely yours,   Woodrow Wilson

TLS (Letterpress Books, WP, DLC).

From Robert Lansing

My dear Mr. President: Washington August 13, 1915.

I thought it would interest you to read the enclosed letter which has relation to certain subjects which we have discussed.¹

Faithfully yours,   Robert Lansing.

TLS (SDR, RG 59, 894.20219/19, DNA).
¹ H. G. Rowe to RL, Aug. 11, 1915, TLS (SDR, RG 59, 894.20219/18, DNA). Henry G. Rowe, editor and proprietor of the Medina, Ohio, *Medina County Gazette*, related an alleged attempt by "an accredited representative of the Japanese government" to purchase extensive American-owned lands located near the northern end of the Panama Canal.

From Edward Mandell House, with Enclosures

Manchester, Massachusetts.

Dear Governor: August 13th, 1915.

I am enclosing you a copy of a letter from Gerard some of which may be of interest. I am also sending one from Lord Bryce and some memoranda which Spring-Rice has given me concerning neutral trade matters.

I had a long conference with him day before yesterday.[1] We talked particularly about the getting of dyestuffs from Germany. They are willing, it seems, to send them through Redfield or anyone we designate. They object to letting it come through Metz.

He indicated if the Germans demanded some cotton in return for the dyestuffs, that this could be arranged.

He is still in communication with Sir Edward concerning cotton. I let him know that Germany was willing to buy 2,500,000 bales if we would guarantee its delivery. This excited him somewhat, and he is pushing his people to meet this proposal.

McAdoo thought it would be of value to have Sir Richard Crawford get in touch with him in regard to the cotton question and I arranged it through Sir Cecil.[2]

A letter from Cobb tells me that his paper will begin the interesting publications on Monday morning.

I closed my answer to Sir Edward's recent letter as follows: "When they are ready, the Central Powers will probably make peace proposals through any government rather than this, but if the Allies will refuse to discuss terms excepting through the United States, they will accept us and it will give us the opportunity we so strongly desire to help in a peace solution that will in a measure justify the awful cost."

Your devoted,   E. M. House

TLS (WP, DLC).

[1] Spring Rice's report of this conversation is C. A. Spring Rice to E. Grey, Aug. 12, 1915, T telegram (FO 115/1920, p. 284, PRO).

[2] McAdoo wrote soon afterward to Spring Rice: "Thank you very much for your note of the 12th instant. I shall be very happy to meet Sir Richard Crawford any time that he cares to confer with me. Mr. Harding told me that he had a preliminary talk with Sir Richard some two weeks ago about the cotton situation but I am not up to date on it. I earnestly hope that a satisfactory solution may be found. It is a pleasure to know of your friendly disposition. I realize, of course, the importance of this matter to you as well as to us." WGM to C. A. Spring Rice, Aug. 15, 1915, ALS (FO 115/1888, pp. 19a-19b, PRO).

ENCLOSURE I

James Watson Gerard to Edward Mandell House

My dear Colonel: Berlin, Germany. July 27th, 1915.

I think the Note marvelous, a veritable masterpiece. I sent a cable advocating some concession and so my conscience is clear. I was afraid that the hate against America here had warped my judgment and now I am glad that the President has taken the strong course.

The Note is received with hostility by Press and Government. Of course, as you have seen, the party of frightfulness has conquered those of milder views, largely owing to the aggressive press campaign made by von Tirpitz, Reventlow[1] and company. The Germans generally are at present in rather a waiting attitude, perhaps wishing to see what our attitude towards England is—but this will not affect their submarine policy. The Foreign Office now claims, I hear, that I am hostile to Germany, but that claim was to be expected. Of course I had no more to do with the Note than a baby, but it is impossible to convince them of that, so I shall not try. . . .[2]

The Emperor is at the front: "somewhere in Galicia." They keep him very much in the background, I think with the idea of disabusing the popular mind of the idea that this is "his war." After all accidents may happen, and after a victorious war there may be a day of reckoning.

The Chancellor went to the front yesterday probably to see the Emperor about the American question.

I am afraid the late Secretary of State mixed matters considerably—certainly he told Dumba and Bernstorff things which were reported here—were told to me and put me and the authorities here a little "off" as to the President's intentions. If we have trouble with Germany he will be responsible. He gave the idea of weakness here.   Yours ever,   J. W. Gerard.

[1] Count Ernst zu Reventlow, feature writer and specialist on naval affairs for the chauvinistic Berlin *Deutsche Tageszeitung.*
[2] Here follow assorted rumors and gossip.

ENCLOSURE II

James Viscount Bryce to Edward Mandell House

Private.

Dear Colonel House: Forrest Row, Sussex. July 30th, 1915.

If you can find time to let me have your views upon any of the current questions, I shall be grateful.

The position of the cotton difficulty causes me some little concern and I gather that the feeling in the South has been growing on it.

As regards Germany, things have taken very much the course I anticipated. She will not recede from her position, but she will try to spin out negociations and if possible play with your Government as long as she can so as to avoid a rupture of relations.

She is at present more externally hopeful than she was three months ago, but I suspect is not really so sanguine as she gives her own people to believe.

Here we are quite as resolute as ever, tho' a section of our press is doing all the harm it can by undervaluing what the fleet has done and what voluntary recruiting continues to do.

I gather that in Russia tho' there has been a good deal of mismanagement (and some say of graft also) in civilian military administration, the people are absolutely united in their purpose to prosecute the war and that the Government could not, if it wished to do so, resist the national will.

I trust the President keeps well.

With our united warm regards to you both, I am,

Sincerely yours,   James Bryce.

TCL (WP, DLC).

ENCLOSURE III

A Memorandum by Sir Cecil Arthur Spring Rice

It is very generally reported in the press that the modified blockade applied by the Allies to restrict German and Austrian commerce is illegal as it does not act equally against all nations alike. It is pointed out that there is no blockade of the Baltic and therefore the United States is discriminated against in favour of Sweden.

The same argument applies to Denmark Norway and Holland. All these countries can trade directly with Germany without making use of the high seas. Between Sweden and Germany it is possible to navigate without passing through the open sea or even through the Baltic. The port of Malmo can for instance communicate with Copenhagen without the possibility of hostile interference as war ships could not conduct military operations in the Sound without an infringement of the neutrality of Denmark and Sweden, if not in law at any rate in principle. Sweden is practically limitrophe with Germany and cannot therefore be blockaded as betwen herself and Germany. The distinction between the situation of Sweden and Denmark or Holland is illusory and can only be advanced from the legal and technical point of view. The material point is whether a neighbour country is or is not being used as an enemy base for facilitating commerce which would otherwise be prevented. If this principle is conceded then Sweden cannot be allowed to supply Germany with foreign goods. If it is not conceded the blockade of Germany is impossible and all trade with her, if not directly carried on through a German port, is legal. There is no middle course.

Notices in the press state that the American note in answer to the British note is ready and will be soon sent off. It is stated that the note will refuse arbitration and will demand the revocation of the Order in Council, that is that it will be a categorical refusal to negotiate.

On a former occasion the Associated Press received from some one nearly connected with the Administration a garbled version of the American note to Great Britain which was telegraphed all over the world.[1] This version was responsible for the impression which prevailed in many quarters that the United States Government which had refrained from any comment on the violation of Belgium attacked the Allies in violent language for a supposed injury to American material interests.

There is little doubt that the same tactics will be repeated and if they are the consequences will be equally unfortunate.

It would be very useful to know where Indians and Germans foregather in New York.

For some time preparations of rather a serious kind have been made in this country for an armed insurrection in India the arms being collected here and sent in small consignments to various points in Asia. Besides this there is reason to believe that Indians are being used for the purpose of arranging for outrages in British Ports and possibly for assassination.

Should these designs be carried out the effect on the relations between this country and the British Empire would be unfortunate as the press would probably attribute what was done to negligence or even to encouragement on the part of American citizens.

T MS (WP, DLC).
[1] About this leaking of the American note to Great Britain of December 26, 1914, see the entry in the House diary printed at Dec. 29, 1914, Vol. 31.

To Edith Bolling Galt

[The White House]

My precious Darling,   Friday, 8 P.M. 13 Aug., 1915

The doctor and I played golf on the Chevy Chase course this afternoon, and, as we were driving back, my thoughts full, as always, of you, I could not help thinking aloud when we reached the point on Connecticut Avenue just above Dupont Circle. "This is the place," I said, "where I first saw Mrs. Galt" "Yes," he said, "and you asked me who she was." We recalled that you were wearing a red rose that afternoon. And then we fell to talking of you,—how could I resist it? The doctor had said this morning that probably no man ever had in a life-time more than one such friend as Col. House, if he were fortunate enough to have one, and so, when we fell to speaking of you, I said that you were another such friend as Col. House, and he agreed very heartily. And it was no mere piece of sentiment on my part, Sweetheart, any more than it was on his. That is my deliberate judgment. I feel about your character and the disinterested loyalty of your friendship just as I have so often told you I felt about House. If I did not love you, I would still utterly trust you and cling to you and value your clear-sighted counsel, in which you would be *thinking for me*, as House does, as I would value that of no one else in the world, not even his. You are talking nonsense, dear little girl,—suffering from the infection of some of Mr. Wilson's nonsense,—when you speak of wishing that you had "the wisdom of a well-informed mind" in order that you might be a 'staff for me to lean on.' I have plenty of well informed minds about me. I can get all the wisdom of information that I can make use of. That is not what I need. What I need is what you give me,—not only "a keen sympathy and comprehension," that you speak of yourself and know that you give me, but an insight into the very needs of my heart that nothing but your sweet love could supply, and the support of *a great character*, in love with reality, vivid with life, rich in all the qualities that inspire and delight. And the *capacity* of your mind is as great and satisfactory as that of any man I know. I have not loved you blindly, and I will not let even you depreciate the wonderful lady whom I love with my mind as well as with my heart. I have dealt with many sorts of persons about many sorts of things, things intellectual and things practical, and I know my equals when I meet them. I know what I say when I say that you are fit to be *any* man's help-mate, the partner of his mind as well as of his heart, and I include men who are far and away my superiors in gifts and capacity and character! I don't think that you realize what pleasure, what delight, you give to every faculty of appreciation I have. You have faults, of course,—though I cannot for the life of me remember what they are,—but I do not "forgive" them: I love you so that I do not see them,—and I love you for cause, because you satisfy everything that is in me and call out all that is best in me. I could not love or admire a blue-stocking or endure a woman politician! So, please, Ma'am, don't try to alter yourself! It's *you* I love and admire and enjoy. It's you who completes me with what she gives of tender love and instant comprehension and frank counsel and a companionship that fills *all* the needs of my thoughts and my affections. And, oh, Sweetheart, these dear letters that you are writing! They contain something that your letters never contained before,—something that makes my heart sing. They make my heart leap with joy by their consciousness of our identification with one another—by their natural and instinctive use of "we"—"when we get home," says this dear letter of yesterday; and they use my *name* as you never used it before. I can hear the sweet accent of it in the written word itself. That is what has made this home coming—this return to the place that has been your home for half your life—so different for me from any former return to the White House—*my* sense of identification with *you*, my joyful consciousness of your entire and happy acceptance of the idea that wherever my home is yours is also, as of course. It's a new place, and this is a new world because you have come to me as you have, generous and whole-souled in love as in everything else,—doing this supreme thing greatly as becomes you and my ideal of you. The way you can love is enough to confirm my conception of what you are. I have seen the wonderful stages of it all and the final consummation is as beautiful,—as full of the sweet profound mystery of self-surrender that belongs to everything spiritual and sacred,—as any poet who really knows the human heart could conceive. I dare not admit how much I miss you, how desperately I long for you—I could not trust myself—but I cannot be *unhappy* now: you have rendered it impossible!

Thank you, my Precious, for your sketch of the way you spend your days with the Roses. It interests me very much. But it is evident that you give much more than you get, and your apparent enjoyment of it is only an additional proof of the quality of your friendship. I am glad they are going to bring you down to Ocean City—glad and sorry; glad because they love you and will take good care of you,—sorry because that is the way of travelling which involves the greatest amount of exposure and the most physical risk from accidents and adventures of the road,

—and when I think of anything happening [to] you you [*sic*] everything goes black before me! I do not wonder that invitations pour in on you for morning, noon, afternoon, and evening. Who that has seen you and been with you would not want you to be their guest? But I like your declining them all. It shows your usual instinctive loyalty and characteristic good taste. My, how I *like* you, Edith, my incomparable Darling. And how you can *hate*, too. Whew! I fancy this very sheet lying before me, on which you have written about Mr. Bryan, is hot under my hand. Isn't it rather risky to use mere paper when you commit such heat to writing? And yet, Sweetheart, I must add, that in my secret heart (which is never secret from you) I love you for that, too. For he *is* a traitor, though I can say so, as yet, only to you.

No, I have not heard from dear little Helen since she went to York Harbor, though I, too, have written to her; but one of the girls heard just a day or two before I left Cornish,—and she was well and "sassy." I wrote her another little note to-day, to tell her of my safe arrival and how much I miss her. Her room, just opposite mine, looks *particularly* deserted and empty, it seems to me, with its door standing always open and no life or movement of any sort within. I keep to my own quarters. These empty rooms are haunted,—though with lovely ghosts.

The day has brought nothing to my desk worth sending you, and I have spent it chiefly in routine, except that I saw Breckinridge, the acting Secretary of War (Garrison having gone to the Jersey coast), about the defence of the Texas and Arizona borders from Mexican raiders, and Burleson about Post Office affairs and the general politics of the United States and the world. My desk was piled high with documents of all kinds awaiting my signature and I signed my name steadily and as fast as I could sign it for a solid hour and a half this forenoon, good Pat. McKenna[1] pulling the documents one by one from under my hand as fast as I could finish them. We have reduced it to a system, he and I.

By the same token, Sweetheart, my hand is very tired and shaky to-night—I've been writing for nearly two hours—and I must stop. It's hard to stop. These are the most precious and most delightful hours of the day for me, these hours when I can sit here, night and morning, uninterrupted, and talk with you, letting my love have sway and my thoughts dwell wholly on you, whom I love with all my heart, purely, passionately, ideally,— as only such a woman *could* be loved. Good night. A lover's kiss and love unutterable sent to you through the night to find you

---

[1] Patrick E. McKenna, clerk at the White House.

as you lie alone in the stately room and make you dream of your lover, who in every thought and purpose is yours. My Darling!

Sat., 7 A.M.

Good morning, my beloved Sweetheart. I hope you slept well and dreamed again that your lover was actually by you. Ah, my precious One, how sweet and comforting this intimate association of our thoughts is. I can't make believe that the separation is not painful, constantly and deeply painful, but there is infinite sweetness even in the pain and no real, fundamental unhappiness possible. For I not only think constantly of you—with thoughts full of tender love that *never* leaves you—but I am conscious of your constant thoughts of me, and your love for me not only comforts and sustains me all the day through but is a source of deep delight,—makes my work go easily and all worries sit light on me. They never get under my skin. My heart is at peace. Your exquisite love has made it so. No one was ever more deeply or more happily in love than I.

And that makes me think of the doctor, and wonder whether he is happily in love,—for I must confess that *as a lover* Miss Gordon is inscrutable to me. She was here when we reached here, but had an engagement that very evening which prevented Grayson from spending the evening with her,—from *seeing* her, so far as I can make out,—until last night. And she is to go off to Wyoming in a day or two to stay two months! But it's none of my business to judge in this matter, and it's entirely unfair for me to do so without knowing more than I do. Grayson is calm, as always, and does not seem unhappy, but I could wish to see him in higher spirits. Being so blessed and happy myself, in the love of a dear Sweetheart who gives her love with generous largess, without thought of limit, I want to see others fare happily—as happily as they can without having a Sweetheart comparable in any way or degree with mine.

The day has come with rather an ardent eye. There's no denying that our dear Washington is hot in midsummer—and to-day promises to live up to specifications, but I have my "naval aide and physician" to testify that I seem to mind the heat and suffer from it as little as anyone he knows, and we are going to play golf this morning notwithstanding the thoughtless weather bureau. My game is picking up a bit now. It suffered collapse after you went away from me at Cornish. I *could* not get my attention concentrated on the ball. My thoughts were "over the hills and far away" and my nerves were, to say the least, not wholly or perfectly under control. Don't you see that you will *have* to come and stay with me at the earliest possible moment—in order to improve my game *in life*? To have the same home in thought and not in act is very stupid. To be thinking in "we"s and acting in "I"s is very confusing—and the acting seems artificial; only the thinking is real. We *are* united, in a very sweet and wonderful way, which nothing can in any essential particular make more real or complete. Everything for us, henceforth, is in terms of "ours." This very house seems full of you, is in fact your home, our home, because it is full of thoughts of you all the day long, and your thoughts dwell in it, too, with me. How hateful and desolate it would be without that! Yes, Hoover had it looking as much like a habitable home as possible, and there were flowers everywhere, but you have no idea how little like a home these upstairs rooms can look when stripped to the bone and habited in white covers. If it were not for you, it would give me the blues in spite of preoccupations of business and everything else. You have saved the situation. Your sweet love can redeem anything. It has transformed this bare official "residence" into the home of our hearts. The rooms you have been in are sweet still with your presence. Every plan, every thought includes you. My heart lives with you even while it waits for you.

Your own   Woodrow

I am perfectly well.

ALS (WP, DLC).

From Edith Bolling Galt

[Geneva, N.Y.] Friday,
My own Dearest: August 13th/1915 11:30 P.M.

I am afraid this has been another wretchedly busy day for you, for I know from the manifold things I found in my *big* envelope today how thoroughly you are going into things. You are a Dear person to take the time to write little sentences on each of the papers you send me—it adds so much to the interest and gives them just the personal touch that would vitalize any subject for me and seems almost as though we had read them together. Just as the mail came I was reading the N. Y. Times' account of the A.B.C. matter—and the letters that had passed between the Mexican heads—and I was so glad to know the original note was to go, as it was first drafted. Thank you my loved Lord for keeping me in close touch with these things that are claiming you and all your efforts. It seems to me if Col. H. has read the cipher message from our representative at Berlin he would advise a change of air for him as more necessary than to Mr. Page.

I could get little out of his message, and it seems to me he was not quite clear about it himself. What about Mr. Hoke Smith's speech in regard to cotton etc.[1] which, the papers state caused the forwarding of a letter to you to ask for the convening of Congress, though stating that all the men from whom the request came stood back of you[2]

Also is it true that you have asked the Secretaries of War & Navy to give you suggestions for preparedness for war, and that you are planning how to finance the increase in war preparedness? Everyone here says this is a splendid move on your part, and I wonder if they know and if you really are doing this. You know I do not mean this for inquisitiveness but just because I know you don't mind telling me—and I am so keen to know of everything you are doing. I felt so queer this afternoon reading all these reports from the different theatres of war—sitting here in my quiet room, away from everything—in a tiny little town beside a calm Lake—I—an unknown person—one who had lived a sheltered inconspicuous existence, now having all the threads in the tangled fabric of the worlds history laid in her hands for a few minutes, while the stronger hand, that quicks the shuttle, stops long enough in its work, to press my fingers in token of the great love and trust with which you crown and bless my life.

I have gotten so that I count on this daily sharing of your work with me, and if the afternoon mail comes with no big envelope, I feel cheated.

See how easily I can be spoiled not content with the most wonderful letters every morning, that fill the day with their wonderful sweetness. I still covet a second message to tell me, even in your hours of absorbing work, I am in your thoughts, and so far hardly a day has passed that I have not found this assurance

Saturday—9:30

Good morning my precious one   Have you had a fine sleep and did you go out early for golf as it is Saturday? I have just finished reading that lovely long letter finished so early yesterday—and it was such a real joy. Your description of the Discussion Club is too funny for words and I wish we could get hold of Mrs. Churchill's paper, and be instructed as to her views. Then I am so pleased to find how often our thoughts run along the same lines—for instance about Hoke Smith. You were answering my question when it was in my mind even before I put it on paper. Doesn't it seem queer, but delicious? I will get the letter you refer to about him by the noon Post, so I shall not be disappointed today. And I will be so interested to see what you refer to.

The package of envelopes came this morning too. Thank you for them, and bless, dear loyal Hoover! He is a most unusual man. Do you give him yours to mail? I am so glad you are feeling so well my precious Woodrow, and if love can make and keep you so, you will never again suffer. Do you know I change my rings when I write because as I hold the pen I can see a little gleaming circle on my finger that thrills me when I remember who it represents and whose dear lips have kissed it.

I am going down town with Mrs. Rose so I have to hurry and finish this for it may be so late when I get back. I am wondering if you get the mail on Sunday—but suppose of course you do. I see in the paper this morning you have consented to go to the camp at Plattsburg sometime in the next 3 weeks. Can't you stop in Philadelphia then, instead of making it a seperate trip? What a shame you should have given your self such a headache on the train by writing to me. I love you for doing it, but hate to think of your suffering.

I am so delighted to know you found everything had gone just as well as if you had been in Washington and feel Mr. Lansing is a real comfort to you.

Now I must run and get my hat on. Goodbye Sweetheart until tomorrow—   Always your own   Edith.

Nothing further from Panama.

ALS (WP, DLC).

[1] Smith, in a speech before a meeting of export and import merchants in New York on August 11, strongly attacked Great Britain's embargo on shipments to Germany and her allies and urged that the Wilson administration proceed as vigorously against British violations of neutral rights as it had against those of Germany. *New York Herald* and *New York Times*, Aug. 12, 1915.

[2] The group mentioned in n. 1 voted to send a petition to the President, urging that a special session of Congress be called to give the administration adequate powers to deal with the situation caused by violations of neutral rights. The petition stressed that its signers had no quarrel with the Wilson administration, but that they wished to see that the government possessed adequate authority to enforce existing international law. *New York Herald*, Aug. 12, 1915.

From Robert Lansing

My dear Mr. President: Washington August 14, 1915.

I am sending you the stenographic report of the Conference on Mexican affairs held in New York on the 11th.[1] The informality of the conference prevented a complete report as frequently several of the conferees were talking at the same time, often the Spanish language was used. I send you this calling your particular attention to the discussion beginning on page 8 and continuing to page 15. I think it is of particular interest in view of our action in regard to Haiti and I hope it meets with your approval. I had prepared, before receiving your telegram, the notes which are embodied on pages 10 and 11.[2]

I also enclose a translation of the communication sent to the various political and military leaders in Mexico.[3]

Faithfully yours, Robert Lansing

TLS (WP, DLC).

[1] "Continuation of the Conference on Mexican Affairs, Biltmore Hotel, New York City, August 11, 1915," T transcript (WP, DLC).

[2] In order to conform to the policy set forth in Wilson's telegram to him of August 11, Lansing almost completely reversed his former position at the conference held on that date. He now boldly argued that the *Carrancistas* were at present the dominant element in the Mexican revolutionary movement and, if they held together, could and would form a provisional government, regardless of what the other American nations might think or do. Above all, the provisional government had to be founded on the revolution. The revolutionaries as a whole had both the right and the power to form the new government, and only they could decide who would be permitted to participate or who would be excluded from participation in it. The "notes . . . embodied on pages 10 and 11," mentioned above, were an amplification of this basic argument. Lansing did concede that the leaders of the various revolutionary factions should unite and recognize the right of all the other revolutionaries to participate in the new government. However, he reiterated that only the revolutionaries had the right to decide the future of the country. In addition to the minutes cited in n. 1 above, see Link, *Struggle for Neutrality*, pp. 491-93.

[3] This enclosure is missing. It is printed in *FR 1915*, pp. 735-36.

From Josephus Daniels, with Enclosure

Dear Mr. President: Washington. Aug. 14, 1915.

Former Governor Metcalf[1] has asked me to do him the favor to give you the enclosed which he had ready to send you when he learned you were leaving Cornish. Governor Metcalf is employed by the Carranza people, but I believe he is sincere in his views and not influenced, at least consciously, by the fact that he is retained for special service.

Sincerely, Josephus Daniels[2]

ALS (WP, DLC).

[1] Richard Lee Metcalfe, journalist, former Commissioner for the Panama Canal Zone.

[2] Wilson sent this letter and enclosure to Mrs. Galt with the following explanation (ALI, WP, DLC): "Metcalfe is an ex-friend of Mr. Bryan's whom I appointed, at Mr. B's solicitation, to an important position in Panama. He is a Nebraska newspaper man. W."

E N C L O S U R E

From Richard Lee Metcalfe

Mr. President: [Washington, c. Aug. 14, 1915]

Having made two trips to Mexico recently for the purpose of doing newspaper work in behalf of General Carranza, I respectfully ask the privilege of submitting several thoughts for your consideration.

I beg you to believe that in sending you this message I am prompted solely by patriotic motive and deep concern for the success of your administration.

Under Carranza peace is coming to Mexico as rapidly as could reasonably be expected. As soon as he has gained military control in a section Carranza has established civil government and there he has put under way the very reforms for which, in our own country, you have taken such a notable stand. He has been the victim of persistent misrepresentation. He is a patriotic man, as devoted to what he conceives to be the best interests of his people as any man in the history of our own country. I am sure that if you were to meet him personally you would be impressed with his good motives and his real ability. Instead of cherishing animosity toward Americans he likes them. He admires our institutions, seeks to copy them and in spite of the misunderstandings of the past he is your friend and admirer. I am sure that with a new beginning and better understanding there would be no trouble in having perfect cooperation between your government and that of Mexico under the Carranza administration.

Your policy of watchful waiting—a policy which has had the approval of the fathers and mothers of America who do not want to needlessly sacrifice their boys on the altar of war—has been vindicated. It has been vindicated with General Carranza's help. The truth concerning his efforts and his successes has not been given to the American people. Neither has it been told to you.

The best tribute ever given a public man was given to you when one of your friends declared that you were the most open-minded man he ever knew and welcomed suggestions from the humblest of men. Because I believe this to be a deserved tribute I am, even though one of your humblest friends, making an appeal to you to give to General Carranza's claims for recognition and cooperation more consideration than some of the influences now at work seem willing to give.

Aside from the terrible consequences of war another danger

is involved in the Mexican situation as it is presented today. I refer to the danger of a religious controversy in our own country such as we have never experienced.

It is already being pointed out by your enemies that Cardinal Gibbons, the recognized head of the Catholic Church in America, has given out several newspaper interviews calling for a war of intervention.[1] Following this remarkable call upon our government to wage war at the command of the Catholic Church came the Latin-American conference. The American newspapers have stated on apparent authority from Secretary Lansing that the fate of Mexico was to be settled at this meeting. No Mexican was allowed to be present at this conference. But Paul Fuller, publicly stated to be the official attorney of the Catholic Church, and a devoted Catholic, was present. Mr. Fuller has not been in Mexico for nearly a year. When he was there he spent less than fifteen minutes in conversation with General Carranza and not one moment of that time was given to an effort to obtain Carranza's ideas with respect to government. Since he was there conditions have materially changed. Under Carranza the Mexican people are rapidly solving their own problems and peace is practically within sight. Governor John Lind made a report based on much longer study of the situation than Mr. Fuller had given to it. Governor Lind is a Protestant. He was present in Washington when this conference was held but he was not invited to become a member of it. While this conference is still being held behind closed doors and veiled in impenetrable secrecy, your administration is suddenly faced with exactly what Cardinal Gibbons has demanded—war with Mexico.

Convinced from personal observation that Carranza is Mexico's hope for substantial peace, I appeal to you to either give him the recognition to which his record and successes entitle him, or to at least continue your policy of watchful waiting while he completes his all but victorious battle for constitutional government.

I am sure you will believe me when I say that I make this appeal as your friend and well-wisher. But I make it also as the father of three boys who will answer any call you may make. In common with millions of other American fathers I would not want my boys to be sacrificed in a war brought on through the connivance of special interests, ecclesiastical or commercial. In common with millions of other Democrats I do not want the arms of my country to be leveled at the breast of the Democrats of Mexico. As a life-long Democrat I solemnly declare with personal knowledge of the fact, that in sorely-distressed Mexico General Carranza represents real and intelligent democracy as faithfully as it has ever been represented in our own land from the time of Jefferson to the time of Wilson.

I feel sure you will accept this purely personal message in the spirit in which it is written and I need not subscribe myself

Your faithful friend and follower,

Richard L. Metcalfe

TLS (WP, DLC).

[1] In an interview on July 31, James Cardinal Gibbons was quoted as follows: "Armed intervention by the United States in Mexico would be deplorable, and I should be sorry to see it, but I believe that some form of intervention is the only solution to the reign of anarchy that has existed there for several years." He further suggested that a protectorate such as the United States had earlier exercised in Cuba might be repeated in Mexico, "although with more difficulty." *Washington Post*, Aug. 1, 1915.

From Edward Mandell House

Manchester, Massachusetts.

Dear Governor: August 14th, 1915.

Sir Cecil was with me today. He says that his Government have definitely agreed to accept the Harding proposal in regard to cotton. They will buy a sufficient amount to keep the price from going below ten cents f.o.b. shipboard.

They are willing to guarantee that neutral countries will get their normal amount of cotton.

He tells me that Sir Richard Crawford is pleased with his conference with Benjamin Strong and Harding and said the suggestions they made in working out the situation, have been invaluable.

Sir Cecil and the Foreign Office are much disturbed over the ramifications of the German propaganda against Great Britain. They are tracing it in the most unlooked for quarters and they are at a loss to know how to combat it. They do not want to create a propaganda themselves and they are waiting in hopes the American people will awaken of their own accord.

Your devoted,   E. M. House

TLS (WP, DLC).

To Edith Bolling Galt

[The White House]

My own Darling, Saturday, 8 P.M. 14 Aug., 1915.

You will be astonished to receive, by parcels post, a box of white and black silk stockings! It is one of four boxes sent by grateful Belgian women to the President of the United States and his family. There is, in addition, one box of silk socks. I fear that they will prove to be miles too big for you, the sizes being *a la Belgique*. If they are, send them back and I will compare them in size with the rest (I *think* I know how) and see if there are not some that are smaller. If there are not, we shall not know what to do with them, for you are as tall as any member of the family—though both Jessie and Nellie have bigger feet, I am sure. It will be jolly if they fit and you like them, for there are three boxes more of them.

I am all by my lee lane this evening. I dined, as my Darling has so often done at 1308, in lonely state. Tumulty has gone to spend the week end with his family on the Jersey coast; Fitz William has gone to Atlantic City at the summons of his new chief, McChord,[1] of the Interstate Commerce Commission, who is there; and the doctor is with Miss Gordon, I am glad to say, who leaves for the West tomorrow afternoon. He was with her last evening, too, till quite late (after eleven), but he seemed grim and out of sorts this morning when we were playing golf—and played carelessly and very badly. He says nothing to me of how his intimate affairs are going, so I can judge and conjecture from external signs and symptoms only. Poor chap! I wish there were some way to help him. He told me that Miss Gordon had got a letter from you,—and certainly you could teach *any*body how to love who was in the least degree teachable—by example, as well as by precept—by *perfect* example, you adorable Darling!

I took a drive, too, all by myself this afternoon—from three to half-past five. My route was, Potomac—Rockville—the Seventh St. pike—the Park, *via* the Miller cottage. Ah, Sweetheart, my precious Edith, what memories crowded every foot of the way! If it had been evening and moonlight, I do not know that I could have stood the sweet pain of it all—and when we (Murphy, Burlasque[2] & I) got to *the* ford I could hardly keep from uttering out loud the longing that was in my heart. I *took* the ride because of its memories and associations—and they were exquisite—*any*thing associated with you is exquisite—I was at first almost sorry I had chosen that way—it made me so *desperately* lonely,—your absence was too nearly intolerable. But at last I was glad, because I got what I had longed for, two hours and a half alone with vivid impressions of you. It was as if you were actually by my side, and *no* one, not even a loved one like Helen or Margaret, to divide

[1] Charles Caldwell McChord, chairman of the Interstate Commerce Commission.

[2] James Burlasque, a general handy man at the White House, who at this point was acting as chauffeur.

our attention, *only* each other and our love to think of, only the sweetness of it and the exquisite certain promise of it. And my thoughts could take back to those actual rides together what was not in them,—the absence of all doubt and all fear that came to my Darling only at Harlakenden, that blessed place of revelation and vision, where what had seemed to my Darling clouds and dark places and obstacles were all dissipated and cleared away and gave place to perfect confidence and—perfect bliss! You can imagine, my precious One, how thoughts like those and the memories of those sacred hours that followed, where we really got a chance to open our hearts without reserve to one another, made the thoughts that thronged upon me on my ride seem trebly sweet and delightful and all but drove loneliness itself away before the drive was over. And the love that filled my heart to overflowing would have endowed a thousand marriages!

I got back to the House before the band concert on the south lawn was over, and heard, I fancy, the greater part of the programme as I sat writing at my desk. At the end, when they played the Star Spangled Banner, I stood up all alone here by my table, "at attention," and had unutterable thoughts about my custody of the traditions and the present honour of that banner. I could hardly hold the tears back! And *then* the loneliness! The loneliness of the responsibility because the loneliness of the power, which no one *can* share. But in the midst of it I knew that there was one who *did* share—*every*thing—a lovely lady who has given herself to me, who is my own, who is part of me, who makes anxieties light and responsibilities stimulating, not daunting, by her love and comprehension and exquisite sympathy. I knew that these things were *not* for me to fear alone, but were *ours* to work out together, your love sustaining me every step of the way, your vision of right supplementing and augmenting mine, the whole divine partnership transforming everything, the Constitution of the United States itself included—and I thanked God and took courage!

You say in this sweet letter received to-day, my own Darling, that you have found yourself wondering from day to day whether I *could* find new words each day into which to put the old, old story that glorifies the world for us and for all who realize, as we do, its overwhelming truth; and you say, bless your dear heart, that the next day always "brings its own message, more full, more rich, more satisfying." You know why, don't you? Your own heart can tell you, for your own letters have the same freshness, as if of a new experience,—an experience renewed, freshened,

extended each day. And that is the fact, is it not, my Sweetheart?
We write every day, not of the same theme, though we constantly use the same words and the same endearments,—not of an
old story recollected and dwelt upon and elaborated,—but of that
day's own realization of what our love and happiness mean to
us. That realization grows fuller, clearer, richer, and never grows
for a moment stale, but is always infinitely fresh and vital. It
is so with me, and I have the most delightful possible proof that
it is so with you, too,—your own letters, which never speak out of
memory but out of the living moment when each word is written,
when your heart is warm with the very love you are putting into
words. That is what makes them so dear to me, and gives me
such a thrill when I read them. I can almost feel the beating of
your heart in them. And it must be that that makes my letters
seem so vital and satisfying to you, and so new each time,—not the
words I use, not the poor attempts to express what is, after all,
inexpressible, but the emotion and the thought that was warm in
me when I wrote them. You know me now, my Darling: you know
my heart,—you know how I love you and the words mean to you
what I mean to you, bless your heart! And then, as I have said,
each day the love in my heart *is* new, *is* fuller and richer and
runs with a mightier tide. I know more fully what you mean to
me; what you are in all your (unconscious) loveliness; how I
enjoy and understand and adore and need you. You own heart
is more clearly revealed to me. I see the beauty and sweetness of
it more clearly and feel more poignantly the delight of you. You
do not know how much your letters reveal and how everything
seems to add, day by day, to the charm you exercise and the
happiness I get in merely thinking about you, or the pride I feel
in realizing that you are mine,—that all this sweetness and delight
has been given to *me*! If my letters thrill you, dear, sweet little
girl, it is because I was thrilled at thought of you when I wrote
them. And you must remember that all the old anxiety has gone
out of me. I am no longer anxious about you, lest you should
not see your way to your own happiness and mine. And so my
heart has free course. There is no weight on it. It runs free and
glad along the way you have chosen to go with it—*because* you
have chosen to go with it. It is sure of its own freedom and delight
and of the fruition of its hopes. And so love grows in it as in
an atmosphere that seems full of the airs of heaven itself. I am
in love with you every day all over again, and every day know
that you are more lovable than I ever realized before. And so my
case is hopeless and I happy.

Sunday, 8.30 A.M.

That story, my Sweetheart, about Lansing's doubting the wisdom of sending battleships to Vera Cruz was a lie made out of the whole cloth. In what paper did you see it, I wonder? It was upon Lansing's suggestion, as you remember, that they were sent down. It was *I* who, on second thought, feared that it was a mistake—though I never breathed a hint of my misgiving to anyone but you. When I got here I found that only two ships, the New Ham[p]shire and the Louisiana, had been ordered down, and that no one had gone too fast or too far—and the ships could still be intercepted if I thought best, for they were at Newport when the orders reached them and it takes a long time to reach Vera Cruz from there. When I left Cornish I thought the ships were at Hampton Roads when they got their instructions. That was one of the many particulars I was not informed about.

Did my last letter from Cornish seem sad, my Darling? I was not conscious of making it so,—I was not conscious, indeed, of being particularly sad when I wrote it. I fancied I was in fine command of myself. It only shows how much that I do not say is conveyed to my little Sweetheart in these letters, in which I lay bare my very soul to her. There was no doubt a subconscious sadness in my heart throughout those last days at Harlakenden, and when the time of actual leaving came I was intensely conscious of it. How could it be otherwise? You were not there, and yet the whole place was identified with you, because it is rich with memories of you of the sweetest kind. Our hearts had found one another there; our happiness had been sealed there by that wonderful mutual revelation; and it was infinitely hard to leave the place where you had said and done such exquisite things as expressions of your perfect love. I seemed for the moment to be breaking some precious tie. Did you have no such impressions as you drove away that morning with the Roses, carrying my heart with you? I could go back, I knew, of course, but you would not be there until next summer. You were with strangers, in a place I did not know, yourself lonely and in need of me. I was going to our home, and yet you would not be there, either, eagerly as our hearts longed that you should be. It was not an easy transition for me to face, little girl; but I am all right now. Indeed I was then, in spite of the sadness I betrayed. I am always all right when I am given a little time for the readjustment,—all right so far as loyal acceptance of the facts is concerned and a glad willingness to do whatever true love demands I should do. I do know what loyal love for you demands of me for the time, and I devote myself to doing it, my Darling, with a sense of deep privilege, even

though, in these familiar talks of ours, I do admit to my Sweetheart, the while, the longing, the *infinite* longing, that is in my
heart. Am I going back to Cornish in September, while you are
here in Washington? Guess! I'll go, if you will. I am going to try
to get back for the week-end including the 28th of this month
because that is dear Jessie's birthday. You will not be here before
the first of September, will you?

I asked you a question, my dear, precious Sweetheart, which
you did not answer. I asked you if you were well and begged you,
with a full heart, to take care of yourself. You promised to take
care of yourself, but you did not say that you were well, and,
though that may have been a mere inadvertence, I fancied it was
not and have been anxious. Have you had a return of those
distressing headaches, or been unwell in any other way? I tremble
to think of your being ill, in the least degree, and I not by to help,
if only by loving sympathy and petting. Please tell me *every*thing
about yourself, so that I may dismiss the anxiety that comes from
surmising. I am perfectly well myself. The weather here is
undenyably hot—"seasonable summer weather"—and the nights
are too close for refreshing sleep, but that does not matter to a
perfectly healthy chap with a happy heart and a reasonably clear
conscience who has so much to live for as I have and is so glad
to live as I am—since you love me. My thoughts are constantly
full of that thought, my own Edith—*that you love me.* It sings
in my heart all day long. It colours everything that I do. It
lightens every fatigue, dispels every anxiety, makes work wear a
touch of romance, lifts the clouds that darken a world at war.
You have blessed and redeemed me, just when my need was
surest, and will make the world complete for me when you are
at last in my arms to stay. I am invincible because I am

Your own   Woodrow

ALS (WP, DLC).

From Edith Bolling Galt

Geneva, N. Y.

My precious One: August 14th [15th] 1915 1 a.m.

I expect you have been in bed for hours, as it is after midnight,
and I have been down on the porch talking to Mrs Rose for nearly
two hours. We had the usual game of "Auction" after dinner, and
at ten 30 Mr. Rose got sleepy and retired. So we sat on the porch,
and the Dr. (Mrs. R's brother) joined us for a while about midnight.

I am not a bit sleepy and can't put the light out until I have talked to you, at least long enough to say goodnight.

The big envelope came at 2 ock, and I am so thrilled at the hint it contains, and want so to know more about it, though, of course, realizing fully, Dearest, that you can not write all you would tell me if we were together. But could you tell me what he means by the "publication" and the fact that it may even lead to War—but still the wisdom of doing it? If you think it better not to put this on paper I will fully understand. But dont mention names. I will understand enough to fill them in.

I came up stairs about four this afternoon and closed my door and read over again your dear, dear letter. This has been one of the days when I have had hard work making myself believe all the things that have happened. I wonder if you ever have that feeling?—as though it were something that had happened to some one else—that it could not be yourself. That the rest of the world goes on the same as it did last year and the year before—and the year before that—and why should I be so changed? Why should the whole order of my existence be revolutionized?

Dont think from this that I am shutting doors, or having one of my dreaded "fits." I am not, only I can't help these occasional waves of amazement that come over me that I can be and am happily in love and eager to be loved, and that out of the whole world I have found *the* one person who comprises the world! Your letter made you real again—made me feel that your dear arms were outstretched for me to nestle in and that your heart was beating close against my own while I whispered into your lips all the unreality of things as they seemed before I came to you.

You know I always got these vagaries when it was sleepy time, and then you would sooth, and pet me until they were all gone and I could go to bed happy. I am going now to put out the light, curl up in your arms and get you to sing to me of your "Four brothers over the Sea." I will go to sleep and dream you are here, and I have only to wake up and find you laughing at some ridiculous conversation we had when I was asleep. Goodnight, Precious

Sunday, 8.30 a.m.

Good morning my dear Lord. Are you going to church for the first time in many weeks? If so, I hope it is cooler and you will not be bored. I suppose I will go just because I want to hear *our* prayer. I have read over this letter, begun last night, and started to destroy it, but know you will understand that I was just a little blue and needed you, but this morning I have readjusted and am ready for the day. I will not have your dear message today, so must be content to know the waiting will be rewarded by two letters tomorrow and that you are near me, perhaps nearer than on other days when your attention is diverted by so many things.

It is a sort of gray day here—after a heavy rain during the night—and the air is dead and unrefreshing. I think we have about decided to leave here on the 20th which is Friday, and, unless we get very bad roads, we should reach Ocean City on Sunday. I have decided to tell Mother and my sister our wonderful secret—as soon as I have the opportunity after we get there. After which I am going to write Randolph—but with these exceptions I will not tell anyone else. I feel sure you will approve of this, don't you?

As to old Mr. Wilson, I wrote him as nice a letter as I could a week ago today and have had nothing from him since. The only thing that could have hurt him is my saying I had nothing to tell him, and no occasion to see him before returning to Washington, so far as I know. But he is so sensative this probably has hurt him, and I am sorry if it is so, but I cannot have my confidence forced. They are calling me for breakfast so I must stop. I will write you a better letter tomorrow. My love must compensate for the lack of interest in this letter, for that is unchanged and goes on in rain or shine, flowing out to my precious one.

Always your own,   Edith.

ALS (WP, DLC).

To Edith Bolling Galt

[The White House] Sunday,
My darling Sweetheart,   8.15 P.M. 15 Aug., 1915.

I beg your pardon for not having told you about the preparedness business;—and, please, dear little girl, don't speak of "inquisitiveness" in asking about it,—or about anything else. There can be no such thing on your part, so far as anything I know or am dealing with is concerned. Whatever is mine is yours, knowledge of affairs of state not excepted,—and that without reserve, except that, as you know, there may be a few things that it would not be wise or prudent to commit to writing. But the preparedness matter is, of course, not one of those. I suppose it had not occurred to me to speak of it simply because it was with me already an old decision before even the summer began. It has been understood among us in the cabinet for some time that I was of course to have a programme to propose to Congress in December; and just before I went up to Cornish last time I told the Secretaries of War and of the Navy that I would like their full advice in the matter, made ready with the assistance of the best experts of their Departments, as soon after my return to Washington as possible. The War Department's report is now on my table, though I have not yet had time to read it even, much less study and digest it and form my own judgment about it (it came only yesterday), and Daniels will have his in a very short time. He has outlined it to me orally already and I know the main lines and items of it. What the newspapers seem to have said (you know I do not read them!) about my studying the method of *financing* the preparedness programme is all their own invention. I have not yet got to that. That will have to be a part of the general revenue and taxation (or borrowing) problem of the next session, induced by the general circumstances of the war and the very great falling off in revenue caused by the immense inevitable decrease in dutiable imports.

You may be sure that I will pay precious little attention to anything these excited (and stimulated) gentlemen from the South suggest. The last thing I should think of doing,—the very last,—would be to call Congress together in special session, to debate the wild schemes of such men as Hoke Smith and Bob Henry. There will be folly enough released and rampant when the regular session of Congress comes in December. I would, as I am sure you will agree, be doing the country a great disservice to bring it on before it is inevitable. In the meantime, it is to be devoutly hoped that some of these trouble-makers will have been exposed or will have hanged themselves by their own voluntary and voluble display of fatuous thinking!

There is another matter I have not told you about which is new. It happens that we are just now necessarily in armed control in Haiti, the present congress and president of the dusky little republic depending entirely on our marines to keep the peace and maintain them in control; and the congress expires by limitation next Tuesday, the seventeenth. We have just rushed a treaty down (within the last twenty-four hours,—by cable) for ratification by the congress which will, if ratified, give us practically complete control of the finances of the Haitian government (the only prize fought for by the many leaders of "revolution" there, and therefore the key to the whole political situation) To ask for its ratification now, when it can scarcely be refused, is nothing less than high-handed, and nothing but the extraordinary circumstances of the time could conceivably justify us in doing any such thing. But the circumstances are unprecedented; the necessity for exercising control down there is immediate, urgent, imperative; it is earnestly and sincerely desired by the best and most responsible Haitians; and our object, of course, is not to subordinate them, but to help them in the most practical and most feasible way possible. I do not like the argument that the end justifies the means, but we should not stand on ceremony now unless we wish this country, as well as Haiti itself, to be seriously and perhaps fatally embarrassed. There is no analogy here to the Mexican case. The "revolutions" of Haiti have no *political* object and no popular aims: they are for plunder purely. Not to interfere and amicably take charge would be to leave them down there a prey to the most sordid chaos. And the effect on "Latin America" of our course down there will not, we think, be serious, because, being negroes, they are not regarded as of the fraternity! The whole thing will presently be known. I shall be curious to hear the public comments.

No, I am not going to Plattsburg. That, too, is an invention of the newspapers. They have me going when I have not yet even received the invitation to go. I shall have an interesting tale to tell you about Plattsburg (a Wood-Roosevelt affair in which we spiked their guns)—it is too much a matter of details for a letter. I ought not to go because a speech on preparedness would be expected of me which Wood and his like would try to use to show that (in another sense) they had "taken me into camp." My speech on that subject ought to me made to Congress—and will be.

Have you seen the articles in *The World* about the German propaganda in this country? The first one appeared this morning. I hope you will get them and read them. It was to these revelations that House referred in the letter (which I think I sent you) in which he speculated that the publication *might* lead to war (I don't go with him there). This is all so private a matter that I hesitate to write it down. Suffice it to say that I know the sources from which *The World* got the material and that they are absolutely reliable.

They got along alarmingly well without me while I was in Cornish! I am not so nearly "the whole thing" as I had foolishly fancied, after all! There is no indispensable man!

But, dear me, Sweetheart, we have been discussing public business all evening (it is now ten minutes to ten!). I have had myself splendidly under control, and have not once let myself look up and tell you how intently, throughout it all, I was thinking of *you* or how much I loved you. You don't want it all business, do you, deeply as you are interested? You would miss the love letters, would you not, and the *other* confidences which concern only us? I am *so* glad to share public matters with you—so anxious to share them with you. It *helps* me to talk them over with you. I could not be happy without this real and vital partnership. But the thing that makes the real difference for me, every day and every hour of every day, is our love. I would share these matters of business with you if you were only my intimate friend and confidante, because you are worthy of all trust and counsel. *But there is so much more in it.* This is only an item. The fountain of it all is something that far, far transcends trust and intimate conference. I love you! I love to be with you. I need,—need more than all else,—the *tenderness* of our *perfect* love. Business fills my days, fills them to weariness,—though it does not weary me to repeat it to you—and I get release from it in letting my thoughts dwell wholly and with undisturbed delight *on you.* I am not misinterpreting what you said in your letter that came to-day, my sweet Darling, about your being disappointed if the *big* envelope did not come as well as the love letter; I am only trying to interpret, if I can, to you the whole method of my thought. It's a stern world, my precious One. The days yield *nothing*, ordinarily, with any *solace* in it. Duty wears a very businesslike mien and requires of one that he forget himself and all his own private interests and affairs and give himself without subtraction or reserve to the service of the hour. When evening comes, and the sweet first morning hour—just after I have waked to find your lovely face just beside my bed in the photograph which I have come to regard as one of my chief treasures—it is life and renewal to me to close the door, shut business for a little while out, and be with my dear One simply as a lover,—filling my whole heart with the consciousness, the delicious consciousness, of you and of our intimate, perfect love

Monday, 7.15 A.m.

I was exceedingly tired last night. That is the only way, so far as I can perceive, that the heat tells on me. I had not had a restful or refreshing Sunday, except for the brief hours I spent with you, morning and evening. John Wilson turned up early in the day—while I was writing to you—and stuck to me every minute that I did not actually close my door against him—talking a blue streak. I love the dear chap, and he loves me so much that I feel it a shame even to imply a criticism of him; but he is anything but restful and when one's thoughts are *very* much preoccupied, as mine were all day, it is little less than distracting to be told the details of the personal politics of Erie County, Pennsylvania, and talked to about like vital matters *all the time*. He even talked a steady stream while I sat (at a distance) and read your dear letter, hearing not a word he was saying, and wishing him in Halifax. In the afternoon I was prevented from taking a long drive by a thunder storm that hung about, like John, indefinitely. But I got a delicious little airing in the park afterwards, and all by myself, during which I read your dear letter again. John, the doctor, and I went to church, like good boys, in the morning, and were rewarded by hearing an admirable sermon by a Mr. Mc-Alister.[1] The doctor was with Miss Gordon during the afternoon and took her to her train at six. He had been with her also both the preceding evenings and at least all of one of the preceding afternoons, and seemed throughout quite peaceful in his mind, I am glad to say.

I am rested this morning, and this dear morning hour, when business has not yet invaded and the house seems to belong to us alone, is the happy part of the day for me,—when everything in me seems at its best. I can satisfy my heart and fortify myself for the day by thinking as I please of the dear one who has made life new for me and rediscovered delight and the companionship that makes the whole world different.

Bless your heart for the little tender touches in your letters, like this of changing the rings on your hands when you write so that the little gleaming circle that stands for our troth and our happiness will be where it moves with the hand that is writing the love words that are to be sent to me. Dear Sweetheart, your letters grow more dear to me every day, not only because I depend on them for solace, but also because they grow more and more tender and intimate and more and more disclose the *little* confidences which mean so much, because it is by the little things that love is made perfect and its quality of happiness made evident.

Yes, Hoover posts my letters for me as well as brings me yours. He posts them in a street box, so that they will not seem to come from this House at all or get, even by chance, into the office handling. He says nothing: he just understands. I think we shall both end by loving him. I could love *anybody* who has had *anything* to do with our affairs these last blessed months, and Hoover already had strong claims on my affection. He needs no instructions so far as we are concerned. There is only one (early morning) delivery of the mail to us on Sundays and your letters do not come by that delivery, but Hoover went himself to the Post Office

[1] The Rev. Dr. James Gray McAllister, professor at Louisville Presbyterian Theological Seminary.

and got it for me later,—and I immediately devoured it, in spite of John (who last night, by the way, went on to New York).

I fear, my precious One,—indeed I can clearly see,—that there is little to satisfy a rich nature like yours in the life the Roses lead; —fond as you are of them, you need more than that. I don't wonder you watch eagerly for the big envelope and feel cheated if one does not come. (You may be sure one will come whenever there is anything to put in it). The zest you find in reading its contents is partly due to the fact that you are now getting what you have always needed (Mr. Wilson is right about that), something big enough, of large enough meaning and consequence, to be worth your while. This is the partnership you have always been fit for. And may I not think, too, my Darling, that the pleasure and excitement of it come also from your intimate knowledge of your partner and your love for him,—from the happiness of being associated with him, in these as in all other—and deeper—matters of his life? It is so with me. Business—burdensome, perplexing business, even—has taken on a new aspect for me since I could share it with you. It is even more *interesting*, because I can know *your* thought about it and feel the comradeship of your mind. When I lay my hand on yours and with the other "turn the pages of history" (as you expressed it in one of your letters) something comes from you to me which is the source of wisdom as well as of joy—perfect sympathy and a love that transforms the world, and makes me better qualified to serve it.

Your own   Woodrow

ALS (WP, DLC).

From Edith Bolling Galt

[Geneva, N. Y.] Sunday, Midnight,
My precious One: August 15th 1915

What a perfectly delicious surprise I had this morning when I came from church! Can you guess what it was? Your letter!!!!!

I mailed a very cross one to you as I went to church. I was blue, it was pouring rain, and I thought I could not possibly have a talk with you before tomorrow—and that seemed an awfully long time off. So I went to church in a blue fog, and nothing cheered me except the fact that all over the country devout people were praying for my beloved Lord at the same time I was and that made my heart warm and comforted.

When we came out of the church behold! the sky had cleared and a brilliant sunshine had followed the rain. We took a short walk, and then came home about 12.30 when, from his office, came Dr. DeLaney with your letter which came, he said, just after we went out. I was so glad to see it I could hardly receive it casually. But as two or three people had come home with us, I had to appear interested in them, and not in the letter, when, as a matter of fact, Sweetheart, I wanted to push them down the steps, and say go home you idiots and let me read the "President's Message"

No such luck—on they sat until lunch was announced. Then they left, but it was too late. I could not read your dear words in a hurry so again I waited, and not until three oclock could I get away and revel in all the tender, exquisite things you said to me.

It is such a lovely letter Dearest, and has made the day so bright for me, and I am so proud and happy that you think me a loyal friend, and, even if you "did not love me, you would still utterly trust and cling to me and value my clear-sighted counsel."

Could any lover yield greater tribute to the lady he has honoured with his choice and into whose keeping he has given his heart?

I love to read over and over those dear words of your letter, and shall never forget them. They shall be a constant inspiration to me, and should I ever fail to respond to such trust and admiration then I will be dead to anything and everything that is fine and stimulating. How you can touch the strings that vibrate through my whole being Sweetheart and make me throb to express all the admiration and love for you that seems the vital part of my life.

Can you realize it is only two weeks tonight since we had our last evening together at Harlakenden? It seems so many more than fourteen days, and I have missed you so! You have been a perfect wonder though Woodrow in keeping up to our determination not to be blue or unhappy. I am awfully proud of you and feel the last of this long month in which we have been seperated will pass comparatively quickly and then I will come and, at least, wave you a glowing salutation should I meet you on that same spot on Conn. Ave. near Dupont Circle.

That can't be any harm, and I can see for myself if you are well, and it will be something to be near you.

Thank you for saying, and thinking all these sweet things of me when you were nearing that spot on Friday—and for telling *me* of them, as well as the Dr.

I am going to read your dear letter one more time now and then go to sleep

Do you feel my arms 'round your neck and my lips on yours while I whisper—goodnight?

Monday, 10.30 a.m.

You dear, precious Sweetheart. What a wonderful mail you had ready for me this morning. Your letter satisfies all the longing in my heart. I mean all the longing that can be satisfied without your very self, and then the two big envelopes full of interesting things, besides this marvelous box from Belgium. What a royal giver you are—a dozen pr. of such lovely stockings. When I saw them I made up my mind that I would have to wear them even if I had to take a tuck in the feet. But they are just the right size and I am so pleased to have them. Thank you my dearest one, and know that you have given me great pleasure. They are beautifully done up aren't they? The box and even the pathetic initial and decoration. It makes me sad—and yet proudly glad—that it is a tribute to you and what you mean to the world. Even a people across the sea whose hearts have been kept from breaking perhaps by the knowledge that there was still in the world such a man and that if anything can be done for them and other sufferers you can and will do it.

I hope you can use the socks and the girls some of the other stockings—it is so like you to think of me and share them first with me. I will have to wait until tomorrows letter to tell you of reading the business papers, for it is already nearly eleven and I am afraid to read them before writing for fear of interruption and not sending my letter in time for the mail to reach you tomorrow.

So this is just an answer to your dear letter. What would I not have given to have been with you on that drive Saturday and have come back and shared the hours in the study, to have put my arms 'round you when the band was playing the last national air, and made you feel how I comprehend your responsibility—your anxiety and tremendous duty—and how I want to share and lighten and help in every way, but also how completely I realize your fitness, your fineness, your unswerving, incomparable ability to quell and steady the tides that are running stronger than ever before in the history of the world. I like in this instance to borrow your belief in regard to the ordering of the universe—the idea that when a man's usefulness is over Fate will let him drop out, and someone else take his place. If this is so, then my precious One is safe indeed from any danger, from any unhappiness, from any disease. For no one can take your place, and the world would be as blank as my life without you.

When I am away from you, I feel as a man full of life and ready for action must feel who is shut fast in a prison, where he can neither use his own strength or help a great cause for which he would give his hearts blood. It is not that he chafes so over the life he is leading, but the fact that time is flying and he is *missing* the vital, the big thing that he might be doing in the world. You are my source, and while I am far from you the waters get clouded—or thin—and I long to come to where they run strong and fresh and sparkling.

Of course I was interrupted here by callers, one of whom said an interesting thing. She is a Miss Webster[1] and said she was in Wash. last winter but only for a week and saw so many lovely things and interesting people but had to leave with her fondest desire ungratified—that of "hearing the President speak." She had met Mrs. T. P. O Connor[2]—she of "I, myself" fame—and she had told her *you* were the only person in America who *could* speak. That she (Mrs. T. P.) had heard every noted speaker in England & America and you compared more than favourably with the former and excelled the latter so far as to be *the only one*. Then she asked if I had heard you—and if I had *read anything* you had written!!!

Now to answer your dear inquiry requiring myself. I did overlook your question purposely for I did not feel a bit well for ten days after I left you. Perhaps it was the change in climate, but I am inclined to think it something more subtle. I had headaches and could not sleep, but for several days I have been quite well again, and will continue to now I am sure. I did not want to tell you until it was over, and this is honestly so, and you must not worry over it. I am so glad you think you can go to Cornish again the end of the month. You will probably be home again by the time I get there and even if you should find you could stay on into Sept. it would *look* well—and do you good. Bless your heart, don't give up a days vacation on my account. Remember I *want* you to go, and when you come back we can have some blessed hours together. Poor Dr. Grayson! my heart aches for him. And if things are still hanging in the balance I must confess a disappointment in her which goes deep, for I have always so trusted and believed in her womanliness. I will try to write him in a few days.

Goodbye my Darling, and thank you for being well and happy and for loving   Your devoted   Edith.

ALS (WP, DLC).

[1] Probably Mary Webster of Geneva, N. Y.

[2] Elizabeth Paschal (Mrs. Thomas Power) O'Connor, the Texas-born wife of the Irish journalist and politician. Her autobiography, *I Myself*, was first published in London in 1910.

To Robert Lansing

My dear Mr. Secretary,   The White House. 16 August, 1915.

The plot thickens![1] This seems to me a very important and serious matter, and I hope that there are channels and means at the disposal of the Department which will enable you to find out whether these negotiations are still in progress and whether there is any way in which we can put a spoke in the wheel. Of course the gentlemen involved do not know that they are playing with fire.   Faithfully Yours,   W.W.

WWTLI (SDR, RG 59, 894.20219/19 DNA).
   1 See RL to WW, Aug. 13, 1915 (second letter of that date), n. 1.

To Lindley Miller Garrison

My dear Mr. Secretary: [The White House] August 16, 1915

I have your letter of August twelfth accompanying the outline of military policy, to which I shall give my most careful attention immediately.

My judgment does not coincide with yours as to the publicity test. There is this danger in that, that a subsequent modification of the suggested policy might be given the color of a difference of opinion between yourself and myself, which I am sure you would not wish any more than I would. If we should differ, I may have the good luck to convince you—I have always found you very open-minded—and I think that a matter of as much consequence as this should, of course, be a matter of common counsel. My judgment is, therefore, that it is best to keep the matter for the present for private consideration.

The desires of the nation, I think, are quite clear in this matter and our duty equally clear, but I think the detail of the policy the country is generously willing to leave to us. It must, necessarily, be a matter of official information and expert opinion.

I hope that you are getting a real refreshment at the seaside.
            Cordially and sincerely yours,   Woodrow Wilson

TLS (Letterpress Books, WP, DLC).

To Florence Jaffray Hurst Harriman

My dear Mrs. Harriman: [The White House] August 16, 1915

I very much appreciate your letter of August eighth which I have read with a great deal of attention.

I think that you will find that there has been a very considerable reaction in the judgment about the whole Eastland business and your friend, Mrs. Robins, has allowed herself to believe a number of things which cannot be substantiated. I think that the whole matter is in a way to be cleared up not only, but that the defects in the law are pretty certain to be corrected very promptly.

I was keenly aware of the apparent public opinion in Chicago at the time of the investigation but I think you yourself will have found now that a different impression prevails.

I am taking the liberty of returning Mr. Norman Angell's paper because I had already read his views in the New Republic. They have interested me very much.

I congratulate you on the approaching end of the labors of the Commission on Industrial Relations. I am afraid you have had a very laborious and trying time.

In haste

Cordially and faithfully yours,   Woodrow Wilson

TLS (Letterpress Books, WP, DLC).

From Margaret Woodrow Wilson

Darling Father,   Cornish, Aug. 16th 1915.

It was *so* good of you to write[1] and Jessie and I just loved your letter.

It gave us terrible heart-aches to have you go, and, oh, how we miss you! I don't like to look into your room from mine because it makes me long so to see you come out of it.

I hope that the effects of your rest will last a long time in spite of the terrible heat in Washington (especially as felt in the landaulet) and the strain you are under.

The Davids have not come yet, though we expected them yesterday. Annie and I will have a fine time wailing when they do come. Her voice, in the lower part of it, is about one third as big again as it was the last time I heard it and she sings much better. I think that she is going to sing unusually well.

The baby *must* be cutting a tooth for he yells half the day and night—poor little thing.

Josephine is full of sympathy for Frank, which she shows in every tone of her voice when she speaks to him. Today she came to me with a blue bow in her hair and said very distinctly "Woodrow has never seen me with my hair this way." It's the first time I ever heard her get your name exactly right, and then she didn't bother about any title before it.

Give my sincerest, warmest love to sweet Edith when you write.

Do you know, I really can hardly wait for her to come and live with us? She left a great big hole when she left. You *know* how I love and admire her don't you, Father dear. I miss Jessie and Nell so terribly and it will seem like having another sister given to me when she comes. She's a darling!

I hope that you have found a comfortable place in which to lie on your side and read this letter.

Everybody sends you dearest love. I love you darling Father, with all my heart and soul.   Your devoted,   Margaret.[2]

ALS (WC, NjP).
  [1] It is missing.
  [2] There is a WWTCL of this letter in WP, DLC, which Wilson sent to Mrs. Galt with the following explanation: "I said, to tease her, that I had to lie on my side to read her handwriting. I made this copy for you for fear you would not know the necessary position in which to tackle the original.   W."

From William Gibbs McAdoo

Dear "Governor,"   [North Haven, Me.] Aug. 16/15

The disclosures in the "World" about Germany and the operations of her Ambassador and agents in this country, which are a gross violation of our hospitality and indefensible from every point of view, convince me that you ought to demand explanations and then ask for the Ambassador's recall & the recall of all of Germany's secret agents & commercial agents in this country. We owe it to our country and to the dignity of our Government, to stop such practices as those of which Germany has been guilty. This is the psychological time to do it (or it soon will be) and it will effectively put an end to further German machination and propaganda here. If we overlook this, we shall have an uncontrollable situation to deal with in the future.

The Department of Justice should carefully consider whether or not our laws have been violated (we now have documentary evidence) and if they have been, prosecutions should be pushed. We ought to pursue a vigorous course in this matter.

The baby is geting along "splendidly" now—has regained all she lost and ought to make a new record soon. Nell gets lovelier every day and joins me in dearest love to you.

Devotedly yrs   W G McAdoo[1]

ALS (WP, DLC).
  [1] Wilson later sent this letter to Mrs. Galt (ALI, n.d., WP, DLC) with the following comment:
  "This is all to-day. The second paragraph refers to certain discoveries of Mac's about the German propaganda in this country and the persons involved which it is not wise for me to put on paper   Oh, for the old talks, my Sweetheart.   W."

To Edith Bolling Galt

[The White House] Monday,
My precious, precious Darling,   8.30 P.M. 16 Aug., 1915

The quiet evening hour has come, the door is closed, and I am alone again with my Love. Oh, how I wish that that were literally true, for my Darling needs me,—this dear, sad letter just received shows it. Bless Hoover's heart: the letter he knew my heart waited for did not come during the day (I suppose it was slow getting started on Sunday) and so he went down to the Post Office after all the deliveries of the day were made, and after dinner,—just a few minutes ago,—handed me your letter! And when I opened it and read it I knew why my heart had so particularly yearned for my Darling the past forty-eight hours and yet had seemed unable quite to reach her and frame a message that would take her complete happiness; and now that I have read the letter the yearning is more intense than ever,—the desire to send her some great heart word that will call her back to her happiness as she would feel it were she really in my arms and I could *say* to her what no written words seem able to convey. My Sweetheart! what shall I say to you? I understand perfectly. I do not wonder that these times come when you seem to lose hold on the reality of the wonderful experience of satisfying love that has come to us. I understand it because I understand you and seem myself to have lived through the experiences and the reactions that you were so generous as to tell me all about, and the long period of settled disbelief in the possibility of love itself, so far as you yourself were concerned. I know that these are not really times of doubt or misgiving,— that you are just as sure of your love for me as you are of my love for you when these times come,—just as sure as when you are in full conscious possession of the dear realities of the present. I understand that what happens is, that in a sense *I* (alas!) do not seem real to you (you say that re-reading my letter made me seem real again) *as compared with what went before in your life*. The exquisite hours we have spent together seem for the moment like a dream because they were so much shorter than the long, weary years that preceded them. The years have in a sense left a deeper impression than these brief three months and twelve days. The years left scars, scars of wounds that, until lately, would never entirely heal. You are more *used* to emptiness than to fullness, to loneliness than to companionship, to self-dependence than to love! And yet, Sweetheart, it is evident that even in the midst of it all you have not in the least lost hold of me. You turn instinctively to me to tell me all about it, and hold

nothing back,—turn to touch me and be sure that the dream was
true. All the while you know that your life lies with me, and not
with those memories that sometimes seek to drive me out. It
would all be so easily dispelled and forgotten by half an hour in
my arms. That is where you belong and where unhappiness and
doubt are seen to be the true unrealities. I know why reading any
one of my letters makes me seem again real to you. When I am
writing them, my Darling, nothing in the world is so real to me
as you are. You seem to be actually in my very arms, my heart
beating close to yours, and every word I write is merely an effort
to share my innermost thoughts with you. I am never more intensely alive in every fibre of me. These are the most vital hours
of the day for me, for everything that is best and happiest in
me is awake seeking to get into communication with you and
make you realize my love for you, make you realize that my life
centres in you, and that every thought in my mind or heart
is turning to you to find its mate. How am I to confine myself
to letters,—how am I to keep away from you,—if you are to lose
hold, even for a few hours at a time, of your happiness? Here,
in this letter, is my whole heart. It is yours. Use it to get hold of
the deepest, most vital reality in all the world,—the reality of love
and of present life. It is a stout heart. It lives by realities. Shams
and mere sentiments choke and smother it. It will bear leaning
on. And it loves you because your heart is like it. Your heart, too,
is incapable of mere sentiment or any kind of sham and knows
reality when it touches it. Your heart, like it, is fit to front the
world with,—and yet fit for infinite tenderness and the sweetest
intimacies. Let this comrade challenge your dear heart, its mate,
to put away all but the present and to go with it and give it cheer
and comfort and joy in the journey of the days ahead. The only
thing we *can* be sure of is our love for one another. The world
is a tumbled chaos. I personally do not feel that anything can
be counted on in circumstance or event or the movement of affairs. The one thing I am sure of is *you*. The one thing that seems
to me fixed in the midst of the welter is our love for one another.
That has come into my life like a great steadying force and a great
redemption from a confusion of purpose that might have bred
weakness,—the weakness of discouragement and the suspicion
that—with all standards crumbling,—nothing was worth while.
Don't you *feel* the challenge, Sweetheart? I am sure you do. *We*
stand together whatever happens! So long as our hearts are
united nothing can daunt them or make them doubt what is real
or right or good. *Can* there be anything more real than the
strength they impart to one another? But I grope for words, try-

ing to utter what is too deep for utterance. The sum of the whole thing is, that I send you myself—every day; and want *you* in return. Come, my Darling, my Treasure, my brave, splendid mate and partner,—come to me every day and lend me your strength, support me with your utter faith and confidence, let me feel your arms about my neck, your kisses on my lips, your exquisite endearments and caresses;—and reality will be all in the present; you will never grope for anything, but just put out your hand and grasp mine and fare along the way. There is happiness, every step of it! I am *so* glad, my precious One, that you are going to tell your mother and sister and your brother Randolph about "our wonderful secret." I not only approve: it is what I have long wanted and hoped you would do. I particularly want your dear mother to know. I hope,—oh, how I do hope!—it will make her happy. I feel cheated that I have not known her before. After you have told her I shall feel free to go to her and try to make her love me. She knows her sweet daughter to be worthy of any man: I doubt if she thinks any man worthy of her sweet daughter. *I*, certainly do not think *this* man worthy of her,—for she is incomparable and altogether lovely; and I shall be abashed and probably not at all at my best when I first present myself to mother. But I shall try hard to make her love me and to overlook my faults because of my great love for you. Do tell me, Sweetheart, *all* that they say. It will be delightful to have them know. And, dear little girl, please tell me in your very next letter, before you forget to do it, what your address in Ocean City will be.

The doctor saw Mr. Clapham to-day. He (Mr. C.) had been making inquiries about Mr. Boyd (who, by the way, was once for a short time connected with the Panamanian legation here), and finds nothing at all against him. He is very handsome, well educated, of an excellent family which is not very popular because considered aristocratic; is one of five brothers; and is a lawyer in good standing. The gentleman of whom inquiries were made is connected with the Panamanian legation himself, seemed to know all there was to be known about Mr. Boyd, and had nothing that was not favorable to say about him. Mr. Clapham had just received a letter from your brother Rolfe which was perfectly cheerful and natural. In it he said nothing at all about his domestic troubles and spoke with a good deal of pride and enthusiasm of recent still further remarkable increases in the deposits and business of the bank. Don't you think we can take a good deal of reassurance and encouragement from that? I think about the dear people down there a great deal. I can't believe that they are not already *my* folks,—I know they are *ours*.

Tuesday, 7 A.M.

Good morning, my own Darling. I hope you had a long, refreshing sleep, that your lover seemed very real to you and all the
world transformed by our love. I stayed consciously with you until
after midnight, awake and aglow with thoughts of you too sweet,
too deep to be interpreted by any words I know. Ah, if you only
could "curl up in my arms," as you said you were going to do,
to chase the blues away, the confusion would go out of your heart
upon the instant. By the time this reaches you, my Precious, all
that little cloud in which you groped for your lover,—never for
a moment, I know, losing hold on your *love*, but only, for a little
while, upon your lover,—will have been dispelled, and you will
have realized that, *for us*, the world does *not* "go on the same as
it did last year and the year before—and the year before that,"—
that for us it has been revolutionized. But, though I am sure the
cloud will be gone, your sweetness in telling me about it gives me
a welcome opportunity to tell you again how much I love you.
In you, "out of the whole world, I have found *the* one person
who comprises the world." And my love seeks you and follows
you every moment of the day, because it is a love for every part
and detail of life. I love you in the little commonplace things of
everyday routine. Nothing that you do can be uninteresting to
me. The details of your toilette are romantic to me. Nothing that
constitutes part of the day for you seems foreign to me. And in
everything there is the stimulation, the strange pervasive stimulation, of intimate and loving comradeship. I love the company of
your mind. Business ceases to be tiresome when I tell you about
it. Generally when a piece of business is concluded, or any part
of it, nothing is quite so tedious to me as to rehash it and go over
it again. But it is not so when I recite the particulars of it to
you. All the life comes back into it, and to take it up with you
while it is current, to get my first knowledge of what is in a despatch by opening it at your side and reading it with you, makes
it seem a vital part of my own life—because you are. And then,
in the midst of business, your eye kindles with some whimsical
thought and your mind breaks into play exactly as mine does,
upon the same suggestion, in the way I most enjoy. Oh, but it is
delicious! We can be children as easily as we can be grown-ups.
Our companionship, our *playmateship*, is perfect. I love to watch
you and enjoy you when we are with other people. You say and
do exactly what I would wish you to do and say, only so much
better than I could have said or done it. It is like watching your
character in action, and every manifestation of your character
makes me admire you just so much the more deeply. I love to

watch you writing or embroidering. You look so like the lovely embodiment of everything sweet and earnest and genuine. I love to look forward to seeing you engaged in simple household duties. Everything becomes you. Everything makes me feel that you are incomparable *to live with*. And, oh, my Sweetheart, what shall I say of the delicious hours that are entirely ours, when all thought of the world and its cares, and business and the errant fortunes of those we love are shut out and there is nothing in our thoughts but love,—when we can look into each other's eyes and see the very deeps of love gleaming there with happy lights that seem to stream from the heart itself; when we can touch each other's lips and let our very life rush together in one single tide of joy and realization! What shall I say of *those* hours except that then we *know* that the happiness has come to us which no one else could give, and that the reality of realities has taken possession of us and made us proof against all fortune except separation. *That* is our only malady, dear One,—separation. And that is easily cured! While it is necessary for us to endure it (and God knows I suffer from it what no physical malady could ever make me suffer) let's take means to defeat it of its triumphs—its temporary triumphs—over our spirits. Let's make the times when it threatens to strike deepest and give us the sorest wounds the times when we specially renew our vows and our intimacy of confession of love, so as to cheat the enemy and make use of him to strengthen the very things he is trying to weaken. We will then simply *pour* out our love to one another. Is it a bargain? Bless your heart, how exquisitely sweet you are! This very letter which makes me yearn almost beyond endurance to come and pet you and stay by you, is itself one of the sweetest love letters that was ever written,—in the very remedies it prescribes for itself and the reassurances it so tenderly gives me, the absent lover to whom you stretch out your dear arms. I am always and altogether   Your own   Woodrow

ALS (WP, DLC).

From Edith Bolling Galt

[Geneva, N. Y.] Monday 11:15 P.M.

My own precious One: August 16th 1915

I dont think there has ever before been a day, when we were seperated, that you have seemed so near me—so a part of myself and as though you were actually sharing all I was doing or thinking. I wonder if you have felt it, or if it is only that your beloved letter of Saturday when you were alone for the drive, for dinner and for the evening, concentrated more on me and made your personality real in the written messenger that brought those loved words to me this morning.

To add to this was also the budget of "work" you let me share—by sending me the many vital things that keep me a real sharer of your thoughts. They all interested me more than I can tell you, and, as usual make me long to talk to you about them. The Metcalf letter is so plausible and his plea such an easy way out of the Mexican trouble that I wish it were true. And it makes me more and more alive to the pitfalls that surround your dear feet on every side. But at the same time quickens my admiration, and adoration for you that you are splendidly steadfast amid the temptations. As to the "Report" of the "A.B.C." proceedings my head was in a whirl when I tried to follow the different conduct of affairs in case one of eight things should happen, and fear, if a reply does not come soon I will get so mixed I will have to get you to straighten me out as to what step will be followed. I think the only very new thing (to me at least) in Metcalf's letter was the Roman C. proposition. Is there anything in what he says, or is it but a spoke in the wheel he is trying to break your present policy on?

I think the letter from Mr. Page[1] the most interesting one I have ever seen from him—but depressing. I was more impressed by what he said regarding the necessity for a terrible battle, such as Waterloo or Gettysburg—to make a climax in this awful state of the world. Yet, at the rate the Germans are winning, it looks now as though such a battle might spell *their* success, so I dare not wish for it. Apropos of this, Mr. Rose was telling me to-day that here in Geneva they are turning out bodies for aeroplanes just as fast as they can get skilled workmen, and they are all ordered by the Curtis people who assemble the parts and ship them abroad—that the foreman in the works here told him the average life of any flying machine was about *48 hours*! Did you ever hear of anything so dreadful.

I found your little note on Mr. Page's letter that you wanted it returned as it must be put on file, so I have fixed up in one package, addressed to Mr. Hoover *everything* you have sent me to date, and will send it by Express tomorrow. I thought in view of the fact that I am going *on the road* again for several days where you won't know where to reach me, something might arise that you would need one of these papers and you could not reach me to ask for its immediate return—and so I had better send them all. I fixed up the package before I began to write, and oh!

[1] WHP to WW, July 23, 1915.

Sweetheart I did hate to take off all the little notes of explanation which you had put there. I would have loved keeping them always just as you sent them to me, but I knew some of them must be kept on file and so I sadly removed each little penciled note and put them together and kept them. Please look over the papers carefully and see that all of them are there. They have been under lock all the time, and I think the Express is perfectly safe.

I will enclose just a note from Rolfe to let you know the latest news from Panama—just destroy after reading—as it is to Randolph and he told me to tear it up.[2]

Tonight we took dinner with Mr. & Mrs. Hutchins of N. York.[3] They have a summer home here and are such old friends of Mr & Mrs. Rose they consented to go there, and they are very genuine, sweet people.

They (as everyone does) had the lovliest things to say of you and, while they were too well bred to ask questions, seemed so anxious to know more about you personally.

Of course they won my heart by saying things about that traitor, "W.J.B." that would not add any feathers to the wing of Peace under which he is hiding. Mrs. Hutchins is the head of the *Anti* Suf. movement in this part of the state and was crazy to know how you stood. I only said just what you said to Mrs. Rose the day they were there to lunch—in regard to your feeling it was a question for the States to settle.

The clock is striking midnight and I must go to bed. I have on my wrapper and am by the window. I also have on one pr. of the lovely white silk stockings, and they are a joy—and make me feel so very rich.

I never had such a luxury before as 12 pr. at once, and I am so pleased with them, and they look so pretty on that I think that is the reason I sat up to write tonight—instead of getting in bed as I usually do.

A fond and very tender kiss my precious Woodrow, before *we* put out the light—and I feel your dear arms fold 'round me.

Tuesday, 9:15 a.m.

The Postman has come and gone Dearest, and left no letter to start the day with. I am sure it is due to a belated train and I will hear by the afternoon delivery, but I am lonely without it and will count the hours until 2.30

It rained nearly all night and is still black and threatening and so cold I have my window down. As I look out the tall bushes

[2] R. E. Bolling to J. R. Bolling, Aug. 4, 1915, ALS (WP, DLC).
[3] Waldo and Agnes Swan Hutchins. Hutchins was a lawyer in New York.

of "golden glow" are bowing and smiling to me as if to tell me there is still *gold* even in black days when I fail to get my morning message.

By the way I find it is easier to send the package by "Insured Registered Mail["] instead of Express so it will go this morning.

I hope it is cooler in Washington and that you are still well and happy. Goodbye until tomorrow. I am with all my heart—

Your very own   Edith

ALS (WP, DLC).

To John Sharp Williams

My dear Senator: The White House August 17, 1915

I have, of course, read with attention the letters[1] you were kind enough to send me about young Mr. Lee, and I have again gone over the matter very thoroughly. My recent letter to you from New Hampshire[2] will show you in what spirit I have approached it and with what attitude towards you.

I know, my dear Senator, that it is not your desire to take a position that appointments of this sort should be made when the President is clear in the judgment that it would be unwise to make them. It would not be like you to hold any such opinion as that, and I cannot escape the judgment that it would be very unwise both for the public service and for young Lee for me to appoint him to the office of Assistant District Attorney. The appointment would be, to say the least, premature, because he has not proved himself sufficiently either in personal habits or in legal practice to justify the appointment.

My desire to appoint young Alexander has already been explained to you. I did not take the idea from Mr. Alexander himself at all, and I knew, of course, that your own relations with Alexander and with his father were such as would make it perfectly evident that the appointment was from the immediate circle of your personal supporters.

I hope, therefore, and urge very earnestly, my dear Senator, and with a very solemn sense of public duty, that you reconsider this whole matter. I want to do whatever is done in the way that would be most acceptable to you.

With warmest regard,

Cordially and sincerely yours,   Woodrow Wilson

TLS (J. S. Williams Papers, DLC).
    [1] These letters in support of Richard Charles Lee, Jr., were sent to the Department of Justice.
    [2] WW to J. S. Williams, Aug. 6, 1915.

From Lindley Miller Garrison

My dear Mr President: Seabright N. J. Aug 17, 1915

Yours of the 16th has just been received.

I will, of course, do nothing further in the matter until I hear from you.

I feel, however, that there are two aspects of the situation which I should call to your attention for careful consideration.

First, this whole matter is the subject of constant discussion at the present time. It will be impossible to keep from publication the conclusions and recommendations of the Department therein. Just how these things get out neither you nor I know; but we both have abundant reason to know that they do.

I think it would be very much the better way to obtain the benefit of a frank disclosure of our position, and of our own presentation thereof, than to have it put out piecemeal, incomplete and without the reasons which led to the conclusions. Furthermore we should move and direct public discussion along sensible lines.

Second: The time between now and the December Session of the Congress is all too short to have the matter properly discussed, digested and understood.

I do not desire to re-open the question of treating as I suggested, but with respect to the reason you give for not agreeing to its wisdom, I have this to say: You as the Chief Executive must exercise the final judgment; those whose duty it is to shape the matter for your decision put forth their facts, reasons and conclusions; you do what to you seems wisest and best under all the circumstances. Any failure to agree would be because of some good reason which directed your judgment. And that is as it should be.

In any event I think you should seriously consider some prompt disclosure of the outlines of whatever is agreed upon, for the reasons above briefly referred to.

Sincerely yours   Lindley M. Garrison.

ALS (WP, DLC).

To Edith Bolling Galt

[The White House]

My precious Darling,   Tuesday evening. 17 August, 1915

Are you really well, entirely well? It startles me a little to find that my precious One has been concealing from me the fact that she was not well,—and apparently keeping it from everybody, exerting herself morning, noon, and night to do what her friends pleased, and letting no one suspect that she was not perfectly fit. It makes me very uneasy. *Please*, my own Edith, *please* tell me in *every* letter whether you are well or not, and with perfect frankness; else I shall conjecture and worry. You are all the world to me and I must know how you are faring if I am to play the game (of separation) with calmness and self-possession. Did you have any symptoms that were novel and that would enable a doctor to help you? Be careful, my Darling. My whole peace of mind is involved. I think I could not bear it if anything were to happen to you!

Ah, Sweetheart, how incomparably you love! The letter I got this morning—the Sunday-Monday letter—fairly intoxicated me with its enchanting sweetness. It is the most wonderful and satisfying love letter I ever read. I have just read it again, for the fourth time; and it has left me all aglow with a joy such as only your love can give,—the love of your dear vital heart. The last letter was exquisite, but pathetic, a little cry for reassurance and comfort, a groping for my hand and my lips in the dark. It drew me as would your arms outstretched, and in the letter I wrote in reply last night and this morning I tried,—oh, so hard,—to respond to the cry and give you my hand,—put my arms around you and hold you close until you could realize me again. And now comes this dear letter full of glad love to fill my heart with its own sunshine. After that sad little epistle this one seems like some elixar to me. It is not I that am making our love vital to you, but you who are quickening me with its full refreshment and invigoration. You speak of your pride in me, my Darling, because I have been so brave and have sustained my spirits so in the face of loneliness and separation: "you have been a perfect wonder," you say, "in keeping up to our determination not to be blue or unhappy,"—but, Sweetheart, I need assistance. It is not easy. For

"Oh, when Nature sinks, as oft she may,
Through long-lived pressure of obscure distress,
Still to be strenuous for the bright reward,
And in the soul admit of no decay,
Brook no continuance of weakmindedness—
Great is the glory, for the strife is hard."[1]

I have many a fight with myself to be patient, to love my Darling unselfishly, worthily, in a way that will make her happy and give her cheer and peace of mind. One passage in this wonderful letter of yours struck a responsive chord in my heart with so direct and

[1] William Wordsworth, "To B. R. Haydon."

true a touch as to make my heart fairly quiver. You say that you "feel as a man full of life and ready for action must feel who is shut fast in a prison, where he can neither use his own strength nor help a great cause for which he would give his life-blood. * * * Time is flying and he is *missing* the vital, the big thing that he might be doing in the world." Ah, my sweet One, my dear interpreter, *that's* the thought that *hurts* and makes it so desperately hard to keep discontent and impatience down. We are *missing* so much. I get enough to make any reasonable man happy through this delightful, stimulating correspondence of ours; for I get daily assurances of your love and of the real union of your heart and life with mine, so perfectly conveyed that I could almost fancy I actually felt your heart beating against mine and actually saw the love-light in your eye and heard the subtle vibrations of love in the tones of your voice. And yet *think* of the hours we *might* be together, the *constant* comradeship of thought and emotion that would be ours if we were always together, the infinite access of joy and vision and contentment that would come from hourly being in touch with one another during these days when we need to have all our powers quickened for each others' sake and for the sake of the great nation whom it is our task to serve! I *did* feel, my Beloved, that you were by me and had your dear sustaining and loving arms about me the other afternoon when the band was playing the national air and I was standing here by this table "at attention," every fibre in me quivering with the consciousness of what it all meant for me—for us; but what if you had been actually here! For each of us the strength of life and of fine purpose would have been doubled,—a great glory of unselfish love would have exalted us; and, sitting down side by side, hand in hand, the day would then and there been made to yield to us life and light. We may make believe as we please, my precious Edith; and it would be unpardonably weak in us, if, having what we have, knowing our love and our happiness in one another, and knowing also our clear duty of temporary self-denial, we should repine or brook any continuance of weakmindedness; but I am free to admit that with me it is the struggle of all struggles to keep steady and hold my heart in restraint. For if I really were to let myself feel the full force of the tide of longing for you that surges through my heart at every thought of you, I would be swept hopelessly off my feet. I *need* you so. Your presence makes me so *perfectly* happy and gives me such strength of heart and clearness of vision, as if I took from your very self all that a man stands in need of to put him in right relation with men and duty,—all the verities as well as all the solaces and stimulations of life,—that I must know,—it would be make believe to deny,—that I stand incomplete and without my full, best force until you come to me and we are actually man and wife. But "great is the glory" just *because* "the strife is hard." And I take this satisfaction in succeeding—that to succeed is to be worthy of you and to fulfil your expectations of me. And yet,— and yet! there is one thing I want you to understand (I am sure you do understand it, for you have your own heart's experience to instruct you) and that is the real *character* of the happiness I manage to maintain without you. It is the happiness of know- ing that you love me and have accepted,—daily accept,—my love with just the feeling of identification with me that I want you to have,—the happiness of a frequent interchange of thought and experience,—the happiness of confident and joyous expectation —but a happiness which, while it lives and sustains in the present, and takes infinite joy from what it has now, relies on the future to bring it to the complete fruition without which it would fall short of its real destiny. But why do I expound these things to you? Your heart, as it speaks to me in these dear letters of yours, as it has spoken to me in whispered confidences which thrilled me with an unspeakable joy, needs no assistance to understand. I think we interpret these things to one another, Sweetheart, just as a delightful means of love-making. It *is* delightful to make love to one another, isn't it, Edith? I never tire of trying some new way to tell you the same thing. It's a lovely, inspiring story when it is true to the very core. You used an expression in your Saturday night letter which pleased me so much—and yet, as you used it there it was touching enough, —you spoke of its being sometimes hard for you to realize that it was you who were "happily in love." In this Sunday letter it is not hard to see that the difficulty is gone and that you do realize it, bless your heart! And I? *How* happily in love I am! My dear One is the most desirable, the most delectable lady in the world, my happiness is made secure by her perfect love!

Good-night, my adorable Darling. I was up very late last night. I must try to get to bed betimes to-night. Give me a lover's kiss and remember that the most delicious thought in the world for me is that you are my own, my very own,—to prove myself worthy of by utter tender devotion,—to serve with infinite love.

Wed. 6.50 A.M.

Good morning, my precious Sweetheart. Did you sleep well and long enough to be thoroughly refreshed? You said that you had not only been having headaches but that you had not been sleeping lately. Please tell me exactly how it is faring with you now. I shall be uneasy until you do. I got a fine rest last night and feel greatly refreshed this morning. I was feeling perfectly well yesterday (as I am to-day) but I was tired and indulged myself with a little loafing. I did not play golf. Colonel Brown is here and I sent him and the doctor out to play (they are very keen antagonists) while I first lay on the lounge in my bedroom and read and then went out for a drive in the secret service car. The heat we have been having since I got here—about 90° every day and little air stirring—passed off during the afternoon and the evening came off cool and invigorating. It has been a perfect night for sleeping. If I could only know that my Darling had fared as well, I could feel that all's well with the world—at least while I sit here talking to her and the cares of the world of affairs are shut out beyond the door.

Speaking of affairs, I did not send you any big envelope yesterday—for the best of reasons: because there was nothing to put in it. I had no communications with the State Department yesterday. They sent me only a small batch of "flimsies,"[2] and they contained nothing but multiplied details—and very small details at that—of the chaos that is Mexico.

I am *so* glad, Sweetheart, that the stockings fitted. They are certainly beauties, and it delights me that you were so pleased with them. Of course I thought first of you! I am in danger of thinking *only* of you! The socks, too, are just the right size (one would suppose they had sent to inquire), but *what*, my Dear, do you think of *my* wearing webby openwork hosiery? What fun for the mosquitoes who have their meal under the table these hot evenings while we have ours from the top of it, out on the west terrace!

So you will see me and greet me with "a glowing salutation" as we approach Dupont Circle, after you get back, will you? You dear Mischief! That will be very delightful: merely to catch a glimpse of you at a distance would make a dark and troubled day bright for me. But what do you suppose *I* will do? I can't tell myself. I think that if I did not at once order Robinson to turn around and follow, I should jump out of the machine and run after you, regardless of the whole world. No, my precious One. I suppose I shall have to endure the pain of occasionally having to let you pass me on the street without a word exchanged or any sign on my part of how violently my heart is a-flutter; but we shall arrange *some* way of seeing each other

2 Copies of telegrams on thin paper.

frequently. My heart would rebel, otherwise. It will be sweet to have you near and know *all* the time how you are and what is in your thoughts—I mean exchange messages that take but a few minutes to transmit, instead of messages that it takes forty-eight hours to receive and answer. You know dear little Helen has promised, of her own accord, to come down in September and lift the embargo. I suppose she can do so as soon as Tumulty's family returns. I find it hard to keep off of Twentieth St. Every time I get in the car I feel like ordering it to take a route that will take me by 1308, so that I may at least look at the house which is made romantic to my thought by the mere fact of being your nest. Ah, my sweet One, it is no longer your home, *is* it?

I am afraid I cannot share your hope that the last weeks of this leaden-footed month will seem to pass comparatively fast. How slow and dull a month it has been! How long it seems since that blessed August first when I was in heaven with my lovely Darling! Ah, Sweetheart, my heart melts within me when I think of you and of all that you mean to me, and of the wonder of your love for me. I am blessed beyond all other men. You are the most adorable person in all the world, the most perfect in charm and sweetness and power to satisfy, and I am with all my heart   Your own   Woodrow

ALS (WP, DLC).

From Edith Bolling Galt

[Geneva, N. Y.]

My dearest One   August 17th 1915 11.10 P.M.

Your letter of Sunday night and yesterday a.m. did come by the afternoon delivery, and I need not add how welcome it was. I was on the porch alone, so I sat right down in a big rocking chair and read it. And for the time Geneva and the Roses were forgotten—I was with you—alone in the brilliant sunshine of a day like October, and you were telling me all the things that are in your mind—of what you were doing in the different difficult situations, in Haiti, in Mexico and abroad—and through it all was running the love song that makes every word you speak or write music in my ears, and I was happy. Yes dearest One, so great is the magic power of love that with this daily record of your thoughts and occupations I can be happy though miles and miles of space divide us.

Thank you for your patience in explaining things to me so fully in regard to the "Preparedness." I so hope the Secretaries of War

& Navy have given you their Reports in such digested form that you will not have to make out the plan, but only decide the method of putting it into action. Goodness knows that is a big enough task, without having to decide the detail. I felt sure, from what you had said about Congress, that you would not call an extra session, but did not know whether this emergency would make you feel it necessary. But I am glad you won't have that body to handle along with other things. I see in the Rochester paper today that you are being urged by all your close associates to return to Cornish by Sept. 1st to get all the rest you possibly can. So I hope this report is true and you will go up for Jessie's birthday and stay just as long as you feel you are not needed in Washington

What you write me about their getting on so well without you makes me very glad, for it means greater ease for you when you are gone, feeling you can rest in the ability of those in charge to carry things on—and then too it means more vacation time for you. So please go Sweetheart, and don't feel you want to be in Washington early in September, because a certain lady will be coming home. She could not see you anyway, and you said yourself it was easier to be away. So write me what day you will go so I can send my letters to the right place. And that brings me to our trip to Ocean City on Friday.

As we expect to leave here about 10 Friday A.M. I would get your letter mailed Thursday, and that will have to last over until Sunday for I would not know how to tell you to find me on Saturday. Mr. Rose thinks now he will go from here to Albany N. Y. spending the first night there. Then as far as we can comfortably on Saturday making the final lap to Ocean City on Sunday. So you can just send your Saturday and Friday messengers together to the "Hotel *Normandie by-the-Sea*" after Thursday, and I would put them in the same envelope. And I will get them on Sunday—if I can get there, or certainly on Monday.

I shall miss you and your dear message on Saturday, but I think it would be useless to try and set any place to have you send a letter, as motoring is such an uncertain thing for fixed plans.

I am so thrilled at your Treaty to Haiti and do hope your enforced action will be understood by the Latin Americans, as any doubt there might embarrass your Mexican affiliations

There is nothing in the papers about it yet, but I shall watch the comments with great interest, and, this being the 17th is the day the Congress expires so they must act. After getting your letter I asked Mr. Rose if he would get the World of Sunday, yesterday & today for me, and I am to have them tomorrow and [will] be so eager to read the articles regarding the German Propaganda.

Wednesday, 18 August

It is now 12.30 Precious One, and I have not had a minute to call my own and now have to write in a rush. Your dear letter, in answer to my blue one of Sunday is full of tenderness and help, and I accept the challenge and promise to keep the faith. How perfectly you understand always and know how to make me *feel* your comprehension   When the Postman came this morning I felt sure your letter would bring me what I wanted and it did. With it came also the Big Envelope, which I will keep until later to read contents, for that will wait and my letter to you must go. What a wonder Hoover really is! His comprehension is almost as keen as your own and his tact wonderful. Besides your letter I got this enclosed one from Rolfe[1] in answer to *our* letter of July 27th, and I feel his worst representations were justified as to the mans ancestry etc. And the only hope is that *he* may not be as bad as the rest of his family.

I hope you will understand my sending you such a disgusting record, but I felt Rolfe's letter explained better than I could, and I am sick at the horror of what may be for Elizabeth in the future. Thank you Dearest for looking up the man in Washington—at any rate his record there is good—and I don't think I should be the one to spread abroad this tragic account of his forebares.

Will you return the letter to me in the next big envelope as I want to show it to Mother. Strange that your account and this should have come together! In regard to what you say about Mother, I will answer in my letter tonight, for I cannot speak of that on the same page with this other awful thing. My heart aches for Rolfe. I only yesterday answered his wife's wild letter and told her to try *tact* and affection in place of force and deception, but I suppose E. will be married before my letter gets there. Goodbye my precious One.

Your own always   Edith

Remember—no more letters here after tomorrow (Thursday)   E.

ALS (WP, DLC).
[1] Wilson returned this letter.

To Lindley Miller Garrison

My dear Mr. Secretary: [The White House] August 18, 1915

Mr. Breckinridge handed me, as I wrote you, the paper containing an outline of military policy and I have now read it with very studious attention. I am sorry to say that it does not contain what I hoped it would. In view of what you wrote me in your letter, it is evident that you were thinking chiefly while preparing it of making the test of public opinion to which you referred. The paper is, therefore, lacking in the detail which is necessary before I can really form a personal judgment about it.

I want to say that the general idea contained in it interests me very much and seems to me a feasible one, but the method by which the thing could be done, I mean by which the training of the citizen soldiery could be carried out, and also the cost, it is of the first importance that I should know.

I learn from Mr. Breckinridge that the War College is now at work on the figures of cost. I hope that it will be possible for you to get them to finish these reckonings at as early a date as possible, and I am going to ask that you will be good enough to have drawn out for me a succinct plan in definite items summing up this paper that I have and sufficiently developing the method of administration to enable me to form a practical as well as a general judgment.

Cordially and sincerely yours,   Woodrow Wilson

TLS (Letterpress Books, WP, DLC).

To Thomas Watt Gregory

[The White House]
My dear Mr. Attorney General: August 18, 1915

I enclose you a copy of a letter which has reached me recently and which was referred to the Department of State. I am sending it to you in order to get your judgment as to whether it affords ground enough for any kind of action or investigation on our part.

If you should think that it does deserve following up, I think it would be wise for the chief of your Secret Service to get into communication with Mr. Flynn, the chief of the Secret Service of the Treasury Department, in order that they may advise with each other in a way that would prevent all crossing of wires in case any investigation should be on hand at the Treasury Department.[1]

Cordially and faithfully yours,   Woodrow Wilson

TLS (Letterpress Books, WP, DLC).
¹ See T. W. Gregory to WW, Aug. 20, 1915.

Two Letters from Robert Lansing

My Dear Mr. President: Washington August 18, 1915.

You ask me for an opinion in regard to the enclosed communication.¹ I hesitate to give one because I do not agree with the premises on which these good people rest their argument for the commencement of a peace movement in this country.

I do not believe that it is true that the civil leaders of the belligerents would at the present time look with favor on action by the neutral nations; and, even if they did, the military branches of the belligerent governments dominate the situation, and, they favor a continuance of the war. It is the latter element which must be won over or we must wait until the civil branch becomes more influential in the conduct of affairs.

It is probable that Germany and Austria, now triumphant in the East and firmly entrenched in the West, would welcome a peace movement by neutrals. I should think that they would, for they are occupying extensive tracts of their enemies territories. While they are losing large numbers of men, the efficiency of their armies remains unimpaired. They are in the best possible situation to make a peace which will give them, in part at least, the fruits of their victories over Russia and their firm hold on the Belgian and French territory which they occupy. They are in a position to demand compensation in territory and treasure. This would unquestionably be their attitude if peace negotiations should be instituted at the present time. It would be the reasonable and logical attitude.

On the other hand the Allies would not, in my opinion, be willing to consider a peace under the present military conditions. Every reason which would induce the Teutons to make peace would make the Allies unwilling. With their enemy successfully occupying their lands they are in no position to make a peace which would be satisfactory to them. They would consider an agreement to negotiate an evidence of weakness, which I do not think they would admit even indirectly. I understand from several reliable sources that their hope is to continue the war in much the same way that it is being carried on now on the theory that Germany and Austria cannot stand the waste of men and resources resulting. The Allies believe that, while this process of wasting is going on, they will on the other hand be gaining in men and munitions and be prepared at the opportune time to force back their exhausted opponents within their own boundaries.

Whether they are drawing right conclusions or not makes no difference if they believe this will be the consequence of continuing hostilities. I am certain that they have this belief.

Manifestly a suggestion to enter into peace negotiations would be inacceptable at the present time to the Allies who are relying on time to equalize the military strength of the belligerents. I think that the attempt now would not only be rejected but resented.

If this estimate of the situation is correct and if we do not wish to destroy our helpfulness when an effort to restore peace offers some prospect of success, it would be folly to approach the belligerents on the subject at the present time.

As to the second premise, the fitness of the United States to initiate a peace appeal at the present time, I think that it is only needful to say that our usefulness for the future as an intermediary would undoubtedly be lost or greatly lessened by such a step, for the Allies would look upon our activity as in the interest of their foes, while the latter would be glad to use us as tools to secure their conquests and not as friends seeking the common good of all.

Holding these views I would strongly favor discouraging any neutral movement toward peace at the present time, because I believe it would fail and because, if it did fail, we would lose our influence for the future.

Faithfully yours,   Robert Lansing.

[1] See RL to WW, Aug. 6, 1915 (second letter of that date), n. 1.

PERSONAL AND CONFIDENTIAL

My dear Mr. President: Washington August 18, 1915.

I have received from Mr. Polk a telegram in which he says that he saw Mayor Mitchel last evening and that he has made satisfactory arrangements with him in case you should decide to act.[1] Mr. Mitchel requests that in case the appointment is made the matter should not be made public for the present.

Personally, I am very much gratified at this information and I hope that you will see your way clear to name Mr. Polk. For the sake of all interested I hope that it will be possible to act speedily in order that they may be advised of the decision.

Faithfully yours,   Robert Lansing.

TLS (WP, DLC).
[1] That is, if Wilson decided to appoint Frank L. Polk as Counselor of the State Department. Polk at this time was corporation counsel of the City of New York.

From Edward Mandell House, with Enclosures

Manchester, Massachusetts.
Dear Governor: August 18th, 1915.

I herewith enclose you copies of a letter from Gerard and the anonymous letter to which he refers.

I am also enclosing you McLauren's letter which you sent me some days ago. The matter is being worked out in another way therefore, I see no need to discuss it with him. He is mistaken about cotton being used in high explosives. It is only used in the propelling power and in torpedoes and I do not think the grade of cotton makes any difference excepting that they would naturally use the lower grade.

Your affectionate,   E. M. House[1]

TLS (WP, DLC).
[1] Wilson sent this letter and its enclosure to Mrs. Galt with the following comment (ALI, WP, DLC): "Gerard's letter will amuse you, at least. I don't think he is in need of a vacation. He has always been that way! W."

ENCLOSURE   I

James Watson Gerard to Edward Mandell House

My dear Colonel: Berlin, Germany. August 3rd, 1915.

I had a conversation last week of one hour and a half with the Chancellor (in German, heaven help me). He sent for me because I had written him to take no more trouble about my seeing the Emperor. He explained of course first that he did not know I wanted to see the Emperor. They keep the Emperor well surrounded. *Now* I do not want to see him. He is hot against Americans and the matters I wanted to talk of are all settled—one way. I cabled an interesting report on the Emperor's conversation *re* America which is *Straight*.[1]

The enclosed copy of an anonymous letter is interesting. This anonymous writer (who writes often) is usually quite correct in his "dope."

The Chancellor is still wrong in his head; says it was necessary to invade Belgium, break all international laws etc. I think however that he was personally against the fierce Dernburg propaganda in America. I judge von Tirpitz has so, through his press bureau, egged on the people that this submarine war will keep on and the Germans will be utterly astonished and hurt when the war is on. After all it is necessary. Von Jagow confessed to me that they tried to get England to interfere with them in Mexico, and Germans "Gott strafe" the Monroe Doctrine in their daily prayers of hate.

Warsaw, as I predicted officially long ago will soon fall. This keeps the Balkan States out.

No great news—we are simply waiting for the inevitable accident.　　　　　　　　　　　　　Yours as ever,　J.W.G.

TCL (WP, DLC); P.S. omitted.
　¹ J. W. Gerard to RL, Aug. 2, 1915, printed as an Enclosure with RL to WW, Aug. 4, 1915.

E N C L O S U R E　　I I

An Unknown Person to James Watson Gerard

Dear Sir:　　　　　　　　　　　　　　　Berlin S. W. 27.8 [1915].

A few weeks ago I had the honor to draw the attention of Your Excellency to the fact that the German Chancellor, Herr von Bethmann, endeavored in vain to counterbalance the aggressive and lawless policy of the Imperial Admiralty, represented by Herr von Tirpitz, with regard to the Lusitania case and the further activity of the German Undersea-boats.

I beg now to congratulate Your Excellency most heartily to the brilliant success, the Foreign Office of the U. S. A. may boast of on behalf of the unswerving attitude of the President and his most prominent colleagues. There is *no doubt whatever, that the German Government must come to terms* in a question, which by the vast majority of all honor liking Germans has been decided in the same just and conciliatory sense as by the U. S. A. legal authorities.

It is a well-known matter of fact, that even German navy-officers, who are independent and enabled to utter judgment, wholly agree with the point of view taken by the U. S. A. Government; *Admiral von Truppel*¹ for instance, the former Governor of Kiaots-Chao in China, who has retired from the service and is now living in Hamburg, *has had the courage of publicly disapproving of the lawless and unjustifiable methods of sea war practiced by the German undersea-boats*, and you may take it for granted that Admiral von Truppel has not taken this step without the plain approbation of the German Chancellor Herr von Bethmann-Hollweg, *who has chosen him as his mouthpiece to the purpose of pressing on the final decision of the Emperor*. The Emperor and Herr von Tirpitz are one and the same thing, *but they shall and must give way*.

　　　　　　　　　　　　　　　　　　Yours truly,　A.

TCL (WP, DLC).
1 Oscar von Truppel.

Two Letters to Edith Bolling Galt

[The White House] 18 Aug. [1915]

I have written the Sec'y of War that this is not what I wanted.[1] It was evidently prepared with a view to publication. What I want is a businesslike statement of actual plans and as full figures of cost as possible. This is a most superficial paper. I am surprised he should have thought to put it off on me. But it is interesting and the idea is not bad.   W.

ALI (WP, DLC).
1 LMG to WW, Aug. 12, 1915, n. 1.

[The White House] Wednesday,
My adorable Sweetheart,   8.15 P.M. 18 August, 1915

Again the faithful Hoover went to the Post Office itself this evening and got to-day's (belated) letter from you, which he has just handed me, and which I have just devoured and been made happy by. I can't imagine what can have made my letter of Sunday-Monday late in getting to you. I am as regular as the clock about getting my letters off. I hand one to Hoover every morning when I go down to breakfast at eight or a little after, and I don't think he ever postpones posting them. This is the last letter I shall send to Geneva; and, unless you wait for the mail on Friday morning, I fear it will not catch you. I shall be anxious about you while you are on the road. Mr. Rose will have under his care my very happiness itself! It thrills me to think that the machine will be headed this way, bringing you every hour *nearer* to me at least; and at the end of the journey you will be in my old jurisdiction. No part of New Jersey ever gave those who had to administer the laws more trouble and anxiety than did Atlantic City and the resorts that flank it, north and south, upon that much resorted to coast. They are not communities at all, made up of responsible citizens, but merely places where people who have laid aside their usual steadying occupations, and who are for the time being idle, are catered to. You may imagine what some of them want—dissipation and distractions of the most exciting kinds; and no sort of law is respected in giving that kind what they are looking for and are willing to pay for. I have had many anxious conferences about Atlantic City and have made many radical speeches there, in audience rooms opening off the board walk. It will please my fancy to think of my dear One in those, to me, familiar scenes, and where once her lover was responsible for the all but impossible processes of government. I have a very soft place in my heart for New Jersey. She has done me great honour, and done it very generously, and I have worked hard and spent the best that was in me to serve her. A man can't help loving a State and a people he has given an important and critical part of his life to. So I hope you will like what you see of the stout little State, though the part you will see is in no respect a typical part. That coast might belong to *any* state,—though I dare say there is no other state *all* of whose coast is devoted to health and pleasure resorts. Thank you, dear Love, for the letter from Rolfe. It tallies, in a way, with the letter I told you Mr. Clapham had received from him. It even seems to me to have in it a certain degree of resignation and willingness to wait and see. Don't you think so? At any rate the hectic excitement of the earlier letters has gone out of it, and it sounds *rational*, even if not hopeful. I suppose the "George" mentioned is Mrs. Bolling's brother who was expected. Heaven send "George" may not lead them into wild courses and get them all into a mad fever again!

Did you, in your enthusiasm for the public business, actually read those eight conjectural cases submitted by the committee of the A.B.C. conference! I did not, and therefore can't answer your question about them. The fact is, I never have had any patience with 'ifs' and conjectural cases. My mind insists always upon waiting until something actually does happen and then discussing what is to be done about that. And so, to tell you the truth, I read only that portion of the discussion which Lansing had run a mark along on the margin. He had given me all the essential points orally, and I am an impatient reader of *words*. But I wanted you to see how the minds of these men work, how dearly they love abstractions and fine-drawn legal points. The idea of spending their time debating the legal lodgement of *sovereignty* in Mexico! They are hopeless legalists,—and all legalists have a very vague and uncertain perception of facts, and no hold on them whatever. How Bryan would have revelled in these discussions of words,—and how well and adroitly Lansing used their own phrases to guide them into the only safe and practical course! Metcalfe's letter *is* a very plausible argument, and it must be said that there may presently be no feasible course left open to us but to recognize that very trying and pig-headed person, Carranza. The other "chiefs" are all in a more or less demoralized condition. Only Carranza has political authority over any considerable portion of the country. The most significant thing that is happening down there just now (if it is safe to believe upon mere newspaper report that it *is* happening) is that the commanders of the several northern districts of the country who have until recently professed to serve under Villa or the shadowy authority still supposed to be exercised by the "Convention," are now saying that they do not intend to fight any more unless attacked, but mean to sit tight where they are, maintain a local authority, and (I suppose) let the future bring what it will. What Metcalfe says about the Roman Catholic church is in large measure true. That church was stripped, before Porfirio Diaz's time, of its legal authority and of much of its property. Diaz permitted it to resume business, so to speak, along the old lines and at the old stands, but did not alter the law, and so kept them (the priests and the hierarchy) dependent on his favour. They exercised practically every privilege of their church *on sufferance*; and the common people hated them for those very privileges. Every revolution in Mexico which has had popular support has had as part of its programme the curbing and subordination of the church. Therefore the alliance of the church is necessarily with the "cientifico" class, the educated, privileged, and propertied class, who are, as with us, owning and running everything, the reactionary class. Hence the wedge in our own domestic politics. I have had no end of trouble with Roman Catholics in this country about Mexico,—and a very large percentage of the thick and thin adherents of the Democratic party in the United States are Roman Catholics. The influence of the hierarchy of that church is, so far as Mexico is concerned, ardently engaged on the side of *reaction*.[1] Mr. Fuller, be it noted, who is active in the A.B.C. conferences, is a representative and very prominent Roman Catholic. And so the complicated plot goes. Fortunately I have discussed affairs and persons and situations in Mexico with so many different persons, guileless and guileful, and from so many different angles that I am tolerably well able, after two years and more of it, to check up such statements as Metcalf, for example, makes. I must say that a great deal of what he says is reasonable and very likely true. The A.B.C. men are all Roman Catholics, I believe, and I think none of them wants Carranza recognized or encouraged.

Yes, my Darling, you are right about Page's letter. It is truly remarkable and terribly depressing. But I can't go with him in thinking that the war must necessarily culminate in some great battle like Waterloo or Get[t]ysburg. I don't see how it *can*,—and it must end! I think it is going to be *a great endurance test* and that

[1] About this last-ditch effort of the Roman Catholic hierarchy in the United States to prevent American recognition of Carranza, see Link, *Struggle for Neutrality*, pp. 640-42.

the Allies are on the whole more likely—being open to the rest of the world, to survive that test than the Teutonic monarchies are. I had a visit to-day, by the way, from Miss Emily Balch, who, like Miss Jane Addams, has been visiting European prime ministers and foreign secretaries in the interest of peace, and who, like Miss Addams, wants me to assemble a conference of neutral nations (which I am expected and invited to "dominate") which shall sit (and I with it, I wonder? I did not inquire about that) continuously till the war ends and all the while, patiently and without sensitiveness to rebuffs, and by persistent suggestion, heckle the belligerent nations about terms and conditions of peace, until they are fairly worried (I suppose) into saying what they are willing to do. I can't see it. And yet I am quite aware that they consider me either very dull, very deep, or very callous. Alack and alas!

And now it is this boy's bed-time, Sweetheart. And here I've been writing for the better part of two hours and have not even mentioned the only subject I've really been thinking about,—my love, my happy and absorbing love, for you, who are the most attractive, the most interesting, the most vital, the most charming woman in the world, and, above all, the most lovely and lovable! I wonder if you are sitting up to-night at your letter-writing to wear your new silk-stockings? You adorable girl! I've no doubt they look lovely on you! They would be a pretty poor sort if they did not. And I wish with all my heart I could see them shown off to such advantage! But I see that you think I had *better* shut up and go to bed. Ah, Sweetheart, I *can't* go till I tell you how much I love you! And yet I can't. I've tried, and it's impossible. When I think of you (as when do I not?) during these evening hours as I sit here alone in the study, and recall those blessed evenings at Cornish, my heart is a little too much for me. You are so exquisitely sweet and lovable, you are such an adorable, enchanting lover, my heart can get so close to yours and every moment that I am intimately with you seems so full of vision and of the revelation of everything that is delightful and of the essence of life and joy, that every instinct in me cries out for you. I can hardly endure the separation from you. *All* the while, my precious One, my thoughts are with you, and now as the day closes they go as if to guard you all through the night and whisper to you of my tender, infinite love for you. I shall go to my bed-room, get out one of those dear photographs, prop it up against the pillow of the bed close to mine, where I shall see it and call it pet names the last thing before I put out the light and the first thing in the morning, and, after say[ing] a prayer from my heart for my

Darling, go to sleep with my arms close about her and lie with happy thoughts because she has accepted my love and I am altogether hers.

Thursday, 7 A.M.

Good morning, precious Darling. I've just come from kissing your picture before locking it up for the day (!) and would give more than could be reckoned to take you in my arms and do the same to you. You wonder why, (when you were writing your Monday-Tuesday letter) I should have seemed so specially close to you, my dear little girl. Have you forgotten that pathetic little letter you wrote me on Saturday and Sunday? I got that on Monday and never since I have known and loved you have my heart and mind, backed by every power and emotion in me, tried so hard to send you a wireless message of love. But, Sweetheart, it is, after all, difficult for me to distinguish between one day and another in that respect. I am always close by you, day and night; my loving thoughts seek you out all the hours through; your heart has at any moment only to stretch out its hand and it will find mine. Your lover is always waiting and longing to take you in his arms and hold you close and tell you all the sweet, intimate things that will make your heart glad. And, oh, with what loving solicitude I shall follow you to-morrow and Saturday and Sunday, on your trip to Ocean City! I hope most earnestly that this letter will not fail to get to you before you start, for it is freighted with love for the journey. Ah, my Love, my Love! I am actually repining that I persuaded you not to come back to Washington in August—though I *know* in my mind that that was best—for I am dying for a sight of you. It would be a delight in the midst of these barren days of mere work only to see anyone as beautiful and altogether engaging as you are, even if I did not adore you,— and to see you and know that love binds us indissolubly together would be bliss, though I could only lift my hat to you and should be under special compulsion to keep our dear secret from all the world. See how inconsistent I am, and how my heart runs away with my head. My head tells me I could not rely on myself to maintain any such magnificent reserve and self-restraint. It calls my attention, in grave tones of friendly warning, to my headlong, impetuous, uncalculating heart, and says, "Woodrow Wilson, you know perfectly well that you could not trust it for a moment. And yet you could hardly blame it (that makes the case all the stronger and the warning all the more necessary) for remember how *perfectly* enchanting and irresistable Edith is! You *could* not pass her on the street without giving yourself dead away." My head is right (it's hateful to be right in such a matter), but my heart is clean daft about you. Any true heart would be that had even half a chance to know what you are,—and mine has had a *whole* chance, has seen to the very depths of the sweetest heart in the world. You are altogether adorable, my Edith; you can love as it would transport any man with joy to be loved; I want you as I want completion of life and I am in everything

Your own   Woodrow

Take care of yourself, my Darling—*please* take care of yourself!

ALS (WP, DLC).

From Edith Bolling Galt

My precious Lord: Geneva, August 18/1915   11:30 P.M.

This has been the most wonderful day, so cool and bracing that one felt new life and energy in the very air, and I went to return eleven calls this afternoon and did not get back until dinner time.

After dinner Mrs. Endicott had asked us to come for a game of "Auction"; and we really had a jolly time. She & her sister Miss Seward are good fun   They, too, live in N. Y. but have a lovely old homestead here.

Geneva is really a very attractive place and has some very nice people. I wonder if you will come here with me sometime, will you?

I am afraid my letter of this morning was so hurried it was not presentable, but I could not do any better, and I was awfully worried about the news from Panama.

I don't wonder Rolfe was so beside himself and wish with all my heart I could have really helped them. Thank you again my dearest one for all you did to help them and me—and for your ever ready sympathy. But I will not fill my letter with that, for there is nothing to be done, and I am thankful George Litchfield got away without doing anything violent. Today at noon I had the sweetest letter from Margaret,[1] and she surely knows the way to my heart when she says such exquisitely sweet things of you. I am going to send it for you to read and get you to send it back to me for I appreciate all she says so deeply and think she has been so wonderful in her attitude toward me. From the very first she has made *me* feel she was glad, and I can't help feeling that her attitude, had it been the reverse of what it is, could not only have made both of us unhappy but would naturally, and unconsciously have influenced the younger girls. And so, I not only love and appreciate her, but I admire her very thoroughly and will always do anything in the world that I can for her happiness.

The more I see and know of these three "little women" the more I realize their superiority and fineness. And I only hope I can make them know how I love them and feel that I never want to come between them and you, but rather to cement the bond that is already so strong between you

When you have any opportunity to impress this fact upon the girls will you Dearest, for they have all been so "big" in their welcome to me, I want them to know they can count on me—and my anxiety to be one with them in my love for you, but never to usurp a place or claim you from them.

I am glad you approve of my telling Mother, Bertha & Randolph. I knew you would, and I am just as sure that they will all love and admire you when they know you and will welcome any opportunity that will let them know you. But as Mr. & Mrs Rose will be there a week I may decide not to say anything until after they go, but I will be guided by circumstances and will, of course, write you everything.

Yes, Dear Heart, it is a bargain—we will cheat seperation of its victory by putting more in our letters than even our lips can say. Really, this is easier than it would seem when we recall how little we do say when we are together. We mostly *know* each others thoughts through the windows of the soul—instead of speech—so when we can not see deep into each other's eyes we have to form these subtle under thoughts into concrete form and make at least a black and white sketch of them in order to convey our meaning.

I am all "trued up" again, and seeing straight, and now that it is 12:30 I must stop and try to go to sleep.

May all the peace that passeth understanding come to you— and keep and bless you!

Thursday, 11 a.m.

Do you know, my dearest One, you have a very dangerous rival I have found here in Geneva. He is the most fascinating person with big brown eyes—soft as velvet—and the most bewitching ways. He lives next door, and whenever I go on the porch he comes over and we have jolly times together which accounts for my delay in getting earlier to my desk this morning—as we have been playing a game. He is only four, but as full of quaint ways and cleverness as little Josephine. I must tell you some of his funny sayings when I see you. Do you remember Miss Waring[2]— Miss Parker's guest at Cornish? Well, she visited Mrs Rose before going there and was very sweet to this small person next door. So yesterday Mrs. Rose asked him if he remembered Miss W. and he said "Yes, I remember how she bored me—but I love Mrs. Galt" which, of course is to show you what a really discriminating mite he is.

I got your dear letter an hour ago—and I am afraid I read through the assurance that you are well [with] just a little doubt. Else why did you not play golf and stay on the sofa loafing? I know what that continued and awful heat is, and don't wonder you felt unequal to effort. But please Woodrow, if you can get away again next week, go. I only wish Cornish was more bracing. I think a week where it was crisp and cold would do you no end of good. How about going up to Harlakenden for the 28th and then motoring to Col. House and stay there a few days? I imagine that is cooler and you might enjoy it. It seems a shame for you to have to resort to the Secret Service car for a ride, and I shall look anxiously for tomorrow's letter telling me the whole truth in regard to yourself and if you really are well. For myself, I can honestly say I am perfectly well, again. I think the cool weather was what I needed, and I have no more headache and sleep from twelve or one to eight without intermission.

We expect to get off early tomorrow morning, and Mr. Rose is still a little uncertain as to which route to take. It is longer to go by way of Albany, but the roads are supposed to be better. However, he thinks if we have no rain today he may choose the shorter way by Watkins Glen. So you see it is impossible to tell you where or in what direction to follow us in your thoughts. But I will mail you a letter tomorrow before leaving and write from our first days destination wherever that may be. But hours are so uncertain in a motor. Should you fail to hear don't be uneasy for I solemnly promise to let you here if *anything* goes wrong—either by telephone or telegraph. Goodbye my Sweetheart. Please keep well.

Always your own   Edith

ALS (WP, DLC).
1 Margaret Wilson to EBG, Aug. 16, 1915, printed as an Enclosure with WW to EBG, Aug. 20, 1915 (second letter of that date).
2 Unidentified.

To Robert Lansing

My dear Mr. Secretary: The White House August 19, 1915
Thank you sincerely for your opinion under date of August eighteenth about the suggestions submitted to you in a letter from

Mr. Oswald G. Villard which you were kind enough to forward to me at Cornish.[1] I need only say that I entirely agree with the conclusions you have yourself arrived at.

Cordially and sincerely yours,   Woodrow Wilson

TLS (WP, DLC).

[1] See RL to WW, Aug. 6, 1915 (second letter of that date), n. 1.

To Lindley Miller Garrison

My dear Mr. Secretary: [The White House] August 19, 1915

I have your letter of the seventeenth in reply to mine of the day before. You always have such good reasons to give for your opinions that I invariably find it difficult to disagree with you, and yet in this instance I do disagree. I think the method of preparedness is something which the country is not prepared to discuss. The demand for reasonable preparedness is clear enough and our own judgments go with it. We are not being driven, but are going of our own accord. It seems to me a very serious matter that there should be leakages of any kind in the War Department with regard to official information, but if that is inevitable, we must endure it and act upon our best judgment notwithstanding. My own judgment is that it is not the best way to go about any difficult job to try our suggestions out before public opinion of their practical and professional side.

That is the reason I took the liberty of suggesting to you in the letter that followed mine of the sixteenth that you send me a different sort of memorandum. I am anxious to get the whole thing onto a very definite basis as soon as possible and to embody it in concrete plan, not only, but also in definite estimates.

With warm regard,

Cordially and faithfully yours,   Woodrow Wilson

TLS (Letterpress Books, WP, DLC).

To William Gibbs McAdoo, with Enclosure

My dear Mac: The White House August 19, 1915

Here is a letter which I think you will be interested to read. It is from Judge Chambers, a very careful and moderate man. I send it with this suggestion, that if you have any way of doing so, it might be well to investigate the facts and whereabouts and the control of the storage of these materials.

Everything is going very quietly here. I am of necessity very lonely but I am not repining, and my thoughts constantly travel to you dear ones in Maine. Give my darling Nellie my warmest love. I hope that the baby is now entirely out of the woods.

In haste   Affectionately yours,   Woodrow Wilson

TLS (W. G. McAdoo Papers, DLC).

E N C L O S U R E

From William Lea Chambers

My dear Mr. President,   Atlantic City, N. J. Aug 17th, 1915

It seems to me that a very dangerous thing may be developing, & if so it would be wise for the Government to know just what is going on.

While the exports of war munitions & accessories are on a large scale, they do not seem to me to be nearly so large as the output by the factories, unless we are greatly mistaken in what we hear of the magnitude of the contracts. It is undoubtedly the case that none of the contracts for German–Austrian–Turkish munitions is being complied with to the point of shipment. What is becoming of these products? Are they (as well may be of some for the Entente Allies) being stored in reserve in this country? And for what reason (if true) are they being so held? We are informed that there [are] 2,500,000 unnaturalized Germanic men of more or less military training in the United States. There are probably an equal number of non Germanic unnaturalized foreigners on our soil. Have we police and Army forces sufficient to adequately control these 5,000,000 men in racial strifes in case war materials are accessible to them? If the Germanic Allies should succeed in the present European conflict, either by conquest or peace negotiations, is it beyond conjecture that they might seize the opportunity of perfect preparedness at home, & the situation that might exist in our own midst to bring the war to our shores?

I appreciate the fact that this letter raises questions that you would not discuss, at any rate, in correspondence, but as a citizen having the highest interest of our country at heart, and in the sincerest loyalty to you and your administration (without parallel in our history) I have felt that I was privileged to communicate my thoughts. My wife,[1] who is an invalid here, has improved sufficiently to be taken home and I am here temporarily for that purpose, and expect to be in my office not later than Monday next.

With great respect,   Very Sincerely   W. L. Chambers

ALS (W. G. McAdoo Papers, DLC).
[1] Laura Ligon Clopton Chambers.

From Lindley Miller Garrison

My dear Mr President: Seabright N. J Aug 19, 1915.

Yours of Aug 18th received.

My initial instructions to the War College were to prepare the desired data as quickly as possible, and I have today sent instructions to let nothing stand in the way of a speedy report thereon.

Just so soon as I can do so I will prepare and present the statement to you. I am gratified to learn that the general idea interests you and seems to you to be feasible.

It is hard to conceive a more difficult question to solve than this one, which has never been properly treated at all.

If we could lay down permanent lines along which real advance could be made we will have achieved something really worth while.   Sincerely yours   Lindley M. Garrison

ALS (WP, DLC).

Emily Greene Balch to Jane Addams

Dedham [Mass.]

Dear Miss Addams,   Thursday afternoon [Aug. 19, 1915]

I *am* so sorry to hear of your bronchitis. Maine is a bad place for that. I trust that you are not seriously ill and that you will soon be well again.

My two letters of Tuesday probably reached you two days ago. I have just got back from my trip to Washington—and my previous letter will have explained how it happened that I went after your telegram suggesting postponement—and I will report on that.

Wilson was very nice and talked with me about an hour. He said definitely that he would not wait to be asked to mediate, if he saw any opportunity to be of use he would take it. This was a comfort as I had feared that he really meant to stand aside.

This is what stands out most positively to my mind from the interview. Most of it went in my report of course.

Speaking of a conference of neutral governments I said that you now felt differently towards this plan, that your mind turned toward an unofficial body. He said that he had heard so and that when you and Miss Wald[1] were with him Miss Wald had wanted you to develope this point but that you had preferred to merely give your report. I can not report even approximately accurately, but it was something like this: With regard to an unofficial body he spoke of some of those who [would] be the natural persons to be on such a body being perhaps not quite well fitted to serve successfully. The out and out pacifist, seeking a solution in terms of right could not understand sympathetically and deal with those who came at the problem from the point of view of military advantage (This is my [memory] roughly approximated to his sense). I asked him whether he would be willing to name those he alluded to. He replied by instancing Pres. Eliot: he had the greatest admiration personally for Pres. Eliot but he could not accept anything as "amoral."

I told him about Dr. Jacobs[2] coming. He said he could not see a foreigner. "What, not a neutral, Col. House had seemed to think there would be no difficulty." He had had unfortunate experiences, newspapers misrepresented any such interview, it was not as if he could see anyone privately. She could tell everything to one of us who could tell it to him (So he implied this sort of interview would be given, at least I think he definitely implied telling not writing) I asked if it would be easier if the interview were nominally with one of us and if nominally Dr. Jacobs just came along. He finally did say that he had not given a final answer and that he would consider it further.

I wonder if it would have been better if my interview had been postponed. I feel such a babe in judgment in all these things.

I am writing Mrs. Catt[3] that I will go on to meet Dr. Jacobs unless you propose some other plan. I told her about what Wilson said and begged her not to let Dr. Jacobs get into the papers if this could be avoided without making a mystery of her arrival which would be the worst of all. I think if she is not known to the papers it will make it easier to get her in to Wilson.

I left memoranda[4] with Wilson as you suggested and he seemed to like to have them. I did not include any written statement of Wallenberg's statement.[5] I also gave him the Survey reprint of the Carnegie Hall speech[6] and offered him Miss Paget's "Peace with Honour"[7] but he had the latter. When he was saying how reporters always gave things wrong I took the opportunity to slip in remarks about the "dope" embroglio,[8] saying how absolutely within the bounds of your information, and how guarded, your statement had been. He seemed very sympathetic and comprehending.

He told me what he would like me to say to the reporters about my interview with him, "not that that would prevent their saying what they liked"

I had begun the interview by asking how many minutes I had and he set no limit. At last he obviously closed the interview. Do you know whether this implies that I had stayed too long? I had many qualms after the interview as to my manners, and my management of the golden moments but that way madness lies so I won't worry.

I hope you can excuse my unsuitable paper and difficult hand writing. As to the first I am away from home and out of reach of supplies, as to the latter I am trying though you may not think it.

Will you give my kindest remembrances to Miss Smith;[9] and to Miss Wald and you, you know that I am always

gratefully and affectionately   Emily G. Balch.

ALS (J. Addams Papers, PSC).

[1] Lillian D. Wald.

[2] Aletta Henriette Jacobs, Dutch suffragist and peace leader. She had issued the call for the International Congress of Women at The Hague and subsequently accompanied Jane Addams on her visits to the capitals of belligerent nations. She was also noted as the first woman physician in the Netherlands and as the founder of the first birth control clinic in the world—in Amsterdam —in 1878.

[3] Carrie Clinton Lane Chapman Catt, long-time leader of the woman suffrage movement in the United States, who was also active in the peace movement.

[4] These memoranda are filed at August 18, 1915, WP, DLC. They include: (1) "Proposal for a Conference of Neutral Governments. Extracts from the report of the delegates interviews with the Governments," T memorandum. These extracts summarized the reactions of the foreign ministers of Great Britain, Germany, Austria-Hungary, France, Belgium, and Russia to the proposed conference. All were noncommittal, although none rejected the idea outright. (2) Emily G. Balch to [Jane Addams, July 3, 1915], T draft LS. Miss Balch summarized informally the results of her delegation's interviews with various high officials in Denmark, Norway, Sweden, Russia, and the Netherlands. The Swedish Foreign Minister was receptive (see n. 5 below), the others noncommittal. (3) "Recommendations as to Conference," T memorandum. The first three recommendations were that the conference be small, that it begin immediately, and that it be "continuous." The final "recommendation" was a list of eight reasons or pretexts which the President of the United States might use for calling a conference at this time. (4) "Scope of Action," T memorandum. This was still another, more general, justification for the calling of a conference. (5) T lists of officials called upon or consulted.

[5] Knut Agathon Wallenberg, Swedish Minister of Foreign Affairs. Actually, the letter from Emily G. Balch to Jane Addams, July 3, 1915 (cited in n. 4 above) did include a summary of Wallenberg's statements during his interviews with the Balch delegation. She commented on the first interview as follows: "The case appears to be that he (Wallenberg) desires to have the conference, when peace comes to be made, held in Stockholm and that he would be glad to play a role in all this. . . . He finally said that he would be willing to take the initiative in regard to a neutral conference if he had sufficient evidence that it would be 'not unacceptable' to the belligerents. We pressed the question of what would be sufficient evidence and got him to say that if 'a lady for instance' brought a little 'billet' from the chief representative of both sides that would be enough." At a second interview some days later, Wallenberg was more cautious: "He said now that he had said he would be willing to act if we brought evidence that the belligerents asked him to but on our stating our remembrance of it . . . he tacitly admitted our version."

[6] This was a reprint of Jane Addams, "The Revolt Against War," The Survey, XXXIV (July 17, 1915), 355-59. This was a stenographic transcript of her speech at Carnegie Hall on July 9, in which she discussed the results of her travels to European capitals in search of peace.

[7] Vernon Lee [Violet Paget], Peace with Honour: Controversial Notes on the Settlement ([London], 1915). This pamphlet was one of numerous anti-war publications during this period by this prolific author, better known for her literary studies and fiction.

[8] In her Carnegie Hall speech, Jane Addams included the following remarks: "And the young men in these various countries say of the bayonet charges: 'That is what we cannot think of.' We heard in all countries similar statements in regard to the necessity for the use of stimulants before men would engage in

bayonet charges—that they have a regular formula in Germany, that they give them rum in England and absinthe in France; that they all have to give them the 'dope' before the bayonet charge is possible" (Jane Addams, *op. cit.*, p. 359). These offhand comments stirred up a furor in newspapers across the country and produced many embittered replies, notably from the well-known war correspondent, Richard Harding Davis, accusing Miss Addams of wantonly attacking the courage and patriotism of those who had died for their countries. See Allen F. Davis, *American Heroine: The Life and Legend of Jane Addams* (New York, 1973), pp. 226-31.

9 Mary Rozet Smith, a close friend of Jane Addams.

Two Letters to Edith Bolling Galt

[The White House] 19 Aug. [1915]

The point of all this[1] is that the British government tries to justify itself in intercepting our trade with the Scandinavian Countries (which has enormously increased since the war began) on the ground (and no doubt they are right) that is [it] was in effect trade with Germany *through* these countries. We countered by asking whether British merchants were not doing the same thing. This is the answer. It does not at all cover the question whether we have not a *right* to ship to Germany through neutral ports.   W.

ALI (WP, DLC).

1 The enclosure is missing in WP, DLC, but it was in WHP to RL, Aug. 16, 1915, *FR-WWS 1915*, pp. 511-15. This memorandum from Sir Edward Grey reported on British and American exports to Holland, Denmark, Sweden, Norway, and Italy during the first four months of 1915, as compared with such exports during the first four months of 1914. It pointed out that, while British exports had increased slightly, American exports had grown immensely—600 per cent in the case of cotton, for example, and 100 per cent on an average.

[The White House] Thursday,

My sweet, my precious Darling,   3.15 P.M. 19 August, 1915

My heart aches with sympathy for you. If I could only take you in my arms and tell you so, it would all be so much easier for both of us! I have just read Rolfe's letter about the Boyds,—and would have known, if your letter had not shown me, what effect it must have had on you, to whom everything in the record is of course especially abhorrent. There is nothing to do, as you say, but to hope that he will prove better than his kind, and, then, if the apparently inevitable happens to poor Elizabeth in the future, of utter disillusionment and unhappiness, to go to her aid to the utmost in whatever way the circumstances may permit. Neither we nor her parents can think for a moment of abandoning her to her fate and if, too late, (i.e. after her marriage) she comes to herself and will *let* us help her, we must go to her, with love and forgiveness, and do for her what we would do for our own. Ah, my Sweetheart, how plainly your pain and mortification are written in these few lines of your letter which are so restrained and reticent as to be better evidence of your wound and its kind than any outpouring could have been; and my heart is full of it all, as if it were happening to my very own—as indeed it is. When *you* suffer the suffering is doubled for me, for the one thing that is most distressing to me is that you should be given pain. And I know how keen this pain is, because I know your nature so well,—its purity, its quick, instinctive revulsion against anything unclean or debased, its aloofness from anything that could demean. I honour you so, and quiver as you do under anything that might make you feel that you or yours had been touched with any sort of dishonour. The whole thing is simply tragical; but, my Darling, my noble Darling, it is just in the presence of tragedy that we must show our strength. Nothing can touch us that we do not do ourselves, and our duty is always love and sympathy and tender pity. It is touching how Rolfe turns to you in loving admiration and dependence, as his tower of strength, who will understand and of course *help.* I can understand his feeling and his confidence there,—for I do the same. You are now *my* help-mate, God be praised! I have strength to give as well as to ask, my Darling, I hope and believe, and I am particularly happy that I have been sent to you to help at this very time, when love and comprehension is the very help you need. You have given me *every*thing that I need, and it is a sweet privilege to be able to give you what you need. There is a sense, my precious Edith, in which I am glad that, if such things must happen to you, they should happen at this time, when I can have the joy of sharing them, and the *pride,*—for I am proud to be partner with you. And, Sweetheart, don't let the thing look to you more tragical than it is. After all, what really matters is what sort of man this particular Boyd turns out to be. If he proves himself straight and honorable and makes Elizabeth happy, I, for my part, think that the rest is a matter we can almost forget. It is *her* fortunes we are interested in; and I cannot help conjecturing that what Rolfe says of the man's antecedents and connections rests largely upon rumour and may come from hostile, or, to say the least, unsympathetic sources. It would be bad enough at best to have anyone we love marry into any Central American family, because there is the presumption that the blood is not unmixed; but *proof* of that seems to be lacking in this case, as I read and interpret Rolfe's letter; and, even if it be so, we must not turn away from and abandon the girl, who is of *our* blood. That is the fixed rule of love, as I read life; and there may be a great many ways in which we can help. It is hard,—it is almost intolerably hard,—to be separated from you at moments when you are disturbed and unhappy. You *need* me, that's enough to make it almost impossible for me to stay away from you. It would be such a happiness to take some of the strain off of my Darling's heart by making her feel, as I held her close, so close, to my heart, that *nothing* hurt *too* much that we could share and go through and think out *together*. I think that at such times, when I realize your need, I also realize my love for you as I do not and cannot at other times. *Then* I know how truly and entirely you have become a part of me, your interests my interests, your feelings mine, all the little shades of your thought mine, too, and my heart utterly yours, with a love that escapes all measure. There is a sense in which a special *happiness* comes to me: for nothing makes me so happy as a sense of *union with you*! Ah, my Beloved, how complete, how sweet, how satisfying and happy it all is! I am only sad that I must write it instead of speaking it, in tones that would really interpret it, into your own dear ears and sweet lips.

6.05 P.M.

I have been out for a ride, Dearest, and return, with such eagerness, to resume my talk with you. When I feel you are in special need of me I simply cannot keep away from you.

I think that Rolfe's head has cleared a great deal since he wrote those excited letters we read at Harlakenden. What he says about the business outlook at Panama is, I think, perfectly true. I doubt whether it would be worth the while of an ambitious man to stay there with a view to a career. When the bank is fully established (and that seems already practically accomplished, or, at any rate, will be by Autumn), it will hardly be worth while staying with it longer, at least with a view to enhancing the reputation deservedly gained in giving it so quick and successful a start. I am going to work with the doctor very earnestly to try and realize Rolfe's hope about the Baltimore bank. If that comes to nothing, I shall inquire whether there is any possibility of getting him into the Treasury Department as a bank examiner or anything of that sort. I only wish I could work directly in the matter of the Baltimore bank, instead of indirectly. In the other matter I shall not hesitate to act directly. Fortunately Rolfe is not *known* to be my brother-in-heart and I am free to work for him! And what a pleasure it will be if I can find something and be the means of his release. I've made his affairs my own,—and am the happier for it—would be made deeply happy by it, if only he were not himself unhappy,—because think what it means! It means that you are my very own and that he is my brother! I wonder if you really *know* what deep down delight such thoughts give me. And I love to help all the more because you are strong, not weak. They all depend on you and take your strength and capacity for granted (how proud of you that makes me!). I am merely adding my strength to yours, for the honour of the association and the sweet meaning of it. Ah, Sweetheart, I get more from the wonderful partnership than you do!

Not to be outdone by my lovely other half (it seems to me as if *all* that I cared for lives in you) and to feel that I am in the fashion, *I* am starting on an automobile trip to-morrow morning. I am going to motor over to Philadelphia and back, to pay my promised visit to de Schweinitz, my oculist. The doctor (and of course my keepers) will go with me. We are planning to take breakfast a little after six and start at seven, for we guess that the ride over there and back will take eight or ten hours. The weather is fine and it will be incomparably less hot and fatiguing to take the journey that way than to go in one of those superheated steel railway coaches. I am going in that way for another reason, too. I want more time to think about my Darling. I shall dream as I go. It will please me all the day through to think that I am having experiences similar to yours and am spending the day as you are spending it,—and that we are speeding *towards* one another at least half the day, though we cannot meet. You speak of the comradeship of heart my letters give you, dear little girl. It *is* infinitely sweet, isn't it, to keep close company with one another's thoughts and hopes, and emotions even, in spite of our enemy, Space,—to feel that we can defy circumstance, in a way, and keep close to one another in spite of every obstacle,—just because we are absolutely one in heart and purpose and desire? Love is the only sovereign thing in the world; and we do not have to debate, as the A.B.C. men do, where *this* sovereignty is lodged! We know. We live under a sovereign whose supreme authority we rejoice to acknowledge. Only while he lives and reigns can we live our full life and live it freely and in complete happiness.

8 P.M.

Here I am again, back to continue my little chat with you, and, oh, so *glad* to be back!

Apparently the Haitian congress did *not* adjourn on the 17th. If it did, we have had no news of its adjournment. The new president of the republic,[1]—a man chosen with our approval and therefore in a sense our man,—said when the text of the proposed

[1] Dartiguenave.

treaty was presented to him that he would expedite its ratification as much as possible, and that is the last we have heard. I was talking about it with Lansing over the telephone this afternoon and he does not know any more about it than that. He is wondering, as I am, why we have heard nothing further. That no report of the proposal of the treaty has come to the newspapers from Port au Prince would seem to be a convincing indication that the attention of the world is so engrossed with other things that what happens in Haiti may pass without comment, even if reported at all.

This afternoon has brought the news of the torpedoing of the White Star liner *Arabic* on her way *out* from Liverpool by a German submarine, without warning, and her sinking within ten or eleven minutes.[2] There are said to have been Americans on board of her and it seems that not all on board were saved;—but the facts will all be known and printed long before this reaches you, so I need not even speculate as to whether any of the American passengers were lost or not,—and, after all, that may not prove to be an essential detail in any case. If they were on board and no opportunity was given for them to escape before the torpedo was fired at the vessel, this would appear to be what we told Germany we should regard as "a deliberately unfriendly act," knowing the significance of the words we used. You may easily imagine, therefore, my precious One, my sweet Counsellor, what sober forebodings are in my mind to-night. As always, I am holding my mind off from decisions until I can know what actually happened, but meantime the news plainly means something very serious for this dear country we love. It is not likely, as you will see, that, with this development, I shall be free to leave Washington and be in Cornish for dear Jessie's birthday, the 28th. But that is a small matter. I did not want to go, except to please you and gratify my dear little daughter. I never want to go back to Harlakenden until I can take or find you there again. The last time I went—the only times I have gone—there this summer you were there. After you left the place was still full of you, for me. To go back now and not find you there, and know that you were not even expected, would be a very sad experience for me. I can't undertake it for my own sake, and I cannot believe that, feeling as I do, it would do me any good or afford me any refreshment. If I go it will be only because my Lady makes a point of it and commands me and because Jessie might not understand. But my Sweetheart will not order me away from my duty here. Certainly the Germans are blood-mad. You notice the *Arabic* was bound *out* from Liverpool.

2 About this torpedoing, see Link, *Struggle for Neutrality*, p. 565.

There can be no plea of destroying arms and ammunition that were intended to be used against sacred German lives. It is just an act of wanton disregard of international law and of brutal defiance of the opinion and power of the United States. Ah, my Darling, my precious Edith, you are now, if that were possible, more necessary, more indispensable to me than ever. As the stress and the responsibility increase, with the seriousness of the situation in Europe and the world, your love and sympathy and counsel become more and more sweet and satisfying and vital to me. By 'vital' I mean necessary to my *life*. And the glorious thing about it is that I *know* that I can absolutely *count* on you for all the inestimable things a noble woman can give by means of her love and companionship and tender devotion. The more perplexing the task, the harder the duty, the richer I feel, and the stronger, because *you* are with me; your love will increase with my need; your eagerness to be with me and sustain me by the utmost gifts of love will respond more and more generously as my calls for you grow more and more earnest; and there is *nothing* that your loyalty will withhold. I could almost stand up and shout with the sense of strength and adequacy and solemn joy that gives me. You, *you*, my incomparable Darling, are *mine*, and nothing else really matters. Oh, how I love you! You are so splendid, so lovely, so sufficient!

Friday 8.10 P.M. 20 Aug., '15

Our motor trip came off, but not exactly as planned! Burlasque, the only driver here now, is a feather-headed person (not that Robinson would be much more *intelligent*) had not taken the least pains to study out the way to get *through* Baltimore and the other big places we had to pass through, and Murphy's attempts to direct him only made matters worse, so that we took an hour and a half longer to reach Philadelphia than we ought to have taken. I wanted very much to be back here not later than eight o'clock; we therefore changed our plans and came back by train, reaching here by 6.40. But the *way* we did everything was out of the ordinary, very much annoyed the secret service men, and constituted the day quite a spree. The oculist pronounced my good eye as in *splendid* condition and its powers of vision even *above* the normal, and said that the bad eye was successfully holding it's own; so that you need give yourself no anxiety on the score of my *eyes*, my precious One. After my consultation with him we went to lunch on the roof of the Bellevue-Stratford,—too late, alas! to mix with many people (it was quite two o'clock), but not too late to see a good many of them and to have escaped from my sacred isolation. The roof of the Bellevue-Stratford is a delightful place on a warm afternoon, and the lunch we had was very good indeed. Meantime, while I was with Dr. de Schweinitz, Dr. Grayson had, at my request, gone down and secured accommodations for us on the ordinary parlour car attached to the 3.30 train for Washington,—a "drawing room," and chairs for the secret service men,—just what I have wanted to do again and again instead of making a stupid, lonely trip in one of those tiresome special cars and paying the railway company an iniquitous price for the privilege. We finished lunch in time to take a walk down Walnut Street and up Chestnut Street before our train was to start. That was not a very pleasant move, as it turned out, for practically everybody on both streets that looked at us recognized me, and before we reached the railway station we were being followed by several hundred people and escorted by a mounted policeman. The doctor overheard a very funny conversation. "What's all this?" asked a big Irishman of some one who was following in our wake. "It's the President," he was told. "The President of what?" "Of the United States, you damned fool." ["]Oh, the hell you say, is *that* so!" The journey back was comfortable and I felt more normal and more like myself, the real W.W., than I've felt on any journey since the 4th of March, 1913. When we reached Washington there was no car waiting for us, of course, for we had left both the landaulette and the secret service car in Philadelphia to find their way back as they went. So we took a "taxi" with glee and completed a day of freedom as it should have been completed! Our cars will get back some time between ten and eleven to-night, I dare say. I am tired, but not too tired to enjoy a chat with you. Shall I ever be too tired for that?

All day long, my precious Sweetheart, my thoughts have dwelt on you and on *The Arabic*, on you even when they were most concentrated on the *Arabic*,—for I think of all public questions—and of all others, too,—now with my hand on yours, as we used to sit on the West Porch at Harlakenden, and seem always to be thinking *with* you, so that you are always present and I am conscious of your sympathy and help whatever my thoughts may be doing. You may imagine, therefore, how blank I felt when I found that no letter had come from you to-day,—not even a belated one! The faithful Hoover, whom I shall always love and value as a personal friend, went down to the Post Office after all the deliveries had been made, but there was nothing there. He is going down again, bless him, and will report again about ten o'clock to-night whether the 9.30 mail from New York has brought me what my heart waits for. It is the first time I have had to go without a letter from my generous Darling, and I must admit I am very blue. It was a most inopportune day for such a disappointment (though I know it cannot have been your fault or neglect, my dear little girl) for it has been a day of special anxiety, of course, in the presence of the apparently "deliberately unfriendly act" of Germany, in sending the *Arabic* to the bottom, and the likelihood that that act has brought us to the final parting of the ways. It was as if I had taken my hand from yours for a moment, to turn a page—a page with the shadow of war upon it—and that when I had sought it again and looked to get the reassurance in your dear eyes you were not there! Besides,—and this disturbs me deeply,—the letter I got yesterday closed hastily and with the shadow of that letter from Panama on it and I cannot but fear that my Darling hesitated to write while the depression of that was upon her, for fear of conveying the pain of it to me! No, no! that cannot be it! She would know how that would hurt me,— holding me away when she most needed me. The letter will come! This is the very time when I most belong to you, my darling Edith. I never before felt quite so intimately identified with you, or more happy in the identification,—more thankful that you had come to me in season to let me share and help. We shall work *some*thing out of this sorrow that will make us know and love each other better still. The only thing that could make it a tragedy for us would be *not* to share it! And you will have something happy to tell your dear Mother and sister as well as this sad story of Elizabeth's tragical blunder! I am *so* glad about that!

Your hand is in mine again now; your dear eyes have cleared and have loving counsel and intimate comradeship in them, and I return to talk of the *Arabic* again. I spoke just now of the shadow of *war* being on the page I was turning, but I must reassure you. That is not *necessarily* so. There are intermediate courses to pursue, if the course is left to our choosing. We can recall Gerard and give Bernstorff his passports, and note the effect of such a breaking off of all dealings with Germany before we go further. In that case *Germany* might declare war and the guidance of our policy be taken out of our hands. Bernstorff will probably, quite apart from this affair, have to be asked for explanations of these matters which have been appearing in *The World*, and *they* may lead to our requesting that he be withdrawn. After breaking off diplomatic relations, if we wished to go further, probably the next step would be to call a conference of neutrals, not to do what Miss Addams and Miss Balch suggested (though it could do what it pleased when once it was constituted), but to consider the present treatment of neutrals by *both* sides in the

war and concert some action, to be taken either severally or
jointly, calculated to make neutral rights more secure. The one
thing that is clear, or, rather, the two things that are clear are
that the people of this country rely upon me to keep them out of
war and that the worst worst [sic] thing that could possibly happen *to the world* would be for the United States to be drawn
actively into this contest,—to become one of the belligerents and
lose all chance of moderating the results of the war by her counsel as an outsider.

I am sending you, in the big envelope, a letter from Lansing[3]
which shows that there are some as yet undetermined facts in this
case of the *Arabic* which *may* be of capital importance as bearing
upon what ought to be done,—which must largely enter into the
determination of the real character of the act. The letter states
the whole case very much as it lies in my own mind at this time,
with the information we have.

Did you notice in the papers the interesting item which said
that so many men were volunteering for enlistment as marines
that the Navy Department could not accept all of them, and that
it was because of the things the marines were being called upon
to do down in Haiti? It would look, from that, as if it were not
probable that we should lack for volunteers if more serious things
should happen.—But God forbid!

Sat. morn., 21 Aug.

I hope my precious Darling is still asleep after her fatiguing
ride yesterday, and that she will not wake up until she is really
refreshed. It must have been a *very* fatiguing ride, if you did go,
as planned all the way to Albany. It is not yet seven o'clock. I will
not say Good morning, for fear I should wake her tempted as I am
to kiss her on the eyelids and lips and make her open those wonderful eyes and look, before she sees anything else to-day, into my
eyes to see the utter love and trust and happiness there. I will
only sit quietly by her without touching her or making any stir,—
as I used to do in the morning room at Harlakenden,—and *think*
my love of her, drink deep of the thoughts of her sweetness and
of all that she has brought me to make *my* spirit steady at least,
and *my* vision serene and clear, in the midst of this perplexed
world of bitter strifes and hatreds. Outside it is raining. The
morning is dark and bleak and without any light of promise in
the sky. But within the room, so long as my Beloved is by me,
there is the sweet light of love which makes it bright and the air
is full of every comforting influence. There is no uneasiness in my

3 RL to WW, Aug. 20, 1915.

heart, except that the letter did not come at all yesterday. Hoover
came in at about half after ten last night with a look on his kind
face which told me of my disappointment before he spoke; and
my fear is that my Darling is not well. I can't ask her till she
wakes, and her face is for the moment hidden. How sweet it is
to sit here and think of what has come to me within the little
space of time that has gone by since the fourth of May,—"little
space of time"! What more could have been crowded into a long
year? That is the time within which the sinister effects of the
war on the United States have been disclosed and the questions—
of life and honour—thrust upon us which it is my grievous duty
to decide. My Darling came to me as a gift from Heaven. I would
have grown old in these few weeks without her. She has put
peace and joy and unconquerable strength into my heart and
made life seem to me as if it had but happily begun. And so the
grey day has no power over me. *Nothing* has any power to sway
me this way or that except her own dear hand, directed by her
love. I sit here with a sort of sweet enchantment on me. That dear
face, for the moment hidden from me, is the very mirror in
which I see my life written. Its beauty, so noble, so vivid, so individual, so radiant with spirit, is but the external and visable sign
of the great nature that sustains me in all its lovely manifestations. There are no waters ahead too dark or too deep to go
through calmly and with lifted head so long as her hand holds
mine and her eyes give me their message of love and faith. I
wonder if my Love knew that I was beside her last night, too,
trying by sheer force of tender thoughts to give her rest and happiness? Before I slept I went to her and spoke all that was in my
full heart. She *must* have heard. My heart was fairly bursting
with the passion of love and devotion that thrilled and shook it.

8.50 A.M.

Just as I was leaving the study to go to breakfast Hoover came
and handed me the missing letter!—my Darling turned her face
and awoke, and the love-light shone in her eyes and made my
heart secure against the whole day—and whatever it may bring.

I will not try to answer the dear letter (which tells of my
rival—*of course* he loves Mrs. Galt!) now, because no envelope
will consent to contain this letter if I make it any longer,—except
to say that I am perfectly, absolutely well, my Darling. I never
was better or stronger in my life. It is your love has made me so.
I pledge you my word to be absolutely frank about how I feel.
You must not be alarmed if I sometimes get *tired*. I am not playing golf this morning because it is raining *and* because there is

too much to do. It makes me so happy that you are well. *Please*
keep so. I love you with all my heart and am always and
altogether   Your own   Woodrow

ALS (WP, DLC).

From Edith Bolling Galt

[Geneva, N. Y.] Thursday,
My precious One: August 19, 1915 11:30 P.M

This is the last letter from Geneva, and I think we have decided
to take the road direct to Albany and then straight down the
Hudson river, skirting New York and going through Trenton. Of
course this is subject to change but is as near as I now know.
At any rate I will send you daily messengers—but oh! how I shall
miss yours! You have been in my thoughts so constantly today
and tonight when I read of the sinking of another ship I knew
how worried and upset you are. I wish so Dearest I could be
there, at least near enough for you to call me should you need me
—when you have new and constant anxieties. You are "playing
the game" so wonderfully and making everyone believe you are
happy even though we are seperated. And I am trying to do the
same thing. But news like this makes me know how you need me,
and I long to come.

Were I there now, even if you were asleep, I would slip in and
kneel by your bed and put my arms so tenderly 'round you. You
would not wake—just sleep more restfully—and when you did
wake instead of a photograph, you would find me smiling down
at you to say with my eyes I love you. Thank you for sending me
the 2 dear letters from Margaret & Helen. Both of which I thoroughly enjoyed, and appreciate their sweet thoughts of me.

Wasn't it funny *our* letters should have crossed each other,
each carrying a letter of that dear little Margarets? What a bundle
of impulse and affection she is—and how she adores you! 'Twas
like you to take the trouble to copy her letter for me, but I think
I could have read the original—but this was much easier. I am
sending you in this little note from Nell,[1] I told you of, and this
very hearty welcome from Mr. McAdoo that came to me this
afternoon.[2] Wasn't it nice of him to write, and of course what he
says about you makes him my friend for life, and I wrote him so
at once. Please let me have both letters back as I want to keep
them. Surely no one ever had a sweeter welcome than all your
loved ones have given me, and I am so touched by it. And you
should feel Sweetheart that it is the evidence of their overpowering love for you that they welcome a stranger just because it

means your happiness. And I am so proud of their love for you and know how richly you deserve it all.

Oh how I want you—*this minute*

I read most carefully the Report of the Sec. of War and while it is interesting and practical as far as the necessity for greater increase goes, it offers no plan and gives no working basis for cost etc. As you say it seems intended for publication and carefully avoids intimate details of what you need and want, but which, of course, could not be given to the public. It is just about what I expected though that you would have to do all the work. I am so glad too to have the Austrian note. I had read it in the papers and think it quite up to your standard. There was such a nice Editorial about it in yesterday's Post[3] I will try to find it to send to you

We are to get up in the morning early and breakfast at 7:30 so I shall not have time to add a word perhaps, so this is to bring you all my love & tell you that which your heart never fails to interpret. You seem to me more worthy of all love every day, and I am the happiest person in the world because I have won your love. Take tender care of your precious self, and remember how I am missing you and loving you Woodrow—and longing to be safe again in your dear arms.   Goodnight   Edith

ALS (WP, DLC).
    [1] Eleanor W. McAdoo to EBG, Aug. 7 [1915], ALS (WP, DLC).
    [2] It is missing.
    [3] "The Reply to Austria," New York *Evening Post*, Aug. 16, 1915, which declared the American note to be "a complete and crushing rejoinder" to the Austrian protest against American arms shipments to the Allies.

From Robert Lansing

PERSONAL AND CONFIDENTIAL

My dear Mr. President: Washington August 20, 1915.

The torpedoing of the ARABIC has created a crisis of a most serious nature. The vessel was outward bound from Liverpool. There could, therefore, be no pretext that the cargo consisted of munitions of war, which was so strongly urged in the case of the LUSITANIA. From our advices up to the present time the submarine attacked without warning. There were from fifteen to twenty Americans on board. Whether any of these were lost is still uncertain. I do not see, however, that that materially affects the case. From the official accounts received the attack seems to have been wanton and from a military point of view needless.

In the newspaper accounts there are two facts stated, which, if true, may have some bearing on the case.

First, the ARABIC was under convoy up to a few moments before she was attacked. Of course it is not required to visit a ship under convoy. If the convoying vessels were still near enough to offer protection the question arises as to whether the submarine was legally bound to visit the ARABIC, that is, compel her to stop and give time for the persons on board to reach a place of safety. This is discounted, however, by the official statement that rescue ships did not arrive for four hours.

Second: In one statement by a survivor it appears that the persons on the ARABIC were, at the time when the torpedo struck, watching another vessel, the DUNSLEY, which was evidently being attacked by a submarine as her boats were being launched. The important part of the statement is that "the ARABIC was *making toward the* DUNSLEY when the streak of a torpedo" was seen. The point is just this. Can the Germans claim, with any show of reason, that they feared that the ARABIC intended to ram the submarine or drive it away? I don't think that it is a very strong argument but it may be raised in defense of the attack without warning.

Until we have full reports I do not wish to express any opinion, but it seems to me that it would be well to have some plan of action in mind in case no real excuse can be urged and the act of the submarine is shown to have been wanton and inhuman.

I proceed on the assumption that we do not want to enter the war, and that the American people do not wish it but are greatly insnesed [incensed] over this last submarine outrage. Outside of the newspapers everybody I have met, official and civilian alike, takes the position that the declarations in our notes are so strong that we must act, that otherwise it will be said that our words have been mere "bluff," and that it would place the United States in a humiliating position to temporize.

It is the attitude of the public mind which makes the situation especially difficult, but I do not think that it can be ignored without inviting widespread criticism. To satisfy public opinion something must be done at once to show the intense earnestness of the Government to maintain the rights of Americans and to show that we view the situation as most grave and critical. Probably the easiest way to do this would be to send out notice for an immediate meeting of the Cabinet and to let it be known that the cabinet is summoned to consider this case. I believe that would convey to the public the impression desired, and would not have a bad effect on the German Government.

Meanwhile the possible course of action could be carefully considered and a definite policy determined in case the official reports confirm the newspaper accounts.

Faithfully yours,   Robert Lansing.

TLS (WP, DLC).

From Thomas Watt Gregory

My dear Mr. President: Washington, D. C. August 20, 1915.

I acknowledge receipt of yours of the 18th enclosing copy of a letter written to you by Austin Flint Denny from Indianapolis, Indiana, and asking whether it affords ground for any action or investigation on our part. I have read it carefully, and discussed it with the Chief of the Bureau of Investigation of this Department.[1]

The letter is of an extremely general character and does not give the name of the individual who made to him the rather imprudent remarks set out in the letter. The name of the writer of this letter will be sent to our representative at Indianapolis with the request that the name of the individual referred to be given to him and such individual be kept under careful observation.

The general matter referred to in the letter is receiving a great deal of attention on our part. We receive reports from various sections of the country telling of the activities of the societies in question, the number of the members, and anything else which would have a bearing on their purposes. I hardly think the matter requires attention at this time.

You asked me on yesterday the name of the German in New York who had the letter box and who was reported to me as being in charge of the German secret service organization in the United States. I find that the name is Paul Koenig and he is head of the Bureau of Investigation of the Hamburg-American Line. He seems to be closely connected with the attache of the German Embassy[2] to whom I referred on yesterday, and there are a number of indications that he is a confidential representative of the German Government.   Faithfully yours,   T. W. Gregory

TLS (WP, DLC).
[1] Alexander Bruce Bielaski.
[2] Franz von Papen, military attaché, or Karl Boy-Ed, naval attaché.

From Josephus Daniels

Dear Mr. President: Washington. Aug. 20th, 1915.

I am very sorry not to have seen you before getting away for a little trip. Mr. Forster told me Monday you would let me know when you could arrange to see me with Admiral Benson. It is my plan to be away for about ten days. Enclosed you will find the confidential preliminary recommendation from the General Board together with a memorandum prepared by Admiral Benson giving the reasons for each class of craft.[1] If you wish to talk this matter over with Admiral Benson, he will come over at any time.

Of course the Navy Department will be in touch with me all the time so that I can return to Washington at any time you desire. I would not go at all but having been here practically all the summer am a little fagged.

Faithfully yours,   Josephus Daniels

ALS (WP, DLC).
[1] C. J. Badger to JD, July 30, 1915, CCL, and [W. S. Benson], "Memorandum," Aug. 19, 1915, T MS, both in WP, DLC. Badger's letter reported the opinions of the General Board as to the necessary increase in the size of the United States Navy. The board stated as its opinion that the American navy should, no later than the year 1925, be "equal to *the most powerful* maintained by any other nation of the world." To achieve such equality (with the British), the board recommended authorization in 1915 of the following craft: four battle cruisers, four dreadnoughts, six scouts, thirty coast submarines, seven fleet submarines, twenty-eight destroyers, six gunboats, eighteen support vessels, dry-docks, etc., and 11,000 men—at an estimated cost of $285,600,000. Benson's memorandum described in some detail the characteristics of each type of vessel mentioned in Badger's letter.

From the White House Staff

The White House. August 20, 1915

Mr. Harding of the Federal Reserve Board, asks if he may see the President briefly concerning the cotton situation, at the President's convenience.

Monday, 23, at 12. (Lever's committee is not coming)[1]

TL (WP, DLC).
[1] WWhw.

To Edith Bolling Galt

[The White House] 20 Aug. [1915]

It is noticeable that those who are getting the worst of it are willing, and that the rest are not![1]   W.

ALI (WP, DLC).

¹ He had enclosed M. Letcher to RL Aug. 18, 1915, T telegram (WP, DLC), transmitting a message from Francisco Villa, saying that he would accept the "good offices" of the Pan-American conferees in arranging a meeting of all the Mexican factions to discuss the establishment of a provisional government.

To Edith Bolling Galt, with Enclosure

[The White House, c. Aug. 20, 1915]

This *is* a dear letter and it comes straight from her heart. It is just like her, bless her heart.   W.

ALI (WP, DLC).

ENCLOSURE

Margaret Woodrow Wilson to Edith Bolling Galt

Dearest Edith,   Cornish, Aug 16th, 1915.

I've been intending to write to you ever since your two dear letters came, but have failed to do so because of a losing race with my accumulating mail. I thought that if I could ever catch up with my semi-business correspondence I would then have time to write my friends real letters. But I'm afraid that real letter writing is not an American art, because leisure time is not an American treasure. So here goes less of a letter than I meant to write, but it is as full of love as hundreds of words would have been.

We have missed you horribly. Really you have no idea what a large hole you left (now don't say that I'm unkind in my metaphor). Please come and fill it up as soon as you can.

We have been doing the same old things, driving, reading, singing etc. Annie and I have singing contests. She usually wins out on the highest notes but when it comes to being chesty on the low notes, she's not in it with me.

We hated so to see Father go away to terrible heat and strain, but he looked wonderfully well and I'm hoping that the rest will mean much to him. Oh I'm so glad that he has your love to help him and support him in these terrible times! The more I see of other men, no matter how fine and interesting they are, the more I realize what of course I knew before, that he is the greatest man in the world. Isn't it thrilling to think that in this world where there are so many misfits, the greatest person is in the greatest place?

Father's prescription for reading my letters is to lie on your side. Try it.

Wilson with Francis Bowes Sayre and Francis, Jr.

Schenectady - N.Y.   August 3rd 1915

Dearest =

I am at my window here at the

"Edison Hotel" overlooking city streets
and ugly brick houses and trolley
cars — But, instead of looking out, I
am dreaming of a big house in the
centre of green terraces, and tall
pine trees — and wondering if a certain
pair of dear eyes are resting on the
peace and beauty of this loved spot!
    I am wondering if Helen and
Jessie and Frank really started

Mrs. Galt's letter to Wilson of August 3, 1915

on their Journey this morning – and if
your Sister came – In fact I have
held you so in my thoughts that each
minute has been filled with questions
I am longing to have answered –

Oh! Sweetheart there are no locked
drawers – or Suit cases now – but instead
all the gates are flung wide – and
a perfect flood of longing rushes
out to you –

I mailed a letter to "Margaret" last
night at Manchester – about 11 – and
then I got to bed about 12.30 ____

This morning Mr. Rose played golf
with 2 N.york men. and said the

course really was lovely – but Tuesday wet from the reartious rains – We had such at 12:30 so as to get off early – and we had but gone 10 miles before it began to pour – So we had to run slowly – but got it away so early ejected 16 comes on here – arriving got 16 gray so early ejected 16 comes on here – arriving entered halfpen hour ago – The roads are fine most of the way – but very slippery – We are going off pretty early tomorrow – Thinking we might reach Greenally might – but it is 180 miles and if it is raining we were enough to make an easy run on Thurs – any.

I see in the paper this morning his spiene and

About the Q.B.C. Conference and Bread are very nice Editorial agent year Wisdom in inviting this Conversation – and I am longing to know what

New things have come to you since my last happy wave never — I don't believe I ever made you feel
how perfectly happy I was when you would let me share your work — and I think well when it comes back
to me now — in the midst of all the whirring of the machinery, that seemed so complicated as to demand
every part of brain and energy — your voice would turn to me with look on your lips, and whisper the material
sweat in the world — and makes me grow with the business — just nothing could crowd me out of your
thoughts —

I had to stop here to

from that moment now it is nearly I'm and I must get
this across — So matter you saw thing being Mrs. R. said
to me tonight in speaking of you and the girls — She said you
and Samuel so devoted to each other — that she wanted if you should
marry again it would make the girls unhappy — adding
that you were so charming and attractive she never would want to fall
in love with you — but adding I'm in earnest true — but

At a World Series Game with Mrs. Galt in Philadelphia

Robert Lansing

Theobald von Bethmann Hollweg

Well I must run to a lesson. Forgive me for not writing sooner. I'm afraid that you will learn from experience that the only decent correspondent in our family is Father. However I should think that daily letters from him would make up for any lack of any kind in the world.

I love you dear Edith, and I love to be with you.

Affectionately yours,   Margaret W. W.

ALS (WP, DLC).

Two Letters from Edith Bolling Galt

[Geneva, N. Y.] Friday [Aug. 20, 1915] A.M. 7.30

Goodby my Precious One. We expect to get off in an hour & I hope to have your dear letter to take with me. The day is bright & cool, and I am feeling perfectly well. *Hope* you are. With all my love   Your own   E.

8.30 P.S.   Telegram just received.[1] Bless your heart. Long live the Tiger!

ALI (WP, DLC).
[1] It is missing.

My precious One: Albany, N. Y. August 20th, 1915 8 P.M.

I did get your dear letter, as I asked Mr. Rose if we could stop at the Post Office (for it was far too early for the Postman) and I was rewarded by your beloved messenger, which I read as we sped along, and was furious when they would interrupt me to look at the scenery.

I will never be able to tell you how infinitely sweet it was to know you were thinking of me and following me in your thoughts across the country.

As you see we got as far as Albany. And, though it lacks only a few miles of 200 from Geneva, we are not a bit tired, for the roads are wonderful and it is cool enough to be bracing. And we all feel so fit we are going out in serch of amusement as soon as Mrs. Rose finishes her letter. I will take this upstairs with me and finish it after rereading your precious love letter, and will mail it in the morning before leaving. We have just finished dinner and are all at different desks writing.

I am so anxious to know how you feel about the 2 Americans lost on the Arabic

I have thought so much of you today and know this must add to your anxieties. In the Albany paper tonight there is a very sensible Editorial about it, and this is the only comment I have seen.

It contends that being on an enemy ship, Germany could not be held accountable for the lives of Americans, that all the U. S. is responsible for are ships under the stars & stripes, and we can not protect Americans on an enemy ship. Is this true? I know it must worry you to repeat so much of public business to me in your letters, but I do enjoy them so and feel so much more in touch with you, that I can't bear to ask you to stop doing it. But always understand I don't want you to do it if you are very weary.

11:30 P.M.?

I had to stop as Mrs. R. was ready and we went to "Proctors" and saw a very poor vaudeville show—left before it was over—and I enjoyed the walk home in the night air. I have had a hot bath and am now in bed, where I have just finished reading your dear, dear letter.

I wanted so to talk to you tonight. If I had thought it possible to get you without anyone knowing who I was, I would have called you up. But I would not let myself think about it, for I knew it would be indiscreet and your *head* would disapprove it, even if your *heart* thought it nice. But there is a phone right at the foot of my bed, and it gives me a delicious feeling to know that I *could* take the receiver off the hook and actually hear your dear voice speaking to me, *here in this very room*. But I expect you are already asleep, so I must not wake you, though "Main No. 6" is an awful temptation.

I guess it was all the memories that came flooding back this morning when I got your dear telegram signed "Tiger"—it seemed so like last summer. I mean *this* summer—see, how, unconsciously, I let you see how long these weeks have been without you.

I shall think of you when I cross into New Jersey and of all the things you say in regard to your associations with her. I know so little of the state, for though I have been to Atlantic City so often I don't feel that to be representative at all—and can easily imagine what a thorn in the side of good government such a place must be.

We expect to get off by 9 tomorrow & I have no idea where we will stop for the night. But I will surely write you, and we certainly hope to reach Ocean City by Sunday afternoon in time for dinner.

You do not mention going to Cornish next week? Unless the sinking of this ship interferes, you will go, won't you Dearest? For I see from your letters you have felt the heat added to the

anxiety about so many things, and one more week away will do
you lots of good.

Kiss me goodnight my precious One, for I am getting sleepy.
My heart is on my lips and goes out to meet its sovereign Lord.

Your own   Edith

ALS (WP, DLC).

To Robert Lansing

My dear Mr. Secretary,   The White House. 21 August, 1915.

I have your letter about the *Arabic*, and find myself in substantial agreement with it.

I do not think that an immediate summons of the Cabinet
would be wise. We should first know all the facts. So soon as
they are known we ought of course to find the views of our colleagues. Haste in the matter would be likely to give the country
the wrong impression, I fear with regard to our frame of mind.

Faithfully Yours,   W.W.

WWTLI (SDR, RG 59, 841.857 AR 1/89½, DNA).

To Edward Mandell House

Dearest Friend,   The White House 21 August, 1915.

I greatly need your advice what to *do* in view of the sinking of
the *Arabic*, if it turns out to be the simple case it seems. I know
that Lansing will be as desirous as I am to learn what you are
thinking.

Two things are plain to m[e]:

1. The people of this country count on me to keep them out
of the war;

2. It would be a calamity to the world at large if we should
be drawn actively into the conflict and so deprived of all disinterested influence over the settlement.

I am sorry if I have been in any degree a marplot in the Scripps
matter.[1] The truth is that, as Rogers says, Mr. Scripps wanted an
inside place of special confidence and privilege which I thought it
would be fatal to our relations with all other papers to accord
him.

We must write to England, and in very definite terms. Do you
think that there is any chance of our getting them to rescind the
Order in Council and depend altogether upon the contraband list
to carry out their policy of keeping from Germany what she can

use again[s]t the Allies? I am to see Harding on Monday and learn all that he knows to be afoot.

What extraordinary stuff Gerard sends us. I must admit I am not helped by it at all.

With regard to Walter Page, I have this feeling: he is undoubtedly too much affected by the English view of things and needs a bath in American opinion; but is it wise to send for him just now, and is it not, after all, rather useful to have him give us the English view so straight?

I am well, but desperately lonely down here. Your letters come like the visits of a friend.

Affectionately Yours, Woodrow Wilson

WWTLS (E. M. House Papers, CtY).
  1 Wilson here referred to EMH to WW, Aug. 19, 1915, TLS, enclosing W. S. Rogers to EMH, Aug. 16, 1915, TLS, both in WP, DLC. Walter Stowell Rogers, secretary to Charles Richard Crane, briefed House on several attempts during the past year by Edward Wyllis Scripps to place a representative of his newspaper enterprises in or near the White House. In Rogers's opinion, what Scripps had in mind was that this person should be neither a reporter nor a press agent, but rather "be taken in as one of the family and given inside facts," which he would use "to work out plans that would lead to favorable publicity." The matter had come up again at this time because Scripps was considering the establishment of a newspaper in Washington.

To William Gibbs McAdoo

My dear Mac.,   The White House. 21 August, 1915.

That was a terribly confident opinion you fired at me the other day about what I ought to do to Bernstorff. I wish the matter looked as simple as that to me.

And, of course, the Arabic affair has come to put the whole thing, so far as any one of the German representatives in another channel entirely. When we are certain of all the facts in this last performance of the submarines, we shall know comprehensively what course to take.

Thank you very much, my dear fellow, for the decision about the War Fund. I was confident that you did not know just what the need of the State Department was.[1]

I am very lonely down here, and my thoughts constantly travel up to darling Nellie and you up there in Maine, and with my thoughts go deepest love.

Affectionately Yours, Woodrow Wilson

WWTLS (W. G. McAdoo Papers, DLC).
  1 A special appropriation by Congress. McAdoo must have written about it on a separate note and enclosed it in his letter of August 16. The note is missing.

To John Sharp Williams

My dear Senator: The White House August 21, 1915

I think not even the case of the Arabic has given me more disturbed thoughts than your distress over the case of the appointment of young Lee to the Assistant District Attorneyship under Mr. George and I know that you will believe me when I say that the decision I have felt obliged to come to is one which I would not have arrived it [at] if I could have seen any right escape from it.

But, my dear Senator, the only possible living programme upon which I can go in administering the Government is to trust the men whom I have chosen for the headships of the departments. I hold them responsible. Appointments such as this are within the choice of the head of the department himself. The Attorney General assures me that he cannot think that it would be best for the public service to put Mr. Lee in this place and I should be acting contrary to every experience I have had in executive office if I should seek to oblige him to make this appointment. The only conceivable way of maintaining a right relation to my colleagues is to trust their judgment if I hold them responsible for the results.

The case distresses me because it distresses you. I have for you such feelings as for few other men in public life and I know I can depend upon your generous understanding of me to interpret my action justly.

With warmest regard,

Faithfully yours,   Woodrow Wilson

TLS (J. S. Williams Papers, DLC).

To Edith Bolling Galt

[The White House] 21 Aug. [1915]

Obregon is principal Carranza general and a man of some capacity.[1]   W.

ALI (WP, DLC).

[1] He enclosed W. L. Bonney to RL, Aug. 19, 1915, T telegram (WP, DLC), transmitting a message from Álvaro Obregón in reply to the Pan-American conferees. Obregón stated that he had sent their communication, directed to him, to Carranza, who alone had the power to reply. Obregón also took the occasion to suggest that the conferees had "completely over-looked [the] solidarity of our movement" and the "perfect control" exercised by Carranza over the entire Constitutionalist army. If the Latin American republics represented at the conference really wished to assist Mexico, they had only to avoid being misled by false information or "unscrupulous influences" and to allow the Constitutionalists to conclude their work of pacification and the establishment of democratic government "without outside influence."

From Joseph Patrick Tumulty

Dictated by Mr. Tumulty over the telephone.

My dear Governor: Avon, New Jersey, August 21, 1915

I intended to return to Washington immediately upon receipt of the news of the sinking of the Arabic but upon second thought determined to remain here until Sunday afternoon. Realizing the seriousness of the situation, I thought that it would be wise to leave you free. My time here, however, is occupied in considering the issue raised by the sinking of this ship. My mind is clear as to the following:

1. The people are very calm and apparently are unmoved by this new situation. But they have an unfaltering confidence in the President and are willing to follow him wherever he may wish to go.

2. There is no jingoistic sentiment among the people.

3. Radical action is not demanded (by radical action I mean a declaration of war and a severance of all relations with Germany).

4. There is, however, a universal demand for the recall of von Bernstorff and the withdrawal of Gerard. If no radical action is intended, the latter course should follow *very speedily after an ascertainment of all the facts in the matter*. The very heart of action of this kind lies in the speed and the expedition in which it is carried out and done.   J. P. Tumulty   C.L.S.

TL (WP, DLC).

Two Letters from William Gibbs McAdoo

Dear Mr. President: North Haven, Maine, August 21, 1915.

Yours of the 19th just received. I shall immediately do everything I can to investigate the matters referred to in the letter of Judge Chambers. It is extremely difficult to accomplish anything in this direction. It is a very serious question as to what extent the sources of supply have been taken over in this country, but I shall get all the information I can.

I feel very guilty about being away from Washington, and hope I am not causing inconvenience to you, or anyone else, by my absence. I have merely transferred my office to North Haven for the time being, I would return immediately, but I don't like to leave Nell and the children here alone. In any case, we expect to move about the first of September.

It will ease my conscience very much if you will telegraph me on receipt of this and say frankly whether or not you prefer to have me in Washington. I can easily make the necessary arrangements, if you desire it. So don't hesitate to call me back immediately if you think I can be of greater service there.

Nell is as well as can be, and the baby is at last making some real progress. You can imagine how much our anxieties have been relieved thereby. All the other children are well. Our warmest love goes to you. You are always the object of our deerest [dearest] thoughts.   Affectionately yours,   W G McAdoo

TLS (WP, DLC).

Confidential.

Dear Governor: North Haven, Maine August 21, 1915

You know how loath I am always to burden you with Treasury affairs, but matters of such great importance have arisen in connection with the financing of our export trade that you ought to know the facts.

Great Britain is, and always has been, our best customer. Since the war began, her purchases and those of her allies, France, Russia and Italy, have enormously increased. Food products constitute the greater part of these purchases, but war munitions, which as you know embrace not only arms and ammunition, but saddles, horses and mules and a variety of things, are a big item. The high prices for food products have brought great prosperity to our farmers, while the purchases of war munitions have stimulated industry and have set factories going to full capacity throughout the great manufacturing districts, while the reduction of imports and their actual cessation in some cases, have caused new industries to spring up and others to be enlarged. Great prosperity is coming. It is, in large measure, here already. It will be tremendously increased if we can extend reasonable credits to our customers. The balance of trade is so largely in our favor and will grow even larger if trade continues, that we cannot demand payments in gold alone, without eventually exhausting the gold reserves of our best customers, which would ruin their credit and stop their trade with us. They must begin to cut their purchases from us to the lowest limit, unless we extend to them reasonable credits. Our prosperity is dependent on our continued and enlarged foreign trade. To preserve that we must do everything we can to assist our customers to buy.

We have repeatedly declared that it is lawful for our citizens to manufacture and sell to belligerents munitions of war. It is lawful commerce and being lawful is entitled to the same treatment at the hands of our bankers, in financing it, as any other part of our lawful commerce. Acceptances based upon such exportations of goods are just as properly the subject of legitimate bank transactions as if based on non-contraband. We have reaffirmed our position about munitions in our recent note to Austria—clearly and conclusively.

If our national banks are permitted to purchase such acceptances freely it will greatly relieve the situation. We can do so without any danger of rendering "non-liquid" even a small part of our present extraordinary large credit resources. But National Banks will not buy such acceptances freely unless they know that they are eligible for rediscount at Federal Reserve Banks.

We have two strong pro-German members of the Reserve Board—Mess[rs] Miller & Warburg. Miller is even stronger (pro-German) than Warburg. He is a far less reasonable and intelligent man and more difficult to deal with. He and Warburg have always been opposed to our banks buying acceptances or accepting for the exportation of munitions, although they know that it is perfectly lawful for the banks (member as well as Federal Reserve) to do so and Counsel for the Board have so advised. The Board has no power whatever under the Fed. Reserve Act, to discriminate between lawful exports or imports or the acceptances based thereon.

While I was ill and confined to my bed, the Board (Fed. Reserve) on April 2, 1915 adopted "regulation J." on Bankers acceptances. Warburg & Miller skillfully injected into these regulations such restrictions and limitations as to, in effect, render ineligible for re-discount in Federal Reserve Banks, a large part of the acceptances based on munitions exports. I never saw these regulations, as I was too ill at that time to consider business, and the other members of the Board seem to have acted without full realization of the effect of the regulations. These regulations (I mean sub-sections C & F) are clearly ultra vires; they should never have been adopted.[1] Five of us favor repeal or modification but it brings the issue sharply and concretely to the front. Mess Miller and Warburg are insisting that the Administration *define* its position or attitude on the question of financing war munitions. It is not necessary for them to do this, i.e. raise such an

[1] As McAdoo indicates at the beginning of this paragraph, sub-sections C and F of Regulation J, though couched in legalistic language, which made no direct reference to war materials, did have the effect of prohibiting bank acceptances based upon exports of such materials. For the full text of Regulation J, see *Federal Reserve Bulletin*, I (May 1, 1915), 45-46.

issue. If they were thinking of our interests instead of Germany's they would not do it. I believe that their purpose is to embarrass, if possible, the Administration and that it is deliberate. It ought to be sufficient that the Administration has declared exports of munitions lawful commerce and that the Federal Reserve Act clearly makes acceptances based thereon lawful business for National Banks and Federal Reserve banks—leaving the policy of buying or dealing in or creating such acceptances to the Officers & Directors of the Banks—National & Federal Reserve—to determine. I think that Mr. Miller & Mr. Warburg both agree to the soundness of this as a legal proposition, although they have succeeded in imposing the limitation on the Federal Reserve Banks to re-discount the acceptances in question by a skillfully disguised definition of "banker's acceptances"—sub-sections C. & F. of the regulations of April 2, 1915. These sub-sections will have to be rescinded. Gov. Hamlin writes me that both Miller & Warburg have intimated plainly to him "that they would both oppose such rescission." I understand that Warburg has gone so far as to say "that financing of war munitions, although legal in form, violates the spirit of neutrality."

The exchange situation in New York had become so serious recently, that it became necessary to call a hurried meeting of the Federal Reserve Board in New York on Aug. 10, to clear up the question of acceptances by National Banks, which, although a matter for the Comptroller of the Currency to decide, it was important for the Reserve Board to concur in so that National Banks could proceed with the knowledge that acceptances so made or bought by them would be eligible for rediscount by Federal Reserve Banks.

Without knowing that Gov. Hamlin has authorized a call for a meeting at the Federal Reserve Bank I directed that the meeting be called for the Sub-Treasury, my idea being that as the questions upon which the Board was asked to rule were presented by the Federal Reserve Bank of New York and it was interested in the result, it would be better for the Board, which is a Government body, with its headquarters in the Treasury at Washington, to meet in the United States Sub-Treasury in New York instead of in the Bank itself which was seeking a decision of the Board.

I could not remain for the meeting, as you know I had to see House promptly about some very urgent matters.

Miller, Warburg & Harding refused to attend at the Sub-Treasury. Hamlin & Williams had to join them at the Bank to make a quorum.

I attach a report of Mr. Williams on this meeting which is very truthful and dispassionate and I wish you would read it.[2] Hamlin also sent a report but Williams' is, on the whole better because more in detail.

I also attach a letter from Mr. Harding.[3] His quotation from Warburg's letter to him is most interesting. Warburg doesn't want England to buy cotton; prefers a *"valorization scheme,"* rather than put ourselves at "England's mercy"!! He seems to favor our buying up the "war materials" produced in this country. Harding's reply[4] demolishes him. Warburg also complains because Hamlin and Delano conferred with Col. House and thinks he ought to be fully informed, but he doesn't offer to inform the Board of his conversations with Bernstorff and Albert (the chief figure in the World exposures) with each of whom he is very intimate—especially with Albert. I hope you may have time, some time, to read Harding's letters to me & Warburg.

Gov. Hamlin writes me: "Mr. Miller is strongly opposed to any acceptances being issued by National Banks or re-discounted by Federal Reserve Banks involving the exportation of war materials. He puts it rather on the ground of policy than any prohibition in the law." But to get back to the meeting: The Comptroller and the Fed. Res. Board agreed on a satisfactory solution of the acceptance problem for *member* banks but the question is yet to be dealt with for Fed. Res. Banks.

I shall insist on the repeal of the restrictive regulations of April 2, 1915 and I shall refuse to say in response to Miller & Warburg that the administration expressly desires Fed. Reserve Banks to finance exports of war munitions; that it is solely for the Directors & Officers of the Reserve Banks to determine that matter for themselves. This being done our export trade will get substantial relief but not nearly enough.

It is imperative for England to establish a large credit in this country. She will need at least $500,000,000. She cant get this in any way, at the moment, that seems feasible, except by sale of short time Government notes. Here she encounters the obstacle presented by Mr. Bryans letter of Jany 20, 1915 to Senator Stone in which it is stated that "war loans in this country were disapproved because inconsistent with the spirit of neutrality" &c and "this Government has not been advised that any general loans have been made by Foreign Governments in this country since *the President expressed his wish that loans of this charac-*

2 J. Skelton Williams to WGM, Aug. 11, 1915, TCL (WP, DLC).

3 W.P.G. Harding to WGM, Aug. 13, 1915, TCL (WP, DLC).

4 W.P.G. Harding to P. M. Warburg, Aug. 13, 1915, TCL (WP, DLC).

ter should not be made.["] The underscored part is the hardest hurdle of the entire letter. Large banking houses here which have the ability to finance a large loan, will not do so or even attempt to do so, in the face of this declaration. We have tied our hands so that we cannot help ourselves or help our best customers. France & Russia are in the same boat. Each, especially France, needs a large credit here.

The declaration seems to me most illogical and inconsistent. We approve and encourage sales of supplies to England and others but we disapprove the creation by them of credit balances here to finance their lawful and welcome purchases. We must find some way to give them needed credits but there is no way, I fear, unless this declaration can be modified. Maybe the Arabic incident may clarify the situation! I should hate to have to have it modified that way.

Notwithstanding Mr Bryan's letter expressing disapproval of foreign loans the German Government openly issued & sold last Spring through Chanler Bros, Bankers, of Phila. & New York $10,000,000. of its short time bonds. England & her allies could sell a small amount of obligations, perhaps $25,000,000, in the face of your disapproval as expressed in this letter, but it would be fruitless. The problem is so huge that she must go "whole hog" & she cant do that unless our attitude can be modified. Perhaps it could be done, if you decided that it should be done at all, by some hint to bankers, although I dont think that would do. In fact England & her allies will have great difficulty in getting the amount of credit they need here even if our Government is openly friendly. I wish you would think about this so we may discuss it when I see you. To maintain our prosperity, we must finance it. Otherwise it may stop and that would be disastrous.

I haven't the slightest fear that we shall be embarrassed if we extend large credits to foreign Governments to enable them to buy our products. Our credit resources are simply marvellous now. They are easily 5 to 6 billion dollars. We could utilize one billion in financing our foreign trade without inconvenience and with benefit to the country.

I wrote Lansing a brief note yesterday about credits to foreign Governments and suggested that nothing be done to emphasize the position, taken in Mr. Bryan's note until I could have a chance to discuss it with you and him.

My apology for writing at such length is my desire to give a clear idea, if possible, of the problem and the situation in the Reserve Board which has within it mischevous potentialities on account of the attitude of Miller & Warburg.

Later on I may submit to you my correspondence with them about their refusal to attend a lawfully called meeting of the Board in New York. Thus far they have evaded the issue and I am without a direct statement from them of the reasons for their extraordinary and inexcusable action.

Affectionately Yours   W G McAdoo

ALS (WP, DLC).

From Robert Lansing, with Enclosure

My dear Mr. President: Washington August 21, 1915.

I am sending for your information copy of a telegram received from the American Minister at Copenhagen,[1] dated August 19th, concerning the proposed purchase of the Danish West Indies.

I am, my dear Mr. President,

Very faithfully yours,   Robert Lansing

TLS (WP, DLC).
[1] Maurice Francis Egan.

E N C L O S U R E

TELEGRAM FROM AMERICAN MINISTER,
COPENHAGEN, dated
August 19th.

In an interview I had with the Minister for Foreign Affairs[1] regarding the sale of Danish West Indies, he stated that he thought that immediate action would seem strange in time of war, but that personally he believed that the Islands ought to be sold. Minister stated that he had had no opportunity of consulting his colleagues or public opinion, but that an offer, generously made, safeguarding the interests of the inhabitants would be seriously considered.

A mail despatch being forwarded today.

T MS (WP, DLC).
[1] Erik Julius Christian de Scavenius.

To Edith Bolling Galt

[The White House] Saturday,
My precious Darling,   5.10 P.M. 21 Aug., 1915

It is Saturday afternoon. Again the Marine Band is playing to a crowd on the south lawn just outside my windows, and I sit

down to write to my Sweetheart with the strange, subtle excitement thrilling along my nerves that music always creates in me.
I do not know how calmly or sensibly I can talk to you in such
circumstances, for my thoughts are restless at best this afternoon. They are roving abroad in search of you. I do not know
where you are,—somewhere on some highway, speeding along
in an automobile. It is strange how *unsettled* it makes all my
thoughts when you are "on the road." I got to-day, following
close upon the letter that *would* not come yesterday when I so
longed for it, the dear little letter written Thursday night and
the pencilled good-bye of Friday morning, just before you started.
And they were a perfect tonic to me, they were so tender and
sweet and intimate. Do you know, I have a certain index of your
state of mind. In the letters you write when you are disturbed
deeply about anything and are not "seeing straight," there is never
any *explicit* word of love. Until these blessed little notes came
to-day, there had not been for several days. There is everything
else: sweet steadfastness, the *implication* of everything that is
intimate and loyal,—as if you were thinking, not separately from
me, but as part of me. I feel the lovely *constancy* which is part
of your very nature; and all through I catch the sweet under-
tone of love,—and musicians say that to enjoy music you must
listen to and learn to catch the tones not actually produced by
the instruments, but latent in the harmony itself. But there is
throughout a strange sort of—what shall I call it?—*reticence*,
as if your heart held back from *words* of love and practiced a
kind of dumb reserve which pained it as much as it cheated me.
Your letters, when written that way, move me strangely. I know
that you need what I feel helpless to give you in letters,—a love
so personal that it can be conveyed only in person. They make
me feel your love, but they make me long to help you release it.
Do you know, I am inclined to think that, in the letters I write
you, I so constantly put our love in all its phases into words,—
or, at least, try to,—that you have a sense of its being fully expressed, rely on me for the interpretation, and feel yourself
relieved of the responsibility. But, oh, my Darling, what of me,
whose heart is waiting so eagerly for the dear words out of your
own lips that set me free of every real care? Do you think *I* had
better be more reticent, and let you feel the challenge? I do not
know whether I could be or not. My heart seems to need to have
its ardour poured out in words when there is no other medium.
It is too full of love for you to contain it. And I have not forgotten,
my adorable Sweetheart, what you told me,—that you had never
before *written* words of love to any one as you have to me; and

I know how much it means that you have written them to me. When you *do* write them,—and you write them in almost all of your letters—they are the most wonderfully beautiful and expressive words ever written,—the very coinage of your heart. Because your heart is incomparable in the way it loves,—the generosity, the deep, womanly strength and single-heartedness, the fresh, untouched purity and sweetness and yet unstinted ardor of it, its loyalty and its depth,—the beauty of the phrases in which you express it is incomparable, and thrills every fibre of me. Do you wonder that I long for them? They are as poignant as they are unstudied. And so, when the reserve comes upon you and you are silent,—only sweet and constant and steadfast, leaving the transcendent thing that is in both our hearts to implication, to be taken for granted,—I know that there is some obscure pain or trouble in your heart. Your love letters are always also your light-hearted letters. I can feel the gayety and high spirits in them,—can almost see the light dance in your eyes and the fascinating, happy smile that would come if I were there,— perhaps does unconsciously come as you write. And you can imagine my joy, my Beloved, in feeling that your love for me is the cause of your light-heartedness and that I have brought you happiness.

8.20 P.M.

I knew, sweet Love, that when you read of the cruel sinking of the *Arabic*, your first instinctive thought would be of how much and how specially I needed you. And oh, how I *have* needed you and do need you, dear little girl! It would all go so easily, if you were here, for the path is clear enough,—all that hurts and disturbs is the loneliness, the lack of the instant touch of your hand. The Secretary of State and I spent an hour together this afternoon and he agrees with me that the course I outlined to you in my last letter is, substantially, at any rate, the course it will prove wise and necessary for us to take. My need of you is proof of the nature of our love for one another, my precious One. The moment these big things happen I am made keenly aware of just what the companionship of your mind and heart means to me; of how perfectly your thoughts fit into mine, with how sure an instinct, or, rather, an *insight*, you know just the support of ideal and feeling I need. Our love is based on a perfect understanding of one another, not only, but upon something deeper,— upon a real kinship of thought and feeling. And I glory in it so, my Love: for I admire you so profoundly and am so proud to feel that in any essential particulars I *match* you and am your counterpart! The more affairs thicken about us, dear little Lady, the shorter must be the time of our partial separation,—the sooner you must come and be always by my side. I cannot wait long to have my strength perfected when such things as now press upon me are every day added to and multiplied and I must be at my best, not only, but not wear out!

Speaking of public matters, I ought before this to have acknowledged the receipt of the package of papers you returned. They came promptly and intact, and the contents complete. Thank you, Darling, for your care of them and the careful way in which you sent them back. Except for the one or two that do not belong to *my* files, I was perfectly willing that you should keep these papers. If you want any of them, you have only to ask for them and I will send them to you.

In the big envelope I am intending to send you along with this letter I am returning the letters from Nellie and Mac. They are sweet and genuine letters; but just wait until they know you as Margaret does and their welcome will be based on enthusiastic love for you for your own sake. It is sweet of you to say that their attitude towards you is chiefly prompted by their love for me and their wish for my happiness, but you cannot say that of Margaret and Jessie, for I *know* that they love *you* and welcome you for your own sake; and I know that it will not be possible for you to say it long of Nellie and Mac. I know Nellie so thoroughly that I am as certain she will adore you as I am that I do now. You are *her kind*, and her enthusiasm for you will know no bounds; and while you are of her kind you are so different, have so individual a variety of lovliness and of all that is delightful in you, that the attraction will be all the more irresistible. It will be great fun to see you together and to enjoy both of you! I copied what you said in one of your recent letters about the girls and sent it to Jessie to-day, in the letter in which I told her how unlikely it was that I could get up to Cornish for the 28th, and asked her to show it to Margaret (as of course she would) and to send it to Nell. You asked me to tell them, and I knew I could never say it so sweetly or so well as you had said it yourself. With what a perfect feeling about it all you come to us to bless us, my adorable Sweetheart!

I am sorry you will have to wait to tell your Mother and sister till the Roses go. I am so anxious for them to know, because I am sure it will add to your peace of mind and happiness so much, and I *hope* it will add to theirs. Please tell them how clearly I know that I am getting the best of the bargain and with what a grateful heart I mean to devote myself to prevent your ever repenting of it.

Sunday, 9.15 A.M.

I am so glad that you liked and enjoyed so many of the people you met in Geneva, my Love. What a pleasure it will be to go back there with you some time and make these friends of yours friends of mine too. Of course I'll go—anywhere you want me to go, whenever I'm free. I fancied that you were under some sort of strain at Geneva,—at any rate during the latter part of your stay,—and I guessed that it was because your thoughts and your day's routine and engagements did not belong together. Your thoughts were governed by the entire change in your life, by the contents of the big envelopes, by your anxieties about dear ones down in Panama, while your engagements and occupations were those of a quiet household who knew nothing of these things and of a little provincial town remote from all the big things with which your mind was teeming—and about which you could say nothing except what they were saying. Is it not so? I know something of the experience myself, for of course *I* can't speak, generally, of the things I know, and have often to let a conversation go along on some false assumption as to the facts. I am so glad you now have a "change of venue" and can be with your own dear ones and let them know at least the most important part of what is going on in your mind and heart, and I hope that you will stay to get thoroughly refreshed by the sea,—and as long as the place amuses you. It diverts me very much indeed. When you tell your Mother and sister, Dearest, will you not, please, give them my love, and tell them that I think you are the loveliest, most interesting, and most adorable woman in the world? My rival, your next-door neighbour at Geneva, must indeed be a most fascinating person. I am glad he is not older! I want to know him!

I wonder if my Darling's journey is over and she is in Ocean City? My letters have, of course, a much shorter way to go now to get to you. The best trains take, I believe, less than five hours,—so that it may be that what I write will some days, if taken from the post box at just the right time, reach you the day it is written. *That* would cheat our enemy, Space! Thank you, Darling, for your sweet promise to cooperate with me to cheat him to the utmost by what we put into our letters of love and endearment. He is a formidable chap and has a most terrible advantage over us. I try to speak my very heart in the words I write you, but there are so many things there that are too subtle for written words. I can often tell you more in a single kiss than I can tell you in a whole epistle. And the *next* kiss I give you,—the next time I hold you in my arms and feel your sweet lips against mine I shall tell you that there is no happiness in all the world like being with you,—that there is no real happiness away from you,—that the whole world is full of light and life when you are with me as my very own. When I woke this morning I thought first of what you had said in that dear letter written Thursday night, that you would love to come and kneel by my bed and put your arms gently about me, that I might sleep the more happily, and wake to find you bending over me, the full light of devoted love in your eyes, and I felt as if I would almost die of joy if that dream were to come true now. I shall *live* of joy, in fact, when it does come true. I love you with all my heart!   Your own   Woodrow

P.S. Your dear, dear letter from Albany has just come, bless your heart, how sweet it is; and what a comfort to know that the first stage of your journey went so easily. I am off for church and shall think and pray of you.   Your W.

ALS (WP, DLC).

From Edith Bolling Galt

Patterson, N. J. August 21st/1915   10:30 P.M.

So, my Dearest you were off early yesterday to Philadelphia? and every hour of the day we were each speeding nearer the other! What a joy if we could meet somewhere on the road! But I suppose by this time you are safely home again, and I trust the Dr. gave you good news regarding those dear eyes. Thank you for going to see about them, and be sure to write me *exactly* what he said. The first thing I saw in the N. Y. Times this morning was that you left the White House at 7:30 yesterday by motor for Phil. And the public supposed it was in order that you might think over this awful "Arabic" tragedy without fear of interruption.

Bless your precious weary heart! At times like this, when I know you are under extra pressure, I can hardly keep away from you.

I think you have been in my thoughts every minute today. And oh! tonight what would I not give to talk to you. The day has been very long dear, my Lord, without a word from you. The daily letters help more than I realized and when I woke this morning with the knowledge that you did not even know where I was—and so of course could not write or even send me a directed thought—

I knew the 21st of August would be as long as June 21st—the day Helen & I left Washington.

I wonder, if, in your many journeys through New Jersey, you ever had to spend a night in this awful place of Patterson? I trust *not*, for really, between us Sweetheart, I am almost afraid to put the light out & go to bed. We got here after seven ock, and Mr. Rose enquired of policemen, garage men etc. for the best Hotel, and we went to three—all worse looking than this—so finally decided on this with the modest name of the "United States," and it is so common & awful I will welcome the dawn. Fortunately Mr & Mrs. Rose are across the hall and I could get them—in case of need—but the one window that my apartment affords opens out on a flat roof, on which face various other windows. So I have let it down from the top for ventilation and moved the bureau in front of it, and put a chair lengthwise between that and the bed. So if it should be moved, it would wake me both with the motion & the noise

Mr. R. is awfully worried we had to spend the night in such a place, but he had 2 tires punctured and it took so long to fix them we were hours later than we expected to be. This was not altogether the tires but the number of "Detours" we found—all of which were over bad roads.

We left Tuxedo—where we got a new tire on—and had a beautiful run of 20 miles over the most wonderful road when lo! the road was blocked and we were told that for nearly 30 miles the roads were being repaired and we would have to *Detour*   This we did, but it threw us so late—and a heavy storm was right behind us. So we all agreed we had better stop here. It is pouring rain now and sounds as though it might keep up all night.

But, unless there is a flood I think we will leave this place D.V. early in the morning

I mailed you a letter this morning before leaving Albany and I hope it will reach you tomorrow. We had an awfully pretty trip down the river road to Kingston and Newburg, and pretty good roads that end of the route.

I trust we can get to Ocean City tomorrow by dinner time. And oh! how glad I will be to find your beloved letter, which I know will be waiting for me.

Are you well, my precious Woodrow? And will you tell me everything about yourself? I am so lonely without you. I want to be where I can help you, where I can see for myself if you are worried, and where, if you are, I can fold my arms so close about you that I will shut out all that is causing you anxiety—and, for awhile at least, make you forget the world and remember only that I am all your own, and that I love you.

Goodnight   Edith

ALS (WP, DLC).

To Edith Bolling Galt

[The White House] 22 Aug. [1915]

The Carranzista position stated in a very dignified way,[1] it seems to me.

W.

ALI (WP, DLC).

[1] J. B. Treviño to RL, Aug. 19, 1915, T telegram (WP, DLC), in reply to the American ministers' appeal to Mexican leaders. Treviño said that the revolutionists would stop fighting when they were "satisfied that the sacrifices the people have made to reconquer their liberties have been crowned with complete success." Treviño also rejected the proposal for a new convention because the Aguascalientes Convention had only made "our internal divisions more pronounced," due to the attitudes of what he called unrepresentative elements. He closed by affirming his allegiance to Carranza—"the incarnation of the aspiration of the Mexican people" and the only leader who could guarantee the accomplishment of the social reforms of the revolutionary program.

Jacinto B. Treviño, Carranza's former chief of staff and secretary of war, was at this time Chief of the Army Corps of the Northeast.

To Edith Bolling Galt, with Enclosure

[The White House] Sunday,
6 P.M. 22 Aug., 1915

My darling Sweetheart,

You see I am getting in the habit of sitting down at any and all hours,—whenever I get a chance,—to talk to you. I have just come in from a three hour ride, with the doctor and Fitz, out to Marlborough and around by "T.B.," and there is a full hour before dinner for a little chat.

I think you said that you had read Stephens' "Demi-Gods."[1] Do you remember the lines I have copied on my typewriter and will slip in with this? They made me think so of your own dear, vital beauty that I thought I would adopt them as a description of your own lovely poise and beauty,—all but the "consciousness" of it. You seem altogether unconscious of it, though you must have a mirror! But you have never seen yourself *move*.

I fancy that my dear Love is just now nearing Ocean City or already in it. My thoughts have followed her every mile of the way. I find myself wishing that I were still governor of New Jer-

[1] James Stephens, *The Demi-Gods* (London, 1914). There is a copy of this book in the Wilson Library, DLC.

sey and might have the privilege of calling at the Hotel Normandie to welcome the loveliest lady in the land to the State and telling her how much more vital and worth serving the old State
seemed so long as she was in it. What fun it would be to pay you
some public honour and tribute of admiration! Never mind; I
hold a greater office now, and just so soon as you say I may I will
pay you the highest tribute of admiration, trust, and honour any
man can pay to any woman; and I shall be *so* glad of the chance
to call the attention of the whole world to your loveliness!

My heart is aglow to-day with that sweet love letter written
from Albany. I have been to Albany once or twice. I have even
spoken (lectured) there, but somehow it has never had any indi-
viduality in my mind (notwithstanding the various kinds of
deviltry that go on there as the capital of the State), but now it
will always be associated in my mind with this little visit of yours
to it. "That is where Edith stopped over night with the Roses and
went to a tiresome vaudeville performance, walked home in the
fresh night air, and hurried into bed to lie and write me a delicious little love message just before falling asleep." Albany is no
longer merely a place on a map: it is a place my Darling visited!

But you came near being corrupted there, young lady, by
Bryanism! The opinions you quote from an Albany paper about
the loss of Americans on the *Arabic* are rank Bryanism. The Germans have admitted all along that they had no right to sink any
ship carrying our flag without first making themselves responsible
for the safety of the lives of those on board,—as they did in the
case of the *Frye*,—even though she carried contraband consigned
to England. The case we based our protest on was that of the
Lusitania, chiefly,—a British ship, and the case of the *Arabic* is
the same in principle and worse in fact. It was your Friend W.J.B.
who took the ground that we must let Americans understand that
they took passage on British ships, or any other ships owned
owned [sic] by belligerants, at their own risk and peril. Beware
of heresies! It may very well be that this Bryan and Albany
doctrine is the more reasonable and practical one, my precious
Sweetheart, but it is not the doctrine of international law, and we
must base our claims of right on the undoubted practice of nations,—for which Germany is showing such crass and brutal contempt. The road is hard to travel, but it lies plain before us. She
has no right whatever to deal with ships owned by *belligerants* as
she has dealt with the *Lusitania* and the *Arabic*, and the *Falaba*
before them, and when our own people are on board we must tell
her so. It was another *Lusitania* incident we told her we should
regard as "deliberately unfriendly."

Don't apologise, my loved One, for asking me to discuss public questions in my letters to you. For some reason (can you guess it?) business never wearies or bores me when I am talking of it with *you*. It seems to take on a new freshness and interest when I share it with you,—and I am so glad that you want me to.

Ah, Sweetheart, my heart went pit-a-pat when you said that you almost yielded Friday night to the temptation to call me up over the telephone! Oh, to have heard your dear voice! It somehow affected my imagination, while you were at Geneva, that no such connection existed between us,—that Mr. Rose had no long distance telephone. It made you seem so much less accessible, so much less within call, so much further away! It is thrilling now to feel that I *could* call you—if I dared or there was necessity—and that I could hear your own dear voice itself in reply. It is *so* long since I heard it,—so long since I saw you! As a matter of fact it will be exactly three weeks to-morrow (when this letter is posted) since you left Cornish, but it seems to me (as to you, bless your heart!) last summer, a blessed season long ago, that we were together and learned to see the very core of each others' hearts. And it will be—how long?—before I shall see you again. I suppose you will not be back literally by the first of September? You say the Roses are going to stay for a week,—that would take you to the 29th or 30th,—and I suppose your dear ones will want to have you to themselves for a few days. You see what I have in mind, don't you? I simply *must* see you as soon as you reach here: I would have the blind staggers if I could not; and I want it to be as near as possible to the time when this White House bachelor arrangement will be coming to an end and Helen's return made as easy and natural as it can be made, and can't you make it come at the end of a week? But that need not hamper you, my Darling. If it cannot be managed as I suggest, just tell me, so soon as it is settled, when you expect to reach here in time for me to ask dear Margaret to come down for a day or two. We must devise means to keep our hearts from *too* great a strain!

The doctor has just gone over to his club, at my request, to call up the Hotel Normandie, at Ocean City, New Jersey, to ask if his friends, Mr. and Mrs. H. L. Rose, of Geneva, New York, have arrived. He is to say that he does not wish to disturb them to speak with him over the 'phone to-night; he merely wants to know whether they have reached the hotel or not. I shall sleep so much more happily if I can know to-night that my dear One is safely at the end of her journey and with her own loved ones again.

The day has gone very quietly with me. After finishing my let-

ter to you this morning, I went to church with the doctor and Fitz
and we heard the same interesting and stimulating preacher we
heard last Sunday. After church we took a turn in Potomac Park;
then came in to lunch, and after lunch took the drive out to
Marlborough and around of which I have spoken, and I came in
to write to you, as I am still doing. We have had dinner since
I began, and it is now about half past eight. (The mosquitoes
had, I think, as much to eat as we did on the terrace). No news
of consequence or of new significance has come in to-day, though
I shall have a few "flimsies" for the big envelope which will be
mailed to you to-morrow. I must admit I am thankful when nothing new comes in. There has been no *good* news on public matters
that I can remember for a year past now. Everything new seems
simply to add to the confusion and increase the darkness amidst
which we are left to thread our way through the confusion. There
seems to be no relieving particular in the *Arabic* incident, such as
Lansing thought there might be when he wrote the letter to me
which I sent you the other day; and, since it is just a clear and
simple case of insolently ignoring the protest and the warning of
our three notes, there seems to be nothing for it but to go forward
and do the things I have already outlined to you. I suppose we
shall be expected first to send Gerard to the Foreign Office in
Berlin to ask von Jagow whether he has anything to say about the
case or not; but I do not see what he *could* say to alter the significance of it. I take for granted that he will neither offer an apology
nor disavow the act of the commander of the submarine,—and
these formalities, gone through with only to satisfy ourselves that
we omitted nothing that might conceivably alter the result, will
do little more than delay for a few days the announcement of our
decision. You understand, of course, my Darling, that the withdrawal of Gerard and the dismissal of Bernstorff will not necessarily lead to *war*. We will not declare it (*I cannot*; only Congress
can), but Germany may (I doubt it—but the hope may be the
father to the doubt), and if she does, we are at last caught in the
maelstrom and our independence of action is lost: I must call
Congress together and we are in for the whole terrible business.
If she does not, we can call the conference of neutral nations of
which I spoke and it is *possible* that what issues from its deliberations may affect the whole course and the ultimate results of the
war. It is our judgment (Lansing's and mine) that it should be
asked to meet, not on the other side of the water, but in Washington, and I take it for granted that I should myself be obliged to
take an active part (if I did not preside) in its deliberations.
These are very solemn thoughts, my precious One, my little part-

ner, and they seem somehow to draw me nearer to you than ever. As things thicken about me I more and more realize what you mean to me, and more and more feel my dependence upon you to keep the *darkness* off, hold the lamp of love for me to walk by, keep the loneliness at bay by your loving, intimate companionship, make me free from everything that could weaken or dismay my heart. With your hand in mine, your head close at my shoulder, your eyes beaming with confidence and reassurance, your lips ready always to speak love and counsel and give the kisses that mean our absolute union, I am fit for anything and can fare through any trial!

Monday, 7 A.M.

It was nine o'clock last night when the doctor called up the Normandie and, since you had not yet arrived I went to bed, I must admit, a little uneasy,—for all the world is centred for me in my darling Edith. It was a brilliant moon-light night, fit for delightful travelling, but I fancied my Darling very weary and I could not go to bed for some time for thinking of that, and that when she did reach her journey's end her lover would not be there to pet and rest her and make her forget everything except his love. I conquered the restlessness and went to my room, but it was hard. After I had locked my door and done the little things that precede undressing, I went to the window by my bed to look out on the brilliant night and something gave me suddenly an irresistible desire to go down on the South Portico,—where I have not been since I came back,—where I had intended not to go until I could take you out there and get you to chase the ghost away. There was an enchanting half light filling the whole space of the place when I got down there—mixed of moonlight and the reflections from the lamps below on the awnings—but not too much for lovers. I sat down in a chair drawn close beside the high-backed chair that stands against the central window of the blue room, and there had a delicious whispered conversation with you which sent me to bed happy. When I first stepped out of the red room window the ghost was there and I was uneasy; but the minute I sat down by you he was gone,—and I do not think he can ever come back again. It was about eleven.

That is but one illustration, my beloved Darling, of how consciously I spend the hours with you. I manage to take from three to four hours every day to actually talk to you, with this pen of mine as telephone, but that does not measure the time I consciously spend with you. You are all in all to me and my spirits suffice for the tasks of the day in proportion to my consciousness that you are thinking of me and loving me with a conscious love that sends your dear thoughts to keep me company and give me cheer. I shall be so glad when I hear that you are safely at the end of your journey. Did you realize that at Ocean City you are less than fifty miles north of Washington? Cape May, which is only forty odd miles south of Atlantic City, is almost exactly on the same parallel of latitude as Washington City. Doesn't that make it seem nearer? It makes me feel easier to realize it! My heart is all the while with you, my adorable Sweetheart, day and night. It waits for you with an *infinite* longing.

Your own   Woodrow.

ALS (WP, DLC).

E N C L O S U R E

"She walked carelessly as the wind walks, proudly as a young queen trained in grandeur. She could run as a deer runs, and pause at full flight like a carven statue. Each movement of hers was complete and lovely in itself; when she lifted a hand to her hair the free attitude was a marvel of composure; it might never have begun, and might never cease, it was solitary and perfect. She was so conscious of her loveliness that she could afford to forget it, and so careless that she had never yet used it as a weapon or a plea."[1]

WWT MS (WP, DLC).
  [1] Adapted from Stephens, *The Demi-Gods*, pp. 63-64.

Two Letters from Edith Bolling Galt

[Paterson, N. J.] Sunday August 22, 8 P.M. [A.M.]

Well Dearest One, I have lived through the night and we will get away now in a few minutes—I hope! This takes you all my love and the hope that you are well and happy.

Always your own   E.

ALI (WP, DLC).

My precious One: Lakewood, N. J. August 22, 1915

As you see from the heading of this we are still 70 odd miles from Ocean City and seventy miles from your dear letter, which my heart is waiting for so eagerly. We left that awful town of Patterson at nine this morning and sailed along to within twelve miles of Princeton when the front tire blew all to pieces. We were carrying 2 extra ones so Mr. Rose put one on and we got into Princeton, just as another one exploded. We left the car at a garage and went to the Princeton Inn for lunch (it seemed right queer that it is just two months yesterday since Helen and I were at Princeton together) and it seems so full of you, although, I never even knew you when you were blessing it with your presence.

We did not get away from there until after three, and while we followed directions and maps, correctly as we thought, instead of coming direct here—as we wanted—we landed in Asbury Park, where the automobiles were thicker than gnats, and we had another tire leak. Mr. Rose got an entire new outfit, tire and tubes for the front wheels so surely tomorrow we should have no trouble, and we hope to get to Ocean City in time for lunch. I called Mother up on the phone when I got here, and they had been expecting us for hours and were awfully disappointed at our delay. Here we are most comfortable, however and, if I had my letters, I should be very content. It is so hard to *really* know nothing of what you are doing and thinking—save what the newspapers give—which I always discount. Still it is a comfort to just read your name and that you are conferring with Secretary Lansing about the German question. If I *had* been a man, Sweetheart, I wonder if you would have given me the appointment as Sec. of State? How I would love just to *demand* an audience with you this minute—and threaten you with divulging *secrets* if you refused.

I am afraid my letter of last night and this a.m. may be very late in reaching you tomorrow for, when I went to post it in Patterson the man at the desk said there was no mail sent out from that awful place on Sunday. So I took it with me as far as Morristown and posted it there.

I think after this one though they should reach you regularly Mr. and Mrs. Rose have gone upstairs to bed—for he was awfully tired. I have really enjoyed the trip—except last night, as I did not have to bother with the tires. But Mr. Rose has had an awfully hard time with them. They are both so sweet to me. I know you will love them for my sake, and they are both so appreciative and enthusiastic about you it warms my heart to the core. They were charmed with Princeton, and every thing there did look lovely

I know this is a very stupid, uninteresting letter, but I am very tired, so you will forgive it.

Three weeks ago tonight we were on the big davenport in the

morning room at Harlakenden, and how many more than three have these 21 intervening days seemed—and how *our* household of that night is scattered. I am just wondering if you will be there again next Sunday, the 28th? I know it will depend on the war developments and that you can't tell yourself this far ahead. But I hope you can go and stay until it is cooler at home.

Goodnight Beloved. My heart is gone in serch of you. And when you feel it warm and pulsing in your hand remember every beat is for you, and that I am all   Your own—Edith

ALS (WP, DLC).

To William Gibbs McAdoo

[The White House] August 23, 1915.

Do not think there is any real necessity for your being here. When all needed information is ontained [obtained] will call Cabinet. Love to all.   Woodrow Wilson.

T telegram (Letterpress Books, WP, DLC).

A Letter and a Telegram from William Gibbs McAdoo

Dear Governor,   North Haven, Me. Aug. 23, 1915

Thank you for your telegrams, also for your letter which I did not expect.[1] As you say the Arabic affair puts a new and all comprehensive phase of the situation before us and action on that will dispose of everything, in all probability.

We are very happy about the baby. She is doing so well at last. Nell almost weeps to think of your being so lonely there and we both hope that it wont have to be for long. We hope to see you soon. We plan now to let Nell & the baby go to Cornish the end of this week. Sally[2] & I will go to Washington. The other children will "scatter" for the time being.

Our dearest love goes to you always,

Devotedly yours   W G McAdoo

ALS (WP, DLC).
  [1] One of the telegrams is the one just printed; the other is missing. The letter is WW to WGM, Aug. 21, 1915.
  [2] Sally Fleming McAdoo, the youngest child of McAdoo's first marriage.

North Haven, Maine, August 23, 1915.

I am issuing statement today about deposit Government fund in the South to help cotton and have directed Cooksey[1] to send you copy[2] immediately so you may have it in mind in anything you contemplate saying to the press. It seems to me most important to get immediately to the South this statement of willingness of Treasury to make Government deposit of gold without interest. I believe it will be most reassuring and help to counteract adverse influence of contraband declaration.[3]   W. G. McAdoo.

T telegram (WP, DLC).
    [1] George Robert Cooksey, private secretary to McAdoo from 1913 to 1917.
    [2] G. R. Cooksey to WW, Aug. 23, 1915, TLS (WP, DLC), enclosing T MS dated Aug. 23, 1915.
    [3] The British government had put cotton on the list of absolute contraband on August 20.

To William Procter Gould Harding

My dear Mr. Harding: [The White House] August 23, 1915
    Thank you sincerely for your letter of August twenty-third.[1] It gives me just the information I desired.
    What interests me most is this: It is evident from what you tell me that the country banks with whom the farmer and other producers directly deal can get money at from four to four-and-a-half per cent. and that the question whether the benefit of this advantageous rate is to be extended to the farmer is in their hands. It is inconceivable to me that those who are responsible for dealing directly with the producers of the country should be willing to jeopard the prosperity of the country itself by refusing to share with the producer the beneficial rates now obtainable for money loans. I think that we can confidently expect that the banks in the cotton states and in the agricultural regions generally will content themselves with a rate not more than one or two per cent. above the rate which they themselves pay. I hope that the facts which you have stated to me will become generally known among the producers of the country so that they may feel themselves free to exact of the banks with which they deal what they undoubtedly have a right to expect.
    Cordially and sincerely yours,   Woodrow Wilson

TLS (Letterpress Books, WP, DLC).
    [1] W.P.G. Harding to WW, Aug. 23, 1915, TLS (WP, DLC).

Sir Cecil Arthur Spring Rice to Sir Edward Grey

Washington   August 23rd, 1915.
    Harding has informed Sir R. Crawford that the President discussed the cotton situation with him this morning and expressed

his appreciation of the re-assuring announcement which accompanied the declaration of cotton as contraband.[1]

The President, who must not be quoted, hopes that you will not allow cotton to drop below 8 cents per lb on farm during the next three months as he regards maintenance of this, i.e. the level, price as essential to prevent unrest in the South stirred up by Senator Hoke-Smith and others hostile to us from becoming troublesome.

Hoke-Smith says that 8 cents on farm is represented by 9 cents f.o.b. New York and about 8.75 cents at New Orleans. Harding gave Sir R. Crawford draft of an address he will deliver with President's approval on August 25th to an audience of cotton growers and Southern Bankers at Birmingham, Alabama, on the situation as affected by contraband declaration.

It is friendly in tone throughout to our action and should calm apprehensions of the growers.

Press comments so far have been on the whole moderate and reasonable.

Announcement had been well discounted last week in the Southern journals largely by excellent articles from Board [pen] of Mr. Theodore Price[2] whose co-operation has been very valuable.

T telegram (FO 382/464, No. 117981, PRO).

[1] The Foreign Office's statement read: "His Majesty's Government have declared cotton absolute contraband. While the circumstances might have justified such action at an earlier period, his Majesty's Government are glad to think that the local conditions of American interests likely to be affected are more favorable for such a step than they were a year ago; and, moreover, his Majesty's Government contemplate initiation of measures to relieve as far as possible any abnormal depression which might temporarily disturb market conditions." *New York Times*, Aug. 22, 1915.

[2] Theodore Hazeltine Price of New York, former cotton broker, currently editor and publisher of the weekly journal, *Commerce and Finance*, and free-lance journalist. Price was acting as adviser to Spring Rice on cotton questions.

To Edith Bolling Galt, with Enclosures

[The White House, c. Aug. 23, 1915]

Of course I shall deal with Germany first.

What an impertinent Prussian Bernstorff is!   W.

ALI (WP, DLC).

E N C L O S U R E   I

From Edward Mandell House

Manchester, Massachusetts.
Dear Governor: August 22nd, 1915.

Do you not think it would be best to leave our controversy with England in abeyance for the moment?

If you should take decisive action in the Arabic case questions now before our Government and the Allies would be automatically settled.

If we question England concerning the rescinding of the Order in Council, they will take it to mean that we intend doing nothing further in regard to the loss of American lives upon unarmed merchantmen that are sunk without warning, and it seems to me it would make a bad impression.

However, if you desire me to do so, I will take it up with Sir Edward by cable.

I am enclosing you a copy of a letter which came today from Bernstorff. I shall answer it in general terms. If there is anything you would like me to say to him, please send a code message and I will do so.   Your affectionate,   E. M. House

TLS (WP, DLC).

E N C L O S U R E   I I

Count Johann Heinrich von Bernstorff
to Edward Mandell House

My dear Colonel House: New York, August 21st, 1915.

Many thanks for your last letter. I am sorry to say we do not seem to be moving on at all. We are still on the same spot and any day some incident may lead to very grave results and create a situation, which makes war inevitable.

Although I am sure that the English version of the "Arabic" incident is made in Great Britain for American consumption, we are nevertheless, so to speak, sitting on a barrel of gunpowder.

I have been endeavoring to get instructions from Berlin for the purpose of beginning confidential negociations with the United States Government, which might lead to a favorable answer to the last American note. I know now that we will certainly make concessions, but German public opinion must be prepared for such concessions. You know well enough that nobody in Germany believes in the impartiality of the American Government.

Before I can do anything in this matter, I must be able to give my people at home some proof of my contention that President Wilson wishes to give us a square deal. The developments of the last weeks will certainly have irritated public opinion in Germany instead of improving it. Our people cannot understand why the British violations of International law—especially with regard to the cotton situation—have not yet led to any measures on the part of the American Government. They, furthermore, cannot understand why nothing is done to protect the German Embassy against the continual unjust attacks by the American press, and last, not least, they would not be able to understand, if England should be allowed to raise an enormous loan in the United States.

Our people are sure to say: when the English cannot make their own ammunition, they get it in the United States, and when in consequence of their inefficiency their credit is tottering, they again receive help in the United States, whilst the American Government at the same time permits every violation of International law by England and tries to prevent Germany from making full use of its submarines against England.

The above remarks may seem very sharp, but it is no good mincing matters, and I think you should know, why it is so difficult for me to push along the policy which you and I have so often spoken of and agreed upon.

Yours very sincerely,   J. Bernstorff.

TCL (WP, DLC).

To Edith Bolling Galt, with Enclosure

[The White House, c. Aug. 23, 1915]

All this is true, only *too* true! I wish he had not put in the sentence I have marked in the margin. It is not of how *I* will stand that I am thinking, but of what it is right to do. You see he does not advise: he puts it up to me!   W.

ALI (WP, DLC).

ENCLOSURE

From Edward Mandell House

Manchester, Massachusetts.

Dear Governor: August 22nd, 1915.

My heart has been heavy since the Arabic disaster and my thoughts and sympathy have been constantly with you.

I have hoped against hope that no such madness would seize Germany. If war comes it is clearly of their making and not yours. You have been calm, patient and just. From the beginning they have taken an impossible attitude which has led them to the brink of war with all nations.

Our people do not want war, but even less do they want you to recede from the position you have taken. Neither do they want to shirk the responsibility which should be ours. Your first note to Germany after the sinking of the Lusitania made you not only the first citizen of America, but the first citizen of the world. If by aby [any] word or act you should hurt our pride of nationality you would lose your commanding position over night.[1]

Further notes would disappoint our own people and would cause something of derision abroad. In view of what has been said, and in view of what has been done, it is clearly up to this Government to act. The question is, when and how?

To send Bernstorff home and to recall Gerard would be the first act of war, for we would be without means of communication with one another and it would not be long before some act was committed that would force the issue.

If you do not send Bernstorff home and if you do not recall Gerard, then Congress should be called to meet the emergency and assume the responsibility. This would be a dangerous move because there is no telling what Congress would do in the circumstances.

If Bernstorff were sent home and Gerard recalled, and later Germany committed some other overt act, Congress would be amenable to your suggestions. It is an unhappy position, but it might as well be faced.

For the first time in the history of the world, a great nation has run amuck, and it is not certain that it is not a part of our duty to put forth a restraining hand. Unless Germany disavows the act and promises not to repeat it, some decisive action upon our part is inevitable, otherwise, we will have no influence when peace is made or afterwards.

The weather is growing cooler and I hope soon to be in Washington.

I am, with deep affection,

Your devoted,   E. M. House

TLS (WP, DLC).
[1] This is the sentence that Wilson marked.

Two Letters to Edith Bolling Galt

[The White House] Monday,

My precious Darling,   12.30 P.M. 23 Aug., 1915

Alas, that any place in New Jersey should have been so inhospitable to you as Paterson was! Your precious little love letter pencilled there has just come, and I am *so* sorry you should have had so hard a time, bless your heart, and I not there to guard and comfort and protect you. The Jersey towns near New York City have wretched hotels, because nobody stays over night there, but all go on to the big city, but I did not know that Paterson was near enough to the octopus to be so affected. Poor, dear little girl! Well, you are out of it now, and with your dear ones at Ocean City, *I hope*,—I have not heard yet, of course, and I have not thought it wise that the doctor should telephone again. (Interrupted)

There has been an apparent conspiracy of incidents and interruptions to-day to keep me away from my Darling,—nothing of importance, but little things without number that could not be thrust aside,—not to keep me away from you in thought (nothing can do that) but to prevent my talking to you. It is now after dinner and almost nine o'clock. I do not see how anything *else* can break in now. The heat has decended on us again—I hope you are unconscious of it by the sea—and I am sitting here in my pajamas comfortable as can be, except for the oil lamp near me, whose light is very grateful to my eyes, but whose heat is rather trying. I can sit here as long as I please, for at least these evening hours are mine, and rest my mind and heart in sweet intercourse with my own darling Sweetheart,—for the only real rest is in refreshment and renewal. No matter how tired my brain is, it wakes and is fresh again the moment it comes into contact with yours, my Love, no matter how far away you are; and I think that if my heart were at the point of breaking with the weight of the sense of responsibility that is put upon me, and upon me singly, by the opinion of the country, a single love message from you would heal it and make it proof against trouble upon the instant. If you were *here*, and I could feel the touch of your hand and look when I pleased into those sweet wells in your eyes from which I have so often drunk life and joy, I could never, even for a little, *feel* as if my heart were under a strain. I love to tell you these things, Edith, my own Darling, because they are of the very essence of me and I want you to know what your love for me means to me.

I hope you found your dear Mother and sister well. I can

imagine how glad they were to see you. And I hope that you have
had a chance to tell them already of the happiness that has come
to us. They must have wondered at the singularly fat envelope
from Washington for you that reached the hotel nearly twenty-
four hours before you did. Were you not a bit overwhelmed by it
yourself? Did you ever before get a letter forty pages long? It's a
safe bet that you never before received a *love* letter that long! I
felt almost ashamed to send it. And yet, in truth, it was not really
a letter. It was just a transcript, as all my letters are, of part of
what I would have said to you had you been here to share with me
my days and my thoughts. Ah, Sweetheart, how sweet, how unspeakably sweet, it will be when we can cast this poor substitute
aside and be always close to one another where we can share
everything, and share it all the time, at every turn of the day!
Your praise of me for the way I have borne our separation and
kept a cheerful front and made everybody I came in contact with
feel that I was in good spirits and in every way in fine fettle, is
very, very sweet to me,—for it has been hard, very hard. I don't
take any credit to myself for it because I was doing it for your
sake, and to prove that, having so much, I was not so poor a
sport as not to be willing to wait, gracefully and cheerfully, for
the full consummation of my happiness. But, my precious One,
I never needed you more than I need you this moment! This is a
time of as great anxiety (of as intense and anxious thought about
my duty) as I have ever known. And think what your presence
and constant, loving companionship would mean to me. Suppose
that, whenever things grew tense, I could seek you out in your
own quiet room, or that you could come to me in my study, and
that, sitting for a few minutes side by side, my arm close about
you, my cheek pressed to yours, I could pour out to you the whole
thought of my heart and receive and give the assurances of love
that are, after all, the sources of vision! Suppose that, when the
evening came, we could shut the world out and make our hearts
young and gay with sheer enjoyment of one another, and that all
through the night we were made conscious of each other's love,
as we would be in a thousand ways! Don't you see how little
burdens would mean to me, what a joy would be in my heart all
the while, with what almost boyish ease and gayety I could carry
the whole day off? It is *painfully* sweet to think of. I would not
dare (especially days like these, when it sometimes seems to me
that I would be willing to give some future *year* of my life for an
intimate week with you—I would if the future year were not to be
with you!) to dwell on the picture in my thoughts if I did not
know that it was a dream that was sure to come true,—the longing

would be intolerable!—I must change the subject for a few minutes, as it is, to let my heart quiet down! "The time has come," the Walrus said, "to speak of many things; of shoes and ships and sealing wax and cabbages and kings"!

Tumulty got back to-day. He has been with Mrs. Tumulty and the children for about ten days. Mrs. Tumulty had some sort of nervous attack early in the week and he did not feel that he ought to leave her; and I am happy to have him a good deal away—to pick up opinion,—which he does wonderfully well. Washington is no place to learn what the *country* is thinking about, and I like to import as large quantities of the genuine article as possible. Please keep your own ears open, my sweet One, and give me *your* impressions of what people are thinking and saying.

Tuesday, 7 A.M.

At this point on the sheet this hand of mine went back on me and I had to let it off from further struggles with the pen. It's all right this morning and I am *so* happy to be talking with you again! I think it must have been the rather hard game of golf I had had with the Colonel and the doctor that had tired my hand and arm,—for I am perfectly well and fit—fit as I shall ever be away from you. I shall keep my promise literally, Sweetheart, and tell you of even my little ailments, so that you need not have the least anxiety lest I am not well and you do not know it. I sometimes wonder at myself. I take things hard, I am afraid,—am indifferent to nothing—and the things that are happening now are of such a kind as, taken hard, ought to break a man's back. And yet I am as well and vigorous as I ever was in my life, and I have been blessed with health always! I verily believe it is because I found you and you gave me your precious love.

To go back to Tumulty a minute, you will find in the big envelope to-day a memorandum he sent me a day or two before he came back.[1] I wanted you to see it because it is characteristic of the careful way in which, after reading all the papers he can get hold of and listening to everybody talk, he seeks to sum up for me his impressions. He has done me a great deal of service in that way—though the contents of this particular memorandum happen to be rather obvious. I am sorry you are not prepossessed in his favour, for your instinct, I have found, is a singularly sure one, and I am made uneasy when you do not wholly trust any one who is very near and very essential to me. I have *proved* Tumulty's loyalty: that will stand any test, the most acid; and where there is absolute loyalty one can dismiss fear. The only errors will be errors of judgment,—and who does not make them?

House's letters which I am sending you explain themselves, or are explained by the little pencilled notes I have attached. Bernstorff is evidently feeling the attacks on him under the skin. His demand that the government stop the newspaper attacks on him shows how little he knows of the country to which he is accredited. This is not Prussia. We cannot tell the newspapers what they may and what they may not print! Of all the trials of the situation, Bernstorff is one of the hardest to bear.

Tell me what you do at the seaside, will you not, my sweet Love? I am unhappy unless I can be with you *all the time*, at least in imagination, and I want to have a chance to follow you with my thoughts all the day through. Do you go in the surf? Does the parade of the idle on the board walk amuse you? Do you take long strolls on the board walk or do you take a chair? And what does your dear Mother do? Does she go about much or does she keep to the hotel,—and do you read to her? How I should love to be there and take care of you all. My love for you, my precious Sweetheart, is a very intimate love,—and it is no mere holiday affair, for fair weather. I am going to devote my life to making you happy,—to taking care of your *heart*, as well as of you. I want to surround you with an *atmosphere* of love that will make all parts and particulars of our lives one consistent experience of devotion and pervading joy. I need you and I want you to need me. I want to make my love such that you will feel that you cannot breathe without it,—as I could not breathe without yours. That is what I every day try to make you realize that [what] I mean when I say that I am your own Woodrow,—and I know that that is the meaning lying at the heart of these precious words that close that dear note from Paterson—"I am all your own and I love you" Bless you, my adorable darling. *That* being true, I am the happiest and freest man in the world!

Your own   Woodrow

ALS (WP, DLC).
  1 JPT to WW, Aug. 21, 1915.

[The White House]

My precious One,   Tuesday, 8.10 P.M. 24 Aug., 1915

Your dear note from Lakewood reached me this morning just *before* breakfast, which makes me hope and expect that your letters from Ocean City will come early each morning, to make the whole day easier and happier. I never feel as if the day had really begun until I have had your messenger and know how it is faring with you,—and every day my heart seems to await it more eagerly

than the day before. There is a peculiar charm for me in having
you write from places I know so well as the New Jersey towns. I
have travelled to and fro in the State so much, on political and
other errands, that there is hardly a place in it which has not
some special association in my thought with interesting people or
incidents, and to have you visiting there seems like having you at
my own home, in my own haunts,—and that is delightful. In Lakewood I had a speaking experience,—in a hall over a garage, by
the way,—that I would like some time to describe to you. It was
unusual and interesting. And it made me very happy that you
had gone to Princeton again. Some day we will go there together.
I will be your guide into the nooks and corners and try to make
the old place live in your thoughts as it lives in mine. But I am
glad your automobile travels are over. For I think of you as very
tired and I want you to have a jolly, care-free rest, with your dear
ones near you,—in a place where there is nothing to do but to loaf
and invite your soul. Perhaps I feel that desire for your ease and
rest the more because of my own sense of fatigue and wish that
I might be let off for a little while. I did not realize until yesterday
and to-day, when the great heat returned, how great a strain this
Arabic affair had put upon me,—because, no doubt, of the conviction, which I could not escape, that the (perhaps all along inevitable) break with Germany had come, and that yet, this "deliberately unfriendly" act notwithstanding, the people of the country
were still demanding of me that I take no risk of war. There is a
little rift of hope in the telegram from Bernstorff which I enclose,[1]
though I so thoroughly distrust him that I suspect some mere
manoevre for delay (until the Balkan States have been forced to
a decision?); but I cannot see how the German government can
deny or explain away the facts and it is not likely that they will
apologise and reprimand the commander of the submarine. You
can imagine how the hot days have made me realize the drain
this anxious matter has been on my vitality. I had hoped, against
hope, as I am sure the whole country had, that, while maintaining their old attitude publicly, the German admiralty had instructed the commanders of their undersea craft to be careful not
to offend the United States; and the disappointment of that hope
came as a great blow. Don't fancy, Sweetheart, that there is anything to be anxious about, so far as my health is concerned. There
is not. I am perfectly well, and haven't a pain or bad symptom of
any kind. I am simply and only more tired than usual when the
day's work is over,—and am taking better care of myself than
usual. This forenoon, for example, when I found that I *could* run

---

[1] It is printed with Wilson's covering note as the following document.

away, I sent for the car and took a ride all round about the Park, all by myself, dozing comfortably almost the whole time I was out, and then, when I got back to the house, lay down on the lounge in my bed room and slept soundly for half an hour more before lunch, with the result that I beat the Colonel at golf very handily this afternoon (the doctor did not play) and feel fine this evening. But the consciousness of strain, which I would not admit to anyone but you, my other self, has made me feel the separation from you more keenly than ever before. One hour with you would relieve and remove it all. If I could only see you and touch you and hear your dear voice, with the tender tones in it that thrill me so, I would forget that I had longed for relief and rest. Merely talking to you here in this quiet place, *on paper*, has worked a great peace and quietness in my thoughts. How truly has your love been my salvation as well as my joy, my own Edith, my blessed Darling.

I was thinking to-day, my precious One, that perhaps I had not set the *Arabic* matter in its full light before you, to enable you to see just what questions are involved and just what facts we are seeking to clear up. Before we act we ought to be sure that the German authorities admit the act as the act of one of their submarines. The people on the *Arabic* saw no submarine, though many of them claim to have seen the torpedo approaching through the water. The *Dunslea*, the vessel seen sinking from the *Arabic*, was, it seems, being *shelled* from some quarter and her captain says it was by a submarine which was concealed behind his vessel from those who were on the *Arabic*, and he says that the submarine passed around his vessel to get clear of her and launch a torpedo at the *Arabic*. What account the Germans will give of the whole matter I cannot conjecture, but Bernstorff's message must mean that their account of it will be different. While it seems clear (and this is the second point) that the *Arabic* was not under convoy at the time she was attacked and sunk, it is not entirely clear that she did not leave the Mersey under convoy. If she did, the German commander may say, with some colour, that he naturally assumed that her convoy was still at hand, and that a convoy rendered her a public vessel (as distinguished from a merchantman) and made it legitimate to attack her and destroy her in any way he could (which is good international law). A third point is, Did she (the *Arabic*) give the German commander any reason to think that she was coming to the assistance of the *Dunslea*? One of her passengers says that she had put about and was heading for the *Dunslea*. Her captain seems to say that she was not. These are points of varying importance, of course, but they are all points upon which the Germans are entitled to be heard, *if they wish to be*. The papers have stated that we have asked the German foreign office for an explanation; but we did nothing of the kind. We merely instructed Gerard to call on von Jagow, as I told you the other day, and ask whether he had received an official report of the incident, and so give him a chance to say anything he may wish to say. No doubt all these points have been obvious enough to you from the first, my Darling, but the newspapers confuse the whole matter with so much that is irrelevant and so much that is false, that I have set them down here for your convenience in keeping step with me day by day and interpreting the flimsies I send you. The big envelope you receive to-day will contain a very extraordinary and alarming despatch from our consul at Moscow;[2] but I must believe that he is under the influence of rumour and panic. It's a bolt out of the blue, so far as I am concerned. I have not heard anything like this from any other quarter. According to him, the Russian defence has gone to pieces and the Russian government itself is thinking of taking refuge in Siberia!

But, enough of public business for this evening. I *must* have a few minutes with my Darling, before I go to bed, like those blessed evenings we had at Harlakenden, when I could think only of my precious Edith and our love,—rejoice in her beauty and sweetness, in her tender endearments, and try by my own tender care of her as she rested on the Davenport to make her feel to the very depths of her dear heart how I loved her and loved to make her happy, every care forgotten and nothing but love remembered in all the world. How the memory of those blessed evenings changes care into joy and fatigue into refreshment for me amidst the anxieties and worries of my long days away from my Sweetheart. They altered the whole aspect of life for both of us, and the magic they wrought has endured. Life can never be intolerable or burdensome again,—for my Darling understands and loves me perfectly and knows all the depths of my love for her. It is those memories—of those nights of perfect revelation following upon days of perfect companionship and partnership in the tasks and problems of life—that have made this separation endurable. Oh, my Darling, my own Edith, I wonder if you can

2 J. H. Snodgrass to RL, Aug. 23, 1915, T telegram (WP, DLC), saying that ten million refugees were moving across Russia in advance of the retreating army, many of them were dying from starvation and exposure, and that people expected St. Petersburg and perhaps Moscow to fall before the year's end. He added that American aid for relief and arms "would create a favorable impression." Wilson sent this (his note is undated) with the following comment (ALI, WP, DLC): "From our consul. Surely panicy and greatly exaggerated—10 millions! W."

possibly realize how happy it has made me to find you again and again reckoning the length of these innumerable days of separation from that last unspeakably happy Sunday evening in the morning room. If it was planned to make me know how much and how tenderly you loved me,—designed, by some tender instinct of your heart, to convey to me a message that would make me deeply, ecstatically happy,—it has certainly succeeded! You are the most adorable lover in all the world! I am going to bed without a conscious care because my heart has received these things from you. Good night. A lover's kiss—and all my heart in it!

Wednesday, 7.10 A.M.

Having gone to bed happy with thoughts of you, my Darling, and having had a fine sleep, I feel as fit as a fiddle this morning. The air grew lighter towards bed-time and sleeping was easy and refreshing. I envied you the sea breezes I hope you are having, but I most of all envied Ocean City and everyone who had had sight of you there. If I could only be by for a moment and see you pass, it would be a delight and a *little* break in the long waiting. If I could exchange glances with you and see the love light gleam in your dear eyes, I would be refreshed and gladdened for the day. If I could have you all to myself for long enough to pour into your ears the full message of my heart to you while I held you close in my arms and interpreted my meaning with kisses, I could face the world like a god! To think of the whole hotelful of people having sight of you and access to you, and I here starving for a glimpse of you. Never mind, Sweetheart, we shall make up for it in the sweet days to come. I hope I shall be generous and let others have a *little* of you *some*times. I shall *try* to behave! The very thought of you makes me happy; the possession of you will enhance my capacity for happiness a hundredfold and my fitness for everything in life that calls for the strength that can come only from zest and joy and self-forgetfulness in the doing of it.

I was offered a job the other day, to be undertaken when my present job is over by the statute of limitations! A man who must have thought me a very easy mark, Mr. Howland, of the *Independent*,[3] came, on behalf of a sindicate of magazines and papers, to ask me to be the editor of a history of the present war, to be written by the generals, on both sides, who have taken part in it! I said Nay with such emphasis that I think he was a little jarred, and told him Roosevelt was the man he wanted; not W.W. He made a wry face and went away. Think of spending precious working days fighting this wretched war all over again, when

[3] Harold Jacobs Howland, associate editor of *The Independent*, 1913-20.

308 AUGUST 24, 1915

everybody ought to be engaged in the healing work of setting up honorable peace and civilization again! And the main idea, of course, was that my name would be a good commercial asset, and enable them, besides, to get more of the participants to contribute to the volumes. He did not know what contempt he bred in me. And, like all the others of his kind, he had sought the interview with me on the ground that his errand (unstated, of course) was of pressing and immediate importance!

The days go very quietly with me, my precious Love, except in my thoughts. I keep my engagements at a minimum and give myself time to do my work thoughtfully and deliberately. There is none of the winter strain of rush and office pressure on me, and I am taking *very* good care of myself. Just love me with all your might and nothing can hurt me. Please tell me that you are perfectly well and that it makes you happy to know that I am

Your own   Woodrow

ALS (WP, DLC).

To Edith Bolling Galt, with Enclosure

[The White House] 24 Aug. [1915]

You will have seen this in the papers. I hope and believe it is a favorable sign.   W.

ALI (WP, DLC).

E N C L O S U R E

Secretary of State, Washington.   New York. Aug. 24, 1915.

I am instructed by my government to communicate the following to you: "So far no official information about the sinking of the ARABIC is available. The Imperial Government trusts that the Government of the United States will not take a definite stand after only hearing the reports coming from one side, which, according to the opinion of my government, cannot possibly correspond with the facts but will give the Imperial Government a chance to be heard equally. Although mu [my] government does not doubt the good faith of the witnesses whose statements have been published by the newspapers in Europe, my government thinks that it should be born in mind that such statements have naturally been made in great excitement which might easily produce a wrong impression. In case Americans should actually have lost their life this would naturally be contrary to the intention of the German Government who would deeply regret this fact and has instructed me to extend its sincerest sympathy to the Government of the United States." May I ask you to be good enough to publish the above or to kindly let me know whether you agree to my publishing it.   J. Bernstorff.

T telegram (WP, DLC).

To Edith Bolling Galt, with Enclosure

[The White House, c. Aug. 24, 1915]

The Colonel evidently regards it as not incredible (so do I, for that matter) that there might be an armed uprising of German sympathizers. Rumours of preparations for such a thing have frequently reached us, but investigation never has disclosed anything, and our tiny army is so scattered (a few hundred here, a few hundred there) that at the first—not knowing *where* to be ready—we would be unable to do anything effective. But for my part I think the fear probably very slightly founded.   W.

ALI (WP, DLC).

ENCLOSURE

From Edward Mandell House

Manchester, Massachusetts.

Dear Governor: August 23rd, 1915.

If our relations with Germany grow worse and if they finally come to a breaking point, are we sufficiently prepared for any outbreak which may occur within the United States?

This is not looked for, but it may come and it seems to me it would be the part of wisdom to prepare in advance. If I were you, I would certainly not have any formal break with Germany without first getting matters well in hand.

Our people would find it hard to forgive the Administration if trouble should arise from within and there were no adequate means to meet it.

Activity in this direction would perhaps be helpful for it might convince the Germans that you are in earnest and it might lead the people to feel something of the seriousness of the situation.

I wish to heaven there was some way out, and there would be with any but a mad people to deal with.

Your devoted,   E. M. House

TLS (WP, DLC).

To Edith Bolling Galt, with Enclosure

[The White House, c. Aug. 24, 1915]

This matches that pe[s]simistic letter of Walter Page's.[1] These constitute the most discouraging features of the present situation. The slight gains at the Dardanelles and the naval success in the Gulf of Riga may put a little ginger into the Allies.   W.

ALI (WP, DLC).
[1] That is, WHP to WW, July 23, 1915.

E N C L O S U R E

From Edward Mandell House

Manchester, Massachusetts.

Dear Governor: August 23rd, 1915.

Page's secretary, Clifford Carver, is the most ubiquitous youngster I know. He goes with everybody in England and numbers among the Ministry many personal friends. Every week he gives me a resume of all the facts and gossip that comes to him. I have a letter this morning and these are some of the things he says:

"The general topic of conversation at the Vice Regal Lodge (Dublin) was the situation in Constantinople and that in Russia. They, as everyone else over here who thinks any, believe that the only hope of the Allies at the present time is at Constantinople. If the attack there fails I really don't know what they will do next."

"I spent the week-end at Lady Paget's[1] and heard several things of interest. The Grand Duke Michael[2] was there and also General Paget. I asked the Grand Duke if any serious effect would be caused by the fall of Riga, and he told me that the situation would remain unchanged.

I heard Sir Arthur tell him that the four new divisions which had been sent to the Dardanelles would in all probability make an effort to break through the lines there in the immediate future, and if no results were accomplished by October the entire operation would have proved a failure and it would be very difficult, if not well nigh impossible, to embark any of the forces now there.

The night before, General Paget, who, as you probably know, has but recently returned from France, told me that the greatest battle of the Allies had been fought at Souchez, and that although the French used over 500,000 men but three kilometres were gained, and in the attack the French casualties exceeded 220,000.

This was indeed the great effort which the French had planned to make in the spring. In conclusion he expressed the firm belief that the Allies could gain absolutely nothing in Flanders, and that the end of the war would find the line constant. Even by adding the grain of salt which is necessary for any of his remarks, this is an interesting and somewhat prevalent prophesy."

"I firmly believe that another trip similar to the one you have already made this year would prove far more profitable than the last. I have heard from several Cabinet people and others, various rumors regarding proffered peace terms here and there. For the moment, I don't think any of these will be considered, but still they are in the air."

Since his letter was written it seems that the Allies have made considerable progress in the Dardanelles. It shows, however, a general spirit of depression in England.

Your affectionate,   E. M.   House

TLS (WP, DLC).
   1 Lady Mary Fiske Stevens Paget, daughter of a wealthy New York family and wife of General Sir Arthur Henry Fitzroy Paget, who commanded the British forces in Ireland from 1911 to 1917.
   2 Grand Duke Michael Mikailovich, cousin of Nicholas II, who resided in England after his morganatic marriage in 1891.

To Edith Bolling Galt

[The White House, c. Aug. 24, 1915]

These poor chaps are between the devil and the deep sea.[1] They dare not offend us, and yet if they yielded to us their enemies would make a great case against them in any subsequent elections. But we must insist. Control of the customs is the essence of the whole matter.   W.

ALI (WP, DLC).
   1 R. B. Davis, Jr., to RL, Aug. 23, 1915, T telegram (WP, DLC), reporting on his ultimatum to President Dartiguenave demanding that the Haitian congress accept the treaty with the United States without modification by August 25, and on the Haitian leaders' threat to resign unless permitted to submit a resolution of intent to "conclude a convention . . . to the best reciprocal interests of the two countries." Davis suspected that the Haitians hoped to change the provision for United States control of the customs service and advised that no changes be accepted.

From Edith Bolling Galt

Ocean City, N. J.

My own precious One: August 24, 1915 9:45 a.m.

There is so much I want to tell you and answer in these dear letters I found waiting for me and the one that has just come, that I hardly know where to begin. But I don't really know a better beginning than that which my heart is calling all the time—I love you. More today than yesterday, and more yesterday than ever before. I could not begin this last night, as I usually do, for Bertha stayed in my room until 2, and it was then too late to begin a letter. So I fell asleep dreaming of you and woke at 6 to read over your blessed letters of Friday and Saturday and early Sunday. My heart was so hungry for them and they were so full and pulsating that nothing could have so filled my need, except your own royal splendid self. No, Sweetheart I was not conscious that my letters had lacked what you waited for, to such an extent. And I understand what you mean. But I always write so assured of your understanding and comprehension that I possibly do leave too much for you to read into them.

But I will remember how I should miss what you never fail to give, and not cheat in my part of the bargain. I am so sorry my letter did not come on Friday when you so needed it, but I promised you that I would always let you know if anything was wrong so you can count on that and feel that if the letters fail it is not because of some misfortune, and I trust the ones of Sunday and Monday came more directly.

I am trying to write this downstairs in a sort of "Lounge" and every two minutes someone comes to talk. But I trust it will be intelligent and bring you the message that is in every line and every word.

Along with the sweetness of your letters came the bitterness of the announcement of Elizabeth's marriag. I will send you the notice that was in the Baltimore paper.[1] I have only a line from Rolfe saying they would not go to the ceremony—and that their hearts were broken.

Poor fellow, I can't get him out of my mind, but all your love and sympathy ease the pain in my own heart and I know would help him—if he only knew our secret and I could send him a copy of what you say about him, and the attitude that it's the only *right* one concerning her. Of course I can't do this, but I love to rest on your strength and comfort my distress with the splendid knowledge of your love.

I feel with all the burden resting so heavily now on you that I should not dwell on any extra shadow that is clouding my horizon, but the truth is Sweetheart the wonderful power of love is so strong that I am almost ashamed to acknowledge how the light of our happiness glows so bright as to make even this

---

[1] She enclosed a clipping from the Baltimore *Evening Sun*, Aug. 18, 1915.

tragedy fade into the shadow. And my heart refuses to mourn, because it has found its own mate and to me "all's right with the world." I hope this is not selfish—I surely don't mean it to be. But I am so happy because we love each other!

I have not yet had a chance to talk to Mother, for we did not get here yesterday until lunch time, and we all were together for the afternoon and evening. After dinner we went to see *Annette Kellerman* in "Neptune's Daughter." Have you ever seen it, for, if one cares for moving pictures, it is very good. And we got out of the theatre about 10.

The Roses & Mother were tired so came home and Bertha and I walked 2 miles up the Board Walk in the moonlight and talked over many things, *not cabbages*—but *Kings*—for she asked me if I minded telling her if I was engaged to you, and I told her I did not *mind* telling her anything, but I wanted to talk to Mother first. Then she said she *knew*, and that she was sorry she asked but she just could not help it. But that she thought you were perfectly delightful, and that after she met you she felt it was a foregone conclusion. That if it meant my happiness she was happy and that she realized so what her life had missed that no one could more fully appreciate the glory of such a love than she. I know as soon as I can talk to Mother they will both write you. I can never make them understand how proud—how splendidly proud I am of you, of your love for me, or make them know what you are. That must wait until the blessed opportunity comes to them to know you for themselves—and comprehend you as no one can through description, even though the description comes from one who adores you and to whom you have poured out the wealth of your golden heart.

They are calling me to come and join them on the walk, so I must hurry. But one more thing—and that is in answer to your question about my coming and about your dear eyes. Woman fashion I reverse the order of discussion and say how charmed I am that you had such a really jolly spree going to Phil. and that the report about your eyes is so eminently satisfactory. Perhaps you shan't mind going oftener—if you have such a good time—and then we can keep closer watch on those eyes that are now mine and which I want very tender care taken of.

Now Sweetheart, I had not written you about my plans for coming home, because I feared if I said I would be home next week you would give up going to Cornish and that I did not want to interfere with—if you felt you could get away and have a rest. Of course now I feel your reasons for not going cannot be gainsaid (I mean the State reasons) and so I will tell you what I am thinking of.

Mr. & Mrs. Rose are going home by way of New York, and are crazy for me to go with them and stay one or 2 days, and they will go early Monday the 30th. If I did this I would get home Wed. or Thursday. On the other hand this place closes the 4th or 5th so Mother & Bertha had arranged to go on Monday, the 30th and the only trains leaving this place are 5 A.M and 4 P.M. They had arranged to take the latter which would arrive in Wash. at 10 at night. In case I should come with them this hour does not suit me very well as my faithful survitor Susie is away on her vacation, and I did not want to send for her until her time is up (i.e. on the 4th of Sept) So I had thought I would just have the man open the house for me & go to Mother's for meals and still get into my own quarters to unpack and get things straight.

So, I rather think I may go to N. York, for that is a far more comfortable trip home than the one from here, as this has 2 changes from one train to another and runs no Pullmans until after leaving Philadelphia. But I have not yet fully decided which to do and wish you would tell me. You will, I trust, have this early tomorrow, Wednesday, and if you would send me an extra line in case you have posted your letter I would have it Thursday. And I will do either you want me to. But precious One, I don't believe (and it breaks my heart to say this) that it would be prudent to have *our* dear Margaret come just as soon as I get home. I do want you so, and want to help you with every fiber of my being, but don't you think people would know, and make gossip about it? I have racked my brain to think of some other way to make it safe to see you—but so far nothing comes. But, if it will help you to know I am home, I will come Monday. But I really thought perhaps it was easier to know I was away. Just as you told me when we were discussing it at Harlakenden. Write me frankly how you feel.

All these pages and not a word about public affairs and now I must stop. But know that I read with vital interest every one of the contents of the 2 big envelopes I found waiting for me here and am thinking of you every minute with the tender hope that in your great wisdom you may yet find a way out of this blackness regarding the Arabic. And please always set me straight, as you did about the Albany Editorial, for I do want to see through these dear eyes I love so.

Another interruption—so this must go in the mail. My heart is with you day and night and I am so glad the ghosts have gone from the South Portico. I knew they would go, but now we can both love that spot, without fear—that brought light and strength in perfect love into our lives.   Always your own,   Edith

ALS (WP, DLC).

To Edward Mandell House

Dearest Friend,   The White House. 25 August, 1915.

I do not know what impression you have got from Bernstorff's request that we suspend judgment until we hear the German side of the sinking of the *Arabic*. I am suspicious enough to think that they are merely sparring for time in order that any action we might take may not affect the unstable equilibrium in the Balkans. Do you think that is too far fetched a suspicion? And how long do you think we should wait? When we *asked* for their version of the sinking of the *Orduna*[1] they pigeon-holed the request and we have not heard yet!

I note what you say about being prepared for a possible outbreak in this country; but *where* and *how*? I have thought of that, of course, and with the greatest solicitude; but, though we have followed up every clue, even the most vague, when reports reached us of alleged preparations for outbreak, we have found nothing definite enough to form the basis for even so much as guessing *where* we ought to be ready. What had you in mind? Does your own thought fix the danger definitely enough at any one point in the country to make it possible to suggest any particular concentration of force, or precautionary vigilance?

The gossip Page's Secretary sends you is quite in line with all that we hear from England, and is the most discouraging feature of the whole situation.

How does his suggestion that you might get a readier hearing now than you got when you were over there before impress you?

Do you give any credence to the report that the German financial authorities are within sight of the end of their rope? I should think they would be, but I take it for granted that if they were they would not say so in public.

I am well, and Lansing is proving most satisfactory. But most satisfactory of all is your watchful and loving friendship.

                    Affectionately Yours,   Woodrow Wilson

WWTLS (E. M. House Papers, CtY).

[1] Commander Walter Schwieger of the *U20* made an unsuccessful attempt to sink the Cunard liner *Orduna*, bound for New York, on July 9, and the State Department asked the German Foreign Office for an explanation on July 24. Von Jagow refused to reply on the ground that the incident involved an enemy ship on which no American lives had been lost.

From Robert Lansing, with Enclosure

My dear Mr. President: Washington August 25, 1915.

As the letter of Mr. James B. Forgan, which is enclosed to me by Mr. Hamlin,[1] deals directly with the general policy of the Government I feel that before answering it I should be advised as to your wishes. I therefore enclose Mr. Hamlin's letter and a copy of Mr. Forgan's.

I think we must recognize the fact that conditions have materially changed since last autumn when we endeavored to discourage the flotation of any general loan by a belligerent in this country. The question of exchange and the large debts which result from purchases by belligerent governments require some method of funding these debts in this country.

Faithfully yours,   Robert Lansing.

TLS (SDR, RG 59, 841.51/266, DNA).
[1] C. S. Hamlin to RL, Aug. 24, 1915, *FR-LP*, I, 143.

E N C L O S U R E

James Berwick Forgan[1] to Frederic Adrian Delano

My dear Mr. Delano: Chicago August 17, 1915.

I want to get some information for a very confidential purpose and it has occurred to me that you may be in a position to help me secure it.

It is, to put it bluntly; I would like to know what the attitude of the government administration in Washington would be towards the flotation of a large British loan in this country. Sometime ago I remember seeing in the press that the State Department had discouraged New York bankers on a proposition to float a British loan in this country, but at the same time it was stated that it was not within the province of the government to veto such a transaction. It would seem to me that the present condition of international exchange would deter the government from entering any objection to the flotation of such a loan in this country, or to the sale by Great Britain of American securities in this country. One or other of these transactions would seem to be a business necessity at the present time. As I am in a bit of a hurry to get the information I would appreciate a telegram indicating what you believe the government's attitude would be. You might send me one of the following telegrams to indicate which of the positions you think the government would take in regard to the flotation of a large British loan in this country and I will understand your meaning:

1. Parties would be favorable to and would encourage such a transaction.

2. Parties would take no action either for or against such a transaction.

3. Parties would discourage such a transaction but would not offer any active interference with it.

4. Parties attitude would be such as to make such a transaction practically impossible.

With kind regards, I am,

Very truly yours,   James B. Forgan.

TCL (SDR, RG 59, 841.51/266, DNA).
1 President of the First National Bank of Chicago.

To Edith Bolling Galt, with Enclosure

[The White House, c..Aug. 25, 1915]

It is a little provoking to have Page do this kind of thing. *Of course* that is the view over there; but we know how crazy they are to have us follow them. This makes one wish to order P. to visit his native land!   W.

ALI (WP, DLC).

E N C L O S U R E

London August 24, 1915.

2686. Confidential for the Secretary and the President. I report the following as indicating public opinion here for whatever it may be worth, if it be worth anything.

Sir William Mather, who you know is a good representative of conservative minded non-political thoughtful Englishman, called to see me yesterday to express the friendly grave fear lest delay in action should deepen the impression throughout Europe that the United States is seeking to maintain peace at the price of humiliation in the face of repeated offences. This fear is becoming more or less general, even among thoughtful men.

The reported intention of our Government published here to give Germany another opportunity to explain and thereby to evade and to cause delay provokes the general opinion that any delayed action on our part will lose much of its moral effect by tardiness.

The tone of the less responsible press is a tone of open ridicule. The tone of the best papers shows surprise at what they regard as an unfortunate delay and a restrained fear lest the United States delay too long.

Several men in official life have expressed opinions such as the opinion that follows. They have so spoken, not to me but in quarters where they knew I should hear from it "the Germans shuffled and evaded and lied to us for ten years and we refused to believe that this was their deliberate policy. The Americans seem slow to learn by our experience. They have a contempt for the United States as they had for England and they hope to keep her writing letters at which they laugh."

The facts about the ARABIC seem so clear here as to leave no doubt of her deliberate sinking by the German submarine without any provocation. The testimony all survivors is identical on all important particulars.   American Ambassador,   London

T telegram (WP, DLC).

To Edith Bolling Galt, with Enclosure

[The White House, c. Aug. 25, 1915]

I don't know why the Sec'y sh. have formulated this opinion and sent it to me just at this time. Perhaps so that we might every day *share* our thinking.   W.

ALI (WP, DLC).

E N C L O S U R E

From Robert Lansing

PERSONAL AND PRIVATE:

My dear Mr. President: Washington August 24th, 1915.

In view of the situation created by the torpedoing of the ARABIC and the danger of being involved in war with Germany in case we should sever diplomatic relations, *which appears probable*,[1] I have been considering the general effect of a state of war between this country and Germany upon the part we desire to play when negotiations for peace may seem practicable.

The position which we have hoped to occupy, was that of a mutual friend to the belligerents, who would act as intermediary in opening negotiations and as a restraint upon either party in making oppressive demands.

As the war has progressed I have become more and more convinced that we were losing constantly the friendship of both parties and that we would have little influence upon either in bringing about negotiations or in moulding the terms of peace. It would take but little to eliminate us entirely in the final settlement.

So far as Germany is concerned, I think that we have lost irretrievably any influence we may have possessed over her Government, and that our participation in any way in the restoration of peace would be resented.

As to the Allies, I believe that their distorted views as to our attitude, which is certainly misunderstood in Great Britain, would deprive us of influence with them.

Now, on the assumption that we sever diplomatic intercourse with the German Government, which responds by a declaration of war, the consequences internationally would seem to be the complete restoration of friendship and confidence with the Allies and the necessary recognition of the United States as a party to the peace negotiations. We would be in a position to influence the Allies, if they should be victorious, to be lenient in their demands and to regain a part of the good will of Germany by being a generous enemy. If, on the other hand, Germany should triumph, we would be included in any settlement made, and Germany would be deprived of the free hand she would otherwise have in dealing with us after she had overcome her European adversaries.

If the foregoing views are sound, it would appear that our usefulness in the restoration of peace would certainly not be lessened by a state of war between this country and Germany, and it might even be increased.

I have endeavored to analyze the situation impartially from the standpoint of our international relations and not from the standpoint of domestic policy. As to the latter standpoint my ideas are less definite. I do not know what effect war would have upon the American people. Of one thing though I am convinced, it will not arouse very much enthusiasm,** however it may be approved by the American people other than those of German birth or descent. Beyond this I do not wish at the present time to express an opinion.

Faithfully yours,   Robert Lansing.

* I suppose he means the severance of diplomatic relations is probable,—is war?

** quite right.

TLS (WP, DLC).
1 Emphasis Wilson's. The footnotes are also Wilson's.

To Edith Bolling Galt, with Enclosure

[The White House] 25 Aug. [1915]

Is not this characteristic of Gerard? Instead of giving full and adequate report of conversation with von Jagow, goes off into his own opinion—"I told you so," in effect. Does he not seem pleased to make things as black as possible?   W.

We are cabling him to-night to send us a complete account in detail of his conversation with von J.

Bernstorff is to see Lansing to-morrow morning (the 26th)

ALI (WP, DLC).

ENCLOSURE

Berlin via Copenhagen Aug. 24, 1915.

2772. Your 2105. According to your instructions saw Von Jagow 6.15 today. When I came in he said, "I have been expecting you every day. I do not understand this ARABIC business." Asked him if they had any report. He said, no; but that it was done contrary to instructions if the boat had been torpedoed as reported. I said, "What were the instructions." He said "Not to torpedo without notice," and so on. I said "You mean passenger ships."

He said he had sent Bernstorff a wireless cipher telling him to ask our Government to suspend judgment, that while not doubting the good faith by [of] the eye witnesses that they might naturally have been excited, and that the Germans regretted the loss of life; he did not know whether Bernstorff had received the wireless, that he had not answered.

Von Jagow gave me the impression of being greatly worried by the occurence; personally I am sure it was done by order of Von Tirpitz who thus wants to make a direct issue with the Foreign Office and Chancellor even at the expense of war with us. The threats of the friends and followers of Von Tirpitz that something of the kind would be done have been too open and continuous; even Von Gwinner, the head of the Deutsche Bank, sent me word by Winslow that if they could catch the MAURETANIA it would be treated like the LUSITANIA.   Gerard, Berlin.

T telegram (WP, DLC).

To Edith Bolling Galt, with Enclosure

[The White House] 25 Aug. [1915]

Foxy Carranza!   W.

ALI (WP, DLC).

E N C L O S U R E

Vera Cruz, Mexico   Undated.
Rec'd August 24, 1915. 8:15 Am

Am requested to send the following textual communication, dated August 21st, received by me this evening:

["]The Honorable Messrs. Robert Lansing, Secretary of State of the United States of America; Dionisio de Gama, Ambassador Extraordinary and Plenipotentiary of Brazil; Eduardo Suarez Mujica, Ambassador Extraordinary and Plenipotentiary of Chile; Romulo R. Naon, Ambassador Extraordinary and Plenipotentiary of Argentina; Ignacio Calderon, Ambassador Extraordinary and Minister Plenipotentiary of Bolivia; Carlos Maria de Pena, Envoy Extraordinary and Minister Plenipotentiary of Uruguay; and Joaquin Mendez, Envoy Extraordinary and Minister Plenipotentiary of Guatemala, Washington.

The Citizen First Chief of the Constitutional Army and in charge of the Executive Power of the Union having read the circular note which your Excellencies were pleased to address to him through the Honorable Mr. John R. Silliman, Confidential Agent of the Department of State of the Government of the United States of America near this Government and in which you tender your good offices for the re-establishment of peace in the Mexican Republic, has seen fit to decide that I apply to you, as I hereby have the honor to do, and beg you to be pleased to inform him whether the said note has been issued by authority of the Governments you worthily represent and in their names or whether you have sent it in your private capacity and without any official character. It is my very great honor to express to Your Excellencies on this occasion the assurances of my respectful and distinguished consideration. Signed Jesus Acuna in charge of the Department of Foreign Relations of the Mexican Republic. I have the honor to make the foregoing known to you and beg you to transmit the note transcribed, hoping that you may be pleased to communicate the answer of the representatives to whom it is addressed. Signed Acuna."   Silliman

T telegram (WP, DLC).

Two Letters to Edith Bolling Galt

[The White House]

My precious Love,   Wed., 25 Aug., 1915

Your first letter from Ocean City was handed to me by Hoover *just* after I had sealed my love letter. My, how it made my heart sing; bless your heart for all the sweet explicit love in it,–but I cannot let myself start on that. This is just a line to answer your question about your plans.

You are right about bringing Margaret down, though I do not see how I am to endure not seeing you at once when you come here. Of that, later. It would be very dreary, added to other things, for you if you were to come down before Susie arrives and just camp out at 1308 or make shift in some other way, and I hope, my Darling, that you *will* go with the Roses to New York. They will give you a good time; you enjoy New York and its amusements; and you will be diverted and refreshed. Go by all means,–but by *motor* again? Let me know what your address there will be.

In rushing haste,–and a heart full of love,

Your own   Woodrow

[The White House]

My own precious Darling,   Wednesday evening 25 Aug., 1915

My, but it was hard to write and advise you to go to New York with Mr. and Mrs. Rose,–turn in the opposite direction again,–and with all the uncertainties of the road,–when you had seemed actually on your way here at last! My heart sank within me as I wrote that little note this morning. But it was clearly the right decision. It would worry me to have you here in an empty house, without even Susie to look out for you—and I cut off; and I know that you will have a good time, and you *need* some real diversion now that the dear folks at Panama have seen their fears realized. I don't wonder the Roses are crazy to have you go to New York with them! There they will try to induce you to go back to Geneva with them. They will not give you up to me until they have to. And in my heart I don't blame them. Who would ever willingly give you up that had ever spent a day with you? But I envy them desperately. You are mine, not theirs; and yet you cannot come to me and can stay with them. How the gods play with us and make sport of us and laugh at the game! Have a good time, my Sweetheart,–a light-hearted, jolly time, for my sake,–because, even in the midst of our loneliness for each other, it will make me happy to think of you at the theatre and going about the gay city as a care-free looker on, merely waiting till you can go to your lover. And I have something up my sleeve. We *can* see one another *just as soon as you get back.* So don't be later in arriving than Susie herself. You are hereby bidden to dinner on the evening of the fourth—note the date and the coincidence! On a certain fourth of the month four months earlier you were bidden to dinner here: I want to continue the conversation begun that evening! Do you accept? Never mind how it is to be managed: the method will be quite unexceptionable, and I am sure you will approve, but don't be late and don't come back from New York on so narrow a margin of time that you will be tired. Ah, how my heart beats to think of it! Do you realize, my precious One, that we have never before, since we first met one another, been separated for so long a time as we have the past endless weeks? Let us see to it that we shall never so long as we live be so long separated again. I can stand *this* only if I never have to stand the like again. Isn't it glorious that we can really form that resolution and be as sure as we can be of anything in this world that we can carry it out? It makes my heart leap with joy,—at the very moment when I know that your face is set in the other direction! We will make a pledge to one another as old and sacred and sweet as love itself: "Intreat me not to leave thee or to return from following after thee: for whither thou goest I will go; and where thou lodgest I will lodge: thy people shall be my people, and thy God my God." Naught but death shall part thee and me. Thy people *are* my people, my Darling, *now*, and mine are yours. You know how I feel about being allowed to share your anxieties about the dear ones at Panama; and I hope with all my heart that there will be some practical way in which you and I can be of service to Elizabeth. Would it not be delightful if we might some day be instrumental in reuniting her to her parents? They are sore now, and a bit hard,—as we often are when deeply wounded,—but their hearts will melt within them before long when they think of their daughter, whom they have so tenderly loved. Maybe, some of these days, before *they* are ready to do it, we can have Elizabeth and her husband come to us, and then induce Rolfe and his wife to come too. Sorry as I am about the marriage, tragical a mistake as it seems, I cannot help feeling a great relief that it was not prevented in any of the outrageous, melodramatic ways that old fool Edwards had suggested and we had feared the doctor brother might try to carry out. What a handsome girl Elizabeth is, even in the poor newspaper print of her photograph which accompanies the article you sent me from the Batlimore paper. I can't help hoping, against all the probabilities, that she will be happy in this wilful marriage, after all. Your own heart, I know, is harboring the same hope

It is *not* selfish, my precious Darling, for you to be happy because of our love, bless your heart, even in the midst of these distresses about Rolfe and Elizabeth. You are not cheating them by it. There is nothing you can do for them,—and certainly your unhappiness would not help them, though your sweet, genuine sympathy does. And, knowing, as I do, how deeply you feel all these things that affect those you love and who have so constantly depended on your love and counsel, you may imagine what joy it gives me to know that our love offsets for you all distresses of every kind, and makes you secure, as it does me, against sorrow or real misfortune. Ah, my Sweetheart, what a love letter this is you have sent me to-day, written though it was amidst the interruptions of the "Lounge." Every line of it is surcharged with the warmth of your own dear heart. When you put your love for me thus into words, it fills me with a delight for which I know no expression except to take you in my arms and say what it seems possible to whisper, but not to write down! I was deeply interested in your Sister's impulsive question and your answer (just like you, you sweet daughter) and her comments. But I don't quite understand what she meant by saying that she *knew* we were engaged, or would be, so soon as she met me,—unless, indeed, she intended an overwhelming compliment to me! She would of course know that I was certain to fall in love with you, but why should it seem to her so certain that you, who she had known to resist all temptations in that direction, would fall in love with me? But, never mind what she meant,—I am only interested in having her and your dear mother love me and think me good enough for their wonderful Edith. I wish I could go to see them the minute they get here, and before you get back from New York. I could face them less bashfully if you were not there, I think, wishing me to appear at my best (!), and, besides, I would like to show them how eager I am to know them and be with them. But I have not yet figured out how I could elude my guards and do it.

I find that I am getting more and more to transfer what I have to say about affairs, my dear Love, to the little slips I attach to the papers I put into the big envelopes, because I think you will like to read my comments and explanations along with the documents themselves. But there is one item about Bernstorff that ought to be added as very interesting (though I am not *yet* clear as to what he is up to). He telephoned Villard, of the New York

Evening Post, that he was disappointed that the papers had not "played up" his message to Lansing about suspending judgment in a more emphatic way,—that it was intended as a disavowal of the act of the submarine commander. And a newspaper man who manages to keep quite intimate with von Bernstorff and to get from him most of what is in his mind telephoned Lansing to-day that he might expect an official disavowal of the act through von B. at their interview to-morrow morning. But such "tips" seldom prove to be worth serious attention, and von B. may be "stuffing" both Villard and his other newspaper friend (a man named O'Laughlin).[1] What *is* clear, however, is that von B. and his superiors in Berlin are seriously disturbed over the possibility of a breach with us, and have determined, at this eleventh hour, to prevent it if they can. The disavowal must be very explicit and must involve a virtual promise that these barbarities will stop.

Don't think, Sweetheart, that I *expect* a comment on all the papers I send you. Most of them merely continue old subjects and are sent only to keep you posted. Don't you see now how comparatively easy it is to keep the threads of even a very complicated public matter in your head when some despatch or memorandum about it turns up almost every day? You used to wonder that I could remember so much of so many things. You no doubt think it easy to do yourself by this time. Are my explanations and comments on the little slips ample for your guidance?

Thursday, 7.10 A.M.

I hope my precious One has had as fine a rest and sleep as I have. I feel fresh and fit for anything,—and largely, I think, because I read my Darling's sweet love letter again just before I put out my light and thoughts of her blessed me all the night through. I did not so much *dream* of her as feel *conscious* of her with an occasional vivid moment when I could actually see her and speak to her, between kisses. These morning hours, my sweet Love, seem hours of specially close communion with you. I am no more intensely conscious of my deep, adoring love for you than when I am trying to teach my pen how to talk to you in the evening, but in the evening the crowding, insistent thoughts of the day will not be wholly dismissed, and I feel, as it were, the whole *confusion* of these anxious times. It would not be so if you were actually with me. Your *presence* eclipses everything for me. Nothing can for a moment compete with your

[1] That is, John Callan O'Laughlin.

charm or your power to absorb my every thought and emotion.
But this very table is a place of business. I cannot lift my eyes
from the sheet I am writing on without seeing some paper lying
within reach of my hand which contains some question of public business I have to consider and settle. If you were here I
would see nothing but you. In the morning the things these
papers about me suggest have sunk into the background; the
silent house has no business astir in it; all its suggestions are
domestic and private; it is a home waiting for you. It seems to
call out to you as my heart does. And so the morning and evening, taken together, are a sort of epitome of what our love
means. In the evening you are the partner of my life, on its public side as well as its private; in the morning you are just the
darling partner of my heart, and nothing dare invade our
privacy. It is delightful,—it has become an indispensable part of
my life,—to have you associated with everything I do or think,—
the day's business would be intolerably empty and burdensome if
you were not in it, in all of it. But I can not *live* on business,
even when you are part of it. I live by your love. The times when
I can be conscious of that and of that alone are my hours of
deepest happiness. Ah, Edith, my adorable Darling, I love you
'more than tongue can tell.' My whole heart and life are wrapped
up in you. Your love has made this a new world.

Your own   Woodrow

ALS (WP, DLC).

From Edith Bolling Galt

Ocean City, N. J.

My precious One: August 25th/1915 12.15 M.

We have just come in from a long ride toward Cape May. It is
very warm, even here, but delightful riding, and I must hurry
and get this ready to mail as the train goes at four.

I found your dear messenger of yesterday ready to greet me
when I went to breakfast this morning (9 oclock) and as Mother
& the Roses had breakfasted at eight and Bertha was not yet
down, you and I had ours together, which was great fun. I really
have no idea *what* we had, for I was so glad to have you all by
myself and talk of all you were thinking and feeling that I paid
no attention to mere food. It is jolly to begin the day together,
and it does make me happy to feel we are so much nearer to each
other. I had no idea Cape May was so near to Washington and we
were within fifteen miles of Cape May this morning. And I felt a

little thrill each time I would read a road sign saying "30 miles to Cape May," "20 miles etc["] and felt each mile was taking me nearer *home*—for each mile was lessening the distance that seperates us. I am anxious to know what you feel about my coming next week. I know you will tell me frankly, and I will do whatever my dear Lord wants me to.

It has cast a shadow over me that I had to write you what I did yesterday about Margaret's coming

I so long to see you, but I must not let that longing make me forget the caution we owe to that awful tyrant, the world, and Bertha tells me a number of people here have spoken to her about things they had heard, just as soon as she said I was coming. And this morning I had a letter telling me the same thing.

I know you need me Dearest, and you know how I want to come, but isn't it easier for you to go on with the seperation, even though I am in Washington, than to see each other for the brief stay Margaret could make, and then begin the seperation all over again

This looks as horrid *written* as it sounds when read. And I might as well tell the whole truth and say that now I know we have ourselves *in hand*—and *I* can go on. If we relax, we probably couldn't. And it can't be *much* longer before the girls are home to stay, and things resume a *normal* footing.

Write me Sweetheart, how you feel about this. Don't be afraid I won't understand, for I will—always as you do me.

I am worried about your dear hand. Please if it hurts you use your typewriter, for I never want to consciously cause you pain. I was so interrupted yesterday when writing and had so much I wanted to tell you that I did not thank you for the really lovely tribute you pay me in saying you think the lines you copied descriptive of me. I think they are lovely but am afraid—in spite of Dr. de Schweintuz's—is that the way you spell him? report about your eyes, that you see through roseatee glasses. But it makes me infinitely happy to know you *do* so see me and I will always try to play under the becoming rosy light.

The two big envelopes that came this morning are still unopened, but after lunch I am coming upstairs and read and enjoy all you have said on the little penciled notes and the matters you refer to. I will be *very* interested in Mr. T.'s report to you of public opinion etc. and want to ask you, Dearest, not to worry over my opinion or intuition concerning him, for I really don't know him at all, and you do and trust him—and besides my idea may be colored by his commonness. But, if he is *loyal* to you nothing else matters, and you have so many other things to worry you it would be a crime to disturb your confidence in him, unless I had grounds for it, which I have not.

You ask me how we spend our days. Well, I spent most of yesterday morning, writing to you. Then we went on the Board Walk but it was too hot to be pleasant so we came in for early lunch and afterwards went to Atlantic City on the car—electric —for poor Mr. Rose had such trouble with his tires—which were new—that he thought he could get others in Atlantic City and send these back for an adjustment as to price. So we wandered 'round while he looked up garages etc. But, I must confess I was awfully bored. It was too hot to walk, and none of the others wanted chairs, because they wanted to look in the shop windows, while I longed to get out to sea and think. We got back about dinner time, after which we played Auction and got to bed about 11.30   This morning we went riding, and I think I will try to make the others play cards or something this afternoon while I finish this and write a few other letters I owe

2:15

I have just come up from lunch and find I will have to take this to the Post Office as there will be no more collections before the 4 ock train. So you and I will enjoy a short walk and I will then get a big double chair and take you for a ride up the Board Walk. There are lots of funny looking people, and it will divert you you precious thing. Oh! What fun you are going to have with me when I have the *right* to tell your "keepers" that I want you and we will go off for a spree as you did in Philadelphia. I am so glad you had a good time there!

I am sending you with this a copy I made of a letter Mother had from Elizabeth.[1] It is a pitful little letter, and there does seem some way should have been found to make her and her father and mother understand each other. At Bertha's and my suggestion Mother sent the letter to Rolfe, for we have had three more heart broken ones from him. I had one this morning saying E. had "given up her country, her religion, her people and her parents"—for that *he* could never acknowledge this man—but he, (Rolfe) wanted to withdraw his request that we have nothing to do with them, that knowing everything we could do as we saw best.

I have purposely said nothing about State affairs, for what can I say my Beloved to help you. It is all so awful. But all that I am, all that you believe me to be is yours, and I am longing to help. I am with you, and you can "make it so" if you feel you cannot bear the strain. I will come on Monday—or any day—for I love you my precious Woodrow and you can rest in that as in your own strength and splendid courage. I have not yet told Mother. She is very depressed about Elizabeth, and I thought (as she does not know you) this might be a sort of shock, until your daily letters, and mine, pave the way. Bertha has just come and asked me to send you her love   Now, get your hat, Sweetheart we are off for the Post Office. A great big kiss to his Excellency Woodrow, Rex from his most loyal subject   Edith.

ALS (WP, DLC).
¹ Elizabeth Bolling to Sallie W. Bolling, c. Aug. 18, 1915, HwCL (WP, DLC).

Two Letters to Robert Lansing

My dear Mr. Secretary,   The White House. 26 August, 1915.

My opinion in this matter, compendiously stated, is that we should say that "Parties would take no action either for or against such a transaction," but that this should be orally conveyed, so far as we are concerned, and not put in writing.

I hope that this is also your own judgment in the matter.
                              Faithfully Yours,   W.W.

WWTLI (SDR, RG 59, 841.51/266, DNA).

My dear Mr. Secretary,   The White House. 26 August, 1915.

I very much appreciated your letter setting forth the pros and cons of the effect of hostilities with Germany. I find that it runs along very much the same lines as my own thought.
                              Faithfully Yours,   W.W.

WWTLI (SDR, RG 59, 841.857 AR 1/91½, DNA).

From Robert Lansing, with Enclosure

PERSONAL AND PRIVATE

My dear Mr. President: Washington August 26, 1915.

Since writing you of my interview this morning with Count Bernstorff¹ I have received the revised telegram which he desires to be sent by wireless to his Government. Please indicate your wishes and send it to me the first thing in the morning.
                              Faithfully yours,   Robert Lansing.

P.S. He also submits another telegram which explains itself. RL.²

TLS (SDR, RG 59, 763.72/2131, DNA).

[1] Lansing's letter is printed as an Enclosure with WW to EBG, Aug. 27, 1915.
[2] It is missing.

ENCLOSURE

MESSAGE IN PLAIN ENGLISH.

No 168

With regard to the confidential negotiations which I hope soon to be able to take up with the American Government, it seems that the last paragraph of the American Frye note of 10th inst.[1] contains a suggestion which may prove useful in the general negotiations concerning Lusitania and Arabic. I understand the suggestion so that we should refrain from attacking passenger ships without warning pending negotiations, which would put the burden on England to refrain from unlawful blockade pending negotiations. It does, however, not mean that we should give up the whole submarine warfare.

T MS (SDR, RG 59, 763.72/2131, DNA).

[1] It read: "If this proposal proves acceptable to the Imperial German Government, it will be necessary also to determine whether, pending the arbitral award, the Imperial German Government shall govern its naval operations in accordance with its own interpretation, or in accordance with the interpretation maintained by the United States, as to the obligations imposed by their treaty stipulations, and the Government of the United States would be glad to have an expression of the views of the Imperial German Government on this point." RL to J. W. Gerard, Aug. 10, 1915, *FR-WWS 1915*, p. 505.

Robert Lansing to William Gibbs McAdoo

CONFIDENTIAL

My dear Mr. Secretary: [Washington] August 26, 1915.

Mr. Hamlin sent me a copy of the letter of Mr. James B. Forgan which you enclosed to me in your letter of the 23d.[1] I sent the letter to the President on the 25th, a copy of my letter to him is enclosed, and I also enclose his reply of today.

I have read your comments upon the matter of loans to belligerent countries and must say that I concur in your opinion—in fact, from the outset, I have held that opinion of such transactions viewed from the legal standpoint rather than from the standpoint of expediency.

While the President did not authorize me to send a copy of his communication to you I feel that he would wish you to know his position.   Faithfully yours,   Robert Lansing

CCL (SDR, RG 59, 841.51/266, DNA).

[1] WGM to RL, Aug. 23, 1915, TLS (SDR, RG 59, 841.51/266, DNA).

To Edith Bolling Galt

[The White House]

My own Darling,   Thursday evening, 26 Aug., 1915

You need not fear that I will for a moment misunderstand your arguments for going with the Roses and not coming back to Washington at once. What you say is sweet, brave, true, and loyal to the uttermost, like everything you think and do. But I must beg you, my sweet Darling, not to attach too much importance to Washington gossip, or to what anyone is saying. If we keep within bounds, as we shall, and give them no proofs that they can make use of, we can and should ignore them. And there are some very big reasons why we should ignore them, within the limits we of course mean to observe. Our happiness is not an ordinary matter of young lovers; it is, for me, a matter of *efficiency*. I hate to argue the matter in my own interest; but I know *you* are thinking of that side of it, too, and will, in your generosity, forgive my speaking of it. I can of course practice self-denial to any extent,—spend any proportion of my energy upon it that is required,—so far as it is a mere question of strength and resolute self-control; but it costs me more than anyone but you and I can know, and I doubt if it is my duty to use myself up in that way any more than is unavoidable. I am absolutely dependent on intimate love for the right and free and most effective use of my powers, and I know by experience,— by the experience of the past four weeks,—what it costs my *work* to do without it to the extent involved in entire separation from you. And so we are justified in taking risks. If during this dreadful week that has just gone by—the most anxious week of my whole term as President, when loneliness sat upon me like a pall—I could have had you actually at my side, if only once or twice a week, I would have *laughed* at the strain and carried it with a light heart. I am not saying these things, my precious One, with the thought that you need to be reminded of them. The whole tone of these two precious notes in which you have spoken of your plans is one of utter devotion to me and readiness to do anything I *wish*, whether it is altogether wise or not, just because if I need you you stand ready to do *any*thing to satisfy that need. I never loved you more tenderly and utterly than I have loved you as I have read these dear letters. I have never felt your love for me beat stronger or purer or in lovelier form than in these sentences that I treasure in my heart. You understand, as always, and you are none the less sweetly and tenderly and self-forgetfully in love because you are trying to *think* for both of us and to choose the best and wisest course. But I know how you wince under gossip—especially, bless your heart, when you think it will injure me—and I know how many people there will be who will be ready and eager to repeat it to you now that you are getting down into this latitude, and I want to help to fortify you against it. We are entitled to go our own way so long as it is dignified and gives the gossips nothing but their own prurient surmises to go on. And we shall be able to see each other rather frequently just so soon as you get down here. I am not going to tell you *how* because,—well, frankly, because I want you to go with the Roses to New York, for the pleasure you will have there, and I am afraid you would give the trip up if I told you now, before you start! I'll tell you in my first letter written to you in New York. Is it a bargain? I *want* you to go. Ocean City is boring you. You have had bad news since you got there. You need a few days of fun and entertainment. And, when you have had them, you will hurry back and dine with your lover at the White House on the evening of the fourth at seven o'clock sharp. Heaven grant he may not have heart failure at the sheer joy of seeing you and being near you again after the loneliest weeks of all his life! I can hardly restrain the excitement of it as I write, though it is still ten long days before it can be!

Thank you, dear Love, for sending me a copy of Elizabeth's letter to her grandmother. It is one of the sweetest and most touching letters I ever read. It makes me like her and believe in her. She believes in the man utterly, and makes me ready to believe in him until there is some reason in his own life and conduct why I should not. Of course her grandmother wrote and reassured her about her continuing love for her, did she not? I feel like writing to her myself,—because I know what love means. Don't you wish that you and I could join in begging her to come to see us and let us make her feel that we were going to give her a show, and more than a show? I am glad, very glad, Rolfe withdrew his request that we should have nothing to do with her. It was not only right that he should but I cannot help hoping that it shows the beginning of relenting on his own part. I wish that Mr. Boyd could move to this country and establish himself here (I don't mean in Washington, but in the United States), chiefly because I know the effect of the tropical climate upon the health of women born and reared in the temperate zone. They can't stand it more than a very few years. It is much worse on the women than on the men. My whole instinct and desire is to take care of Elizabeth. Since reading that letter I feel as if I had had a glimpse of her real self and the glimpse attracts me. I wonder why I am always so much drawn to the outlaw?

I don't know *what* to make yet of the German situation (you see it is evening and my head still teems with the business that has been taxing it all day,—and the business is inextricably mixed up with thoughts of you, because every moment of special perplexity is always a moment of special need of you and special loneliness because you are not here). I am going to send you in the big envelope which will go to you to-morrow the account Lansing has sent me this afternoon of his conversation this morning with Bernstorff, and also Gerard's latest cable. It is evident enough that the German authorities are *very* anxious to effect an amicable settlement with us. The Associated Press despatch from Berlin in this afternoon's papers about the interview with von Bethman-Hollweg[1] is significant of that,—the more so as it was allowed to pass the censor. But what is *not* yet clear is, whether they understand what we will expect of them as Lansing set it forth (not a whit too strongly) in what he said to Bernstorff. But there's no use conjecturing and wondering. We must wait and see. It would be indecent, when they have begged for time to explain, to be too impatient and to seem to wish to force things to an issue as quickly as possible,—as we justly criticised Austria for doing in dealing with Serbia at the outset of this terrible war. I feel like a pilot who has been so long at the wheel that he longs to be relieved so that he may relax his attention, and his muscles, for a while, but who knows that he has come to the most difficult part of the passage, where he is not even sure of his chart and holds his breath lest any moment the vessel under him should strike a reef. The 'watch' is not half over. He would be near to fainting but that ever and again a love message from the one he loves best in all the world is laid on the little ledge by the compass and he can again and again turn to

[1] The Imperial German Chancellor talked with the Berlin correspondent of the Associated Press on August 25 and, although he refused to be quoted, he issued a formal statement about his government's attitude toward the *Arabic* case. The dispatch interpreted Bethmann Hollweg's informal remarks as friendly toward the United States, citing as evidence his appeal to the American people to keep open minds until the facts of the case were established and his frequent references to the instructions given to submarine commanders after the sinking of *Lusitania*. In his formal statement, the Chancellor pointed out that no one yet knew whether a mine or a German torpedo had sunk *Arabic*. However, he continued, if it were shown that a submarine commander violated his instructions, "the imperial government would not hesitate to give such complete satisfaction to the United States as would conform to the friendly relations existing between both governments." The dispatch appeared in afternoon papers of August 26. The *Washington Post* carried the formal statement in the morning papers of that day and the full dispatch on August 27.

the words in which she pours out her heart to him and cheers him with her exquisite, tender sympathy and renews his strength and his flagging spirits with the sweet assurance, by which he lives, that she is thinking of him and loves him. If she could only come and stand, in her own sweet, radiant person in the pilot house beside him, and sometimes actually lay her dear hand on his tired arm and sometimes smile into his tense face with that wonderful smile he knows and loves so well and longs for all the long watches through, his whole frame and temper would respond. All the fatigue would go out of him. He would steer with a new instinct for the channel, and smile back at her like a boy steering his pleasure boat for her refreshment and delight! Ah, Sweetheart, all thoughts, all needs, all desires lead straight to you. I love you more and more every hour, and need you in proportion to the love. Bless your heart for saying "I love you more than I did yesterday, and loved you yesterday more than I ever did before." It not only made me deeply happy, but it so exactly expressed my own experience. I am more and more deeply in love with you every day of my life. I don't know, I can't imagine, where it is going to end. I suspect it will never end at all, but that all the rest of my life I shall go on from love to love as I know my Darling better and better. She grows more and more lovely the more I see of her, the more intimately I know her. I love her so that it is hard for me to tear myself away even from a sheet of paper on which I am making love to her, no matter what o'clock it is. But there is another day of work ahead of me, and I must, in conscience, say Good-night. Ah, if she only knew how I was thinking of her this moment, I wonder if she would not forget all her surroundings and run to me and nestle close in my arms and give me a long, long lover's kiss, and send me to bed the happiest man in all the world. My Darling, my Darling! Good night.

Friday, 6.40 A.M.

Good morning, my precious One! I love you with all my heart, and it is sweet to be closeted here again alone with my thoughts of you,—the sweetest, most delightful thoughts a man's heart could desire. The day is overcast: apparently we are to have rain, and there is a decided chill in the air; but I hope that it is bright and full of tonic air where you are. And I hope you do not know it yet,—that you are still sound asleep, and will be these two hours to come. For I'm worried about the small amount of rest and sleep you take. I wish with all my heart it were much more. I wonder if I can teach you better habits? Ah, if I could only steal in and sit by your bedside and watch you as you sleep and throw loving thoughts about you to make the sleep sweeter, as I used to do in the half light by the Davenport in the morning room! I would not touch you: that would startle you, for you would not be expecting me. I would only sit and watch that lovely face that is in my heart all day long, every day, and think unutterable thoughts of tender love,—thoughts too deep and tender to be put into words,—very stuff of my life. And then, when at last you stirred, and opened those dear eyes with the wonders in them that I dream of,—I wonder what you would do! I know what I would do. I would take you in my arms and smother you with kisses, striving at the same time to pour out in half formed whispered sentences all the longing and loneliness of the weeks that have held us apart. What would I not give for such a privilege this very minute—and what would it not mean to me! The House is very quiet. Out in the streets the town is waking up. Trucks are lumbering by to their early work, the negro drivers calling to their teams; but inside I do not hear a sound. The Colonel is a good sleeper and I generally take breakfast before the doctor and Tumulty are down. It is practically an empty house so far as anything like domestic life is concerned,—just a place where four men sleep and take their meals; and meal-time is like business-time, so far as the talk is concerned. I live my real life inside myself, as if the others were not here. I hope and believe that they do not know it,—for I try to play the game and play it generously; but I could not stand it if I *really* lived with them. The world I live in (I've peopled my own world ever since I was a boy) is full of the most delightful persons in the world. No one is admitted whom I do not love. And the centre of that world is an adorable beautiful woman whom I love more than aught, more than *all*, else in the wide world, and who, in her sweet grace, loves me and has changed the world for me. She moves about this little kingdom within me, which I lovingly maintain until it may be established in fact as well, with a sweetness, a self-forgetfulness, a charm of perfect womanliness, a vivid power to dominate without self-assertion, by the mere divinity of her own adorable self, like a queen and yet a simple friend and lover. Thoughts of her change the whole aspect of the day, make me glad to be alive, and alive for her. She is my own, incomparable Love, and I am   Her own   Woodrow

ALS (WP, DLC).

From Edith Bolling Galt

Ocean City, N. J.

My own precious Sweetheart: August 26, 1915 9:20 a.m.

I have just read your dear little note in regard to my home-coming. And do you know it is the very first letter that has ever come directed by your own hand to me *without* a cover, and it does make it seem more personal some way. Don't think me a foolish sentimentalist, but it is sweet to feel no one else had any part in it. But, you dear thing, it is not a real answer to my question. You say "go by all means" but you don't say what would be your wish in the matter. I mean under the existing circumstances. I so wanted to know what you really felt, but I appreciate your thinking only of my comfort and pleasure instead of your own. And I'll tell you a secret—if I thought I could see you the minute I get home *nothing* would induce me to postpone one second longer coming. But as things are I thought you might rather I would go. I will think the matter over until tomorrow, but I believe I will go and will surely send you my address in N. Y. and will not be later than Thursday coming home.

I paused here to read your real message of the day that was finished yesterday before the other was begun. Thank you, my Dearest, for writing me so fully all the correct reasons for explanations and waiting Germanys statement. I had read much of it—but not so clearly put, or so free from comments that confuse. You are infinitely patient to do this, for you are so weary that just to reherse all these matters is an added strain. But it is such a real joy to me, and I am hoping it will not be necessary to *write* it all out—for very much longer. I knew you were feeling the strain, although there was not a word in your letters about it. Somehow there seems a subtle something that brings me strong impressions of just what is going on concerning you—in heart, in mind, in physical being. Oh! if I could come and give you what you are pleased to tell me I do give—new life and strength.

Can a letter charged with all the love and tenderness of my adoring heart take my place? If so, you truly will never lack for the Elixir that will keep you young and strong and radiant.

I am perfectly well my precious One, and you can draw without fear on my vitality itself if such a thing is possible.

Bertha and I took a long walk last night, when the others went upstairs at 10. We went out the Board Walk beyond the glare and noise of the lights and crowds, where we could see only the water with the tide coming in with great white foaming billows, and the moon above throwing a path of light straight across the dark waters. It pleased me to believe that that path of light led straight to you, and I sent my spirit with flying feet across it—straight into your own room at the White House, where it hovered near you all the night—bringing a message of love and longing. Did you feel it, and did it bring a fresh, salt current of health giving air to brace your weary nerves? Why can't you get away for even one day on the Mayflower and run down the River far enough to get new air in your lungs

I wish you would do this Why not, it would be at least a break in the monotony of days.

Oh! how I would like to be a stowaway and come up and find you on the deck where we have been together! But I must not think of that.

Yesterday after I got back from *our* walk to the Post Office I wrote Dr. Grayson a letter and then sat down by myself and read the contents of the big envelope and was so crazy to sit right down and discuss this with you. But of course I had to be with the others and talk of *uninteresting* things which, of course you with your uncanny intuition know, bores me—and now they are waiting for me and I have to touch these big things with only the sketchiest sort of reference. The telegram from Bernstorff in your letter is a ray of hope, and I do hope for once he is honest and see from the morning paper you are still waiting to hear what they have to communicate. I was so boiling mad when I read the account of that villain's speech about you (I mean T. R.) at Plattsburg[1] that I could hardly eat my breakfast. Did you stoop to read it? I just wish for a few minutes I was a man as big as old Ollie James. I would go and make him eat his words or [knock] his disgusting teeth out. Perhaps both, for someone ought to thrash him for the honour of the *men* in America. But you will tell me again I am an incendiary if I dont hush.

I am glad the English cable has been cleared up by Mr. John

---

[1] Theodore Roosevelt, speaking at Plattsburg on the evening of August 25, set off a controversy between the Wilson administration and General Leonard Wood, who oversaw the military training camp. Roosevelt, while advocating military preparedness, attacked the administration's policies toward the war. "For thirteen months America has played an ignoble part among the nations," he said, because it substituted elocution for action. As Roosevelt left Plattsburg, he gave reporters a more pointed statement in which he said that no one owed allegiance to the President unless the President showed loyalty to the country. Secretary Garrison, in a telegram to Wood, rebuked the General for permitting controversial subjects to be introduced at the training camp. Garrison gave this telegram to the press on August 26. See the *New York Times*, August 26 and 27, 1915; and J. G. Clifford, *The Citizen Soldiers*, pp. 83-88.

Wilson's letter,[2] and did you decide to see him? I am so sorry that after all I never succeeded in getting but one N. Y. World with the "Propaganda Matter." So am a little in the dark when I read things about the M. P. But don't bother to write all this out for I remember you thought it wiser not to, and you will tell me about it when the blessed time comes that we are together.

Mr. Tumulty's data was interesting and concise—and I am trying to see him through your eyes. I see the Haitian Government is still allowed another day to answer, and I will look eagerly for the paper tomorrow to see what they decide. Yesterday was the first time I have seen it in the paper, but it actually seemed correctly stated.

I hope if Col. House comes to Washington, which he implies in the letter you sent me, I will see him. I know I am wrong but I can't help feeling he is not a very *strong* character. I suppose it is in comparison to you, for really every other man seems like a dwarf when I put them by you in in [sic] my thoughts. I know what a comfort and staff Col. House is to you Precious One and that your judgment about him is correct, but he does look like a weak vessel and I think he writes like one very often. This is perfectly unnecessary for me to tell you this but it is such fun to shock you and you are so sweet in your judgments of people and I am so radical. Never mind I always acknowledge my mistakes and take a secret joy in finding you right and stronger than I am in every way.

The big envelope with the Moscow trouble has not yet been opened, though it is on the desk as I write. But I will see that later, and everything must wait when I can talk to you

Tell me how you feel about the Mexican situation. As you say in your little note Carranza's attitude is dignified, and one must admire him for that, at least.

All the others seem only too glad to confer as suggested. But will it be worthwhile, unless they all come—and Carranza's seems

2 Wilson, on August 21, had received a mysterious telegram from a "Major Miller" of the British Expeditionary Force, which said: "I have an important diplomatic matter to report personally to Your Excellency. Please cable me direct if audience will be accorded." Wilson gave the telegram to Lansing, who showed it to Spring Rice. The latter, in turn, sought information about Miller from the Foreign Office. In the meantime, John A. Wilson, the President's cousin, had been called to the house of his friend, General Charles Miller, father of the Major. General Miller had received a similar telegram from his son. John A. Wilson wrote to the President conveying the Major's request for an interview. Wilson replied to his cousin that he had not known Miller's identity when the telegram arrived and had felt obliged to deal with the matter through the British Embassy. Wilson had sent the correspondence to Mrs. Galt. C. Miller, Jr., to WW, Aug. 21, 1915, WWTC telegram; C. Miller, Jr., to C. Miller, Aug. 21, 1915, T telegram; RL to WW, Aug. 21, 1915, ALS; J. A. Wilson to WW, Aug. 21, 1915, ALS; WW to J. A. Wilson, Aug. 23, 1915, T telegram (Letterpress Books); and J. A. Wilson to WW, Aug. 23, 1915, TLS, all in WP, DLC.

the strongest power. I hate to go but I must. Goodbye until tomorrow   Keep a stout heart my precious Woodrow and remember
how I love—love—love you   Edith

ALS (WP, DLC).

To Edith Bolling Galt, with Enclosure

[The White House] 27 Aug. [1915]
Don't you think Lansing does these things well?   W.

ALI (WP, DLC).

E N C L O S U R E

From Robert Lansing

PERSONAL AND PRIVATE

My dear Mr. President: Washington August 26, 1915.
Count Bernstorff at my request called upon me this morning.
I informed him that I wished to see him about the proposed wireless code message which he desired us to send for him to his
Government. I pointed out to him the objectionable feature of
making any reference to the ABABIC in connection with negotiations; that the ARABIC could not be considered in the same way as
the LUSITANIA in view of what had passed between the Governments since the latter vessel was sunk; that he must appreciate
that the torpedoing of the ARABIC might interrupt further
negotiations, since a condition of their continuance was the cessation of destroying passenger vessels without warning and opportunity to reach a place of safety.

The Ambassador replied that he realized the situation had
changed and that he would take the proposed wireless message
and rewrite it. As soon as he sends it to me in revised form I
will send it to you.

I then asked the Ambassador what the statement of his Government, which he had telegraphed to me and had made public,
meant in regard to instructions to submarine officers, that I
would like to know what those instructions are.

He replied that he had not been told but supposed they
referred to warnings and opportunities to leave ships attacked.

I asked him, if such instructions had been given, how there
could be any doubt about their violation in the case of the
ARABIC?

He said that the facts seemed uncertain and he hoped to have an explanation from his Government.

To this I answered that we had received evidence from Americans on board the ARABIC showing the vessel was torpedoed and that a German submarine had shelled the DUNSLEY and was seen by the survivors of that vessel after the ARABIC foundered, and that there was practically no doubt at all but that the vessel was intentionally attacked without warning. I said to him that to advance any excuse of mistake by the submarine commander would be absurd and would irritate rather than relieve the situation.

He asked me if we were willing to await a report of the affair from Berlin, because he felt sure there was some explanation.

I replied that I could not see how any explanation could be given which would be satisfactory; and that our experience in awaiting reports of submarine attacks was not encouraging. I then pointed out the case of the ORDUNA, in which we had waited for a report for a month without reply. The Ambassador seemed greatly surprised and said that he could not understand it.

I said that any considerable delay could not be thought of, that, while the public feeling here was less demonstrative than it had been after the sinking of the LUSITANIA, I believed it to be far more intense.

He said that he realized this, but hoped that some time would be given so that his Government might have opportunity to make reparation if its officer was at fault.

This is the substance of our conversation.

The Ambassador seemed to be worried over the situation and was, for him, in a very serious mood. He is, however, optimistic that the affair can be amicably arranged. I did not indicate to him that I shared his optimism but rather tried to give him the impression that I considered the situation most critical and that Germany would have to act quickly to avoid the consequences of the torpedoing of the ARABIC, even if it were possible to do so.

Faithfully yours, Robert Lansing.

TLS (WP, DLC).

To Robert Lansing

My dear Mr. Secretary, The White House. 27 August, 1915.

It does not seem to me that the Ambassador states our position fully enough here, and I should very much dread seeing his Government misled. Our point is, not merely that no passenger ships should be attacked without warning, but that care should be taken to make adequate provision for safe-guarding the lives of non-combatants. Mere warning on a stormy sea, mere putting of passengers and crew into open boats, might be as brutal as giving them no warning at all. "Without warning and provision for the safety of the lives of non-combatants," if he would accept the phraseology, would cover my point.

Faithfully Yours   W.W.

WWTLI (SDR, RG 59, 763.72/2139½, DNA).

From Robert Lansing

PERSONAL AND PRIVATE

My dear Mr. President: Washington August 27, 1915.

I had a conversation this morning with the German Ambassador in which I told him of the objectionable feature of his proposed wireless message to Berlin. He appeared to appreciate the force of the objection and I accordingly returned him his letter of yesterday with the draft of message. I have now received another letter with a revise of the message.[1]

If this meets with your approval please return it at once so that it can go forward to Berlin. I think that it practically eliminates the objectionable features of his former dispatch although, of course, he has in it the sentence—" * * *which would put the burden on England to refrain from unlawful blockade pending negotiations." I think, however, he is entitled to express this view which is his own.

Faithfully yours,   Robert Lansing.

TLS (SDR, RG 59, 763.72/2140½ A, DNA).

[1] J. H. von Bernstorff to the Foreign Office, received Aug. 28, 1915, T telegram (Der Weltkrieg, Unterseebootkrieg, geheim, Vol. 2, p. 71, GFO-Ar), repeating the text as enclosed in RL to WW, Aug. 26, 1915, with the revision proposed by Wilson in WW to RL, Aug. 27, 1915, to read: "I understand the suggestion to be that pending negotiations we should refrain from attacking passenger vessels without warning and provision for the safety of noncombatants, which would put the burden on England to refrain from illegal blockade pending negotiations." Bernstorff's telegram was sent in English.

To Robert Lansing

Dear Mr. Sec'y.   [The White House, Aug. 27, 1915]

Thank you. I am willing that this should go forward.

W.W.

ALI (SDR, RG 59, 763.72/2140½a, DNA).

Two Letters to Edith Bolling Galt

[The White House] 27 Aug. [1915]

Gerard is here a little more coherent than usual, and the two despatches taken together give a rather clear and vivid impression of the contest between the foreign office and the military crowd.[1]   W.

ALI (WP, DLC).

[1] J. W. Gerard to RL, Aug. 25, 1915, 4 P.M. and 5 P.M., T telegrams (WP, DLC). The first reported on a conversation with Von Jagow, who said that, if *Arabic* had been torpedoed, the act would be disavowed, and that the Emperor, not the Admiralty, made decisions about whether to disavow actions of submarine commanders. The second was a report saying that Gerard had been informed that Von Jagow had spoken at the direction of the Chancellor, who had taken his stand on the *Arabic* case "on his own initiative." Gerard urged Lansing to appreciate "what a bold step has been taken by the Chancellor and Foreign Office" and to "make their road to disavowal and reparation as easy as possible," lest Von Tirpitz again gain the upper hand.

To Edith Bolling Galt

[The White House]

My lovely Darling,   Friday evening, 27 Aug., 1915

How do you manage, you little magician, to get so much of your fascinating self into these adorable love letters that make me so happy? You ask, you Darling, "Can a letter charged with all the love and tenderness of my adoring heart take my place?" No, Sweetheart, it cannot. Nothing can. But it brings me so much that is exquisitely sweet and comforting and stimulating that I ought to be ashamed ever to *complain* of *any* lack while you are absent,—and I shall try never to do so again,—except as a means of letting you know how I love you and long for you. Your letters do bring "the elixir that will always keep me young and strong and radiant" because they bring so much of you, and you are my life. This dear letter that came to-day—came early enough to brighten all its grey clouded hours—seems literally a part of your own bewitching self. I can almost fancy as I press my lips against it that it is warm with your own heart blood, so truly and vitally has your sweet love got into its tender phrases. If I could do the same by these sheets, you would be aglow with happy blushes and happy, happy thoughts the moment you took it into your hand. I know I cannot, but I know that the love that beats through my heart and along every fibre of me as I write is as deep, as pure, as devoted, as happy, as full of every sweet thought and joy and tender longing, as ever a man gave any woman! There is no other possible way to love *you*! You not only satisfy but delight everything in me. It stirs every sweet ideal in me to think of you. I love you with an enthusiasm that is the satisfaction of what I had longed for in dreams. You are so real and vital, and yet you seem to have come to me out of some "dream of fair women," where the poet had pictured women, not as they are, but as their lovers would have them be. Yes, Sweetheart, I *did* feel the "message of love and longing" you sent to me across the water Wednesday night. As I went to bed there came over me the happiest feeling that you were thinking about me, that you loved me (that *always* makes me light-hearted!) and that all was well with the world, bless your heart! There is something very wonderful, my darling Edith, about this invisible actual bond that love has made between us,—and something very delightful! How it has changed all the world. I often speak of being wretchedly *lonely*, but I do not mean that I feel for even a moment, nowadays, that I've lost touch with you, but only that the very vivid consciousness of you that so pervades my days and nights itself makes the longing for your actual personal companionship just so much the more intense. I feel so cheated because I cannot have you actually beside me when I know that you are there in thought and in every wish of your dear heart. And do you think I could think me "a foolish sentimentalist" because you want my own handwriting on the envelopes of my letters as well as in the letters themselves? Why, my dear little Girl, I love to have you feel that sort of sentiment and to want everything you get from me to be as directly and wholly personal as it can be made. I'm that sort of a "sentimentalist" myself; and I wouldn't give a fig for a lover who wasn't. I can't even tear up a piece of paper I know you have handled,—a blank sheet, for example, to keep the writing from being legible through the envelope! And there's no reason, when I come to think of it, why I should not write the address on all my envelopes with my pen rather than with my typewriter. They do not know my handwriting where the letters are sent. Don't worry about my pen hand, by the way, my sweet One. It is often hard to manage and the writing is sometimes cramped and queer, but it seldom gives me any *pain* to write with it; and I hate to use anything but my pen in writing to you as much as you dislike to have me. The handwriting is of course more personal and individual, and we want to keep as close to each other as we can even in the mechanical part of our messages. I *love* to write to you. Perhaps it's just as well that with me it is a rather slow and laborious process: if it went fast and easily when could you find time to read the letters I would spin out?

Of course you knew I was feeling the strain of the last week or so (bless you for your sweet divination; it is the most subtle and convincing proof of your perfect love that my heart could desire), but all the same I'm a bit ashamed that proof of it, and even explicit confession of it, crept into my letters. Why should it, I wonder? When I am writing to you I am happy. Those are the times when I am *released* from the strain and feel the strength and peace and joy that come with every thought of your love. There ought to be nothing except light-heartedness in my talk to you—and an occasional, unavoidable confession of longing. I suppose it's the sense of partnership, the instinct and desire to share *every*thing, and the very, very human and natural desire for sympathy—that all-sufficing sympathy that comes from perfect love and perfect comprehension. At any rate, my dear Love understands. She knows that I am not giving way to the strain, that it is no sign of a lack of stout heart that I call out to her; but only one of many ways in which I show how, and how confidently, I depend on her and what infinite strength and reassurance I draw from her. Ah, my blessed little partner, how I adore you! It's a pity I can't find words also for the other things I get from you in such transcendent abundance! I have such *fun* thinking about you, as a boy has in thinking about a girl who loves him and who, he is convinced, is an angel and an exquisite, delicious playmate to boot. I so *enjoy* you, and there is so much gay play and mere irresponsible high spirits and carefree zest in the thought of what we are and what we shall be to one another. Your whole nature is so delightful to me and is so wonderfully fit for holidays. You are as fit for pleasure as for work, and I love pleasure and get untold refreshment from it. We have had and are going to have such *good times* together. We have really never been free to go on a frolic together yet: when we are we are going to have the time of our lives. We shall enjoy the same things and enjoy them intensely—and as if we were not more than ten years old. I sometimes wonder, Sweetheart, whether you really have any idea how much *fun* I have in me or how I dote on fun. I fancy you have seen in me, so far, chiefly the intense and serious side,—not only because I was in the midst of very serious things and was inevitably very much preoccupied with them, but also because I was so intense in my love-making, knowing that all that I hoped to do or be depended on my winning your love. But now that you have put your hand in mine and given me your heart in such exquisite fashion and with such wonderful surrender of all your sweetness and strength to me, I shall show you my other side more fully than you can yet have seen it. I feel somehow that you have never, for long at a time at any rate, given full leave to your power of enjoyment, your capacity for enjoyment, and I have had little occasion of late. *Wont* we have a glorious time just *letting* go and giving our happiness a chance to express itself in careless merry-making, my precious little playmate! No one need ever *know* the thrills we indulge in, so long as we keep a straight face in public when we must, and let only each other know the full ecstacy of our fun together. For my part, I have never fully grown up. Things that amused and pleased me when I was a boy please and amuse me still. I play as hard and fast as I work, and with *more* interest! And you are simply an incomparable playmate! How can I *wait*? That's the only trouble. But why wait, after all? We are sure of one another, and can be irresponsible children without assistance,—can't we?

Speaking of frolicking, I cannot frolic alone and nobody seems *worth* frolicking with now but you. Honestly, Sweetheart, *everybody* seems to me so tame in comparison with you. But this is only a preface to answering your question about the *Mayflower*. It would be awfully dull and lonely now to go on her without you. And, besides, she has been ordered South for target practice; and, during the last few weeks the Berrys[1] have been having a pathetically hard time. Her baby was born prematurely—at five months—and, though the tiny mite lived long enough (a week or two) to give them hope, he died the other day and she, poor lady, is very much prostrated. The Captain *must* leave her for duty but I could not take him away for pleasure.

Speaking of distress, Mr. John Skelton Williams, whom Grayson was consulting to-day about Rolfe, told the doctor something I could hardly credit. He said that a Mr. Sands[2] (is that the name?), connected with the Commercial National Bank, had told him that in a recent letter (he did not say to whom) Mrs. Bolling had spoken as if they were much more "composed" (that was the word he used) about the marriage and that Rolfe and she were calmer and Rolfe again alive to the interest there was to be got in his business. Do you think that can be so? He repeated, too, a number of very favorable and creditable things he had heard about Mr. Boyd, too. That Baltimore place does not materialize as yet, but I feel, from what he said to Grayson to-day, that Mr. Williams is genuinely interested and really determined to find something for Rolfe that will yield at least as much salary as he is getting now. Grayson has told him of

[1] Lieutenant Commander Robert Lawrence Berry, commanding officer of the presidential yacht, and his wife, Lucy Lindabury Berry.

[2] Tucker K. Sands, vice-president, cashier, and a director of the Commercial National Bank of Washington.

my interest in the matter and I am sure he will not lose sight of it.

Saturday, 7 A.M.

It is raining this morning, my Darling, and it looks as if it meant to make a day of it. It was preparing all day yesterday. But rain makes it all the more snug and cozey to be shut in with my precious One for a good quiet talk. My only fear is, that this is a general rain over all this part of the continent and that my Darling is going to be shut in to "auction" and conversation, like a glorious bird in a little cage! I had intended, when I sat down to write to you last night to speak of many public things that you mentioned in your Thursday letter: T.R. (whose speech I did not read), Tumulty, House, Mexico; but I could not resist the temptation to spend the whole evening making love to you, and now this blessed morning hour alone with you has come and I *can't* think of business until after breakfast! And yet it is not fair to leave you in the dark about what I have in mind about Mexico. I don't wonder you ask. It seems a blind alley. But Lansing and I hope that it will be possible to bring all the elements *except* Carranza's into conference and get them to agree upon some terms of accommodation with Carranza which we take to him and use our utmost influence to get him to accept. If he will not, we can put the screws of a thorough-going and effective embargo of the sale of arms and ammunition to him or to any of the rest of them.

I think one reason I am getting impatient of discussing public questions in my letters to you is that your return is now near enough at hand to make me feel that writing is so unsatisfactory and talking so much better. I can with difficulty restrain my excitement at the thought that you will soon be here. It's hard to be content with writing at all, about *anything*, and my love for you so fills my whole heart and mind that nothing else seems a tolerable subject for my writing to you. I am sending a few "flimsies" to-day, my Sweetheart, and they are rather more than usually interesting, but I shall not try to get any big envelopes to you in New York: the risk of their not reaching you is too great,—don't you think so? I will have all the *World* articles collected and saved for you to look over when you get back. I'm sorry you missed them. And now let me tell you something,—the thing that means most to me in all the world: *I love you,*—I can never in words tell you how much; and the most inspiring ambition I have is, to prove myself in some degree worthy of the great love you have given me. You are a very royal person, my adorable and adored Sweetheart! Everything you do is done royally and with all the rich greatness of your nature. I *knew* that, when you once let yourself go, you would love royally and without limit, and all the sweet things I imagined of you have come true. It was hard for you to begin—hard for you to unlock the door, but when you did unlock it you threw it wide open and stood with open arms and shining eyes to receive your lover into the very holy of holies. He knows, my Darling, how sacred the sanctuary is into which he has been received and where he has been welcomed as only you could welcome him, and he will never lose his sense of reverence and high obligation to prove in some sort worthy. But, oh, Sweetheart, my present sense is that of the happy lover, and *that* I shall never lose. I am carried away with the sweetness and charm and utter loveliness of my Edith and quite out of my head with joy that she is mine, —that I am actually to have her for my wife and Darling for the rest of my days! And next week she will be here, and I can tell her the joy that fills my heart to overflowing,—and the pride and the high resolution!   Your own   Woodrow

ALS (WP, DLC).

From Edith Bolling Galt, with Enclosure

My precious One: Ocean City, N. J. August 27, 1915 10:a.m.

I have just finished a long letter to Randolph telling him that which is nearest and dearest to my heart of all other things in the world.

Yesterday just after we all came from a morning on the Board Walk, I found a good opportunity to tell Mother and Bertha together of the great happiness you had brought into my life, and Mother, in her own quiet way, was (as she has always been) full of sweet interest and thought for me. I think she was quite unprepared for an announcement so definite and said, if it was for my happiness she was happy, but that of course she did not know you save by reputation, and that certainly nothing could be finer than that is, and she would welcome you more than anyone else—but she could not help a feeling of sadness. I told her that was only because she did *not* know you, that if she did her sadness would turn to joy and thanksgiving, for you were the most splendid person in the whole world and she would be so proud to know you loved me as tenderly and strongly as I love you.

Did I tell you Precious One, that Mother is as shy as a girl sixteen and can never express what she feels. When you meet her you will understand better than I can explain her peculiar *suppression* of all emotions.

It has always been so, and if I did not know and completely understand her I would often feel almost hurt. But she is pure gold and would give her life to help any of us.

You will find her hard to know, at first, and dont try to discuss intimate things with her, for she simply can't do it. If you feel like writing to her, do it, and in that way you will reach her better than by speech. I am afraid this is a sort of formidable picture I have drawn, but she is the least formidable person I know—only very reticent and easily embarassed.

You can say anything you want to in writing, sure of her understanding receptiveness, and on any subject but personalities you will find her responsive and eager to talk to you. And all this is just a sidelight, for knowing your uncanny way of finding things out without being told, as soon as you meet a person, I think these past two pages superfluous.

Bertha was as sweet as she has always been about anything concerning me and is writing to you herself—which I will enclose in this—and I know you and she will be the best of chums—for she is already half in love with you for my sake and the other half for your own.

Your dear letter has just been read, and I am wondering *how* you propose to arrange for me to come to dinner on the 4th. It is mean of you to keep such a secret "up your sleeve" and being a very discreet (?) person I can't accept unless you tell me. Am I not a villain to conceive such a plot to make you tell me?

But it does sound jolly and I *hope* I will be able to approve your plan. At any rate I will keep the date open until I hear from you.

I understand in this godly state you used to govern there is no mail on Sunday either out-going or in-coming, so my letter tomorrow will reach you Sunday but there will be none early Monday, for I suppose they will not begin work in the Post Office before midnight.

Thank you for your dear wish expressed in your first letter sent me here—to honour me before the world. Surely, Sweetheart, you have already done this by giving me your blessed heart and I will treasure that as my greatest possession

I must go after just one more thing.

Another letter from Rolfe last night—said E. was married on the 18th but instead of the ceremony being at 5 *a.m.*, as they had expected[,] Mr. Boyd was too ill to come to the church until 4 P.M. and was too ill to go on the trip so they were with his people there and he, Rolfe, knew nothing more about them.

That Annie, E's mother, "could not desert her—so went to the church with her and stood by her during the ceremony but did not speak to him or his family."

I think Annie was right to "*stand by her*" and am sorry Rolfe did not do the same. Thank you for all the dear things you say about helping them and your feeling of identification with all those I love. Your own "people have become my people" already Sweetheart, because I love them. They have made me so completely welcome that my heart yearns over them, and I want to do everything for their happiness as well as yours you precious thing. Of course, if you

I had to stop here and cant remember what that sentence was to be. But it may come to me later.

I am so happy over the possible way out of Germanys problem that the papers have stated this morning and that your letter confirms.

If *you* have really done this thing for America every soul in it ought to love and reverence my Lord and Master as I do. But oh! no one else can have you for their very own, or be all yours as I am. Goodbye—I love you,   Edith

E N C L O S U R E

From Bertha Bolling

My dear Mr. President: Ocean City, N. J. 26 August, 1915.

Edith has told us the beautiful secret which my heart somehow told me was a foregone conclusion when you met—your love for each other!

All our lives—since we were little bits of girls—she has been my idol; she has always accused me of thinking that "every man she met would fall in love with her,"—a willing captive to her irresistible charm and *power*. And I have not often been mistaken! My love and admiration of her have only deepened as the years have passed; and I think her still the most beautiful, the sweetest, wisest and strongest woman I have ever known, taking them all in all! Having told you of my constant joy in her dear companionship, it is needless to add how rich I think you in the tender possession of it for life.

Even did I not so truly admire and believe in you, my utter trust in her and her judgment, would make me proud and happy in her choice; and the doors of my heart are wide open to welcome you; and to pledge you its truest love and loyalty.

Faithfully and affectionately *yrs*. Bertha Bolling.

ALS (WP, DLC).

To Emily Greene Balch

My dear Mrs. Balch: [The White House] August 28, 1915

I have your letter of August twenty-seventh.[1] I am sure you know my friendly and cordial disposition towards seeing Doctor Jacobs, but your letter leads me to say this: It is absolutely impossible to avoid publicity about any visit made to me and I clearly foresee that it will be practically impossible for Doctor Jacobs to accomplish her mission as she desires if she comes to the White House.

It would be perfectly possible for her, however, to see the Secretary of State or to see Mr. House who is now at Manchester, Massachusetts. Either of these gentlemen would receive her message in perfect confidence and transmit it to me with the greatest fidelity.

I am sure you will appreciate the motives which prompt me to say these things. I want to serve Doctor Jacobs, not throw obstacles in her way.

In haste

Cordially and sincerely yours,   Woodrow Wilson

TLS (Letterpress Books, WP, DLC).
  [1] It is missing.

To Edith Bolling Galt

[The White House]

My own Darling,   Saturday evening 28 Aug., 1915

I was *so* glad to learn that you had told your dear mother of our great happiness, and it was sweet and thoughtful of you to tell me of her shyness, so that I might understand her as you do, and love her comprehendingly as you do. And a great deal of your own singular power to understand and interpret those you love came out in the explanation. You are singularly frank and just and discriminating. Your mind sees clearly and yet your heart interprets tenderly. You are yourself as fine in your judgments as your judgments are fearless and impartial. I feel that I know the dear lady whom I already regard as my own mother as you yourself know her, and I am ready to love her as much as she will let me. I have only this uneasiness about her first impressions of me after I meet her: I, too, am intensely shy with shy people. If they are not demonstrative, I cannot be. If they do not put their feelings into words, and suppress their emotions, I follow suit, almost inevitably. You must coach me in my dealings with her,—for it would make me very unhappy if I did not win her love and succeed in making her think of me as really her son. Your sister's note was altogether lovely. She has completely won my admiration and affection already. What she said about you was as beautiful as it was true, and what she said to me by way of welcome made me deeply happy. She has made me feel her sincerity and her generosity and I am proud as well as grateful that she should be willing to entrust me with the happiness of the lovely sister whom she adores. I love her words about you, "her irresis[t]ible charm and *power*,"—"the most beautiful, the sweetest, wisest, and strongest woman I have ever known,"—and, subscribing to these words as I do, with all my mind and heart, knowing you as the one woman who satisfies my love of beauty, my love of womanly tenderness, my love of firm, quick, complete intelligence, my love of quiet, unconscious dignity and strength, my love of exquisite grace and charm, it *thrills* me to think that *you*, who have all these things in such abounding measure, should love and give yourself to me. Bertha speaks of my having "the tender possession" of your "dear companionship" given me for life, and the very phrase in which she speaks of it,—a phrase made warm by her love for you,—comes to me like a challenge to try to be worthy of the wonderful gift. Bless you, my precious One, how I love you, how I admire you, how I adore you; and how deeply happy it makes me that in the sweet years to come I am to have the opportunity to render you every tender and devoted service! You have brought me, too, into a family which I know I am going to love.

You *are* a little hard on some of my friends, you Dear,—House and Tumulty, for example; but I understand and am able to see them, I think, with your mind as well as with my own. Besides, you do not know them and have not been faithfully served by them, and therefore your heart is not involved in the judgment as mine is. Take Tumulty. You know that he was not brought up as we were; you feel his lack of our breeding; and you do not like to have me represented by any one less fine than you conceive me to be. You think that my Secretary, the man who must speak for me in most of the dealings and transactions of my office, ought to be a gentleman in the same sense that I am one, with tastes and manners that will commend him to the finer sort of people that come to see me. To your fastidious taste and nice instinct for what is refined, he is common. And all of that is true. I share your judgment up to a certain point, and *feel* it as perfectly as if it were my own,—though there are fine natural instincts in Tumulty and nice perceptions, which you have not yet had a chance to observe. *But* the majority, the great majority of the people who come to the office are not of our kind, and our sort of a gentleman would not understand them or know how to handle them;—neither are the majority—or even a considerable minority—of the men at the capitol, in either House; neither, I need hardly add, are a majority of the voters of the country. Tumulty does understand them and know how to deal with them, —much better than I would, and I need the assistance of just such a man. He is absolutely devoted and loyal to me,—of that I have abundant evidence every day. He hates what is crooked just as heartily as you and I do, and ferrets it out much more quickly and shrewdly than we could. He tells me with almost unfailing accuracy what the man on the street,—the men on all streets,—are thinking (for example about T.R.). In this particular job of serving the country through political action to which we are just now devoted a great diversity of talents is indispensable, and the greatest possible variety of breeding. An administration—an office—manned exclusively by 'gentlemen' could not make the thing go for a twelvemonth. The only thing we can afford to have uniform in the administration of the affairs of a democracy, the only uniform requirement for office we can wisely insist on, is morals—a sound character and enlighted principles, and Tumulty has these. Moreover, he is only technically common, not essentially. Wait until you know him and like him, as you will.

And, then, dear House. About him, again, you are no doubt partly right. You have too keen an insight and too discerning a judgment to be wholly wrong, even in a snap judgment of a man you do not know! House *has* a strong character,—if to be disinterested and unafraid and incorruptible is to be strong. He has a noble and lovely character, too, for he is capable of utter self-forgetfulness and loyalty and devotion. And he is wise. He can give prudent and far-seeing counsel. He can find out what many men, of diverse kinds, are thinking about, and how they can be made to work together for a common purpose. He wins the confidence of all sorts of men, and wins it at once,—by deserving it. But you are right in thinking that intellectually he is not a great man. His mind is not of the first class. He is a counsellor, not a statesman. And he has the faults of his qualities. His very devotion to me, his ardent desire that I should play the part in the field of international politics that he has desired and foreseen for me, makes him take sometimes the short and personal view when he ought to be taking the big and impersonal one—thinking, not of my reputation for the day, but of what is fundamentally and eternally right, no matter who is for the time being hurt by it. We cannot require of every man that he should be everything. You are going to love House some day,—if only because he loves me and would give, I believe, his life for me,—and because he loves the country and seeks its real benefit and glory. I'm not afraid of the ultimate impression he will make on you,—because I know you and your instinctive love and admiration for whatever is true and genuine. You must remember, dear little critic, that sweetness and *power* do not often happen together. You are apt to exact too much of others because of what you are yourself and mistakenly suppose it easy and common to be.

About T.R., now, we are entirely and enthusiastically in accord! But what's the use wasting good serviceable indignation on him? He is too common a nuisance to bother our minds about and the best way to vanquish him is to take no notice of him whatever. I wish Garrison had taken that course, richly as Wood deserved the rebuke he gave him. Bless your dear heart, how I love you for getting so furious with T.R. for his assault on me! I could almost warm my hands at those flaming hot sentences in your letter of Thursday morning!

The weather to-day, as well as yesterday, has been very dismal. I am afraid it must have been so with you, too. We have not been able to play golf since Thursday. I got restless this afternoon—after reviewing the National Guard of the District in the rain (in an old silk hat and my enormous leather-lined automobile coat!), and went off with my keepers (the doctor and Colonel being nowhere to be found) to the National Museum and wandered among the paintings and the stuffed animals and the snakes and insects and Indians as long as I could stand them and my fellow countrymen who stopped me to shake hands. I enjoyed the pictures as long as I could make them last,—there are some beautiful landscapes in the gallery, I think,—and many of the other things were interesting, but I was a bit bored by my fellow men and wished it were raining hard enough to drown my tiresome keepers. Upon my word, I think I will order them off to some other job (they are needed to look after German mischief-makers) and regain my freedom and self-respect!

Sunday, 29 Aug., '15

It's plain from the last sentence above that the visit to the Museum did not dispel for me the gloom of an in-door day of rain and no refreshing exercise! It is still damp and overcast this morning, but I've had a fine sleep, all business is out of my head, and there is no one in the world for me but my Darling whom I love with all my heart, and who has given her wonderful love to me. A world in which she reigns alone cannot but be full of sunshine and her own radiance. Sunday has always been for me a day when I could shut out-of-doors all business and everything that was not of my own personal life, and so I can spend it *wholly* in your company, Sweetheart,—as I did at Harlakenden. I will carry you in my heart with me to church, presently, and all through the service I shall be worshipping with you,—I fear I shall be chiefly worshipping you. All elevated thoughts, all high purposes, everything pure and lovely and good for the soul, are easy to associate with you. You are of their kind and company. And to-day begins the last week of our separation! Before it is over I shall see you again! My exile will be over, and the hand again in mine which will guide me to peace and happiness and joy through the rest of my life. I think I will try to get hold of Randolph to-day. I want to talk to somebody about you to whom I *can* talk, with the brakes off. When I can see Bertha it will be jolly. Her note to me proves that she knows *how* to talk about you in the way that will satisfy even my heart,—though I know the depths of your sweetness and the power of your exquisite charm as even she does not. I wonder what Randolph is thinking of me, now that he has received your letter of Friday? Perhaps I had better find out, from you, before I tackle him. I know perfectly well that he does not think me good or fine or great enough for his incomparable sister,—because he is a man of sense and I am *not* fine or good or great enough to be her mate and equal. But I can match her in *love*, in ideal love! As I write, my precious One, the sun is breaking through the clouds, as it did in my heart this morning when thoughts of you came with my waking. That exquisite smiling picture of you was by my bed. It was the first thing I saw, by the half light of the dawn, when I first opened my eyes, and its smile seemed to bring me some dear message from you (I could not make out the words, but I knew the meaning). I turned over and went to sleep again like a child, with the peace and quiet joy in my heart that are there still. To love you and be loved by you is the way to happiness—and how sweet it is to tread it!

I am *so* glad Elizabeth's mother went with her to the church

and stood by her at the wedding, and I wish, with you, that Rolfe
had done the same. Poor Elizabeth! Being myself, by nature, an
insurgent, I find myself more and more inclined to judge her—
not at all. And wasn't it pitiful that Mr. Boyd should be ill and
spoil, or at least mar, the little happiness that it had been possible
for them to plan for that day,—the trip, &c. By the way, I understand that Mr. Boyd has forty thousand dollars in his own name
in (I believe) Rolfe's bank. He can evidently afford to support
Elizabeth as she ought to be supported. How my heart dwells on
those dear folks!

By the time this reaches you, my Darling, you will be about to
start on the road again in Mr. Rose's machine, in which my
imagination has so often tried to follow you. I know many of the
roads that lie between you and New York and perhaps you will
not be quite so hard for me to find as before; but, dear me, I wish
the trip were over. I can't get rid of the anxious thoughts altogether. At any rate, the bore of the Board Walk is over, and of
aimless days in a hotel—and presently, thank God! your face
will be turned *home*ward, and the endless day of separation will
be over. My heart overflows with unutterable love for you, my
Edith, and I am altogether   Your own   Woodrow

Please write to E. yourself and tell her you love her and will try
to help.

ALS (WP, DLC).

From Edith Bolling Galt

Ocean City, N. J.
Saturday, August 28/1915

My own precious Wonderful Sweetheart   9.30 a.m.

I have just read your message of Thursday night and early
yesterday (I was awake at 6 and could not go to sleep again) and
I read into it all the weariness I feared you felt from this awful
crisis we are facing. Your letter is so full of everything my heart
longs for, but tells me so little of your self. I know the days are
pretty much the same with you, but I long to know everything
you do and if you find anyone to really interest you. It almost
alarms me how you "intute" my feelings. I am bored here—
dreadfully bored—and can't find things to fill the hours of waiting
between the blessed early morning hours I spend with you. The
rest of the day and night is just an inevitable sequence—and
necessary to make possible the next morning.

What a wretch you are not to tell me by what magic you have arranged for me to come on Saturday.

I have thought of everyone and can settle on nothing that seems likely. But you have promised to write me to New York so I suppose I must wait. Send your precious letter tomorrow here, as I would get it before leaving and the one of Monday hold until I can tell you where we will stay in N. York. Mr. Rose said he would like to stay uptown as it is easier to get in and out and they will decide on the Hotel today

If they do before train time I will tell you in this—or if not, surely you would get a letter sent after midnight tomorrow in time on Monday to send me a letter which would reach me on Tuesday.

I am so glad it is cooler in Washington. We had just the same sort of gray day yesterday, but I loved the fresh coolness in the air, and Bertha Mr. R. and I took a long walk before lunch, and after lunch Mr. R. took us to Atlantic City in the car, and it was really *cold* driving. Last night we played "Auction" until ten, when the Roses went to bed and Mother, Bertha and I talked until midnight and I told them something of our happy days together this summer.

I was so interested in the clipping you sent about the most wonderful person in the world—and think it will do good to keep before the public all you have done—though the *real* history of it must wait for the future. Whenever I read things like that I long to add the many things left out—but even I could never do you justice

I am almost sorry I wrote you what I did yesterday about Col. House, but I can no more keep things from you than I can stop loving you—and so you must forgive me.

I know he is fine and true, but I don't think him vigorous and strong—am I wrong?

I will look for the promised big envelope that will probably not come until tonight. There is another Wash. mail at 7.36 at night.

I will enclose a letter I got yesterday from *old* Mr. Wilson.[1] You see he is still trilling on the same note, and I don't know how I can keep him bluffed much longer. But I dont want to tell him yet.

Yes, my precious One, I do understand that we will have to stand gossip and try to be callous to it and do not mean to make your burden heavier by useless heed to such stuff. But I thought right now when the country thinks you are giving every thought to the complications of the Government it might be particularly bad to have you discussed   But I know you would not suggest anything that would not be dignified, so I will live in the radiance of the thought that we will be together a week from today. It seems a long time, but, in comparison to these past four long weeks it will be short.

You are the tenderest person in the world. What you write about your feeling for Elizabeth makes me feel your *bigness* as I always do in grave matters, and her letter was as pathetic as anything I ever read.

I must confess her wedding and his illness fill me with new forebodings, and I pity the child more and more.

I have never heard a word in reply to the letter I wrote her from Geneva and don't know whether she read it or not. And so I don't know whether to write her again. What do you think? How naturally I have learned to turn to you for counsel and help—and oh! no one *could* know what it means to me and how sure I am of help and wisdom.

It is impossible in this place to get away from people, and I write my letters under difficulties so please pardon them. Mr. Rose has just come by, and I asked him about the Hotel in New York and he says the "Algonquin"—I think it is 44th Street—so it is not so high up after all.

Unless we have more tire trouble we expect to get to New York Monday night, have Tuesday there, and leave on Wednesday—they going to Geneva and I to *you*, where my thoughts and heart are always.

They are begging me to go all the way home with them (as you surmised) but I will not think of doing it and would come straight home, if I could be with you and help you.

My precious weary Pilot, I will come and hold those dear strong hands that steer the ship in both my own, and kiss the tired eyes that have strained so to see the right course through the blackness ahead, and try to shut out the tumult that is raging 'round you on every side by whispering in your listening ears these tender words—"I love you, my precious Woodrow.["] And I will stand by though the waters dash over the ship, and carry out your orders knowing that, if devotion to duty, strong purpose and intelligent guidance count for anything in such a storm the good ship will ride the waves and stand in all her white splendor fixed and calm in the still waters that follow after storms, and send her lifeboats to rescue and succor those vessels that have gone on the rocks around here—and all because of the strong hand that guided her wheel and the brain that directed her course.

Now I must go. I am so longing for you, and had I found you

by me yesterday when I woke nothing could have had power to hurt or distress me.

I am, my Dearest *all* all   Your own, Edith.[2]

ALS (WP, DLC).
  [1] It is missing.
  [2] There is a WWT copy of this letter attached to the ALS.

From Cleveland Hoadley Dodge

Riverdale-on-Hudson N Y

My dear President   August 29th 1915

I do not suppose that you have accomplished quite all that you are striving for, with Germany, but you have done so much that I cannot hold myself in any longer, and must tell you how devoutly thankful I am. It all seems like a miracle, as two weeks ago Germany's present attitude seemed impossible. It is a glorious triumph and makes T.R.'s vaporings seem like 30 c.

I have just been writing to my good old friend Richard C. Morse[1] felicitating him on having secured John Mott as his successor to the General Secretaryship of the Y.M.C.A. movement, after Mr Morse's wonderful 45 years of service. I told him that the great quality in him, which had enabled him to accomplish such great results, was his Patience—the most marked quality of both Washington & Lincoln. It is the most difficult of all the virtues, and as I do not possess it, I can probably appreciate all the more its possession by others. I do not think that anyone with Scotch-Irish blood was ever born with it, but you have cultivated it to such a beautiful extent, that it has given you the greatest weapon which any statesman could possibly have.

Please forgive this moral effusion but I daily read the papers, with growing admiration of what you are doing, in spite of all the wild criticisms of cranks & partisans. Thank God, the great solid strength of the country is with you.

With warmest regards from all the family

Ever your devoted friend   Cleveland H. Dodge

ALS (WP, DLC).
  [1] Richard Cary Morse, Princeton Theological Seminary graduate, Presbyterian minister, and general secretary of the international committee of the Young Men's Christian Association from 1869 to 1915.

To Edith Bolling Galt

[The White House] Sunday evening, 29 Aug., 1915

My sweet, my precious, my incomparable Darling, how shall I tell you what this dear letter, written yesterday and received to-day, has meant to me? The love that is in every line of it has driven weariness and anxiety and every kind of distress away and made me *feel* all day your sweet, radiant, comforting, inspiring presence in the pilot house. Your dear hand *has* been laid on my tired arm, and the fatigue has gone out of it. The fog has lifted; the ship runs free and steady under my hand; and all's well. My guardian spirit has come aboard! Bless your heart, how instantly, how divinely you understand, and how perfectly you love! And I shall *see* you *this week*. Ah, what an age it has been,—I hope the week will not linger with *too* leaden feet!

The secret is very simple, my Sweetheart. Helen will be here on Wednesday morning, to stay with me till the others return, bless her dear heart. She does not read the papers up there, it seems, and did not hear of the sinking of the *Arabic* until a day or two after it happened. The minute she did hear of it she sat down and wrote me the sweet letter I enclose.[1] I could not resist the temptation to let her come. Indeed, I instinctively felt that it would deeply hurt her if I did not, so I telegraphed her to wait for a letter and wrote asking her to come down early this week, so as to give her the full time she had expected to have with her friends at York Harbor and yet bring her home at "the psychological moment." Isn't she a *darling*? I only hope I can make her believe how thankful and how delighted I am to have her back *for her own sake*. She will be the greatest comfort in the world to me, and make this empty house seem habitable once more. I love the dear little girl, as you know, and she is a delightful companion,—and she will make it possible for us to see one another!

You say, my precious One that my recent letters have told you little or nothing about myself, and that you long to know everything I do, and if I find anyone to really interest me. You surmise the right reason, Darling. My days here, without a family, are all alike. There is little variety. My "work" consists chiefly of *thinking*, and that I share with you in every letter, —when there is anything the least new in the thinking; and the hours I do not spend at work or in the blissful indulgence of writing to you I spend for the most part out-of-doors, in the motor or on the golf course. And the guess that is latent in your question hits upon the real difficulty. I see very few people, you know, and there is no one about me just now who really interests me out of business hours. Colonel Brown has been here for over a week, and is a most interesting and intelligent and likable man. I am genuinely fond of him. But he does not hold my attention,

1 Helen W. Bones to WW, Aug. 23, 1915, ALS (WP, DLC).

or stimulate me at all. I know what his view of a thing is going
to be before he states it, and he does not state it with any degree
of originality. And so our talk is just chat: comment on persons
and on the news of the day, humorous chaff, talk of golf, specula-
tion as to the course of this, that, or the other man in politics, &c.
The dear doctor you know. He has every sterling quality, and his
mind thinks good, sound sense. He is full of right and generous
feeling. He is a restful and most satisfactory companion and a
loyal friend. He every day wins anew my warm affectionate regard. He is true gold. But he is not intellectually stimulating.
He does not wake my mind up and quicken its paces. As for
Tumulty, he is all business. Outside of these I see practically
no one except on public affairs. I am not exacting, Sweetheart,
and I enjoy these men very much. They wear well, too, and
stand the severe test of constant association. Until you asked
the question, I had not been aware just what was making the
days tedious except that they lingered so and were so long in
bringing *you*. Now that you ask, I have to admit that there is
no one here who really interests me in the sense that he gives
the day vitality, gives me something fresh or of his own coinage to think about, or makes such an impression on me that I
think of him when I sit down to write to you. I must admit that
I am often bored. Take to-day, for example: Went to church and
heard an excellent sermon; took a turn afterwards around
Potomac Park with Brown and Grayson, looking out, the while,
in my mind's eye, for a perambulator bearing the number 2023;
had lunch; took a three hour ride out through Marlborough with
Grayson and FitzWilliam Woodrow, during at least a third of
which we all three *slept*; came home and had dinner on the
terrace. The only time to-day that my faculties have been really
awake and I fully conscious of the tide of life in me has been
the hour I spent with you before we went to church and the
time since I came to the study this evening to be again alone
with you. And other days are much the same, except that there
is business to settle in the forenoon, when I must be awake and
my faculties alert, and golf, instead of a motor ride, in the afternoon The whole thing is *suitable* enough. I regard these summer
weeks, during which I am camping out here with a man or two,
as negligible intervals in my private life, periods of a sort of
suspended animation, so far as the vivid thing called *Life* is
concerned. It is with me as you tell me it has been with you:
the only parts of the day that *counted* have been those which
I spent with you, reading your precious love letters, and trying
to pour out to you in written words everything that was in my

mind and my heart—chiefly the great love for you which now seems to me the whole of my personal life. The rest of the day has been, as you say, merely what lay between! You tell me, my Darling, that your letters from Ocean City have been unavoidably written where you were subject to constant interruptions, and add, "so please forgive them." Why, they are the most vital letters I ever read,—because your heart was in them,—that wonderful, loving, generous heart that has made me rich in everything that bestows life and strength and joy. When you were writing—interruptions or no interruptions—was the only part of the day when, by your own account of it, you were really alive and happy, and I feel the pulse of everything that is sweet and fine and genuine and spontaneous in every line of what you have written. I can't tell you, my sweet One, what an impression your letters make on me! It is as if the very atmosphere of your own dear self were in their pages. I seem to take from them as direct intimations of what is passing through your mind or affecting your spirits, *but not expressed*, as I take from the tones of your voice and the look in your eyes and your whole bearing and demeanor when I am with you and sensitive to every subtle movement of your body. And that proves so much that makes me happy. It proves how intensely conscious of me you were when you were writing, how vividly you realized me and your intimate loving connection with me, you blessed Darling. They are the breath of life to me, lacking you yourself. And the love in them!—oh, my own darling Edith, how shall I ever tell you the unspeakable happiness that gives me! It is very wonderful love, exquisite with the flavour of your own incomparable heart. And the love I give you in return, my Love, my little Queen, is the love of my whole nature. There is no part of me that is fine that does not love you with an utter devotion, and rejoice in you as the most adorable, the most enjoyable, the most desirable and wholly lovable woman in the world,—and such *fun*, so interesting. I really don't need anyone else to interest me. I ask of others only that they will leave me alone and let me think about you.

Monday, 7.10 A.M.

When you told me that after the Roses went to bed on Friday night you and your dear mother and Bertha sat talking till midnight and you "told them something of our happy days together this summer," I can't tell you, my darling Sweetheart, what a distinct and delightful consciousness I had of belonging with that little family group, which I could so easily picture in my imagination (though I have never even *seen* your mother, you know), or how I longed to have been with you and shared the intimate talk. Best of all would have been to hear you tell of our times together. What would I not have given to hear! I love to hear you tell of *any* experience, you do it so well, and pick out with so perfect a choice the parts best worth telling about, but to have heard *that* reminiscence would have been a joy indeed: it would have been like living those dear days over again with you! What infinitely sweet and *interesting* days they were, my Darling: how much we learned about one another and how wonderfully and beautifully our love grew from day to day. We shall have times together much more satisfying and delightful even than these, times of *perfect*, unhampered, uninterrupted communion and happiness, at the thought of which my heart leaps, but we shall never forget the joy of this summer. It will always be a shining part of the story of our love making. Your question about whether I found anyone who really *interested* me and took the tedium in some part away from these lonely days I have been forced to spend without you, made me realize more than I ever had before, I think, my wonderful Sweetheart, how much *you* interest me. Quite apart from my love for you is my enthusiasm for you as a companion gifted with an infinite variety, never commonplace, never dull, *even when silent*, because always alive in every fibre, always vital and genuine and real and individual,—not *like* anybody else in the world, and always quick to respond, and respond delightfully, to every suggestion of thought or feeling or playful diversion. No wonder they wont let you alone long enough to let you write an uninterrupted letter to your waiting, longing, eager lover. They want the stimulation and delight of you, that *no*body else can give them. How dull and empty No. 10 Park Place will be for the poor Roses when they get back to it, after having had you in it for so many vivid days, and how *very* tedious it will be for them getting there! It will be like water after wine! And how different this town will be with you merely *in* it,—the most engaging and interesting and lovable person in the world! Merely to know that you are *here* will transform it for me. I was deceiving myself when I said that, if we could not see one another, it would be easier for me if you were away. I now know that I have been happier since you got to Ocean City than I was while you were in Geneva (until I saw how Ocean City bored you!) simply because you were nearer and our messengers were not so long on the way; and I am keenly aware that my heart will be less at ease to-night, when you will be in New York, than it was last night—because New York is further off and you will be riding all day long *away* from me. Oh, how I do want you safe back *here*, where I can at least find out *at any hour* how you are faring! And you will never go away again without me,—will you, my precious One?

I love you past all power of words to express, and wait for you with an eagerness and longing that are almost more than I can bear. With *all* my heart,   Your own   Woodrow

P.S. Will you start for Washington Wednesday night or Thursday morning? Of course you understand *nothing* further has developed about the course Germany is to take. We are simply waiting for the word she asked us to wait for.   W.

ALS (WP, DLC).

To Sallie White Bolling

[My dear Mrs. Bolling,   The White House, Aug. 29, 1915]

I am so glad to have an opportunity to speak to you of the great happiness that has come to me because of your daughter's love, which I could not help seeking eagerly and with all my heart so soon as I came really to know her; for I want you to know how proud and grateful I am to have won it and to have won the privilege of having such a mother as I know you will be to me as well as to her. Edith has told me so much about you that I feel that I cannot be at ease in my heart until I have won your love, too. I shall try hard to deserve it, in the way I am sure can be the only way, by trying to be worthy of her love.

I need not tell you what I have found her to be; but I should like to. I have found her to be altogether lovely, and witty, and strong, and admirable, and inspiring. My love for her is compacted of everything that makes me better as well as happy: of reverence and faith and tender devotion. Her character is as altogether beautiful as her person. My love for her is dictated by the best things in me, and the happiness and wonderful love for me she has given me is my strength and my life for the future.

May I not say that my earnest hope is that you will love me and accept me as your own son. Your confidence and your willingness to entrust your incomparable daughter to my care would fill my cup to overflowing. May I not, with sincerest respect and admiration, subscribe myself

Affectionately yours   Woodrow Wilson

T transcript (WC, NjP) of WWsh (WP, DLC).

To Bertha Bolling

My dear Miss Bolling,   [The White House, c. Aug. 29, 1915]

Thank you with all my heart for your letter, which Edith sent me. It was very lovely, and it made my heart very warm that you should give me such a generous welcome. I can imagine what your adorable sister has been to you: your words about her give the judgment of my own heart proof. She is everything that is lovely and inspiring, and I count myself the most fortunate man in the world to have won her love, which she gives royally, like the royal person she is.

I wanted to talk to you about her, and about nothing else, the day you took tea with us on the south portico, but forced myself to talk about other things, which presently you made easy because you were yourself so interesting about other things. We have so many tastes in common, you and I, that I am sure it is going to be great fun to be brother and sister. And it is the more delightful to look forward to because you are so big hearted and fine in the way you receive me.

I know that you cannot think anyone worthy of your sweet sister: I know it because I think the same thing. But you may trust me to try very hard to make her altogether happy. If unbounded love can make a man worthy, I can claim to be worthy of her. But the love will be proved in the test, not in the word.

Looking forward with the greatest pleasure to the friendship I hope and believe we shall offer as brother and sister,

Affectionately yours   Woodrow Wilson

T transcript (WC, NjP) of WWsh (WP, DLC).

From Edith Bolling Galt

Ocean City, N. J. Sunday,
My own precious One: August 29, 1915 12:30 m.

Last night I was playing "Auction," when the boy brought me the perfectly lovely letter from you that has made every hour since bright and my heart sing. I just could not help reading it there and then, and it was more like a real touch of you than anything that has happened since we said goodbye four weeks ago tomorrow. It had been exactly thirteen hours since your dear hand rested on the page when I could touch the same place with mine and feel it was sacred. There is a sort of reverence in my heart for you Dearest, unlike any I have ever felt for anyone—and every word on those white pages filled me with a joy that passes understanding. I blush truly at your words of loving admiration and yet I love them so I read them over and over again, and I went to sleep with your beloved two letters of yesterday under my pillow, and the last thought when I put out the light at 2 a.m. were *your* thoughts, and the blessed assurance that we belong to each other.

How can you say such ridiculous things about my letters, you dear flatterer for *no* one ever wrote such letters as yours. And I feel when I read them that I am cheating the world in keeping them as my sacred own—that other people ought to be allowed to know you in such a wonderful revelation of your exquisite self. And how the words express that which is to most people inexpressible.

Bertha and I have just come from a long walk on the Board Walk. We went clear to the end, and the ocean is perfectly wonderful today—the surf splendid and long combing waves breaking almost over each other. We went beyond the crowds and stood just where nothing could mar the grandeur and beauty of the water.

I wished so for you and pictured you in church—wondered if you felt my thoughts keeping step with yours and longing to have yours fly free across the space that seperates us and soar together through the life-giving freshness of this salt tonic air. I am stealing a minute to write you before lunch as afterwards we are going for a ride with Mr. Rose.

Yesterday we had the same rain you did, only it did not begin until midday. So we could not get a ride but stayed in, and of course, played cards. But I did not mind anything after your letter came. I could have played all night and not minded it for my thoughts were so far away I was not conscious of what my hands and brain were doing. I think, if you have read the full page article in the "Philadelphia Inquirer" this morning about you, Margaret Helen and me,[1] you will be as furious as I was at first and still realize how completely I do love you that even such things as this have no power to make me long unhappy, and it is worth it all—to have you love me. Poor innocent little Margaret to have two such scheming creatures as Helen and I to take her place—but it is a comfort that you "make no effort to conceal your pleasure when you see our lovely faces"!! Such twaddle—it is not worth worrying over, except that it shows how everything is being watched and noted.

Should we let it affect next Saturday? Bless your heart, I

love you, and I am willing to give up seeing you if it is wisest. And, on the other hand if you need me I am ready to stand such things as this and come and help you.

For *this* in itself would bring me perfect happiness

6:15 P.M.

I am just back from a lovely ride and must finish this and get ready for dinner after which I must see a lot of Mothers friends and then pack   So this must be the last word from Ocean City

I will get the mail before leaving in the morning, and we hope to get started by nine. I will certainly send you a line from the "Algonquin" tomorrow when we get to N. Y., or if we should be held up on the road from wherever we spend the night. I am perfectly well Sweetheart and love to think I will so soon be near you.

God keep you for me—and all the rest of the world.   Always
Your own,   Edith

ALS (WP, DLC).
¹ This article appeared in the Sunday supplement of the *Philadelphia Inquirer*, Aug. 29, 1915. No copy of the supplement is extant.

To Edith Bolling Galt, with Enclosure

[The White House] 30 Aug. [1915]

I always send you Gerard's despatches with a question in my own mind whether it is worth while. They never get anywhere; but they are part of the day's business   W.

ALI (WP, DLC).

E N C L O S U R E

Berlin (via Copenhagen) August 28, 1915.

2789. August 28, 1 p m. FRANKFURTER ZEITUNG states that German press is not making the mistake of not taking the sinking of the ARABIC seriously but appreciates the fact that until an official report arrives, which may take days, German public will not take a definite stand. The Foreign Secretary's conversation with the American Ambassador will have left no doubt of the good will of the government to clear up the matter, nor of the fact that it is not the intention of our submarines to cause the death of American passengers. The paper then quotes with unfavorable comment an article in NEW YORK TRIBUNE of July 24th concerning the shooting club on the ARABIC.[1]

Gerard, Berlin

T telegram (WP, DLC).
[1] "Plotting U-Boats New Sea Sport for Arabic Crew," *New York Tribune*, July 24, 1915. It described the crew's rifle club and its daily practice of shooting astern at rafts and kites which simulated submarines and planes. Club members insisted that they had organized simply for pleasure and claimed that the club, not its members, owned the rifles, so as not to break the British Board of Trade's regulation prohibiting crew members to have weapons on board liners.

To Edith Bolling Galt, with Enclosure

[The White House] 30 Aug. [1915]

Apparently the Haitian authorities are seeking to play fast and loose with us. I am wondering whether to blame them or not!   W.

ALI (WP, DLC).

E N C L O S U R E

Port au Prince August 28, 1915.

Fears expressed in my August 23, 4 p.m. materialized on yesterday when Minister of Foreign Affairs submitted written reply of Haitian Government to treaty submitted. Practically every stipulation of original treaty is either omitted or so changed as to defeat its purpose.

I have this morning replied to the same and after reminding Minister of Foreign Affairs that I had been repeatedly assured that we were in accord as to all principles involved differing only as to slight matters of detail as the basis my August 25, 6 p.m. I declined to discuss the same and requested an expression of opinion as to acceptability of the draft as originally submitted.

Davis.

T telegram (WP, DLC).

To Edith Bolling Galt, with Enclosure

[The White House] 30 Aug. [1915]

Isn't this one of the most unspeakable performances? I need add nothing to what Lansing says. It's horrible!   W.

ALI (WP, DLC).

ENCLOSURE

From Robert Lansing

PERSONAL AND PRIVATE:

My dear Mr. President: Washington August 30, 1915.

You have undoubtedly read the flimsy of Mr. Page's 2716, August 29, two p.m. relative to the attack on the NECOSIAN and the events which followed.[1] To me the conduct of the British naval authorities is shocking, and I sincerely hope that this matter may not become public, as it would seriously affect public opinion in Germany and might result in retaliatory measures of a most rigorous character.

Faithfully yours,   Robert Lansing.

TLS (WP, DLC).
   [1] WHP to RL, Aug. 29, 1915, *FR-WWS 1915*, pp. 528-29. Page reported the testimony of two American muleteers on board the British steamer *Nicosian* about the attack by a German submarine against that vessel on August 19. They further testified that a British Q-boat, *Baralong*, disguised as an American merchant vessel, arrived on the scene. *Baralong*'s crew lowered the American flag once the ship had neared the submarine and then opened fire, sank the submarine, and sought out and shot the crew of the submarine.

To Frank Lyon Polk

My dear Mr. Polk: [The White House] August 30, 1915

Thank you most sincerely for your letter.[1] You may be sure that it gave me the greatest pleasure to acquiesce in Mr. Lansing's suggestion that you should be offered the Counsellorship of the Department of State, and I look forward with the greatest pleasure and satisfaction to being associated with you here.

With warm regard,

Sincerely yours,   Woodrow Wilson

TLS (Letterpress Books, WP, DLC).
   [1] F. L. Polk to WW, Aug. 26, 1915, ALS (WP, DLC), accepting appointment as Counselor of the State Department.

From Edward Mandell House, with Enclosures

Manchester, Massachusetts.

Dear Governor: August 30th, 1915.

I am enclosing you a copy of a letter from Sir Edward Grey and one from Bernstorff.

I believe it is now time to show a disposition to meet Germany half way. It may be their intention to create differences between America and England, and probably is, nevertheless if I were you, I would adopt a distinctly more cordial tone towards them.

I spent Saturday night with Charles R. Crane at Wood's Hole. Richard Olney was there. He takes the view that modern warfare makes it necessary to recognize the submarine, and he does not believe we should go further than to demand of Germany that notice be given before torpedoing merchantmen.

On the other hand, it is his opinion that the Allies are within their rights to try and keep foodstuffs and raw materials out of Germany. He believes that the stand you take in these matters will later become international law, and he thinks you should look at the situation in that light and not altogether in the light of precedent. This is an interesting viewpoint.

I also met Hamlin at Crane's. I urged him to try and smooth over the differences in the Federal Reserve Board. He does not believe that either Warburg or Miller will go counter to the other members of the board in regard to foreign acceptances.

He says the friction in the Board is caused almost wholly by the feeling that it is being made an adjunct of the Treasury Department instead of an independent body. He says they each made great financial sacrifices to accept a place on the Board in the belief that it was one of independent importance.

The question of precedence has also offended their sensibilities because they have been told they must rank below Assistant Secretaries of Departments. I told Hamlin that the country at large did not know whether they walked in next to you or after the elevator boy and did not care, that it was the work that counted and the country would appraise them according to their accomplishment.

The answer to that was, that unless the position was made of importance, first class men would not accept it. Hamlin thinks a little attention paid to them in this direction would smooth all differences and would make them work harmoniously and enthusiastically.

I had a talk with Houston also, who knows from McAdoo something of the differences in the Board, and he too thinks that the power for good will be destroyed and the whole act imperiled if a break should come at this time. I am merely giving you this for your guidance.   Your affectionate,   E. M. House

TLS (WP, DLC).

ENCLOSURE   I

Sir Edward Grey to Edward Mandell House

Dear Colonel House,   London, S. W. August 10th, 1915.

Mr. Bell, of the "Chicago Tribune,"[1] asked through my Private Secretary that I should see Mr. Swinge of his newspaper,[2] who had been in Berlin and lately had a talk with Bethmann-Hollweg, in which the latter had spoken of peace, and had said certain things to Mr. Swinge which he had authorized him to repeat to me, though it was to be understood that Mr. Swinge was not an envoy from the German Chancellor.

I saw Mr. Swinge a few days ago, and what Bethmann-Hollweg said amounts to this: There might have been peace last February, if we had made proposals then; and Germany might still make peace with England, but it was a question of days as to when the opportunity might pass. The terms on which Germany might make peace with England would be the restitution to Germany of all her Colonies, the restitution of Belgium to independence, and the payment of a war indemnity by England to Germany. It would also have to be clear that the independence of Belgium was real, so that she could not be the catspaw of England.

I said that it was an insult to propose a war indemnity to a country that had not been conquered. A war indemnity meant that, until it was paid off, the people of the country paying it must work like slaves for a foreign country.

Mr. Swinge admitted that he had rather shuddered when Bethmann-Hollweg mentioned a war indemnity, but he supposed that it was regarded in Germany as payment to Germany for giving up Belgium. Even so, he regretted that it has been mentioned.

We then had a good deal of talk of the usual kind, in the course of which I said that we could not discuss any terms of peace except in consultation with our Allies, according to our agreement of the 5th of September 1914 and our Alliance with Japan, as was publicly known; but I was quite certain that we would fight on with all our strength until Belgium was restored.

The question of reparation to Belgium was mentioned, and Mr. Swinge said that it would be very difficult to impose on Germany a payment to Belgium: it would be like a war indemnity. I said that I would not commit the folly of proposing that Germany should pay a war indemnity before she was beaten, as Bethmann-Hollweg had proposed with regard to us; but, if everything else was satisfactorily settled and the question of reparation to Belgium remained as the only obstacle to peace, I personally thought that it could then be settled by referring to an impartial and independent Tribunal the following three questions:

Was reparation due to Belgium? If so, what ought the reparation to be? By whom should it be paid? If the German allegations about Belgium were true, no reparation at all was due to her; or if any was due, it should come from France and us. But if, as we knew to be the truth, Belgium had never trafficked with her neutrality; had never lent herself to any design for helping France or us against Germany; and had been perfectly innocent, then most cruel wrong had been done to her, and great reparation was due her from Germany.

We knew this to be the truth, and I should like to bring out before an International Tribunal every document that had passed between Belgium and the Allies, so that the examination of the documents might perhaps bring home to the German people, when blood had cooled after the war, what the truth really was.

I have been much harassed by commercial matters during the last month. I think it quite possible that the Germans have got all the cotton they need to make munitions; but cotton plays such a very large part in the making of munitions that we are bound to prevent it from going into Germany, and any Government here that did not do so would be regarded as failing in their duty to their own people. As it is, we are much blamed for not having stopped cotton from going into Germany during the first seven months of the war.

It is quite indifferent to us how we stop cotton: whether we detain it and pay for it, as at present, or whether we make it contraband and put it into the Prize Court. But hitherto I have hesitated to declare it contraband, for fear of making the feeling in the United States worse instead of better. In any case, we are prepared to enter into an arrangement that will make the price of cotton stable and prevent its collapse.

The general situation is too obscure and uncertain for comment. I think that the Germans hope to force peace by next October; but I do not see how either side is to be brought by that date to accept terms that will be tolerable to the other side.

On the other hand, the general exhaustion of the whole Continent is such that the war cannot last indefinitely, though the end is not yet within sight.

My own mind revolves more and more about the point that the

refusal of a Conference was the fatal step that decided peace or war last year, and about the moral to be drawn from it: which is that the pearl of great price, if it can be found, would be some League of Nations that could be relied on to insist that disputes between any two nations must be settled by the arbitration, mediation,.or conference of others. International Law has hitherto had no sanction. The lesson of this war is that the Powers must bind themselves to give it a sanction. If that can be secured, freedom of the seas and many other things will become easy. But it is not a fair proposition that there should be a guarantee of the freedom of the seas while Germany claims to recognize no law but her own on land, and to have the right to make war at will.

I suppose the United States will have no rupture with Germany now unless Germany provokes it by another incident. The Lusitania discussion was bound to have an inconclusive ending, if it dragged on for any length of time, and I recognize that the President cannot be less patient than his people. But the conclusion of the discussion (if it be concluded) is not satisfactory.

Yours sincerely,   E. Grey.

TCL (WP, DLC).
  1 Edward Price Bell, London correspondent for the Chicago *Daily News*, 1900-23.
  2 Raymond Swing, Berlin correspondent for the Chicago *Daily News*, 1913-17, who changed his name to Raymond Gram Swing upon his marriage in 1920. Swing's account of the interview with Grey appears in his memoir, *"Good Evening!"* (New York, 1964), pp. 53-56.

E N C L O S U R E   I I

Count Johann Heinrich von Bernstorff to Edward Mandell House

My dear Colonel House: Washington. August 28th, 1915.

Many thanks for your letter. Since I received it you will have noticed a great improvement in the political situation and will have seen that I was right in telling you that my Government was ready to make concessions in order to meet the President's wishes.

You know that I have been urging this policy all along. I myself, do not quite know as yet how far my Government is ready to go, because my information, on account of bad communication with Germany, is still very fragmentary, but it seems that the American Government received more information from Mr. Gerard than I have at present. However, the general negociations about "the freedom of the seas" must anyhow be put off for the present, as the American Government wishes to settle the Arabic incident first, before proceeding to the Lusitania case and the general negociations.

I do not doubt that we will be able to arrange the Arabic question satisfactorily. As to the general negociations, you will realize that it has caused me some trouble to induce my Government to take up the policy which you and I have spoken of so often. It would certainly not have been possible for me to push this matter along at all, if my Government had not, on the ground of my reports, regarded the last American Lusitania note as a pledge of the President to take up the negociations about "the freedom of the seas," if we met his wishes regarding the Lusitania etc.

I certainly feel very hopeful now and will always gratefully remember the help and advice you have kindly given me and the friendship you have shown me in trying times.

Very sincerely yours,   J. Bernstorff.

TCL (WP, DLC).

From William Procter Gould Harding

Dear Mr. President: Washington August 30, 1915.

Permit me to thank you for your letter of August twenty-third and for your permission to use it in connection with my address before the Alabama Merchants Association. There were nearly two thousand merchants and bankers present at the meeting and practically all of the cotton growing states were represented. Your letter produced a deep impression and I am satisfied that the result will be a greater measure of cooperation between the merchants, farmers and bankers this Fall than ever before. I am glad to report a disposition on the part of the bankers with whom I talked, to be reasonable in their interest charges on commodity loans, and the whole situation in the South looks better to me than it did a week ago. The rank and file of our people are with you heart and soul, and the great applause that is always brought out by the mere mention of your name before an assemblage, is most gratifying, and is spontaneous evidence of popular affection for and confidence in you.

Respectfully and sincerely,   W P G Harding

TLS (WP, DLC).

To Edith Bolling Galt, with Enclosures

[The White House] Monday,
My precious, lovely Darling,   8.10 P.M. 30 Aug., 1915

Did you ever read a sweeter, lovelier letter than this of Jessie's that I enclose? Bless her heart! You can easily imagine with what emotions I read it, and with what love for her. I tremble, some-times, to think of the wonderful love that has been given me,—because I am so painfully conscious that I do not deserve it. Think of getting on one and the same day this letter of Jessie's and also the one you wrote yesterday,—which Hoover has just fetched me from the Post Office direct! What makes this last letter of yours so wonderful and so delicious, my Darling, is the impression I get from it so vividly that you love me just as I want to be loved,—without rhyme or reason—*just because you love me*! Every *reason* you give,—and you have first and last given a good many, bless your generous heart!—seems to me disputable. I do not recognize the picture you paint of me (just as you ques-tion the picture I draw of you); I demur to this item of praise or that item of admiration; but all the while, whatever I may think of the reasons, I know that you love me, and have the deep joy of feeling that it is just because you find, by being with me, that I am the kind of fellow you love and want to spend your life with. I'm a good deal of a boy about it all. Because I am a mature man and have seen a good deal of the world and mixed with all kinds of men and women, and had a chance to test their brains and their quality, I know how unusual you are, how ex-ceptionally gifted in every way, and that in describing what you are I am telling the simple truth and not being duped by either my heart or my imagination; but, all the same, I know that I would have found you irresistible and loved you whether you had been these things or not,—simply because you *suit* me exact-ly and delight me altogether,—simply because I couldn't help it, because I knew I could not do without you. And it delights me to feel that you love me the same way,—not because I possess this, that, or the other gift or quality or excellence that you think you discover upon critical analysis and examination, but because I am wholly to your taste, because, whatever the analysis may disclose, you love me and want me for your chum and hus-band. Does this sound to you like nonsense? I know it does not. I know it because of this letter I have just read with such profound joy. It's the letter of a dear, fascinating girl, happily in love, written in response to the letter of her lover written with the same happiness and enthusiasm. All her sweet heart is in it. It is warm with her blushes *and* her kisses. Ah, my adorable Edith, you know what I mean. You have a mind that would deeply interest me, whether I cared for you or not; you can give counsel after a fashion that would make me resort to you, as so many friends and all of your family do, whether you engaged my heart or not—and I would resort to you about more things than they know about; you are perfectly beautiful and delightfully entertaining and I might quite conceivably perceive that you were without falling in love with you,—as probably many men have. But men who truly and deeply fall in love do not fall in love by a mere process of admiration. There is something besides—who shall say what it is or give any intelligible account of it?—which says to them 'this woman is kin to my heart, can give me more joy and more genuine companionship than any other woman in the world, is my mate and delight, if she can but recognize and love me as I have recognized and love her.' It is instinctive, not rational. That is what I meant when I said that I recognized in you my natural playmate and found such zest and fun in being with you and doing things with you. When I am with you and share with you all the things of all the day I not only feel as if every faculty in me were at its best but that a great deal were added of what I would like to be, because *you* are what I would like to be. I feel almost as if I partook of your vitality and charm and expressed what I would like to express through your personality. I know what you think before you put it into words, because I feel that it is what I would have thought had I been you.

But, dear me, I am attempting the impossible! I am trying to put into words what has always eluded them and always will elude them—*Love itself*, the recognition and desire of one heart by another, the ineffable thing that binds the lives of a man and a woman together in a happiness that nothing can equal and nothing disturb. And all this because I wanted to say how happy I was to find you loving me in a way that I knew to be what my heart desired because I perceived that there really was no reason for it except the best,—that you found yourself happiest with me! *You* know, Sweetheart,—you *must* know—that all this about my being a great man, and the rest—is all nonsense. Nobody loves a man because he is great. You know that my heart entertains great ideals—has always entertained them and lived with them,—and that what is in me is simply what is in all gently bred men who have been nurtured among fine people, but raised to a high power, so to speak, by the influence of what my heart has always conceived most beautiful and desirable;

and *I* know that in you I have found the things that I have always loved, carried by a kindred spirit. *I* know that, whether I am at work or at play, you exactly fit into my every taste and faculty, and give me exquisite satisfaction. And I find myself regretting that I am bound fast every day, day in and day out, to such serious, such portentously serious, things—things some of which seem to involve the very destiny of nations—and that you must always for the present find me under the influence of these things and sobered by them, when there is so much irresponsible gayety in me which I long to share with you. But the time will come. No matter what my nominal age may be, the boy in me is never going to die,—nor the girl in you, and we are going to have the time of our lives together. You understand and respond to everything there is in me and I can keep step without trying to every movement you make, in your dear mind or in your sweet heart, and the days we shall spend together will seem to us fuller of sheer life and contented joy than we ever supposed mere days could be out of children's story books!

It has made me very happy to find out—a few minutes ago—that you are safe in New York. At my request, Grayson went out, about nine, to a telephone booth outside the House—I think at his club—and called up the "Algonquin," to ask if Mr. and Mrs. H. L. Rose, of Geneva, New York, had arrived; and he has just been in to say that the clerk at the hotel reports that they arrived at about six. I think it safe to assume that the most beautiful and most lovable woman in the world arrived with them. It relieves my mind immensely. I cannot help being anxious when you are on the road and I know that an accident might darken the whole world for me by bringing you harm. How intensely I have been thinking of you all day, my Darling! It has not been a particularly busy day. Business seems to have come to a standstill while we wait to see which set of his counsellors the Kaiser will heed. I have had the sort of leisure to-day that I have come to love,—the leisure to let my thoughts be with you without any consciousness of playing truant somewhere else. I love you,—love you more and more! There is a welcome awaiting you here that ought to satisfy the most exacting lover,—ought to satisfy even your great heart, which itself knows so perfectly how to love.

It is ten o'clock, Sweetheart, and I feel it *mighty* hard that I cannot go down to meet your mother and Bertha. How I would love to! I am going to send flowers to them early to-morrow morning. I was afraid if I sent them to-night there would be no one to arrange them and their being there would only add to what they would have to do before going to bed. I wish I could at least call them up and say 'howdy.'

Tuesday, 7.08 A.M.

Please, my precious Darling, try to go to bed earlier and not stay awake till the small hours of the morning. It frightens me the liberties you take with that splendid vitality of yours. You tell me, in your sweet generosity, that it is mine to draw on, but how shall I ever dare to put any extra strain on it, or draw on it at all, when I see you spending it so recklessly and so uselessly. Please, *please* take care of yourself. *N*obody can go on indefinitely like that, and you are all the world to me. Think what it would mean to me if you were to break down in *any* way or degree. This is a plea from the bottom of my heart. I can't bear to think of your even reading my letters at two in the morning, exquisite as is the dear love you give me as you read them and deeply as it delights me to think that you are consciously with me in those quiet, intimate hours. Will you try? You can't make yourself sleep at first—you have been bad too long!—but you can if you keep on trying and remembering that it is *for love*. Suppose you were to get dark rings under your lovely eyes, like Helen, and look at your lover full of weariness in the morning. But I know you'll do it for my sake. You *can* when you get here.

What are my orders, Sweetheart, about my letters during the day or two before Susie returns and No. 1308 is really open? Am I to send them to the *Cordova*, in your mother's care?

I read Mr. Wilson's letter with a great deal of interest. Yes, he is still on the trail, but not quite as hot as before. You've thrown him off a little and I think can manage him for a little while yet. Why not tell him, when you see him, that a delightful intimacy *has* grown up between us; that you find yourself deriving a great deal of pleasure and profit (!) from it; and that it pleases you to think that perhaps you are in a way performing a certain service by giving me opporturnies to relax and enjoy a friendship which has nothing to do with politics,—and let it go at that for a little while? Modest way for *me* to suggest putting it, isn't it? No charge, madam, the profit is yours without grudging!

No doubt you have seen in the papers of the last day or two the lie, at once silly and malicious, that I have broken with House and taken up with some other 'favorite.'[1] It has made me so indignant that I have given instructions that the repre-

[1] There were wild front-page stories about this in, for example, the *New York Tribune*, Aug. 30, 1915, and the *Chicago Daily Tribune*, Aug. 30, 1915.

sentative here of the paper that started it (the New York *Herald*) be excluded from the office until his paper has disciplined the man who wrote it.[2] These things are very hard to bear.

I did not see the article in the Philadelphia *Inquirer*. It is a paper of only local circulation and of no influence whatever. It distresses me beyond measure to have you annoyed, or *talked about at all*; but I am sure we shall know how to carry ourselves, Darling, and make the path of the gossip a barren one. You take *just* the right attitude towards it all, bless your dear heart: we will do what is right and necessary for each other's happiness and let the rest take care of itself. Any other course would be weak and would gain us nothing but wretchedness.

Ah, my Beloved, you are beyond all words adorable. Your love makes my heart so light that the world seems to me all right when it is most obviously all wrong. There is no way to thank you for that blessed love letter you wrote just before leaving Ocean City or for this dear, dear homesick little note dashed off in New York last night—(which Hoover has handed me since I wrote the last sentence) except to take you in my arms and kiss you till you have breath for no more. *Of course* I kissed you at eleven fifteen Sunday night! I had just gone to bed, and lay there kissing that exquisite smiling photograph of you as if it were your very self. My *Darling*! I am *so* glad you are homesick. Will it never be Saturday! How *can* I wait?

Your own Woodrow

I slip in a sweet, characteristic letter of Helen's. W.

ALS (WP, DLC).
² George Laughlin of the Washington bureau of the *New York Herald*, which on August 30 and 31 had printed his reports recounting rumors of a split between Wilson and House over the latter's conviction that Carranza should be recognized. The first dispatch conceded that the rumors were "not generally believed" and concluded that House's "personal relations with the President are still most cordial." The second dispatch added the rumor that Oswald G. Villard had replaced House as Wilson's closest adviser.

E N C L O S U R E   I

From Jessie Woodrow Wilson Sayre

Cornish, New Hampshire

Darling, darling Father,   August 28th, 1915

Your adorable telegram¹ came this morning and made such a bright and beautiful beginning for the day that I must write at once and thank you for it. I miss you, of course, but the thought of you is so sweet that there is happiness for me even when I am away from you.

I am so grateful that I am your daughter and that I have had the joy and privilege these twenty eight years of knowing and loving you. It is such an inspiration to think of you, even, dearest Father!

I wish that I could be of some service to you. I am jealous of Cousin Helen. I want to be the one to make things smoother and easier for you now. It is a pleasure to look forward to the new year and to see there new happiness for my darling Father. Give my love to Her and to yourself all my heart's deepest love and gratitude

> Devotedly your ever loving daughter   Jessie.

ALS (WP, DLC).
1 It is missing. This was Jessie's birthday.

E N C L O S U R E   I I

From Helen Woodrow Bones

Dearest Cousin Woodrow,   York Harbor, Me. August 27, 1915

Thank you so much for letting me have my way: as you know, I like nothing better!

My berth on the Federal Express leaving Boston at five next Tuesday evening is bought, so you can't change your mind now; I'll reach Washington at some hour on Wednesday—Hoover will know what.

I'm very happy to be coming; the only cloud in my sky is Fitz William. Is he to stay on indefinitely? He will be quite a problem in our making of plans. You certainly have the nerviest lot of relatives I've ever known; often I wonder whether after all I'm one of the worst—probably, because I am so hard in my judgment of the others! Of course I am selfish in my wish to get rid of F.W. for to me he is like one of the plagues of Egypt; or the afflictions of Job—his only cause for being—around—seems to me an unpleasant kind of discipline; but I really don't see just what *you* are going to do about him, for he is very curious as well as ever present.

I hope by now Mac has appeared *without* Nell and Ellen. I think he surely cannot have taken the latter to Washington, at least! The plan was for him to send them both to Cornish, from Boston, where he was to start them on their way.

Good-night. How good it is to think I shall see you on Wednesday!   Yours lovingly   Helen

ALS (WP, DLC).

From Edith Bolling Galt

My precious One: Manhattan August 30th/1915 6:35 P.M.

Here I am safe and sound and whistling to keep my courage
up, for, just to you, I will confess I am homesick. But you will
laugh at me for cowing when I say that, but I must own up.

Never mind I have your dear letter to comfort me that came
to Ocean City this morning and the "big envelope" which I have
not yet opened, but I read your dear letter en route and loved
every word in it. We left at 9:30 and had a lovely trip but came
rather slowly as there had been such heavy rains. Between Ocean
City and Lakewood we ran into an awful storm, but it cleared
after that and I hope tomorrow will be bright. Mother & Bertha
got your really lovely notes this morning, and we all read them
together. And they both said they were the sweetest, tenderest
messages they had ever read—and I was overcome by all you
said of me.

Thank you Sweetheart for every word of them which I know
came from the truest heart that ever beat.

I need not coach you any further with regard to Mother   You
have found your way instinctively and need no further guidance
to her heart. Be your own dear self—when you meet her—and
there need be no shyness on either side. I am writing in such
a tearing hurry for we did not get here until ten minutes of 6
and we want to have dinner & go to the Theatre. I have unpacked, dressed after a bath and written Mother a card—all in
40 minutes. And now I must run, as we are to meet at quarter
of seven.

I will send you a real letter tomorrow—this is just a scrappy
little note to tell you how I love you.

Always your own   Edith

Did you kiss me at eleven 15 last night? Just suddenly I felt
your lips on mine, so *really* that I could not believe it was not
you your very self. I had gone to bed, and the light was out, and
I was half wake, half sleep, when I knew you were there. Think
of it—you will tell me in your letter tomorrow *how* I can see you.
And Saturday will *never* come—it will seem so long.   E.

ALS (WP, DLC).

An Announcement by Joseph Patrick Tumulty

August 31, 1915

The President has instructed me to refuse admission to the White House to any representative or representatives of the New York paper responsible for publishing the stories with reference to an alleged break in the pleasant relations between Colonel House and himself. This, of course, carries with it a denial of any privileges which accompanies the right of access to the White House Offices. This order will continue in force until the paper publishing this story disavows it or makes public apology to the President.

T MS (WP, DLC).

Two Letters to Edward Mandell House

My dearest Friend: The White House August 31, 1915

Of course you have known how to interpret the silly, malicious lies that the papers have been recently publishing about a disagreement between you and me, but I cannot deny myself the pleasure of sending you just a line of deep affection to tell you how they have distressed me. I am trying to bring to book the men who originated them. The only things that distress me in the malicious work of the day against us are those things which touch, not me, but those who are dear to me.

Affectionately yours,   Woodrow Wilson

TLS (E. M. House Papers, CtY).

Dearest Friend,   The White House. 31 August, 1915.

I have your letter of the thirtieth of August, enclosing copies of letters from Sir Edward Grey and Bernstorff.

Of course our reply to Germany's overtures of conc[i]liation will have to depend a great deal on the terms in which they are actually made. Bernstorff has only stated the principle which will be accepted, and you know I trust neither his accuracy nor his sincerity. But it certainly does look as if a way were opened out of our difficulties, so far as Germany is concerned.

That only makes more perplexing our question as to how to deal with England, for apparently we have no choice now but to demand that she respect our rights a good deal better than she has been doing. Shall we insist that she open the door to neutral trade to Rotterdam and Scandinavia, for example, which she is quite right in believing is in effect trade with Germany? Bernstorff is now demanding of us, in a note from his government, that we insist on Germany's getting our cotton "for the use of her civilian population." Germany has at last come to her senses and is playing intelligent politics. She is seeking to put us, and is likely to succeed in putting us, into a position where we shall have to play to some extent the role of catspaw for her in opening trade to her.

You are right about the Reserve Board imbroglio. And I think MacAdoo thinks so too, now. Indeed, I think he raised the question about the action of certain members of the Board about that meeting only to get a leverage for something bigger, the proper handling of acceptances and discounts.

If this cool weather takes a notion to stay, it would be jolly to have you come down some time early next week, after your lease at Manchester has expored [expired].

Always   Affectionately Yours,   Woodrow Wilson

WWTLS (E. M. House Papers, CtY).

From Robert Lansing

My Dear Mr. President: Washington August 31, 1915.

I enclose a report sent to us by the Department of Justice in regard to Mexico which you will find interesting.[1] Will you kindly return it as it is our Department copy?

Faithfully yours,   Robert Lansing.

TLS (R. Lansing Papers, DLC).
[1] A. M. Allen, "Mexican Revolution, Neutrality Matter," T memorandum, Aug. 23, 1915 (R. Lansing Papers, DLC). It described a meeting with "informant Shorb" about rifle shipments to Mexico, the presence of various Mexican officials in San Francisco, a request from Villa supporters that Shorb return to Mexico and incite a mutiny against the *Carrancistas*, and an agreement between Carranza and Frank A. Vanderlip. Under this agreement, the National City Bank of New York would finance Carranza's operations and receive an exclusive concession for the mining of anthracite coal in the state of Coahuila and a concession for opening a bank in Mexico City, with branches throughout the country.

To Robert Lansing

My dear Mr. Secretary,   The White House. 31 August, 1915.

This is extremely interesting.

Is there not some way in which we can properly make inquiry as to the truth of a portion of this, by having the National City Bank told what we have heard and asked direct if it is true? It is very important indeed that we should know, and extremely important that we should prevent private agencies of this order from guiding and determining affairs in Mexico. The country ought to be made to realize and accept the fact that this Government is in charge.

Faithfully Yours,　Woodrow Wilson

WWTLS (R. Lansing Papers, DLC).

From Robert Lansing, with Enclosure

Personal and Private.

My Dear Mr. President:　　　　Washington August 31, 1915.

I send you the original of a telegram which I have just received from Vera Cruz. You will understand that it is from the man who went there recently.[1] Will you kindly give me your views as to what reply should be made? You will perceive that the matter requires immediate attention if it is considered desirable to give any instructions.

Faithfully yours,　Robert Lansing.

TLS (SDR, RG 59, 812.00/16014½, DNA).
[1] David Lawrence. Lawrence had gone on a secret mission, for which he adopted the code name Laguirre, to Carranza to urge his acceptance in principle of a peace conference leading to a coalition provisional government and to its recognition by the United States. See Link, *Struggle for Neutrality*, pp. 630-32.

E N C L O S U R E

Vera Cruz Aug. 29, 1915.

CONFIDENTIAL. For the Secretary only. Laguirre sends following: "Had pleasant, friendly interview of two hours with Carranza, outlining to him that I have volunteered to clear up misunderstanding and that I had insisted on having no official character so as to be (#) service to both sides, and was thoroughly conversant with Washington viewpoint. Explained dangers of preferring one armed faction to another, because of resentments which might thereby result, and urged that harmonizing elements meant surer domestic peace as well as minimizing chances of foreign intervention. He said he did not believe the minority element in revolution, which would be ignored if he were recognized, could provoke trouble and that in three weeks he expected to completely dominate country. He rejected idea of even accepting in principal conference as proposed, because it implies acceptance of foreign mediation in internal affairs. I endeavored to explain that recognition was international ques-

tion and he said he was willing to discuss it but not through
such a conference because this would not lead to internal agreement. I suggested his calling of conference of his own initiative. He was impressed by suggestion but would not state
specifically if he would do so. He said that his answer to our note
would reveal his course, that he had not yet decided what to say
and was waiting a reply to his inquiry to Latin American diplomatists which he said was very important to him because if
the ministers acted individually he could not accord them the
same consideration as acting on behalf of their governments. I
dissipated erroneous impressions he had from press as to our
intentions through Pan-American conference, emphasizing that
its sole purpose was to determine what elements in Mexico
seemed capable of creating a government that could satisfy
international obligations. Carranza then said his chiefs had all
replied that he alone was competent to treat such customs [ques-
tions], thereby demonstrating that he held the executive power in
Mexico. I asked for his programme. He said he would grant an
amnesty and would convoke congress by an immediate election
and then reforms would be carried out, this followed by a presidential election within six months; he himself would retain title
of first chief and would consider himself eligible to be presidential candidate. I outlined what seemed to me method by
which he could obtain recognition, suggesting that his note be
written so as not to offend any signatories and that some kind of
conference be called and if no agreement could be reached more
powerful faction probably would be chosen, provided it gave
promise of satisfying international obligation. He said that he
was willing and anxious to treat questions international but not
internal. I assured him our policy was simply the international
question of recognition. He suggested that if I were invested with
official character of some kind he could so phrase his note as to
assist in solving situation. I said I feared in the midst of negotiation with Latin American countries United States could not undertake this. He said subject would be kept confidential and informal. I said I would inquire as to Washington wishes but they
would be influenced by impression my suggestions had made.
He authorized me to say in general terms that what I have said
had impressed him well but that it must be understood that in
any course that was followed he could not make compromises.
He was willing to give guarantees and political rights to all except military persons accused of crimes but no participation in
his government. He asked that Silliman be instructed to say that
I spoke in the name of the Secretary of State. I said I thought

this would be too official. My own suggestion is that you send message to Silliman to be shown to Carranza saying while I am not commissioned by government I know its point of view, having discussed these questions exhaustively in Washington and that Carranza could feel assured that the views I expressed were identical with those held by the Secretary of State because of my general familiarity with the situation. Found it necessary to advise Silliman of situation because likelihood Carranza open up subject with him. German situation not troublesome and no intention to expel any more diplomatists. Please expedite answer as boat sails Thursday and wish to accomplish as much as possible in brief time." Canada.

T telegram (SDR, RG 59, 812.00/16014½, DNA).

To Robert Lansing

My dear Mr. Secretary,   The White House. 31 August, 1915.

It does not seem to me that our friend has got anywhere in particular in his representations to the stiff-necked First Chief or made any impression on him that is likely, if confirmed, to lead to cooperation on his part with the United States; and therefore it does not seem to me wise that we should do more than this: send word to Silliman that our friend does come fresh from conversations with you and is in a position to know what the real sentiments and purposes of the Government of the United States are. Any sort of official recognition of him would be a mistake, and quite out of keeping with the understanding upon which he went down there, as I am sure you yourself think. Silliman could be told what I have suggested as if it had been communicated to him in reply to inquiry on his part.

Faithfully Yours,   W.W.

WWTLI (SDR, RG 59, 812.00/16015½, DNA).

From Robert Lansing, with Enclosure

Personal and Private.

My dear Mr. President: Washington August 31, 1915.

I have just received another despatch from Vera Cruz, which I enclose. I believe that the situation there is fairly summarized. As to the course advised, I am much in doubt as I feel that the Pan-American Conferees would be strongly opposed to following it. Perhaps you would be willing to give me your opinion after having had your interview this afternoon with General Scott. Until I hear from you in regard to this second telegram, I do not think it advisable to send any word to Vera Cruz.

Faithfully yours,   Robert Lansing

TLS (SDR, RG 59, 812.00/16016½, DNA).

E N C L O S U R E

Vera Cruz Aug. 30, 1915.

CONFIDENTIAL   For the Secretary only.

Laguirre sends the following: "Situation here with respect to the representation of United States Government is indescribable, (?). Our influence is virtually zero. We do not even get our protests or messages before Carranza. Silliman privately told me situation seemed hopeless; Canada takes same view. Carranza told me in conversation that Canada was enemy of his cause, sending bad reports to Department of State, but that Silliman was all right. Investigation among authoritative and well informed persons shows Canada has told truth. Carranza has not granted audience to Silliman in nearly three weeks. Yesterday when Silliman had appointment with Carranza latter instead went parading with his troops leaving word that foreign secretary[1] was authorized to take up anything Silliman had. Foreign secretary is inexperienced boy. Even your most urgent representations are handled in this indirect and fruitless way. Carranza has taken advantage of his old friendship with Silliman to turn him down repeatedly and Silliman is not the forceful kind of personality who would insist on an audience in the name of his Government. Carranza complained to me that his representative in Washington was not received. I explained that the purpose was to avoid receiving Mexicans of so many factions but he was not impressed. Silliman has worked faithfully and loyally but tells me privately he is discouraged and believes our recent strong notes and Latin-American appeal have caused strained relations. I think Silliman would welcome a change in handling these questions. He told me the point had been reached where threats of force and strong notes only aggravate Carranza and that he is not afraid of us because he is confident we do not dare to intervene.

In this connection I offer the following plan for your consideration:

First. That new representative be sent here fully conversant with Government point of view so that Carranza will understand that this representative is fully supported by the Government at every stage. Second. That if Latin-American plan of conference is not accepted as certainly *seems to be* United States will look to Carranza as the head of the most powerful faction to establish government and will recognize him. Third, that recognition is accorded with the understanding that thereafter the constituted government automatically is invested with full responsibilities and duties to protect the lives and properties of foreigners throughout entire territory of Mexico, and that failure to do so will be considered as violation of our treaties and lead, not to interference in internal concerns, but to satisfaction of international rights. Fourth. That the United States suggests that, in order that rights of foreigners everywhere in Mexico be respected, a friendly and harmonizing disposition be shown by Carranza toward those opposed to him, but that if this is not done the full responsibilities still attach to the recognized government for everything done by all rebels in field and the United States will insist to its full powers on obtaining satisfaction from Carranza whenever rights violated.

Both Canada and Silliman to whom I have outlined above agree with it heartily. Such a programe gives a fair chance to Carranza to demonstrate that he is able to rule Mexico. Might be suggested discreetly to him and might influence his reply to Latin-American notes causing him to begin to assert the dominance which he claims by calling conference of his own initiative of chiefs in his control irrespective of what our future policy is to be. The situation here would seem to demand that some one be selected who will talk earnestly, forcefully, insistently, to Carranza and who will not hesitate to inform Carranza whenever the occasion arises that his refusal to receive the representative of the United States bearing urgent communications would be considered as indication of desire not to remain on friendly terms with United States. Canada has gotten results by this method and is respected by Carranza but is not persona grata now. Some new representation should be made. This filed before receipt of any reply to my first message of August 29."

Canada

T telegram (SDR, RG 59, 812.00/16016½, DNA).
1 Jesús Acuña, in charge of the Department of Foreign Relations.

To Robert Lansing

My dear Mr. Secretary,   The White House. 31 August, 1915.

I do not think any part of this advice good. The usual thing has happened: a man is sent down to explain our exact position and purpose and within a day or two sends us a comprehensive plan of his own entirely inconsistent with what he was sent to say.

I think it is best to make no reply at all to this, and simply to let it go at what we replied to the first communication.

It is a great pity, but it is clear that nothing can be done either with or through Carranza. I have no doubt that your conversation with General Scott strengthened this impression in your mind, as it did in mine.   Faithfully Yours,   W.W.

WWTLI (SDR, RG 59, 812.00/16017½, DNA).

To Lucius William Nieman

My dear Mr. Nieman: [The White House] August 31, 1915

You have several times made me very happy by the editorials appearing in the Journal, but none has given me greater comfort and encouragement than the one published in your issue of August twenty-sixth.[1] May I not tell you how genuinely grateful I am for such appreciation, greatly as it exceeds my deserts?
        Cordially and sincerely yours,   Woodrow Wilson

TLS (Letterpress Books, WP, DLC).
    [1] "Woodrow Wilson's Work," *Milwaukee Journal*, Aug. 26, 1915. It praised Wilson for his "patience, dignity, firmness and power" under extreme domestic and international pressures. "The darts and javelins hurled at him in fits of passion by men whose first thought may not be of America, but whose welfare, whose very lives, he is wisely safeguarding, have not turned him a hairbreadth from his course."

From Edward Mandell House

                                        Manchester, Massachusetts.
Dear Governor: August 31st, 1915.

I wonder if you realize what a great diplomatic triumph you have achieved in your negotiations with Germany.

If it comes through as now seems probable, there will be nothing in history to compare with it. Everyone is talking of it and to the great satisfaction of your friends.
                    Your affectionate,   E. M. House

TLS (WP, DLC).

Francis Burton Harrison to Joseph Patrick Tumulty

My dear Mr. Tumulty: Manila, August 31, 1915.

As the time for the convening of the new Congress is drawing near, I am taking this opportunity to write you about our Philippine legislation. Knowing your great interest in Philippine matters, I have often wanted to write you about affairs out here but have hesitated to do so through a desire not to add to your already great burdens of office. The present situation, however, is one which I consider so serious for the success of our administration out here that I hesitate no longer as to writing you.

As you of course know, there was a tremendous expectation on the part of the Filipinos when the new administration came into power, and no doubt they had their minds fixed upon the first Jones Bill containing a fixed date for independence as the probable legislation they might expect; when it became clear that Congress did not intend to pass the first Jones Bill, a successful effort was made to secure the support of the Filipinos for the second Jones Bill, which omits the fixed date and yet states clearly in the preamble the intention of the United States to give them ultimate independence. The failure of the second Jones Bill in the last days of the last Congress, owing to threats of filibuster by a few of the minority Senators, left the situation in an unsatisfactory condition out here, but the President's splendid message to the Filipino people of March 5th[1] reassured them completely as to the outcome of the legislation, and they have with much dignity and patience and good will accepted the prospect of passage by the new Congress of the Bill which failed for lack of time. With the support of the President and of the Chairmen of the Senate and House Committees and the apparent cooperation of most, if not all of the Democratic leaders, I have every hope that the Bill will pass and pass soon. It is not too much to say that the final success of the Democratic administration in the Islands will depend upon the passage of this Bill.

I make this last statement in spite of the fact that entirely outside of the matter of the Jones Bill, our administration in the Philippines has succeeded in securing the confidence and good will of the Filipino people for the United States; has materially improved the relations between Americans in the Islands and Filipinos; has given the Filipinos already extensive grasp of local self-government; and has pulled the treasury out of an impending bankruptcy and put the finance of the country on a firm foundation. But, in spite of all this, I feel confident that the failure of the Jones Bill now would do away with all confidence on the part of the Filipino people in the intentions of the United States towards them, and would be construed by them as a repudiation of what they always understood to be the policy of the United States towards the Islands. This would hopelessly prejudice the good name of our country in its relations with the Filipinos, and would make it exceedingly difficult for any administration or any set of men to govern these Islands successfully for the balance of the time remaining before our country decides to grant the Filipinos their independence.

I presume that the President expects to make some reference to the Philippine legislation in his message to Congress as he has so kindly done on several previous occasions, and hope that he will think it desirable to talk to General McIntyre upon his return from the Islands; McIntyre will leave here in a few weeks and is, I believe, delighted with conditions as he finds them here. As far as we can tell at this distance, the Republican attack against our Philippine policy will not be based upon open opposition to ultimate independence but will probably consist of an attempt to show that Filipinization has destroyed the efficiency of the Government out here. While I am inclined to believe that they have already worn this feature of their attack threadbare and have been unable to substantiate it in any of their declarations as to our impairing the efficiency of the administration out here, and while all of their predictions of the past two years have failed to materialize, I am decidedly anxious that something should be done to dissipate this method of attack. My opinion is that we have not impaired the efficiency but have increased it by bringing the Government into touch with the people and by securing the cooperation of the people in the execution of administration policies as well as in the administration of the laws themselves. However, it may seem to you that I am attempting to blow my own trumpet in this matter; therefore, I will leave it to General McIntyre's statement of the situation when he returns—he can hardly be said to be a partisan in this matter, since he has served through the preceding administration as well as in this one. While it appears to me that our opponents have for the time being worn themselves out along the old line of attack, they had without doubt a well organized and well supplied camp, and judging from home newspapers, they made a good deal of progress at first; they supplied news information to Mr. Taft and to many other persons at home, and Mr. Taft, with his usual gullibility, allowed himself to be made the mouthpiece of this attack. For the last six or eight months, however, businessmen in the Philipines have come to see that, compared with other countries of the world at the present time, they have been doing exceedingly well. In fact, they have had, perhaps, a greater share of prosperity than they might have expected during the time of the great world war. Both business matters and the finances of the Government are now in a most creditable shape, in fact, better than they have been for a long time, and the businessmen, I think, have come to believe that this administration has done and is doing as much for them as it legitimately can, and as much or more than has ever been done for them before. Consequently, most of them are in good humor towards the Government here with the exception of those representatives of the "invisible government" which existed here previously for the benefit of a special few.

Anticipating, however, that the same old attack of "destroying efficiency" will be made in the present Congress and, probably, in the Republican platform next year, I wish to suggest that some means be taken to offset it and, if possible, spike their guns before they can use them.

We have had a few Congressional visitors here this summer, and of these the only one who seems determined to make mischief at home is Representative Miller of Minnesota,[2] whose evident intention is to try to make a reputation at the expense of the administration here and also at the expense of the facts.

Commissioner Quezon is leaving the Islands on his return trip and will no doubt call upon you about the time this letter arrives there. His work in the Islands this summer has been most effective in promoting good feeling between the Filipinos and the Government here, and he is immensely popular in the Philippines.

With cordial regards,

Yours sincerely,   Francis Burton Harrison.

TLS (WP, DLC).
¹ See WW to F. B. Harrison, March 8, 1915, quoted in LMG to JPT, Oct. 19, 1915.
² Clarence Benjamin Miller, Republican.

To Edith Bolling Galt

[The White House] (29)

My precious Darling,   Tuesday evening, 31 Aug., 1915

I haven't the least idea where I am to send this letter. Perhaps my dear Lady's letter from New York which ought to reach me to-morrow morning will give me instructions. You spoke of leaving New York on Wednesday, but whether that meant in time to *get* here that day or leaving by the night train and getting here in the morning, I don't yet know. As the blessed day approaches when I am to see my Darling again, I grow more and more impatient of *writing*. That seems a symbol of the slavery of separation! Do you know what the figure in parenthesis at the top of the first page of this letter means? It means that this is the twenty-ninth day since my Darling drove away from Harlakenden with the Roses, and seemed to take the very light of the day itself with her. The days are all numbered on the calendar that stands here before me on my table. And they have been the longest days in all the year. Each has been longer than the day that preceded it, and the days of *this* week seem nothing less than interminable. Saturday will be the thirty-third since we parted, and the one hundred and twenty-third since I told you of the deep love that is in my heart, like a new life. What a wonderful experience has been crowded for us, my precious One, into these one hundred and twenty-three days. Did anything more beautiful ever happen to two human beings? And it is so delightful to me to know that in that blessed time I have been able to make you realize what my love for you is,—of what sort and how great. I not only love you—I am *in love with you*, as I was trying to expound to you last night; and there is a deep romance in it all that thrills me. I am deeply moved whenever I think of you,—you *delight* me so,—and I am as homesick as you are! Ah, Sweetheart come,—come quickly. I want you, I long for you, I cannot do without you! I have *tried* to fill the day so as to keep off impatience, but I have been aware all the while that I was merely marking time. I had one really vital conversation, with Gen'l Hugh Scott, the Chief of Staff, who has just come back from the Mexican border, with very definite impressions which he was stating to me in his laconic, soldierly way, and to whom I could state (because I have known him a long time and know him to be utterly loyal and trustworthy) what I wanted from the War Department, by way of a programme of preparedness, much more satisfactorily and with much greater assurance that I would be entirely understood and entirely and intelligently obeyed, than I could to that self-opinionated politician, the Secretary of War, who is a very able person but who concentrates his entire attention on his own opinions and does not listen to mine, and who is, if the plain truth must be spoken, a solemn, conceited ass! I think my conversation with Scott will bring results. At any rate, he knows how to obey orders, and comprehends them when he hears them.

Senator Kern, the leader of the majority in the Senate, was

in, too, and I discussed with him the advisability of calling an extra session of the Senate alone, to convene in October and discuss executive business. It is imperative that the Senate's rules of procedure, which, as they stand, permit the minority, and indeed any individual Senator, to block action on any matter indefinitely, should be altered before the regular session begins in December, so that at that session something definite in the way of legislation may be accomplished. It will take not less than six weeks or two months, the Senators whom I have seen think, to fight the changes through. There are some treaties, too, notably the one with Colombia, that ought to be pushed to ratification. I can call the Senate into extra session without the House, for the consideration of matters in which the House has no part, and when Congress adjourned in the Spring I had a sort of tacit understanding with some of the leading Senators that I would do so. But the acute difficulties with Germany which have developed since then and the likelihood that some mischief-makers like Hoke Smith of Georgia would add to the delicacy and difficulty of the situation by intemperate speeches and ill-considered proposals if they were given the vantage ground of the floor of the Senate to speak from, and the thought that probably my hands had better be left absolutely free (which is devoutly to be wished), had made all of us hold back a little on the plan; and I was begging Kern to-day to take the question up afresh with some of the men we had consulted before, to advise me what they think wise in the changed circumstances. If the communication about the *Arabic* affair for which the Germans have asked us to wait ever comes & is satisfactory, so that the air clears, that will remove our doubts, and I shall have the delectable privilege of an extra two months association with the Senators of the United States. I want the German crisis to clear away, but—!

I am putting up a bluff, Sweetheart. I am *writing* about plans for preparedness and information concerning the Mexican border and arguments for and against calling the Senate in extraordinary session, but I am not *thinking* about them. I am *thinking* about you and about Saturday! I can *talk* about other things, and decide them (I have decided several rather important matters of public business to-day) and yet all the while have my mind so full, so delightfully full, of you that nothing seems even to have interrupted my loving thought of you! Will Saturday *never* come?

I am eagerly looking forward to dear little Helen's coming in the morning. It will change the whole aspect and atmosphere of the house and be such a tangible and visible evidence that the exile is over! She is a most companionable, and a most comprehending small person, and we can concoct all sorts of delectable schemes together; and on the days when I can't see you *she* can see you (maybe you will resume your walks in the Park) and bring me word direct how you are and what you are thinking about. I am already meditating a plan for an afternoon tea to which your mother and Bertha might be induced to come and at which I could happen in—instead of peeping through the window of the Green Room to catch a bare glimpse of the most beautiful lady in the world. Is there *no* way, I wonder, in which I might escape from this prison and call on those dear ones at the *Cordova*? I would give my head to do it. Here they have been in Washington all day to-day, I assume, and I have not been free so much as to speak with them over the telephone, much less to stop by and see how they fare and send you word. I feel rebel[l]ious not only, but also like a bit of a coward, or a fool, for not kicking over the traces and going anyhow! It's intolerable!

Mac. got back from Maine—and Cornish—this morning—alone. He took Nell and her baby to Cornish last week and they got there on dear Jessie's birthday and helped to celebrate it—wasn't that jolly? The baby stood the journey admirably and is now in fine shape again, entirely well and flourishing. Frank is back from Newfoundland, so that the little family circle lacked only (!) you and Helen and me. If only we could all have been there! Mac. has come down ahead for several reasons, one of the chief being that they have taken a new house, I am ashamed to say I do not know exactly where, and he wants to get their things all moved and everything ready for the family before Nell comes back with the baby. Apparently Nona is of no use in such circumstances or did not offer. The house on Massachusetts Avenue proved much too small, for, when all together, they are a big family. When the boys[1] came in, from school and college, they had to farm them out for sleeping and the dining room was so small that they could hardly crowd in even for meals. I don't know that Nona will be much less of a problem in a larger house than she has been in the small one. But fortunately she is a great deal away, having a good time somewhere on a visit; and it may be that some adventurous youngster, deluded by her beauty, may marry her soon! That's a hateful remark, I admit, and I apologize, but everything that is in my mind will *out* when I'm talking to you, and it must be said that Nona is *not* an admirable person.

[1] William Gibbs McAdoo, Jr., a student at Princeton, and Robert Hazlehurst McAdoo, at St. Paul's School.

I am *so* delighted, my Darling, that your mother (would you feel that I was going too fast if I simply said "Mother"—it would be very delightful to me if I might, at least in speaking to you?) and Bertha were pleased with my letters to them and read in them what I was really trying to say. My letter to Bertha didn't compare with hers to me, which I thought exceptionally lovely in its revelation of her love and admiration for you, her wonderful sister, and its generous offer of her affection to me. I shall try to prove to her how I appreciate that, and that I know how to respond in the same spirit. But I want to see them! It is hard to believe that, in such thraldom, I am free, white, and twenty-one!

(30) Wed., 7.05 A.M.

You readily see, my Love, from what goes before, what a "state of mind" I was in last night. Impatience to see you had so got hold of me last night that it was hard to make my heart behave at all. I loved you so intensely that I scarcely dared trust myself to speak of it. This morning the longing is no less intense, and a deep excitement has taken hold of me because of the possibility that you may be here in Washington *to-day*; but I am fresher and have better command of myself, and can, I hope, make love to you without making the time of my seeing you and holding you close in my arms again seem a whole year off! Make love to you! It seems to me I do nothing else, and *want* to do nothing else. All day long my thoughts are following you with love, with a love that is beyond measure or expression, and that is full of the playful, yearning, *courting* tenderness that springs from a happy, joyful devotion and a perfect delight in companionship. You are as real a *presence* to me all the day and night through as if you were, in some queer intangible way, actually present in the house, in the motor, on the golf course, wherever I go, and I find myself very often, when no one else is by, speaking to you out loud,—almost feeling that I hear your sweet response, as it comes so often in your wonderful letters, and might stretch out my hand and touch you. You seem to me the only real, effectual personality in the world, and I seem to be waiting to be *completed* because I am so deeply aware that you are mine,—that you are what I lack, that you are what I am waiting for to supply what I need, intellectually and spiritually and emotionally. How abstract and thin it sounds when I write it down in such words,—the only words I can find! But I am speaking to your heart, my precious Darling, not to your ear: I am whispering these things through a lover's kiss, and I am as sure that you understand and send me back a similar message of need and longing as I am that I am speaking the deepest truth of my heart. When you come to me and our lives are in fact united (I can't write those words down without setting my heart pounding with the most exquisite excitement!) I shall be able to recover other people—get them solidly back into my consciousness, but not till then. Now they are a bit like automata that bring me the news of the day and the tasks of the day in some way quite familiar to me and perfectly intelligible, and I can deal with them in the usual way. There is nothing *unreal* about them. They are as concrete, as agreeable or disagreeable, or as negligible, as ever, and the business they bring me grips me as usual and is performed with real and close attention to its details; but *they* do not grip me. I am waiting for the one radiant, satisfying person who can fill my heart with life. Ah, my Darling, my Darling, it isn't possible to tell you how or how much I love you. We will have a *great* deal to say to one another, either silently or in words, when you come, will we not? We have found out a great deal about our love for one another, during these interminable weeks of separation, that we never realized before, haven't we? And it has all been in glorious confirmation and enhancement of our love, hasn't it my own sweet Darling? I shall *try* to tell you what it has meant to me.

My Darling, my heart beats so I can hardly keep my pen steady! You *are* in Washington! Hoover has just handed me your little note telling me. Hurrah! I can't tell you how happy it makes me. I love you with an unspeakable love and delight! Welcome, you blessed Darling.   Your own   Woodrow

ALS (WP, DLC).

From Edith Bolling Galt

My precious One,   Manhattan August 31st/1915 2 P.M.

When you read this I shall probably be at *home* Think of it—really in Washington again!! I have just decided to take the midnight train and should be there by seven. I am going up to the Cordova to breakfast with Mother and afterwards to my own nest. I wonder if I can wait until Saturday to see you—but, at least I will know you are near.

Do tell me you are glad I came without waiting to tell you. I just decided while we were at lunch. As Mr. Rose said they wanted to make an early start tomorrow morning, and would I mind if they left before I did.

So I just said, No, indeed, not in the least, I will take the night train and be home early tomorrow morning. So I went right out and telegraphed Randolph. How I wanted to wire you too, but I knew I must not. So I will leave the address for your precious letter to be forwarded to me tomorrow and skip off without a regret. I am so excited over it—and know you will be.

Thank you for sending me Helen's letter. It is just like her, and I know she meant every word of it—bless her heart.

They are waiting for me so goodbye my precious One. Hurrah —no more letters for I am coming!!!!   Edith

P.S. I got your dear letter this morning—it has made my day bright

ALS (WP, DLC).

To Cleveland Hoadley Dodge

My dear Cleve: The White House September 1, 1915

It is so next to impossible down here as I struggle with the tasks of every day to get any kind of perspective on the work I am doing that I need just such letters as yours of August twenty-ninth to keep me going. You must certainly have some wireless way of knowing when I am in need of a word of cheer and affection, for your letters always come just at the right time.

I am deeply grateful to you, my dear fellow. What you tell me is valuable to me and I thank you with all my heart.

Are you not coming down this way some time soon, so that I might catch a glimpse of you? Don't come down without letting me know.

With warmest affection,
                    Your devoted friend,   Woodrow Wilson

TLS (WC, NjP).

From Robert Lansing

Personal and Private.

My Dear Mr. President: Washington September 1, 1915.

Yesterday morning I had an interview lasting nearly an hour with Dr. Aletta Jacobs of Amsterdam, Netherlands, and Miss Emily G. Balch of this country in regard to a proposed conference of neutrals to offer to the belligerent governments "continuous mediation," which was the plan adopted by the Women's Peace Conference at The Hague.[1] The interview was in accordance with your letter of August 30th to Miss Balch.[2]

The purpose of the interview was to induce this Government to invite the Goverments of the Netherlands, Denmark, Sweden, Norway, Switzerland, and possibly Spain to name delegates to a conference, which should make proposals to the belligerents as opportunity offered. Failing to prevail on this Government to take the initiative these ladies desired to obtain a statement that the United States would send a representation[3] to a Conference if invited to do so by another neutral government (presumably the Netherlands).

Dr. Jacobs held herself out to be the unofficial representative of the Prime Minister of the Netherlands and to substantiate this she had a third person statement (unsigned) by the Netherlands Minister.

I told the ladies in the first place that even unofficially I could not express the views of this Government on credentials of that sort, that the Netherlands Government, if it desired to know our views, could approach us through the Minister unofficially and confidentially, and that, while I appreciated their zeal and motives, it seemed to me that it would cause less embarrassment to follow the usual channels of informal intercourse between Governments. They seemed to disapprove heartily of this idea and said that the Netherlands could not do that, but were unable to explain the reason.

I shall not bore you with an account of the conversation which took place. I tried to have them explain what they meant by "continuous mediation," but they seemed rather vague as to its meaning. I said that we had offered our services and that the offer still stood. They replied that the mediators should make proposals to the belligerents as a basis for peace. I asked them to whom the mediators would propose the payment of a war indemnity? To Germany or to the Allies? They said that would have to be decided later.

I have said enough to show you the futile character of the interview. These ladies impressed me as most earnest in purpose and inspired by humanitarian motives but as failing to view the situation practically. The perversity and selfishness of human nature are factors which they have left out of the problem.

I told them, however, that I would submit to you the questions: Would this Government send a delegate or delegates to a Peace Conference of Neutral Powers? If so, would the United States take the initiative? If not, would it accept an invitation to participate?

I am afraid the ladies left me with the impression that I considered their plan at present impracticable, and that, if it were practical, it should be taken up by the Governments rather than by outside parties. I felt that it would be unwise to encourage this movement at the present time, because its rejection now by the belligerents might close the door to an offer of mediation when a more propitious time should come.

However, they will ask me what you said in regard to their proposal, so I hope that you can make some sort of reply which will discourage them from renewed efforts to secure action by this Government.   Faithfully yours,   Robert Lansing.

TLS (R. Lansing Papers, NjP).
    1 About this organization, see n. 2 to remarks at a press conference printed at April 13, 1915, Vol. 32.
    2 He referred to WW to Emily G. Balch, Aug. 28, 1915.
    3 He presumably meant "representative."

To Robert Lansing

The White House.

My dear Mr. Secretary,   31 August, 1915 [Sept. 1, 1915].

Thank you for your account of your conversation with Dr. Jacobs and Miss Balch. I had surmised that their errand was what it turned out to be, and I had already discussed with Miss Balch the proposal for a Conference of Neutrals.

I would be obliged if you would say to Dr. Jacobs and Miss Balch, that I highly appreciate the whole spirit and purpose with which they have acted, and need not say that my interest in bringing about peace, when that is possible, and in any way that may prove feasible, is profound. But I do not feel that at this time it would be wise for the United States to take the initiative in calling such a conference, and that the question whether we should respond to such a call, if made upon the initiative of some other nation is one which I do not feel I can wisely answer beforehand. It would necessarily depend on the occasion and on the whole European situation as it stood at the time of the call. I am sorry to give them a reply to their suggestions which will, I fear, appear to them so unsatisfactory, but, all things considered, I might be misleading them were I to give any other.

Faithfully Yours,   W.W.

WWTLI (R. Lansing Papers, NjP).

From John Lowndes McLaurin

PERSONAL

Mr. President: Columbia, S.C. Sept. 1, 1915.

I am enclosing an address to the farmers, commenting on the statements of yourself, Secretary McAdoo and Mr. Harding.[1]

Such boldness and generosity is something new to the South. It almost took my breath away. I never expected to live to see a Federal Administration go so far in doing justice to our people. The banks here have lived by usury. Eight per cent. discount is their uniform rate, and about twenty per cent. to the tenant class, borrowing fifty to two hundred dollars. Two-thirds of the crop is produced by this class of people, and we must reach the cotton of the producer who has no personal credit. It was for this purpose that I devised the State warehouse system. When that is accomplished, not only will we have prosperity, but better political conditions in this and other Southern States. Just discontent with industrial conditions is now the fertile breeding ground of the dangerous demagogue.

Sincerely,   Jno. L. McLaurin

TLS (WP, DLC).

[1] "To Finance Cotton Receipts," in J. L. McLaurin, *Warehousing Cotton and Financing Warehouse Receipts* (Bennettsville, S. C., 1915), pp. 2-7 (WP, DLC). McLaurin urged producers to keep cotton off the market until prices had risen and chastised banks for failing to extend credit on reasonable terms to farmers.

Count Johann Heinrich von Bernstorff to Robert Lansing

My dear Mr. Secretary: Washington, D. C., September 1, 1915.

With reference to our conversation of this morning I beg to inform you that my instructions concerning our answer to your last Lusitania note contained the following passage:

"Liners will not be sunk by our submarines without warning and without safety of the lives of noncombatants, provided that the liners do not try to escape or offer resistance."

Although I know that you do not wish to discuss the Lusitania question till the Arabic incident has been definitely and satisfactorily settled, I desire to inform you of the above because this policy of my Government was decided on before the Arabic incident occurred.

I have no objection to your making any use you may please of the above information.

I remain, my dear Mr. Lansing,

Very sincerely yours,   J. Bernstorff

TCL (WP, DLC).

Robert Lansing to Frank Arthur Vanderlip

PERSONAL AND PRIVATE:

My dear Mr. Vanderlip: [Washington] September 1, 1915.

A report has come to the notice of the Department that the National City Bank has under consideration the question of financing the Carranzista movement in Mexico. As this rumor, if true, might be a serious embarrassment to the Government in its international relations, I would appreciate it if you could advise me personally and confidentially, by letter or by interview as to the truth of this reported action on the part of the National City Bank.[1]   Yours very sincerely,   [Robert Lansing]

CCL (R. Lansing Papers, DLC).
[1] Vanderlip replied that there was absolutely nothing to the report that he or the National City Bank was making arrangements to supply money to Carranza in return for concessions. F. A. Vanderlip to RL, Sept. 2, 1915, TLS (R. Lansing Papers, DLC).

Hugh Lenox Scott to Leonard Wood

My dear General Wood: Washington. September 1st, 1915.

I was called to the White House yesterday afternoon about Mexican affairs, and took the liberty when the President mentioned the camp at Plattsburg to say to him that I felt certain that you had no intention of transgressing the proprieties, and I was in hopes that he would not hold anything up against you in his mind. He showed some resentment and said some of your speeches he did not like—one in particular in which you spoke of the "ignorant multitude." I asked him if he would have any objection to my mentioning this and he said "No; go ahead." . . .

I find so much to do that I will not be able to go to Plattsburg during this class but hope to go to the next.

Ever sincerely yours,   H L Scott

TLS (L. Wood Papers, DLC).

To the Editor of the *New York Herald*[1]

My dear Sir: [The White House] September 2, 1915

You were recently imposed upon by a story of a breach between me and my friend, Mr. House, which came to you through one George Laughlin, connected with your service here. The story was an invention out of the whole cloth and was originated with what motive I can only conjecture. I note that Mr. Laughlin is associated here with the Mr. Craig who uttered so inexcusable a libel not long ago against the Secretary of the Treasury.[2]

I write to request that you withdraw Mr. Laughlin from service in Washington. Until he is withdrawn, we cannot be sure that you will be honestly informed of what is going on here and I should very much regret anything which would prevent complete confidence in our dealings with the New York Herald.

Sincerely yours,   Woodrow Wilson

TLS (Letterpress Books, WP, DLC).

1 Josiah Kingsley Ohl.

2 Donald Alexander Craig, head of the *New York Herald's* Washington bureau, later wrote to Tumulty saying that Laughlin, after learning late in the evening that the story about the Wilson-House break was being telegraphed to other newspapers, had sought to verify it. Failing to reach Tumulty, he had written the article as an unconfirmed rumor and had added that it was not generally believed. D. A. Craig to JPT, Sept. 14, 1915, TLS (WP, DLC).

In a letter to Wilson, Craig explained that he had not written the "inexcusable libel" against McAdoo (it related to McAdoo and the ship purchase bill and was published "last winter"), that he had personally apologized to McAdoo, who had generously accepted his apology, and that the reporter who wrote the story was no longer on his staff. D. A. Craig to WW, Sept. 13, 1915, TLS (WP, DLC).

Wilson commented on the foregoing, as follows:

"I do not find the enclosed at all convincing as to the justification of sending the story about House from the Herald office here without so much as extending to us the courtesy of an inquiry as to whether it was true or not, and every word of it is grossly false. It is full of pure invention.

"But I am glad to have Mr. Craig's true relation to the libel on McAdoo explained to me and I hope you will say to him that I am sorry that I was misled in the matter." WW to JPT, c. Sept. 14, 1915, TL (WP, DLC).

To Oswald Garrison Villard

My dear Mr. Villard: The White House September 2, 1915

Mr. Tumulty has just shown me your letter to him of yesterday[1] and I hasten to drop you a line to assure you that it never for a moment entered my head that you were in any way responsible for the stories to which you refer. I would have known that that was impossible. I am only sorry that you should have been distressed by being put in a false position.

May I not thank you with all my heart for the generous articles you have recently been writing about me?

Cordially and sincerely yours,   Woodrow Wilson

TLS (O. G. Villard Papers, MH).
¹ O. G. Villard to JPT, Sept. 1, 1915, TLS (WP, DLC), saying that he had had nothing whatever to do with the stories about himself and House, had never exploited his friendship with the President nor claimed superior knowledge on the basis of his friendship, and that he had "sought to take my trick with you and the others like a regular Washington correspondent."

From Robert Lansing, with Enclosure

Personal and Private.

My Dear Mr. President: Washington September 2, 1915.

You have undoubtedly read the flimsy of the strictly confidential despatch from London, No. 2732, September 1, 7 P.M., in which there is a copy of a letter signed by Ambassador Dumba and which was taken from Archibald¹ who was carrying it to Vienna.

It seems to me that the conduct of the Ambassador is of a very serious nature and that we should consider at once what steps should be taken in regard to it.

Faithfully yours,   Robert Lansing.

TLS (SDR, RG 59, 701.6311/141, DNA).
¹ James Francis Jewell Archibald, an American journalist in the pay of the German embassy, sailed for Europe on August 20, carrying documents to Berlin and Vienna, which British naval authorities at Falmouth seized. Among them was the letter printed below.

E N C L O S U R E

London Sept. 1, 1915.

2732.   GREATEST URGENCY/STRICTLY CONFIDENTIAL.

My 2722, Aug 31, 4 p.m. This afternoon at the Admiralty Bell¹ was shown in confidence one of the despatches which Archibald was bearing to Vienna. It is from Dumba to Baron Burian, Austro-Hungarian Minister for Foreign Affairs, and is entirely in long hand. Bell was allowed to keep possession of the document long enough to make a rough translation which I append, and take photographs of the document which will go forward in the next pouch.

Letter reads as follows:

"Excellency: New York, August 20, 1915.

Yesterday evening Consul-General Von Nuber² received the enclosed memorandum from the chief editor of the SZABADSÁG, an influential paper, after having had an interview with me on the previous day, in which are defined his proposals with regard to the arrangements for a strike in the steel and munitions factory at Bethlehem (Schwab's) and in the middle west. Today at 12 o'clock, Mr. Archibald, who is well known to Your Excellency, leaves for Berlin and Vienna on the ROTTERDAM. I wish to take this rare and safe opportunity of recommending the proposal to Your Excellency's warmest consideration. I have the impression that we could if not actually prevent at any rate very much disorganize the manufacture of munitions of war at Bethlehem and in the middle west and hold it up for months which the German military attache states is of great importance and would considerably outweigh the relatively small cost. But even if the arrangement does not succeed it is probable that we should compel favorable conditions of work for our poor oppressed countrymen through the crisis. These white slaves now work at Bethlehem for twelve hours a day on seven days of the week. All the weaklings go under and get consumption.

As far as German workmen exist under these sweated conditions a means of escape will be provided immediately. A private German employment bureau has also been established which obtains fresh employment for such persons as have voluntarily ceased work and which is working very well. We will take part in this and give it the widest support.

I beg that Your Excellency will kindly tell me by wireless whether you agreed to the contents of this letter as it is urgent. With all esteem signed C. Dumba."

The enclosure which is in Hungarian has not yet been translated.

Archibald is due to arrive tomorrow morning at Rotterdam on the ROTTERDAM.   American Ambassador London.[3]

T telegram (SDR, RG 59, 701.6311/141, DNA).
    [1] Edward Bell, secretary of the American embassy in London.
    [2] Alexander Nuber von Pereked, Austro-Hungarian Consul-General in New York.
    [3] For a discussion of the so-called Dumba affair, see Link, *Struggle for Neutrality*, pp. 645-46.

From Robert Lansing

My dear Mr. President: Washington September 2, 1915.

I have just received the following telegram from Mr. Bryan:

"Please accept for yourself, and convey to the President my hearty congratulations upon the successful settlement of the submarine controversy."

I have also received from David R. Francis, Esquire, the following:

"Germany's conceding our contention is great diplomatic achievement for America and merits hearty congratulations which are sincerely tendered."

I have received other communications of a similar nature but these two I thought, would be of particular interest to you.

Faithfully yours,   Robert Lansing.

TLS (WP, DLC).

Three Letters to Edith Bolling Galt

[The White House]

My own Darling,   Thursday morning, 6.30   2 Sept., 1915

These are the papers I forgot to bring you last night.[1]

May I just smuggle this line in to say that I love you with all my heart; that it is a great comfort to have you so near; that I am well; and that I do not know what to do with myself this morning?

With all the devotion of a very full heart,

Your own   Woodrow

ALS (WP, DLC).
[1] The enclosures are missing.

[The White House, c. Sept. 2, 1915]

Is not Gerard extraordinary? He repeats nothing but gossip[1] —and *seems* to intimate that we are being taken in.   W.

ALI (WP, DLC).
[1] J. W. Gerard to RL, Aug. 31, Sept. 1, 12 noon, 1 P.M., and 2 P.M., 1915, T telegrams (WP, DLC), sending various unofficial messages about events in Berlin. In the first, Gerard repeated a rumor that the Germans wanted to keep the *Lusitania* and *Arabic* cases separate because they could more easily make concessions in the latter; in the second, he speculated that the Germans were only working for a delay until the Balkan situation was in hand and suggested that, the sooner the United States made its demands, the greater was the probability of their acceptance. Gerard had also heard that Walter Niebuhr, editor of the *Daily Courier* and president of the Courier-Herald Co. of Lincoln, Ill., had seen the Emperor. Gerard guessed that, since Niebuhr was "undoubtedly in the pay of the propaganda," he had probably told the Emperor that the United States was "only bluffing" and would not dare to enforce its rights. In the last telegram, Gerard reported remarks made by the wife of a German official to a woman at the American embassy to the effect that the United States would not break with Germany, "knowing too well that it would be to her disadvantage." Gerard concluded that this represented Foreign Office thinking on the subject.

[The White House]

My precious Sweetheart,   Thursday 10.40 A.M.   2 Sept., 1915

I could not talk to you as freely last night as if we had been alone. I was sorely puzzled by your decision that we ought not to interchange letters on the days when we cannot see one another. That would be giving up our *only in*conspicuous means of keeping in touch with one another because we would have to avoid frequent use of the conspicuous ways. But I loyally accepted your decision, as I am bound and most willing to accept any decision that will relieve you of distress—whatever distress it may cause me.

I am breaking your rule now only because I found I could not bear to be *more* cut off from you on this my day of apparent triumph than I was when you were hundreds of miles away and were every day helping me to bear days of deep strain and anxiety. I send you the enclosed[1] because I want you above all things to share my successes. Nothing means anything to me unless you share it with me. I do not care for it a moment unless you can. My heart is full of you—and of nothing else, and I am, though for the moment disobedient,

Your own   Woodrow

ALS (WP, DLC).
 [1] J. H. von Bernstorff to RL, Sept. 1, 1915.

From Edith Bolling Galt

[Washington] Thursday Sept 2, 1915

How can I resist sending you just a tiny little note this morning when I have just gotten that perfectly blessed letter you sent me to New York. Could anyone ever write a more perfect symphony of love, and to think I have seen you again Sweetheart and you are *really*, *truly* more wonderful than I remembered—and yet you love *me*! I was so excited last night for fear you would not like me as well as you thought you did, that perhaps your memory had played tricks, and you pictured me more interesting and lovable that [than] I am. And this letter (although it was written of course before you saw me) seems a sort of answer to my fears.

It is like a steady hand holding my nervous excited ones and has the same affect that your dear presence had last night. When I was all aquiver at the things that had happened during the day and, after being with you, clasping your dear hands and feeling the protection of those tender arms fold 'round me, the trouble seemed to melt away and I came home, serene, secure, and happy.

I was afraid, my precious one, that you went away with a little ache in your heart, not only that you thought I was worried but, well, that I did not seem responsive. Am I right? If I am, I want to set it right and know you will understand. I just can't discuss intimate things before anyone else—even our dear, loyal, little

Helen. It is not that I doubt her affection or interest, but I can't do it except to you, and, even if the intervals of seperation are far apart when it will be possible to see you just by ourselves I would rather wait. Do you mind? I hope you don't—and perhaps I will get used to a third party—but just now I would rather talk of general things than the precious ones that mean nothing to anyone but you and me.

5 P.M.

Dearest, Dearest I had to stop here, and now I have just gotten your little note written at 10.40 this morning. Bless your heart for writing it and saying just what you did. Am I not breaking my own rule. Surely I can't blame you for doing the same thing.

Oh! Sweetheart all day I have wanted to throw prudence to the winds and come straight to your arms, there to nestle and pour out all my love and pride in this day of triumph and all the longing that is eating into my heart.

Instead I am here—away from you—hearing that you are too tired to play golf—and have gone to ride instead.

And besides not being able to come and help and rest you, I have the hateful feeling that something I did last night has caused you pain. I am just as unhappy as I would want even old W.J.B. to be at this minute—and I love you so that even that is a pain.

Please write to me, and pay no attention to what I said. Love me all you can—   Edith.

ALS (WP, DLC).

From Margaret Woodrow Wilson and Others

Windsor, Vermont, September 2, 1915.

Great joy here over todays news. The Smith's join us in deepest love.   Margaret, Jessie, Nell, Frank.

T telegram (WC, NjP).

To Edith Bolling Galt

[The White House] 3 Sept. [1915]

I tremble a little bit over this 'triumph'[1]—we have not yet seen the *terms* of Germany's concessions, though Bernstorff professes himself certain what they will be   W.

ALI (WP, DLC).
[1] The enclosure is missing. However, it was one of many editorials or letters hailing Wilson's "triumph" in winning the so-called *Arabic* pledge.

To Robert Lansing

My dear Mr. Secretary,   The White House. 3 September, 1915.

The contents of the strictly confidential despatch from London, No. 2732, September 1, 7 P.M. are certainly serious enough, and I entirely agree with you that we shall have to take some decided action with regard to the activities of Dumba as well as those of Bernstorff. But when, and how?

I take it for granted that we shall first wish to make sure of Germany's concessions and of their exact terms before dealing with either of these allied Ambassadors about the other matter. So much for the When.

As for the How, what do you think would be the best course, a private intimation to each of them which would allow them to ask to be relieved, without public rebuke, or a direct request on our part to their Governments? I do not know the practice in these matters.   Faithfully yours,   W.W.

WWTLI (SDR, RG 59, 701.6311/145½, DNA).

From Robert Lansing, with Enclosure

PERSONAL AND PRIVATE

My dear Mr. President: Washington September 3, 1915.

I send you a telegram which has just come to my desk.

After reading it will you please return the telegram as no copies have been made and this is the only one in the Department.   Faithfully yours,   Robert Lansing.

TLS (SDR, RG 59, 812.00/16187½, DNA).

E N C L O S U R E

Vera Cruz, Mexico September 1, 1915.
CONFIDENTIAL. For the Secretary only.

Laguirre sends the following:

"After the receipt of your message through Silliman, I had four hours conversation with Carranza alone but could not change his point of view on the subject of conference or attitude towards opponents. Succeeded in the interest of future relations in removing from his mind deep-rooted conviction that President and yourself were personally prejudiced towards him and I think now he feels better disposed. He explained his ideas and programme at length and emphasized frequently desire to reach an understanding with United States. I told him that in event of no reply from Latin American[s] he could assume that they acted officially. His point seems to be to locate responsibility for what he considers unnecessary interference and attempt to deprive his revolution of triumph it was about to obtain. He claims much resentment stirred up among people on account Latin American plan and that irrespective of whether or not he was eliminated tomorrow this nationalism would continue. Assured me, however, reply to note would not offend and would not embarrass subsequent relations, though would decline conference. Toward end of conversation he showed better disposition to understand our real purpose and made several suggestions as to how by personal negotiation International questions could be resolved in way that would bring peace. Will relate this in person when arrive. He urges in main, however, that if American Government will give him month or six weeks more without complicating situation in any way, he can promise complete triumph and generous treatment of opponents. He outlined plans for handling claims, loans and concessions, promising equitable treatment of all. He was very friendly and cordial.

Leaving tomorrow, Thursday, night, arriving Washington next Wednesday noon."   *Canada.*

T telegram (SDR, RG 59, 812.00/16187½, DNA).

From Herbert Clark Hoover

Dear Mr. President,   London, 3rd September, 1915.

I should like to convey to you on behalf of myself and all my colleagues in this Commission the sincere gratitude which we feel to you over the success of the German negotiations. We are certain, from intimate contact in Germany, that this has only been accomplished with the extraordinary appeal which you formulated to justice and humanitarian sentiment in Germany as well as the firmness you displayed, and that in any less able hands the situation would have drifted us into the appalling result of war.

While the work of this Commission would undoubtedly have been continued by the help of other neutral Governments, even in that contingency it would have most certainly diminished in efficiency. More especially is this true now than some months ago as we are about to expand our operations greatly by the import of raw material and export of manufactures from Belgium, in the hope that we may stem the tide of destitution through productive labour.

This is, however, an infinitesimal matter compared to the infinite disaster to the American people which would have been involved in engaging in this conflict, and it is a condition which no good American could for one moment consider except as the last alternative to continued transgression.

Also we feel that the great success which you have had in this negotiation is of the widest possible import in the matter of the rehabilitation of a sense of the responsibility for international engagement. That this rehabilitation has got to come before there can be any hope of successful peace negotiation is obvious. Incidentally we have the view that no peace can be hoped for until the bitterness of hatred on all sides has been somewhat diminished, and it is our further view that the bitterness at present existing is more the result of war directed against civilians on all sides than it is from original causes or the losses by military operations, and that every step which tends to diminish the amount of impact on civilians will contribute materially towards letting down public feeling to a point where a peace proposal might be possible of execution. At the present moment it is obvious that no European statesman could carry peace with his own people on any terms which would be within the range of possibility.

I take the liberty of sending you herewith a copy of our recent report,[1] covering a period of eight months' work. I do not assume you will have time to look it over but at least if you have such a leisure moment we should feel honored if you would do so.

Your obedient servant,   Herbert Hoover
Chairman

TLS (WP, DLC).
    It is missing in WP, DLC.

From Josephus Daniels

Personal

Dear Mr. President: Washington. Sept. 3. 1915.

Upon my return to the city, before taking up the accumulated correspondence, I must tell you of my happiness in the complete vindication of your policy with reference to Germany. Even the able men who felt that a note of like tenor ought to have been sent at the same time to both Germany and England will rejoice that you had the wisdom to put the protection of life far above the protection of property, important as that is.

Upon my trip I had the opportunity to talk with men of prominence of all parties in New England and was entrusted with many messages of congratulation and approval. There is but one voice and that is your tempered firmness has secured the most notable diplomatic victory of half a century. This universal approval must be most grateful to you and compensate for the long days of stress and anxiety, an anxiety which we shared in common.

It makes me happy to be associated with you in these epoch-making times.

Sincerely and faithfully,   Josephus Daniels

I will be ready to come over and discuss naval expansion when it suits you. JD

ALS (WP, DLC).

From Franklin Knight Lane

My dear Mr President,   Washington [c. Sept. 3, 1915]

Just a modest leaf that I wish to add to the wreath that is being woven in appreciation of the triumph of your "instructed idealism." I will never forget the pain upon your face the night of the last note to Germany. I hope that you will now allow yourself to feel some of the glory of this "impossible" victory.

It is a constant and increasing joy for me to know that I am a "hand" on your ship.

Sincerely & faithfully   Franklin K Lane

ALS (WP, DLC).

From Oswald Garrison Villard

My dear Mr. President: New York September 3, 1915.

I thank you most warmly for your kind note of September 2, and for the autographed picture of yourself, but I do not think it does you justice, or is as good as the one which the Evening Post blazoned on its front page last night. It will always be one of my most valued possessions.

I could not refrain from telegraphing you yesterday to express to you even slightly my deep feeling of gratitude as an individual citizen, and more than that, my profound satisfaction as a friend, that my certain faith, beginning with the Lusitania episode, that you would find a way out in peace, was justified. And now I am praying with all my heart that you will set your face against any surrender to the advocates of militarism. I see your letters this morning to Mr. Daniels and Mr. Garrison, and I do trust that you will deem it wise, after all the facts are before you, to postpone any recommendations as to preparation for war until the war in Europe is over. Beginning with next week, I am going to devote myself to writing on some of the phases of this whole question. I hope they will be constructive articles showing what is wrong with the services today, and I shall hasten them as rapidly as possible and shall take the liberty of bringing them to your personal attention, particularly a brief as to the dangers involved in the bill to pay the Militia for services rendered gratuitously since the foundation of the republic.

Again with renewed and heartiest thanks, and warmest congratulations,

Sincerely yours,   Oswald Garrison Villard.

TLS (WP, DLC).

From Mary Allen Hulbert

Dear Friend: Los Angeles. Sept. 3rd [1915]

I have received the documents regarding the mortgages, through Mr. Clark. Of course, the property is really Allen's, and he left them in my name in event of any emergency arising when I might need funds, and he was too far away to supply them. As it is Allen's business, it seemed better that it be done through Mr. Clark, who is sales-manager in the new enterprise. If you can *conveniently* buy them, we will not only be most appreciative but it will help much in carrying the venture to a successful issue— if you *do* so decide. You should know that although Mr. Squires, A's lawyer who made the investment for him, considers the property as having appreciated in value, others, chiefly Mr. Clarence Davies, a Jew real estate man and an authority in Bronx property, reports them as over valued. I only asked Mr. Clark to go to you when I, and he, had in turn tried every means to convert them into cash in time to secure the property here. Also— if you can take them, kindly deduct $600.00 with interest to date, before sending the check. I think this is all in the way of business I have to say. And hope when I report again, to have a glowing one to make.

We are very busy, and I am *very* happy. Happier than I've ever been in my life. More deeply content would perhaps better describe my feeling. Allen is up at five every morning, busy the whole day, in bed at eight thirty does not touch anything in the way of spirits, is thoughtful and tender of me. And seems—awake —at last.

They have bought a motor-car, with trailer for use in the business, and when he can do so, Allen takes me out on these wonderful drives for an hour at night, usually from half after five to 6:30. Virginia Kilgour invited me last week to go to Coronado with her for three days—and I was fortunate enough to be there through the hottest weather we have had. Allen was in the San Fernando Valley, where his property is located and the temp. rising to 110° he was obliged to stop work and come in. They tell us that the continued heat is unusual. We are both well, in spite of it.

I am alone part of the week now, and have much time for reading, and study(?) The little apartment is very pleasant and we have a wonderful view. I still have the sense of all former things having "passed away." It is fortunate I am on *fairly* good terms with myself, or living so alone would be disastrous. The terrible daily monotony of war news affects me as it does the rest of the world. And I pray God it may soon cease. It is too terrible.

I know all true patriots thank Him, that you were given us at this time. May He bless and keep you, and give you strength for the almost intolerable burden. My love to your dear ones. When you can, send just a line to

Your devoted friend,   Mary Allen Hulbert.

ALS (WP, DLC).

Two Letters to Edith Bolling Galt

[The White House] Friday morning, 8.   3 Sept., '15

Why, my Darling, my Darling! "Love you all I can"? Why I love you with the passion of my whole heart. There seems to be nothing in my heart—and no room for anything—but love, love, love for *you*, the most precious, adorable woman in the world. I felt *dumb* Wed. night, I was so excited, so *overcome* with the delight of finding you more wonderfully beautiful and sweet and adorable than I had remembered or even yet conceived. I have just received your little letter of yesterday. It has so delighted and overjoyed me that I cannot make this pen go straight. I will write you a real letter later to-day when I can behave.

I love you past all thought   Your own   Woodrow

[The White House]

My precious, incomparable Darling,   Friday, 3 Sept., 1915

By what sweet and wonderful magic of love do you manage to interpret the longings and the infinite love of *both* of us in your letters? I can manage my pen again now—*pretty* well. Your dear letter written yesterday filled me with such a sudden *passion* of gratitude and joy that I could scarcely write legibly when I scribbled that little note I sent by Helen just now (she has just left the house to go to you—oh, how I envy her!) Yesterday *was* a day of pain for me, my blessed Sweetheart, though I am ashamed now to confess it,—but *not* because I did not understand,—only because you had seemed to me upset and distressed Wednesday night, and not happy, and it had made you a little constrained and unresponsive while I was overcome with joy at seeing you. I knew that the slight constraint came from the most natural and sufficient causes, but I could not help being a little affected by it, and what gave me the *pain*, then and all day yesterday, was nothing that you could help (Love interprets *you* to me now perfectly) but the *separation*, notwithstanding your actual presence. The presence of a third person, though it was our darling Helen, restrained me, too, and of course prevented my taking you in my arms and applying the only cure possible for our distresses—the pouring out in words and kisses of our perfect love and intimate confidence. And then I had to *leave* you and endure a whole day and two nights without a chance to know what you were thinking or let you know what I was thinking! I wanted to tell you that when I saw you Wednesday night the whole wonderful glory of you came upon me with a new revelation,—not only your exquisite beauty of person and unspeakable charm but your meaning to me. I realized as I had never realized before not only how perfect and overpowering my love for you was but how absolutely necessary you were to me to give me complete life and joy, and how your very presence gave both and gave them instantly—gave them all the time I was with you, and would leave me when I left you! I have no words in which to express the pride and joy and adoration of my love for you or what came to me when I saw you again. Surely, for one thing, you never *were* so beautiful before.

I understand *perfectly*, my Beloved, your preference to talk of general things, and not of our own precious intimate matters, when *anyone* else is present and I will respect the preference scrupulously hereafter. The other night I was foolish. It had been so long since I held your dear hands in mine that I could not govern myself.

We have been *two* foolish persons, my precious Darling, these last thirty-six hours. I'm not ashamed of it—it makes me glad, rather,—*especially* glad that you were as foolish as I was—for it shows how much, how delightfully deep, we are in love. We have both been unhappy with longing and because we could not completely reveal our feelings to each other. And does that not prove that the only way we can be sure of being sensible and keeping steady is by *writing* on the days on which we do not see one another? The mails, sent through the P.O., tell no tales to gossips; and we've *got* to risk the gossips anyway, if we are not to long ourselves sick. Write as much or as little as we please, we can at least let each other know *every day* the state of our minds and hearts. It grieves me so that my precious Edith should have been unhappy yesterday because of *me*—because she feared she had put some sort of ache into my heart, when all the while my heart was overflowing with love for her and what I needed what [was] what she was supplying in that blessed exquisite letter!

Ah, my Sweetheart, my own Darling! Your love is what I want and you give it in such fashion as makes me *know* that you are mine and that my happiness is full and running over, but send it, or bring it, to me every day to keep the sun in heaven, and, in return I will send you—though you know you have it—the love and devotion of a heart that contains nothing but you. I love you more and more every minute I live!

Your own   Woodrow

ALS (WP, DLC).

From Edith Bolling Galt, with Enclosure

My own precious One: Sept 3rd, 1915 2:45 P.M.

I can't understand why you are not the proudest man in the whole world, for certainly not one word of praise in these papers is strong enough for what you have done and what the people, the country and the world owe you. It just thrills me so to read them —and to *know* that they are *all true*!

Oh! Sweetheart, I can't find words to express my own pride in you and the almost awesome wonder that I feel whenever I realize that you have given me your splendid heart and self.

Can I just be worthy of the power you have given me—in giving the right to help you. This position is one in which I can be such a help—or such a hindurance. Help me Dearest to learn *how* to help you. I am still ashamed of worrying you so Wednesday night about these wretched newspaper people and I promise not to go up in the air so again. It was just the combination of *you* and the Reporters in one day! Last night Randolph and I had our first real long talk since I got home, and he asked me if he could write you a note and say just what he felt, and I told him, I would be so glad if he would. He has just phoned me he was sending a note to me, and I know it is really to you, so I will enclose it and get our dear little Helen to take it to you. Helen has come so I must stop. The Postman brought me your promised *real* letter just this minute which I will keep and read when I am alone.

I can hardly wait—but I will.

Thank you for sending me the papers and sharing your triumph with me. Certainly your own heart tells you nothing could be sweeter than such a partnership.

I am so glad you went to the Theatre last night. How I wanted to go and sit in a far away corner and look at you. But I had promised a gentleman to go for a ride in his new car, and we did not get back until after eleven. Don't turn *green*   Randolph went with us.

With all my hearts love,   Your own   Edith

ALS (WP, DLC).

ENCLOSURE

From John Randolph Bolling

Dear Mr. President: Washington, D. C. September 3d, 1915.

Edith wrote me last Saturday, telling me of her engagement to you.

Could I have reached you, I should certainly have come immediately to express to you, in person, the great happiness it will give me to claim you as a brother.

The love and affection—and the perfect understanding—that exists between Edith and me, is one of the most beautiful things in my life. Your coming to us, I feel sure, will only serve to strengthen this very sweet and tender relationship.

I want so to know you better, and I hope I can—very, very soon. God bless you both!

Faithfully,   John Randolph Bolling

ALS (WP, DLC).

From Robert Lansing, with Enclosure

PERSONAL AND PRIVATE:

My dear Mr. President: Washington September 4, 1915.

I have just received a letter from the German Ambassador, a copy of which I enclose to you.

I do not feel that we should wait very long for an explanation in regard to the ARABIC and I am inclined to answer the Ambassador to that effect. What would be your impression of letting him know that the at[t]itude of the German Government might be stated hypothetically on the evidence which we have received from the survivors of the ARABIC and the persons who were on board the DUNSLEY? This, of course, would be based on the fact that the German Admiralty is not in receipt of a report within a short time.

I will not reply to Count von Bernstorff until I hear from you as to your wishes. Faithfully yours, Robert Lansing

TLS (SDR, RG 59, 841.857 AR 1/51, DNA).

ENCLOSURE

Count Johann Heinrich von Bernstorff
to Robert Lansing

My dear Mr. Secretary: Cedarhurst, L. I., September 3, 1915.

This evening I received a wireless message from my Government stating that the only German submarine which according to the sphere of operation might have sunk the "Arabic," has not returned home and that consequently an explanation of the case is, for the present, impossible.

As the principle underlying this question has been satisfactorily settled, I hope the delay will not cause you any annoyance.

I remain my dear Mr. Lansing,
Very sincerely yours, J. Bernstorff

TCL (SDR, RG 59, 841.857 AR 1/51, DNA).

To Edith Bolling Galt

[The White House]

My precious Darling, Sat. 4 Sept., 1915

I am *so* sorry that the dear head continues to ache,—my heart aches so long as it does not get well—all the more because my place is at your side to pet and comfort and love you—and perhaps draw the pain out by the sheer force of the love in my fingers.

Is anything (Panama, for example) worrying you? If it is, wont you please dismiss it till to-night and then share it with your lover?

This is just a message of tender love, love that already passes all measure and yet grows with every day & hour.

Your own   Woodrow

ALS (WP, DLC).

To Edith Bolling Galt, with Enclosure

[The White House, c. Sept. 5, 1915]

For once Gerard has sent something interesting and important. The reference to German-Americans seems to me very significant.   W.

ALI (WP, DLC).

E N C L O S U R E

Berlin via Copenhagen, Sept. 4, 1915.

2832. Leading article in FRANKFURTER ZEITUNG last evening states that the prospects of a peaceful settlement of the difficulties arising out of the sinking of the LUS[I]TANIA and the ARABIC are exceedingly welcome to Germany, although this may be quite the reverse of what her enemies expected. The reasons why are far reaching and sufficient weight to overcome the feelings aroused in every German by the American business in arms and ammunition, the attitude of a large part of the American press and other symptoms.

Germany could not contemplate unmoved the approach of conflict with America on account of the millions of German blood residing there, although Germany readily assumes their loyalty whether their attachment to the U. S. be one of years or generations would be placed in a most painful position the tragedy of which could not fail to effect our own feelings. We have learned to recognize the value of the sympathies for the fatherland aroused again in the hearts of the countless numbers in America and hope for great results from this sympathy in the future.

War, however, which would force German Americans to take up arms against the land of their fathers, would be productive such bitterness as to be fatal to good relations between the two countries for years to come. Sympathy with us in America is going to be of great value to us in economic matters after the war. The military situation is so favorable that neutrals are bound to acknowledge at least that no one can deprive us of ultimate victory now. It does not become us to assume an absolutely unbending attitude. Those highest in command are best able to judge what concessions are wise in the interests of the whole country and we have full confidence in them. We agree to concessions to America and believe it not vain to expect that peaceable relations with Germany will favor the influence against the trade in arms which undeniably forms an element of deep Bitterness among our people. Berlin TAGEBLATT surmises that consideration for the Balkan situation prompted the concessions to America and quite approves settlement of the difficulty. The radical press of course can scarcely contain its rage, but the muzzle is on.

Many papers rejoice because they think English and French intrigues will be defeated by the understanding between Germany and America.   Gerard, Berlin.

T telegram (WP, DLC).

To Edith Bolling Galt

[The White House]

My own precious Darling,   Sunday, 9.40 A.M. 5 Sept., 1915

I had the best, most peaceful and restful sleep last night that I have had since you drove away that day from Harlakenden with the Roses, and all because you had come back, I had seen straight into your dear heart again, and had found there everything to delight and satisfy me,—all that was there that blissful Sunday night before you left *and more*, as you were generous enough to say in your exquisite loving sweetness. What was in my heart I have not the words to tell—supreme unbounded love and joy! I could not *help* being happy in spite of your having to leave me, to go away from your real home,—and yet how empty the house seemed with you out of it! Ah, my adorable Sweetheart, how tenderly, how utterly I love you, and how hard it is to do without you for a single hour—how different the house will seem until you are in it again!

And yet, Sweetheart, there never will come a time when you need feel your liberty lost or curtailed. You will *always* be free to go and come as you please,—and I promise never to misunderstand, no matter how lonely I may get. I shall never seek to put any harness on you of any kind or demand anything that is not given gladly and of your own free will. I would not want or accept anything not so given. What I said the other day in a letter about your never again going away without me, I said under a misconception: I thought I was interpreting the desire of your heart as well as of mine. I was not trying to exact a promise. You shall be as free as your heart desires, and when your heart desires it I shall try to understand, and I think I can, for I love and trust and believe in you perfectly. You shall never feel hampered even.

I hope last evening made my Darling's heart as full to overflowing as it made mine with perfect joy and the realization of everything her heart desired.

With all my heart's love   Your own   Woodrow

ALS (WP, DLC).

From Edith Bolling Galt

                                          [Washington] Sunday
My precious One: [Sept. 5, 1915] 12.20 m.

Helen has just phoned me she is coming up and I can't resist the temptation to send you a little word of love. You are the dearest, most precious thing in the whole world, and being with you last night was like finding you all over again. The time went so fast there and goes so slowly this morning.

I have been in bed until just a few minutes ago reading "Nancy Stair"[1] and even that made me happier because you *sent* it to me   Are you feeling rested and better this morning? I do so hope you are and if being loved can bring you rest and happiness then my heart has found a cure for any strain or and anxiety that will ever come to you.

Helen has come, and I have your precious note. What a dear you are to put all my foolish requests into writing so soon, and how completely you do whatever you undertake. You were interpreting my own heart with your own, in the letter you wrote when I was away. But this is just in case any "wings" get cramped and I have to fly away for a minute so as to keep them in working order

Oh! Sweetheart how I love you, and how I want to come back with Helen. You said you envied her sometimes. Have you ever thought how I envy her? But I am so happy she is with you. Goodby, and remember I am all   Your own—Edith

After you see the picture Helen is bringing you will believe I was an ugly little girl.

ALS (WP, DLC).

1 Elinor Macartney Lane, *Nancy Stair: A Novel* (New York, 1904).

From Robert Lansing

PERSONAL

My Dear Mr. President: Washington September 6, 1915.

Doubtless Secretary McAdoo has discussed with you the necessity of floating government loans for the belligerent nations, which are purchasing such great quantities of goods in this country, in order to avoid a serious financial situation which will not only affect them but this country as well.

Briefly the situation, as I understand it, is this: Since December 1st, 1914, to June 30, 1915, our exports have exceeded our imports by nearly a billion dollars, and it is estimated that the excess will be from July 1st to December 31, 1915, a billion and three quarters. Thus for the year 1915 the excess will be approximately two and half billions of dollars.

It is estimated that the European banks have about three and half billions of dollars in gold in their vaults. To withdraw any considerable amount would disastrously affect the credit of the European nations, and the consequence would be a general state of bankruptcy.

If the European countries cannot find means to pay for the excess of goods sold to them over those purchased from them, they will have to stop buying and our present export trade will shrink proportionately. The result would be restriction of outputs, industrial depression, idle capital and idle labor, numerous failures, financial demoralization, and general unrest and suffering among the laboring classes.

Probably a billion and three quarters of the excess of European purchases can be taken care of by the sale of American securities held in Europe and by the transfer of trade balances of oriental countries, but that will leave three quarters of a billion to be met in some other way. Furthermore, even if that is arranged, we will have to face a more serious situation in January, 1916, as the American securities held abroad will have been exhausted.

I believe that Secretary McAdoo is convinced and I agree with him that there is only one means of avoiding this situation which would so seriously affect economic conditions in this country, and that is the flotation of large bond issues by the belligerent governments. Our financial institutions have the money to loan and wish to do so. On account of the great balance of trade in our favor the proceeds of these loans would be expended here. The result would be a maintenance of the credit of the borrowing nations based on their gold reserve, a continuance of our commerce at its present volume and industrial activity with the consequent employment of capital and labor and national prosperity.

The difficulty is—and this is what Secretary McAdoo came to see me about—that the Government early in the war announced that it considered "war loans" to be contrary to "the true spirit of neutrality." A declaration to this effect was given to the press about August 15, 1914, by Secretary Bryan. The language is as follows: "In the judgment of this Government loans by American bankers to any foreign nation at war is inconsistent with the true spirit of neutrality."

In October, 1914, after a conference with you, I gave my "impressions" to certain New York bankers in reference to "credit loans," but the general statement remained unaffected. In drafting the letter of January 20, 1915, to Senator Stone I sought to leave out a broad statement and to explain merely the reasons for distinguishing between "general loans" and "credit loans." However, Mr. Bryan thought it well to repeat the August declaration and it appears in the first sentence of division 13 of the letter, a copy of which I enclose.

On March 31, 1915, another press statement was given out from the Department which reads as follows:

"The State Department has from time to time received information directly or indirectly to the effect that belligerent nations had arranged with Banks in the United States for credits in various sums. While loans to belligerents have been disapproved, this Government has not felt that it was justified in interposing objection to the credit arrangements which have been brought to its attention. It has neither approved these nor disapproved—it has simply taken no action in the premises and expressed no opinion."

Manifestly the Government has committed itself to the policy of discouraging general loans to belligerent governments. The practical reasons for the policy at the time we adopted it were sound, but basing it on the ground that loans are "inconsistent with the true spirit of neutrality" is now a source of embarrassment. This latter ground is as strong today as it was a year ago, while the practical reasons for discouraging loans have largely disappeared. We have more money than we can use. Popular sympathy has become crystallized in favor of one or another of the belligerents to such an extent that the purchase of bonds would in no way increase the bitterness of partisanship or cause a possibly serious situation.

Now, on the other hand, we are face to face with what appears to be a critical economic situation, which can only be relieved apparantly by the investment of American capital in foreign loans to be used in liquidating the enormous balance of trade in favor of the United States.

Can we afford to let a declaration as to our conception of "the true spirit of neutrality" made in the first days of the war stand in the way of our national interests which seem to be seriously threatened?

If we cannot afford to do this, how are we to explain away the declaration and maintain a semblance of consistency?

My opinion is that we ought to allow the loans to be made for our own good, and I have been seeking some means of harmonizing our policy, so unconditionally announced, with the flotation of general loans. As yet I have found no solution to the problem.

Secretary McAdoo considers that the situation is becoming acute and that something should be done at once to avoid the disastrous results which will follow a continuance of the present policy. Faithfully yours, Robert Lansing.

TLS (SDR, RG 59, 811.51/2624a, DNA).

To Edith Bolling Galt

[The White House]
Monday, 9.15 A.M. 6 Sept., 1915

Well, my precious Darling, the great "triumph" did not last long, did it? Apparently nothing can last long which depends on Germany's good faith. Of course we do not know all the facts yet, and it is *possible* that the facts, when fully disclosed, will put a different face on the sinking of the *Hesperian*,[1] but it seems to me a very slim possibility. And of course my first thoughts turn to you, my blessed Sweetheart, by means of whose love I am able to face *any*thing with a steady heart. I need you more every day of my life, and every day you give more and prove yourself the royal partner I knew you would be. Since Saturday night my heart has been singularly at peace. I have had two of the finest, sweetest night's rest I have had in a long time—because all the while *conscious* of your loving thought hovering near me. Even last night, after hearing the first rumours of the *Hesperian*, I slept the better part of eight hours,—*all the while* conscious of you! And now I turn to you, my precious One, in such happy assurance that you will give me the loving help I need. I must share everything with you.

It was sweet of you to let Helen bring me that picture; I delight in it! "Ugly" little girl, indeed! Why I perfectly adore the cross little solid mite. She is fascinating—and my love now dates back to her. I *dote* on the little petulant darling!

This is just a message of tender, adoring love, my own sweet Edith. I just had to speak my heart to you. I shall look forward with such joy to seeing you this afternoon.

With a full heart, in which you are all in all,

Your own   Woodrow

ALS (WP, DLC).

¹ An explosion ripped the side of the liner *Hesperian*, bound for Montreal, and killed eight passengers, none of them American, on the night of September 4. The ship's crew believed, on the basis of fragments thrown up on the deck, that a torpedo had caused the damage, but the Germans, after refusing to answer American inquiries because the ship was armed, said the ship must have hit a mine because no submarines were in the vicinity. See, Link, *Struggle for Neutrality*, pp. 652-53, 665.

From Edith Bolling Galt

Dear, my Lord: Monday, Sept. 6, 1915 9:30 a.m

How I long to come to you instead of writing, for words and paper and ink can never express what is in my heart. I want to put both arms 'round you and kiss your eyes and whisper all my love and tell you how I am sharing this new anxiety that I have been reading of in the papers this morning. Some way last night I felt you were worried—and I was here at my desk writing to those forlorn ones in Panama, when I felt I must go to you—I mean go where I could see the house and if there were still lights in the study. I telephoned Bertha to know if she would like to go for a ride and got the "Purambulator" and rode straight down where I could see your windows. It was ten thirty, and everything was lighted and seemed alert.

Oh! my precious Woodrow how I wished I were "Peter Ibettson" or some such psychic person and could make you feel my nearness. I told Bertha nothing except that I preferred to ride round the street and just back of the White House instead of the Potomac drive, because it was growing late

Don't worry Sweetness any more than you can help. I know it will all come right just as the Arabic affair did that seemed so much more hopeless. I am coming to Tea this afternoon and we will find a minute to look into each others hearts.

Do you remember the little picture you gave me that was sent you in Cornish? It is framed—with a little printed expression from the "Saturday gossip" of you as the man of the century. Well I just could not help hanging it up, and I have it right by my bed by the side of one of father and mother—and it gives me the sweetest sense of protection and nearness to you.

Then I have also boldly put one of your *real* pictures here in the living room—on the music rest of the piano. Isn't it jolly you are President and I can appear to strangers just as a patriotic person—and to myself as an adoring worshiper of my precious One. Oh! by the way, will you dearest send your picture to Annie Litchfield.[1]

I think right now it would lighten the gloom for her more than anything in the world, and I will so appreciate it. If you don't mind putting your name on it or something she would be doubly pleased, but don't bother about it if you have no pictures available. I will write the address and you can get Hoover to see to it for you.

AL (WP, DLC).
[1] Her sister-in-law, Mrs. Rolfe E. Bolling.

To Robert Lansing

My dear Mr. Secretary,   The White House. 7 September, 1915.

The sinking of the *Hesperian* has for the time arrested everything, and therefore an answer to the enclosed[1] is perhaps too much belated to be of any use to you. But this is clear, that we should let the German Government know that it was not wise to wait too long to state their attitude and the course they intend to pursue with regard to the sinking of the *Arabic*.

However, we shall not be certain of anything until we hear all the facts about the *Hesperian*.

Faithfully Yours,   W.W.

WWTLI (SDR, RG 59, 841.857/32½, DNA).
[1] J. H. von Bernstorff to RL, Sept. 3, 1915, printed as an Enclosure with RL to WW, Sept. 4, 1915.

To Edward Mandell House

Dearest Friend,   The White House. 7 September, 1915.

I send this to greet you on your arrival at Roslyn, and to carry you my greeting of deep affection. It's jolly that you are making your way in this direction. I am very eager to see you.

I am sure that you understand why I do not reply to each of your letters, and that I am greatly helped by all that they contain. I ponder them and they enter into all my thought concerning the great matters we are now threading our way through. Would you prefer that I should acknowledge them as they come, so that you may be sure that each one reaches me?

I see no escape from asking the Austrian government to replace Dumba with someone who will know better what he is privileged and what he is not privileged to do? Do you? And yet, if Dumba, why not Bernstorff also? Is there any essential difference? And the request that both of them be withdrawn would have to be managed mighty well if the implication of a diplomatic breach is to be avoided.

My thought just now is full, of course, of this *Hesperian* business. It looks, I fear, as if it were going to be extremely difficult to get at any real facts in the case; and yet the facts are essential to any intelligent handling of the case. Shall we ever get out of the labarynth made for us all by this German "frightfulness"?

Please give my most affectionate regards to Mrs. House and the Mr. and Mrs. Auchincloss.

Affectionately Yours,   Woodrow Wilson

WWTLS (E. M. House Papers, CtY).

To Josephus Daniels

My dear Daniels: The White House September 7, 1915

I ought to have thanked you when you were here the other day for your generous letter of September third. I have come to expect such letters from you because you are always so thoughtful and generous, but they none the less seem to me in each instance a delightful evidence of your thoughtful friendship. The evidences of your confidence that you have given me make me more and more as the days go by

Your affectionate friend,   Woodrow Wilson

TLS (J. Daniels Papers, DLC).

To Thomas Dixon, Jr.

My dear Dixon: [The White House] September 7, 1915

I must frankly say to you that I am sorry after reading the synopsis of your new enterprise, because I think the thing a great mistake.[1] There is no need to stir the nation up in favor of national defense. It is already soberly and earnestly aware of its possible perils and of its duty, and I should deeply regret seeing any sort of excitement stirred in so grave a matter.

I would not feel at liberty to ask the Secretary of the Navy to make an exception as you suggest.[2] I think you can have no idea of the complications exceptions lead to, what misunderstandings and heartburnings and general confusion. If you did, I am sure you would realize that I am justified in saying that I do not think it wise for me to make such a suggestion.

Sincerely yours, Woodrow Wilson

TLS (Letterpress Books, WP, DLC).

[1] It is missing, but it described the play, "The Fall of a Nation," which had its movie premiere in June 1916 and appeared as a novel later that year. Dixon later described the story, which attacked pacifists, as "a study of the origin, meaning and destiny of American Democracy by one who believes that the time is ripe in this country for a revival of the principles on which our Republic was founded." Thomas Dixon, *The Fall of a Nation: A Sequel to the Birth of a Nation* (New York, 1916), preface.

[2] T. Dixon, Jr., to WW, Sept. 5, 1915, TLS (WP, DLC), asking that his crew be allowed to film target practice on the navy's battleships, even though the General Board had prohibited all cameras in such cases.

To Robert Lansing

My dear Mr. Secretary, The White House. 7 September, 1915.

I enclose this[1] for your files, as you suggested.

I have the feeling that our friend is finding out what we already know, and yet it may be that he has been serviceable in removing some erroneous impressions from Carranza's mind.

Faithfully Yours, W.W.

WWTLI (SDR, RG 59, 812.00/16188½, DNA).

[1] The Enclosure with RL to WW, Sept. 3, 1915.

To Franklin Knight Lane

My dear Lane: [The White House] September 7, 1915

Thank you from the bottom of my heart for your generous letter about the turn in affairs regarding Germany. This Hesperian business has given all our thoughts and hopes a setback, but it is incredible that they should not clear it up if they did indeed authorize Bernstorff to say what he said to us. It is a great pleasure, my dear Lane, to have you think such thoughts of me and you may be sure that they are returned in full measure.

Faithfully and affectionately yours, Woodrow Wilson

TLS (Letterpress Books, WP, DLC).

To Oswald Garrison Villard

My dear Mr. Villard: The White House September 7, 1915

I am sincerely obliged to you for your letter of September third and I hope that you will believe that I shall value very highly the articles you are planning to write with regard to national defense.

I do not think there need be any fear that the country will go too far in the policy to be adopted. I think its thought is, on the whole, very self-restrained and judicial and that it will wish to see a course pursued that lies between the extremes in every particular.

Cordially and sincerely yours,   Woodrow Wilson

TLS (O. G. Villard Papers, MH).

A Memorandum by Joseph Patrick Tumulty

[Avon, N. J., Sept. 7, 1915]

The sinking of the Hesperian brings to an immediate test a question which involves the good faith or bad faith of Germany. In treating with the questions arising out of the Lusitania and Arabic incidents it is my firm opinion when all of the facts in this regrettable incident are disclosed that no lack of good faith on the part of Germany will be shown. In my opinion this incident in its finality will serve to strengthen the attitude of the President in accepting in good faith the statement of the German Government conveyed through Count Von Bernstorff "that the German Government would not sink any liners without strict compliance with the rules of international law." The whole question involved is a question of good faith on the part of the German Government. It is my firm opinion that the communication of the German Government of last week was proof of a fundamental change of policy on the part of the German Government with reference to submarine warfare, a change which must have been a cause of deep humiliation to her own people in Germany and to her supporters in this country. Having taken the stand she did, it would be foolish for her to abandon it now. Skeptics among our own people will be inclined to state that the advantage derived by the Administration by the happening of last week will be lost by reason of this incident. I do not believe it. The sinking of the Herperian will immediately afford us an opportunity whereby the good faith of Germany can be tested and immediately decided and the issues arising out of it determined. In its ultimate result, I think it will be helpful. Unfortunately, the Dumba incident will aggravate the Hesperian matter.

I think it would be unwise for the Secretary of State to allow the Dumba matter issue to come in conflict with the Arabic, Lusitania, and Hesperian matters. It seems to me that the disposition of the Dumba charges should be held in abeyance until these very much more important matters are out of the way. I think that the time for an early, full, complete and sincere disavowal on the part of the German Government covering the Arabic, and Lusitania matters is at hand.

T MS (WP, DLC).

From Robert Lansing

PERSONAL AND PRIVATE:

My dear Mr. President: Washington September 7, 1915.

Ambassador Dumba has just left. We went over quite thoroughly the situation created by his letter to the Foreign Office. In substance his defense is set forth in a memorandum which he left with me and which I enclose to you.[1] I do not think that I can add anything of value to it, though he did elaborate to an extent in conversation.

I also called his attention to the employment of Archibald as a messenger, and pointed out to him the impropriety of a diplomatic representative in this country using one of its citizens, who carried an American passport and was entitled bo [to] protection by this Government, as a bearer of official dispatches which were to pass through enemy territory. He seemed surprised at this complaint; said that he had never thought of it; that he had never used an American citizen before, and never should again for such a purpose. He also said that it should be realized that conditions of communication with his Government were very difficult and that they took any practical means to send their official dispatches. I told him that I would like to have him think the matter over and if he desired to furnish a memorandum on the subject.

I further gave him the decided impression that you were much concerned, I think I might say irritated, over what had occurred and that I would report the substance of our interview to you and that he would hear from me in a few days.

He is evidently very much distressed because of what has occurred, but I do not think he really repents of his action; he only deplores the fact that he was found out.

Faithfully yours,   Robert Lansing.

TLS (SDR, RG 59, 701.6311/146½, DNA).
[1] C. T. Dumba, "Memorandum," Sept. 6, 1915, T MS (SDR, RG 59, 701.6311/

146½, DNA). Dumba explained that he had a responsibility to help Austrian and Hungarian subjects in the United States avoid the stiff penalties imposed by their government for producing war materiel in neutral nations to be used against Austria-Hungary. This was the reason why he had proposed to subsidize foreign-language newspapers, organize labor unions among his fellow countrymen in order to protect themselves against inhuman working conditions, and establish a labor bureau to find jobs for persons leaving the munitions plants. He closed by asking the United States Government's help in finding work for his countrymen in order to "save no end of misery to my countrymen and prevent trouble and unrest in the labour conditions of this country."

From Mary Allen Hulbert

My dear Friend: [Los Angeles] Sept 7th [1915]

The feeling that my letters to you must be of telegraphic brevity sometimes results in my writing less than necessary. The other day I did not tell you of our *deep* appreciation of your help in regard to the mortgages, nor how much it will further our interests if you buy them. It is a *big* thing Allen is working on, and we are doing it on small capital. It is clean fine good business, and in three months we should have the first returns. He is working, happy and interested from 5 a.m. to six in the evening. I go tomorrow to take a course that will make me a more able assistant. I am here every night, as Allen does not think I would be comfortable in the tent. I *would.* When you can, send me just a line or ask Helen to do so, of her goodness. The thyroid gland trouble has nearly disappeared, and save for an occasional blue period, when I am over tired, I am a cheerful old soul. I miss my mother. I want her so at times it seems as though she *must* come. You know I am sorry to trouble you about the mortgages, but its "make or break" this time, and it will be *make*, I know. You are more wonderful to us, every day, so wonderful as to seem not quite human. That sounds queer. You know that I mean superman, etc. Forgive me for taking so much of your time.   Always yr. devoted friend,   Mary Allen Hulbert.

ALS (WP, DLC).

To Edith Bolling Galt

[The White House] Tuesday, 9.45 A.M.
My own precious Darling,   7 August [September], 1915

I am ashamed to have kept you waiting so long for these articles in the *World*.[1] I hope that you will forgive me and that you will not find them stale. What Dumba has just been caught at gives them fresh interest and importance.

My precious Love, what deep, deep happiness those few minutes with you yesterday gave me! How few they were, and yet how
perfectly they revealed you to me in all your ineffable sweetness
and charm and power to bless, and what a delicious sense they
gave me of the real union of our hearts and lives. My heart and
all that I am or can be is absolutely yours, my precious One, and
I live in your love.

I came upon a little poem yesterday, Sweetness, that partly expresses what I tried to write you the other day:

"Mine to the core of the heart, my beauty!
Mine, all mine, and for love, not duty:
Love given willingly, full and free,
Love for love's sake—as mine to thee.
Duty's a slave that keeps the keys,
But Love, the master, goes in and out
Of his goodly chambers with song and shout,
Just as he please—just as he please."[2]

And, oh, to see him enthroned in your eyes *for me*, to hear him
speak in your voice, to receive his sovereign touch through your
lips, has made me supremely happy and supremely safe against
all the world!   Your own   Woodrow

ALS (WP, DLC).
[1] That is, the *World*'s articles about Albert and his activities.
[2] From "Plighted," by Dinah Maria Mulock Craik (1826-87). Often reprinted,
the poem was first anthologized by the author in *Poems* (London [1859]).

From Edith Bolling Galt

My precious One: [Washington] Sept. 7, 1915

I am so glad you went to the Theatre last night and had something to divert and cheer you. We all enjoyed the "Tea Party"
so yesterday and Mother is in love with you—said she did not feel
the least bit embarrassed or formal with you that, on the contrary, she felt she had known you always and knew she was
going to love you (as if anyone could help loving you when once
they *really* know you) and Bertha was distressed that she had no
opportunity to say all the sweet welcoming things she wanted to
say to you. I was so proud of you Sweetheart and always expect
to be. It was right funny that after dinner last night Randolph
said, "Let's all go to Keiths," and I said I was too tired to do it
and came home at nine thirty and went to bed. I wonder if I
would have felt braced enough to go had I known you were
there?

I have been down town all morning and seen to a lot of things that had to have my personal attention. I hear *old* Mr. Wilson is back, so I must brace myself for another campaign. Helen says she will come at 2, so this is just a hurried line to tell you my precious Woodrow how I love you and how I am missing you.

Don't stay in the sun too long if you go to the Golf Club. It seems to me terribly hot   Mrs. Rose sent me the enclosed[1] Please keep it for me. Always your   Very own—Edith.

ALS (WP, DLC).
[1] A cartoon entitled, "How to Find the Size of the Average American, Split the Difference." It depicted Wilson on the left with a line descending from his head to the top of a figure labeled "Daniels" about one third the size of Wilson on the right. Halfway between them was an outline figure of a man whose height was half the difference between Wilson's and Daniels's. The Editors have been unable to identify the source of this cartoon.

From Robert Lansing

Personal and Private.

My Dear Mr. President: Washington September 8, 1915.

I enclose herewith a telegram to Ambassador Penfield relative to Dr. Dumba. If it meets with your approval I would suggest that it would expedite it to send it directly to the telegraph room of the Department of State.[1]

Faithfully yours,   Robert Lansing.

TLS (SDR, RG 59, 701.6311/145a, DNA).
[1] RL to F. C. Penfield, Sept. 8, 1915, T telegram (SDR, RG 59, 701.6311/145a, DNA), printed in *FR-WWS 1915*, pp. 933-34. It declared that Dumba was *persona non grata* to the President and requested his recall.

Two Letters to Robert Lansing

My dear Mr. Secretary,   The White House. 8 September, 1915.

I have no doubt that our oral discussion of this matter[1] yesterday suffices. If it does not, will you let me know that you would like a written reply?   Faithfully Yours,   W.W.

WWTLI (SDR, RG 59, 811.51/2624a, DNA).
[1] That is, RL to WW, Sept. 6, 1915, concerning the administration's policy toward private loans to belligerents.

My dear Mr. Secretary,   The White House. 8 September, 1915.

I have no doubt that the memorandum handed you by Ambassador Dumba has made the same impression on you that it has made on me. I see no alternative but to follow the course we decided on yesterday. And I think it would be well to apprise

Dumba and the press of what that course is to-day, unless there seems to you to be an impropriety in mentioning it before our cummunication has reached the Foreign Office in Vienna.[1]

Faithfully Yours,   W.W.

WWTLI (SDR, RG 59, 701.6311/147½, DNA).
[1] The telegram to Penfield was sent to Vienna at 4 P.M. on September 8.

From Seth Low

Dear Mr. President: Albany, N. Y. September 8, 1915.

The Constitutional Convention at Albany has kept me so busy that I have not been able until now to write to you, as I had hoped to do, to congratulate you upon the acceptance by Germany of your point of view in regard to attacks upon liners. I am hoping that the "Hesperian" incident will not complicate the situation still further, and that you may have the immense satisfaction of having stood not only bravely but successfully for a principle in which the welfare of humanity itself was at stake.

Busy as I have been at the Convention, I have still found time to think of you often in these anxious days, and of the great burden which you are bearing for us all. I do pray that you may be led to see the right, and to be true to it in every emergency. I almost hesitate to express an opinion on the matter so important as the Dumba incident when I have at command only information that is available to the public. In the hope, however, that it may be of service to you in dealing with this new problem, I venture to say that it seems to me the incident ought to terminate his services in this country. The most distressing side of the War as it affects ourselves to me has been the evidence that so many of our naturalized citizens have been willing to speak and act as though the interests of the home land were superior to the claims of their adopted country. To pass over the indiscretion, to use a diplomatic phrase, of the Austrian Ambassador, would seem to me to justify all such half-hearted citizens in the attitude which they have taken. Whatever betide, therefore, it seems to me essential to the well being of this country that this incident should be dealt with as was the much less serious indiscretion of Sackville-West.[1]   Very sincerely, yours,   Seth Low.

TLS (WP, DLC).
[1] Sir Lionel Sackville-West, British Minister in Washington from June 1881 until October 30, 1888. He was summarily dismissed by President Cleveland after writing a letter in Cleveland's favor during the campaign of 1888 to a correspondent who said that he doubted that any man of English sympathies could vote to re-elect the President. The correspondent, who had written under a pseudonym in order to entrap the British Minister, sent the reply to Republican newspapers, which published it a few weeks before the election.

To Edith Bolling Galt

[The White House] Wed., 7.05 A.M.

My precious One, my lovely Darling,   8 Sept., 1915

Was ever there a more blissful ride together than we had last night! The ecstacy of it made all the world seem compact of nothing but peace and happiness. Your tender, sweet, intimate, demonstrative love, with its unspeakable gentle charm and earnestness, gave me a delight that passed all words to express and excited in me a love so deep, so tender, so touched with joy and adoration, that it seemed almost as if I had never loved you before, by comparison, and could never love you enough to pay my debt of happiness. Ah, Sweetness, I do not understand how this glorious gift of your wonderful love came to fall to *me*, unless it be that I can give a love and devotion in return which even yours cannot excel and can give you, too, the tribute of *every* power that is in me to prove that I know what sovereign grace and power of true womanhood there is in you and what *homage* is your due. With what feelings I left you!—the pang of turning away from you and leaving you standing there alone, after such an evening, full of such sweet revelations and promises as sweet, —the irony of *leaving* you there when we absolutely belong to one another!—the *longing* to take you or to stay,—and, along with all that, and in spite of it, a sense of exquisite elation, of having been blessed and rendered secure against any kind of *real* anxiety or suffering, the consciousness of having found *completeness* in the satisfaction of a love that unites me to the one exquisite woman in all the world who has all the qualities I most admire and most enjoy and take inspiration from every time I have the joy of being with her. It was an evening, for me, my incomparable Darling, not only of joy and delight, but of *consecration* also, to the happy task of filling your life with love in all its forms, little and great, and making a home for you that will be worthy of what you have brought to it already and will bring to it in full abundance. I love you past all thought! Are you well this morning?   Your own   Woodrow

ALS (WP, DLC).

To Joseph Patrick Tumulty

Dear Tumulty,   The White House. 9 September, 1915.

Thank you warmly for your memorandum. I have thought about it a great deal since I read it.

I hope, and believe, that you are right about the attitude of the

German government: at least I try to believe it, notwithstanding that we have had nothing yet direct from Germany and have only Bernstorff's word to go on,—no text of an actual communication from Berlin (we are asking Gerard what it means).

But as to the Dumba matter, I do not see how that can wait. It ought to be got out of the way, so as to centre public attention on other matters. And it is my judgment that a firm attitude on that, showing that we will take no nonsense of that kind, will have a helpful rather than a harmful effect in Berlin. The case is made up, besides, and there is hardly any excuse available for a delay.   Affectionately Yours,   Woodrow Wilson

WWTLS (J. P. Tumulty Papers, DLC).

From Robert Lansing

PERSONAL AND SECRET:

My dear Mr. President: [Washington] September 9, 1915.

I enclose you a telegram which has just been received from Ambassador Page, in London,[1] which, as you see, is of a strictly confidential nature.

I confess that it conveys to me an impression that the British Government and British public are desirous of having us "pull their chestnuts out of the fire."

As I assume this telegram is intended for you especially, I wish you would indicate, if you will be so good, what answer, if any, should be made to it.

Faithfully yours,   Robert Lansing

CCL (SDR, RG 59, 763.72/2106, DNA).
[1] WHP to RL and WW, Sept. 8, 1915, printed as an Enclosure with WW to EBG, Sept. 10, 1915 (second letter of that date).

From Robert Lansing, with Enclosures

PERSONAL AND PRIVATE:

My dear Mr. President: Washington September 9, 1915.

I enclose to you three letters which I have received today from the German Ambassador, and to which I have made no reply. Please return them at your earliest convenience.

Faithfully yours,   Robert Lansing.

TLS (SDR, RG 59, 841.857/28, DNA).

E N C L O S U R E S

Three Letters from Count Johann Heinrich von Bernstorff to Robert Lansing

My dear Mr. Secretary: Cedarhurst, N. Y., September 8, 1915.

With regard to the Arabic incident I am authorized to inform you confidentially that *since several months* the commanders of our submarines had orders not to attack the large ocean liners without warning and safety for non-combatants. Therefore, if the Arabic was attacked without warning, this would have been done contrary to the instructions given to the commanders of the submarines. These orders have now been modified, so as to comprise all liners. These instructions are and will remain in force pending the negotiations with the Government of the United States, which as we hope will in the end lead to a complete understanding on all questions of maritime warfare.

I remain, my dear Mr. Lansing,
Very sincerely yours,   J. Bernstorff

TLS (SDR, RG 59, 763.72/2102, DNA).

My dear Mr. Secretary: Cedarhurst, N. Y., September 8, 1915.

I have been waiting to hear from home about the Hesperian incident, but have as yet not received any information, which seems natural, as the submarines engaged at the time of the sinking of the Hesperian must first return home. Till then it will not be possible to know, whether the Hesperian was sunk by a German submarine or a German or British mine. How ever this may be, I wish to inform you, that this case in no way changes our general policy with regard to submarine warfare.

I further desire to draw your attention to the fact that according to all reports the Hesperian was armed. This seems exceedingly important as the whole controversy between the United States and Germany turns on the subject of "unarmed merchant vessels." Therefore, in my opinion, the case of the Hesperian has no bearing at all on the question we have been discussing.

I remain, my dear Mr. Lansing,
Very sincerely yours,   J. Bernstorff

TLS (SDR, RG 59, 763.72/2101, DNA).

My dear Mr. Secretary: Cedarhurst, N. Y., September 8, 1915.

I just received the following wireless message from Berlin:
"According to information available here it seems highly im-

probable that Hesperian was torpedoed. Much more likely boat ran on mine. Foreign Office."

I remain, my dear Mr. Lansing,

Yours very sincerely,   J. Bernstorff

TLS (SDR, RG 59, 841.857/28, DNA).

From Franklin Knight Lane

My dear Mr President,   Washington [Sept. 9, 1915]

The newspaper boys have a report that you have asked for the dismissal of a New York Herald man named Laughlin whom I dont know. He was I believe one of the authors of that story that you and Col. House were no longer friendly. That was an infamous yarn & I have been trying to find out who started it. It appears that it was created by several imaginations, and that Laughlin was not alone responsible, probably less responsible than some others.

I beg to suggest the hope that you may not find it necessary to ask for Laughlin's discharge because the reaction among the newspapermen will not be beneficial.

Most sincerely yours   Franklin K. Lane

I have just heard from one of my men that the Chicago Tribune claims that it has justification of the story in a letter written by Col. House to John Lind to the effect that he (House) had suggested that you recognize Carranza but that you had not thought favorably of the idea. And out of this the story came.

ALS (WP, DLC).

To Edith Bolling Galt, with Enclosure

[The White House] 9 Sept. [1915]

I have a sneaking sympathy for these resisting Cabinet members who have resigned and yet I believe what we have proposed to be necessary for Haiti's salvation.   W.

ALI (WP, DLC).

E N C L O S U R E

Port au Prince September 7, 1915.

I have just returned from a conference with President and cabinet which began at three this afternoon at which time I had demanded a definite answer regarding treaty. Minister for

Foreign Affairs and Minister of Public Works refused to accept financial adviser which, however, declared to be essential. Whereupon the President requested and accepted their immediate resignations. Remainder of cabinet agreed to accept the treaty substantially as submitted. The President then asked me to allow him a short delay to enable him to fill vacancies in the cabinet to which I agreed. He then requested a conference with me tomorrow morning to discuss appointees. Resignation of Minister for Foreign Affairs removes cause of previous delays and will doubtless enable the President to expedite signing. President's action today seems to indicate that he now realizes the necessity for action without further delay and that he has determined to use all means to attain this end.   Davis.

T telegram (WP, DLC).

Two Letters to Robert Lansing

My dear Mr. Secretary,   The White House. 10 September, 1915.

The only present comment necessary on these letters,[1] obviously meant to be reassuring, is that my original error in speaking of "unarmed" vessels when I should have said "unresisting" is now rising up to embarrass us, for which I am very sorry.

The reply about the *Arabic*, if correctly outlined in the newspapers this morning,[2] is not very promising of a fulfilment of what Bernstorff indicates as the attitude of his government in these letters.   Faithfully Yours,   W.W.

WWTLI (SDR, RG 59, 841.857/30½, DNA).
[1] That is, Bernstorff's letters printed as Enclosures with RL to WW, Sept. 9, 1915.
[2] That is, the German note of September 7, printed as an Enclosure with WW to EBG, Sept. 10, 1915 (first letter of that date). The newspapers, e.g., the *New York Times*, Sept. 10, 1915, printed a long summary and the complete text of the note.

My dear Mr. Secretary,   The White House. 10 September, 1915.

I do not think any answer to this despatch[1] is necessary.

It is no doubt useful to know what opinion is on the other side of the water. After while even Englishmen will begin to understand (I wonder if they really ever will?) that what we are guided by is our sense of what is just and right and not our sensibility as regards what other nations think about us.

          Faithfully Yours,   W.W.

WWTLI (SDR, RG 59, 763.72/2140½, DNA).
[1] That is, WHP to RL and WW, Sept. 8, 1915, printed as an Enclosure with WW to EBG, Sept. 10, 1915 (second letter of that date).

To Edith Bolling Galt, with Enclosure

[The White House] 10 Sept. [1915]

This seems to me so obviously disingenuous that I am still further impressed with the feeling that Bernstorff has been misleading us. What is there for the the Hague under the terms of this note? W.

ALI (WP, DLC).

ENCLOSURE

Berlin (via Copenhagen) September 7, 1915.

2855. Foreign Office sends me the following report of the sinking of the ARABIC with the request that it be brought to the knowledge of the American Government:

"On the nineteenth of August a German submarine stopped the English Steamer DUNSLEY about sixty nautical miles south of Kinsale and was on the point of sinking the prize by gun fire after the crew had left the vessel. At this moment the Commander saw a large steamer making directly towards him. This steamer which, as developed later, was identical with the ARABIC was recognized as an enemy vessel as she did not fly any flag and bore no neutral markings. When she approached she altered her original course but then again pointed directly towards the submarine; from this the Commander became convinced that the steamer had the intention of attacking and ramming him. In order to anticipate this attack he gave orders to have the submarine submerge and fired a torpedo at the steamer. After firing he convinced himself that the people on board were being rescued in fifteen boats.

"According to his instructions the Commander was not allowed to attack the ARABIC without warning and without saving lives unless the ship attempted to escape or offered resistance. He was forced however to conclude from the attendant circumstances that the ARABIC planned a violent attack on the submarine. This conclusion was all the more obvious as he had been fired upon at the great distance in the Irish Sea on August 14th, that is a few days before, by a large passenger steamer apparently belonging to the British Royal Mail Steam Packet Company which he had neither attacked nor stopped.

"The German Government most deeply regrets that lives were lost through the action of the Commander. It particularly expresses this regret to the Government of the United States on account of the death of American citizens. The German Government is unable however to acknowledge any obligation to grant indemnity in the matter even if the Commander should have been mistaken as to the aggressive intentions of the ARABIC. If it should prove to be the case that it is impossible for the German and the American Government to reach a harmonious opinion on this point the German Government would be prepared to submit the difference of opinion as being a question of international law to the Hague tribunals pursuant to Article 38 of the Hague Convention for the pacific settlement of international disputes, in so doing it assumes that as a matter of course the arbitral decision shall not be admitted to have the importance of a general decision on the permissibility or the converse under international law of German submarine warfare. Berlin, September seven, 1915."

Respectfully suggest that if ARABIC was bow on toward submarine torpedo would not have hit ARABIC on side, and am convinced that situation here is such that if demands are not made quickly there is little chance of a favorable settlement.

Gerard, Berlin.

T telegram (WP, DLC).

To Edith Bolling Galt, with Enclosure

[The White House] 10 Sept [1915]

I wish Page could feel a little more strongly that we are acting upon our own convictions and not upon English opinion. Of course they want us to pull their chestnuts out of the fire.   W.

ALI (WP, DLC).

E N C L O S U R E

London, Sept. 8, 1915.

2771. Strictly confidential. For the Secretary and the President only.

The feeling even of conservative men here seems hardening into the conviction that the United States is losing the fear and therefore the respect of foreign governments and of foreign opinion. The sinking of the ARABIC and the apparent acceptance of Bernstorff's assurance of the cessation of submarine attacks on passenger ships created a bad impression because the assurance was not frank and specific and because no mention was made of the LUSITANIA. Fear of the same acquiescence in the torpedoing of the HESPERIAN is provoking ridicule and is fortifying the belief that we will desist from action under any provocation. This feeling is not confined to those who would like to have us enter the war but it exists among our best friends, who think we ought to keep out of actual war. They seem to construe our attitude as proof of weakness and there is danger that whatever we may say hereafter will be listened to with less respect. I think I detect evidence already of a diminishing respect for our communications. The impression grows that the "peace at any price" type of man has control of American opinion. Dumba's remaining would certainly tend to deepen this feeling into a permanent conviction.

You must read this not as my opinion but as my interpretation of responsible opinion here. Men here are, of course, likely to form judgments on partial selfishness, but I have tried to leave out of account the ordinary temporary selfish section of public opinion and to include only that which looks as if it may become the permanent English judgment of the American democracy. Thinking men persist in regarding the United States as a more or less loose aggregation of emptied nationalities without national unity, national aims, or definite moral qualities.

American Ambassador, London.[1]

T telegram (WP, DLC).
[1] Page repeated these observations in WHP to WW, Sept. 9, 1915, ALS (WP, DLC).

To Edith Bolling Galt, with Enclosure

[The White House] 10 Sept. [1915]

Ordinarily our Ambassador ought to be backed up as of course, but—this ass? It is hard to take it seriously.   W.

ALI (WP, DLC).

E N C L O S U R E

Berlin (via Copenhagen) September 8, 1915.

2857. Hear again definitely that Emperor refuses to see me as long as America delivers arms. To emphasize matter Emperor has lately received an American propagandist named Nilbuhr [Niebuhr] and an American spy named Doctor Marx[1] who hangs about Hotel Adlon and is a medium of communication between American correspondents here and General Staff, lending correspondents money and otherwise corrupting them. (I beg?) you to back me up and notify Bernstorff that President will not see him or allow him to enter White House until Emperor receives me. It is customary here that foreigners must be presented by their Ambassadors. I also want authority in my discretion to take up passport of Doctor Marx giving him emergency passport to United States. Above is not fault of Foreign Office or Chancellor but of military who surround Emperor and keep him out of Berlin.   Gerard, Berlin.

T telegram (WP, DLC).
¹ Dr. Lewis Hart Marx, a young American physician, who worked for the German government, according to Gerard, in a variety of medical and political ways. See J. W. Gerard to RL, Dec. 7, 1915, TLS (SDR, RG 59, 763.72/2343½, DNA).

To Thomas Nelson Page

                                                    The White House
My dear Mr. Ambassador: September 10, 1915

I know that you are so generous and so thoughtful of the many tasks I am carrying that you do not expect acknowledgment of your interesting letters, but I must occasionally give myself the pleasure of sending you a line of genuine appreciation and of warm thanks for the services you are rendering the country in the interesting post at Rome.

Your letters throw many side lights, as well as many direct lights, on the European situation which it is very valuable to me to have. They enable me to see my own course more clearly and to feel the European situation more intimately. It is fine to have one so capable not only to observe, but to interpret what is observed, to stand at my elbow and tell me what I could otherwise find no means of knowing.

My thoughts often go out to you in the warmest appreciation of the services you are rendering.

Please give my warmest regards to Mrs. Page.
            Cordially and sincerely yours,   Woodrow Wilson

TLS (T. N. Page Papers, NcD).

To Franklin Knight Lane

Personal.

My dear Lane: [The White House] September 10, 1915

Thank you sincerely for your note about the newspaper men and the offence of Mr. Laughlin. I feel that it was a particularly malicious offence,—I do not know what else to call it,—and I do not for a moment believe what comes from the Chicago Tribune about the matter. Even if Mr. House did write such a letter to Governor Lind, which I very much doubt, it could furnish no sort of excuse for the story that was published. There has appeared to be a systematic effort recently to make ugly personal situations, since there is no other successful way of attacking the administration, and I feel very strongly about the matter.

The Herald people are investigating the action of Laughlin for me very thoroughly, or at least promised to do so, and I shall, of course, await their report. I don't want to do anything extreme but that office in particular has taken liberties with the reputation of members of the administration which I don't think we ought to submit to.

Always

Cordially and faithfully yours,   Woodrow Wilson

TLS (Letterpress Books, WP, DLC).

To Walter Hines Page

My dear Page: The White House September 10, 1915

I do not often acknowledge your interesting letters, but that is not because they are not of vital interest to me but only because I have nothing to write in return which compares in interest with what you write to me. Practically all that happens on this side of the water is on the surface and, though the accounts of events and policies here which our newspapers give are ridiculously inadequate when they are not absolutely erroneous, you have so long been a reader of American news that you know how to make the discounts and additions, and any personal details which may be lacking I am sure others like House supply you with.

Your letters are of real service to me. They give me what it would not be possible for me to get in any other way, and if it is not too great a tax upon you to write them as often as you do, I hope that you will not leave out a single line or item which is interesting your own thought. It is only in this way that I can get the atmosphere, which, after all, is quite as important as the event because it is out of the atmosphere that the event rises.

I am delighted to be reassured as to your health. I was afraid that the all but intolerable strain you must be under was beginning to tell upon you. When it does begin to tell, I beg that you will let me know, because you ought to have a rest. My own

444 SEPTEMBER 10, 1915

judgment was that it would create a misapprehension if you should come home just at this time, and I am very glad indeed to find that your own instinctive feeling about the matter was the same. It would be jolly to see you and have a long talk with you, and I think it would refresh you to get into the freer and cooler mental atmosphere of this country of ours, where the majority are not half so much off their poise as a small minority seem to be, but we must postpone that pleasure for a little while.

In the meantime, believe me, with grateful appreciation,

Your sincere friend, Woodrow Wilson

TLS (W. H. Page Papers, MH).

From Robert Lansing, with Enclosure

My Dear Mr. President: Washington September 10, 1915.

The enclosed telegram has been received from Ambassador Fletcher. Will you kindly indicate to me what are your wishes in the matter?   Faithfully yours, Robert Lansing.

TLS (SDR, RG 59, 710.11/202, DNA).

ENCLOSURE

Santiago, Chile September 9, 1915.

CONFIDENTIAL. I believe Chilean Government can be brought to accept substantially the President's plan. Minister for Foreign Affairs is ready to open negotiations with me with that end in view. I have read the telegrams exchanged between the Foreign Office and Suarez on the subject and the Minister has offered to place all the papers in my hands. Would the President and the Department like to have me proceed with the negotiations here.

Fletcher.

T telegram (SDR, RG 59, 710.11/202, DNA).

From Joseph Patrick Tumulty

Dear Governor: Avon, New Jersey September 10, 1915.

In the Hesperian matter, I have been very much interested in the expression of opinion I have found in some of the leading newspapers throughout the country. I am sending you some of the editorials which I know will prove to be mighty interesting reading.

The Baltimore Evening Sun, summing up the situation, says that the admission of the officers of the Hesperian that a six-inch gun was mounted on her stern alters the whole incident, so far as it relates to us.[1]

The Springfield Republican, one of the most conservative papers in the country, says that "it must appear to the majority of the American people that no diplomatic rupture with Germany could be justified in a case like that of the Hesperian." Saying further that "we could never be warranted in extreme action because a British-Canadian liner carrying a mounted cannon had been torpedoed, even with the loss of American lives."[2]

It seems to me that the safe position for us to take is outlined in the leading editorial in the New York Tribune of today, entitled, "Making a Vague Pledge Vaguer."[3] It says, "What is needed is a clear, full, indisputable interpretation of the vague promise of September first. How far is Germany really prepared to go in accepting the principle of neutral rights as laid down in this government's notes? To what extent will she forego submarine warfare which is in contravention of international law? Until these points are cleared up, it will be premature to congratulate ourselves on having argued Germany into reasonableness or on having won any real victory in our fight for civilization and international justice."

Our only safety lies, in my opinion, in confining Germany to an interpretation of what she really meant in the instructions conveyed through Count Von Bernstorff on September first. I am still hopeful that Germany will see the wisdom of strictly adhering to the principles laid down in this communication. If she does not, it seems to me that we have reached the parting of the ways.

A view at variance with that expressed by the Springfield Republican is found in the editorial which I am sending you from the Philadelphia Public Ledger.[4]

I hope you can read the editorials from the New York Times, the New York Tribune, and the New York Press[5] touching on this question.   Affectionately yours,   Tumulty.

TLS (WP, DLC).

[1] The editorial in the Baltimore *Evening Sun*, Sept. 9, 1915, went even further and said that submarines were entirely justified in torpedoing armed ships.

[2] The editorial in the *Springfield*, Mass., *Republican* Sept. 8, 1915, concluded: "As neutrals, we cannot now make an effective protest against the sinking of the Hesperian because the ship's absolute noncombatant character as against submarines cannot be established."

[3] The editorial in the *New York Tribune*, Sept. 10, 1915, was mainly a commentary on the German note of September 7 about the *Arabic* case. "If it is to be left to the commander of each German submarine to excuse himself for torpedoing a merchantman without warning, on the plea of self-defence, the von

Bernstorff guarantee is whittled down to a pale and ineffectual distraction . . . a hollow mockery. It gives the United States no guarantee worth having against recurrences of the Lusitania and Arabic outrages." Then followed Tumulty's quotation.

⁴ "Armed for Defense," undated clipping from the Philadelphia *Public Ledger*. This short editorial said that *Hesperian* was well within the law in carrying a gun for defense, and that acceptance of the German contention "would be another indication of a strange infirmity of purpose where Germany and the lives of American citizens are concerned, in startling contrast with the insistence upon the letter of the law regarding merchandise which has characterized the correspondence with Great Britain."

⁵ They, along with other editorials, were all printed in the New York *World*, Sept. 10, 1915, and all demanded Dumba's dismissal. The *Tribune* said that there was increasing apprehension in the country lest the country and the administration were getting uncomfortably close to cowardice. The *Times* said that it doubted rumors that the administration would be lenient with the Ambassador. Germany and Austria had been inclined to look upon the United States as a sort of Belgium. "No self-respecting nation can put up with such effrontery, with such brazen defiance of its interests and its laws." The *Press* exclaimed that Germany was making "a spectacle" of the United States and its foreign policy. Now Austria was playing the same game by Dumba's fomenting riot and sedition. "How long can it go on? How long will the country be flouted and jeered and made a mockery before the world? How much more will Washington stand?"

To Edith Bolling Galt

[The White House] Friday, 7.15 A.M.
10 Sept., 1915

My own precious, lovely Darling,

Don't think, because I am at my desk so early, that I did not sleep well. I slept delightfully, with the sweet influences of our wonderful day together acting on my spirits in such a way as to put my heart absolutely at ease. Surely no lovers ever came to a sweeter understanding of each other's hearts than we came to yesterday. I felt *glorified* by it: for it let me see *all* of the loveliest heart in the world and made me realize more completely than I ever did before that it had been given absolutely to me, in all its exquisite beauty. I waked early only because so deeply moved by sweet thoughts. It was delightful to lie there in bed with your picture before me and think of what you are and what you mean to me, but I could not keep my thoughts to myself: I could not resist the impulse to come here to my table and renew my vows to you of utter love and allegiance. The love welled up in my heart too strong to be given no vent. The only way I could at all satisfy the deep longing that all but overcame me was to come and pour out my love to you: the only way I could begin the day with steadied spirits was to come here and put the worship that is in my heart into words. For, my Darling, it *is* worship that is in my heart this morning,—worship of the exquisite woman who has given herself to me. Every intimate view I get of you, my wonderful, my adorable, my incomparable Sweetheart, deepens my adoring love, not only, but also my delight in your character, my admiration, my enthusiasm for the traits and charms and

gifts of heart and mind I discover. It is beyond measure delightful to be with you and see what I see; for I see some new charm,
or some familiar one more fully displayed, each time I am with
you; and always the same thing happens: I am more deeply and
more happily in love with you than ever. And that is what I got
up to tell you: I am more deeply, more happily, more rejoicingly
in love with you than ever. I glory in you! You are *altogether*
lovely and desirable!   Your own   Woodrow

I will write you about Boyd after I see him and send the note
to you with the big envelope I forgot to hand you last night.   W.

Well, Sweetheart, I have had twenty minutes with Mr. Boyd.
He had a real mission which he stated with clearness and force.
He is very pleasant in appearance,—not in any way unwholesome;
has the manners of a man of education; and talks excellent English. Elizabeth is in New York. He will bring her to present her
thanks for the invitation to Cornish on their return from San
Francisco. It will be fun to tell you all about him to-morrow!

ALS (WP, DLC).

From Edith Bolling Galt

My precious One: [Washington] Friday: Sept. 10, 1915
I am so happy this morning, all because of the complete happiness of yesterday. It came like the benediction that follows
after prayer, for my heart was so hungry for you and your wonderful love, and nothing could have been tenderer or more comprehending than you were
I am writing in a tearing hurry as Helen is coming but if I
covered pages with written words they could only reiterate what
is singing in my heart—I love you, I love you, and I am perfectly
happy because you love me.
                         Always your very own   Edith.

My love to the Dr. and the hope he is better this morning—
and thank him again for asking me to stay to dinner. I had such
a good time   E.

ALS (WP, DLC).

To Robert Lansing, with Enclosure

My dear Mr. Secretary,   The White House. 11 September, 1915.
For your information I send you the enclosed from Dave.
Lawrence.   Faithfully Yours,   W.W.

WWTLI (SDR, RG 59, 812.00/16190½, DNA).

ENCLOSURE

From David Lawrence

Dear Mr. President: Washington *Friday* [Sept. 10, 1915]

Arredondo, Carranza's representative here, told me today he had received three days ago a cablegram from Carranza advising him what had taken place in my conversations at Vera Cruz and expressing in conclusion the opinion that he had been very much impressed by the ideas I had brought as to the attitude of the American government. He said that in his reply he would express a disposition to discuss "international questions" with the several governments. This follows a suggestion which I made to him *as a last resort* but on which he did not committ himself at the time that he enter a conference of some kind whether it was called for the discussion of international or internal or other questions but so that there might be some formal means of bringing a government into being in Mexico. Speaking of this suggestion in his message to Arredondo, Carranza indicated that his note would tell why he could not discuss internal affairs but would leave the way open for a conference on international matters. Arredondo himself volunteered the opinion to me that in such a conference, which would be secret, of course the line between international and internal would background to this of which I will tell you when I see you on Monday at 2 o'clock as arranged. Sincerely, David Lawrence

TLS (SDR, RG 59, 812.00/16189½, DNA).

To Robert Lansing

My dear Mr. Secretary, The White House. 11 September, 1915.

I am so exceedingly anxious to push this matter to an early settlement that I hope that you will authorize Fletcher to go ahead by all means, if you think we can do this without discourtesy to Suarez, through whom we have been able to do virtually nothing in this affair.

I regard it as of the utmost importance that these negotiations be completed and carried to a successful outcome at this particular time.

Am I right in understanding that Brazil has assented in all essential particulars? Faithfully Yours, W.W.

WWTLI (SDR, RG 59, 710.11/205½, DNA).

Three Letters from Robert Lansing

Personal and Private.

My Dear Mr. President: Washington September 11, 1915.

I have received a note from the German Ambassador dated the 9th, asking me whether I wish to discuss with him the Arabic case.[1] I have not replied to the note as I thought it well to have an understanding as to what our course is to be before I see Bernstorff, if I do see him at all, on this matter. I am sending you in another letter a rather full discussion of the Arabic case and my views as to the probable course we will have to adopt.

The Ambassador added in his letter the following:

"As you know I also have instructions to discuss our answer to your last Lusitania note with you as soon as you consider the Arabic incident closed."

Faithfully yours,   Robert Lansing

TLS (WP, DLC).
    [1] J. H. von Bernstorff to RL, Sept. 9, 1915, TLS (SDR, RG 59, 841.857 AR 1/62, DNA).

PERSONAL AND PRIVATE:

My dear Mr. President: Washington September 11, 1915.

I have been through the German note on the ARABIC case,[1] and also the affidavits which we have received from London and Liverpool given by survivors of the ARABIC and of the DUNSLEY.[2]

I consider that the German note is most unsatisfactory; that in fact we are back where we were before Count von Bernstorff communicated to us the German admission of principle in submarine warfare.

From the evidence I think that the following facts are conclusively established:

(1) The ARABIC was never nearer the DUNSLEY than two miles;

(2) The ARABIC was pursuing a zig-zag course, which is a customary maneuver when the presence of a submarine is suspected.

This method of avoidance must have been known to the submarine commander so that the changes of course by the ARABIC could not have been mistaken by the commander as an attempt to ram, though the ARABIC might have been headed for him at one or more times during her approach to the DUNSLEY.

(3) The submarine, on observing the approach of the ARABIC, submerged;

(4) The submarine was never seen by any person on board the ARABIC. If it had been seen, the presumption would be that the ARABIC, being at least a mile or more away, would have turned from and not toward the submarine, as the ARABIC carried no armament.

(5) The torpedo was not seen by persons on board the ARABIC until it was about two hundred yards away from the vessel. There was evidently no time to swing the vessel to any considerable extent after the torpedo was seen. Yet the torpedo appears to have struck the ARABIC almost at right angles, not far from the vessel's beam. Judging the location of the submarine by the direction from which the torpedo came, the submarine commander could not, at the time the torpedo was released, have had the slightest reason to suppose that the ARABIC was attempting to ram his vessel.

(6) The unavoidable conclusion seems to be that the submarine commander did not believe the ARABIC was attempting to attack him, but that he wantonly torpedoed the vessel without warning and with utter disregard for the lives of persons on board.[3]

I would submit the following comments on the German note:

The statements as to what occurred do not purport to be by the commander of the submarine. Every allegation might easily be constructed from the press reports of the incident. The only fact alleged which appears to be solely within the knowledge of the officers of the submarine, is the alleged attack in the Irish Sea on August 14th, five days before the ARABIC was sunk, and this may have been reported to the German Admiralty before the ARABIC incident occurred.

The question arises—Did the submarine commander make any report? If he did, why does the note fail to say so, and why does it not give the language of the report as to the facts?

Reference is made to the instructions issued to the Commander of the submarine. Why is not the language of the instructions given?

The failure to admit liability for indemnity for the lives of American citizens lost amounts to a justification of the commander. If the commander is justified in drawing such a conclusion, as it is alleged in the note the commander of the submarine did draw from the facts in this case, then the lives of persons on board merchant ships are in as great danger as they were before the instructions were issued.

The note proposes to submit the question of liability to The

Hague for arbitration, expressly withholding the question of the legality of submarine warfare in general.

The whole tenor of the note is a cold and uncompromising declaration that the commanders of submarines have practically a free hand though bound, technically, by some general form of instructions, and that if they make mistakes, however unwarranted, their Government will support them. It seems to me that we must reach a conclusion that the Bernstorff statement of principle is valueless and cannot be relied upon as a protective measure.

If the foregoing analysis of the evidence as to the facts is true, and the comments on the German note are justified, it would seem as if a course which this Government might pursue is to inform the Berlin Government that the note is highly unsatisfactory both in its declarations and in its tone, and a demand that the act of the submarine commander who torpedoed the ARABIC, being deliberately unfriendly, be disavowed, that the officer be punished for his wanton and illegal conduct, and that a formal declaration be made that the sinking of the ARABIC was contrary to the instructions issued to submarine commanders, of which instructions this Government was notified by the German Ambassador here.

If the foregoing course is not adopted, I see no alternative other than to announce that the German note is entirely unacceptable as an explanation of the conduct of the submarine commander, and that as the German Government supports the commander, this Government must consider that the German attitude is one of deliberate unfriendliness and, therefore, the United States must sever diplomatic relations with Germany.

I regret very much that the present situation has arisen which seems to preclude further negotiations, as continued discussions of this subject would, I believe, be contrary to the dignity of the United States and would invite general criticism from the American people. I further think that we should reach a decision promptly.   Faithfully yours,   Robert Lansing.

TLS (WP, DLC).
  1 Printed as an Enclosure with WW to EBG, Sept. 10, 1915 (first letter of that date).
  2 WHP to RL, Aug. 23, 1915, FR-WWS 1915, pp. 518-20.
  3 Lansing's conclusions were correct. See Link, Struggle for Neutrality, p. 565.

PERSONAL AND PRIVATE:

My dear Mr. President: Washington September 11, 1915.

I enclose herewith a letter which I think you may find of interest.[1] It appears that Dr. Dumba dined at the Hotel Plaza on the evening of the 8th with the Austrian Consul-General, and with a third person who is supposed to be Capt. von Papen.

Faithfully yours,   Robert Lansing

TLS (SDR, RG 59, 701.6311/150½, DNA).

[1] Anna R. Gilford to RL, Sept. 9, 1915, TCL (SDR, RG 59, 701.6311/150½, DNA). It briefly reported on what she had overheard of the conversation of Dumba and his companions at the Plaza Hotel on September 8. Actually, she caught only stray words such as "Schwab," "Pittsburgh," and "Carnegie." However, she also heard "Wilson," followed by laughter, a tap on the neck, and the further words "zwei Jahre."

To Edith Bolling Galt, with Enclosure

[The White House] 11 Sept. [1915]

This is at least rational and intelligible,—thanks to the naval attaché.   W.

ALI (WP, DLC).

E N C L O S U R E

Berlin (via Copenhagen) September 9, 1915.

2860. Following memorandum is based largely on opinion of our naval attache[1] with which opinion I agree. His deductions are founded upon careful observations and reliable information.

The remarkable change in the German attitude between Bernstorff's statement and the last German note regarding the ARABIC arises from a decision having been reached to follow naval policy rather than the policy of the Foreign Office and to give no guarantees that the submarine warfare will in any way be modified. The reasons for this I believe to be as follows:

One. Of the group of submarines of which one sank ARABIC three boats failed to return and have been given up for lost, namely, U-27 and two others. This constitutes by far the greatest loss sustained by the submarine fleet at one time although I believe that sixteen have been lost since the beginning of the war of which only ten have been publicly announced.

Two. It is reported by one returning submarine that on August eighteenth when trying to carry out order to give warning before torpedoing an English merchant vessel she was fired on by this ship and escaped only by diving.

Three. English reports of destruction of the submarine U-27 as received by the German Navy Department are as follows. "It is reported with certainty in England that a German submarine was sunk by an English destroyer after the sinking of the ARABIC in the vicinity of the scene of the latter's destruction. The submarine which had come to the surface was in the act of stopping and sinking a steamer with a load of mules en route from New Orleans to Liverpool when an English destroyer, which had been hidden from sight by the steamer, hastened to the scene and destroyed the submarine with gun fire before it had a chance to submerge."

Backed up by these reasons the German Navy Department was in a position to tell the general government that to follow the policy laid down for submarine warfare would mean total failure of that method of warfare involving the destruction of the German submarine fleet. I believe that these facts were used by the Navy to influence the government and that they were successful in reversing the policy as laid down by Bernstorff in his conversation and note.

The above statements could not have been applicable to the sinking of the ARABIC or HESPERIAN. They apply only to the attitude adopted in the German note of September seventh.

Gerard, Berlin.

T telegram (WP, DLC).
1 Commander Walter Rockwell Gherardi, U.S.N.

To Edith Bolling Galt, with Enclosure

[The White House] 11 Sept. [1915]

Who can fathom this? I wish they would hand this idiot his passports!   W.

ALI (WP, DLC).

E N C L O S U R E

Berlin, via Copenhagen, Sept. 9, 1915.

2861. Reported that Admiral Bachmann, Chief of Naval Staff and always at general headquarters with Emperor, and a Tirpitz man, has been replaced by Admiral Holzendorf.[1] Latter has a brother who is director of Hamburg-American Line and right-hand man of Ballin. Reported that von Tirpitz angry at appointment of Holzendorf, and that last ARABIC note was a concession to von Tirpitz. Von Jagow told me that his conversation with me about ARABIC, reported in my 2777, August 25th, 4 p.m., was for consumption of American Government only and that he meant if possible to keep it secret here, as public opinion here had to be considered. The whole matter is complicated with internal politics and intrigues here and von Tirpitz seems able to overrule Chancellor and Emperor.   Gerard, Berlin.

T telegram (WP, DLC).

1 Admiral Henning von Holtzendorff, new chief of the German Admiralty.

Two Letters from Robert Lansing

PERSONAL AND PRIVATE:

My dear Mr. President: Washington September 12, 1915.

We have for several days held at Norfolk a British merchant vessel "Waimana" because she had on board a mounted 4.7 gun, endeavoring meanwhile to have the British Admiralty direct its removal before the vessel left our port.[1]

We are now advised that the British Admiralty declines to remove the gun and asserts, correctly, that the vessel has complied with our declaration of September 19, 1914, as to armed merchant vessels.[2] Up to the present time the British Admiralty as a result of an informal understanding have kept guns off British merchant vessels entering American ports. For a year, therefore, the question has not been discussed as no case has arisen.

Meanwhile submarine warfare has developed as a practical method of interrupting merchant vessels. At the time we issued the declaration as to the status of armed merchant vessels this use of the submarine as a commerce destroyer was unknown, and the declaration was based on the means employed prior to that time.

I feel in my own mind that these changed conditions require a new declaration because an armament, which under previous conditions, was clearly defensive, may now be employed for offensive operations against so small and unarmored a craft as a submarine. On the 4th of this month the German Ambassador called my attention to the fact that on two occasions German submarines were attacked and fired upon by British passenger steamers. While these may be isolated cases the fact that such vessels are attacking submarines makes it difficult to demand that a submarine shall give warning and so expose itself to the heavy guns carried by some of the British passenger vessels.

As to the effect of these cases on our declaration, it would seem to me that we ought to amend it by asserting that in view of the successful employment of submarines as commerce destroyers and the possibility of offensive operations against them by a merchant vessel carrying an armament regardless of the number, size or location of the guns composing it, this Government will hereafter treat as a ship of war any merchant vessel of belligerent nationality which enters an American port with any armament.

The assumption of this position has another advantage and that is that the term "armed" instead of "unresisting" will be justified, and as it was used I feel that we ought to stand by it.

In the particular case of the vessel at Norfolk I think that we should be less rigid on account of our former declaration. A proposed note to the British Ambassador is enclosed treating the case specially and leniently.[3]

I enclose also the entire docket in the case directing your attention in particular to Count von Bernstorff's note of the 4th instant, and our declaration of September 19, 1914, which immediately follows it.   Faithfully yours,   Robert Lansing.

TLS (SDR, RG 59, 763.72/2142½ B, DNA).
  [1] Treasury Department to State Department, Aug. 24, 1915, T memorandum (SDR, RG 59, 763.72111/2777, DNA); A. J. Peters to RL, Aug. 26, 1915, TLS (SDR, RG 59, 763.72111/2778, DNA); RL to C. A. Spring Rice, Aug. 25 and Sept. 4, 1915, CCL (SDR, RG 59, 763.72111/2777, DNA); and RL to C. A. Spring Rice, Sept. 11, 1915, CCL (SDR, RG 59, 763.72111/2954, DNA).
  [2] C. A. Spring Rice to RL, Sept. 10, 1915, TLS (SDR, RG 59, 763.72111/2954, DNA).
  [3] The proposed note, which was not sent, and the documents mentioned in the next paragraph, are missing.

Personal and Private.

My Dear Mr. President: Washington September 12, 1915.

I enclose the reply of Carranza to the communication of the Conference of diplomats.[1]

The position taken by Carranza is not unreasonable though it seems to me to be unwise since he fails to seize an opportunity which would give him exceptional advantage, and especially so in view of the desperate situation of the Villistas, who seem to be entirely disorganized and incapable of offering united resistance to the advancing Carranzista army.

Of course his invitation to meet in conference on the border to discuss Mexican affairs from the international standpoint with the sole object of determining whether the government, of which he is the head, is entitled to recognition as a *de facto* government cannot be accepted. The place of a meeting for such purpose could not in any event be Mexican territory. If Carranza had named Washington it might be at least worthy of consideration.

The proposal, however, shows a better disposition, it seems to me, than any previous action by Carranza. He says that he is willing to discuss the facts on which must be determined whether or not his government should be recognized. That necessarily involves the questions of its ability to restore peace, its stability, and its international responsibility. As a result such a conference would in fact review the entire domestic state of Mexico including the power of the factions and their complaints against one another.

The Carranzistas are undoubtedly stronger and more cohesive than they have ever been. In fact I have almost reached the conclusion that they are so dominant that they are entitled to recognition. If they are not recognized, I cannot see what will be gained by recognizing any other government, since the present war would continue and be prolonged by strengthening the opposition to Carranza, who, I feel certain, would win in the end.

The situation has changed materially since the communication was sent to the Mexican chiefs. Villa's power has rapidly waned, his forces have disintegrated, and many of his ablest lieutenants have abandoned him or are quarreling with him. As long as the Villista faction was capable of offering stubborn resistance to the Constitutionalists the desirable thing was to stay the strife by harmonizing the factional differences. That was the purpose of the proposed conference of leaders. Now, it seems to me, the problem is whether or not peace in Mexico will not be more quickly restored by giving moral support to the triumphing faction of Carranza.

The difficulty we are in is that we proposed a conference of Mexicans to determine a course of action. The weaker factions other than the Carranzistas have accepted the invitation. Can we consistently or honorably refuse to call such a conference? If we do call it, what will be the practical value of its deliberations? With the utter demoralization of the enemies of Carranza it would be absurd to assert that any government, which they could set up, represented the sovereignty of the Mexican people.

The conference might meet, however, to formulate the grievances, which the participants have against Carranza and which could be laid before him. Of course such a course would entirely change the purpose of the conference, but then conditions have materially changed in favor of Carranza.

I think, in any event, it is necessary to call the Ambassadors and Ministers together and lay before them the replies of the Mexican chiefs and also the present state of affairs in Mexico and the continuing successes of the Carranzista arms. But before doing this I would like to be prepared to present a course of action for consideration which would be practical and expedient in the circumstances.

As this involves the whole general Mexican policy I think that I should be advised as to your wishes in the matter.

Faithfully yours,   Robert Lansing.

TLS (SDR, RG 59, 812.00/16988, DNA).

   1 J. R. Silliman to RL, Sept. 10, 1915, T telegram (SDR, RG 59, 812.00/16988, DNA), printed in *FR 1915*, pp. 746-48. Carranza, speaking through his Foreign Minister, Jesús Acuña, declared that he could not "consent to a discussion of the domestic affairs of the Republic by mediation or on the initiative of any foreign Government whatever." Acceptance of the Pan-American offer would gravely prejudice Mexican independence and set a precedent for foreign intervention in the settlement of internal questions. Moreover, Carranza was the leader of a true political and social revolution in Mexico; therefore, he could not sit down at the peace table with men who had attempted to corrupt and destroy that revolution, nor could he allow these men to take part in the new government. The truth of the matter was that the revolution was at the point of culmination: the strife was now nearing an end, with "the reactionary faction" (Villa, Zapata, and their followers) now being confined to a few isolated areas of the country. Although Carranza had to refuse the Pan-American invitation, he would be willing to meet the would-be mediators at one of the border towns held by his forces, with the understanding, however, that the discussions there would have the sole object of determining whether the mediators should conclude that Carranza and his government were entitled to *de facto* recognition.

Two Letters to Edith Bolling Galt

[The White House]

My own Darling,   Sunday morning, 12 Sept., 1915

   I want you to know the real character of my love for you, and I am eager to do anything to make you realize it,—its reality, its tenderness, its depths upon depths, its delight in you as it actually finds you. You are constantly struggling—I had almost said *agonizing*—to make me understand 'what you really are,' as if to prove to me that it is not the woman I have been loving, but another, whom I could not, as you imagine, continue to love; and when you have finished the 'confession' and put the case as unfavourably as you can against yourself, the same thing always happens: I understand you *without trying*; the problem you present to me, with deep trouble and shame in your dear eyes, seems to me no problem at all, but merely the struggles of a noble heart with itself; *and I love you more than ever*,—with an unspeakable longing to give you love in such abundance and in such ideal, unselfish fashion that everything but joy and confidence will be driven out of your thoughts forever. For I love you, not some ideal woman whom I have constructed out of my imagination or out of a silly, blind love—as an inexperienced boy might. I am a mature man, sensitive beyond measure to impressions of character; and you have revealed yourself to me as you never revealed yourself to anyone else,—have taken pains to put into words the innermost secrets of your nature. And the result? Love, *love*, unbounded, joyous love! Explain it how you will, it is *you* I love, just as I have found you; and not only love but trust and admire and adore. I am so impatient to devote my life to you and give you every day just the sort of love you want *that day*, so eager to prove to you that I know you and because I know you want you, that the waiting, if much longer continued, is likely to become intolerable. You are the companion I want (*nobody* satisfies my mind or my fancy as you do), the counsellor I want (nobody steadies me as you do), the sweetheart I want (nobody delights me as you do), the wife I want (nobody can glorify or complete my life or give me happiness as you can). I am writing this, my Love, with a solemn intensity of self-examination and a solemn realization of the full meaning of every word I write, that should make it serve you as that precious document you wrote on the West Porch[1] has served me, as you have from week to week put a deeper meaning into it. I feel it all so deeply that I am obliged to write with extreme slowness to control my pen hand at all. Keep this, my own Darling, as if it were written with my heart's blood (I feel as if it were!) and turn to it whenever doubts of any sort assail you, to open your eyes again to the real love and character of   Your own   Woodrow

ALS (WP, DLC).
[1] EBG to WW, June 29, 1915, Vol. 33.

[The White House] 12 Sept. [1915]

This is the letter[1] that filled my mind with such grave thoughts yesterday. I am not in agreement with all parts of its conclusions as to what we sh. do, but something practically equivalent we can hardly avoid.

I attach the other letters because I am sure they will interest you.

Please, Sweetheart, return these by messenger this afternoon some time, and tell me in a few lines at the same time that Mr. Wilson has not had business to put before you that has disturbed you over much or that I cannot help in.   W.

ALI (WP, DLC).
[1] That is, RL to WW, Sept. 11, 1915 (second letter of that date).

From Edith Bolling Galt

Dearest:

[Washington] Sunday,
Sept. 12, 1915 9:30 a.m.

I was up two hours ago and wrote you a hasty little note to tell you that "all's well with the world," but I have just read it over and did not like it so tore it up and can now give even a better account of myself. The enclosed note from Mr. Wilson explains itself and why I can take another blessed half hour to talk to you.[1]

I can *honestly* say Sweetheart, all the *kinks* have got straight, and I had a much better night. Do you know why? Well, it was because you love me and made me feel it in the sweetest, tenderest way. Bless your heart you will leave no room for doubts or fears when I can always be with you, for before they get hold of me, as they do now, I can go and put my arms 'round you and tell you of them and you will shield and protect me from them and bring me back to happy belief in my self again and the blessed assurance that I have your love—perfect, complete.

Last night was a happiness, and I am only sorry so many of the precious minutes together had to be spent in chasing shadows. Sometimes I can run faster than they can catch me, but other days (as yesterday) I can not outdistance them until I have your dear hand to steady and guide me. Then I am safe—nothing can really hurt. I suppose you will go to church this morning, and I will go with you in spirit, while my outward, material self sits here at my desk—sending out checks etc. to clear up things that have gone over since the summer. Mother[,] Randolph & Bertha will come to lunch with me, and perhaps later I will go for a ride.

Just here your note has come and as the messenger is waiting I cannot really *answer* it.

I can *never* do that except with my lips on yours and my heart beating against your breast. But—oh Dearest I can't find the words that I want—and so I leave the page white, and pure as the best answer, for you will fill it with your own beautiful thoughts and read my heart and find there the adoration, the trust, the love of my life.

All the rest must wait until I am in your arms again

Your own—*Proudly*   Your own,   Edith.

ALS (WP, DLC).
   [1] N. Wilson to EBG, Sept. 12, 1915, ALS (WP, DLC), saying that he had suddenly been called out of town.

Two Letters to Robert Lansing

My dear Mr. Secretary,   The White House. 13 September, 1915.

I have read this carefully.

I think the course we orally outlined this morning is the best one:

To let this particular vessel go upon a promise by the British Admiralty and a bond by the owners of the vessel that he[r] arms will in no case be used for offe[n]ce;[1]

And to prepare the general regulation you suggest, but not publish it or put it into effect until we see what we are going to be able to work out of this Arabic business.

Faithfully Yours,   W.W.

WWTLI (SDR, RG 59, 763.72/2143½, DNA).

[1] As it turned out, the British decided not to make a test case out of *Waimana*'s gun. The ship landed the gun on September 21 and sailed the following day. About this whole episode, see Link, *Struggle for Neutrality*, pp. 668-71.

My dear Mr. Secretary,   The White House. 13 September, 1915

We have already gone over this matter orally; but perhaps it is best for me to put down what I understand our course of action is to be:

We are to call our Latin American colleagues together and suggest to them a conference with representatives of Carranza at Washington, on substantially the basis he proposes, to discuss the advisability of recognizing him as the *de facto* head of the Republic; having it clearly understood that we think the acceptance of the Revolution absolutely necessary.

We are also to keep faith with the leaders of the other factions, who have accepted our proposal for a conference on Mexican affairs, and are to call such a conference of their representatives to be convened and held in Mexico; with the understanding that we wish from them any proposals they may wish to make, but with the intimation conveyed to them in some proper way that the best and most helpful thing for them to do is to let us know confidentially the terms upon which they will submit to Carranza in view of the probable necessity we shall be under, because of the utter alteration of conditions since our suggestion of a conference was conveyed to them, of recognizing him as the head of the Republic.   Faithfully Yours,   W.W.

WWTLI (SDR, RG 59, 812.00/16989½, DNA).

Two Letters from Robert Lansing

PERSONAL AND SECRET:

My dear Mr. President: [Washington] September 13, 1915.

The interview with the German Ambassador on the ARABIC case took place at noon today. I believe that he fully appreciates the gravity of the situation and is very anxious about the outcome. I also believe that he will do anything in his power to have his Government take the steps necessary to change the situation.

We discussed the German note on the ARABIC and I pointed out to him very explicitly the objectionable features which made it impossible for us to reply to it in its present form. I told him that the attack upon the ARABIC and the unconditional support of the submarine commander's conduct by his Government made the Ambassador's acceptance of the principle insisted upon by the United States as valueless. He replied that he understood perfectly that such must be our feeling; that he had done all he could to prevent such a crisis as the present; and that he was greatly disappointed at what had occurred. He said that all the information which his Government had, of course, was the report of the submarine commander and that he wished they might know of the evidence which we possessed, and which I had read to him. I told him that in view of the critical state of affairs the Government was disposed to transmit for him a cipher message to his Government in order that he might explain fully the situation, and that we would send to Ambassador Gerard, at von Bernstorff's request, a summary of the evidence which we had in regard to the ARABIC.

I pointed out to him at the same time that the ARABIC note did not disclose that any report had been received from the submarine commander, and if the statements were based on such a report I thought that his Government should so inform us.

I said that the instructions to the submarine commander had never been revealed to us except in the most general terms, and, therefore, we did not know what discretionary powers had been conferred upon the commander.

The Ambassador seemed particularly grateful for our willingness to transmit a message for him and said that he would impress upon his Government the seriousness of the present situation.

I also said that such a mistake as was made by the officer who attacked the ARABIC made this Government very doubtful as to the efficacy of the instructions.

He said that he realized that that must be so and that he was very much distressed at what had happened; that he was not sure that he could accomplish what was desired; but that he would use every effort to do so.

I also said to him that I thought the German Government should broaden its declaration so as to include all merchant vessels and not be limited to passenger steamers; that in the past the practice of the German submarines has been to warn freight vessels and I could not see why an exception should be made in their case as to the general principle, since some of these freighters might have American citizens in their crews. He replied he would do what he could to obtain such an extention of the principle which his Government had announced.

We also spoke of the matter of arbitration and I said to him that I thought it was valueless at the present time to discuss it because I considered the evidence was so clear in the case of the ARABIC that we could not arbitrate the justification of the submarine commander and that the only question left was the amount of indemnity; that I thought his Government should admit that the mistake was without justification and disavow the act of the officer; and that it would then be a proper time to discuss whether or not we could arbitrate the amount of indemnity which Germany should pay.

The whole attitude of the Ambassador was conciliatory and an evidence of willingness to do anything to avoid a rupture between the two Governments. I think I may say he was extremely "docile." There was none of the aggressiveness which he has shown on other occasions. He seemed to be much depressed, and doubtful as to what he could accomplish with his Government.

He did not mention his desire to have an audience with you and I did not think it worth while to inform him that at present it would be impossible for you to see him.

Faithfully yours,   Robert Lansing

CCL (SDR, RG 59, 841.857 AR 1/91½B, DNA).

Dear Mr. President: Washington September 13, 1915

With reference to several conversations which the American Minister at Copenhagen has had with the Danish Minister for Foreign Affairs, concerning the proposed purchase of the Danish West Indies by this Government, I beg to transmit, herewith, a copy of a despatch dated August 18, 1915, giving the substance of the Minister's latest conversation with Mr. Scavenius regarding the matter.[1]

I remain, my dear Mr. President,

Very sincerely yours,   Robert Lansing

TLS (WP, DLC).

[1] M. F. Egan to RL, Aug. 18, 1915, TLS (SDR, RG 59, 711.5914/32, DNA), printed in *FR 1917*, pp. 593-95. Egan had once again sounded the Danish Foreign Minister on the possibility of the sale of the Danish West Indies to the United States. Scavenius had replied that, while it was "a rather delicate matter" to discuss during the present war, he believed that his government would consider seriously any offer which was financially "generous" and would give assurance that the black population of the islands would be treated "in the most kindly and liberal way." It was, however, up to the United States to submit a proposal; Denmark would not do so.

To Edith Bolling Galt

[The White House]

My precious Darling,   Monday morning, 9.50. 13 Sept., 1915

The weight of public matters rests rather grievously upon me this morning and I have been obliged to fill the morning with many important engagements,—beginning with the Secretary of State in half an hour,—but there is one resource for me always: I can turn to you (what would it not be worth to me if I could *go* to you!) and all the burden will fall away with the realization of your love and vital, comprehending sympathy. The Secretary of State and I will be obliged this morning, I fear, to make some decision that *may* affect the history of the country more than any decision a President and Secretary of State ever made before, and it gives me such a steadiness and added *balance* in my thinking that you have come to my side and put your hand in mine and given me your splendid life to sustain mine. Each day I know better, more fully than I knew the day before what your love means to me in strength and confidence and firmness of step. I did not sleep well last night; but in the middle of the night I got the first volume of Morley's *Life of Gladstone* and the tonic of sound thinking and acting I found there helped to take my thoughts off what was worrying me not only but brought the iron back into my blood. I had a most unexpected attack of pain (in my digestive organs) in the midst of my wakefulness, as has so often happened to me as the result of anxiety, and was in dire need of a loving visit from my Darling—the mere sight of her would have cured me—but I pulled through all right despite the loneliness and feel tolerably fit this morning.

And I am so deeply, deeply in love! I love you with a love that rules my life and *contains* it!

Your own   Woodrow

ALS (WP, DLC).

From Edith Bolling Galt

Dearest: [Washington] Sept 13, 1915

You left me last night with the feeling that you sternly disapproved of me and thought me willful—I am so sorry.

I did not take the ride! This is the day that you said would be full of grave anxiety for you—and that a word from me would help lighten the burden. I wish instead of a written word I could come and stand by you—ready to help in any and every way. Even if it is only to kiss your eyes and whisper I love you.

This is not an "s.m.s."[1] but it comes near being an s.m.h.[2] because I want to dispel any disappointment or disapproval I caused last night. Please don't worry about me in any way Dearest One. I am well and strong and love you so that I will try to give up my nocturnal rides if they cause you an anxious moment.

I do hope the German question will take a more hopeful color today. This is your lucky *thirteen*, so it is encouraging. And all through the day, Sweetheart remember I am with you in my thoughts

I have just had a note from Dr. Smith of St Thomas[3] in reply to mine.

I am answering it and will show you both when I see you. Randolph is better this morning, and all the Cordova family are coming to lunch with me.

I shall see you tonight, and it will be a queer sensation to be near you and yet so far. It will be as Browning puts it

The little more, and how much it is.

The little less, and what worlds away.[4]

Our love can bridge any distance Beloved and just to see you will be a joy.   Your own   Edith.

ALS (WP, DLC).

[1] Save My Soul?

[2] Save My Heart?

[3] That is, the Rev. Dr. Charles Ernest Smith, rector of St. Thomas's Episcopal Church in Washington. The note is C. E. Smith to EBG, Sept. 13, 1915, ALS (WP, DLC). Smith's letter was a response to a letter from Mrs. Galt saying that she was withdrawing from his church. He wrote that he thought that Mrs. Galt

did not want to tell him her reasons for leaving his church because she did not want to hurt his feelings. The tone of Smith's letter showed that he had been deeply hurt by Mrs. Galt's letter.

⁴ Robert Browning, "By the Fire-side," stanza XXXIX.

To Edith Bolling Galt

[The White House] Monday, 3.30 P.M. 13 Sept., 1915

No, no, my precious Darling, *not* "stern disapproval," or any kind of disapproval that involved *blame*: I understand you too perfectly for that; but just loving anxiety, about your personal safety from danger or any sort of insult, and, now that you are, alas! so much under observation, from misconstruction of any kind; and distress that you should ever find it easier to wander about at night instead of seeking sweet sleep that would preserve your bloom and your splendid vigour. I dread to think of my sweet One as so restless and unable to find peace and rest, with all the responsibilities she has to carry. I thought that that was what my love had brought her—peace and happy thoughts, and hoped that she would no longer have to run away from herself or from shadows or from *any*thing! That was my whole thought, my own precious Sweetheart. There was no disapproval, bless your sweet heart, but only deep, loving, tender solicitude. It's all love, Edith, my Darling. There's nothing else in my mind or heart for you. I am feeling all right this afternoon, tho. it seemed more prudent not to play golf in this intense heat. I've just been out buying you some golf sticks.

I want you to carry this to the theatre with you to-night as the message of utter love and trust and admiration   I want you to have [it] in your thoughts there to offset the pain of our seeing one another and yet being unable to speak a word of what is in our thoughts. I love you with my whole heart and thought, and your love has redeemed this anxious day for me. I could not live or work now without it. I saw Lansing this morning and we agreed to tell Bernstorff practically what Lansing had said to me in the letter you saw. L. has just telephoned me that he found B. very much disturbed, very "docile," and eager to do all in his power to bring his government to a different attitude. He is going to send me a full report of the conversation between them to-day (at noon) (the conversation was at noon) and I will send it to you, my precious Darling. I need the companionship of your mind and spirit every minute in this critical business, need it more and more every day of my life. Yes the 13th ought to be a lucky day for me, but it may be a very memorable day some time as we look back on this extraordinary crisis of the world.

What would I have done without the wonderful love you have given me,—and the delight in you which has brightened these months of my joy! You are all the world to me. There is perfect, unclouded love in my heart for you,—and there can be nothing else.   Your own   Woodrow

Your letter has made the day over for me.

ALS (WP, DLC).

From Oswald Garrison Villard

My dear Mr. President: Washington, D. C. Sept. 14, 1915.

It is because I thought that I detected a note of fatigue and discouragement in your little talk of yesterday to the Manassas delegation[1] that I want to send you this word. I sincerely hope that your wonderful patience and store of good will are not yet exhausted, and that you will be patient a little longer. I cannot believe that the great victory which seemed to have been won last week has been lost, or is going to be lost. The next ten days will, of course, show, but I have been so much encouraged by my talks with the Ambassador that I share his cheerful hopefulness and would like to pass some of it on to you. Of course, if he is wrong, we shall all be disillusionized shortly—and permanently, but meanwhile in this final trial I trust it will be of help to you to recall how many thousands of your fellow-citizens are sympathizing with you hourly and wishing you well and are most eager in their efforts to help you bear the burden. They are not impatient; they are quite ready to wait and they are certain that you will find a way out by that patience which to so many has recalled that of Lincoln.

Please do not trouble to answer this letter; it is merely a message of gratitude and sympathy from one who would like nothing better than to be of help to you in this fresh trial, if he could.
                    Faithfully yours,   Oswald Garrison Villard.

TLS (WP, DLC).
[1] A delegation of Virginians led by Congressman Charles Creighton Carlin called on Wilson on September 13 to ask him to visit Manassas Battlefield on September 30. Wilson declined on the ground that he could not leave his post in the present critical state of American foreign relations. "My thoughts are mortgaged beyond recall for the present," he said. "We are all hoping and praying that the skies may clear, but we have no control over that—on this side of the water—and it is impossible to predict any possible course of affairs." New York *World*, Sept. 14, 1915.

To Edith Bolling Galt

[The White House] Tuesday,
My precious Darling,   7.40 A.M. 14 Sept., 1915

What a delight it was to see you and to hear your voice last night! A tantalizing delight, of course, because I could not go to you in the theatre, as I longed to do, and because I could not speak my heart out to you over the telephone, but a vast deal better than nothing. You looked so lovely and were such good chums with Randolph, whom I envied and yet for whose sake I was glad. What must it not mean to him to have such a sister! When you smiled, Sweetheart, it seemed to me to fill the whole atmosphere of the theatre with sweetness,—for you were the only person in the room, for me,—the only person I *could* think about or wished to look at. I wonder if you were conscious of how intensely I *was* thinking of you and loving you? The play[1] really did not make any difference, except that it was silly and vulgar, and I hated to have anything vulgar associated with you *even in space*, particularly when its vulgarity touched some of the most sacred and beautiful things in the world. I did not have to think about the play, and did not think about it. I thought only of you, and the air of the place was pure. Bless your heart! You are a divinity who can bless and beautify any place or circumstance for me, by your mere presence, and I was deeply thankful for those two hours and a half during which I could look at you and feel that you were there. I wonder what you were thinking.

The Browns came last night, Darling, and Tumulty is back, but I *beg* that you will come to dinner to-night. I cannot see you alone, but we can make it one of the old *reading* evenings, if you would like that, and it will mean such a delight to me to have you here, part of the circle,—the whole of it, so far as I am concerned. You will come, wont you? It will mean so much to me to spend a few hours where you are, here in your own home where my heart waits and longs for you day and night, and every hour is empty that does not contain you.

Please, my own lovely, Darling, to cheer and sustain

Your own   Woodrow

[1] "The Only Girl," book by Henry Blossom, lyrics set to music by Victor Herbert, which had opened the Belasco Theatre's season. The play was about a young librettist (and a woman hater) who was working on a new play. He hears music coming through his window, sends for the player, and discovers that she is a girl. They agree to collaborate on "business terms." He, of course, falls in love with her.

To Edith Bolling Galt, with Enclosure

[The White House] 14 Sept. [1915]

The letter from Bernstorff is ominous of the worst. If his attitude towards the evidence of those on board the *Arabic* is what it seems to be, that will also in all likelihood be the attitude of his government, too, and they will stand by the wholly incredible statement of their submarine commander. What a *Prussian* letter Bernstorff's is! 　　　　　　　　　　W.

ALI (WP, DLC).

ENCLOSURE

Count Johann Heinrich von Bernstorff
to Edward Mandell House

My dear Colonel House: 　　　　　New York, September 11, 1915.

The press reports about the Arabic case are so allarming that I will have to go to Washington again, although Mr. Lansing has not yet expressed the wish to see me. If there is any truth to the newspaper reports, the situation looks very serious, and I will as "ultima ratio" have to try to see the President again. Now that we have accepted the principle for which the President is contending, our people at home would certainly not understand another sharp American note, and I am convinced that such a note would inevitably lead to war. It is all very well for the press to talk lightly about breaking off diplomatic relations. The newspapers should remember that diplomatic relations succeeded in bringing about an agreement on the principle and that as soon as they are broken off, every British ship will be torpedoed. It is only in deference to the United States that we limit our reprisal against England,—a reprisal which she most fully deserves for her unlawful and inhuman blockade.

As far as I can see, there is nothing in the Arabic incident now, but a question of conflicting evidence, and it would be terrible, if such a difference should bring about war after the question of principle has been settled. I have not seen the evidence against us and only know it by the newspapers. If it is not better than what the press gives us, it is very weak. A passenger never knows what the captain has back of his head. On the other hand, it is universally known, that the captains of British merchant vessels have received orders to destroy the German submarines whenever they can. One of them received the Victoria cross for being successful in doing so. If you look at the matter in this way, it seems much more probable that an English captain should have obeyed these orders, than that a German naval officer should have disobeyed his. German discipline is too well known to assume the latter possibility. The American press has never given us a square deal, but I have always hoped that the Government would. I still cling to this hope, although I am beginning to fear that I will be disappointed.

Yours very sincerely, J. Bernstorff

TLS (E. M. House Papers, CtY).

To Mary Allen Hulbert

Dearest Friend, [The White House] 14 September, 1915.

Only imperative things that I could not turn away from have prevented my reply sooner to your letters of September third and seventh. I know that you will understand and pardon. It gives me real pleasure to purchase the mortgages, and I am enclosing a draft on New York for seven thousand five hundred dollars. I did not know how to make the deductions Mr. Clark suggested, and of course did not care to. I hope with all my heart that your hopes about the new business will be realized in all their completeness; and it delights me to see that you are so happy in your new surroundings and your new work. It is fine. Your letters have a full ring in them.

You know by the papers all that I am doing, and of course a vast deal that I am not doing. You will know how to distinguish the true from the false. I am well; hope to have the family back from Cornish by the first of October (Helen is here now); and all goes as well as I have any right to expect in the midst of such world-wide anxieties and perplexities. It would be almost selfish to be free from deep cares when all the world is in travail.

Helen joins me in affectionate messages.

Your devoted friend, Woodrow Wilson

WWTLS (WP, DLC).

From Edith Bolling Galt

Dearest and Best: [Washington] Sept. 14, 1915 11:20 a.m.

Your note came to me at 9 just as I was starting to get Mother to take her down town, and I only lingered long enough to read it and then had to fly. My first idea was that perhaps 'twould be better not to come to dinner tonight—in spite of my longing to see you. But I have just come in and read your note again and have decided to come. You want me, and what does the rest of the world count? Bless your precious heart, how I long to sweep away all that troubles you and bring back days and weeks of refreshing absolution from care.

I could not say what I wanted to on the phone last night, but perhaps I will get a chance to whisper it to you to-night. Remind me to tell you the "germ of a great idea" (to quote from that horrid play) concerning a telephone.[1] Oh! there are so many things I want to tell you—they come up every day—and it will be such fun when I can run in and talk them over without waiting. You did not tell me how you are today, and it worries me

Don't play golf unless you are perfectly fit. Did you really mean you went to look at golf sticks for me? You precious person. I am afraid—in spite of the Browns and Mr. Tumulty[—]I will have to put my arms round you and tell you how I love you. But I will try not to be indiscreet   Always   Edith.

I must post this or it will not reach you.

ALS (WP, DLC).
[1] It was to run a private wire between her home and some private location in the White House.

To Lawrence Crane Woods

My dear Woods: The White House September 15, 1915

I am returning the Outlook article.[1] I have read it with a pain-ful sort of interest. It carries my thoughts back to the distress which constantly comes over me about the University and its whole tendency. Unfortunately, almost all of the article is true. I wish that it were not.

In haste

Cordially and sincerely yours,   Woodrow Wilson

TLS (WC, NjP).
[1] "The Confessions of an Undergraduate," *The Outlook*, CX (July 28, 1915), 711-14, enclosed in L. C. Woods to WW, Sept. 11, 1915, TLS (WP, DLC). The anonymous author (later revealed to be Thomas King Whipple, Princeton 1913) strongly criticized American colleges, declaring that they gave their graduates only an inability to work and a habit of conformist thinking. The inability to work grew out of a research-oriented faculty uninterested in teaching, the dis-tractions of extracurricular activities, and the "ridiculously small" amount of study necessary to graduate, even with honors. The conformist thinking came from the pressures to be taken into a desirable social club or fraternity. The author did have some favorable things to say about his intellectual development in college, but he concluded that most of it occurred in spite of the system rather than because of it.

To Robert Lansing

My dear Mr. Secretary,   The White House. 15 September, 1915.

Thank you for letting me see this letter.[1] I hope, with you, that the withdrawal of Dumba takes away the king pin from this structure of intrigue.   Faithfully Yours,   W.W.

WWTLI (SDR, RG 59, 701.6311/151½, DNA).
[1] See RL to WW (third letter of that date), Sept. 11, 1915, n. 1.

From Joseph Patrick Tumulty, with Enclosure

Dear Governor: The White House. September 15, 1915.

I had a very distressing talk with Craig of the New York HERALD last night. He informed me that the contents of your letter to the HERALD had been forwarded by cable to Mr. Bennett,[1] and that his dismissal as head of the HERALD Bureau in Washington would inevitably follow. I am satisfied from what Craig told me that he had no hand in the House yarn, and that perhaps a grave injustice will be done him. In a case of this kind which involves so much doubt, I know that you will move slowly before you take any final action which may cause the loss of Craig's position. I hope you will read this letter from Tom Pence.

                                    J.P.T.

TL (WP, DLC).
[1] James Gordon Bennett, proprietor of the *New York Herald*, who still lived in Paris.

ENCLOSURE

From Thomas Jones Pence

                                    Washington, D. C.
My dear Mr. President: September 15, 1915.

Mr. Joseph K. Ohl,[1] Managing Editor of the New York Herald, has acquainted me with the fact that you wrote the Editor of The Herald regarding the publication of the story attempting to show the existence of a breach between you and Colonel House. I learned from Mr. Ohl you are under the impression that Mr. Donald Craig, the head of The Herald Bureau in Washington, was responsible for the story.

I have investigated this matter and have ascertained that the publication appeared in several newspapers, and probably in more exaggerated form than in The Herald. Mr. Craig knew nothing of the yarn, which was originally handled by one of the young men in his office as a "cover" story. That is a newspaper shop expression, which related [relates] to the use of a story it is known other papers will print.

I know the publication of an invention like this gets on one's nerves, and I appreciate how you, with all your many worries must have felt about the publication of such a false article. I too, was indignant. I have no patience with a man who will invent and give circulation to a story of this kind, but I want to let you know that I do not believe Mr. Donald Craig, whom I have known for many years, would be capable of such an offense. He was not the author of the story that gave offense to Mr. McAdoo, and I think Mr. McAdoo was satisfied by the assurances made by Mr. Untermeyer and others that Mr. Craig bore him no ill will. I have worked with Mr. Craig and I know that he has nothing but admiration for you and your Administration, and I have heard him speak more than once in high praise of Mr. McAdoo. To my knowledge he has been fair in handling news stories with reference to you and the cause you represent. In fact, he has been a good friend on a number of occasions. I am sure you have obtained a wrong impression with regard to Mr. Craig, and under the circumstances I felt it my duty to trespass long enough upon your valuable time to give you this information.[2]

With every good wish, I beg to remain,

Sincerely your friend,   Thos J Pence

TLS (WP, DLC).
[1] Josiah Kingsley Ohl.
[2] Wilson conferred with Ohl and Craig at the White House at noon on September 17. It must have been a friendly meeting, for Craig retained his position.

From Robert Lansing

PERSONAL AND PRIVATE:

My dear Mr. President: Washington September 15, 1915.

I enclose copies of the papers which Mr. Naón drafted and which I think are pretty well done. The first is a resolution to be adopted by the Conference on Saturday,[1] and the second is a statement to be given to the Press.[2]

You of course appreciate what I said today, and that is the extreme desire of the Latin-American to be consistent with previous action, and I should have added the fact that they are not at all indifferent to publicity.

I would be pleased to have any comments which you may wish to make on these two documents.

Faithfully yours,   Robert Lansing

TLS (SDR, RG 59, 812.00/16989½A, DNA).

1 [R. S. Naón], T MS, n.d. (SDR, RG 59, 812.00/16989½A, DNA). The resolution stated that, in view of the inability of the Mexican factions to reach agreement on a provisional government, the diplomatic representatives participating in the conference on Mexico had agreed to recommend to their respective governments the recognition, "as soon as possible," of a *de facto* government in Mexico, provided that such government had "sprung from the independent and exclusive action of the Mexicans" and possessed the capacity to protect the lives and property of nationals and foreigners"; that each nation should be its own judge of what that *de facto* government was and should extend recognition whenever it deemed proper; and that the conferees would invite the "two principal factions in Mexico" to send representatives to confer separately with the Secretary of State and the other diplomats so that the latter might hear any statements that would be helpful to them in deciding on the recognition of a *de facto* government.

2 [R. S. Naón], T MS, n.d. (SDR, RG 59, 812.00/16989½A, DNA). This press release restated the resolution summarized above.

Aletta Henriette Jacobs to Jane Addams

Dear Miss Addams,   Moylan [Pa.], Sept. 15th, 1915

I saw the President at noon. I told him what I had to say and asked him the several questions. He was very kind and manlike as well as gentlemanlike. His answers were very diplomatique. In short it was: "The U. S. were now in such great difficulties with the belligerents that a definite answer in one way or another was impossible. The Pres. was very thankful for the informations I brought, but about his attitude towards peace he could not say a word. Every-day that attitude could be changed, according to the circumstances and even a quite unofficial statement in one way or another could bind him in a certain degree. He want to remain free to act in the best way as he sees the things himself." . . .

With my best wishes for your health,

Cordially yours   Aletta H. Jacobs.

ALS (J. Addams Papers, PSC).

To Lucy Marshall Smith

Dear Cousin Lucy,   The White House. 15 September, 1915.

Thank you with all my heart for your card. It made my heart warm to the core. I have thought, I cannot say how often, of you and dear Cousin Mary up there with the dear ones, and wished with all my heart that Helen and I could join the beloved circle. But things of many serious sorts hold me here, and Cornish seems like a paradise lost. My comfort is in the delightful expectation that you will come down with the others when October comes and that we shall have a delightful reunion here that will make up, for me, for the things I cannot have now. Unfortunately there is no present prospect of a clearing in this complicated German matter. Apparently they do not know how to keep faith with anybody, and we are walking on quicksand.

Helen seems well and content and sends lots and lots of love to you both and to all. I am well, and the only weight to business lies just now in its character rather than in its amount: it's the anxiety, not the labour, that gets under one's skin and hurts.

A telegram has just come from Stockton this morning, from Chicago, saying that he will be here on Thursday in time for dinner. Is not that jolly? We had not heard from him in months, and I had sent a telegram in search of him.

Colonel Ed. Brown was quite ill for about a week in New York. Grayson went up to him, and sent word to Mrs. Brown, who came on post haste from Ohio. But he pulled out all right (it seems to have been a touch of pneumonia), and both he and Mrs. Brown are now here. He is quite over the attack, but still feeling very weak and looking a bit pale and interesting. They will be here for several days,—I do not know exactly how long. Will it not be a pleasant surprise for Stock. to find Mrs. Brown here?

There is no news except public news, and Heaven forbid I should weight a letter of affection with that!

Bless you for your sweet thought of me. You don't know how it helps. Give my warmest love to Cousin Mary, keep as much for yourself, and tell the other dear ones that I long for them every day.   Affectionately Yours,   Woodrow Wilson

WWTLS (WC, NjP).

To Edith Bolling Galt

[The White House]
My precious Darling,   Wednesday, 15 Sept., 1915

What a delight it was to have you here last evening! It gave me the feeling (always lacking when you are not here) that this was *home*. And after our little talk alone, when you had put your dear arms about me and told me what you had been doing and thinking, and I had put into hurried words the need of my own heart for you, I was absolutely made over! All the ache had gone out of my mind that had been brought by the anxieties of the day, and my heart had been so comforted and exalted that I felt like a care-free boy. There's magic in your love, you adorable Darling. I *enjoy* you more and more the oftener I am with you;

and your sweet, tender, understanding love makes me too happy for words.

Dr Smith's letter, Sweetheart, gives you, it seems to me, an excellent opportunity and justification for letting the whole thing drop, as a piece of concluded business, about which there is nothing more to say. Summed up, what he says is this: If you state all there is that you care to say now, of course "let the subject, as you wish, be closed." If there has been any misunderstanding, or if you have been told anything that has given you offence, he would like a chance to explain, and feels confident he could explain; but, "if there be nothing of this kind, then the subject can be closed from this point of view also." There *has* been "nothing of this kind," therefore the subject is closed. If you were to write (as, I gather, he does not expect) it would be only to say that. Don't you think so? How sweet it is to have you make your affairs mine also, my adorable little partner. All these sweet intimacies make me very happy. And I was *so* glad you were so much pleased with the golf bag and clubs. Bless your heart, what a delight it is to give you any sort of pleasure! For the fact is I love you with all my heart, with an ever increasing tenderness and pride and delight. The more I see into your dear heart the more altogether lovely I find you.   Your own   Woodrow

ALS (WP, DLC).

Two Letters from Edith Bolling Galt

My precious One: [Washington] Sept. 15, 1915 9:40 a.m.

Did you feel my love all night as it poured out from the depths of my heart? And are you better today and ready to take up the great burden of affairs? My dear Lord, how perfectly radiant it makes me to feel that in this struggle I can be of help. Nothing could be sweeter than that knowledge, and you make me feel it so completely.

It was harder than ever to leave you last night, and I am counting the hours now until I can see you again and find out with my first look in your splendid eyes if things are going straight.

There was so much to talk about and the minutes flew so that I feel I did not say half I wanted to about your going out in the heat to get my golf sticks

They are such beauties and I will always have the tenderest association with them and feel when I hold them it is a real touch of your own dear hand. I ought to play much better with them than even your own clubs, and I am as pleased as a child with a toy. Don't you think you should keep that wonderful bag and give me your old one?

I feel like such a pig to take it but love you for wanting me to.

Old Mr. Wilson is coming in ten minutes so this is a flurry message as usual. I am wondering whether to mail it now or wait and add to it after he goes. I expect it will be a long session, so I had best send this along. I read Gardner's "President Wilson"[1] after I came home, and even he does not do you justice. Goodbye Precious. Please be well and happy and remember how I love you.   Edith

[1] Alfred George Gardiner, *The War Lords* (London, 1915), pp. 310-17. There is a copy of this book in the Wilson Library, DLC.

                                              [Washington] Wednesday,
My precious One,   2:45 [Sept. 15, 1915]

I have done the deed. I have told old Mr. Wilson! And if you could have seen the dear old man you would have loved him. I had not decided before he came just what I would do. But when he got here and was so distressed and worried over those awful newspaper things (that even upset me you remember) I thought it was wisest to tell him. And Sweetheart, he was so genuinely pleased that the years seemed to really fall away from him as he listened to all I said of you.

Had he been my own father he could not have been more tender, more happy for my happiness, or more concerned that everything should be made smooth—and nothing arise to block our days of happiness together.

It is too long to write you, but I will keep it fresh in my thoughts to tell you. He was so pleased when I told him I had let you see some of his letters and that you said he knew me through and through. He said, "Did he agree with my opinion of you?" and I said "Yes." To which he replied, "Well, if he knows you as I do, and thinks of you as I do, I have no further fear for your happiness"

I told him what sweet things you had said of him and that you wanted to know him, and his eyes lighted up with enthusiasm as he said, Well, I should be proud to know any man you loved, but this man's friendship would be unlike that of any other man in the history of this time. I then told him how impossible it was now for me to ask you both here to dinner to know each other, but I hoped some day to have that real happiness.

Then we talked over my business affairs, and he spoke of my

obligations etc. And I told him I had told you exactly the state of my affairs, and that until I could see my way clear to discharge personal obligations, I did not feel I could come to you.

He looked at me curiously a minute and said, "I felt perfectly sure you had done that. It is what I expected of you—and of course he respected your feeling—but thought it foolish pride, didn't he?" Then I told him just what you had said and his answer was, Well, I agree with him. This must not interfere, but we must find a way out. Then he stopped and thought a long time and finally said, "I am perfectly satisfied things are as they should be, and it seems too perfect to be a reality in this world—it seems more like a beautiful dream. And it is a dream I have had for months—that was beyond anything dear to me["]

ALS and AL (WP, DLC).

To Oswald Garrison Villard

Personal.

My dear Mr. Villard: The White House September 16, 1915

It was very gracious and thoughtful of you to write me your kind letter of September fourteenth and I appreciate it very deeply.

I must admit that I have at no time recently had any feeling of confidence that the German Government would sufficiently yield to our demands to clear the situation, but you may be sure I have not lost patience and that I shall give the matter abundant time for proof.

Of course, wear and tear are inevitable and the fatigue of this sort of anxiety is very great, but I am still quite fit, I am happy to say, and do not doubt that I shall have the strength to stick it all out.

Cordially and sincerely yours,   Woodrow Wilson

TLS (O. G. Villard Papers, MH).

From Franklin Knight Lane

Personal.

Dear Mr. President: Washington September 16, 1915.

I am a bit troubled about one or two things that Mr. Bryan said to me this afternoon at this office, and think probably that it is my duty to advise you of them.

The thing of most moment that he spoke of was his purpose to have Congress take up the question of passing a law forbidding Americans from sailing from either side of the water excepting on American ships, or from entering, even on American ships, within the war zone. I asked him if it would not be entirely satisfactory to him if Germany made good on the promise that Bernstorff volunteered. He said that was good as far as it went, but that it left too much to contingencies. His idea apparently was that the law should prohibit passengers sailing on foreign ships, and if they did, they did so at their own risk and that we would not be bound in any way to protect them or even protest against their being blown up. I pointed out to him the peril of such a question being raised in Congress, and his answer was quite characteristic—that it was better to have a blow-up in Congress than a war. I told him that it might lead to agitation for a declaration of war and counter agitation for an embargo on munitions, but all these things he regarded as of trivial importance. His one purpose, he said, was to insure in every way practicable against our being drawn into the war.

He spoke in very strong opposition to the proposed English and French loan of a billion dollars which the Allies are attempting to make here. This, he said, was furnishing money to the Allies with which to buy munitions to destroy their enemies. I should judge that he was quite willing to engage in agitation against any such flotation of bonds.

I asked him if he was going to Europe, and he said that he would give a hearing tomorrow to the representatives of foreign-speaking newspapers, and if he was convinced that he could in any way find out the terms upon which the nations would agree to peace, that he would go to Europe. My best guess is that he won't go, but if he felt that he could put England and France in the position of being unwilling to set terms of peace that he would think he had accomplished something. The burden than [then] would be upon them for continuing the war.

I spoke with gratification over the change in the public tone towards Secretary Daniels. He looked as if I had mentioned the name of one who had fallen from grace. He said "I am not so sure about Daniels." I think Daniels can make up his mind that if he favors any larger expenditure than that made this year for the Navy, that he is to be regarded as no better than a worshipper of Baal. As to Garrison, he is quite hopeless.

Faithfully yours,   F.K.L.

TLI (WP, DLC).

To Edith Bolling Galt

My precious Darling,

[The White House] Thursday,
7.05 A.M. 16 Sept., 1915

How sweetly you kept in touch with me yesterday, and how much it *helped* me all day long! Every day you show more fully that you know *how* to love and to help and my heart goes out to you in a gratitude and adoration that quicken every source of strength and confidence in me. I am so glad you told Mr. Wilson. Your account of the interview was not only delightful, it also filled me with a new affection and admiration for him. He sees so straight and feels so truly. You told him that you did not feel that you could come to me until you had discharged the personal obligations connected with your business, but you did not tell him that you had promised me that that feeling should not stand in the way of our happiness (a promise that has been the source of untold peace and confidence and security in my heart, my adorable Darling), and he said just what he ought to have said, that, knowing your spirited strength and independence as he does, that is exactly the feeling he would have expected you to have, but that the pride was a mistaken and foolish pride, and could not and should not come into competition with a love like ours. It was not necessary for you to tell him of the promise not to be guided by it: he knows your heart as well as he knows your splendid strength and he knows where it would render its chief allegiance; and he seems to have divined my own feeling exactly. How I should have loved to be present, unseen, at the interview: to love you for all that you said and to get the full taste of his fine quality! I can imagine just the sweet frankness and delicacy of it all on your part and (because you know so well how to give the spirit of a conversation in your account of it) just the glow and interest and affectionate solicitude and affection of the dear old man. He is my personal friend already and I am impatient for an opportunity to show him how truly and warmly I am his.

You will come to dinner Saturday night will you not, my Darling? I need you—I cannot do without you. When I see you to-night I will tell you some things about the Browns that will, I am sure, remove entirely any embarrassment or uneasiness you may have felt about them. The other day you wrote, "my first idea was that perhaps 'twould be better not to come to dinner to-night, in spite of my longing to see you" (bless you!) "but I have just come in and read your note again and have decided to come. You want me, and what does the rest of the world count?" Ah, my precious Love, you will never know what such sentences of self-forgetting love mean to me. For one thing, they mean your glorious self,—the most adorable, enchanting, and altogether satisfying lover in all the world. Indeed I do want you! I more than want you, I *need* you, sorely and all the while. That was an exquisite treasure of a little love letter that you wrote me yesterday morning, my Darling: it made all the weary day bright for me inside my heart. It is harder every day to live *between* messages and *between* meetings, and such words of love help so —*such* words,—such as apparently only you can write,—with magic in the simplest phrase! The vividness of you yourself seems to steal out upon the page through your pen,—a personality more wholly compact of charm and sweet power to stimulate and inspire and bless than any other in the whole realm of lovely women. And to think that it should have been given to me to make my life full and complete. Ah, Sweetheart, my heart is as full of thanksgiving as of longing. It is harder, much harder, to part each time we meet, but there is a sweet side to the hardness, for it means that we each time realize more fully than we ever did before how inseparably our hearts have become united, how deep and intimate and of the very essence of our lives our love for one another is, how we lose our sense of completeness and of unalloyed joy when we are separated from one another. It is proof of our growing love and mutual dependence. How wonderful you are, and how I adore and hourly long for you, my incomparable Darling.

Don't worry about my health. I am perfectly well again, and the serenity of heart your exquisite devoted love gives me will keep me so. When you are actually with me every day I think I shall probably be and look a boy again. I feel myself one whenever I am with you. You are my strength and delight.

Your own   Woodrow

I like the telephone idea.

ALS (WP, DLC).

From Edith Bolling Galt

You dear "Tiger":   [Washington] Sept 16, 1915 3:30 P.M.

I know you hate these cards but I am just sending it to tell you how I love you and what a lot of things I want to talk to you about tonight, and how I have kept you in my heart all these weary hours we have been away from each other. The golf balls are the first gift from a real *live* Tiger I have ever had, and I love him for them. Thank you Sweetheart for all your dear thoughts of me. I am so interested in the little note from dear *old* Miss Smith and like her already for what she says of you.

I agree with you about the memo.[1] I can't trust him. Apropos of this I will send you a letter I got from an old friend in N. Y. this morning—to let you see the "other fellows" point of view. I also had another long talk with Mr. W. this a.m. All my love & longing for 8:15 to come quickly.   Your own   E.

ALI (WP, DLC).
[1] The Editors know nothing about this matter. Perhaps it referred to her business affairs.

To Franklin Knight Lane

My dear Lane: [The White House] September 17, 1915

Thank you very warmly for your letter about your talk with Mr. Bryan. I cannot say that I am surprised because, after all, these are just the views which he expressed in Cabinet, but, of course, I am genuinely sorry that he intends to extend his agitation before Congress.

In haste   Faithfully yours,   Woodrow Wilson

TLS (Letterpress Books, WP, DLC).

To William Gibbs McAdoo

My dear Mac: The White House September 17, 1915

I did not realize you were off to your own house yesterday. We miss you very much.

I enclose a telegram from Senator Chamberlain[1] which I think makes it important that his misapprehensions should be corrected, or, rather, that he should be shown the real significance of this loan, namely, the maintenance of international exchanges whose breakdown would be absolutely disastrous to the United States. I wonder if you could not get the information conveyed to him without its seeming like an administration announcement in this matter with which we really have nothing to do?

Affectionately yours,   Woodrow Wilson

TLS (W. G. McAdoo Papers, DLC).
[1] It is missing in both the Wilson and McAdoo Papers in the Library of Congress. McAdoo's letter to Chamberlain is printed as an Enclosure with WGM to WW, Sept. 22, 1915.

From Lindley Miller Garrison

My dear Mr. President: Washington. September 17, 1915.

I herewith transmit to you two documents. One is the statement of military policy recommended by the War College Division of the General Staff.[1] The other is that which I recommend should be adopted and submitted to Congress for enactment.[2]

In the "Outline of Military Policy"[3] heretofore transmitted to you, I stated the cogent reasons which induced my conclusions, and of course shall not indulge in any useless repetition thereof.

In order that you may consider this whole question, properly enlightened, it is necessary for me to give you certain information.

The War Department, on its administrative side, in addition to the Secretary and his Assistant, has various Bureaus and Staff Departments; such as the Quartermaster General, in which is the commissary, transportation, and pay; the Ordnance Department; the Engineer Department; etc.

To assimilate our military administration with that of other countries in which this matter has been given great attention, there was, in 1903, added a General Staff. The avowed purpose of this legislation was to furnish to the Secretary of War a body of officers selected from the Army to study and report on various matters. This General Staff now consists by law of 34 officers, ranging in rank from captain to colonel, inclusive, with two officers of the grade of general and two officers of the grade of general attached as ex-officio. The two general officers first referred to are the Chief of Staff[4] and the Assistant Chief of Staff,[5] who is also the Chief of the Mobile Army Division of the General Staff.

I very much doubt whether the framers of this legislation and the advocates of its efficacy realized that in the countries from which they took their model there was a very large number, amounting into the thousands, of officers above the grade of colo-

---

[1] "STATEMENT OF A PROPER MILITARY POLICY FOR THE UNITED STATES: Prepared by the War College Division, General Staff Corps, In compliance with instructions of The Secretary of War, March, 1915," T memorandum (WP, DLC). This thirty-page document provided a detailed rationale for the recommendations which Garrison summarizes in the above letter. Appended to it was a one-page cost estimate, dated Sept. 11, 1915, and prepared by Brigadier General Montgomery Meigs Macomb, president of the Army War College, which Garrison also summarizes above.

[2] This document is missing but it was undoubtedly a version of what came to be known as the Garrison plan, which will be thoroughly documented in Vol. 35.

[3] See LMG to WW, Aug. 12, 1915, n. 1.

[4] General Hugh L. Scott.

[5] General Tasker H. Bliss.

nel whose experience and práctical knowledge as well as theoretical training well qualified them to perform certain functions which could not be expected to be similarly performed by a general staff which of necessity would be largely composed of officers of junior grades and which could not have on it more than three or four officers of the grade of general. I refer to this because, unless considered, there would be a natural disposition to place the same reliance upon recommendations from a general staff under all conditions, whereas in fact the conditions are so variant that such would not be the proper and considerate treatment of the matter.

For the study of the technical matters of military science, I consider our General Staff efficient, and that for that purpose it fully justifies itself; but I do not consider that a general staff, composed as ours of necessity must be, can be expected to furnish the wisdom, experience, accumulated theoretical information, and knowledge of practical matters, necessary to formulate, lay down and justify a military policy for the Nation.

The plan proposed by the War College Division of the General Staff, herewith submitted, calls in general, as will be seen, for a standing army aggregating 281,000 officers and men, at an annual cost the first year of $258,960,000, and of a continued annual cost thereafter of $249,973,000, in addition to which their plan calls for an expenditure for the National Guard of $7,000,000 annually, and for the continental or citizen army the first year of $87,500,000, with certain variants for the second and third years and a permanent annual appropriation thereafter of $62,500,000, in addition to which large sums would be required for the additional physical accommodations of the new army, the accumulation of the necessary reserve materiel and the necessary expenditure upon seacoast defenses and ammunition for its arm. So that, conservatively stated, the first year's annual expenditure for these purposes would consist of the following items:

Regular Army,	$258,960,000.00
National Guard,	7,000,000.00
Citizen Army,	87,500,000.00
Reserve materiel,	132,676,100.95
Total,	$486,136,100.95
To which must be added the requirements of the coast defense fortifications, of	20,000,000.00
Making a grand total of	$506,136,100.95

Under their plan of accumulation of reserve materiel, as set forth on page 22, there would be a constant increase of expense up until the eighth year, and thereafter there would be a reduction, but such reduction would still leave the annual appropriations for the Army surely over $325,000,000.

I do not feel the necessity of indulging in any extended statement of reasons as to why I could not adopt and submit with my approval to you or to Congress this plan.

I approached the consideration of the matter from the standpoint and in light of the considerations set forth in the "Outline of Military Policy" heretofore sent you. I actively worked with the assistance and cooperation of the Chief of Staff, General Scott; the Assistant Chief of Staff, General Bliss; the Assistant Secretary; and the various Bureau chiefs and Department heads above referred to. I kept in constant touch with the War College Division and held frequent conferences with representative members designated by them for the purpose. I was not able to concur in their final conclusions, and they apparently felt that their final conclusions expressed their views of what the situation required and of what they should respond as a statement of what was needed.

What I submit to you has the approval of the Chief of Staff, the Assistant Chief of Staff, the Assistant Secretary, and myself. I am convinced, without being properly authorized to specifically so state, that others of the general officers of the Army, both Bureau and Department heads and in the line, likewise favor the plan as proposed.

I feel convinced that if this plan, in substance, is adopted, a vitally important and meritorious step will have been taken in the right direction. I fear that if the other plan is put forward, so many obstacles will immediately arise as to chill, if not effectually destroy, any opportunity to obtain real progress.

With respect to considerable of the expense which it is necessary for us to incur, it must be realized that we are simply making up for the omissions of previous years. If this vitally important subject had been properly treated, there would from time to time have been additions of personnel and materiel, comparatively insignificant in cost but in the aggregate sufficient to have materially benefitted the situation and relieved us now of the necessity of supplying the omission and neglect thereof.

In conclusion, I again take the liberty of suggesting that as soon as you can properly do so, you make or authorize a statement of your general plan in substance. There is no one matter, in my judgment, which is so prominently in the minds of our best citizenship at this time as this one. They await your determination with respect thereto; and if, prior to the meeting of Congress, you have, in general and in substance, acquainted them with your conclusions, I think there will gather behind you and under your leadership the very best elements of our community, with the result that their representatives in Congress will enact their will into law.

Sincerely yours,   Lindley M. Garrison

TLS (WP, DLC).

To Edith Bolling Galt

[The White House] Friday,
My precious Darling,   7.15 A.M. 17 Sept., 1915

I am up early this morning (I have been up for about an hour) because when Helen and I came in last night I found several communications from the State Department which called for immediate attention, and there was nothing for it but to get the work on them done before office hours this morning. We found the Browns, Stockton Axson, Tumulty, and the doctor all out on the South Portico, talking and fighting mosquitoes, so we sat down with them and joined the pastime till midnight. Net result: a very brief night's sleep for your humble servant. But, though still sleepy, he is well and all right,—rejoiced to turn away from State Department matters to talk to you, his lovely Sweetheart. It is dreary to think that I shall not see you again until to-morrow evening, but it is churlish of me to grieve, with the magic of you last night still fresh upon me. It is nothing less than magic, the way you affect me: your irresistible charm, your fascinating tenderness, now playful, now deep as your dear wonderful heart! You are so exactly what I want you to be, only infinitely more delightful than I would have had the genius to originate if I could have had you made to fit into my heart and mind. It's absurd that you should ever be taken for anyone else! You are not in the least like anybody else. No one else in all the world is half so lovely as you are, or so altogether delightful. I do not know how I am going to *endure* waiting days and days for an evening alone with you: there are so many things to say, so many things to consult you about, so many sacred secrets of my heart waiting to be poured out to you. One reason why I appear constrained (as I fear I did for a little while last night) when we are together, but not alone, and can yet go a *little* way into the matters that are nearest our hearts—as we can when that darling Helen is with us—is that I cannot speak out what is really in my heart, and feel pent up and unnatural. But I am sure you understand: that is one of the wonderful gifts of your heart,—to see into mine and understand—understand at least this: that there is nothing in my heart but a passion of love for you, a longing for you that fills my whole life, and a purpose to make you happy which I am eager to put to the test of constant service. Ah, how I do love you!

Your own   Woodrow

ALS (WP, DLC).

From Edith Bolling Galt

Dearest One: [Washington] Sept. 17, 1915

We did have breakfast together this morning after all, for I found your big Envelope on my breakfast tray waiting for me when I emerged from my bath. I am *so* sorry you have had such an unrestful night and want you to try to get a little nap before lunch. It will set you up, and then if you go for a game after lunch come back in time to rest half an hour before dinner, and you will enjoy the Theatre.

How I wish I were there to see that all these directions were followed out. And to sit by you while you slept and make your waking radiant with my love. I knew last night you were discouraged and weary and that to talk (as we must talk with even Helen) was an effort. All the things I had wanted to say to you went unsaid, and I could only *play* when my heart was yearning to go deep into yours and touch and sooth the ache and longing there.

I know how Helen tries to fill and anticipate all your needs, and I love to feel you have her. She is so very generous and sweet to me.

I am sending back the paper about that Traitor with an Editorial from the Post this morning.[1] His impertinence passes understanding, and should he embark on even an American vessel for Europe and get blown up I would be the first one to beg our government not to insist upon indemnity from Germany, but to send the Commander of the Submarine our highest commendation and decoration. I suppose it is wrong to wish for such a deliverance but it would greatly strengthen my belief in eternal justice

As to the interview with Von B.,[2] I am speechless at his manifold plots and underhand dealings and know your splendid patience is strained to the breaking point.

Oh! Dearest how I want to help and serve you.

Do I make you feel how really splendid I know you are. Do I express the reverance, the pride, the deep adoration that is in my heart for all you are, and all you are giving to the world? I am afraid I seem like a thoughtless child sometimes but deep down, where no one but you can fathom there is profound tenderness and comprehension of all your need.

Last night, Randolph and I went right out for a ride, and as I passed 17th St. I met Robertson[3] with your car, so I was very close behind you. And I went 'round back of the White House and wondered if you knew I was only a few yards away and if you were in the study or your bed room. I did not think of the portico, for you usually don't care for that. We got some ice cream and brought it home and then tried the music to the "Only Girl" Randolph had gotten, so it was pretty late when I got to bed. But I did not get up until 8, so I am way ahead of you and feel perfectly rested. Mother & Bertha are coming to lunch and we may go to the matinee afterwards, and tonight you will probably see the same thing. Doesn't it seem queer that we are really so close and yet so utterly seperated at *times*. But there are *other times* that make these forgotten, and the future looms bright with the happiness of being together. Do as I ask about resting please and remember how I love you.

Your own Edith

ALS (WP, DLC).

[1] The enclosures are missing. However, the editorial was "Mr. Bryan and $10,000,000," *Washington Post*, Sept. 17, 1915, ridiculing a report that Henry Ford proposed "to turn over $10,000,000 to Mr. Bryan for the purpose of financing peace in Europe."

[2] Wilson had undoubtedly told Mrs. Galt that Bernstorff had requested an interview with him and that he, Wilson, had refused the request.

[3] She of course meant Robinson.

From Robert Lansing, with Enclosure

PERSONAL AND PRIVATE:

My dear Mr. President: New York City, September 18, 1915.

We have just finished the Mexican Conference, and I am sorry to say that we failed to carry out in full the program embodied in the Argentine Ambassador's Resolution which I sent to you. The failure was due to the Brazilian Ambassador who is apparently opposed to all the revolutionary factions in Mexico to the extent that he is unwilling to be in any way responsible for the recognition of any of them. I believe, however, that in case this Government determines to recognize a *de facto* government in Mexico he will advise his Government to follow our course.

The split came over notifying the representatives of the factions to meet us separately in conference. The Argentine Ambassador and the Ministers from Bolivia and Uruguay supported strongly the proposal. The Chilean Ambassador was not in entire accord but I believe would have submitted if da Gama had agreed. The Guatemalan, though he said nothing was evidently favorable.

As a consequence, we got no further than to agree to recommend to our respective Governments the recognition of a *de facto* Government in Mexico as soon as possible. I enclose for your information, copy of the agreement.

It was further understood that independently we should collect all the evidence we could as to the facts showing which Government in Mexico, on account of stability, was able to give adequate guarantees to perform its international obligations. It was recognized there were various sources of information as to these facts. I expressed the view that I thought the two principal factions should have the opportunity to present by personal representatives the reasons why one should be recognized over the other, and that I thought it might be well for me to invite the Chiefs of those factions to send such representatives to Washington, before our next conference in order that I might have an interview with them and with any other members of the Conference who desired to participate.

Since the Conference adjourned I have been thinking it might possibly be better to orally communicate with the representatives of the two factions already in this country, and ask them for an interview of this sort. In this way we would not get into difficulties which might arise if we formally addressed either Carranza or Villa. I told the Conference that I should have to submit the question of such interviews to you for your approval before I took such a step. If you approve the latter of these plans of obtaining the facts as to the situation in Mexico, I would suggest that Mr. Polk ask Arredondo and Llorente to come and see him, and to tell them that I desire to see them in about two weeks, in order that they could present their case for recognition to me orally and in writing. In case the more formal method is adopted, I think telegrams should be sent to the *de facto* Ministers of Foreign Affairs of Carranza and Villa, asking them to send delegates to meet me at the time I suggest. Meanwhile, I think we should telegraph our various Consuls in Mexico as to the exact situation in their localities.

I am disappointed, naturally, that the plan that we had agreed upon was not carrited [carried] through, but as it has failed, to an extent, I think we should follow out some such scheme as the one above proposed.

Faithfully yours,   Robert Lansing.

TLS (WP, DLC).

E N C L O S U R E

In view of the answers to the telegraphic appeal sent to the political and military chiefs of the factions struggling in Mexico, on the 11th of August last, the representatives who signed that appeal believe that the time has arrived to carry out the conclusion agreed upon in their last meeting in order to recommend to their respective Governments the recognition as soon as it will be possible of a Government in Mexico that shall have sprung from the independent and exclusive action of the Mexicans and that possess the material and moral capacity to protect the lives and property of nationals and foreigners.

T MS (WP, DLC).

To Edith Bolling Galt

[The White House]
Dearest,   Sat. afternoon 18 Sept., 1915
There is something, personal to myself, that I feel I must tell you about at once,[1] and I am going to take the extraordinary liberty of asking you if I may come to your house this evening at 8, instead of your coming here to dinner. You will understand when I have a chance to explain, and will, I believe, think even this extraordinary request justified, and yourself justified in granting it. I love you with the full, pure passion of my whole heart and *because* I love you beg this supreme favour.

With a heart too full for words.

Your own   Woodrow[2]

ALS (WP, DLC).
[1] See the entry from the House diary printed at Sept. 22, 1915. This is very important for understanding the immediate sequence of events.
[2] Wilson's handwriting reveals that he was in a state of great agitation.

Two Letters from Edith Bolling Galt

Dearest One: [Washington, Sept. 18, 1915]
Of course you can come to me, but what is the matter? I feel so worried that anything should trouble you. May I ask one thing

precious One—and that is that you ask Dr. Grayson to come up with you? I know he will have intuition enough not to stay, and it will look better if anyone should see you. And it is also a protection to you.

Don't think me foolish and know that my heart will wait for you and be made happy by your coming. Of course you have told Helen to make some excuse for my not coming to dinner. And if you think it better for me to tell her over the phone, ask her to make some excuse about telling me about the car, and call me, and then I will give some reason why I can't come.

Are you better and more rested bless your dear heart. What ever is troubling you, bring it to me and let me share it and try to help.   Your own, Edith

ALS (WP, DLC).

Dearest: [Washington] Sept. 19, 1915

The dawn has come, and the hideous dark of the hour before the dawn has been lost in the gracious gift of light

I have been in the big chair by the window, where I have fought out so many problems, and all the hurt, selfish feeling has gone with the darkness. And I now see straight—straight into the heart of things—and am ready to follow the road "where love leads"

How many times I have told you I wanted to help, and now when the first test has come I faltered. But the faltering was *for* love—not lack of love. I am not afraid of any gossip or threat, with your love as my shield. And even now this room echoes with your voice as you plead, "Stand by me," "Dont desert me!"

This is my pledge, Dearest One, I will stand by you—not for duty, not for pity, not for honor—but for love—trusting, protecting, comprehending Love. And no matter whether the wine be bitter or sweet we will share it together and find happiness in the comradship

Forgive my unreasonableness tonight (I mean last night, for it is already Sunday morning) and be willing to trust me.

I have not thought out what course we will follow for the immediate present, for I promised we would do that together.

I am so tired I could put my head down on the desk and go to sleep, but nothing could bring me real rest until I had pledged you my love and my allegiance   Your own   Edith.

ALS (WP, DLC).

Two Letters to Edith Bolling Galt

[The White House] Sunday,
My noble, incomparable Edith,   7.20 A.M. 19 Sept., 1915

I do not know how to express or analyze the conflicting emotions that have surged like a storm through my heart all night long. I only know that first and foremost in all my thoughts has been the glorious confirmation you gave me last night—without effort, unconsciously, as of course—of all I have ever thought of your mind and heart. You have the greatest soul, the noblest nature, the sweetest, most loving heart I have ever known, and my love, my reverence, my adoration for you, you have increased in one evening as I should have thought only a life-time of intimate, loving association could have increased them. You are more wonderful and lovely in my eyes than you ever were before; and my pride and joy and gratitude that you should love me with such a perfect love are beyond all expression, except in some great poem which I cannot write. But I am equally conscious that it is anything but pride and joy and gratitude or happiness that the evening brought you: that it brought you, instead of a confirmation of your ideal of me, an utter contradiction of it, dismay rather than happiness, uneasiness in the place of confident hope, —the love that is solicitude and pity, not admiration and happy trust,—and that intolerable thought has robbed me of sleep. When it was the deepest, most passionate desire of my heart to bring you happiness and sweep every shadow from your path, I have brought you, instead, mortification and thrown a new shadow about you. Surely no man was ever more deeply punished for a folly long ago loathed and repented of,[1]—but the bitterness of it ought not to fall on you, in the prime of your glorious, radiant womanhood, when you embody in their perfection, for all who know you, the beauty of purity and grace and sweet friendship and gracious, unselfish counsel. I am the most undeservedly honoured man in the world and your love, which I have least deserved, is the crowning honour of my life. I have tried, ah, *how* I have tried to expiate folly by disinterested service and honorable, self-forgetful, devoted love, and it has availed only to lead the loveliest, sweetest woman in all the world, for whom I would joyfully give my life, to mortification and dismay. May God forgive me as freely as he has punished me! *You* have forgiven me with a love that is divine, and that redeems me from everything but the bitterness of having disappointed you. For all but a little space I have tried for a whole laborious life-time of duty done to be worthy of such love; but the little space defeats the life-time and brings me to you stained and unworthy. I humbly sue for leave to love you, as one who has no right to sue, and yet I know all the time that I am offering you a love as pure, as deep, as void of selfishness and full of utter devotion as any man ever offered any woman, worthy even of your acceptance. I know I have no rights; but I also know that would break my heart and my life if I could not call you my Darling and myself

Your own   Woodrow

ALS (WP, DLC).

¹ The forthcoming study of Wilson's personality by Edwin A. Weinstein, M.D., will include a full analysis of Wilson's relationship with Mrs. Peck (Hulbert) and its impact upon him personally and politically. For other sensitive accounts, see John M. Mulder, *Woodrow Wilson: The Years of Preparation* (Princeton, N. J., 1978), pp. 246-50, 257-58, 261-63; and Frances W. Saunders, "Love and Guilt: Woodrow Wilson and Mary Hulbert," *American Heritage*, XXX (April/May 1979), 68-77.

[The White House] Sunday

My precious Darling,   9.10 A.M. 18 [19] Sept. [1915]

Thank God there is such a woman and such love in the world. Your note has just come and I could shout aloud for the joy and privilege of receiving such a pledge, conceived by such a heart. A nobler, more wonderful, more altogether lovely, loyal, adorable there could not be. I pray God may give me strength to love and serve you as you should be loved and served

Your own   Woodrow

ALS (WP, DLC).

From Robert Lansing

PERSONAL AND PRIVATE: Henderson Harbor, N. Y.

My dear Mr. President: September 19, 1915.

I see by the morning papers that Count von Bernstorff's statement that he now has charge of the negotiations is confirmed by press reports from Berlin. If that is so it may be necessary to see him shortly, if he so requests. In view of the fact that Gerard has not, as yet, had an audience of the Emperor I assume that you would not be willing to see the Ambassador. I am writing to advise you that it will not be an inconvenience for me to go from here to New York at any time to meet him, if you think advisable. I can leave here late at night and arrive in New York the next morning.   Faithfully yours,   Robert Lansing.

TLS (WP, DLC).

To Edward Mandell House

Dearest Friend,   The White House. 20 September, 1915.

Thank you with all my heart for your letters, and for the copies of Bernstorff's letters. He is a most extraordinary person. In his letters to you he [is] one person, in his interviews (particularly in his confidential interviews) with the newspaper men he is quite another. I wish I knew which, if either, is the genuine Bernstorff.

I wish with all my heart that this heat *would* pass. There are so many things which can be made clear only in conversation; and circumstances alter with each day, so that an interchange of letters seldom catches them in any kind of fixed condition.

Bernstorff is evidently anxious to get his government off from any explicit or formal disavowal of the Arabic offence; but I do not see how we can with self-respact do that. The country would consider us "too easy" for words, and any general avowal of a better purpose on their part utterly untrustworthy. Do you not think so?

They are moving with intentional, and most exasperating slowness in the whole matter. I fear that when they have gained the time they need, for example in the Balkans, they will resume their reckless operations at sea, and we shall be back of where we started.

The country is undoubtedly back of me in the whole matter, and *I* feel myself under bonds to it to show patience to the utmost. My chief puzzle is to determine where patience ceases to be a virtue.

Mr. Bryan is here, as you see, and is now seeking an interview with me. Since he can no longer be counted on to be scrupulous about the way in which he uses interviews, or any other material that comes to his hand, I greatly regret the necessity of seeing him.

I have not been feeling very well the last week or so, but am getting straightened out now, I believe. I have not been kept away from my work, but have done only what was necessary.

With the most impatient desire to see you,
                    Affectionately Yours,   Woodrow Wilson

WWTLS (E. M. House Papers, CtY).

To Herbert Clark Hoover

My dear Mr. Hoover: The White House September 20, 1915

It was a real pleasure to receive your letter of September third. I have for a long time wanted to express to you the great admiration with which I have followed the extraordinary work that you have been doing as chairman of the Commission for Relief in Belgium. It has been a work wonderfully done and my thought has followed you very constantly in it.

I warmly appreciate your thought of me as expressed in your letter and thank you for it from the bottom of my heart.

Cordially and sincerely yours,   Woodrow Wilson

P.S. Thank you also most sincerely for the report which you were thoughtful enough to send me.

TLS (H. Hoover Papers, CSt-H).

To Edith Bolling Galt

[The White House] Monday,
My precious Darling,   7.30 A.M. 20 Sept., 1915

I slept like a little child last night. I was just going to bed, as you were, when I called you on the telephone, and the sound of your dear voice was just the touch of love and home I needed to bring me complete rest of body and spirit. I ventured to say much more over the telephone than I had ever said before—my heart was so full, and had been all day—that I could not for the life of me have said less,—but, oh, the things I did *not* say that welled up in me when I felt your beloved presence at the other end of the wire—that I *cannot* say until I have you safe in my arms again, my blessed Darling! A new chapter has opened in our wonderful love story; the meaning of the whole thing has deepened; a new and greater happiness has come to me, and a more comprehending love,—a greater happiness, despite the poignant sorrow that underlies it, because a truer knowledge of the miracle of love that has been wrought for my redemption,—a more comprehending love because you have been revealed to me in your full beauty and nobility. I know you as I never knew you before—know you capable of love not merely, the sweetest love ever given by a woman to a man, but of *heroic* love, love that rises serene above suffering, perfect in its self-forgetfulness. You faltered only for a moment, my Darling, and I understood even in the midst of my pain; and when you did find yourself you found the most glorious woman in all the world, a woman capable of "trusting, protecting, comprehending love." I cannot even copy those words without tears of joy in my eyes. The other night a dry, dumb misery was upon me; tears would have taken the tense, terrible strain off my heart. But they did not come till I read that blessed note you wrote yesterday in the dawn,—and then they were tears of unspeakable joy and thanksgiving that sprang from the depths where my very life lies, hidden from all but you. Sweetheart, how shall I tell you what that note meant to me,—how shall I *ever* tell you except by a life-time of devotion? A more wonderful pledge of perfect love was never conceived or written: it is the very image of the heart I love beyond my life and everything that life has ever contained. It has brought me a happiness that exalts and strengthens and purifies. Deep and solemn as the meaning of this new chapter in our love is, it is the beginning of a new happiness for us, my Love, because of a new comprehension of our love and our comradeship. We can both say "no matter whether the wine be bitter or sweet, we will share it together and find happiness in the comradeship," and if we can say that we have said all. I shall put that little note written at dawn with the lines you wrote on the West Porch at Harlakenden as the most precious of all my possessions,—and how much more this new pledge means than the other—how much more *every*thing means now that your love is *perfectly* revealed to me, in all its depth and loveliness,— a "love that *passeth* the love of women." I feel that I am consecrating myself to the high endeavor of being in some sort worthy of such love when I sign myself, with love unspeakable,

Your own   Woodrow

ALS (WP, DLC).

From Edith Bolling Galt

[Washington] Sept. 20th, 1915 7:45 P.M.

This is just a little line to bring you my love and the tender wish for a *good* night. I will try to find those dear arms that you said would be waiting for me. And even, if in my darkness, I cannot find them, the thought that they are *there*, held out, will comfort and protect me. Oh! Woodrow I never wanted so to think only of myself, but I would not be worthy of your love if I did not think first for, and of you, and it is that which makes the way hard. Do you think it was easy to turn my back and leave you tonight, when everything that was feminine and meek cried out to go back and throw myself in your arms and give up the fight for reason and expedient [expediency]. It is so easy to yield to love—to be "reckless" as you put it. But I must not. We must both try to sleep and get back to normal and think only that this earthquake has left our love untouched and that we must rebuild our City of Dreams on such a firm foundation that no other can shake it—or cause the occupants to quake or tremble. I love your splendid defiant courage, but even that may not lead to the wise road. So, Sweetheart, with our hands close grasped and our hearts beating in perfect accord we must find the way.

You have promised to get another man's point of view, and I have promised to let things go on as before. This will steady us both and bring rest to our aching hearts, and we will wait until we have all the help we can get before we choose a course My eyes are queer and I can scarcely write but as soon as I can I am going to bed. Please try to sleep   Goodnight

Your own   Edith.

ALS (WP, DLC).

An Outline and Two Drafts of Statements[1]

[c. Sept. 20, 1915]

Analysis of the Statement.

Admission.

Even while it lasted I knew and made explicit what it *did not* mean.

It did not last, but friendship and genuine admiration ensued. Now.

❖

These letters disclose a passage of folly and gross impertinence in my life. I am deeply ashamed and repentant. Neither in act nor even in thought was the purity or honor of the lady concerned touched or sullied, and my offense she has generously forgiven. Neither was my utter allegiance to my incomparable wife in anyway by the least jot abated. She, too, knew and understood and has forgiven, little as I deserved the generous indulgence. But none of this lessens the blame or the deep humiliating grief and shame I suffer, that I should have so erred and forgotten the standards of honorable behavior by which I should have been bound.

I do not understand by what principle either of common honor or of Christianity the theft[2] and publication of these letters can be justified by those who have brought this humiliation upon me and this embarrassment upon the lady who is made also to suffer despite her entire innocence of all responsibility for the liberty I took. But they have been published, and a public man has always to remind himself that he owes it to those who have trusted him to make frank admission of so much as is true when such disclosures come, and attempt neither denial nor self-justification. When he alone is responsible, he must not shield himself. That the thing is past and gone, the offense repented of and forgiven, does not relieve him of the obligation.

❖

These letters are genuine, and I am now ashamed of them—not because the lady to whom they are addressed was not worthy of the most sincere admiration and affection, but because I did not have the moral right to offer her the ardent affection which they express. I am happy to remember that the only thing that at all relieves the pain and shame with which I now read these letters is the recollection that nothing associated with this correspondence could even in the least degree affect the honor of the noble lady to whom I then had the distinction and happiness to be married.

T transcripts (WC, NjP) of WWsh MSS (WP, DLC).
   1 The date assigned to the following documents is somewhat conjectural, but it seems likely that Wilson wrote them before or after writing the letter to Mrs. Galt that follows them. The shorthand, as the text illustration of Wilson's draft of the statement beginning "These letters," reproduced on pages 498 and 499, makes clear, reveals his high state of agitation.
   2 A nice way of exonerating Mrs. Hulbert from any blame.

To Edith Bolling Galt

Dearest,

[The White House] Tuesday,
7 A.M. 21 Sept., 1915

I slept last night because I had at last found my real self. As I look back I am amazed that I should have been so long about it. It was, I think, because my thoughts were going a round instead of going straight. That talk with you yesterday—which is now one of the many, many things, generous and true and dictated by love, that have made me your debtor for the vital forces of life itself—did me a double service: it gave me a new insight into your love and it brought to me the startling, humiliating discovery that I was allowing myself to be dominated by fear and the desire to conceal something which no doubt everybody who has trusted and believed in me probably has a right to know, unless I am to play the hypocrite. That discovery set me free. I had not realized the real situation. I had looked at every other aspect of it except that, that I had [been] acting the part

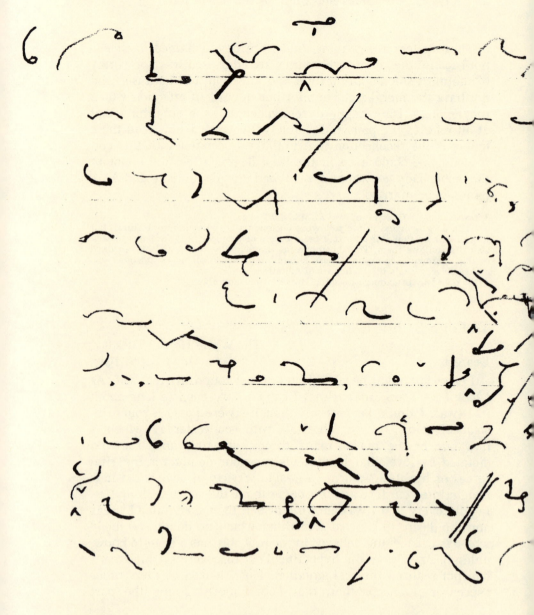

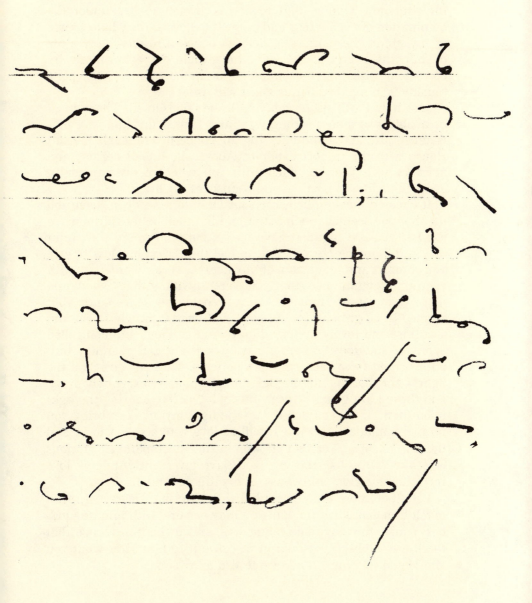

of coward. To realize that was an instant emancipation. I am not a coward,—that's the one thing about myself that I am certain of and have proved—and it's no great boast at best! I am mortified that I should have played the part. And now that I see straight I shall take steps to show what I really am. I suppose I dreaded the revelation which seemed to be threatened because I knew that it would give a tragically false impression of what I really have been and am,—because it might make the contemptible error and madness of a few months seem a stain upon a whole life. But now I know that to permit myself to live under the domination of such a fear and allow it to govern the whole course of my life in the matters of deepest concern to me—deprive me of happiness and peace of mind—would be even more inconsistent with my true character than the offence itself. The remedy is in my own hands and I will use it.

Just how I will use it remains to be determined. There must be a right way and a wrong way, and I must find the way that is most just and honorable for all concerned. I shall consult House with the utmost candour. Above all, I shall consult and at every turn keep in touch with you who are my partner in every thought and purpose and counsel of my life.

It cheered me so much, precious One, to have dear Helen tell me that you seemed much better and in much better spirits when she left you last night. It gave me untold pain to see you suffer as you did during our talk and to feel that I was helpless to give you comfort and relief, though my heart was fairly breaking with yearning, longing love—that you were unwilling that I should do more than sit in front of you and hold the dear hands that seemed to be groping for support. You were infinitely sweet and steadfast and lovely in your dignity and candour and controlled agony of emotion. You are always wonderful and adorable. But, oh, it would have been so much better if you had "given up the fight,"—for there is nothing left to fight against except shadows, and those I am going to sweep away by merely pouring the light upon them. Until you do give up the fight my love can bring you no real happiness and joy. It will be love with a shiver in it; and there is no place for fear in wonderful, incomparable, glorious love like yours, like the love you have given me. And my love for you is the glory and power of my life. It *is* my life!

I shall do more than be cordial with Grayson, Dearest; I mean to tell him candidly (though, you may be sure, with infinite kindness) just what my real feeling was, and make him realize that there was nothing personal in it. I owe it to him after what you and Helen told him;—and owe it also to myself.

Ah, Sweetheart, it is hard to sit here and write with my heart full of you without knowing how the night went with you or what your thoughts and wishes are this morning. Have you found solid foundations for our "House of Dreams"? *Not* of *dreams*, my Darling, but of life, of reality, of blessed love—"trusting, protecting, comprehending" and joyous love,—joyous because without fear or bounds or questions of any kind.

Your own   Woodrow

ALS (WP, DLC).

Two Letters from Edith Bolling Galt

Dearest: [Washington] Sept. 21, 1915 12:30 M.

I had to go out so early with Mother this morning I did not have time to tell you of the night. I got to bed a little before one and went to sleep almost at once and did not move until five minutes after seven! That tells the story Sweetheart, and I will only add—I love you   Your own   Edith.

I do hope you will go out for a game this afternoon and that you took the walk, as you promised, last night

Our ride was so lovely, but your absence made even the beauty of the night unsatisfying

Dearest One: [Washington] Midnight, Sept 21 & 22/1915

Did you ever know a more inconsistent bundle of complexities than I? It is just an hour since I left you, and my heart is aching to come back and do away with all the pain I caused. Oh! Sweetheart I was too much of a coward to tell you the cause of my unhappiness because I could not bear to see the pain it would bring to your loved eyes. But I think it is better to tell you that it *is* the awful earthquake of Saturday night that has caused doubt of the *certainty* of anything.

I don't mean doubt of *you* (nothing is farther from my thoughts) but doubt of the permanent fixedness of happiness.

I have been so blindly happy these past weeks since I came home and found you that I have not felt one of the old misgivings, but just the exquisite luxury of loving and being loved, when, in the midst of this radiance, fell like a rocket from the unseen hand of an enemy the blow from which I am still staggering

It seemed to shut out the sun for a little space, and then the shadow lifted. Love was still on the throne, but pale and bleeding trying to smile through his tears and say the blow did not really hurt.

It hurts so that I am ashamed to confess it even to you, and the only ease it finds is in *pretending* it doesn't hurt. Of course it shows how blindly I loved you that I thought nothing could ever have touched you of the clay of which I am made.

Just as you said tonight of the proud joy one feels in just the association with and appreciating of beautiful things, so I felt about you—that you were so fine I could breath[e] better in your atmosphere, that the very air was charged with purity and that this heart of gold had been given into my keeping. It is, I know, far better that I should have been awakened from this dream of, almost, idoletry and made to look at the unreality of such a possible finite being. But it takes time to readjust such things and Love can do any miracle

So we will trust Love to lead us and help me to a new and stronger knowledge of all the greatness and sweetness of your heart, and make me forget the *super*man my love created in the vital, tender, *normal* man in my precious Woodrow.

I mean this as a confession of faith in you Dearest—faith that your *love* is all and more than I could ever create—but that I had thought the human tenement was as perfect as your love for me. And now I know the truer proportion of things.

When I get this fixed in my heart, as it already is fixed in my mind there will be no more "torture" for either of us, and the ocean of our love will be untroubled in its depths. Help me as only you can, and I will not turn away or sit idle, but will walk in the light and know at last my City of Dreams is founded upon the rock.

Goodnight—and may the day dawn on us with no shadow between.

I love you, and I want you to bring me back out of the shadow into the light of fearless certainty.

Always your own   Edith.

ALS (WP, DLC).

To Edward Mandell House

The White House Sept 22d 1915

Delighted you are coming Shall hope and expect to bring you directly to us

Woodrow Wilson

Hw telegram (E. M. House Papers, CtY).

To Robert Lansing

My dear Mr. Secretary: The White House September 22,1915

I have your letter of September nineteenth about your willingness to run down to New York to see Count von Bernstorff if it should become necessary and greatly appreciate it. I hope with all my heart that you are getting a refreshing rest and the sort of recreation that takes one's mind off heavy responsibilities.

Cordially and faithfully yours,   Woodrow Wilson

TLS (SDR, RG 59, 763.72/2174½, DNA).

To Frank Lyon Polk

My dear Mr. Polk,   The White House. 22 September, 1915.

May I suggest the following as a message to Penfield? It is along the line of your own.

Please explain to the Minister for Foreign Affairs that there were only two courses open to this government in the case of Dr. Dumba, either to hand him his passports or to request his recall. It chose the latter course as the more considerate. The fact is that Dr. Dumba is persona non grata. His immediate recall does not imply condemnation of him by the Austro-Hungarian Government but only his unacceptability to this government, and we are at a loss to understand why a report from him should be awaited. In the circumstances we can only repeat the request of this government that Dr. Dumba be recalled immediately.[1]

I hope that this form will seem to you a full expression of our meeting.   Faithfully Yours,   W.W.

WWTLI (F. L. Polk Papers, CtY).
[1] Dumba was recalled on September 24, 1915.

From William Gibbs McAdoo, with Enclosure

Dear Mr. President: Washington September 22, 1915.

I beg to hand you herewith copy of a letter I have just sent to Senator Chamberlain in reply to his telegram to you of the 15th instant.   Faithfully yours,   W G McAdoo

TLS (WP, DLC).

William Gibbs McAdoo to George Earle Chamberlain

Dear Senator: [Washington] September 22, 1915.

The President has sent me your telegram of the 15th instant, because it relates to finance. The Government has no power to interfere with the negotiations now going on between representatives of foreign governments and bankers in New York. The proposed arrangements relate, as I understand it, to the establishment of credits in this country for the purpose of facilitating and financing the purchase of supplies and commodities from our people. The arrangements, if made, will be with bankers and private citizens of the United States, just as the supplies and commodities will be purchased from private citizens of the United States. The Government has no power to prevent national banks from extending credits or making loans permitted by the national banking laws, and of course it has no power to interfere with loans made by private individuals or corporations not under its jurisdiction.

Perhaps you may remember that the French government and the German government each made a public offering last spring of their short-time obligations in this country and sold large amounts of them to our people, and that no objections were raised thereto.

Believe me, with kind regards,

Sincerely yours,   [W G McAdoo]

CCL (WP, DLC).

From William Phillips

Dear Mr. President: Washington September 22, 1915.

The Secretary asks me to take up with you the appointment of a new Minister to Liberia, to succeed Mr. George Washington Buckner who has recently resigned.

The principal candidate for the position is Mr. James L. Curtis, colored, attorney and counselor at law, 5 Beekman Street, New York City, who has the endorsement of Senator O'Gorman and Senator Kern, and more especially of Bishop Alexander Walters of the African Methodist Episcopal Zion Church. Bishop Walters has been to see me several times, has introduced Mr.

Curtis to me, and has given me the following brief synopsis of Mr. Curtis's career:

Born Raleigh, N. C., July 8, 1870; graduated from Lincoln University, Pennsylvania, 1889 with first honors; graduated from Northwestern University Law School, 1893, as honor man of his class; engaged in practice of law in Chicago, Minneapolis, and New York since 1893. Member of Bethel A.M.E. Church, New York, and member of Board of Managers, Colored Branch of the Y.M.C.A.

As of possible interest I am enclosing copies of endorsements of Mr. Curtis which have been filed with Senator O'Gorman.[1]

I should be glad to know whether you have anyone in mind to fill the vacancy created by the resignation of Mr. Buckner, and if not, whether you desire to consider the appointment of Mr. Curtis.

With assurances of respect, etc., I am, my dear Mr. President,
Faithfully yours,   William Phillips

TLS (WP, DLC).
1 These enclosures are missing.

From the Diary of Colonel House

[Roslyn, L. I.] September 22, 1915.

The weather has turned cool and I sent the President a telegram last night saying I would go to Washington today. I saw Grayson before leaving. He was much disturbed over the situation in Washington. He described both the President and McAdoo as terribly upset because of their personal affairs. The President is anxious to have his engagement announced and is waiting for me to come in order to discuss it with me. Grayson says it is clearly up to me to decide this question.

When the German Ambassador asked for an interview I replied that I could give him not more than ten minutes and that he must come at once. The interview with him was short, but full of interest. He had received instructions from his Government that in future no passenger ships would be torpedoed without warning and *that the benefit of the doubt would be given the ship.*

He said the question of disavowal was more difficult, that they did not want to make one, but were willing to agree to leave the matter to an international commission to sit at the Hague, and they would abide by any decision this commission might make. I promised to take the matter up with the President and would let him know when I returned from Washington. . . .[1]

Washington [Sept. 22, 1915].

I had a pleasant and restful trip to Washington. I was met by a White House carriage and driven there. The President was playing golf and I therefore went to the Treasury to talk with McAdoo. He was terribly concerned about the President's private affairs which he knew nothing of excepting by inference, but which the President told me of in the evening and of which I will write later.

The President and I went into his study after his return a little after six o'clock and remained for an hour. We first discussed the message which Bernstorff had sent him through me. He thought it would be difficult to satisfy our people without some sort of disavowal and it was agreed that I should tell Bernstorff this and try to work out something that would be satisfactory.

Much to my surprise, he said he had never been sure that we ought not to take part in the conflict and if it seemed evident that Germany and her militiristic ideas were to win, the obligation upon us was greater than ever. We discussed this situation at great length, I telling him something in detail of the mistakes I thought the Allies had made and which might easily have been avoided. There was one thing I thought particularly unfortunate and that was in not having a strong man at the head of the British Government. Asquith has ability, but he lacks force. The President remarked that this seemed to be true of all the other belligerents. I thought Sir Edward Grey had made a mistake in not bringing the personel of the British Diplomatic Corps to a higher level. I believe he has followed the same course in the Balkans as he has here, but the result has been more disastrous.

We dined at 7.15. The others present were Miss Bones, Colonel Brown, who is a relative from Georgia, and Dr. Axson, a brother-in-law. Almost immediately after dinner we went to the study and resumed our conversation which continued until ten o'clock.

The President at once took up his most intimate personal affairs. I could see he did it with reluctance, but with a determination to have it over. It showed remarkable courage, in which he is not lacking. He said many years ago the family had met at

[1] Bernstorff's report of this conversation was conveyed in J. H. von Bernstorff to the Foreign Office, Sept. 22, 1915, T telegram (Weltkrieg, Unterseebootkrieg gegen England, ganz geheim, Vol. 13, p. 54, GFO-Ar).

Bermuda a lady who was then Mrs. Peck. He had gotten to know her quite well. That there had never been anything between them excepting a platonic friendship, though afterward he had been indiscreet in writing her letters rather more warmly than was prudent. He understood there was much talk about his friendship with her and he wanted me to know the whole story.

He said quite recently her son had gone into business in Southern California raising fruit, and that Mrs. Peck, who is now Mrs. Hurlburt, wrote him, the President, saying as they were in need of money she had been trying to sell some mortgages which they owned but had been unsuccessful. The President of his own volition and without being asked, offered to take up these mortgages. They amounted to $15,000.00.

Stories have been rife concerning Mrs. Hurlburt and the President for many years, just as stories are always rife concerning public men. McAdoo knowing of these rumors, and having heard that the President had sent Mrs. Hurlburt $15,000, was very much disturbed, and in trying to find some way by which he could get the President to discuss it with him, told the President he had received an anonymous letter from Los Angeles saying Mrs. Hurlburt was showing his letters and was doing him much harm. The President did not respond to McAdoo's bait and he does not know now that the anonymous letter was not genuine. However, he spoke to me about it with the greatest concern, telling me it was contrary to his idea of Mrs. Hurlburt and that he thought she must have fallen under some evil influence. He did not know that I knew the entire story both of the money having been sent and of the anonymous letter, and in order to protect McAdoo I could not explain.

I advised him not to worry about it, for I was sure she was not showing his letters or attempting in any way to blackmail him. He showed me some of her letters so as to give me an idea of their tone. I was more convinced than ever that McAdoo was entirely wrong and that no trouble was brewing.

I have never seen a man more relieved when I gave him this assurance. To illustrate how honest he is, he had told Mrs. Galt every detail concerning the matter. He expressed the desire, if any trouble were to come to him because of this indiscretion, he would like it to come now, and he would not, in any circumstances, allow anyone to blackmail him. They might publish if they pleased every letter he had ever written, and that while he might be humiliated in spirit, yet that would be preferable to having a sword continually hanging over his neck. He has shown throughout a splendid courage. Taking his exalted position, his past career, his present and his future, it makes the courage the more notable.

When McAdoo told me what he had done about the anonymous letter, I did not realize what a cruel thing it was to do.

We then discussed his prospective marriage, the time the announcement should be made, the character of the wedding, and many other details. The decision was placed squarely up to me and upon my shoulders the responsibility was set. I accepted it cheerfully as I always do where a friend such as Woodrow Wilson seeks my advice. We tentatively agreed upon the middle of October for the announcement and for the wedding to follow before the turn of the year.

I wish to explain here while I am upon this extremely delicate subject that I believe the President's affection for Mrs. Wilson has not lessened. I have never seen a man more dependent upon a woman's companionship. He was perfectly happy and contented with his wife. They had an ideal married life, as all her relatives will readily testify and have, indeed, to me. But his loneliness since her death has oppressed him, and if he does not marry, and marry quickly, I believe he will go into a decline. Dr. Grayson shares this belief. None of his family are with him, and his loneliness is pathetic. With the weight of the burdens upon him, it seems but a small concession which public opinion might make in behalf of this man not to criticize him too much for doing what one in a humbler station of life would be able to do without comment.

We went to bed at eleven o'clock and I could see that I had lifted a load from him.

T MS (E. M. House Papers, CtY).

To Edith Bolling Galt

[The White House]
Wednesday, 7 A.M. 22 Sept., 1915

I love you, my Darling, love you, the incomparable lady of my dreams,—love you with a pure, chivalrous, trusting, protecting, comprehending love, in which there is no fear, but only eagerness and joy, and to which there is no limit but the powers of life itself. I need you,—your sweet presence, your direct help in everything, big or little, your counsel, your confiding, intimate love,— at every turn of every hour, and am desolate and robbed of the best part of my strength whenever I must face the world without you. I long for you with a longing in which everything that is finest and best in me speaks with the passion of my whole life. At any moment you need me, at any place you need me, in what-ever way you need me, great or trivial, for joy or for comfort or for heart's ease, merely for pleasure or for the deepest uses of your spirit, I am always and altogether

Your own   Woodrow[1]

ALS (WP, DLC).
[1] There is a WWT draft of this letter in WP, DLC.

From Edith Bolling Galt

Dearest: [Washington] Sept. 22, 1915

Helen and I have just come back from our game, and it is the first time I have used my clubs—and they are *such* splendid light ones. Of course I did not play well, but my equipment was an untold joy, and I mean to work up to its standard in my game. It was such a wonderful morning and I so wished you were with us. I don't suppose I would ever have hit the ball, if you had been —but what fun to have you laugh at me.

We will go together sometime, and I hope you won't then be ashamed of me. Do go out this afternoon after you get through with that Traitor, for you will need fresh pure air in your lungs after being with him, and I only hope he will not bring you any new problems.

As you see my hand is so tired I can hardly write, so this is just a message of love—to nestle close to your heart and tell you how I miss and want you.

Helen says Col. House will be here tonight. Please let him help you in every possible way. And remember we are both strong enough to do the *right* thing—no matter what it costs. I wrote you for an hour after coming home last night, but decided not to send it this morning. The mood has passed, and when I come again you will find a new spirit—more at ease and less "imperious." Thank you for your dear note and all its tender manifestations. You have the wonderful faculty of making me *feel* your love, and it eases all the pain in my heart.

Always your own,   Edith

ALS (WP, DLC).

From the Diary of Colonel House

September 23, 1915.

We breakfasted at eight. After breakfast Tumulty talked to me for nearly an hour. The President rescued me and took me up to his study. We discussed Mexico. He laughingly said that Carranza had once or twice put it over us and in a very skillful way. He thought when the A.B.C. Conference resumed on the 8th of October we would perhaps have to recognize Carranza. We were both of the opinion that General Obregon was responsible for the accelerated fortunes of Carranza and that he would perhaps finally turn out to be the "man of the hour" in Mexico. We agreed if Carranza was to be recognized, he must first guarantee religious freedom, give amnesty for all political offenses, institute the land reforms which had been promised, give protection to foreigners, and recognize their just claims.

To Edith Bolling Galt

[The White House] Thursday,
My precious Love,   7 A.M. 23 Sept., 1915

I had a *fine* talk with House last night, which cleared things wonderfully, and I am *so* glad I am to have a little while with you before lunch to tell you about it. It would be most unsatisfactory to write it, because it needs to be discussed. He is really a wonderful counsellor. His mind is like an excellent clearing house through which to put one's ideas and get the right credits and balances. I am sure that the first real conversation you have with him, about something definite and of the stuff of judgment, you will lose entirely your impression that he lacks strength. It is quiet, serene strength, but it is great and real. I am impatient to have you know him,—and still more impatient to tell you what he said last night, after I had purposely laid our problem before him in the baldest way, as if it were a question of business or of politics, and not of the heart at all. I wanted a perfectly cool-blooded judgment and I'm sure I got it.

How empty the day was without you, my precious Darling— how empty all days are without you, and how hard! And yet yesterday was full enough of interesting happenings. I had a call from Mr. Ford—*the* Mr. Ford—who is a friend of ours politically and who is going to help us study the motors in our submarines. I amused myself talking ideas to him—in the vein of that essay of Gardiner's on Bernhardi[1]—and observing how ideas took no root in his mind, which did not stir till you gave it a fact. And then came W.J.B. (yclept "The Traitor," by a lovely lady I know and love—and love partly for the enemies she makes, for herself). It was a most surprising interview. It seemed to have no definite object. He was perfectly natural and at ease,—as I was, too, for that matter. It was as if he was still in the cabinet and, without having any particular piece of business to lay before me, had dropped in to tell me what he was thinking about and learn what I was thinking about. He had the air of one who feels himself at home and a member of the family. It was amusing and amazing. We spent a third of the time, I should say, telling stories and discussing matters that had no connection whatever with public affairs. I need not tell you that when politics became the subject of conversation, he got nothing out of me whatever except what all the world already knew. He looked extraordinarily well and seemed quite happy. I cannot, I am glad to say, understand such a person

Ah, how it thrills me, my Sweetheart, to think that in a few hours I am going to see you. My heart follows you every moment of the day and *lives in you*. I love you beyond all measures of word or thought. I am *so* glad the golf clubs are so satisfactory. I wish that every time you touch one of them you might feel the warmth and depth of the love with which they were chosen for your use and I like to think of any gift of mine held close in your dear hands and made use of for your pleasure. How I shall envy Col. Brown all morning—and what fun we shall have in the sweet days to come playing together. Bless you for wishing for me and missing me. I long for you with a longing as deep and as constant as the life in me, with a love and longing that *are* my life.

Your own   Woodrow

ALS (WP, DLC).
[1] Gardiner, *The War Lords*, pp. 248-67.

To William Phillips

My dear Mr. Phillips: The White House September 24, 1915

My own inclination would be to appoint Bishop Alexander Walters himself to the post in Liberia if he were willing to accept it.

I, of course, know nothing about Mr. James L. Curtis but would be perfectly willing to consider his appointment if you and the Secretary think that my idea about Walters is not wise or practicable.[1]

Always   Faithfully yours,   Woodrow Wilson

TLS (SDR, Applications and Appointments File, DNA).
[1] Curtis was appointed on October 25, 1915.

To William Gibbs McAdoo

My dear Mr. Secretary: [The White House] September 24, 1915

Thank you sincerely for the copy of the letter you recently addressed to Senator Chamberlain. It seems to me to meet the case admirably.

Always   Faithfully yours,   Woodrow Wilson

TLS (Letterpress Books, WP, DLC).

To Samuel Gompers

My dear Mr. Gompers: The White House September 24, 1915

I have read your letter of September twenty-second with close attention and a great deal of interest, and realize the force of what it urges.[1] I, moreover, have the greatest respect for your own personal judgment in matters to which you have devoted your attention. I can only say in reply to your letter that it will form a valuable part of my thought with regard to a very perplexing matter, and I hope sincerely that we are near a solution of the difficulties of our relationship with Mexico.

Cordially and sincerely yours, Woodrow Wilson

TLS (photostat in RSB Coll., DLC).
  [1] S. Gompers to WW, Sept. 22, 1915, TLS (WP, DLC), urging, on behalf of the executive council of the American Federation of Labor, that Wilson recognize Carranza, whom Gompers regarded as a champion of the Mexican working people.

To Ellison DuRant Smith

My dear Senator: [The White House] September 24, 1915

I thank you sincerely for the frank expression of opinion and advice contained in your letter of September twenty-first.[1] I fear that there is a great deal of weight in what you say. Indeed, it has been very much in my mind from the first. My thought was that the whole business of the next session will be embarrassed and delayed and perhaps thrown out of gear if the rules of the Senate were not altered or if the time of the regular session were taken up in the attempt to alter them, and I was inclined to think, though I had reached no conclusion in the matter, that it was best to risk a good deal to effect so desirable and, indeed, imperative an object.

Cordially and sincerely yours,   Woodrow Wilson

TLS (Letterpress Books, WP, DLC).
  [1] It is missing.

From the Diary of Colonel House

September 24, 1915.

We breakfasted at eight as usual. The President and I went to his study and talked with but little interruption until eleven o'clock. We discussed foreign affairs, Mexico, and his personal affairs. He said he had about made up his mind to live in Washington when his term of office was over, and it was his intention not to meddle or to speak about public matters. He thought it would be a good example to the country. He believed Roosevelt and Taft were making a mistake in injecting their personalities into every question that arose. He said if the American public utilized the services of their Presidents as long as they could be of service that was one thing, but when they condemned them to two terms of four years each and then to oblivion, he thought the President should accept their decision and remain silent. There was a quiet and refined circle in certain parts of Georgetown where he thought he would find much congenial society. He thought he would do this and live in Europe five or six months of the year, writing and doing other things that had been denied him during his official tenure.

I spoke of the lies told of me in that part of the press antagonistic to the Administration. He advised paying no attention to them and not to dignify them by notice. This is in line with my own judgment and inclination. He thought a lie could not survive any length of time. I do not agree with this for I think many survive the centuries.

I told the President that I understood Tumulty would speak to him soon and ask him for an appointment on the Appraisers Court in New York made vacant by the death of Judge Summerville.[1] I advised him to accept Tumulty's resignation if offered and assured him we could better the situation with another man. Much to my surprise, he did not argue to the contrary, but merely said "I think you and I have agreed already to accept any resignation offered and not to urge continuation in office."

He asked where I thought Tumulty had failed. I replied that he did not work well with other people. He wished to know whether this was jealousy or an inherent inability to do so. I thought both, that none of his, Wilson's close friends had been able to work with Tumulty since he had held office, and it was a serious handicap to the Administration. I expressed sincere regret that I had urged Tumulty upon him in the first instance, and admit-

---

[1] Henderson Middleton Somerville, member of the Board of General Appraisers of the Customs Service in New York, who had died on September 15, 1915.

ted I was wrong and that he had been right in thinking a man of different temperament would have been more suitable. He asked whom I now had in mind and I told him Frank Polk would be an ideal Secretary to the President. McAdoo and I had also thought of Robert Woolley who is now Director of the Mint.

Another difficulty about Tumulty was his utter inability to retain information when once it came into his possession. The President admitted this and said, to his mind, it was his most serious fault, and now he never told him anything until it was ready for publication.

We spoke of the question of defence, of how much the Army should be increased and how much the Navy, and in what directions. He showed me a memorandum from the Secretary of War giving his opinion as to what should be done. The President asked me to be careful not to let this be known, and said he had kept it from Tumulty for fear he might tell it. We discussed the Navy at greater length than the Army because we both think, for the moment, it is the more important.

The President thought we should rely at first upon a large number of submarines, and that we should plan more for defence than for attack. I called his attention to the fact that if we were at war with either Japan or Germany we should want the fleet to go out and meet their fleet for we should not want them to prey upon our commerce.

It seems that he and Secretary Daniels had taken his view and the Naval Board had taken the other and more aggressive view. I suggested that he allow me to write Balfour in confidence and get his opinion as to the most effective naval program we could follow at the moment. Our interests and England's are so closely allied in this matter, and my relations with Balfour are so cordial that I am sure he would give a disinterested opinion and one that would be of value. I explained that we had no expert adviser with the British Navy who was worth while. He had made a mistake in not sending our best men there so as to get information at first hand; that we were now proceeding largely upon theory and undertaking to spend a great sum of money without actually knowing the conditions as they exist today. He accepted my suggestion provided I could reach Balfour in a way that would be absolutely safe.

Between eleven and twelve I saw many newspaper men who were desirous of talking with me. I also saw the Vice President and discussed public matters with him for fifteen or twenty minutes. Our talk concerned the proposed Special Session of the Senate as well as pending legislation.

At twelve Huston Thompson of the Department of Justice came to tell of the various happenings since we met. One was that Mr. Bryan had returned to Washington very angry with the Administration. He had seen Governor Folk, perhaps his closest friend, and had begun a tirade against the Administration, claiming it had instigated attacks upon him. Folk replied that he had talked with me and I had eulogized him, Bryan, to such an extent that he knew positively the Administration had no such feeling as he believed. Bryan was visibly affected and repeated several times, "did House say that? I am much gratified for that puts a different phase upon the situation."

I repeated this to the President later. Oswald Garrison Villard came at 12.30. He is full of himself and of the work he thinks he is doing in behalf of international peace.

McAdoo came to lunch and afterward we went upstairs to my room and had an hour's talk, principally about the Treasury, the Federal Reserve Board etc. He said Tumulty had asked him to keep open the appointment of Judge in the Appraisers Court in New York, and thought he would ask the President to let him take it. McAdoo, like every other member of the Cabinet, with the exception of Garrison, is delighted with the thought of getting rid of Tumulty.

Phillips came again at three, and I was able to tell him the President's views as to the Diplomatic Service, which was in effect that in exceptional cases he would appoint first counselors or secretaries of embassies to legations. The difficulty in doing this was the insistence by members of Congress upon using these places for patronage, and also because these places were becoming increasingly important and the President thinks, as I do, that the best service cannot always be obtained through the Diplomatic Corps. England is suffering from this now. The most conspicuous success they have had in recent years was James Bryce as Ambassador at Washington and he had had no previous diplomatic training.

Frank Polk followed Phillips. I told Polk what the President had in mind for Dumba. He expressed sympathy for Dumba which I shared, but it was not a question of sympathy but a question of policy, and Dumba should not be given any consideration, and the President shared in this view. Polk said, "Then I suppose he must be given his passports unless his Government recalls him." I thought that was the proper course to pursue.

I told him it was quite within the possibilities that Tumulty would resign within the next thirty days and I had suggested his name to the President as his successor. The President was willing to accept my judgment in the matter and would offer it to him provided he would accept it in a way that would relieve the President of any embarrassment. The President does not desire Polk to make any sacrifice or to think he was making any in his, the President's behalf.

Polk heard this with mingled feelings. His delight at the thought of getting rid of Tumulty was softened by the thought of the sacrifice he would have to make if the matter was put up to him in that form. He wished time to consider it. It is my opinion that Tumulty is making a "grandstand play" and will not resign and we will hear nothing more of it.

After Polk the Attorney General came to take me driving. We drove for an hour and I returned to the White House for another engagement at five. Gregory and I talked largely of departmental matters; the appointment of a Federal judge in Nebraska, a district attorney in Mississippi and matters of this sort about which he wished advice.

At five o'clock Mrs. Galt came to the White House by appointment for tea so that we might have a more intimate talk than we had yesterday. She seems delightful and full of humor, and it makes me happy to think the President will have her to cheer him in his loneliness.

I took occasion to tell her something of the President's work in the near past and what I hoped he might accomplish in the immediate future. She asked if I did not think it would be just as well for him not to run for a second term. My opinion was that in the event he could accomplish during the remainder of this term the things we had in mind it would be well not to stand for re-election. To do so after four such brilliant years would be something like an anti-climax. She said the President spoke of me with affection and said that "his mind is so lucid that when I bring matters to him, it is like a clearing house. Things were assorted, placed in their proper niches and the situation cleared of its complexities."

He had told her of our first meeting and of the delight it was to find one whose mind ran parallel with his own upon public questions. I thought if our plans carried true, the President would easily outrank any American that had yet lived; that the war was the greatest event in human history excepting the birth of Christ, therefore, if the President were able to play the part I hoped for, I was in favor of his retiring at the end of the present term.

We took a short drive together in her ele[c]tric runabout and I returned to the White House to meet Huston Thompson and

Robert Woolley to discuss the organization of a committee to make public the different achievements of the Administration.

After dinner the President, Helen Bones, Dr. Axson and I went to the National Theater to see May Irwin.[2] The other boxes were largely filled by Cabinet Members. The President insisted upon my taking a front seat to emphasize, so he said, the fact that we were not at outs, as had been recently stated. After the theater we drove to the White House and the President insisted upon going to the train with me, although it was then after eleven. I urged him not to do so for I had several notes I wanted to write and which I could not do because I did not wish to keep him waiting. We drove to the station and I left him at 11.30.

[2] In a comedy entitled *33 Washington Square*. May Irwin claimed to be the author.

To Edith Bolling Galt

[The White House] Friday,
My precious, precious Darling,   7.15 A.M. 24 Sept., 1915

I did not get up early this morning because I was wakeful, but because I was so eager to pour out my heart to you in love and gratitude. I have had a sound and restful sleep, full of perfect peace, and feel fresher and more fit this morning than I have felt for weeks. But, now that I am here, at this desk where I have so often tried to put into words the great love that is in my heart, I know once more that there *are* no words that can carry the message as my heart conceives it. Moreover, my heart is so full of joy that what I want to say is shot through with every kind of happiness and sweetness and can be said only into your sweet lips between kisses. You have set me *free* and made my full happiness, not merely a confident hope, but a *plan*.[1] You have swept every sort of interrogation point from my path and given me certainties to deal with, and my *mind*, as well as my heart, is at peace. Above all, you have brought my supreme happiness *near* and have promised me unhampered, unembarrassed comradeship in the mean time. I can go to you; I can take my papers and my problems to you; I can have you by my side when I am full of thought and when I am thinking only of play; I can read to you and play golf with you and pour out to you all the dreams and theories and plans that fill my mind when it is free, as it is now; I can show you *all* sides of me instead of only one; and I can make love to you without fear of embarrassing you! You have never disappointed me, my splendid Darling. Your love is as great and as generous and as full of vision as you are,—a perfect woman, nobly planned, to love, to comfort, and command,—to delight, to fill the man she loves with every high desire and quickening inspiration. Your love means life to me, my own lovely, incomparable Darling, and my whole heart is full of the infinite sweetness and power to bless and strengthen and make complete that it gives. I love you,—love you with what happiness, what joy and sense of having won *every*thing that makes life beautiful and complete, it is impossible to put into words! My Darling loves me and is coming to me *soon*, in all her glorious lovliness, and the whole world is changed!

Your own   Woodrow

ALS (WP, DLC).
  1 That they would announce their engagement on October 15.

From Edith Bolling Galt

Dearest One: [Washington] Friday, Sept. 24/1915 8 P.M.
  I cannot let this day end without a word of love to you.

It has been such a full day that now, when I am waiting for *old* Mr. Wilson, is the first minute I could claim to tell *young* Mr. Wilson how proudly happy I am to have you tell me, as you did in that note (written so early this morning) how at rest and content you are. I will forgive your getting up early this one time —but hereafter you *must* not do it. Even to tell me you love me. You need the rest Sweetheart, and I would rather you showed your love by taking care of yourself than any other way—and you can find a moment later in the day. Or, if that is impossible you know I will always understand.

I could not read your note today until we got back from golf, but it was a happy sensation to feel it was there waiting to unfold its sweetness

10:40

Mr Wilson came, and we have had a long interesting talk and then I would take him home—in spite of his protests—and quite enjoyed the little ride. The moon is perfectly wonderful, and you are missing it all sitting in the Theatre. But I hope you are having good fun, and I will tell you tomorrow night all Mr. W. said—and how pleased he is you want to *know* him. Dear old gentleman! He is starting off early tomorrow morning to bring his wife home from Williamstown. She has been taken ill there.

I did have such a nice talk with Col. House, and he is just as nice and fine as you pictured him, and his admiration for you is sufficient to establish my faith in his judgment and inteligent perceptions. I shall wait and tell you some of the things he said—and you will tell me honestly if he *liked* me. Helen said he said nice things about me but you will know if he meant them or if he was just *trying* to mean them for your sake. He told me you knew I was coming for Tea, and I was divided between pride at your strength of mind in playing golf and mortification that I had such a dangerous rival in the game—that you did not *even hurry* back! Goodnight—and my love and tender thoughts now, and always, Your own Edith.

ALS (WP, DLC).

From Robert Lansing

Henderson Harbor, N. Y., September 25, 1915

Confidential. Received today the following telegram from German Ambassador in New York City:

"I understand that President wishes me to speak with you when you pass through New York on your way back."

Have you indicated such a wish? Do you desire me to see him. I expect to be in New York next Saturday morning and to spend the day there. Robert Lansing.

T telegram (WP, DLC).

To Edith Bolling Galt

[The White House] Saturday,
My own Darling, 7.10 A.M. 25 Sept., 1915

Don't you think I was a true and loyal sport to stay away from the house yesterday afternoon when I knew that you were here? My, but it was hard! I did not keep my eye on the ball a dozen times, and got beaten all to pieces! But it was a joy to see House afterwards and talk to him about you. I never saw him so enthusiastic about anything as he was about you. He said he had not words in which to express his admiration for you,—that the sum of the matter was that you were a wonderful and delightful person and that it seemed to him that it was the best and most fortunate thing that could have happened, for me or for the country, that I had won such a partner and comrade and helper. I wish I could give you some impression of the way in which his face glowed when he spoke of you. You made the same impression on him that you make on every man of parts to whom you show your real qualities of mind and heart. Their attention is first caught and held by your grace and beauty and charm of manner and by your vivid personality, and then they find that, besides all that, you have a mind that makes you their equal in any kind of intercourse, and a wit that makes them feel a keen pleasure in the talk; you are so stimulating and such good fun, and in every way so rewarding and worth while. I love him more than ever—the true, loyal friend—because he has become, from the moment of seeing and knowing you, as much your friend and partisan as mine. I hope you liked and admired and trusted him a tithe as much as he did you! Ah, what a luxury it is to be free to talk about you,—and yet I cannot tell anyone but you what is really in my mind and heart about you. It is a delicious mixture, little girl, of romantic love and intellectual delight. There is no part of me that you do not satisfy and give delight to,—so that, whatever my mood or my occupation or my need, whether I am at work or at play, you are the one person I need and enjoy most. And now I shall be free to be with you and claim you and make myself secure in heart and mind! I am to be acknowledged as

Your own   Woodrow

ALS (WP, DLC).

From Edward Mandell House

Dear Governor: New York. September 26th, 1915.

Bernstorff came to see me very promptly this morning. He said he had an intimation from Washington, indirectly through Tumulty, that you wanted him to hasten the Arabic matter and to see Lansing when he passes through New York before he reaches Washington.

This is what he would like to know.

(1) Do you want anything done before he sees Lansing? He reiterates that what he can do now is to give additional assurances directly from his government that no passenger vessel will be torpedoed in the future without notice, and that the ship will have the benefit of the doubt.

(2) They are willing to submit the Arabic case to an international commission and accept the principle of indemnity for the loss of life.

If this is not satisfactory, he will take the question up with his government as to some form of disavowal based upon American evidence. But if his government makes the disavowal they would want to refer the question of reparation to the Hague.

(3) If you decide a disavowal must be made, do you want him to make an effort at once, or would you prefer that he wait until after he consults Lansing?

I have told him I thought I could get him this information by Tuesday morning.   Your devoted,   E. M. House

TLS (SDR, RG 59, 841.857, AR 1/103½, DNA).

To Joseph R. Wilson, Jr.

My dear Brother,   [The White House] 26 September, 1915.

Something very delightful has happened to me which I am not yet at liberty to tell others but which I want you to know among the first. A great happiness and blessing has come to me in the midst of my loneliness. Mrs. Norman Galt, a lovely woman whom I met first in April last through Helen, who had become her fast friend, has promised to marry me. When you know her you will know why it was inevitable that I should love her, for she is wholly delightful and lovable. She lives here in Washington and is known for everything that is fine and for nothing that is touched with the small spirit of Washington society folk. You would think that it was only love that was speaking if I were to tell you what she really is, but you will find out for yourself how truly wonderful she is in gifts both of heart and of mind.

Please for the present keep this as an absolute secret. We are not yet ready to let others know of it, though we shall, of course, in due time make public announcement of it.

With love from all to you all,
                    Your loving brother,   Woodrow Wilson

WWTLS (WP, DLC).

To Annie Josephine Wilson Howe

Dearest Sister,   [The White House] 26 September, 1915.

A great happiness has come to me, of which I am not yet at liberty to speak to others, but which I want you to know among the first. Mrs. Galt, whom you met here and who, you will remember, was one of our party on the *Mayflower*, has promised to marry me. When you really know her you will know why it was inevitable that I should love her, if you do not know already. You would think that it was only love that was speaking if I were to tell you what she is, but you will find out for yourself, I know, how truly wonderful she is in gifts both of head and of heart. Her love for me has changed a very desolate world into a very bright one full of hope and reassurance.

Please, dear Sister, keep this for the present as an absolute secret, even from Wilson and George and other members of the family. We are not yet ready to let any but the circle of loved ones immediately about us know, though we shall, of course, in due time make public announcement of the engagement.

We are all well. I hope that it will be only a week or so now before our little household here is reestablished. And the Smiths will come down for a visit.

Helen joins me in warmest love to you all three. I hope that the work goes well.

Your devoted brother, Woodrow Wilson

WWTLS (WP, DLC).

To Mary Eloise Hoyt

Dear Cousin Mary,   [The White House] 26 September, 1915.

Something very delightful has happened to me which I am not yet at liberty to tell others but which I want you to know among the first. A great happiness and blessing has come to me in the midst of my loneliness. Mrs. Norman Galt, a lovely Washington woman (born in Virginia) whom I first met in April last through Helen, who had become her fast friend, has promised to marry me. When you know her you will know why it was inevitable that I should fall in love with her, for she is wholly delightful and lovable. She is known here for everything that is fine and for nothing that is touched with with [sic] the small spirit of the society folk of the place. You would think that it was only love that was speaking if I were to tell you what she is like, how endowed and made distinguished in her loveliness, but you will, I am sure, find out for yourself how truly wonderful she is in gifts both of heart and of mind.

Please for the present keep this as an absolute secret. We are not yet ready to let others know of it, though we shall, of course, make public announcement of the engagement in due time.

We have been very anxious for recent news of dear Florence. I hope with all my heart that you are encouraged about her and that she has regained in the hospital all, and more than all, of what she had lost.

Please give her and Margared [Margaret] our love. We expect the little household here to be reestablished her[e] by the return of the Cornishites in a very short time now, and are happy in the prospect.   Affectionately Yours,   Woodrow Wilson

WWTLS (received from W. D. Hoyt, Jr.).

To Margaret Randolph Axson Elliott

Dearest Madge,   [The White House] 26 September, 1915.

Something very delightful has happened to me in the midst of my loneliness and anxiety which I am not at liberty to tell others yet but which I want you to know among the first. Mrs. Norman Galt, a lovely Virginia woman long resident here in Washington, whom I first met in April last through Helen, who had become her fast friend, has promised to marry me. When you know her you will know why it was inevitable that I should fall in love with her, for she is wholly delightful and lovable. She is known here for everything that is fine and for nothing that is touched with the small spirit of the society folk of the place. You would, I fear, think that it was only love that was speaking if I were to try to tell you what she is like in person and character, how endowed and made distinguished in her loveliness, but you will, I am sure, when you know her, find out for yourself how truly wonderful she is in gifts alike of heart and of mind.

Please, dear Madge, just for the present, keep this very carefully as an absolute secret. We are not yet ready to let others know it, though we shall of course, in due time, make public announcement of the engagement.

Stock is here and we are enjoying him thoroughly. We have not seen him for a long time, and it is delightful not only to have him here but to see him so well. He has made us happy by telling us how wonderfully you have improved in health.

Only Helen is with me just now, but the others will be down from Cornish in a few days I hope. I am sure they would join with me, if they were here, as Helen does, in warmest love to you both. I am well but very tired.

Affectionately Yours,   Woodrow Wilson

WWTLS (WC, NjP).

To Edith Bolling Galt

[The White House]
My precious Little Girl,   Sunday morning 26 Sept., 1915

The love message that goes with this this morning is full of unspeakable tenderness and desire for nothing so much as your happiness. What I want, and want above all things else in the world, is to devote myself to making you happy. When, through stupidity or any lack in me, I fail, the pain to me is infinitely greater than any I can cause you. For I love you truly and with all my heart and am always and altogether

Your own   Woodrow

ALS (WP, DLC).

From Edith Bolling Galt

[Washington] Sunday,

My precious One   Sept. 26/1915 8:30 a.m.

I have just gotten up after a restful, undisturbed night, and have come straight to my desk to talk to you and tell you how happy I was with you last night and that the pain that had eaten so deep because of the "Earthquake" has gone, and that I feel steady again with my feet once more on firm ground. What a week of emotions this has been since you came to me here with your dear heart on fire with perplexities, and then, how the sky gradually cleared and we found the path that leads to happiness again.

I am trying to get rid of all the interogation points that so distress you, and with your dear arms around me they slip back into the shadows, and sometime they will be driven back so far they will never find their way out again—and I will be safe with you.

Don't feel hurt or disturbed because I was nervous last night. I love you and I am trying every day to be as straight and steadfast and fine as you believe me, and if I fail I know your love will never fail to understand

I hope you are well and happy this brilliant morning my precious one, and that you will feel my love for you all through the day. For it is there, warm, and pulsing—and I am longing to come and tell you instead of writing it.

Always your own   Edith

ALS (WP, DLC).

To Edith Bolling Galt

[The White House] Sunday evening,

My precious, darling Little Girl,   8.25 26 Sept., 1915

That sweet note that came this morning was a true mirror of your dear loving heart and brought me deep comfort and joy. I know that you *are* "trying to get rid of all the interrogation points that so distress" me; and I have not the least real fear that you will fail to get rid of them altogether. I have no apprehension as to the outcome. You *are* "straight and steadfast and fine," and I understand the struggles you are having with yourself as well as if they were taking place in my own heart: for love has given me an insight into your dear heart which has never failed. To witness the struggle sometimes pains me very deeply, because it is a struggle against shadows, not realities, and a struggle for your own happiness; and the pain is never so great as when I feel that something that I seem to you to be or something that I have blunderingly done, has thrown you for a little while back into the toils of doubt and misgiving again. I love you so without limit, with so perfect a comprehension and so unhesitating a love of you *as you are*,—a love so entirely without misgiving as to anything except my own worthiness, and I know so well the unspeakable joy of loving without questioning the love, that it disturbs me beyond measure to see you fighting with what I know to be unrealities and yet be unable for the time to show you how you have but to stretch your hand out and accept a happiness that will be without fear or alloy,—the happiness that you have missed and are yet more capable of enjoying in its fulness than anyone else I ever knew. But it is splendid to see, after all, for you are successfully fighting through to your emancipation and freedom, and to the complete realization of what you have waited for and never expected to see all these years,—have already fought through, if you but knew it! And you are so noble and beautiful in all that you do in the course of the struggle,—so noble and beautiful even at moments which are in themselves almost tragical,—beautiful in what you unconsciously reveal of the ideals after which you are striving, of the standards you think you ought to hold yourself to,—in all the negative as well as positive proofs you give of what you really believe in and love!

Yes, indeed, my Darling, if you will but continue to go straight forward in the way of love which you are treading with such sweet resolution of devoted loyalty, *all* the interrogation points will be "driven back so far they will never find their way out again" and you will be utterly safe in the love that has so wonderfully grown up in your heart. You need only trust me, my precious One, and let my trust of you suffice to give you confidence in yourself, and believe steadfastly in the sovereign power of love itself, and the sweet miracle will be wrought. Please, my darling little girl, put your hand in mine and let me lead you along the path of love. I promise to guide you to the happy place of peace and certainty you seek, if you will but trust me to find the way and go with me, looking, not at the road, but in my eyes and, through my eyes, into my heart. I trust you utterly, and with a love that has never had the least shadow of doubt in it of any kind. I love you with joy, with thanksgiving that such a glorious love and comradeship as yours should have been given me. I am so eager and so proud to be your guide! And the only thing that makes me competent to guide is my love, which is not greater than yours but more confident, with its eyes turned to the future, not to the past.

Monday, 7 A.M.

The morning has come with a peculiar bloom of tender light on it, and with it the sweetest thoughts that could fill a man's heart. I am feeling fine and fit, and my whole heart is full of the glory and sweetness of our love for one another. That sweet sentence in your note of yesterday, "The pain that had eaten so deep because of the 'earthquake' has gone and I feel steady again with my feet once more on firm ground," sings in my heart. For I am happy only when you are. The world seems full of *you*, in all your loveliness and adorable charm. It is such a delight to think of you always, as you really are (and you have revealed your whole self to me), but this morning thoughts of you fill me with a peculiar joy, as if, with the new week, we had found a new confidence in one another,—as if the shame for me and the suffering for you that made last week dark for us both,—though the light came steadily back from the first—were all gone (though the shame will never be entirely gone for me) and there lay before us now only the certainties and rewards of true and tested love. Henceforth, my precious Sweetheart, our love will not ask questions, but accept the joy and life that are to make the days to come so full of everything that we long for and know how to enjoy. We are going to enjoy each other's minds, each other's tastes, each other's whims and fancies, each other's quick sympathies, and be the chums we were intended to be without further misgivings. And *what* a desirable chum you are, my fascinating Darling! How *intensely* I enjoy you, when your dear heart is free from pain! Your mind *interests* me so, your heart delights and satisfies me so! Our *plans* are going to settle themselves. We are going to do the *natural* thing, and that, and that alone, will be the wise and dignified thing.

The love I send you this morning, my precious Darling, is as full of confident joy as it is of adoration of you, the loveliest little girl in all the world, and the most delightful. The strength that is in me this morning is the strength of love and happiness; and all the happiness comes from you,—because you love me and I can devote my life to you!   Your own   Woodrow

You will come to-night—wont you?

ALS (WP, DLC).

To John Worth Kern

My dear Senator: [The White House] September 27, 1915

Thank you sincerely for your letter of September twenty-second.[1] I think your own judgment is the sum of the whole matter. If our foreign affairs clear sufficiently, I think that we ought to have an extra session of the Senate and I hope and believe that we can remove that "if" within the next week or two.

I am sincerely obliged to you for the care you have taken to canvass the opinion of members of the Senate, and your letter is of great assistance to me.

With warmest regards to Mrs. Kern and love to the boys,
          Cordially and sincerely yours,   Woodrow Wilson

TLS (Letterpress Books, WP, DLC).
    [1] J. W. Kern to WW, Sept. 22, 1915, ALS (WP, DLC). Kern reported on the results of his correspondence with Democratic leaders in the Senate to determine if they favored a special session of that body for the purpose of revising its rules. Kern found that six senators favored it, two were uncertain, and four were opposed. Kern himself was in favor, provided that Wilson felt that the "war situation" made it safe to call a special session.

To Robert Lansing

The White House, September 27, 1915

Would be obliged if you would arrange for interview on your way down at New York as suggested in the message you quote.
          Woodrow Wilson.

T telegram (SDR, RG 59, 763.72/2175½, DNA).

To Edward Mandell House

The White House Sep 27 1915

Your letter of twenty sixth received. Answer to question one no, question three yes, when interview occurrs that should be the assumption. Party passes through New York on Saturday and will arrange interview.   Woodrow Wilson.

T telegram (E. M. House Papers, CtY).

From Robert Lansing

PERSONAL AND SECRET   Henderson Harbor, N. Y.

My dear Mr. President: September 27th, 1915.

I have received from Mr. Page in London, the following message—Number 2866, September 25th, two p.m., which was repeated to me in the private code which we use and which was not deciphered at the Department:

"Referring to package papers forwarded in Department's pouch to Berlin which you instructed Gerard to return to you personally,[1] I transmit the following telegram written by Kirk,[2] Third Secretary of Berlin Embassy, who has come here under Gerard's oral instructions to send it as it could not safely be dispatched from Germany. Kirk remains here pending your instructions. Papers are in my safe.

" 'Package in question which has been placed with other official notes pending receipt of instructions from the Department was inadvertently opened by Mr. Gerard himself and as importance of contents was instantly perceived almost complete papers were examined. Package found to contain statements in duplicate of accounts of German Embassy in Washington together with supporting vouchers in the original or certified copies. Vouchers show that five thousand dollars were paid to Archibald for propaganda; four thousand five hundred dollars to Marcus Braun, Editor of Fair Play; three thousand dollars to Miss Ray Beveridge[3] for a lecture tour and one thousand dollars to _____ Emerson[4] for traveling expenses. In addition statements from the Western Union Telegraph Cable Company contain names of persons in the United States and elsewhere to whom messages were sent by the German Embassy, as well as purpose of message, whether propaganda or official business. These statements show also the bill for cables Bogotá from April first to the tenth amounted to over four thousand dollars, and to Guatemala three thousand, and to Shanghai two thousand. Large sums spent in cables to Mexico City, Manila, Honolulu, Haiti and (#) (#) (#) (#) [Buenos Aires in that paper] appear to furnish authentic list of all kinds German agents in the United States and elsewhere and also indicate extent and direction of German propaganda.

" 'In this connection Mr. Gerard considers that Department would be justified in examining papers in question especially in view of all the facts in the case since the beginning of the war. American Embassy in Berlin has found it necessary to direct seventeen notes to German Foreign Office protesting against (#)

[opening of] mail addressed to the Ambassador. These protests have for most part been ignored where [while] in the single case where a letter to another chief of mission in Berlin was opened, an official apology (∗) [was made] before protest was lodged.

" 'Mr Gerard, in accordance with his custom in opening correspondence, did not tear envelope or break seals of this (cipher incomplete) [parcel] but detatched bottom flap of envelope without it.

" 'In view of nature of documents it did not seem advisable photograph them in Berlin or to entrust them to regular courier.' American Ambassador, London."[5]

(#) group makes no sense

(∗) apparent omission.

You will recall the circumstances of a package, addressed to the Foreign Office at Berlin, enclosed in another wrapper addressed to the American Ambassador at Berlin, and sent in our Government's pouch to the Embassy. Upon receiving information of this, Mr. Gerard was instructed to return the package and at the same time an investigation was on foot when I left the Department, to find out how the package came to be in our mail pouch. I believe Mr. Phillips was conducting the investigation in the Department.

It seems to me that the package should be forwarded to Washington—the only question being whether it should be sent by our pouch from the London Embassy or by a messenger. From the brief statement contained in the Ambassador's telegram it would seem that the information is of a very important character and that we might well avail ourselves of it.

I have not sent a copy of the Ambassador's telegram to Mr. Polk as I do not wish to have more than two copies in existence. I think, however, it might be well to show it to him and instruct him about having the package forwarded from London.

Of course it is possible when opportunity is given to examine the papers, they may not prove to be so serious as they appear from the Ambassador's telegram.

I am planning to leave here Friday for New York and will be at the Hotel Biltmore for Saturday. My impression is that I have already written or telegraphed this to you—I am, however, as I said before I left Washington, entirely at your disposal.

Faithfully yours,   Robert Lansing.

TLS (WP, DLC).

1 That is, a package sent by Ambassador Bernstorff to the German Foreign Office, transmitted in the State Department's diplomatic pouch to the United States Embassy in Berlin.

2 Alexander Comstock Kirk.

³ American-born actress and singer who had spent much time in Germany. She had recently made a lecture tour in the United States collecting money for the German Red Cross.

⁴ Edwin Emerson, born in Germany of American parents, journalist and war correspondent.

⁵ This telegram is printed in *FR-WWS 1915*, pp. 942-43. Editorial emendations from this copy.

From David Lawrence, with Enclosure

Dear Mr. President: [Washington] Sept 27th [1915]

I am enclosing for your information a copy of a letter I have just sent to Secretary Lansing who asked me to keep him advised about Mexican developments. It includes the text of a telegram which Carranza sent to Arredondo today for his own information but which Arredondo gave me in confidence at my request.

                    Very sincerely yours,   David Lawrence

TLS (WP, DLC).

E N C L O S U R E

David Lawrence to Robert Lansing

PERSONAL

My dear Mr. Secretary: [Washington] Sept. 27th [1915]

Thank you for your letter of the 21st; through it I was able to dissipate the story of our alleged support of Obregon before it got momentum or caused mischief among the Carranza people. In accordance with your request that I keep you advised of the situation, I am including in this letter the substance of a talk I had with Luis Cabrera, Carranza's Minister of Finance, with respect to loan negotiations that seem to be in progress already; some details of the military situation in Juarez and vicinity; and a copy of a telegram received by Arredondo today from Carranza which I am permitted confidentially to give you.

Cabrera told me that he had been approached indirectly by several big banking houses and that a great many people of the class that seek brokerage commissions etc., were after him constantly. He said he had asked Carranza by cable what steps he should take and that the First Chief had advised him to be cautious about committing himself to any proposal whatsoever until after recognition shall have been extended. Such offers as had been made, I understand, were for a loan at 70 and 75, the amount desired, according to Cabrera, being about $500,000,000. Cabrera believes they can sell their bonds at 85 or 90 if recognition comes and anticipates stiff terms by the American bankers.

Cabrera amplified to me the idea of a constituent assembly which Carranza mentioned to me when I visited him at Vera Cruz. Cabrera says it is Carranza's own plan and seemed to him the only way to reestablish the constitutional order. The constitutent assembly, it seems, when convoked would determine whether Carranza should be First Chief or Provisional President and whether or not he shall be in charge of the executive power if a candidate in the elections ensuing.

Cabrera has submitted an amnesty plan which he feels confident Carranza will put into effect. It seeks, briefly, to make every case stand on its merits enabling thousands of Mexicans who never took part in politics to make inquiry as to whether or not there is any charge against them and accepting them back into the country on pledge of loyalty to the constituted government.

Arredondo tells me that the garrison at Juarez in charge of Gen Ornelas,[1] the Villista officer, will turn over to Obregon as soon as the latter reaches Chihuahua or it is apparent there is no danger of a retaliatory move by Villa who is withdrawing into Sonora on the confident expectation that he can continue to use Juarez as a base of supplies.

I find Arredondo's appreciation of our viewpoint improving daily. His vision may not be as broad as might be desirable but fundamentally he is honest and I feel that I can rely on what he tells me. He told me very confidentially a few days ago that he believed Carranza would make him Minister for Foreign Affairs. I think this would be of great benefit to us because Arredondo seems more reasonable than any of the Carranza people I have met and certainly is an immense improvement over Acuna, Carranza's present minister of foreign affairs.

Arredondo has dealt with me with all cards on the table, has shown me his messages to Carranza and replies from the First Chief, and has divorced himself absolutely in all this business from connection with the Carranza attorney, Douglas, or other members of the so-called junta. A few days ago I impressed upon Arredondo that at present the situation as between Vera Cruz and Mexico City seemed to belie the Carranza control of that region and that some information as to what Carranza was doing about it would be worth having; also that very soon, as you informed me, it would be desirable to get some very definite pronouncements on the subject of treatment of the clergy, property and interests of foreigners, and the handling of international obligations generally. Arredondo communicated the substance of this to Carranza and today received the following message in cipher, which (at my request), he gave me for your confidential information.. The translation is my own, verified by Arredondo:

"Vera Cruz Sept 26th

"Received your cipher message of yesterday. The military campaign which the Constitutionalist Government proposes against the Zapatistas will be prosecuted even to the smallest bands that are marauding in various places. They do not constitute the nucleus of resistance nor are they able permanently to cut communication with Mexico City or deprive it of food, water or light. The irregularity of railroad traffic is really due to a lack of rolling stock for which there is an extraordinary demand not only by the merchants who want cars to transport their freight but by the Constitutionalist government which is anxious to transport the provisions it has obtained to alleviate the situation in the city of Mexico. It is untrue that the Zapatistas actually interrupt traffic; only in isolated cases have they attacked our lines of communication because we have ordered that all trains shall now run only with strong escorts for their protection.

"The manifestos which I made in December of last year and again in July of this year addressed to the nation include the complete program of the Government that I propose to follow to the reestablishment of constitutional order and in these documents are comprehended the specifications which the First Chieftainship makes to satisfy the national public opinion and to obtain the respect and consideration of foreign countries.

"I confirm hereby the instructions which I have given respecting this confidential agency; it is the only authoritative medium of communication of the First Chieftainship able to treat all classes of business with the Department of State of the United States. I beg you to express to Mr. Lawrence my appreciation of his good offices.   "Venustiano Carranza"

Mr Arredondo, when the appropriate time comes, will have detailed instructions with reference to the proclamations referred to above and assures me there will be no difficulty in getting the guarantees desired by the American government.

I suggested to Arredondo that Carranza's continued presence in Vera Cruz when he had possession of Mexico City was subject to the construction that he feared to go to the capital and that it would no doubt have an important moral effect on public opinion in the United States if before October 9th, Carranza were to go to Mexico City and establish himself there. Arredondo cabled a message of inquiry on this subject to Carranza today transmitting what I had said. I find Arredondo amenable and he confidentially assures me that since Carranza will now have opportunities to show his real friendship for the United States, he will not hesitate to manifest this in the proper way.

Very sincerely yours,   [David Lawrence]

TCL (WP, DLC).
[1] General M. S. Ornelas, one of the more obscure of Villa's "generals."

From Edith Bolling Galt

[Washington]

My precious One: Monday afternoon, Sept 27, 1915

I did not answer your dear note this morning, because I knew I could tell you so much better tonight, when I see you, the things that are in my heart.

It pleases and also awes me, sometimes, to feel how you interpret me even when distance seperates us. Just what you express in your note of last night and early this morning really happened —yesterday during church—after I had written you earlier. All the strain seemed to break, and I positively *felt* you by me and knew things were straight at last and I could trust myself in something the same way I trust you—though not in the same degree.

This is to take to you tonight but not to be read until tomorrow for you will go away so early in the morning I would not be able to get a note to you, and I want this to be in your pocket close to your heart to warm and cheer you with my unquestioning love all through the day. What a record of pain you have gone through with me Sweetheart, but I hope it is all past now and I am going to bring you nothing but joy. Do take care tomorrow and let nothing happen to you   How I wish you could go with us as far as Baltimore—but of course you can't. But the days are few now before the world can no longer demand our absence from each other, and we can have such fun together.

I am just starting down to have a talk with Mr. Bergheimer,[1] which I will tell you of tonight.

I was made so happy this morning by your blessed note for it actually *sang* with joy—and that has made my day complete. I will follow you all day tomorrow and love you, love you, love you.

Your own   Edith.

ALS (WP, DLC).
[1] Henry Christian Bergheimer, manager of Galt & Bro.

An Address to the Grand Army of the Republic[1]

[Sept. 28, 1915]

Mr. Chairman,[2] gentlemen of the Grand Army of the Republic, ladies and gentlemen: I bid you a very cordial welcome to the capital of the nation; and yet I feel that it is not necessary to bid you welcome here, because you know that the welcome is always warm and always waiting for you.

One could not stand in this presence without many moving thoughts. It is a singular thing that men of a single generation should have witnessed what you have witnessed in the crowded fifty years which you celebrate tonight. You took part, when you were young men, in a struggle the meaning of which, I dare say, you thought would not be revealed during your lifetime. And yet more has happened in the making of this nation in your lifetime than has ever happened in the making of any other nation in the lifetime of a dozen generations.

The nation in which you now live is not the nation for whose union you fought. You have seen many things which have made this nation one of the representative nations of the world with regard to the modern spirit of that world, and you have the satisfaction which, I dare say, few soldiers have ever had—of looking back upon a war absolutely unique in this, that, instead of destroying, it healed; that, instead of making a permanent division, it made a permanent union.

You have seen something more interesting than that, because there is a sense in which the things of the heart are more interesting than the things of the mind. This nation was from the beginning a spiritual enterprise, and you have seen the spirits of the two once divided sections of this country absolutely united. A war which seemed as if it had the seed of every kind of bitterness in it has seen a single generation put bitterness absolutely out of its heart. And you feel, as I am sure the men who fought against you feel, that you were comrades even then, though you did not know it, and that now you know that you are comrades in a common love for a country which you are equally eager to serve.

This is a miracle of the spirit, so far as national history is concerned. This is one of the very few wars in which, in one sense, everybody engaged may take pride. Some wars are to be regretted; some wars mar the annals of history; but some wars contrasted with those make those annals distinguished, show that the spirit of man sometimes springs to great enterprises that are even greater than his own mind had conceived.

So it seems to me that, standing in a presence like this, no man, whether he be in the public service or in the ranks of private citizens merely, can fail to feel the challenge to his own heart; can fail to feel the challenge to a new consecration to the things that we all believe in. The thing that sinks deepest in my heart, as I try to realize the memories that must be crowding upon you, is this: You set the nation free for that great career of development, of unhampered development, which the world has witnessed since the Civil War.

But, for my own part, I would not be proud of the extraordinary physical development of this country, of its extraordinary development in material wealth and financial power, did I not believe that the people of the United States wished all of this power devoted to ideal ends.

There have been other nations as rich as we; there have been other nations as powerful; there have been other nations as spirited. But I hope we shall never forget that we created this nation, not to serve ourselves, but to serve mankind.

I love this country because it is my home, but every man loves his home. It does not suffice that I should be attached to it because it contains the places and the persons whom I love, because it contains the threads of my own life. That does not suffice for patriotic duty. I should also love it, and I hope I do love it, as a great instrument for the uplift of mankind. And what you gentlemen have to remind us of, as you look back through a lifetime to the great war in which you took part, is that you fought that this instrument, meant for the service of mankind, should not be impaired, either in its material or in its spiritual power.

I hope I may say, without even an implication of criticism upon any other great people in the world, that it has always seemed to me that the people of the United States wished to be regarded as devoted to the promotion of particular principles of human right.

The United States was founded, not to provide free homes—but to assert human rights. This flag meant a great enterprise of the human spirit. Nobody, no large bodies of men, in the time that flag was first set up, believed with a very firm belief in the efficacy of democracy.

Do you realize that, only so long ago as the time of the American Revolution, democracy was regarded as an experiment in the world, and we were regarded as rash experimenters? But we not only believed in it; we showed that our belief was well founded and that a nation as powerful as any in the world could be erected upon the will of the people; that, indeed, there was a power in such a nation that dwelt in no other nation unless also in that other nation the spirit of the people prevailed.

Democracy is the most difficult form of government, because it is the form under which you have to persuade the largest number of persons to do anything in particular. But I think we were the more privileged to undertake it because it is difficult. Anybody can do what is easy. We have shown that we could do what was hard. And the pride that ought to dwell in your hearts tonight is that you saw to it that that experiment was brought to the day of its triumphant demonstration.

We now know, and the world knows, that the thing that we then undertook, rash as it seemed, has been practicable, and that we have set up in the world a government maintained and promoted by the general conscience and the general conviction.

So I stand here, not to welcome you to the nation's capital as if I were your host, but merely to welcome you to your own capital, because I am, and am proud to be, your servant. I hope I shall catch, as I hope we shall all catch, from the spirit of this occasion, a new consecration to the high duties of American citizenship.

T transcript (WC, NjP) of CLSsh (C. L. Swem Coll., NjP).

1 Wilson spoke at Camp Emery in Washington at the opening session of the forty-ninth annual encampment of the Grand Army of the Republic.

2 William Frederick Gude, a Washington florist and chairman of the citizens' committee for the encampment.

From Edward Mandell House

Dear Governor: New York. September 28th, 1915.

Bernstorff came this morning and I read him your telegram in answer to my letter of the 26th.

I find that question number 3 really involved two questions, therefore your affirmative is not altogether clear. We both took it, however, that you meant he was to do nothing until he saw Lansing, and he will wait until Saturday unless you advise otherwise in the meantime.

Rathom of the Providence Journal was here this morning. He has been with Justice Hughes at a fishing camp in Maine. He believes that Hughes will accept the republican nomination if tendered. This I consider interesting and important if true.

Mr. Dunlap has telephoned concerning the Daniels article that he is preparing for the November number of his magazine.[1] He thinks that it should be done by Franklin Roosevelt instead of himself, and he would like to know what you think of the suggestion.   Affectionately yours,   E. M. House

TLS (WP, DLC).

[1] John Robertson Dunlap, editor of *The Engineering Magazine*, had volunteered to conduct a public relations campaign to improve Josephus Daniels' public image.

Two Letters to Edward Mandell House

Dearest Friend,   The White House. 29 September, 1915.

Many things make us feel the embarrassment of keeping the announcement until the fifteenth of October, and I wonder if there is any conclusive reason in your mind why we should not make it earlier, say, next week? I know you will give me your candid opinion about so important a matter. Is there anything to be gained by delay that is of sufficient importance to be weighed against the freedom that would be given me by an earlier announcement,—freedom from all sorts of minor inconveniences and embarrassments connected with our seeing one another and planning all the things that lie ahead of us in the near future? We will both await your advice with eager interest,—I in particular, for of course I have to admit that I will be the chief gainer by an early emancipation from concealment of the most important fact in my personal life.

We join in the most affectionate messages.

Your devoted friend,   Woodrow Wilson

Dearest Friend,   The White House. 29 September, 19,5.

I feared at the time that my telegram was not very clear. What I meant was that I did not think it necessary for Bernstorff to do anything further before having a full and frank conference with Lansing on Saturday; and that when he saw Lansing I hoped that the inference or, rather, the understanding in their conversation would be that we would find it difficult to get to a satisfactory understanding with Berlin without a disavowal of the act of the submarine commander in sinking the *Arabic*. I do not think that opinion in this country would sustain a settlement based on anything less.

I agree with you about Rathom's information about Mr. Justice Hughes. It is important *if true*.

In answer to Dunlap's question, it is my opinion that an article written by Franklin Roosevelt, Daniels' colleague would have less weight than an article written by Dunlap himself.

Affectionately Yours,   Woodrow Wilson

WWTLS (E. M. House Papers, CtY).

To Altee Pomerene

Confidential.

My dear Senator: [The White House] September 29, 1915

Thank you for your courtesy in repeating to me in your letter of September twenty-fifth[1] the views you expressed to Senator Kern about an extra session of the Senate. I have been giving the matter a great deal of anxious thought. My present feeling is that perhaps an extra session of the Senate would be inadvisable unless we can before the date for which it would be necessary to call it feel sure that at least the most critical of our foreign difficulties are out of our way. Would you not think in those circumstances that the situation was altered?

In haste, with warmest regard,

Cordially yours,   Woodrow Wilson

TLS (Letterpress Books, WP, DLC).
[1] It is missing.

To Edith Bolling Galt

[The White House] Wednesday,

My own precious Darling,   7.40 A.M. 29 Sept., 1915

What a happy, peaceful day you gave me yesterday by means of that precious little note you gave me to carry with me! It was a perfect expression of what we both felt Monday night,—only I think that, if you had written it *after* that blissful evening, instead of just before it, you would have said, not that you 'hoped,' but that you knew that all the pain was past now and *all* the misgivings, and that you could trust yourself henceforth as entirely as you trust me. For *I* know that you can trust yourself to love and be happy as I trust you. I have seen the sweet miracle wrought and am as sure of its efficacy as I am of your utter loveliness. Ah, Sweetheart, if you only know how *adorable* you were Monday night! That was one of the most wonderful experiences we have had together, for its unalloyed happiness and joy in one another. There were moments when I felt that my heart was too full of delight to bear the thought of letting you go from my side even for an hour, and ever since we sat there by the fire, your dear form nestling close to me as I leaned above you and looked into your dear loving eyes and kissed your sweet lips, I have felt, somehow, as if we were united by bonds sweeter, more intimate, more tender than ever. The joy of it all has remained with me like an inspiration and everything has looked brighter to me than it ever was before; every task has been easier and has seemed to have the exquisite light of your love upon it. There entered my heart as we sat there an *assurance* of strength and happiness which I know can never leave it. And, oh, my Darling, the promise you gave me! It has made the whole world different to me! The session of Congress, to which I had been looking forward with a sort of dread, I now anticipate without the slightest sense of burden or anxiety. I am to have my lovely Darling by my side and *nothing* can oppress my spirits or weigh me down. Your love has redeemed me and made me proof against discouragement,—for it is love such as only you can give! I love you, I *love* you, my own darling little girl!

Your own   Woodrow

ALS (WP, DLC).

To Robert Lansing

My dear Mr. Secretary,   The White House. 30 September, 1915.

I enclose for your information a letter from House,[1] which explains itself.

I replied that I was willing to wait until Bernstorff could see you in New York on Saturday, and that when he did see you I thought it best that he should take it for granted that we would have to insist upon a disavowal of the action of the submarine commander in sinking the *Arabic*. I said that I did not think that public opinion in this country would be in the least satisfied with anything short of that.

You will know better than I can as yet just what line to take with the Ambassador when you see him.

I hope that you have had a real and a very refreshing rest. We shall all be mighty glad to see you back. Polk has been doing finely.   Faithfully Yours,   Woodrow Wilson

WWTLS (SDR, RG 59, 841.857 AR 1/104½, DNA).
[1] EMH to WW, Sept. 26, 1915.

To William Spry[1]

The White House [Sept. 30, 1915].

Respectfully ask if it would not be possible to postpone execution of Joseph Hillstrom, who I understand is a Swedish subject, until the Swedish minister has an opportunity to present his view of the case fully to your Excellency.[2] Woodrow Wilson.

WWT telegram (WP, DLC).

1 Governor of Utah.

2 Wilson was responding to a telegram from the Swedish Minister in Washington (W.A.F. Ekengren to WW, Sept. 29, 1915 [WP, DLC]), requesting postponement of the execution of Hillstrom, scheduled for October 1. Spry replied on September 30, saying that he had granted a reprieve, but only because the President had requested it, and urging the Swedish Minister to come to Salt Lake City to make his own investigation. W. Spry to WW, Sept. 30, 1915, cited in Gibbs M. Smith, *Labor Murder: Joe Hill* (New York, 1969), pp. 154, 223.

Hillstrom, who was born Joel Hägglund, better known in the United States as Joe Hill, was a member of the Industrial Workers of the World, an itinerant laborer, and well-known for his I.W.W. songs. He had been arrested for the murder of two grocerymen in Salt Lake City in January 1914, convicted of murder on flimsy circumstantial evidence, and sentenced to death by shooting in June 1914. The I.W.W. then appealed his case through various courts, and it became an international *cause célèbre*. The standard work on this subject is Smith, already cited; however, see also Melvyn Dubofsky, *We Shall Be All: A History of the Industrial Workers of the World* (New York, 1969), pp. 307-13.

From David Lawrence, with Enclosure

My dear Mr. President: [Washington] September 30, 1915

Thank you for your note of today.[1] I have been reluctant to send you copies of these letters fearing I might be burdening you with detail. I infer that you are anxious to keep informed and shall endeavor to confine myself to developments that have a direct bearing on the situation.

I enclose, therefore, a letter to Mr Lansing embodying a conversation with the Argentine Ambassador today, at his request and initiative, and a later talk with the Chilean Ambassador which resulted in a suggestion that may influence the situation if approved by the Secretary.

                    Very sincerely,   David Lawrence

TLS (WP, DLC).
1 It is missing.

ENCLOSURE

David Lawrence to Robert Lansing

My dear Mr. Secretary: Washington Sept 30, 1915.

The Argentine Ambassador invited me to lunch today in order that, as he explained, he might outline to me the situation among the Latin-American conferees with respect to the next conference on Mexico. He told me that all seemed to favor the recognition of Carranza except the Brazilian and Chilean Ambassadors. He finally asked me if I would not use my personal influence with da Gama and Suarez to convince them of the necessity of according recognition to Carranza. I promised to call on both and give them the benefit of such information as I had.

I talked with Suarez of Chile for nearly two hours today without mentioning of course the suggestion or interest of Naon in this matter. I found Suarez very uncompromising at first. He told me in confidence that he personally was disposed to go to the next conference prepared to avoid the assumption of any responsibility for the recognition of Carranza. He said Carranza had failed to give guarantees and wanted to make himself dictator. I asked what policy he would suggest. He said he favored keeping hands off absolutely and leaving the thing alone completely. He saw no necessity for intervention or any other move. I argued with him that even assuming the wisdom of such a course, which in itself is open to argument, the conference had by its acts and declarations already committed itself to assist in some way in solving the situation and that nothing had occurred since the last conference to justify a sudden throwing off of the task originally undertaken. I suggested also that a passive policy might result in such disintegration that foreigners would have to be protected eventually by force of arms. He said he was sure we would not intervene but recognized we had a right and would not be opposed in Latin-American sentiment if we acted only in behalf of our nationals though he said this would be "war" and not "intervention"; to the former he had no objection.

After further discussion, I learned that he doubted whether Carranza was in actual control in the states he claimed and believed that "ten revolutions" would start the day Carranza was recognized. As to the latter point, which is the burden of the argument being made by the Villista delegates here, I think I convinced Suarez that with an embargo on arms a constituted government would have no difficulty in crushing armed opposition. As to the actual control, Suarez said he intends to depend on the information which you will present to the conference.

I asked then what would be his course assuming that the physical facts as to control were established beyond doubt. He said that Carranza's record was so bad as to the protection of private property that not only this but a "full amnesty" must be given. I made to him the argument already familiar to you on the amnesty question showing that for a time—until the government shall have been firmly established—Carranza believed it would be suicidal to admit all the political intriguers whose activity in the United States was substantial evidence of what they would do to undermine a government founded on revolutionary principles. He said he realized this and would not object if Carranza made exceptions in his amnesty declaration specifying "persons guilty of non-political crimes" and even if he announced that amnesty for political offenders would not go into effect until say three months or so from the date of recognition so as to give Carranza the opportunity he desired to make the central government strong.

I made then this suggestion: suppose Carranza should address to the conference a note setting forth his program with reference to the clergy, amnesty, the protection of foreigners etc., what would Suarez think about that? He said frankly this would satisfy him and his government and afford a basis for according recognition. I said this could be suggested to Arredondo and communicated thereby to Carranza. Suarez said he was agreeable that his name be used as the originator of the suggestion if necessary. I promised to sound Arredondo on the advisability of this and said I would let Suarez know in a few days. Before, however, approaching Arredondo in this connection, I want your opinion and advice for while the plan has the merit of definitely placing Carranza on record so that in replying thereto with formal recognition we could place on record before the world and our own public opinion the understanding that we have of the purposes of the government recognized, I feel that this step should have first your consideration. In fact I think it might well follow after you have discussed with the other factions their grievances so as to afford a broader view of what might be desirable as a basis for according recognition.

The Brazilian Ambassador reached here tonight to spend a day or two. I have an engagement with him tomorrow and will advise you as to his feeling etc.

Very sincerely,   [David Lawrence]

CCL (WP, DLC).

Louis Wiley to Joseph Patrick Tumulty

PERSONAL

Dear Mr. Tumulty: [New York] September 30th, 1915

As you know, I am strongly in favor of the enfranchisement of women. Some of the ladies identified with the movement in this city, who are eager to obtain the President's support, wish to send a delegation of New Jersey women to Washington to request him to make a declaration which will be helpful to their campaign in New Jersey and New York. They, however, do not wish to take such a step unless it will be entirely agreeable to the President. They realize that he is pressed for time and is now engaged in meeting some of the most important problems in the life of the nation. They have consulted me on the subject, and I have advised them to take no action in the matter for a few days.

Meantime, I write to you confidentially, to see whether or not such a course will be annoying to the President. Possibly, if he decides to make a statement, he will prefer to do it in some other way. I shall be glad if you will write me frankly.

With regards,   Very sincerely yours,   Louis Wiley

TLS (WP, DLC).

A Dialogue

Thursday, 7 A.M. 30 Sept., 1915

A DIALOGUE

Dramatis Persona: The Imp Anxiety.
                    w.w.

Scene: A dark bed-room

Time: 4 A.M.

Imp. (squatting on w.w's solar plexus) "Did you notice that half sad, half absent look on Edith's face when you came out into the city's light last night?

w.w. Indeed I did. I could not have gone to sleep at all last night for thinking of it if I had not been so tired that exhaustion was stronger than my heart. There was the same aloofness and a sort of gentle constraint in her manner when she said good night. My heart ached from it, and aches still.

Imp. What caused it? What had you said to her?

w.w. There's the trouble. I don't know, and I *ought* to know. My intuition is generally infallible in understanding what is going on in her dear heart, but this time it was and is at fault. My own heart was never more full of tenderness and eager love. It is always a mistake for me to be with those I love when I am worn out and discouraged; I suppose because I am then most selfishly absorbed in myself. And yet it is just then that I need them most. I ought to have been able to read that look on Edith's face, but I was not. It was not quite like any other expression I ever saw on it. It made her face exquisitely beautiful and yet it was as if the beauty were not for me!

Imp. May it have come from something Helen had been saying?

w.w. I tried to think so; but her slight constraint of manner was with me, not with Helen, so far as I could perceive; and there was the same tone in her voice when she spoke to me over the telephone a few minutes later.

Imp. What had you been talking about?

w.w. Helen had been trying to persuade her to announce our engagement at once.

Imp. Didn't you see how she shivered at the idea of being conspicuous and being talked about? Had she not already generously promised that she would announce the engagement two weeks from now, and had you not already frightened her by talking about the articles that would have to appear in the papers?

w.w. Yes, and I had no right to urge anything. Perhaps I should have taken her part against Helen in the argument—but really my heart's desire got the better of me. And I could not help agreeing with Helen that Edith will be happier when the announcement is made and all possibility of *unpleasant* publicity past than she is now with everything under cover—under very uncertain cover.

Imp. Well, what are you going to do about it?

w.w. I am going to tell her how my heart aches to have disturbed her and that my love for her seems to be the only thing my heart contains, seems to be the whole substance of my life.

Imp. And are you going to let her alone when you are tired and unfit to love her as she ought to be loved?

w.w. You don't know her! That's the very time she *wants* to comfort and help. She is the sweetest lover in the world. But I have, I hope, at last learned a lesson,—to love less selfishly, and particularly to guard myself when I am tired and forlorn—wounded, as at Princeton, worn to a frazzle as yesterday at Washington.

    Curtain: 5 A.M.

Correct report. Attest Woodrow Wilson

My precious Darling,

    My heart is yours,—to do with what you will. I have no wish but your happiness.   Your own   Woodrow

WWhw MS (WP, DLC).

From Edith Bolling Galt

[Washington]

My precious One: Thursday, 11 a.m. Sept. 30, 1915

I am so sorry you were unhappy last night because of me and this "Dialogue with the Imp" is a perfect nightmare—and caused by your own weariness and depression. I don't mean that I had no responsibility about it, for I knew I suddenly grew silent, and you felt the change. But, if you had been at par yourself you would not have troubled over it.

I was cross and half sick last night or my feelings would not have been hurt by your quickly agreeing with Helen that the Smiths' coming should settle the day of announcing things, regardless of me. You first were eager to have it the 5th as Helen suggested. Then when she said oh! the Smiths will then see it in the papers before you tell them, and you said, "Oh! yes. Well, we will wait until they come, *whatever* day that is, and then announce it" without even a word to me—and frankly, it hurt my feelings and made me feel I was treated as a child.

Then at the door when I said to you, impulsively, "Oh! I am so tired having to ask people things, and now even have to get the Smiths permission to announce our own engagement," you still did not seem to think it important or to comprehend my meaning.

I know it is better to tell you plainly how I felt—though it will worry you which I never want to do. But it all comes from the fact that I have never had to ask permission to do things in my whole life. I have always just done them, and that ended it. And I have seldom even discussed what I was going to do. Now, while I know it must be different, when things are all discussed and consulted over I get impatient and restless, and, if I did not love you, would be off with the bit in my teeth and showing a clean pr. of heels to anyone who dared try to catch me. There, I feel better already just to have told you about it. And I won't sulk any more.

Please go and play golf this afternoon and clear away all the undigested G.A.R.'s, the Princeton disappointment, and my own share in your depression, and know that I still love you enough to walk up to the harness and put it on though I may kick it all to pieces if you don't know the trick of handling the ribbons so as to guide without my knowing it.

Helen and I have just come back from a ride. If you could have gone with us we could have cleared up everything.

I missed you and wanted you and love you, and nothing can change these facts. Thank you for letting me see the letters from your brother and Miss Hoyt.[1] As you said, last night, hers is charming in its genuine wish for your happiness, and no other thought but that. I will send you Mrs. Dumonts[2] letter I spoke of. All the reference to her husband's coming to Wash. would be in awful taste if she knew the true state of things—but she does not know I even know you—and for over 2 years she has been writing just this same thing about their coming to Wash. and her anxiety to have him get some position where he could do his best work. They are very interesting people and he is capable and she helps him all the time. Now I will kiss away all the weariness from your dear eyes and fold you in my arms to make you know I love you.   Always yours own,   E

ALI (WP, DLC).
  [1] J. R. Wilson, Jr., to WW, Sept. 27, 1915, TLS (WP, DLC), and Mary E. Hoyt to WW, Sept. 28, 1915, ALS (WP, DLC).
  [2] Mary Wolfe (Mrs. Frederick Theodore Frelinghuysen) Dumont. Dumont was American consul at Florence, Italy.

INDEX

NOTE ON THE INDEX

THE alphabetically arranged analytical table of contents at the front of the volume eliminates duplication, in both contents and index, of references to certain documents, such as letters. Letters are listed in the contents alphabetically by name, and chronologically within each name by page. The subject matter of all letters is, of course, indexed. The Editorial Notes and Wilson's writings are listed in the contents chronologically by page. In addition, the subject matter of both categories is indexed. The index covers all references to books and articles mentioned in text or notes. Footnotes are indexed. Page references to footnotes which place a comma between the page number and "n" cite both text and footnote, thus: "624,n3." On the other hand, absence of the comma indicates reference to the footnote only, thus: "55n2"—the page number denoting where the footnote appears.

The index supplies the fullest known form of names and, for the Wilson and Axson families, relationships as far down as cousins. Persons referred to by nicknames or shortened forms of names can be identified by reference to entries for these forms of the names.

All entries consisting of page numbers only and which refer to concepts, issues, and opinions (such as democracy, the tariff, the money trust, leadership, and labor problems), are references to Wilson speeches and writings. Page references that follow the symbol Δ in such entries refer to the opinions and comments of others who are identified.

In this index, we have omitted, under WOODROW WILSON, the entries, "Press Conferences," and "Public and Political Addresses and Statements." These are fully listed in the Table of Contents. We will follow this practice in future volumes.

N.B. In the entries for Woodrow Wilson and Edith Bolling Galt, we have not attempted to note their expressions of love for one another. Except for the first letters that they exchanged, all of the letters between Wilson and Mrs. Galt were love letters. The letters are of course indexed for subjects, names, events, and so on.

Two cumulative contents-index volumes are now in print: Volume 13, which covers Volumes 1-12, and Volume 26, which covers Volumes 14-25.

INDEX